Deploying and Troubleshooting Cisco Wireless LAN Controllers

Mark L. Gress, CCIE 25539

Lee Johnson

Cisco Press

800 East 96th Street

Indianapolis, IN 46240

Deploying and Troubleshooting Cisco Wireless LAN Controllers

Mark L. Gress, CCIE 25539 and Lee Johnson

Copyright© 2010 Cisco Systems, Inc.

Published by:
Cisco Press
800 East 96th Street
Indianapolis, IN 46240 USA

Printed in the United States of America

Third Printing: May 2012

Library of Congress Cataloging-in-Publication data is on file.

ISBN-13: 978-1-58705-814-1

ISBN-10: 1-58705-814-6

Warning and Disclaimer

This book is designed to provide information about the Cisco Unified Wireless Network (CUWN) solution pertaining to understanding and troubleshooting wireless LAN Controllers (WLC) and access points (AP). The information contained in this book, in conjunction with real-world experience, also provides an excellent self-study resource for the CCIE Wireless exam. Every effort has been made to make this book as complete and as accurate as possible, but no warranty or fitness is implied.

The information is provided on an "as is" basis. The authors, Cisco Press, and Cisco Systems, Inc. shall have neither liability nor responsibility to any person or entity with respect to any loss or damages arising from the information contained in this book or from the use of the discs or programs that may accompany it.

The opinions expressed in this book belong to the author and are not necessarily those of Cisco Systems, Inc.

Trademark Acknowledgments

All terms mentioned in this book that are known to be trademarks or service marks have been appropriately capitalized. Cisco Press or Cisco Systems, Inc., cannot attest to the accuracy of this information. Use of a term in this book should not be regarded as affecting the validity of any trademark or service mark.

Feedback Information

At Cisco Press, our goal is to create in-depth technical books of the highest quality and value. Each book is crafted with care and precision, undergoing rigorous development that involves the unique expertise of members from the professional technical community.

Readers' feedback is a natural continuation of this process. If you have any comments regarding how we could improve the quality of this book or otherwise alter it to better suit your needs, you can contact us through email at feedback@ciscopress.com. Please make sure to include the book title and ISBN in your message.

We greatly appreciate your assistance.

Corporate and Government Sales

The publisher offers excellent discounts on this book when ordered in quantity for bulk purchases or special sales, which may include electronic versions and/or custom covers and content particular to your business, training goals, marketing focus, and branding interests. For more information, please contact: U.S. Corporate and Government Sales   1-800-382-3419   corpsales@pearsontechgroup.com

For sales outside the United States please contact: **International Sales**   international@pearsoned.com

Publisher: Paul Boger	**Cisco Representative:** Eric Ullanderson
Associate Publisher: Dave Dusthimer	**Cisco Press Program Manager:** Anand Sundaram
Executive Editor: Mary Beth Ray	**Technical Editors:** Dmitry Khalyavin and Fabian Riesen
Managing Editor: Patrick Kanouse	**Copy Editor:** Karen A. Gill
Senior Development Editor: Christopher Cleveland	**Proofreader:** Jovana San Nicolas-Shirley
Project Editor: Mandie Frank	
Editorial Assistant: Vanessa Evans	
Cover and Interior Designer: Louisa Adair	
Composition: Mark Shirar	
Indexer: Ken Johnson	

CISCO.

Americas Headquarters
Cisco Systems, Inc.
San Jose, CA

Asia Pacific Headquarters
Cisco Systems (USA) Pte. Ltd.
Singapore

Europe Headquarters
Cisco Systems International BV
Amsterdam, The Netherlands

Cisco has more than 200 offices worldwide. Addresses, phone numbers, and fax numbers are listed on the Cisco Website at **www.cisco.com/go/offices.**

CCDE, CCENT, Cisco Eos, Cisco Lumin, Cisco Nexus, Cisco StadiumVision, the Cisco logo, DCE, and Welcome to the Human Network are trademarks; Changing the Way We Work, Live, Play, and Learn is a service mark; and Access Registrar, Aironet, AsyncOS, Bringing the Meeting To You, Catalyst, CCDA, CCDP, CCIE, CCIP, CCNA, CCNP, CCSP, CCVP, Cisco, the Cisco Certified Internetwork Expert logo, Cisco IOS, Cisco Press, Cisco Systems, Cisco Systems Capital, the Cisco Systems logo, Cisco Unity, Collaboration Without Limitation, EtherFast, EtherSwitch, Event Center, Fast Step, Follow Me Browsing, FormShare, GigaDrive, HomeLink, Internet Quotient, IOS, iPhone, iQ Expertise, the iQ logo, iQ Net Readiness Scorecard, iQuick Study, IronPort, the IronPort logo, LightStream, Linksys, MediaTone, MeetingPlace, MGX, Networkers, Networking Academy, Network Registrar, PCNow, PIX, PowerPanels, ProConnect, ScriptShare, SenderBase, SMARTnet, Spectrum Expert, StackWise, The Fastest Way to Increase Your Internet Quotient, TransPath, WebEx, and the WebEx logo are registered trademarks of Cisco Systems, Inc. and/or its affiliates in the United States and certain other countries.

All other trademarks mentioned in this document or Website are the property of their respective owners. The use of the word partner does not imply a partnership relationship between Cisco and any other company. (0805R)

About the Authors

Mark L. Gress, CCIE 25539, is an escalation engineer at the Cisco Systems Technical Assistance Center (TAC) in Research Triangle Park, North Carolina, where he has worked since 2005. He has been troubleshooting complex wireless networks since the birth of the Cisco Wireless LAN Controller (WLC) as a TAC engineer, a technical lead for the Enterprise Wireless team, and now as an escalation engineer supporting the complete Cisco line of wireless products. Mark has diagnosed problems in some of the largest Cisco wireless deployments and has provided training for TAC teams around the world. He has also contributed to numerous design guides, application notes, and white papers. As one of the highest contributors of identifying and assisting in defect resolution, his work has led to increases in overall product quality and stability. Mark graduated summa cum laude with a bachelors of science in both computer information systems and business management from North Carolina Wesleyan College. For more than ten years, Mark has been professionally involved in the networking industry.

Lee Johnson is currently a wireless specialist on the RTP Wireless TAC team at Cisco. He has been troubleshooting wireless networks, including both autonomous and controller-based infrastructures, since 2006. Lee troubleshoots complex wireless issues in Cisco customer networks around the world. He has been dispatched to customer sites to address critical accounts and represented Cisco at Networkers. He also provides training and documentation for fellow Cisco engineers in both wireless and nonwireless TAC groups. Lee works closely with the wireless development group at Cisco to improve product quality and the customer experience with the WLC. He holds a bachelor of science degree in biology from the University of North Carolina at Chapel Hill.

About the Contributing Author

Javier Contreras Albesa, CCIE Security, is a member of the escalation team for the Wireless Business Unit, at Cisco Systems in Spain, where he has worked since 2005. Since the introduction of the Wireless LAN Controllers, he has been an escalation engineer on the TAC in Belgium and now interfaces between post-sales support and development responsible for supporting the European region. Javier has been involved on most support cases for the region and several priority cases worldwide. He has been a significant contributor to quality improvement on different wireless products. He has published several whitepapers and application notes and is the main developer on the WLC Config Analyzer, a tool used to simplify the support on WLC deployments. Javier graduated in computer information systems in Venezuela. For more than 12 years, Javier has been involved in networking, security consultancy, and the wireless industry.

About the Technical Reviewers

Dmitry Khalyavin is the lead engineer in Cisco's Wireless Network Business Unit escalation team. He has six years of experience working with design, implementation, management, and troubleshooting of the complete line of Cisco's wireless product offerings. He holds a bachelor's degree in computer science from Polytechnic Institute of New York University.

Fabian Riesen is Technical Leader at Cisco Systems' TAC in Switzerland. He joined Cisco in 1999 as a project engineer. He owns a Swiss-Engineer degree from the University of Applied Sciences Winterthur/Zurich* with specialization in Software Engineering and Transmission Technologies. He is CCIE ISP-Dial and CCIE Wireless No. 6268.

Dedications

I would like to dedicate this book to my loving wife, Kameron, and children, Taylor, Trinity, and Tanner. They are the root to my strength and dedication that constantly moves me forward in life. They have dealt with me through tough times and made personal sacrifices so I could achieve more. No matter what, they have always been there for me, and for that I will always love them and be extremely grateful.

I would also like to make a special dedication to my doctor, one of the best in the world, Dr. David Paul Adams. With his medical expertise, he has assisted me in accepting the physical limitations I have struggled with throughout this process, giving me my life back so I can continue to accomplish special tasks and achieve what others cannot. I truly do not know where I would be without his understanding, compassion, and support.

I would also like to make a special dedication to my brother, Michael Gress. I am very proud of him for everything he has achieved and hope one day that I can be as good as a person as he is.

Finally my father, Larry Gress—not only is he a terrific father but also my best friend! Thank you for bringing me into this world and all your help!

—Mark L. Gress

I would like to dedicate this book to my wife, Lisa, and children, Tyler and Kasey. Without your love and support, I might never have been able to finish it. Lisa, thanks for putting up with me and taking care of the family while I was engrossed in this project.

—Lee Johnson

Acknowledgments

Mark and Lee would like to thank both Fabi Riesen and Dmitry Khalyavin for providing their expert technical knowledge in reviewing this book. Their comments and suggestions were invaluable in making this book complete and accurate. Thanks for keeping us on our toes with the latest features and configuration settings.

Thanks to Fabi Riesen for his contributing work. Fabi is a great technical resource and certainly helped lighten the load for us to make sure this book reached completion in a timely manner.

We also want to thank the Cisco Press team for this book. Mary Beth Ray, Christopher Cleveland, and Mandie Frank kept us on track and inline to get this work done. Thanks for putting up with us!

Lee would like to thank Mark Gress for approaching him and giving him the opportunity to work on this book. It was definitely a learning experience!

Mark and Lee would like to thank Jason Fitzgerald, manager of the RTP Wireless Technical Assistance Center, for giving us the opportunity to prove we are the best of the best at what we do! Without his encouragement and support, this book would not have been possible.

Contents at a Glance

Contents

Icons Used in This Book

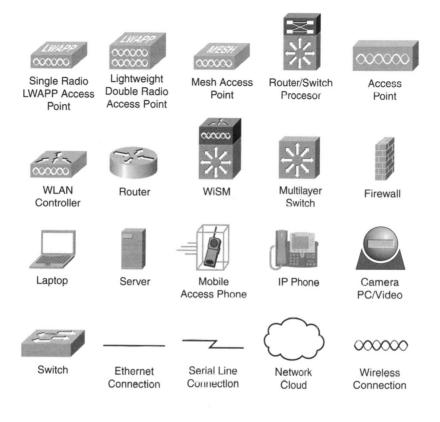

Command Syntax Conventions

The conventions used to present command syntax in this book are the same conventions used in the *IOS Command Reference*. The *Command Reference* describes these conventions as follows:

- **Boldface** indicates commands and keywords that are entered literally as shown. In actual configuration examples and output (not general command syntax), boldface indicates commands that are manually input by the user (such as a **show** command).

- *Italic* indicates arguments for which you supply actual values.

- Vertical bars (|) separate alternative, mutually exclusive elements.

- Square brackets ([ ]) indicate an optional element.

- Braces ({ }) indicate a required choice.

- Braces within brackets ([{ }]) indicate a required choice within an optional element.

Introduction

Wireless networking is a fast-evolving technology. Long gone are the days when companies view wireless access as a perk. Along with a dial tone, more and more companies view wireless connectivity as a given network resource. Information technology (IT) professionals are required to fully understand the latest wireless products and features to properly implement a wireless solution. Companies and standards bodies are designing and offering certification programs so candidates can prove their wireless knowledge and benefit the organization.

The Cisco Unified Wireless Network (CUWN) solution is a bleeding-edge wireless technology platform that most wireless professionals need to be familiar with to properly install, configure, and troubleshoot.

Goals

The goal of this book is to give you the necessary knowledge to install, configure, and troubleshoot Cisco wireless controller–based networks in a technically proficient and concise manner. Although this book tries to cover the topics in an in-depth manner, it would be impossible to cover all possible network scenarios that might exist. You should be able to take this information and apply it to any network issue and determine the underlying cause and resolve it. A wireless problem is going to fall into one or more of the following categories: configuration mistake, radio frequency (RF) issue, client issue, wired network issue, or bug. Basic wireless knowledge is assumed in this book, so some wireless topics are glossed over at a high level.

Although not specifically designed to help you pass the CCIE Wireless written and lab exams, this book does provide you with real-world configuration and troubleshooting examples. Understanding the basic configuration practices, how the products are designed to function, the feature sets, and what to look for while troubleshooting these features will be invaluable to anyone wanting to pass the CCIE Wireless exams.

Who Should Read This Book?

This book is designed for senior wireless networking professionals who will be installing, configuring, and maintaining Cisco wireless controllers and access points (AP).

How This Book Is Organized

Although this book can be read cover to cover, it is designed so that you can flip directly to the particular chapter that discusses the topic you are interested in. Chapter 1, "Troubleshooting Strategy and Implementation," provides the basis on how to develop a solid troubleshooting method that you can apply to any of the following subjects covered in the remaining core Chapters 2 through 15. The appendixes provide a list of debug commands, payload information, and information on the next generation of Cisco wireless controllers.

The core chapters, 2 through 15, cover the following topics:

- **Chapter 2, "Wireless LAN Controllers and Access Points"**: This chapter discusses the different wireless controller and AP models and the differences between them. It also covers hardware and software requirements.

- **Chapter 3, "Introduction to LWAPP"**: This chapter discusses the basic concepts behind the Lightweight Access Point Protocol (LWAPP).

- **Chapter 4, "The CAPWAP Protocol"**: This chapter covers the Control and Provising of Wireless Access Points (CAPWAP) protocol, including session establishment, troubleshooting the discovery and join process, and CAPWAP communication.

- **Chapter 5, "Network Design Considerations"**: This chapter covers physical and logical install and design considerations for the controllers and APs. It covers controller failover, access layer, distribution layer, service block controller installations, WAN considerations, and dense access point deployments and location.

- **Chapter 6, "Understanding the Troubleshooting Tools"**: This chapter covers the options and possibilities for troubleshooting wired and wireless issues within your deployments.

- **Chapter 7, "Deploying and Configuring the Wireless LAN Controller"**: This chapter explains how to deploy and configure the Wireless LAN Controller (WLC) for connectivity with APs using multiple AP-Managers and link aggregation (LAG). The chapter also covers how to troubleshoot some of the more common WLC issues.

- **Chapter 8, "Access Point Registration"**: This chapter covers the AP registration process for a controller and the methods for AP discovery and troubleshooting.

- **Chapter 9, "Mobility"**: This chapter discusses intra-, inter-, Layer 2, and Layer 3 controller roaming and troubleshooting. It also covers AP mobility between controllers.

- **Chapter 10, "Troubleshooting Client-Related Issues"**: This chapter covers general client information, client associations, debugs on the client, use of wireless and wired sniffer traces, local AP debugs, and interpreting the output of **debug client** on the controller command-line interface (CLI).

- **Chapter 11, "Wireless Voice"**: This chapter examines proper voice deployment guidelines, configuring the controller for voice depolyments, common voice-related troubleshooting methods, and proper quality of service (QoS) for wireless voice deployments.

- **Chapter 12, "Radio Resource Management"**: This chapter examines the auto-RF feature of the controllers and how RF groups and group leaders are elected. It also covers dynamic channel assignment, transmit power control, coverage hole detection, and Radio Resource Management (RRM) guidelines, enhancements, and troubleshooting.

- **Chapter 13, "H-REAP"**: This chapter covers Hybrid Remote Edge Access Point (H-REAP) configuration and troubleshooting, differences between REAP and H-REAP, Split MAC versus Local MAC, H-REAP modes of operation, configuration, and troubleshooting.

■ **Chapter 14, "Guest Networking":** This chapter covers web authentication and how it works, auto-anchoring (guest tunneling), wired guest access, guest profiles, QoS profiles for guest users, and custom web authentication pages and certificates and how to troubleshoot them.

■ **Chapter 15, "Mesh":** This chapter discusses wireless mesh APs, the different mesh code releases, deployment guidelines, mesh routing, parent selection, configuration, Ethernet bridging, and troubleshooting.

■ **Appendix A, "Debugging Commands":** This appendix covers Comprehensive debug command list and usage guide for WLCs covering all versions of code. The debug commands also include Remote AP debugs and other debugs that will aid in troubleshooting almost every issue possible!

■ **Appendix B, "LWAPP and CAPWAP Payloads":** This appendix is a comprehensive list of specific payloads and their uses. The Vendor Specific Payload message element is used to communicate vendor specific information between the WTP and the access controller (AC). Also included are payloads sent in LWAPP messages and the corresponding ones that will be sent in CAPWAP messages.

Chapter 1

Troubleshooting Strategy and Implementation

When you think about a wireless network, especially one involving Lightweight Access Point Protocol (LWAPP) or Control and Provisioning of Wireless Access Points (CAPWAP), the topology can be profoundly large. The challenge of troubleshooting a wireless issue can be intimidating to any seasoned engineer. The issue might not even be wireless, but ultimately it can affect all wireless connectivity or the quality of the connection. The question is a simple one, but at this point, it might be the most difficult: Where do I start or how do I begin?

Developing a Troubleshooting Strategy

Developing a troubleshooting strategy can be a life saver. Usually strategies work well on issues that have been around for awhile or that are intermittent. Depending on the issue, your strategy might change to best suit what is currently going on. No matter which way you look at it, the best choice is to have a plan ready to go. You can always modify your strategy if the parameters of the problem change while you're troubleshooting. It's easier to be in a situation in which your strategy needs extensive modification than to be without one.

Production Versus Nonproduction Outages

A network problem typically falls into one of the following two types of categories, either of which can fit into a production or nonproduction outage:

- **Outage renders the network completely useless or inoperable:** Believe it or not, this does provide some positive aspects to troubleshooting. Network activity that would usually require a maintenance or change window can now be accomplished at any time because the network is down. A network-down scenario is usually easier to identify and fix because the issue is constant.

- **Outage renders the network partially impaired:** Issues that fall into this category are usually smaller in magnitude, but not always. For example, your wireless laptop users might be able to access all network resources with the exception of the printers. Another example would be if your 7921 voice users have degraded voice quality. Users can still receive and place calls, but it might be difficult to understand the other party.

Step 1: Gathering Data About the Problem

No matter what issue you encounter, the one resource that helps any situation is information about the issue and knowledge of the environment. Information aids in your understanding of what you are potentially dealing with—the scope, magnitude, and other facets that could be influencing the issue at hand. No matter what problem you start to troubleshoot, information gathering should always be the first step. In most cases you do not even realize you have done that.

Step 2: Identifying the Problem

Identifying and isolating the problem can be a major headache in itself, especially in a centralized wireless network using LWAPP and CAPWAP.

Wired networks alone can encompass quite a few network resources. Figure 1-1 shows an example of what you might see in a typical wireless network setup.

If you add the components of a wireless network to a wired network, you have a rather large plethora of network resources:

- Multiple LANs
- Large LANs
- Multiple VLANS (Inter-VLAN routing)
- WANs
- Routing protocols
- Multicast
- Hot Standby Routing Protocol (HSRP)
- Ether Channel

This list is just a small example of the wireless network resources and issues you need to investigate on top of the existing wired devices. Do not forget that this is a wireless deployment and that you also have to look at the wireless pieces:

- Interference
- Access points (APs)
- Controllers
- Antennas

- Authentication equipment (RADIUS servers, APs, or Wireless LAN Controllers [WLC], and so on)

- Client-related problems

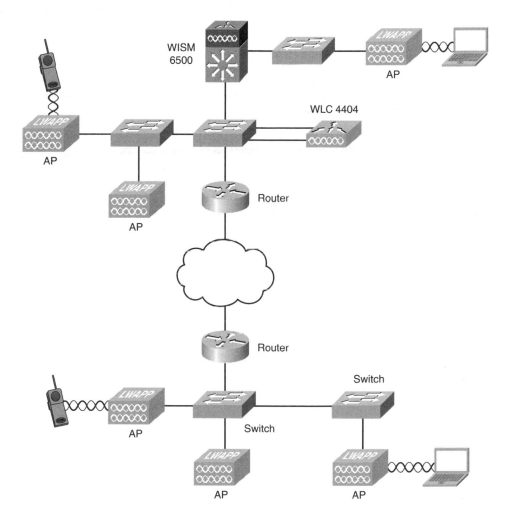

Figure 1-1 *Resources in a Typical Network*

Step 3: Isolating the Problem

A key piece of troubleshooting is to potentially identify the source of the issue. A networking topology can be a valuable tool in assisting you to do so. Judging from all the items listed previously, you have a lot of work cut out for yourself. You should always keep in mind that, while narrowing the list of possible culprits, you should never permanently rule out anything. At some point you might have to revisit the same resource that you looked at initially. Anyone who has been involved with troubleshooting networking-related issues for some time has been a part of a problem that was misdiagnosed or at some point had to claim responsibility for an incorrect action or identification of the problem.

A valuable piece of advice to remember is to always look at the big picture when searching for the root cause of the problem. Never let the symptoms of the problem mislead you.

Network Topology

A network topology can be a great visual roadmap of all the routes and equipment that are used. A network topology can isolate the issue even further and once again inform you of what pieces are or are not involved.

One of the most important steps is to develop a network diagram of the current network on which you are troubleshooting the issue. This can really put the network and its components into perspective. To build your network topology, use network diagram drawing software such as Microsoft Visio, SmartDraw, or similar tools. After the foundation is built, you can update it when needed. This can prove to be useful, especially if you have to contact a third-party support vendor. Your network topology is at your disposal and benefits others. Ideally, when troubleshooting, this drawing is already present or is included in any service requests.

What does the network diagram need to contain? The answer to this question can vary depending on the network size and type. This assists in tracking and being able to quickly connect to any device in the network. What is going to be useful in helping you solve the issue? Consider the following commonly used items:

- Device type diagrams (routers, switches, and so on)
- Model numbers
- IP addresses
- Subnets, VLANs, and so on
- Routing areas
- Protocols (Frame Relay, ATM, and so on)
- Interfaces, port numbers, and so on
- Software version
- Passwords

In addition, for the wireless portion of the network, you might need the following to generate a comprehensive topology:

- Mobility groups
- Radio frequency (RF) groups

- Radiation patterns of APs

- Access point channel information

- Access point power information

- Physical barriers or RF barriers

- AP group VLANs (if applicable)

Note   AP group VLANs, along with WLAN override, have replaced the AP group functionality in version 5.2.

You can also generate this information by using a Wireless Control System (WCS) if you have one. The WCS and the Wireless Location Appliance, as seen in Figure 1-2, can be useful in many ways. The Cisco 3300 Series Mobility Services Engine is a combination of hardware and software. The Mobility Services Engine is an appliance-based solution that supports a suite of software services to provide centralized and scalable service delivery. The Mobility Services Engine transforms the wireless LAN into a mobility network by abstracting the application layer from the network layer, effectively allowing for the delivery of mobile applications across different types of networks.

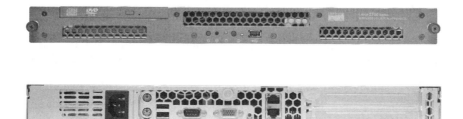

Figure 1-2   *Cisco Wireless Control System and Wireless Location Appliance*

Note   The 2700 (wireless location appliance) has been deprecated and is being replaced by the 3300 Series Mobility Services Engine.

The WCS contains useful information and can be quite helpful.

However, because of the real-time necessity of information gathering, WCS can be suboptimal at times when troubleshooting. WCS takes snapshots at configured intervals to update its database. If any changes are made, the administrator has to wait until the next update interval or manually submit an update to see the change. WCS is not needed for a wireless network. WCS is a management standalone database that operates on a server. It acts as a third-party device and is passive unless used otherwise for configuration changes and so on. Figure 1-3 demonstrates how WCS is integrated into networks.

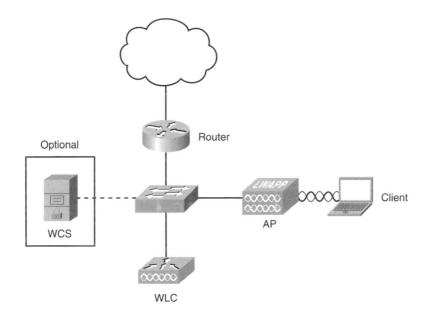

Figure 1-3 *Cisco Wireless Control System Integrated into a Network*

Depending on the size of the network, you might have multiple topology pages and maps. Always remember that there is nothing wrong with this—having too much information is not a bad position to be in. Obviously, everything listed is not required or set in stone; items are listed to give you a good starting point or items additional options to consider. You should always get as much information as needed to troubleshoot your issue.

Gathering General Information

Information is valuable in any form or fashion and is always vital. The best way to determine what information you might need for your network issue is to imagine that you are talking to someone over the phone. That is usually the most challenging environment because you are not physically there. Imagine what questions you would ask to educate yourself so you could provide the next course of action(s) or help solve the problem. This list can give you an idea of the potential information that is going to be needed. If you are the network administrator/owner, you must obtain the following information:

- Details about what the user actually experienced or is currently experiencing

- Information about the scope of the issue and how many users are affected

- Frequency of the issue

- Configurations of devices

- A network topology

- Any error messages, message logs, or sys log information

- Debug requirements

- MAC addresses/IP addresses for debugs or any other utility/application that might need them

- Any additional information/resources for the next troubleshooting steps

This is a good list to get you started. By no means is this list set in stone; you should modify it to fit the issue. If you have to contact a third party for support, it is beneficial to have this information, and in many cases, this information can decrease network outage time. It all comes down to what works for you.

You will encounter network issues that you simply will not have sufficient or the right kind of information to even begin troubleshooting. In many cases, you will need multiple tools set up or in place so when the problem happens again you can collect all the necessary elements. The key element is that in many network issues, additional work will be needed to gain the informational components to proceed to the next step in troubleshooting. This step might be acquiring additional informational resources or corrective action of the issue.

Frequency of the Issue

When discussing time with regard to a problem, you must consider a few factors. Time can be a valuable asset when trying to troubleshoot an issue. The frequency of the problem is important if the entire network is not down. Some issues that you can run into might occur only once a month. This can help set expectations on what information to acquire during the time the issue exists. The problem duration is also valuable because you know what can and cannot be done during this time frame.

In summary, you need to answer four questions in the most accurate and efficient manner:

- How long has the problem been going on?

- When did it start?

- How often does it occur?

- When the problem occurs, how long does it last?

The answers to these questions provide valuable information for the troubleshooting process. They also direct action for the next step you need to take in solving the problem. A subsequent question might be this: Were there network changes before or at the time the problem started? You open the door for numerous other questions while educating yourself, taking one step closer to the problem solution.

Step 4: Analyzing the Data Collected About the Problem

Now that you have collected data from various sources, you must analyze it to find the root cause or workaround for your problem. In many scenarios, you will find that your support vendor will ask or obtain this information to aid in efforts to troubleshoot. If part of your plan is to engage your support vendor, it is a good idea to have already gathered this information. This saves you quite a bit of time in the long run. In addition, it decreases the overall time to locate and resolve the issue you are having. For any piece of hardware, get to know your supporting vendor and what this person might or might not ask.

> **Tip** Get to know your vendor and what this person might ask to help solve your issue. Having this material ahead of time reduces troubleshooting and resolution time.
>
> Another good idea is to get experience and knowledge of the common troubleshooting tools that you might use to aid in problem resolution. An example of this is using sniffer tools to read packet captures or the debugging system of the WLC.

Narrow the List of Possible Causes

After you analyze the collected information data from monitoring tools, logs, and so on, you are in a position to logically narrow the list of possible causes of your problem. It is usually a good idea to start large and then work your way down to something more manageable. When problem identification is at a point that you can reasonably apply additional test methods, you can thoroughly investigate that particular cause and really put it to the test. In many cases, it is as easy as using common sense to reduce the list by 50 percent to 75 percent.

Determining the Proper Troubleshooting Tool

A plethora of troubleshooting tools is available. Most products sold on the market usually contain their own troubleshooting tools, debugs, or some form of diagnostic system. The large number of troubleshooting tools can make it extremely difficult to select which ones are best suited for the job. This book lays out the best tools, debugs, and troubleshooting tips to help you solve most issues that may arise. That way you are better prepared for whatever problem might surface—expected or unexpected.

Summary

Most network issues are reported with a generic description. For example, "All users on the wireless network are experiencing slow response to an application." You must be logical when reporting and troubleshooting the problem. It will be difficult to troubleshoot every user if someone reports that all users are experiencing latency. In many cases, there will be a working model and a nonworking model. A few examples would be a problem on a particular switch. If you had multiple switches in your network, you could compare the working switch to the switch that had the issue. The nice approach to this model is that even if you do not have any idea what is occurring, you can always take a packet capture of the working and nonworking switch and compare packet to packet. In another example, you could look at a problem with a client PC. You would start by listing the difference between the working and nonworking machine.

Tip   When comparing equipment, try to find pieces that are close or identical.

You want to try to find machines that are inherently close to each other. The differences between each piece of equipment could invalidate your research and results.

After you have the list of differences between a working and nonworking PC, examine each difference by itself. You do this by removing the differences one at a time. If you remove more than one, you run the risk of solving the problem, without knowing which difference was the cause. One major flaw in the strategy is that you do not always have an accurate picture of the correctly running machine.

Troubleshooting methodology is critical when any network problem arises. You need to have the quickest and most efficient method in your head and at your fingertips. The difference could cost you resources and considerable time.

Chapter 2

Wireless LAN Controllers and Access Points

Cisco access points (AP) provide a way to extend wired networks or install network components where normal physical wiring cannot be installed. APs also provide an alternative solution to networking at a fraction of the cost. Cisco wireless solutions offer secure, manageable, and reliable wireless connectivity with exceptional range and performance. Cisco wireless solutions are offered in two mechanisms:

■ A standalone device that interacts directly with the wired network.

■ A two-part system that relies on a controller. APs talk directly to a controller or central-based piece of equipment, and this device interacts directly with the wired network.

Each mechanism is Wi-Fi certified for interoperability that offers support for various client devices. Both deployment mechanisms support 802.11a/b/g/n connectivity for indoor and outdoor environments. Many controllers and APs exist, a good portion of which were the creations of the autonomous or the controller technology. By the end of this book, you will have learned what product was intended for what solution and what will suit your business needs. However, you need to dig in and learn a little about the history before you begin.

Wireless LAN Controller Platforms

A range of models can work with any platform you have. The idea of the Wireless LAN Controller (WLC) is to simplify the deployment and operation of wireless networks. It is intended to offer a higher level of security, AP radio frequency (RF) management, single point of management, and mobility services.

The WLC also offers a variety of services, some of which are specific to the model of the controller. Later on in this chapter, you will learn about the functionality differences between the platforms. The main solution is data and voice networks. Within these networks, the WLC can provide wireless and wired guest services, location tracking, quality of service (QoS), and other varieties of 802.11a/b/g/n services. Everything mentioned here and more will be discussed in the future pages of this book.

Current Production WLCs

The controller models differ by their uplink interface size/speed and the number of APs they support. They also vary to a degree with the type of equipment that they interface with. The sections that follow briefly describe the current line of WLCs.

Cisco 5500 Series WLCs

The Cisco 5508, as pictured in Figure 2-1, is the most powerful WLC to date. It offers reliable performance, enhanced flexibility, and zero service loss for mission-critical wireless. This WLC platform was developed with the new 802.11n standard that offers up to nine times the performance of 802.11a/g networks.

Figure 2-1   *Cisco 5508 WLC*

The main improvements and new capabilities that the Cisco 5508 offers over the other controllers are as follows:

■ Maximum Performance and Scalability:

Support for up to 250 APs and 7000 clients

Nine times the performance of 802.11a/g networks

Ability to manage 250 APs simultaneously

■ Improved Mobility and Services:

Reliable connections even in the most demanding environments

Larger mobility domain for more simultaneous client associations

Uninterrupted network access when roaming

Consistent streaming video and reliable, toll-quality voice

■ Licensing Flexibility and Investment Protection:

Option to add additional APs and feature licenses over time

Optional WPLUS software, which supports the Cisco OfficeExtend solution and Enterprise Wireless Mesh

Cisco Catalyst 6500 Series Wireless Services Module

The Wireless Integrated Service Module (WiSM), as shown in Figure 2-2, is a card that fits in the 6500 chassis and actually houses two 4400 controllers on one blade. Each WLC actually supports 150 APs, allowing for a total of 300 APs. Each WLC in the WiSM has its own console port for access. This was the added benefit of purchasing a WiSM over two separate standalone 4404s—the additional 100 APs. This was the largest controller made until production of the 5508 WLC. Of course, there are plans for devices supporting far greater numbers of APs, such as the 5508.

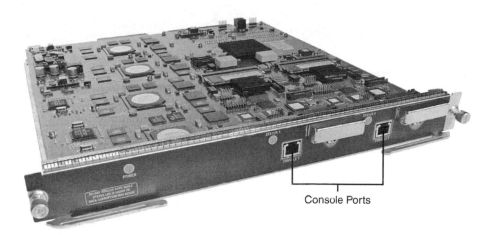

Console Ports

Figure 2-2   *Wireless Integrated Service Module*

The WiSM is typically referred to as the replacement for the Wireless LAN Services Module (WLSM). Cisco offered a trade-in program when the WiSM first came out as a way to increase migration to the WiSM.

Cisco Catalyst 3750G Integrated WLC

The WLC integrated 3750G takes the same approach as the WiSM but on a smaller scale. It is a single 4404 built into a 3750G switch. It is often referred to as the foxhound. The switch has 24 Ethernet 10/100/1000 ports with IEEE 802.3af and Cisco prestandard Power over Ethernet (PoE). It supports up to 50 APs. Figure 2-3 shows the 3750G integrated WLC.

Figure 2-3   *3750G Integrated WLC*

Cisco 4400 Series WLCs

The 4400 series WLCs come in two models—the 4402 and the 4404, as shown in Figure 2-4. The 4402 has two gigabit connections, whereas the 4404 has four. The 4402 is sold in variants that support up to 50 APs, whereas the 4404 supports up to 100 APs.

Figure 2-4   *4402 and 4404 WLCs*

Cisco 2100 Series WLCs

There are three models of the Cisco 2100 series WLCs shown in Figure 2-5. Each model correlates to the number of APs that it can support—2106, 2112, and 2125. The 2106 supports six APs, whereas the 2125 supports 25. There was a large architectural change between the old 2006 controller and the 2100 series controllers. The 2106 is now built on the ASA5505 platform. This offers much more functionality and capability than the 2006.

Figure 2-5   *2100 Series WLC*

Cisco Wireless LAN Controller Module

The Cisco Wireless LAN Controller Module (WLCM), shown in Figure 2-6, supports up to 25 Cisco Aironet APs and is supported on the Cisco 2800 and 3800 ISRs and 3700 series router. The WLCM is basically a 2106 sitting on a card that slides into a router. The WLCM is offered in four models: one that supports 6, 8, 12, and 25 APs.

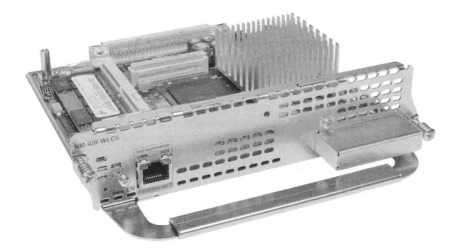

Figure 2-6   *WLCM*

Previous WLCMs

To understand how and why the current models were produced, you need to know the history of the products and the companies they came from. The acquisition of Airespace marked the Cisco entrance into the centrally controlled managed solution, which was selling and gaining ground much faster than the standalone AP approach. These models can be identified with the Airespace labeling even though they were sold as Cisco units. The units eventually were sold with the Cisco branding.

The newer brands are a bit different from their older counterparts. When Airespace introduced its line of controllers, one of its intentions was for the WLC to function like a switch. Customers were to use these controllers to plug their APs directly into the controller's ports. This design had its benefits and flaws. The design of these models restricted the overall design and implementation of wireless because you had to plug the APs directly into the unit. This is why you no longer see models like the 2000 or 4000 series WLCs.

This limited scalability from the product line was one of the major selling points and advantages over the typical standalone IOS-based APs. When applying this concept, the APs had to be located close to the controller and were limited to the length of the Ethernet cable.

The scalability factor is the understanding that you can have a network of any size and plug the APs into the network at any location regardless of geography. One AP might be located in Ohio and another in North Carolina. As long as they have IP connectivity back to the WLC, they establish communication with the controller and register. We will discuss the registration process in more detail in Chapter 8, "Access Point Registration."

Cisco 3500 Series WLCs

The 3504 WLC was the first generation small controller. It is similar to the 2006 in design, but it does not have the same hardware resources as the 2006. It contains less memory than the 2006 and similar models. The 2006 was a direct replacement for the 3504 and had improved hardware, although both were cosmetically identical. You have probably never run across these models unless you have been buying this equipment since Airespace started.

Tip   You can install a 3504 image on a 2006, but you cannot install a 2006 image on a 3504 because the 2006 contains more memory than the 3504.

Cisco 4000 Series WLCs

The 4000 series had a few different models, including the 4012 and the 4024. The 12 and 24 were actually the number of 10/100 Ethernet ports that were located on the front of the box. These units did have one or two gigabit ports on the back of the box: 2-port SX or 1-port TX. The ports were also PoE, which was a nice feature. In addition, the units had console, service, and utility ports. The utility ports were always reserved for future users but ended up never providing functionality.

Cisco 2000 Series WLCs

The 2006 was the only model of 2000 series WLCs. The 6 referred to the number of APs it supported. This was and still is the smallest controller built as far as the number of APs supported. The 2006 had a 10/100 uplink that you could plug into a switch, enabling it to function like a larger WLC. The 2006 also had four Ethernet ports, a console port, and a utility port. What was unusual about the 2006 was the idea behind it. The model was built with the idea that people did not have to have a switch for it to work; they could plug the APs directly into the unit. Of course, it is difficult to do this when only four 10/100 Ethernet ports exist. Furthermore, one of the Ethernet ports had to be used as an uplink back to provide network connectivity, leaving only three ports. The 2006 did not have network processing units (NPU); it was more software based and limited to what it actually could do. The 2006 drawbacks were addressed with the release of the 2106, which is discussed in more detail in Chapter 5, "Network Design Considerations."

Cisco 4100 Series WLCs

The 4100 series WLC was the first hybrid or migration over to the 4402 or 4404s that exist today. Having numerous Ethernet ports all over the box and plugging the APs directly into the box were finally abandoned. These changes were definitely huge benefits because they affected scalability to a high degree.

The 4100 series had one or two ports: one active and one standby. The 4400 utilized SFP modules instead of the 10/100 Ethernet ports.

Functionality Differences Between WLCs

There is actually a great deal of functionality difference in software depending on the model of the controller. If you do not understand the terminology or feature at this point, you will learn more as you progress through the book.

These software features are not supported on the 2000, 2100, and Network Module Controller (NMC) series controllers. The majority of these features *are* supported on the other WLC models:

- PoE for 2100 series controllers. PoE has only two designated ports.

- Service port (separate out-of-band management 10/100-Mbps Ethernet interface). The 2000 and 2100 series WLC does not contain a physical service port.

- Multicast is not supported on APs that are connected directly to the local port of a 2000 or 2100 series controller.

- VPN termination (such as IPsec and Layer 2 Tunneling Protocol [L2TP]) is not supported. IPsec is supported only on 3.2 code on the 4100/4400 models with a VPN module.

- Termination of guest controller tunnels is not supported. (Origination of guest controller tunnels is supported.) This is also known as a *mobility anchor*. The smaller WLC models cannot function as an anchor.

- External web authentication web server list is not supported.

- Layer 2 Lightweight Access Point Protocol (LWAPP) Transport mode is not supported. The 2000 series, 2100 series, and NMC are only L3 capable.

- Spanning tree is not supported.

- Port mirroring is not supported. This feature was originally designed for the multi-port WLC platforms in mind. It is similar to a span session on a switch.

- Cranite is not supported.

- Fortress is not supported.

- AppleTalk is not supported.

- QoS per-user bandwidth contracts is not supported.

- IPv6 pass-through is not supported.

- Link aggregation (LAG) or ether channel is not supported.

- Multicast unicast Replication mode is not supported.

The Foxhounds (the 3750s with the built in 4402s) and WiSMs are only capable of link aggregation (LAG). This is also known as EtherChannel. Another point to remember is that the EtherChannel is not capable of channel negotiation; I am referring to Link Aggregation Control Protocol (LACP) or Port Aggregation Protocol (PAgP).

Tip   LAG on the WLC does not support LACP or PAgP. Its mode is simply on: "Channel group mode ON." Also, the load-balancing algorithm is src-dst-ip:

```
switch(config)#port-channel load-balance src-dst-ip
```

The channel group mode is simply in the "ON" state. If your WLC is running LAG or ether channel, it must be in Layer 3 mode. All the 2000, 2100, and NMCs are only capable of Layer 3 mode. When Layer 2 or Layer 3 is referred to in the context, it is referring to the lwapp transport mode, and it is strictly a controller function. For now the only point of interest you need to know about Layer 2 and Layer 3 LWAPP transport mode is that in Layer 3 mode an AP-Manager interface is needed/created. The exception is the 5500 series, which does not require an AP-Manager. The management interface handles the AP communication. In addition, the transport mode is specific to LWAPP and has nothing to do with Control and Provisioning of Wireless Access Points (CAPWAP). In Layer 2 LWAPP mode, the APs do not require IP addresses but must be in the same subnet/network as the controller. There is also no AP-Manager interface configured on the WLC.

Note   Layer 2 and Layer 3 WLC transport modes are specific only to LWAPP. CAPWAP operates only at Layer 3.

WLC Hardware and Software Requirements

The size of the wireless network you want to have determines the requirements. The first piece of hardware is a controller. You have to decide on the number of APs you want to have in your network. You also need to plan what applications you want to support over wireless. Some controller models support the same number of APs, but the hardware underneath is somewhat different. For instance, Cisco produces a WLC2125 and a WLC4402-25. Therefore, the question comes down to 4402 versus 2125, because both support 25 APs. The 4400 has two network processing units (NPU) and additional resources that the 2100 does not. The 2100 does not have an NPU but in its place has a smaller processor, and for the most part everything is handled in software. There is a phenomenal difference as far as the packet processing rate between the 4400 and the 2100. Neither video nor voice applications on a large scale would be possible for the 2125. The uplink is a 10/100 Ethernet cable, so you are restricted to this bottleneck. Chapter 5 goes much more into architecture of the devices, but the general idea is that a controller is required.

After you choose a controller, you choose an AP model. Again, what you are trying to accomplish determines the type of AP to go with. If your idea is to build a small wireless network, you can do so with a 2000/2100 series WLC and a single AP. You then have to connect this into your existing network. If you have a large wired network, the same principle basically applies. You can purchase a 4404 and connect the gigports into your switch infrastructure. Then you can connect the APs throughout your network. Finally, there has to be IP connectivity between the APs and the WLC. After you configure the controller, your wireless network is up and running.

Controller Requirements

The controller GUI requires the following operating system and web browser:

- Windows XP SP1 or higher or Windows 2000 SP4 or higher

- Internet Explorer 6.0 SP1 or higher

- Mozilla Firefox 2.0.0.11 or later

Note   Internet Explorer 6.0 SP1 or higher is the only browser supported for accessing the controller GUI and for using web authentication.

Software Requirements

The Cisco WiSM requires software release SWISMK9-32 or later. The Supervisor 720 12.2(18)SXF2 supports the Cisco WiSM software Release 3.2.78.4 or later, and the Supervisor 720 12.2(18)SXF5 (Cisco IOS Software Modularity) supports the Cisco WiSM software Release 4.0.155.5 (with Cisco IOS Software Modularity). If you want to use the Cisco WiSM in the Cisco 7609 and 7613 Series Routers, the routers must be running Cisco IOS Release 12.2(18)SXF5 or later.

The Cisco WLC Network Module is supported on Cisco 28/37/38xx Series Integrated Services Routers running Cisco IOS Release 12.4(11)T2, 12.4(11)T3, and 12.5.

If you want to use the controller in the Catalyst 3750G WLC Switch, the switch must be running Cisco IOS Release 12.2.25.FZ or 12.2(25)SEE.

The 2112 and 2125 controllers are supported for use only with Software Release 5.1.151.0 or later.

Lightweight AP Models

The lingo for the APs can be tricky, but overall it is simple. APs come in two types or groups. Simply put, one group requires a controller to operate, and the other group does not. The APs that do not require a controller to operate also utilize IOS as their operating system. The exception to this rule is Remote-Edge AP (REAP) and Hybrid Remote Edge Access Point (H-REAP), which are discussed in the 1030 Section of this chapter. Table 2-1 summarizes the differences between lightweight and autonomous APs.

Table 2-1   *Typical Naming Conventions Based on Wireless Technology*

Lightweight	Autonomous
Thin	Thick
LWAPP/CAPWAP	IOS
Controller Based	Standalone
Airespace	Aironet

Cisco Aironet APs

Cisco Aironet APs provide secure, manageable, and reliable wireless connectivity with exceptional range and performance. Wi-Fi certified for interoperability with a variety of client devices, these APs support robust 802.11a/b/g connectivity for indoor and outdoor environments.

These lightweight APs—APs that have been converted to run LWAPP—operate with Cisco WLCs to address the security, deployment, management, and control issues facing large-scale enterprise wireless LANs (WLANs).

As key elements of the Cisco Unified Wireless Network—an integrated, end-to-end wired and wireless network solution—Cisco Aironet APs offer comprehensive capabilities, including the following:

■   Wireless voice over IP

- Guest access

- Wireless intrusion detection and intrusion prevention

- Scalable Layer 3 roaming

- Location services

Aironet 1250 Series

You can deploy existing wireless technologies with the confidence that your network investment will extend to support emerging and future wireless technologies. The Cisco Aironet 1250 Series AP is a modular platform designed to make field upgrades easy and to support various wireless capabilities.

The Aironet 1250 Series is the first enterprise-class AP to support the IEEE 802.11n draft 2.0 standard. These APs do the following:

- Offer combined data rates of up to 600 Mbps to provide users with mobile access to high-bandwidth data, voice, and video applications regardless of their location. Keep in mind that the 1250 AP really only provides optimum performance data rate at approximately 300 Mbps.

- Use multiple-input multiple-output (MIMO) technology to provide reliable and predictable WLAN coverage.

- Improve user experience for both existing 802.11a/b/g clients and new 802.11n clients.

The Aironet 1250 Series is part of the Cisco Unified Wireless Network, a comprehensive solution that unifies the wired and wireless network to accomplish these tasks:

- Deliver a common set of services and applications

- Provide a single experience for any mode of network connectivity

- Offer simplified operational management

Aironet 1240 Series

Cisco Aironet 1240AG Series IEEE 802.11a/b/g APs deliver the versatility, high capacity, security, and enterprise-class features that WLAN customers demand. Designed specifically for challenging RF environments such as factories, warehouses, and large retail establishments, it has the versatility associated with connected antennas, a rugged metal enclosure, and a broad operating temperature range.

The Aironet 1240AG Series is available in three versions:

- A lightweight version

- An autonomous version that can be field-upgraded to lightweight operation

■ A single-band 802.11g version for use in regulatory domains that do not allow 802.11a/5 GHz operation

The product comes complete with all the mounting hardware necessary for a secure, rugged installation. The mounting bracket locks the AP as well as the Ethernet and console cables in place to prevent theft and tampering.

Aironet 1230 Series

The Cisco Aironet 1230AG Series delivers the versatility, high capacity, security, and enterprise-class features required in more challenging RF environments. It is designed for WLANs in rugged environments or installations that require specialized antennas, and it features dual-antenna connectors for extended range, coverage versatility, and more flexible installation options. The Cisco Aironet 1230AG Series combines antenna versatility with industry-leading transmit power, receives sensitivity, and delays spread for high multipath and indoor environments, providing reliable performance and throughput for the most demanding requirements.

Aironet 1200 Series

The Cisco Aironet 1200 Series AP is a single-band lightweight or autonomous AP with dual diversity antenna connectors for challenging RF environments. It offers the same versatility, high capacity, security, and enterprise-class features demanded by industrial WLAN customers in a single-band 802.11g solution. The modular device provides the flexibility to field-upgrade to a dual-band 802.11a/g network by adding a CardBus-based 802.11a upgrade module that can be easily installed into Cisco Aironet 1200 Series APs originally configured for 802.11g. The device is available in either a lightweight version or an autonomous version that can be field-upgraded to lightweight operation.

Aironet 1100 Series

Extend security, reliability, and scalability to the WLAN with an integrated wired and wireless framework. The Cisco Aironet 1100 Series offers customers an easy-to-install, single-band 802.11b/g AP that features enterprise-class management, security, and scalability. The device is available in an autonomous or lightweight version and is ideal for deployment in offices and similar environments.

Aironet 1130AG Series

The Cisco Aironet 1130AG Series packages high capacity, high security, and enterprise-class features delivering WLAN access for a low total cost of ownership. Designed for WLAN coverage in offices and similar RF environments, this unobtrusive AP features integrated antennas and dual IEEE 802.11a/g radios for robust and predictable coverage, delivering a combined capacity of 108 Mbps. The competitively priced Cisco Aironet 1130AG Series is ready to install and easy to manage, reducing the cost of deployment and ongoing maintenance.

Aironet 1140N Series

The Cisco Aironet 1140N is the next generation dual-band AP targeting indoor, carpeted area RF applications that are typically found in the ideal office space. The primary function of the 1140N series AP is that it is a dual-band AP with integrated 802.11n radios and integrated antennas.

Aironet 1300 Series

The Cisco Aironet 1300 Series Outdoor AP/Bridge is a flexible platform with the capability of AP, bridge, and workgroup bridge functionality. The Cisco Aironet 1300 Series provides high speed and cost-effective wireless connectivity between multiple fixed or mobile networks and clients. Building a metropolitan area wireless infrastructure with the Cisco Aironet 1300 Series offers deployment personnel a flexible, easy-to-use solution that meets the security requirements of wide area networking professionals. Typical applications for the Aironet 1300 Series are as follows:

- Network connections within a campus area

- Outdoor infrastructure for mobile networks and users

- Public access for outdoor areas

- Temporary networks for portable or military operations

The Cisco Aironet 1300 Series supports the 802.11b/g standard—providing 54 Mbps data rates with a proven, secure technology. Cisco makes the maintenance and installation of the 1300 Series easy by integrating it with your wired network. Based on the Cisco IOS operating system, the Cisco Aironet 1300 Series has advanced features such as Fast Secure Layer 2 Roaming, QoS, and VLANs. This series has the following key benefits:

- Configurable for AP, bridge, or workgroup bridge roles

- Support for both point-to-point or point-to-multipoint configurations

- Enhanced security mechanisms based on 802.1x standards

- Ruggedized enclosure optimized for harsh outdoor environments with extended operating temperature range

- Integrated or optional external antennas for deployment flexibility

Aironet 1400 Series

The Cisco Aironet 1400 Wireless Bridge creates a new benchmark for wireless bridging by providing a high-performance and feature-rich solution for connecting multiple LANs in a metropolitan area. Building a metropolitan area wireless infrastructure with the Cisco Aironet 1400 gives deployment personnel a flexible, easy-to-use solution that meets the security requirements of wide area networking professionals. Designed to be a cost-effective alternative to leased lines, it is engineered specifically for harsh outdoor environments.

The Cisco Aironet 1400 Wireless Bridge is the premier high-speed, high-performance outdoor bridging solution for line-of-sight applications, providing features such as these:

- Support for both point-to-point or point-to-multipoint configurations

- Industry-leading range and throughput, supporting data rates up to 54 Mbps

- Enhanced security mechanisms based on 802.11 standards

- Ruggedized enclosure optimized for harsh outdoor environments with extended operating temperature range

- Models with integrated antennas or models with connectors (must purchase an antenna, which is sold separately) for flexibility in deployment

- Designed specifically for ease-of-installation and operation

Aironet 1500 Series

Cisco Aironet 1500 Series lightweight outdoor mesh AP provides the security, manageability, reliability, and ease of deployment to create high-performance WLANs for outdoor wireless networks.

The Cisco Aironet 1500 Series operates with Cisco WLCs and Cisco Wireless Control System (WCS) Software, centralizing key functions of WLANs to provide scalable management, security, and mobility that is seamless between indoor and outdoor deployments. Designed to support zero-configuration deployments, the Cisco Aironet 1500 Series easily and securely joins the mesh network and is available to manage and monitor the network through the controller and WCS graphical or command-line interfaces (CLI). Compliant with Wi-Fi Protected Access 2 (WPA2) and employing hardware-based Advanced Encryption Standard (AES) encryption between wireless nodes, the Cisco Aironet 1500 Series provides end-to-end security.

Aironet 1520 Series

The Cisco Aironet 1520 Series wireless broadband platform is a high-performance outdoor wireless mesh product for a cost-effective, scalable, and secure deployment in outdoor environments such as municipalities, public safety environments, and oil and gas or other outdoor enterprises.

The Cisco Aironet 1520 Series delivers design innovation for radio versatility and provides flexibility for deploying wireless mesh networks in dynamic environments.

This platform has the following key features and benefits:

- **Versatile:** Provides a platform that enables mobility regardless of the frequency band required, with universal slots that allow for rapid development and integration of radio technology

- **Extensible:** Enables the broadband wireless infrastructure to easily and securely extend services to third-party devices such as IP cameras and automated meter readers in the harshest environmental conditions

- **Fortified:** Provides the highest standard of security with a secure rugged enclosure and the Cisco Self-Defending Network architecture

The 1520 Series wireless broadband platform operates with Cisco WLAN controllers and Cisco Wireless Control System (WCS) software, centralizing key functions of WLANs to provide scalable management, configuration, security, and transparent mobility between indoor and outdoor environments.

Airespace APs

This is the only portion of the book referring to Airespace and the 1000 series APs. Cisco acquired the company in early 2005 and consolidated the product line into the Aironet series. The premise behind the Aironet wireless network was that the APs would be in a standalone mode. Airespace took a different approach and developed a smaller and cheaper AP, often referred to as a thin or lightweight AP, which relied on a controller to function. The Airespace product line did not need as much hardware because it had a controller performing the majority of the functionality for the APs. For instance, the Aironet APs had faster processors and more memory because they had more tasks to perform and had to operate as a standalone unit.

Cisco found out it was able to develop the best AP by taking the benefits of both AP product lines and merging them. In addition, Cisco had already sold large numbers of the standalone AP models and needed a way for existing wireless customers to take advantage of this new technology. The solution here was to provide a conversion method for existing wireless customers. For these customers, Cisco developed code and a conversion utility so people had the option of converting their wireless network to a controller base network without purchasing all new equipment. As far as hardware, existing customers only needed to purchase a controller and convert their old IOS APs, and they had the new controller-based wireless technology. The new technology worked out for everyone in the long run, but it was even better for customers who had the original IOS-based APs. These units ended up being the core AP that Cisco would market and support. They also supported H-REAP, whereas the 1000 series could support only REAP.

The 1000 series APs are supported up to the 4.2.x software train. The older 1000 series APs are also labeled as AS1200. The AS letters referred to the Airespace company prior to Cisco acquiring the company. This model line, which is almost identical to the 1000 series, is last supported in the 4.0.x train. With that said, this chapter is going to briefly discuss the 1000 series; it will be the last reference to this series in the book. However, this does not mean to stop reading here if you do have a wireless network with the 1000 series APs. The functionality will still apply up to the versions mentioned earlier. You will still benefit greatly from this material, and much of it is still applicable to your current setup.

1010 Series APs

The 1010 offers two internal antennas and is the basic entry-level AP offered. This AP with the internal antennas was strictly for indoor applications.

1020 Series APs

The 1020 AP has two internal antennas and two connectors for the use of external antennas. This allows placement of antennas in environments that were not possible with the 1010 AP. The AP with external antennas allowed indoor and outdoor access.

1030 Series APs

The 1030 AP has two internal antennas and two connectors for the use of external antennas. This allows placement of antennas in environments that were not possible with the 1010 AP. The AP with external antennas allowed indoor and outdoor access. This device is also capable of performing a feature known as REAP. The idea behind a REAP is that it can be placed at branch offices to communicate with centrally located WLAN controllers. The REAP transverses the WAN to get to the centrally located controller. When the WAN connection breaks, the AP is still up and operational to provide wireless services. However, this service has limitations, which will be discussed in the AP 1000 Series Limitations Section.

AP 1000 Series Functionality Differences

The main difference between the 1010 and the 1020 is that the 1020 comes with external antenna adapters, whereas the 1010 does not. The 1010 has to use the internal dual omni-directional antennas that are built into the AP. The 1030 AP is comparable to the 1020 AP because it also contains external antenna adapters. The main difference between the 1020 and the 1030 is that the 1030 has the ability to perform REAP. This allows APs in remote offices or locations to remain active if the link to the controller goes down. REAP does have limitations, however, which is why H-REAP was developed. This will be discussed in the AP1000 Series Limitations Section and also in Chapter 5.

AP 1000 Series Limitations

The main requirement for the 1000 series AP is that it must run on controller version 4.2 or earlier. The support as far as software ends with 4.2.

The 1030 AP has REAP, Remote Edge Capability; with this in mind, there are limitations as outlined in Table 2-2.

Table 2-2 shows the various REAP mode features.

Table 2-2   *REAP Mode Features*

		REAP (Normal Mode)	REAP (Standalone Mode)
Protocols	IPv4	Yes	Yes
	IPv6	Yes	Yes
	All other protocols	Yes (only if client is also IP enabled)	Yes (only if client is also IP enabled)
	IP Proxy ARP	No	No
WLAN	Number of SSIDs[1]	16	1 (the first one)
	Dynamic channel assignment	Yes	No
	Dynamic power control	Yes	No
	Dynamic load balancing	Yes	No
VLAN	Multiple interfaces	No	No
	802.1Q support	No	No
WLAN Security	Rogue AP detection	Yes	No
	Exclusion list	Yes	Yes (existing members only)
	Peer-to-peer blocking	No	No
	IDS[2]	Yes	No
Layer 2 Security	MAC authentication	Yes	No
	802.1X	Yes	No
	WEP (64/128/152bits)	Yes	Yes
	WPA-PSK	Yes	Yes
	WPA2-PSK	Yes	No
	WPA-EAP	Yes	No
	WPA2-EAP	Yes	No

[1]*SSID = Service Set Identifier*

[2]*IDS = Intrusion Detection System*

(Continues)

Table 2-2 *REAP Mode Features (Continued)*

		REAP (Normal Mode)	REAP (Standalone Mode)
Layer 3 Security	Web authentication	No	No
	IPsec	No	No
	L2TP	No	No
	VPN pass-through	No	No
	Access control lists	No	No
QoS	QoS profiles	Yes	Yes
	Downlink QoS (weighted round-robin queues)	Yes	Yes
	802.1p support	No	No
	Per-user bandwidth contracts	No	No
	WMM	No	No
	802.11e (future)	No	No
	AAA QoS profile override	Yes	No
Mobility	Intra-subnet	Yes	Yes
	Inter-subnet	No	No
DHCP	Internal DHCP server	No	No
	External DHCP server	Yes	Yes
Topology	Direct connect (2006)	No	No

Lightweight Compared to Traditional Autonomous APs

There are immense differences between lightweight and traditional autonomous APs. This chapter touches on some of the major functionality differences, but the complete explanations are discussed in remaining chapters. Although the autonomous AP is an effective solution, it does lack some of the benefits of the controller-based solution. In certain niches, autonomous systems thrive. However, as the controller-based solutions continue to develop, these niches are disappearing. The Home Office AP will eliminate many of the drawbacks because it will offer a VPN solution without the necessity of an onsite controller.

Scalability

As you will see, one of the strongest advantages of the controllers is all the levels of scalability they can offer. You can easily integrate them in virtually any type of network. This does not mean you have to console or Telnet into the device and configure the unit prior to connecting to your network. The scalability factor offers you the benefit of placing an AP straight out of the box onto your network. The controller itself then configures and provisions the unit. If you want to further manage the AP, you can do so straight from the controller or from a WCS application.

Note   APs placed in different Layer 3 subnets of the controller require a discovery mechanism.

RRM

Radio Resource Management (RRM) allows the controller to dynamically control power and channel assignment of APs. Controllers can work together to ensure that your wireless network operates as smoothly as possible. RRM is quite comprehensive, so this book does not go into further detail until Chapter 12, "Radio Resource Management. RRM allows self-healing to take place if an AP fails. It also allows for the wireless network to adapt to RF interference or environmental issues.

Caution   RRM is *not* a substitute for a site survey.

General Overview of RRM

Along with the marked increase in the adoption of WLAN technologies, deployment issues have similarly risen. The 802.11 specification was originally architected primarily with a home, single-cell use in mind. The contemplation of the channel and power settings for a single AP was a trivial exercise, but as pervasive WLAN coverage became one user expectation, determining the settings for each AP necessitated a thorough site survey. Thanks to the shared nature of the 802.11 bandwidth, the applications that are now run over the wireless segment are pushing customers to move to more capacity-oriented deployments. The addition of capacity to a WLAN is an issue unlike that of wired networks, where the common solution is to throw bandwidth at the problem. Additional APs are required to add capacity, but if they are configured incorrectly, they can actually lower system capacity because of interference and other factors. As large-scale, dense WLANs have become the norm, administrators have continuously been challenged with these RF configuration issues that can increase operating costs. If handled improperly, this can lead to WLAN instability and a poor end user experience.

With a finite spectrum (a limited number of nonoverlapping channels) to play with and the innate desire of RF to bleed through walls and floors, designing a WLAN of any size has historically proven to be a daunting task. Even given a flawless site survey, RF is ever-changing; what might be an optimal AP channel and power schema one moment might prove to be less than functional the next.

Enter the Cisco RRM. RRM allows the Cisco Unified WLAN Architecture to continuously analyze the existing RF environment, automatically adjusting the AP power levels and channel configurations to mitigate such things as cochannel interference and signal coverage problems. RRM reduces the need to perform exhaustive site surveys, increases system capacity, and provides automated self-healing functionality to compensate for RF dead zones and AP failures.

Self-Healing Mechanism

Another huge benefit of the WLC is the automation of the self-healing process. When an AP radio fails, the other APs power their radios up and adjust channel selection of neighbor APs to compensate for the lost wireless coverage. You will learn more about this feature and others related to the self-healing mechanism in Chapter 12, but this determination is made when neighbor APs no longer see RF neighbor messages from the suspected failed AP. Although this sounds like a good idea in theory, deployment plays a major role for this feature to work. The system must be designed to support self-healing capabilities. Specifically, APs must be placed so that the system has at least one power level available to move up if RF self-healing is activated. If the deployment were too dense, a failing AP might actually be a benefit. On the other hand, if the deployment were not dense enough and the APs were already at the highest power level, powering up or changing channels is not going to benefit anyone.

WLC Features

The controller-based solution offers a range of features. With each passing day, more and more functionality is added to make the life of a wireless administrator easier or to allow more flexibility with the current networks. For instance, following are some of the newest features currently available:

■ **40-MHz channelization:** In controller software releases prior to 5.1.151.0, dynamic channel assignment (DCA) supports only those radios using 20-MHz channelization. In controller software Release 5.1.151.0, DCA is extended to support 802.11n 40-MHz channels in the 5-GHz band. 40-MHz channelization allows radios to achieve higher instantaneous data rates (potentially 2.25 times higher than 20-MHz channels).

Caution   DCA does not support radios using 40-MHz channelization in the 2.4-GHz band.

You can override the globally configured DCA channel width setting by statically configuring the radio of an AP for 20- or 40-MHz mode on the 802.11a/n Cisco APs > Configure page. If you ever change the static RF channel assignment method to Global on the AP radio, the global DCA configuration overrides the channel width configuration that the AP was previously using.

Caution   Cisco recommends that you do not configure 40-MHz channels in the 2.4-GHz radio band because severe cochannel interference can occur.

- **AP failover priority:** Each controller has a defined number of communication ports for APs. When multiple controllers with unused AP ports are deployed on the same network and one controller fails, the dropped APs automatically poll for unused controller ports and associate with them. Starting in controller software release 5.1.151.0, you can configure your wireless network so that the backup controller recognizes a join request from a higher-priority AP and if necessary disconnects a lower-priority AP as a means to provide an available port.

Caution   Failover priority takes effect only if the number of association requests following a controller failure exceeds the number of available backup controller ports.

- **EAP-FAST/802.1X supplicant:** You can configure 802.1X authentication between a Cisco Aironet 1130, 1240, or 1250 series AP and a Cisco switch. The AP acts as an 802.1X supplicant and is authenticated by the switch using EAP-FAST with anonymous PAC provisioning.

  The following switches and minimum software releases are currently supported for use with this feature:

  Cisco Catalyst 3560 Series Switches with Cisco IOS Release 12.2(35)SE5

  Cisco Catalyst 3750 Series Switches with Cisco IOS Release 12.2(40)SE

  Cisco Catalyst 4500 Series Switches with Cisco IOS Release 12.2(40)SG

  Cisco Catalyst 6500 Series Switches with Supervisor Engine 32 running Cisco IOS Release 12.2(33)SXH

- **NAC out-of-band integration:** The Cisco NAC Appliance, also known as Cisco Clean Access (CCA), is a network admission control (NAC) product that identifies whether machines are compliant with security policies and repairs vulnerabilities before permitting access to the network. In controller software releases prior to 5.1.151.0, the controller integrates with the NAC appliance only in in-band mode, where the NAC appliance must remain in the data path. For in-band mode, a NAC appliance is required at each authentication location (such as at each branch or for each controller), and all traffic must traverse the NAC enforcement point. In controller software release 5.1.151.0, the controller can integrate with the NAC appliance in out-of-band mode, where the NAC appliance remains in the data path only until clients have been analyzed and cleaned. Out-of-band mode reduces the traffic load on the NAC appliance and enables centralized NAC processing.

- **WAN link latency:** You can configure link latency on the controller to monitor the round-trip time of the LWAPP heartbeat packets (echo request and response) from the AP to the controller and back. This time can vary based on network link speed and controller processing loads. You can use this feature with all APs joined to the controller, but it is especially useful for hybrid-REAP APs, for which the link might be a slow or unreliable WAN connection.

For a more complete list of features, please consult the Cisco Command reference guide or the controller configuration guide.

Central Management

The WLCs offer much easier and varied device management than the conventional stand-alone or autonomous AP. A WLC can offer to management anywhere from 6 to 150 APs from a single WLC or a single connection. Currently, you can access the WLC using the following methods:

- Telnet

- Secure Shell (SSH)

- HTTP

- HTTPS

- Console

- Service Port (if applicable)

- Management VIA Wireless

As you can imagine, if your task were to configure IP addresses and host names on 100 APs, you would need to manually access each device or use network management software such as WLSE. However, WLSE offers a different kind of management and is limited in what it can do. This configuration request and much more can be accomplished from a single WLC that the APs are registered to. If more than one controller is in use, the WCS can come into play, which is discussed in more detail in Chapter 6, "Understanding the Troubleshooting Tools."

Cisco WCS

Cisco WCS is an ideal software application that is used for WLAN planning, configuration, and management. Cisco WCS provides a powerful foundation that allows IT managers to design, control, and monitor enterprise wireless networks from a centralized location, simplifying operations and reducing the total cost of ownership.

The Cisco WCS is an optional network component that works in conjunction with Cisco Aironet Lightweight APs, Cisco WLCs, and the Cisco Wireless Location Appliance. With Cisco WCS, network administrators have a single solution for RF prediction, policy provisioning, network optimization, troubleshooting, user tracking, security monitoring, and WLAN systems management. Robust graphical interfaces make WLAN deployment and operations simple and cost-effective. Detailed trending and analysis reports make Cisco WCS vital to ongoing network operations.

Cisco WCS includes tools for WLAN planning and design; RF management; location tracking; IDS; and WLAN systems configuration, monitoring, and management.

> **Note**   WCS is *not* a necessary component for a wireless network. WCS has no effect on the controllers or APs. Certain actions you perform on WCS can affect service; nevertheless, the WLC (hardware) does not depend on WCS (software).

Cisco Wireless Location Appliance

The Cisco Wireless Location Appliance is the first location solution in the industry that simultaneously tracks thousands of devices from within the WLAN infrastructure, bringing the power of a cost-effective, high-resolution location solution to critical applications such as these:

■ High-value asset tracking

■ IT management

■ Location-based security

This easy-to-deploy solution smoothly integrates with Cisco WLAN Controllers and Cisco lightweight APs to track the physical location of wireless devices to within a few meters. This appliance also records historical location information that can be used for location trending, rapid problem resolution, and RF capacity management.

The Cisco Wireless Location Appliance facilitates the deployment of new and important business applications by integrating tightly with a spectrum of technology and application partners through an open application programming interface (API). This integration helps enable the deployment of powerful location-based applications such as the following:

■ Enhanced 911 (E911) services

■ Asset management

■ Workflow automation

Customers deploying this solution include government organizations and enterprises in the health care, finance, retail, and manufacturing industries.

Cisco WCS Navigator

The Cisco WCS Navigator delivers an aggregated platform for enhanced scalability, manageability, and visibility of large-scale implementations of the Cisco Unified Wireless Network. This powerful, software-based solution gives network administrators cost-effective, easy access to information from multiple, geographically diverse Cisco WCS management platforms.

The Cisco WCS Navigator supports partitioning of the unified wireless network at the management level. It supports up to 20 Cisco WCS management platforms with manageability of up to 30,000 Cisco Aironet lightweight APs from a single management console. It runs on a server platform with an embedded database.

The Cisco WCS Navigator centralizes the operational control and management of multiple Cisco WCS management platforms. This easy-to-use platform delivers the following cross-system capabilities:

- Network monitoring

- Aggregated alarm notifications

- Automated browser redirect

- Simplified setup and configuration

- Quick and advanced searches

- Location tracking of client, Wi-Fi, and rogue devices

- Inventory reports

- Secure administrative access

In summary, the WCS Navigator manages multiple installations of WCS. It is the same approach as WCS monitoring and managing multiple WLCs. To understand the place of Navigator in a network, refer to Figure 2-7.

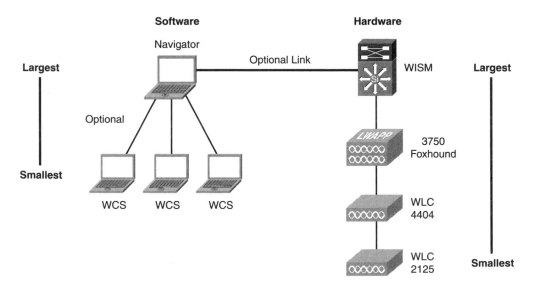

Figure 2-7   *Device Hierarchy*

Note   Navigator is just like WCS in that it is neither necessary nor affects the uptime of your wireless network if it is not functional or present.

Summary

As far as industry trends are considered, wireless networks are certainly in high demand and growing at a phenomenal rate. The wireless technology is also expanding at an astounding rate. The standardization of 802.11n and Outdoor/Indoor Mesh adds yet another chapter to wireless technology. Mesh networks allows cities to deploy wireless networks citywide. Mesh networks were designed primarily for private city use, but this is changing. Some cities have already proposed providing free wireless networking to the public. As time goes on, you will see continual deployments of wireless networks and further developments of the technology. Wireless networks are here to stay.

The wireless transport has certainly changed within the past few years. The introduction of LWAPP and the standardization of CAPWAP have drastically changed wireless. Prior wireless deployments were deployed as "Autonomous" systems. The downside to Autonomous systems was that they were standalone devices requiring configuration on a per-unit basis. In a hospital environment, for example, configuring and deploying more than 300 APs could take some time. Technology such as WLSE, WLSM, and WDS made these deployments a little easier; however, it still required a great deal of labor to install and tweak (adjust to the RF in your environments) a wireless network. This is usually one of the greater challenges. Although controller-based solutions did not eliminate this step, they certainly made it easier. On the plus side for the autonomous system, if you are installing wireless in a small site that requires only one or two APs, the autonomous system is a much more cost-effective solution. Since the controller-based wireless solution started becoming popular, it developed technologies such as REAP and H-REAP to cover this limitation; this book will discuss these concepts in Chapter 5. Regardless of the wireless system, a site survey is always recommended.

Chapter 3

Introduction to LWAPP

Traditional wireless LAN (WLAN) deployments used X number of access points (AP) spread across the premises that needed wireless coverage. With standalone, each AP was an individual entity that needed configuration, monitoring, provisioning, and so on. If these tasks were required for only a few devices, they would be manageable; however, when you are talking about a full enterprise WLAN that might be offering advanced services such as Voice over Wireless, the management of each AP becomes daunting.

You can add additional complexities to an enterprise WLAN, such as radio frequency (RF) management (dynamically adapt to changes in the environment) and security, which is critical in wireless because of the broadcast nature of the medium.

Unless some kind of coordination is put in place, enterprise WLANs will hit scalability and practical limitations sooner or later. The Lightweight Access Point Protocol (LWAPP) was designed to overcome those limitations and expand the feature set and uses of WLANs without increasing the management burden or weakening the security standpoint of the enterprise.

LWAPP is not a "general" solution. In some scenarios, a traditional AP is best—for example with Point to Point bridging, where no coordination or RF monitoring is needed because of the characteristics of the controlled environment for this deployment.

Defining LWAPP

Given the explosion in growth for wireless networks and the ubiquity that these services have in the current enterprise, vendors have implemented multiple approaches to simplify the operation and deployment of wireless services.

Proposed as a potential way of simplifying the operation of wireless networks, LWAPP has been implemented across the Cisco Unified Wireless Networks set of products (Wireless LAN Controller [WLC], APs, and related devices) from their initial software release until version 5.1. New versions, in particular 5.2, are using Control and Provisioning of Wireless Access Points (CAPWAP) as the base protocol.

Formally speaking, LWAPP is described in several drafts of the Internet Engineering Task Force (IETF) CAPWAP working group, the latest of which (at press time) is Version 4 (draft-ohara-capwap-lwapp-04.txt). Cisco Systems, Inc. submitted this draft for standardization in 2004, and through a protocol evolution, CAPWAP is the end result. Chapter 4, "The CAPWAP Protocol," covers CAPWAP in greater detail. Even though LWAPP never became an RFC standard like CAPWAP (http://www.ietf.org/rfc/rfc5415.txt) has, LWAPP is still a relevant and widely used protocol.

The ideas behind LWAPP are as follows:

- Move the traffic forwarding, certain security functions such as authentication, and policy functions from the edge (AP) toward a centralized point.

- Simplify the AP, because higher-level functions are now done separately, which reduces AP complexity and cost.

- Provide an encapsulation and transport mechanism for wireless traffic.

- Centralize AP configuration and management.

LWAPP is a way for an AP to communicate directly with a management entity—the WLC. This new approach to the wireless networks was designed to have nodes or points of presence throughout a network. These node devices would not require configuration and would rely on a master device for their configurations and instructions. These nodes would exist to provide a point in the network to which a wireless user can connect. After a user connects, all traffic going to this node would be sent to the master device. The master device would then determine where in the network or on what virtual LAN (VLAN) the packet needed to go. This approach offers many advantages over the single device configuration setup but requires a protocol to provide constant connectivity and direction for these devices to operate. LWAPP provides the solution.

Although in official standard documents the APs are referred to as wireless termination points (WTP) and the WLCs as access controllers (AC), this book uses the more commonly known terms AP and WLC, or controller, to refer to the "wireless" and "aggregation" points respectively, to make it easier to follow the discussions throughout the book.

In Chapter 13, "H-REAP," we will discuss that the forwarding model of "all traffic" is sent from the AP to the WLC, is true only for a particular mode of operation of LWAPP, and has additional hybrid modes to solve several design needs.

Quick Protocol Overview

Briefly, LWAPP operation is as follows:

Step 1.　AP tries to discover a list of valid WLCs with which to associate or *join*.

Step 2.　When this discovery process is successful, the AP selects a WLC and then tries to join it.

Step 3.   Upon join, the AP checks to see if the software version it is running matches that of the WLC. If it does not, the AP initiates an upgrade process (*image*).

Step 4.   If an image process was done, the AP reloads and goes through the discovery/join process again. If the AP now has the correct software version, it receives the configuration from the WLC.

Step 5.   Depending on the configuration received, the AP might need to do a reload (for example, the AP mode is changed) and pass through the discovery/join steps again.

Step 6.   After newly joining and confirming that it now has the correct configuration and image, the AP transitions into *run* status and starts servicing clients.

Step 7.   During this run status, the AP periodically sends RF and security monitoring information to the WLC for aggregation and processing.

LWAPP has two main traffic types, as seen in Figure 3-1:

■ **Control:** Management traffic between AP and WLC. It is a control channel for configuration, session management, firmware management, and so on. Traffic is encrypted and authenticated.

■ **Data:** Wireless traffic, encapsulated, sent between AP and WLC. You can make an analogy to a GRE-Tunnel.

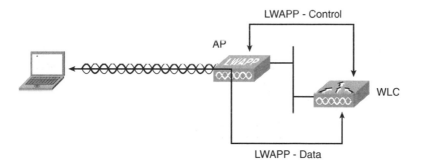

Figure 3-1   *LWAPP Traffic Types*

As Figure 3-2 and Figure 3-3 illustrate, LWAPP has two encapsulation types:

■ **Layer 2:** All communication between the AP and WLC is done on top of native 802.3 Ethernet frames, with an Ethertype of 0xbbbb or 0x88bb, depending on the release.

■ **Layer 3:** LWAPP is carried over IP/User Datagram Protocol (UDP), using port numbers 12222 and 12223 (data and control, respectively).

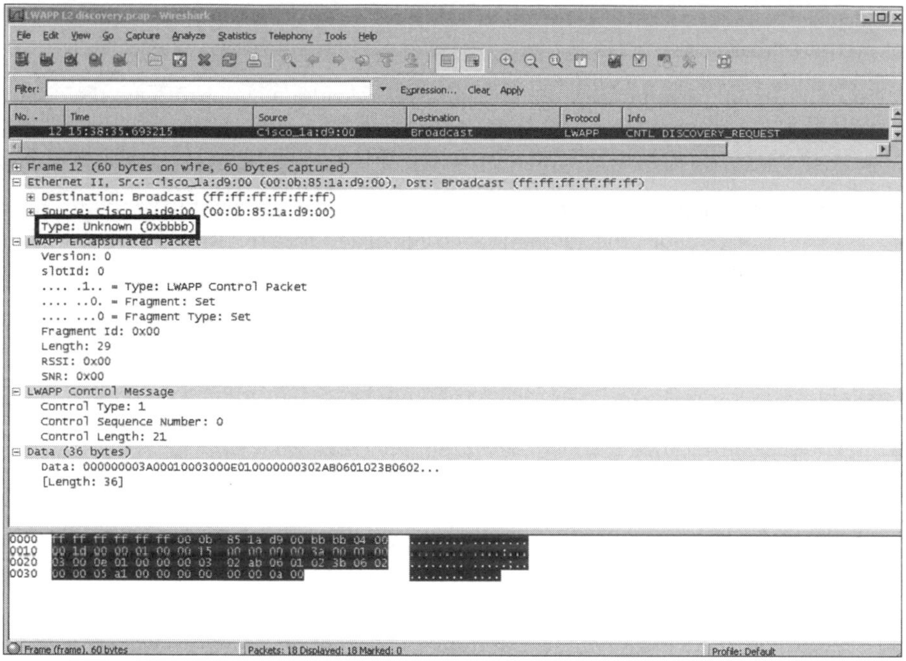

Figure 3-2 *LWAPP Layer 2 Encapsulation*

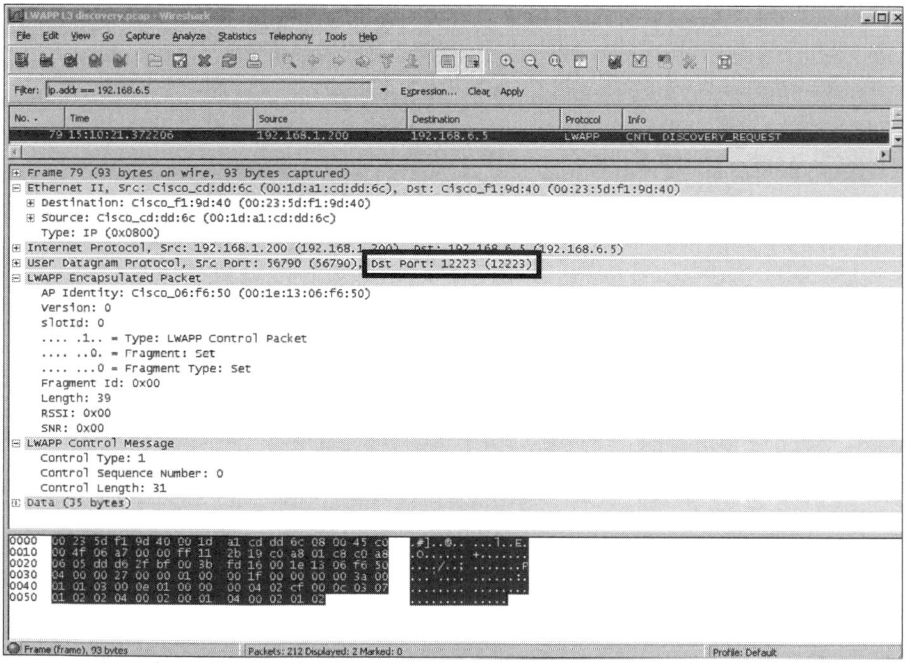

Figure 3-3 *LWAPP Layer 3 Encapsulation*

Layer 2 is mostly for legacy deployments; it is not supported on newer APs. It is depre-cated in code Releases 5.2 and higher, and it suffers from scalability issues. Layer 3 is the recommended mode of operation, where the WLC and APs have IP addresses.

Although LWAPP State Machine has several states, the most important ones are as follows:

■ **Discovery:** The AP is trying to learn a list of valid WLCs to join.

■ **Join:** The AP has determined the preferred WLC and is trying to join it.

■ **Image:** The AP has detected that it is not running the same version of software as the WLC, so it is updating its firmware.

■ **Configure:** The AP has joined a WLC and is now receiving new operating parame-ters/configuration.

■ **Run:** The AP has joined, is configured, and is using the same software version as the WLC. This is the normal state of operation.

LWAPP divides the work between the AP and the WLC and assigns different functions to each component (Split MAC Architecture):

■ **AP:** In charge of beacons, probe response, power management and buffering, sched-uling, queuing, 802.11 auth response, and encryption.

■ **WLC:** In charge of association processing, traffic forwarding to the network, reasso-ciation processing, classifying, 802.1x/EAP, and key handling.

Note Split MAC Architecture was the name initially used for LWAPP, using the acronym of SPAM, which you can still find in WLC debug messages such as the following:

```
Thu Aug 27 08:07:34 2009: 00:1d:a1:cd:dd:6c Length: 8/8 bytes (spamControlMsg_t)

Thu Aug 27 08:07:34 2009: Send AP Timesync of 1251360454 source MANUAL

Thu Aug 27 08:07:34 2009: 00:1d:a1:cd:dd:6c Length: 8/16 bytes
(spamEncodeTimesyncPayload)
```

For obvious reasons, the protocol was later renamed LWAPP, but in the code, you will still see SPAM as the name for the component handling LWAPP. This is not so easy to change.

The Split MAC Architecture is covered in more detail in Chapter 13.

LWAPP Advantages

As mentioned in the introduction to this chapter, as enterprise wireless networks grow, administration and management needs increase. You also need to keep a handle on the security of the wireless network as it grows. The infrastructure needs to be easily scala-ble to allow for painless, or nearly painless, growth.

Because LWAPP allows the 802.11 functionality to be split between the AP and the WLC, it provides a solution to each of these factors, as discussed in the following sections.

Management

AP management is one feature of LWAPP that is a huge departure from previous ways of doing things.

Originally, if a wireless network was composed of hundreds of APs, distributed across different floors in a building, each one needed individual monitoring, configuration, and RF coordination. This was a difficult task, and some products were designed to simplify this, like the Wireless LAN Solution Engine (WLSE), for example. WLSE offered a simplified view; however, APs were still "individual" units.

The emerging presence of WLCs and LWAPP provides a much easier method of AP management. In simple terms, the idea is that each WLC can offer management of anywhere from 6 to 150 APs. The WLC is a single point of aggregation, where

- Configuration is generated for all devices.

- All APs can forward raw operative data for aggregation.

- It is possible to enforce coordination between different RF parameters across all APs.

A WLC has a higher processing capability than an individual AP, which allows you to offer an even higher level of coordination among multiple WLCs. (Chapter 9, "Mobility," and Chapter 12, "Radio Resource Management," cover this in detail for mobility groups and RF groups, respectively.)

Of course, given a maximum capacity of 150 APs in current LWAPP-based WLC models, aggregation of operative data across each WLC must be available. The Wireless Control System (WCS) and WCS Navigator allow you to manage multiple WLCs from a single server. WCS and WCS Navigator are outside the scope of this book.

Note   5500 series WLCs can support up to 250 APs, but they require 6.0 code, which uses CAPWAP instead of LWAPP. To stay in line with LWAPP features, the maximum AP capacity of an LWAPP-based controller is 150.

Scalability

With AP management simplified, the wireless network can now be looked at from an operative point of view with WLCs in place of APs. This substantially reduces the number of individual units that must be administered.

Because LWAPP offers a separation between the existent LAN traffic and the "new" wireless traffic, it simplifies network planning and traffic handling.

Adding capacity to an existing wireless network can be seen as a process of physically studying the RF environment that needs to be covered (to properly add and place the APs) as well as adding WLCs to the mobility group to handle the added load. Through the inherent capabilities of LWAPP, the WLC will offer AP load distribution and failover features. AP load balancing and failover are covered in depth in Chapter 9.

Note Never forget a proper RF site survey.

WLCs using Radio Resource Management (RRM) can compensate for environmental changes and "fix" coverage problems, but they can never correct an RF deployment that was performed incorrectly in the first place.

Security

LWAPP-based systems offer several advantages over traditional individual deployments, including the following:

- Wireless traffic enters the network over a single point (WLC) instead of multiple ingress points (APs), making traffic inspection easier.

- The WLC is now responsible for acting as an authentication point (authenticator), so you now have to configure a single device instead of 100 to take care of authentication.

- An AP does not have a full configuration that can be extracted if someone has physical access to it. Also, no one can tamper with the configuration because it can only be configured from the WLC, using encrypted and authenticated LWAPP control messages.

- The WLC can authenticate the APs that try to join the wireless infrastructure to prevent the introduction of rogue APs with malicious intent.

This list accounts only for the inherent security features of LWAPP and not the different security processes that use LWAPP as encapsulation, such as rogue detection or Intrusion Detection Systems (IDS).

Mobility

Given a simplified deployment and management model, wireless systems became pervasive across the enterprise, opening new working models and applications where users and devices can have permanent network access all the time, in all areas. This opens a full range of new possibilities.

LWAPP systems believe it is critical that this new mobility is kept across different areas and inside the enterprise. Because the APs return all the RF and client information to their respective WLCs using the LWAPP tunnel, inter-controller communication allows all controllers in a mobility group to have information about the entire RF environment and the wireless clients. Several additional protocols allow interaction between standalone controllers, keeping the scalability and providing seamless roaming.

Table 3-1 summarizes the wireless network administration advantages that are inherent with an LWAPP-based wireless infrastructure.

Table 3-1   *LWAPP and Standalone AP Comparison*

	LWAPP WLAN	**Standalone AP WLAN**
Management	Centralized; can manage/configure up to 150 APs from a single controller.	Decentralized; have to touch each AP individually.
Scalability	Can easily add APs to the network. As soon as the AP is registered to the controller, it can start servicing wireless clients. Basically plug-and-play. AP failover and load balancing. Sharing of RF information.	Each new AP must be configured individually. Without WDS[1], WLSM[2], or WLSE, no sharing of RF information.
Security	Single network egress/ingress point for client traffic on the network. (Note that with H-REAP[3] deployments, this is not necessarily the case.) An LWAPP AP that is not connected to a controller cannot service wireless clients. WLC can authenticate APs to prevent rogue LAPs[4] from being on the network.	Multiple egress/ingress points. Each AP bridges client traffic to the wired network. Someone with physical access to the AP can reconfigure it for their own use.
Mobility	Client devices can L2/L3 roam seamlessly within the wireless network.	Must have a WLSM for L3 roaming.

[1]*WDS =Wireless Domain Services*

[2]*WLSM = Wireless Integrated Service Module*

[3]*H-REAP = Hybrid Remote Edge Access Point*

[4]*LAP = lightweight access point*

LWAPP Mechanics

To be able to find where an LWAPP-based system is failing, it is critical to understand how the underlying protocol works, because this lets you reduce the scope of investigation when a complex problem is reported.

This section covers two main parts:

- **LWAPP control path:** Covers AP discovery, join, maintenance, and states in detail.

- **LWAPP data path:** Covers client traffic. Because this is closely related to wireless client states, this will be covered in detail in Chapter 10, "Troubleshooting Client-Related Issues."

The discussion of the control path uses the LWAPP state machine as seen on APs and WLC, which is a simplified view of the one found on the LWAPP draft. Figure 3-4 illustrates the LWAPP state machine.

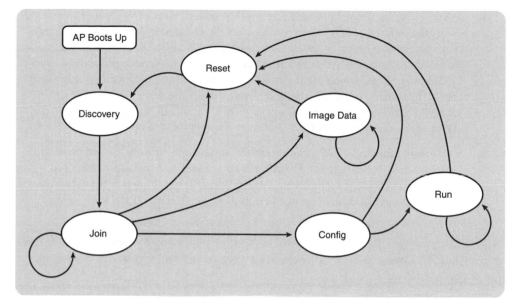

Figure 3-4   *LWAPP State Machine*

Discovery Process

The discovery process forms part of the "hunting" state. It covers several steps, and you might see variations depending on the AP model and software version.

The idea is that the AP will do the following:

Step 1.   **Make a list:** Obtain a list of possible destinations (WLCs) to send a discovery request.

Step 2.   **Send discovery:** On each of the possible available methods (described in the list that follows), the AP will send a discovery request.

Step 3.   **Wait for answers:** Collect the potential answers from the different methods used.

The conclusion of the discovery process is a list of potential destinations that will be passed down to join, after selecting the best candidate.

Discovery can use the following methods:

- **Local Broadcast Layer 2:** Used on 10x0 and 1510 APs that support the LWAPP Layer 2 protocol.

- **Local Broadcast Layer 3:** Supported by all APs, this discovery method uses UDP with destination 255.255.255.255.

- **Option 43:** Sent via Dynamic Host Control Protocol (DHCP) offer, it has a potential list of candidates (controller management IP addresses).

■ **DNS:** Taking the Domain Name System (DNS) servers from a DHCP offer or statically configured, the AP can try to resolve the CISCO-LWAPP-CONTROLLER hostname to obtain a list of the potential management IP addresses as destinations for a discovery request. The AP must have the correct domain name to properly query a DNS server. When using DHCP, this is Option 15. Without the proper domain name, the AP incorrectly queries for the fully qualified domain name (FQDN) CISCO-LWAPP-CONTROLLER. For example, if your DNS domain was company.com, the AP needs to query DNS for CISCO-LWAPP-CONTROLLER.company.com.

■ **Previously known:** The AP can "remember" up to 24 previously learned controllers and send discoveries to them. The AP will learn about any controllers from the mobility group configuration of the controller it is presently registered with. A single mobility group can contain up to 24 controllers. See Chapter 9 for more information.

Note   APs do have a good memory. From the WLC graphical user interface (GUI), if you select **Clear All Config** from the **Wireless > AP** page, the AP still remembers the previously known controllers.

One way of making the AP forget all previously known controllers is to use the **debug lwap console cli** command and then issue the **erase /all nvram:** command. The default username and password to access the AP CLI is "cisco" and "Cisco" respectively.

■ **Statically configured from WLC:** Beginning with Release 4.2, you can configure an IP address for the primary/secondary/tertiary controllers. Using this "priming" method, you can configure a WLC outside the present mobility group as a secondary/tertiary controller for the AP. Starting in Release 5.0, you can also configure global primary and secondary WLCs.

■ **Over the Air Provisioning (OTAP):** APs put the radios in "listening" mode to try to hear neighbor exchanges between nearby APs, learning a potential WLC destination IP address.

■ **Statically configured from AP CLI:** Accessing the AP CLI via the console port, you can configure the following static parameters:

```
lwapp ap ip address ip-addr subnet-mask

lwapp ap controller ip address ip-addr

lwapp ap hostname ap-hostname

lwapp ap ip default-gateway ip-addr
```

Be aware that the ability to enter these static commands from the AP CLI is disabled after the AP has joined a WLC. You have to clear the APs configuration to re-enable them.

Some of the discovery steps have dependencies. For example, you must obtain an IP address to be able to use LWAPP Layer 3 discovery. In addition, an AP will not use DNS if no DNS information is received in a DHCP offer or statically configured, so the actual steps the AP performs might change depending on the network configuration.

In the discovery request from the AP, an element identifies the discovery mechanism that the AP used to locate the controller. The value of the IE 58 parameter indicates the discovery type:

- **0:** broadcast (L2/L3)
- **1:** configured
- **2:** OTAP
- **3:** DHCP server
- **4:** DNS

Example 3-1 shows the output of **debug lwapp packet enable** from the WLC CLI for an AP that is trying to register with a WLC.

Example 3-1   *debug lwapp packet enable Command Output*

```
(Cisco Controller) >debug lwapp packet enable
Tue May 23 12:37:50 2006: Start of Packet
Tue May 23 12:37:50 2006: Ethernet Source MAC (LRAD):      00:0B:85:51:5A:E0
Tue May 23 12:37:50 2006: Msg Type      :
Tue May 23 12:37:50 2006:     DISCOVERY_REQUEST
Tue May 23 12:37:50 2006: Msg Length    :   31
Tue May 23 12:37:50 2006: Msg SeqNum    :   0
Tue May 23 12:37:50 2006:
IE            :   UNKNOWN IE 58
Tue May 23 12:37:50 2006:   IE Length    :   1
Tue May 23 12:37:50 2006:   Decode routine not available, Printing Hex Dump
Tue May 23 12:37:50 2006: 00000000: 00
```

The IE 58 parameter value in Example 3-1 is 1, indicating that the AP was configured with this particular WLC management IP address.

The following sections discuss the LWAPP discovery methods in more detail.

Layer 2/Layer 3 Broadcast Discovery

With Layer 2 LWAPP discovery, the important fact to remember is that this is hardly ever used anymore and is LWAPP only. It is mentioned here because it is part of the LWAPP discovery process and can be seen in traces and debugs. It occurs on the same subnet as the AP and uses encapsulated Ethernet frames containing MAC addresses for communications between the AP and the controller. Only Cisco 1000 Series LAPs support Layer 2 LWAPP mode. Also, Layer 2 LWAPP mode is not supported on Cisco 2100 Series WLCs or Wireless Integrated Service Modules (WiSM). These WLCs support only Layer 3 LWAPP mode.

This is the first method that a LAP uses to discover a WLC. The LAPs that support Layer 2 LWAPP mode broadcast an LWAPP discovery request message in a Layer 2 LWAPP frame, as you saw in Figure 3-2. If there is a WLC in the network configured for Layer 2 LWAPP mode, the controller responds with a discovery response. The LAP then moves to the join phase of the LWAPP state machine.

The **debug lwapp events enable** command output shown in Example 3-2 shows the sequence of events that occur when a LAP using Layer 2 LWAPP mode registers with the WLC.

Example 3-2   *debug lwapp events enable L2 Discovery*

```
!--The WLC receives the L2 discovery request from the AP. You can tell
!  this is an L2 discovery because the destination is the broadcast
!  MAC address ff:ff:ff:ff:ff:ff


Thu Sep 27 00:24:25 2007: 00:0b:85:51:5a:e0 Received LWAPP DISCOVERY REQUEST
from AP 00:0b:85:51:5a:e0 to ff:ff:ff:ff:ff:ff on port '2'


!--The WLC responds with the LWAPP discovery response.


Thu Sep 27 00:24:25 2007: 00:0b:85:51:5a:e0 Successful transmission of
LWAPP Discovery-Response to AP 00:0b:85:51:5a:e0 on Port 2


!--The AP enters the Join state of the LWAPP state machine and sends a join
request to
!--the WLC.


Thu Sep 27 00:24:40 2007: 00:0b:85:51:5a:e0 Received LWAPP JOIN REQUEST
from AP 00:0b:85:51:5a:e0 to 00:0b:85:48:53:c0 on port '2'
Thu Sep 27 00:24:40 2007: 00:0b:85:51:5a:e0 AP ap:51:5a:e0:
txNonce  00:0B:85:48:53:C0 rxNonce  00:0B:85:51:5A:E0
Thu Sep 27 00:24:40 2007: 00:0b:85:51:5a:e0 LWAPP Join-Request MTU path from
AP 00:0b:85:51:5a:e0 is 1500, remote debug mode is 0
Thu Sep 27 00:24:40 2007: 00:0b:85:51:5a:e0 Successfully added NPU Entry for
AP 00:0b:85:51:5a:e0 (index 48)Switch IP: 0.0.0.0, Switch Port: 0, intIfNum 2,
vlanId 0AP IP: 0.0.0.0, AP Port: 0, next hop MAC: 00:0b:85:51:5a:e0


!--The WLC has added an NPU entry for the AP and sends the join response.


Thu Sep 27 00:24:40 2007: 00:0b:85:51:5a:e0 Successfully transmission of
LWAPP Join-Reply to AP 00:0b:85:51:5a:e0


!--The AP registers to the WLC.


Thu Sep 27 00:24:40 2007: 00:0b:85:51:5a:e0 Register LWAPP event for
```

```
AP 00:0b:85:51:5a:e0 slot 0
Thu Sep 27 00:24:40 2007: 00:0b:85:51:5a:e0 Register LWAPP event for
AP 00:0b:85:51:5a:e0 slot 1
12:03 PM 3/1/2009
```

The next discovery mechanism, Layer 3 LWAPP discovery, occurs on different subnets from the AP and uses IP addresses and UDP packets rather than the MAC addresses used by Layer 2 discovery. This is the more common method and should be referred to as the standard.

Example 3-3 shows the output of **debug lwapp events enable** during a Layer 3 discovery by an AP.

Example 3-3   *debug lwapp events enable L3 Discovery*

```
(Cisco Controller) >debug lwapp events enable
!—-Notice how the discovery request is sent to a specific MAC address as opposed
to the
!—-L2 broadcast MAC ff:ff:ff:ff:ff:ff.

(Cisco Controller) >Thu Aug 27 08:07:20 2009: 00:1e:13:06:f6:50 Received LWAPP
DISCOVERY REQUEST from AP 00:1e:13:06:f6:50 to 00:1f:9e:9b:3e:40 on port '1'
Thu Aug 27 08:07:20 2009: 00:1e:13:06:f6:50 Successful transmission of LWAPP
Discovery Response to AP 00:1e:13:06:f6:50 on port 1


!—-Although deprecated, the L2 broadcast discovery from the AP is seen in the
debugs.


Thu Aug 27 08:07:20 2009: 00:1e:13:06:f6:50 Received LWAPP DISCOVERY REQUEST from
AP 00:1e:13:06:f6:50 to ff:ff:ff:ff:ff:ff on port '1'


!—-The rest of the discovery and join process continues until the AP is regis-
tered to the WLC.


Thu Aug 27 08:07:20 2009: 00:1e:13:06:f6:50 Successful transmission of LWAPP
Discovery Response to AP 00:1e:13:06:f6:50 on port 1
Thu Aug 27 08:07:32 2009: 00:1e:13:06:f6:50 Received LWAPP JOIN REQUEST from AP
00:1e:13:06:f6:50 to 06:0a:10:10:00:00 on port '1'
Thu Aug 27 08:07:32 2009: 00:1e:13:06:f6:50 AP AP001d.a1cd.dd6c: txNonce
00:1F:9E:9B:3E:40 rxNonce  00:1E:13:06:F6:50
Thu Aug 27 08:07:32 2009: 00:1e:13:06:f6:50 LWAPP Join Request MTU path from AP
00:1e:13:06:f6:50 is 1500, remote debug mode is 0
Thu Aug 27 08:07:32 2009: DTL Adding AP 0 - 192.168.6.11
Thu Aug 27 08:07:32 2009: 00:1e:13:06:f6:50 Successfully added NPU Entry for AP
00:1e:13:06:f6:50 (index 0)
Switch IP: 192.168.6.6, Switch Port: 12223, intIfNum 1, vlanId 0
AP IP: 192.168.6.11, AP Port: 56790, next hop MAC: 00:1d:a1:cd:dd:6c
```

(continues)

Example 3-3 *debug lwapp events enable L3 Discovery (continued)*

```
Thu Aug 27 08:07:32 2009: 00:1e:13:06:f6:50 Successful transmission of LWAPP Join
Reply to AP 00:1e:13:06:f6:50
Thu Aug 27 08:07:32 2009: 00:1e:13:06:f6:50 spam_lrad.c:1486 - Operation State 0
===> 4
Thu Aug 27 08:07:32 2009: 00:1e:13:06:f6:50 Register LWAPP event for AP
00:1e:13:06:f6:50 slot 0
```

DHCP Options 43 and 60

Any DHCP server can pass this option to an AP, including Cisco switches and routers.

When an AP requests an IP address from a DHCP server, the DHCP discover from the AP contains a Vendor Class Identifier (VCI). If the DHCP server has Option 60 and 43 correctly configured, the DHCP offer includes one or more IP addresses for the management interface of a WLC(s). Option 60 on the DHCP server is configured to correspond to the VCI string of the AP model that you are using. When the DHCP server receives a DHCP discover or request from an AP with the correct VCI string matching that of Option 60, it knows to return Option 43, which is the WLC management IP address, to the AP in the DHCP offer.

Although you can use pretty much any DHCP server for this discovery method, you will learn here how to set up Option 60 and Option 43 using a Cisco switch as the DHCP server. For more DHCP server configurations, please see Cisco Document ID 97066, "DHCP OPTION 43 for Lightweight Cisco Aironet Access Points Configuration Example" at Cisco.com.

The Cisco 1000 Series APs use a string format for DHCP Option 43, whereas the Aironet APs use the type, length, value (TLV) format for DHCP Option 43. DHCP servers must be programmed to return the option based on the AP DHCP VCI string (DHCP Option 60). Table 3-2 lists the VCI strings for Cisco APs that can operate in lightweight mode.

The format of the TLV block is as follows:

- **Type:** 0xf1 (decimal 241).

- **Length:** Number of controller IP addresses * 4 (number of octets).

- **Value:** List of WLC management interfaces. Remember that this is the IP address of the management interface, not the AP-Manager IP address.

Example 3-4 shows configuring DHCP Option 43 and 60 on a Cisco IOS switch for 1240 series AP. Without configuring Option 60, the DHCP server would never pass Option 43 to the AP. Look at Option 60 as a condition. If the device requesting an IP address is this type of device, the DHCP offer will include the IP address in the Option 43 field.

Table 3-2 *Cisco AP VCI Strings*

Access Point	Vendor Class Identifier	Option 43 Format
Cisco Aironet 1000 Series	Airespace.AP1200	ascii
Cisco Aironet 1100 Series	Cisco AP c1100	hex
Cisco Aironet 1130 Series	Cisco AP c1130	hex
Cisco Aironet 1200 Series	Cisco AP c1200	hex
Cisco Aironet 1240 Series	Cisco AP c1240	hex
Cisco Aironet 1250 Series	Cisco AP c1250	hex
Cisco Aironet 1300 Series	Cisco AP c1300	hex
Cisco Aironet 1500 Series	Cisco AP c1500[1] Cisco AP.OAP1500[2] Cisco AP.LAP1505[3] Cisco AP.LAP1510[4] Cisco AP c1520 Airespace.AP1200[5]	ascii for 1500, hex for 1520
Cisco 3201 Lightweight Access Point	Cisco AP C3201 WMIC[6]	hex
AP801 (embedded in 86x/88x series ISRs[7]	Cisco AP 801	hex

[1]*Any 1500 Series AP running 4.1 software*

[2]*1500 OAP AP running 4.0 software*

[3]*1505 Model AP running 4.0 software*

[4]*1510 Model AP running 4.0 software*

[5]*Any 1500 Series AP running 3.2 software*

[6]*WMIC =Wireless Mobile Interface Card*

[7]*ISR =Integrated Services Router*

Example 3-4 *Cisco IOS Switch DHCP Option 60 and 43 Example*

```
ip dhcp excluded-address 192.168.6.1 192.168.6.10
!
ip dhcp pool vlan6    network 192.168.6.0 255.255.255.0
   default-router 192.168.6.1
   option 60 ascii "Cisco AP c1240"
   option 43 hex f104.c0a8.0605
```

In this example, DHCP Option 60 is correctly using the VCI string for the 1240 series AP. The Option 43 line is the TLV. As you can see, the Type is F1, the Length indicates 1 WLC IP address ($1 \times 4 = 04$), and Value is the WLC management IP converted to hex, c0a80605. The WLC IP is 192.168.6.5.

Note   The Cisco IOS DHCP servers allow only one Option 43 definition. This means you can have only one device type for each DHCP address pool, so only one AP type can be supported for each DHCP address pool.

You can configure DHCP servers to return WLC IP addresses in vendor-specific Option 43 in the DHCP offer to lightweight Cisco APs. When the AP gets an IP address through DHCP, the AP looks for WLC IP addresses in the Option 43 field in the DHCP offer. The AP sends a unicast LWAPP discovery message to each of the WLCs that are listed in DHCP Option 43. WLCs that receive the LWAPP discovery request messages unicast an LWAPP discovery response to the AP. Each of the WLCs that receives the LWAPP discovery request message replies with a unicast LWAPP discovery response to the AP.

Figure 3-5 shows a DHCP request with Option 60 and the DHCP over with Option 43.

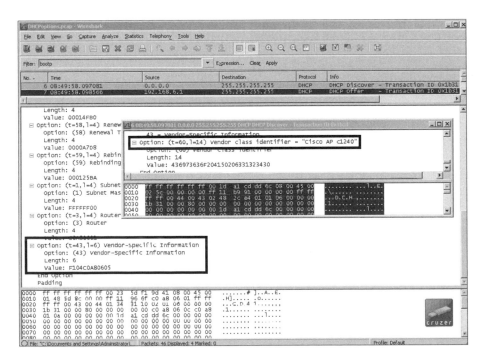

Figure 3-5   *DHCP with Option 60 and 43*

In Figure 3-5, you can see both the DHCP discover (inset) from the AP and the DHCP offer from the switch. Notice the Option 60 VCI string in the DHCP discover packet.

Because the DHCP server received Option 60 from the AP, it returns Option 43 in hex. The AP converts this hex value to the IP address of 192.168.6.5.

DNS

The AP can discover controllers through your DNS. For the AP to do so, you must configure your DNS to return controller management IP addresses in response to a DNS query, nslookup, for CISCO-LWAPP-CONTROLLER.localdomain, where localdomain is the AP domain name, that is, company.com. When an AP receives DNS server information and the domain name (Option 15) in a DHCP offer, it can perform an **nslookup** to resolve CISCO-LWAPP-CONTROLLER.localdomain. When the DNS response returns a list of controller management IP addresses, the AP sends discovery requests to the controllers.

Priming

If the AP was previously associated to a controller, the IP addresses of the primary, secondary, and tertiary controllers can be stored in the nonvolatile memory of the AP. This process of storing controller IP addresses on an AP for later deployment is called priming the AP. Some deployments might have limitations in which you cannot configure DNS or DHCP options. In these cases you can place an AP in a network where the controller is already configured and can join it easily. After the AP joins the WLC, you can configure it as needed and even add a static IP address. You can configure the AP with primary/secondary/tertiary controller information using either the WLC GUI or the CLI. To configure this using the CLI, use the following commands:

```
config ap primary-base WLC System Name AP Name WLC Mngt IP
config ap secondary-base WLC System Name AP Name WLC Mngt IP
config ap tertiary-base WLC System Name AP Name WLC Mngt IP
```

The key element here is that the controller it is going to join must be a member of the current WLC mobility group.

OTAP

If the OTAP feature is enabled on the controller (on the Controller, General page), the controller will accept AP discoveries with an IE 58 value of 2. All associated APs transmit wireless LWAPP neighbor messages, and new APs receive the controller IP address from these messages over the air. This feature is disabled by default and should remain disabled after all APs are installed.

Note   You can find additional information about OTAP at http://tinyurl.com/knofho.

Controller Details Learned During the Discovery Process

In the discovery responses, the AP receives several details that it will use later in the join process:

- Controller system name

- Controller type

- Max AP capacity

- Active APs

- AP manager address or addresses (see Chapter 7, "Deploying and Configuring the Wireless LAN Controller")

- AP load per AP-manager interface

- Master controller flag

The "Dissecting the Discovery Response" section, later in this chapter, reviews the fields sent in the discovery response. Those fields can be quite useful for troubleshooting.

The WLC evaluates several conditions before answering the discovery request:

- **Invalid VLAN:** If broadcast discovery requests are received via a VLAN in which the WLC does not have a management interface, they are discarded. The exception is for WLCs in link aggregation (LAG) mode; if the AP-Manager and management interfaces are on different VLANs, the WLC accepts broadcast discovery frames on the AP-Manager VLAN. Chapter 7 explains LAG in detail.

- **Resource conservation mode:** If the WLC is doing AP upgrades, it limits the number of APs that can join, regardless of the platform limit.

- **MAX AP reached:** If the maximum number of supported APs is reached, new APs are rejected. In code Release 5.1 and higher, you can, however, configure AP join priorities so that if critical APs need to join, the WLC can drop an AP with a lower priority so the higher priority AP can join. The WLC CLI command to set the priority is as follows:

  ```
  config ap priority { 1 ¦ 2 ¦ 3 ¦ 4} AP Name
  ```

A priority of 1 is the lowest, and a priority of 4 is the highest.

> **Note**   To avoid high CPU or memory utilization problems, during resource conservation mode, the WiSM/4400 will handle a maximum of 10 simultaneous APs. The 2100/NM-WLC will handle a maximum of 5 simultaneous APs.

Join Process

At the end of the discovery process, the AP has a list of potential WLC candidates that can be selected for the join process.

The AP selects the WLC using the following criteria, in order of precedence:

- If the AP has primary/secondary/tertiary or global backup WLC names configured, it tries to match them to the system name provided in the discovery response, in that order.

- If none of the system names match or none of them have been configured, the AP sees if any of the WLCs it has learned about through the various discovery methods have the "Master Controller" flag set. If so, the AP sends a join request to the Master Controller.

- If no WLC is found with the master flag set, the AP selects the WLC with the most available capacity from its list of discovered WLCs.

> **Note**   The name selection is done against the system name, not against a DNS name for the WLC. The distinction is quite important, and it is a common configuration mistake. You can see the system name in the home page of the GUI, or you can do a **show sysinfo** command as shown in Example 3-5.

Example 3-5 *WLC System Name shown in show sysinfo Command Output*

```
(Cisco Controller) >show sysinfo

Manufacturer's Name............................. Cisco Systems Inc.
Product Name.................................... Cisco Controller
Product Version................................. 4.2.207.0
RTOS Version.................................... 4.2.207.0
Bootloader Version............................. 4.0.217.0
Build Type..................................... DATA + WPS


System Name.................................... Cisco_9b:3e:43
System Location................................
System Contact.................................
System ObjectID................................ 1.3.6.1.4.1.14179.1.1.4.3
IP Address..................................... 192.168.6.5
System Up Time................................. 0 days 0 hrs 36 mins 21 secs


Configured Country............................. US  - United States
Operating Environment.......................... Commercial (0 to 40 C)
Internal Temp Alarm Limits..................... 0 to 65 C
Internal Temperature........................... +38 C
!--remaining output omitted for brevity
```

The join request contains the AP certificate, AP name, location, and radios installed. It is normally large, so it will be fragmented in at least two frames when it is sent from the AP side.

The WLC evaluates several conditions before answering the join request:

- **Resource conservation mode:** If the controller is doing AP upgrades, it limits the number of APs that can join, regardless of the maximum limit of the platform.

- **MAX AP reached:** If the maximum number of APs is reached, new APs are rejected. Again, AP join priority can override this in 5.1 and higher code releases.

- **AAA:** If AP authorization is enabled, the controller tries to authenticate the AP MAC against the Authentication, Authorization, and Accounting (AAA) subsystem.

- **Certificate validation:** In the LWAPP join request, the AP embeds a digitally signed X.509 certificate. When the certificate is validated, the WLC sends an LWAPP join response to indicate to the AP that it is successfully joined to the controller. The WLC embeds its own digitally signed X.509 certificate in the LWAPP join response that the AP must validate. Make sure you have configured the time, date, and year correctly on your WLC or the certificate validation will fail.

Image Process

This is an optional phase, where APs download a new image from the WLC. This is normally triggered if the AP software version number does not match the version number that the WLC provides.

For 1000 series and 1510 APs, you might see that after a network down situation, or on stranded mesh APs, this family of APs might trigger a software download, even if no WLC software change has taken place. These APs can downgrade to a previous software version (backup image) if the discovery process has failed a number of times. On the next successful join, these APs will download the AP image version from the WLC again.

The transfer is done inside the LWAPP control tunnel using a single packet window protocol with sequence number validation. In some situations, you can see sequence number errors, which is normal if the AP is doing retransmits per timeouts.

Before using the image, the AP does a checksum validation to make sure that it received the entire image and that the image is not corrupted.

Config State

After joining, the AP does a configuration request to obtain the current configuration from the WLC.

Caution During the configuration request process, the wireless regulatory domain is validated. A WLC answers a discovery request for APs of different regulatory domains (for example, a U.S. AP trying to join a European WLC), but fails to answer a join request if the country/domain validation fails.

The AP sends the following information in the configuration request:

- Regulatory domain for each of the radios

- AP serial number

- Current administrative status

- AP group (if configured)

- Radio details (configuration, power levels, antennas, and so on)

The WLC answers with a configuration response. The response includes the H-REAP RADIUS group, deletes mismatched override WLANs and AP groups, and provides a list of other WLCs in the current WLC mobility group.

Normally, depending on whether an AP is newly added to the WLC or if the configuration has changes, the WLC starts a set of configuration commands to bring the AP to the current status. Based on some of the performed changes, an expected AP reload might occur. An example of a configuration change that results in an AP reload is if the 802.11g network status had been enabled or disabled since the AP last joined the WLC.

Run State

After an AP has joined the WLC, has the correct configuration, and has the same image version as the WLC, it remains in the run or maintenance state. This is basically a working AP, joined to the WLC.

During the run state, the AP might be subject to several LWAPP control processes:

- **Configuration updates:** The WLC might send changes to an AP (AutoRF, admin triggered, and so on). The AP acknowledges with a configuration response.

- **Statistics update:** The AP sends periodic status updates involving AutoRF metrics, rogue reports, and so on.

- **Echo response/request:** The AP sends an echo request to the WLC every 30 seconds by default. The WLC should answer with an echo response. In case of timeout, the AP then sends five echo requests at 1-second intervals to check for WLC availability and triggers a new discovery process if needed.

  Periodically, the WLC triggers a key update request to change the security key used for LWAPP Control messages.

- **Reset request:** The WLC can send a reset request, which the AP answers with a request response before reloading.

- **Event request/response:** The AP can send asynchronous events to a WLC as a reaction to a nonscheduled event, such as a duplicate address, Message Integrity Check (MIC) error, or rogue on wire detected.

Remember that every LWAPP control packet contains a sequence number. The sequence number matches request/response packet exchanges. The sequence number in the response packet is the same value as the request packet.

When an LWAPP control frame is sent, the device monotonically increments its internal sequence number and eventually wraps back to 0. This ensures that no two pending requests have the same sequence number.

Dissecting the Discovery Response

This section takes a deeper look into what goes into a discovery response packet. This knowledge can help your understanding of what could be going wrong in an AP join process to a WLC. Keep in mind that a sniffer program cannot dissect the information in a discovery packet. The WLC dissects the packet; you can watch this from the WLC CLI using **debug lwapp packet enable**.

Figure 3-6 shows the most significant fields in a sniffer trace view of a Layer 3 discovery response.

- **IP Header:**

  Source (Src) is the management IP address.

  Destination (Dst) is the AP IP address that sent the discovery request.

  DSCP value (not shown) is normally 0x46. If the interface is tagged with a VLAN ID, the 802.1p UP is 7. This is important if QoS policies are enabled on the network. (LWAPP control is quite important.) A 0 value indicates an incorrect QoS configuration on the switching infrastructure.

- **UDP Header:**

  The source port is 12223.

  Destination is the ephemeral port the AP uses. (It remains the same for the duration of the LWAPP session.)

- **LWAPP Header:** The first byte is a bit field including the following:

  Version (2 bits): This is always 0.

  Radio ID or SlotID (3 bits): This is 0 for discovery.

  Control message (1 bit): This is 1 for the LWAPP control.

Fragment (1 bit): This indicates whether the message is a fragment; this is 0 for discovery.

Fragment Type (1 bit): This indicates whether this is the last fragment of the sequence. A 0 indicates it is.

Fragment ID: This is a one-byte counter, increased monotonically for each group of fragments. It is kept by each AP/WLC relationship.

- **LWAPP Control Message Header:**

  Control type: This will be 2 for discovery response.

  Control Sequence Number: This is always 0 for discovery request/response.

  Control Length: This is the byte count of the transported data.

- **Data:** This contains information about the WLC, including the software version, maximum AP allowed, current number of AP joins, and AP manager IP address.

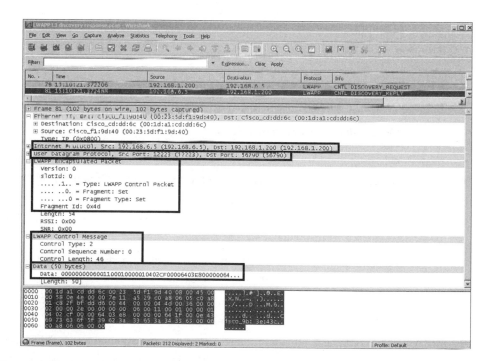

Figure 3-6   *Discovery Response Dissection*

Manually Dissecting the Discovery Response

In a discovery response, you can manually analyze the frame if a debugging of LWAPP packets from the WLC is not possible. Consider the example in Figure 3-7.

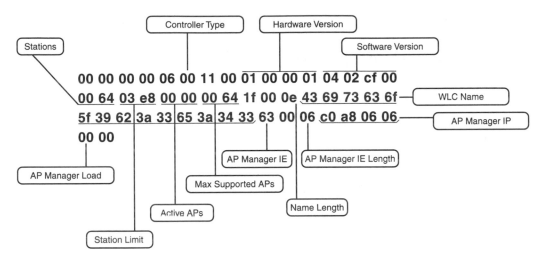

Figure 3-7   *Manual Analysis of Discovery Response Data*

In Figure 3-7, you can see the following information in the Data field of the discovery response from the WLC:

■ **Controller type:** 1-byte value indicating the operating mode of the WLC.

0x00 for a normal WLC.

0x01 for WLC with the master mode set.

As you can see, this WLC is in the normal operating mode.

■ **Hardware version:** 4-byte value representing the hardware version number of the WLC.

■ **Software version:** 4 bytes indicating the WLC software version. In the example, it is 04 02 cf 00, which corresponds to 4.2.207.0.

■ **Stations:** 2-byte value representing the number of clients currently associated with the WLC. In this case, there are none.

■ **Station limit:** 2-byte value representing the maximum number of stations the WLC supports.

■ **Active APs:** 2 bytes indicating how many APs are currently joined to the WLC. Zero in the example.

■ **Max supported APs:** 2-byte value indicating the maximum number of concurrent APs supported on the WLC. This is hardware model dependent. In the example, it is 100 (0x64).

■ **Name length:** 1-byte value indicating the length in bytes of the WLC system name to follow. (This is important to know if you are analyzing the frame manually.) In this example, the length is 14 bytes.

- **WLC name:** 14-byte value in this example indicating the system name of the WLC. This is what will be used to make the join decision. In the example 0x 436973636f5f39623a33653a3433, you can use the sniffer software to translate to ASCII:Cisco_9b:3e:43. This a variable byte length that is not zero terminated.

- **AP manager information element (IE):** 1-byte value. This is 0x63, which marks the beginning of the AP manager list. The type is 99 (63 converted to decimal), which indicates it is an IPv4 address.

- **AP manager IE length:** The number of AP manager addresses. For LAG WLCs, it is 6 (4 for address + 2 bytes for capacity), as shown in the example. For WLC configurations, you might have multiples of 6 indicating how many AP manager interfaces are configured in the WLC.

- **AP manager IP:** 4-byte value indicating the address in hex. In the example, this is c0 a8 06 06, which corresponds to 192.168.6.6.

- **AP manager load:** 1-byte value indicating how many APs are joined currently on this AP manager address. It is 0 in the example.

Summary

Using LWAPP for AP/WLC communications allows for many features that are not possible with traditional, standalone AP deployments. Without LWAPP, central administration and management of the wireless network are not possible. When an LWAPP AP boots up, it goes through the LWAPP state machine to eventually reach the run state, where it can start servicing wireless clients. An AP can learn about potential WLCs that it can join in several ways. You can statically configure WLC IPs, use DNS and DHCP, prime the AP on an existing WLC on the network, and even rely on existing APs to tell new APs about their respective controllers. Understanding the LWAPP discovery and join processes used by the APs to register with a WLC is key to troubleshooting any AP join issues. Chapter 8, "Access Point Registration," covers troubleshooting AP discovery and join issues in detail.

Chapter 4

The CAPWAP Protocol

Control and Provisioning of Wireless Access Points (CAPWAP) is a standard and interoperable protocol that enables a Wireless LAN Controller (WLC) to manage access points (AP) or wireless termination points (WTP). CAPWAP is based on the Lightweight Access Point Protocol (LWAPP). This chapter describes the changes in controller and AP software to enable CAPWAP support and to enable an upgrade from LWAPP to CAPWAP. The chapter covers a good amount of the protocol, but for those who want to get a deeper understanding, refer to the CAPWAP RFCs. Figure 4-1 gives a brief overview of the different RFCs the CAPWAP protocol involves:

- RFC 4564 defines the objectives for the CAPWAP protocol.

- RFC 5418 covers the threat analysis for IEEE 802.11 deployments.

- RFC 5415 defines the actual CAPWAP protocol specifications.

The CAPWAP protocol does not include specific wireless technologies; instead, it relies on a binding specification to extend the technology to a particular wireless technology. Those binding specifications for the IEEE 802.11 wireless protocol are defined in RFC 5416.

Last but not least, Datagram Transport Layer Security (DTLS), defined in RFC 4347, is used as a tightly integrated, secure wrapper for the CAPWAP protocol, whereas DTLS relies on Transport Layer Security (TLS) 1.1 (RFC 4346).

Reading the RFCs also places you in a position to better digest the material covered in this chapter. You should read Chapter 3, "Introduction to LWAPP," before this chapter, because understanding LWAPP is a key component to understanding CAPWAP.

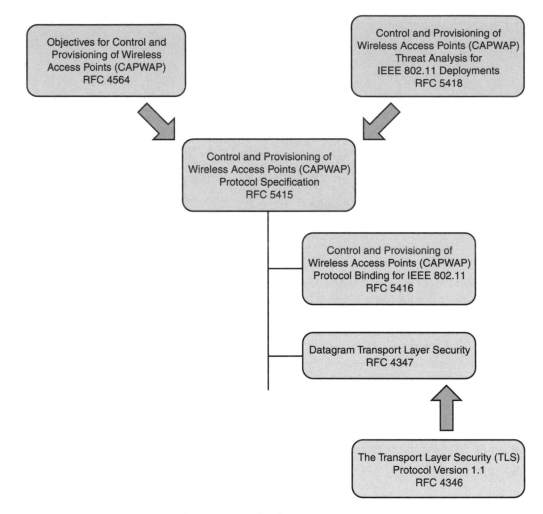

Figure 4-1   *Important Wireless RFCs and Relationships*

Overview of CAPWAP

CAPWAP support starts in controller Version 5.2. The upgrade transition from LWAPP to CAPWAP is typically transparent to the end user. The process by which an AP discovers a controller, validates firmware, and downloads firmware and configurations does not change. The only exception is in the scenario in which a customer has an LWAPP Layer 2 deployment. CAPWAP does not support Layer 2; this should be a null issue because the customer base using Layer 2 LWAPP deployments is minimal or nonexistent at this point. One of the reasons for such little support is that the deployment is restricted to a Layer 2 boundary. Another reason is that during the transition period when Cisco started supporting LWAPP conversions of autonomous APs, one of the requirements for a WLC to communicate with a converted AP was that the WLC must perform all communications in LWAPP Layer 3 mode.

Note   Layer 2 LWAPP has no AP-Manager interface, and the APs do not utilize IP addresses.

Differences from LWAPP

The discovery process changes from LWAPP to CAPWAP are transparent to most users; however, they are indeed different. One of the main differences is the use of DTLS.

As you see from Figure 4-2, the overall deployments are identical between LWAPP and CAPWAP. The only difference is the protocol being used between the AP and the controller. DTLS is used as a tightly integrated secure wrapper for a CAPWAP packet.

Figure 4-2   *LWAPP and CAPWAP Comparison*

Table 4-1 outlines the primary differences between CAPWAP and LWAPP.

Table 4-1   *LWAPP and CAPWAP Comparison*

Feature	LWAPP	CAPWAP
L2 mode support	Yes	No
Security	AES-CCMP	AES-CCMP with DTLS protocol
Control plane encryption	Yes	Yes
Data plane encryption	No	Optional, depending on hardware; 5500s only.
Fragmentation and reassembly	IP fragmentation	CAPWAP fragmentation
MTU discovery	No	Yes
Protocol control ports	12222	5246
Protocol data ports	12223	5247

Because of the similarities, deployments can contain mixtures of CAPWAP and LWAPP software-based controllers. This is not a recommended scenario for a few different reasons the first being if an AP were to move from one controller utilizing LWAPP to another utilizing CAPWAP. In that case, the AP would take longer to join because the code versions would obviously be different. Each time the AP would have to download firmware when moving from one controller to the next with different code versions. When an LWAPP AP discovers a CAPWAP controller, the AP is automatically converted to CAPWAP and vice versa when an AP discovers an LWAPP controller. Overall convergence for the APs to come online will take longer in this scenario. This would be a similar scenario to two controllers running different versions of code. The CAPWAP-enabled software, Version 5.2, will allow APs to join a controller running CAPWAP or LWAPP. However, another disadvantage is that only controllers supporting CAPWAP will be present in the same mobility group. For this reason, mobility is limited to the protocol being used—CAPWAP only or LWAPP only. The exception is 6.0 MR1 code, which will support mobility for 4.2 MR3 code. Otherwise, there will be no support for a combination of both LWAPP and CAPWAP controllers in the same mobility group.

You might encounter a deployment scenario as in Figure 4-3, where you have a mixed deployment. This might happen when you are upgrading to a CAPWAP-supported version, for example. In this scenario, you must ask how much LWAPP support is on a CAPWAP version of code. It is assumed that at any point in time the AP will run only CAPWAP or LWAPP. If it is running an image before CAPWAP support, it will be able to discover

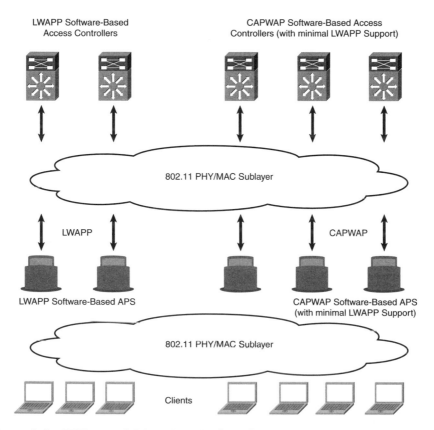

Figure 4-3   *LWAPP and CAPWAP Mixed Deployment*

controllers using LWAPP only. If it is running an image with CAPWAP support, it will be able to discover controllers using CAPWAP or LWAPP. However, LWAPP support is limited—in the sense that LWAPP will be supported only until the AP is able to download an image from an LWAPP controller—for downgrades. At the controllers, LWAPP support in a CAPWAP-enabled image is available to the extent of allowing the existing LWAPP APs to communicate with the controller using LWAPP and being able to download a CAPWAP image. An AP running a CAPWAP-supported image behind Network Address Translation (NAT) will work as it does today with LWAPP. There will be no support for an LWAPP data path in a controller or an AP that is running a CAPWAP-supported image.

CAPWAP Session Establishment/AP Joining Process

As mentioned earlier, the CAPWAP session is similar to LWAPP. The main difference is the use of DTLS for authentication (DTLS-handshake) and tunnel encryption (DTLS-application data). The following is an overview of the session establishment process:

Step 1. Discovery request (optional)

Step 2. Discovery response

Step 3. DTLS session establishment; all messages below will be encrypted (DTLS application data)

Step 4. Join request

Step 5. Join response

Step 6. Configuration status request

Step 7. Configuration status response

Step 8. Run state

Figure 4-4 outlines the detailed CAPWAP packet flow.

Figure 4-5 shows the complete CAPWAP protocol state machine. Use it as reference while reading CAPWAP debugs. You will find the actual states printed in the CAPWAP debugs on the controllers or APs.

You can find a detailed description of the various state transitions and the events that cause them in section 2.3.1 of RFC 5415 at http://www.ietf.org/rfc/rfc5415.txt.

For simplicity, Figure 4-5 uses the same transition index (ASCII character) as has been used in RFC 5415.

Certain debugs such as **debug capwap event enable** are printing the CAPWAP state in cleartext:

```
*Aug 19 20:01:53.038: 00:1f:ca:83:b3:70 CAPWAP State: Join
*Aug 19 20:01:53.134: 00:1f:ca:83:b3:70 CAPWAP State: Configure
*Aug 19 20:01:53.254: 00:1f:ca:83:b3:70 CAPWAP State: Run
```

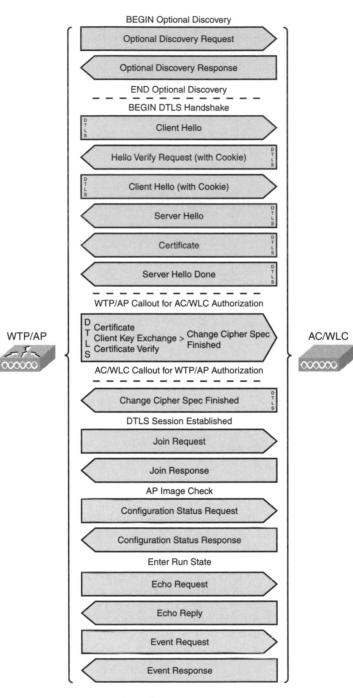

Figure 4-4 *CAPWAP Packet Flow*

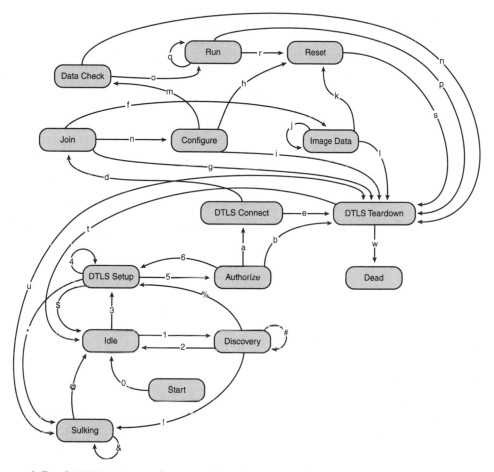

Figure 4-5 *CAPWAP Protocol State Machine*

Other CAPWAP debugs such as **debug capwap detail enable** are printing the internal used state-ID only:

```
*Aug 19 20:24:23.992: 00:21:55:f3:50:50 Msg Type = 9 CAPWAP state = 11
```

Use Table 4-2 to find the corresponding CAPWAP state.

If you compare those states with those in LWAPP (see Chapter 3), you will see that the only difference between CAPWAP and LWAPP is the fact that CAPWAP uses DTLS encryption, which also includes a handshake negotiation.

Table 4-2 *CAPWAP State ID in Controller Debugs*

ID	CAPWAP State
0	NO STATE
1	INIT
2	DISCOVERY
3	DTLS SETUP
4	DTLS TEARDOWN
5	JOIN
6	SULKING
7	IDLE
8	CONFIGURE
9	RESET
10	IMAGE DATA
11	RUN

Discovery Process

Before delving further into DTLS-handshaking, you need to understand the discovery process. Take a look at Figure 4-6, and you will be able to see the entire CAPWAP session establishment in a wire trace. This example uses the following addresses:

- **WLC Management Address:** 10.0.102.254

- **WLC AP-Manager Address:** 10.0.102.253

- **AP Address:** 10.0.102.109

If you look at the discovery response in more detail, you will see that the AP-Manager address is returned to the AP. The AP then starts the join process communicating directly with the AP-Manager. How can you determine this was a discovery response? Look at Figure 4-7 and open the CAPWAP control packet portion of the packet. The CAPWAP message type informs you exactly what it is.

In future versions (6.0 and beyond) and next-generation WLCs such as the 5500s, there will only be a management interface, so the destination address for discovery packets will be the same as for the following DTLS-handshake, join packets. Figure 4-8 is expanding the message elements from the same Discovery Response Packet shown in Figure 4-7. The selected message element is the **CAPWAP Control IPV4 Address**, which is the AP-Manager IP address.

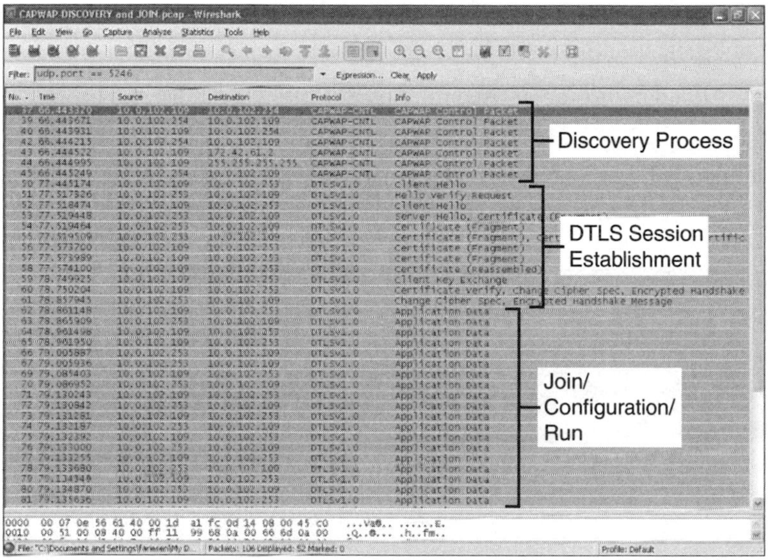

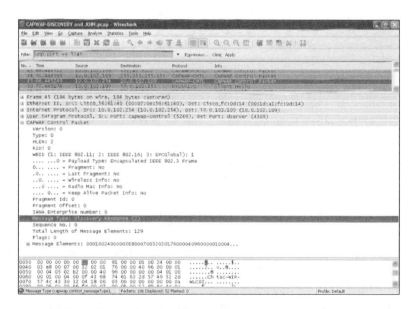

Figure 4-6   *CAPWAP Session Establishment Overview*

Figure 4-7   *CAPWAP Discovery Response Packet*

DTLS Session Establishment

The DTLS protocol is based on the TLS protocol. TLS is the most widely deployed protocol for securing network traffic. It defines four record protocols:

■ **The handshake protocol:** Used to negotiate security parameters and authenticate

■ **The change cipher spec protocol:** Triggers to enable the encryption that has been negotiated by the handshake protocol

■ **The application data protocol:** Used to transport actual data that has been encrypted

■ **The alert protocol:** Notifies if something went wrong (such as an invalid certificate)

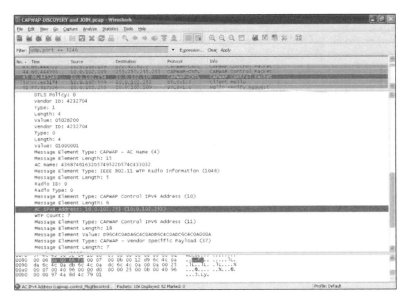

Figure 4-8 *CAPWAP Discovery Response Packet*

TLS must run over a reliable transport channel—typically Transport Control Protocol (TCP). Therefore, it cannot secure unreliable datagram traffic such as User Datagram Protocol (UDP), which is exactly where DTLS kicks in. The basic design philosophy of DTLS is to construct "TLS over datagram." CAPWAP uses all those functions from DTLS/TLS.

Therefore, right after the optional discovery request/response sequence, the first step is establishing a secure CAPWAP connection in the same manner as in a normal DTLS session. Figure 4-9 shows the complete DTLS handshake.

Step 1. **ClientHello:** The client (in the CAPWAP scenario, it's the AP) is sending in the client hello a list from all its supported cryptographic algorithms as well a random value that is used later to calculate the key material used for the CAPWAP encryption.

Step 2. **HelloVerifyRequest/ClientHello (with cookie):** Upon receiving the client hello, a stateless cookie exchange happens to prevent denial of service (DoS) attacks (required because it runs over UDP).

Step 3.   **ServerHello/Certificate:** The server (in the CAPWAP scenario, it is the WLC) selects the cryptographic algorithm from the provided list and replies together with its certificate and a random value to the client (AP).

Step 4.   **Certificate/ClientKeyExchange/ChangeCipherSpec:** Upon cipher suite negotiation and certificate validation, the client (AP) sends the ClientKeyExchange followed by the ChangeCipherSpec record protocol. ChangeCipherSpec notifies the other party that all subsequent records will be encrypted by the just-negotiated ciphers and key material.

Step 5.   **Server–ChangeCipherSpec:** The server responds with a ChangeCipherSpec, which means that from now on, records sent in both directions are encrypted. The DTLS session is now fully established.

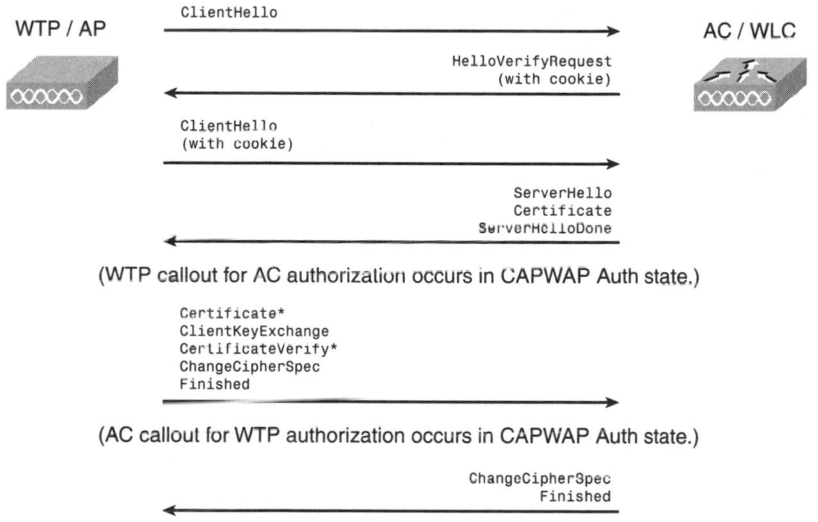

Figure 4-9   *DTLS Session Establishment*

Example 4-1 shows **debug dtls trace enable** on the controller, from which you can see the progress on the DTLS-handshake. The relevant parts to match the DTLS session flow in Figure 4-9 are highlighted in the debug output.

Example 4-1   *DTLS Debugs Taken on a Controller*

```
 (Cisco Controller) >debug dtls trace enable
(Cisco Controller) >show debug

Debug Flags Enabled:
  dtls event enabled.
  dtls trace enabled.
(Cisco Controller) >
```

(continues)

Example 4-1 *DTLS Debugs Taken on a Controller (continued)*

```
*Aug 28 10:50:06.531: dtls_secret_pki_init: Called...
*Aug 28 10:50:06.601: dtls_secret_pki_add_idcert: Called...
*Aug 28 10:50:06.602: acDtlsCallback: Certificate installed for PKI based
  authentication.
*Aug 28 10:50:06.602: openssl_dtls_process_packet: Callled...
  for connection 0x1791b964
*Aug 28 10:50:06.602: local_openssl_dtls_record_inspect:
  record=Handshake epoch=0 seq=0
*Aug 28 10:50:06.602: local_openssl_dtls_record_inspect:
  msg=ClientHello len=44 seq=0 frag_off=0 frag_len=44
*Aug 28 10:50:06.602: openssl_shim_info_callback: SSL state = 0x6000;
  where = 0x10; ret = 0x1
*Aug 28 10:50:06.602: openssl_shim_info_callback: SSL state = 0x6000;
  where = 0x2001; ret = 0x1
*Aug 28 10:50:06.603: openssl_shim_info_callback: SSL state = 0x2110;
  where = 0x2001; ret = 0x1
*Aug 28 10:50:06.603: openssl_shim_cookie_generate_callback: Called...
*Aug 28 10:50:06.603: openssl_shim_info_callback: SSL state = 0x2113;
  where = 0x2001; ret = 0x1
*Aug 28 10:50:06.603: openssl_shim_info_callback: SSL state = 0x2100;
  where = 0x2001; ret = 0x1
*Aug 28 10:50:06.603: openssl_shim_info_callback: SSL state = 0x2111;
  where = 0x2002; ret = 0xffffffff
*Aug 28 10:50:06.603: openssl_dtls_process_packet: Handshake in progress...
*Aug 28 10:50:06.603: openssl_dtls_send: Sending 60 bytes
*Aug 28 10:50:06.603: 00000000: 16 fe ff 00 00 00 00 00  00 00 00 00 2f 03 00 00
............/...
*Aug 28 10:50:06.603: 00000010: 23 00 00 00 00 00 00 00  23 fe ff 20 c0 a8 01 17
#.......#.......
*Aug 28 10:50:06.603: 00000020: a0 bc 12 34 56 78 9a bc  2b b9 d1 82 bf 49 e2 b4
...4Vx..+....I..
*Aug 28 10:50:06.603: 00000030: 4e e1 f4 82 95 cf 2a bf  ab fd 95 77
              N.....*....w
*Aug 28 10:50:06.603: openssl_dtls_send: No data to send
*Aug 28 10:50:06.604: openssl_dtls_process_packet: Callled...
  for connection 0x1791b964
*Aug 28 10:50:06.604: local_openssl_dtls_record_inspect:
  record=Handshake epoch=0 seq=1
*Aug 28 10:50:06.604: local_openssl_dtls_record_inspect:
  msg=ClientHello len=76 seq=1 frag_off=0 frag_len=76
*Aug 28 10:50:06.604: openssl_shim_cookie_verify_callback: Called...
```

```
*Aug 28 10:50:06.604: openssl_shim_info_callback: SSL state = 0x2111;
  where = 0x2001; ret = 0x1
*Aug 28 10:50:06.604: openssl_shim_info_callback: SSL state = 0x2130;
  where = 0x2001; ret = 0x1
*Aug 28 10:50:06.605: openssl_shim_info_callback: SSL state = 0x2140;
  where = 0x2001; ret = 0x1
*Aug 28 10:50:06.605: openssl_shim_info_callback: SSL state = 0x2160;
  where = 0x2001; ret = 0x1
*Aug 28 10:50:06.605: openssl_shim_info_callback: SSL state = 0x2170;
  where = 0x2001; ret = 0x1
*Aug 28 10:50:06.605: openssl_shim_info_callback: SSL state = 0x2100;
  where = 0x2001; ret = 0x1
*Aug 28 10:50:06.605: openssl_shim_info_callback: SSL state = 0x2180;
  where = 0x2002; ret = 0xffffffff
*Aug 28 10:50:06.605: openssl_dtls_process_packet: Handshake in progress...
*Aug 28 10:50:06.605: openssl_dtls_send: Sending 544 bytes
*Aug 28 10:50:06.605: 00000000: 16 fe ff 00 00 00 00 00  00 00 01 00 52 02 00 00
  ............R...
*Aug 28 10:50:06.605: 00000010: 46 00 01 00 00 00 00 00  46 fe ff 48 b6 82 de d7
  F.......F..H....
*Aug 28 10:50:06.605: 00000020: 95 ac 56 cb 27 66 ae 64  96 d1 4d 66 dd ae 22 1e
  ..V.'f.d..Mf..".
*Aug 28 10:50:06.605: 00000030: c9 ac 99 1b e2 57 4d 0b  2c 00 4b 20 f8 79 65 7a
  .....WM.,fK..yez
*Aug 28 10:50:06.605: 00000040: a5 b4 31 e1 e5 fa a2 f5  77 1d ee 6d 55 27 ae cf
  ..1.....w..mU'..
*Aug 28 10:50:06.606: 00000050: 61 bc 5f 53 ee bc 02 80  dc 9b d7 a1 00 2f 00 16
  a._S........./..
*Aug 28 10:50:06.606: 00000060: fe ff 00 00 00 00 00 00  00 02 01 b4 0b 00 04 83
  ................
*Aug 28 10:50:06.606: 00000070: 00 02 00 00 00 00 01 a8  00 04 80 00 04 7d 30 82
  .............}0.
*Aug 28 10:50:06.606: 00000080: 04 79 30 82 03 61 a0 03  02 01 02 02 0a 4d 86 12
  .y0..a.......M..
*Aug 28 10:50:06.606: 00000090: 06 00 00 00 05 74 16 30  0d 06 09 2a 86 48 86 f7
  .....t.0...*.H..
*Aug 28 10:50:06.606: 000000a0: 0d 01 01 05 05 00 30 39  31 16 30 14 06 03 55 04
  ......091.0...U.
*Aug 28 10:50:06.606: 000000b0: 0a 13 0d 43 69 73 63 6f  20 53 79 73 74 65 6d 73
  ...Cisco.Systems
*Aug 28 10:50:06.606: 000000c0: 31 1f 30 1d 06 03 55 04  03 13 16 43 69 73 63 6f
  1.0...U....Cisco
*Aug 28 10:50:06.606: 000000d0: 20 4d 61 6e 75 66 61 63  74 75 72 69 6e 67 20 43
  .Manufacturing.C
```

(continues)

Example 4-1   *DTLS Debugs Taken on a Controller (continued)*

```
*Aug 28 10:50:06.606: 000000e0: 41 30 1e 17 0d 30 36 31   31 30 37 31 35 31 38 32
   A0...06110715182
*Aug 28 10:50:06.606: 000000f0: 32 5a 17 0d 31 36 31 31   30 37 31 35 32 38 32 32
   2Z..161107152822
*Aug 28 10:50:06.606: 00000100: 5a 30 81 98 31 0b 30 09   06 03 55 04 06 13 02 55
   Z0..1.0...U....U
*Aug 28 10:50:06.606: 00000110: 53 31 13 30 11 06 03 55   04 08 13 0a 43 61 6c 69
   S1.0...U....Cali
*Aug 28 10:50:06.606: 00000120: 66 6f 72 6e 69 61 31 11   30 0f 06 03 55 04 07 13
   fornia1.0...U...
*Aug 28 10:50:06.606: 00000130: 08 53 61 6e 20 4a 6f 73   65 31 16 30 14 06 03 55
   .San.Jose1.0...U
*Aug 28 10:50:06.606: 00000140: 04 0a 13 0d 43 69 73 63   6f 20 53 79 73 74 65 6d
   ....Cisco.System
*Aug 28 10:50:06.606: 00000150: 73 31 27 30 25 06 03 55   04 03 13 1e 41 49 52 2d
   s1'0%..U....AIR-
*Aug 28 10:50:06.606: 00000160: 57 4c 43 34 34 30 32 2d   35 30 2d 4b 39 2d 30 30
   WLC4402-50-K9-00
*Aug 28 10:50:06.606: 00000170: 31 38 62 61 34 39 63 66   34 30 31 20 30 1e 06 09
   18ba49cf401.0...
*Aug 28 10:50:06.606: 00000180: 2a 86 48 86 f7 0d 01 09   01 16 11 73 75 70 70 6f
   *.H........suppo
*Aug 28 10:50:06.606: 00000190: 72 74 40 63 69 73 63 6f   2e 63 6f 6d 30 82 01 22
   rt@cisco.com0.."
*Aug 28 10:50:06.606: 000001a0: 30 0d 06 09 2a 86 48 86   f7 0d 01 01 01 05 00 03
   0...*.H.........
*Aug 28 10:50:06.606: 000001b0: 82 01 0f 00 30 82 01 0a   02 82 01 01 00 d5 4a 6b
   ....0.........Jk
*Aug 28 10:50:06.606: 000001c0: c9 cd 56 4d 9e f3 aa d6   8d 61 14 76 1d 9f d9 74
   ..VM.....a.v...t
*Aug 28 10:50:06.606: 000001d0: 72 e0 fd 90 8c ff fd 97   b0 fa be 77 ba 07 1d b1
   r..........w....
*Aug 28 10:50:06.606: 000001e0: 91 91 4e a9 a0 a8 96 ca   f3 93 66 7b ba 89 77 b0
   ..N.......f{..w.
*Aug 28 10:50:06.606: 000001f0: c8 81 af 7f f7 f9 46 da   da d2 db 86 d4 f0 6f 66
   ......F.......of
*Aug 28 10:50:06.606: 00000200: 1d c7 15 87 23 c1 86 75   d7 e1 9a dc 32 9c d6 10
   ....#..u....2...
*Aug 28 10:50:06.606: 00000210: f7 f1 6b ce 8f 82 51 71   4b 32 f4 d5 64 88 8d 86
   ..k...QqK2..d...
*Aug 28 10:50:06.606: openssl_dtls_send: Sending 544 bytes
*Aug 28 10:50:06.606: 00000000: 16 fe ff 00 00 00 00 00   00 00 03 02 13 0b 00 04
   ...............
*Aug 28 10:50:06.606: 00000010: 83 00 02 00 01 a8 00 02   07 93 7e 3b 4a 28 5c fc
```

```
          ..........~;J(\.
*Aug 28 10:50:06.606: 00000020: 6a e0 bc a5 6f d0 eb 0a  2a 9e 5c 78 48 58 f6 4c
          j...o...*.\xHX.L
*Aug 28 10:50:06.606: 00000030: 13 c8 4a 32 fa cb 70 93  c1 a7 a4 51 5e 0c 40 3d
          ..J2..p....Q^.@=
*Aug 28 10:50:06.606: 00000040: 6e f1 e8 d0 98 04 bc 50  ce 67 80 43 fe 5c f7 3f
          n......P.g.C.\.?
*Aug 28 10:50:06.606: 00000050: 3c ce 28 dd b5 52 25 47  7e 79 e8 14 d9 a5 3e 25
          <.(..R%G~y....>%
*Aug 28 10:50:06.606: 00000060: 18 11 28 04 73 e3 dd ad  ac 2b 13 09 a1 9d c3 22
          ..(.s....+....."
*Aug 28 10:50:06.606: 00000070: 86 4b 75 7c 16 6e 4b 9b  47 c8 a3 af 29 19 1c fd
          .Ku¦.nK.G...)...
*Aug 28 10:50:06.606: 00000080: bf 66 38 9a 1f 3c 09 f6  50 7a 11 a6 aa 85 26 b6
          .f8..<..Pz....&.
*Aug 28 10:50:06.607: 00000090: 66 47 64 ec e0 b4 d9 f9  e6 c6 bc d1 d1 b7 72 8f
          fGd...........r.
*Aug 28 10:50:06.607: 000000a0: c4 04 d8 dd 49 b9 37 e9  7b a6 34 a2 9b 7b 0a 78
          ....I.7.{.4..{.x
*Aug 28 10:50:06.607: 000000b0: 0f a5 07 31 e1 51 02 03  01 00 01 a3 82 01 21 30
          ...1.Q........!0
*Aug 28 10:50:06.607: 000000c0: 82 01 1d 30 0b 06 03 55  1d 0f 04 04 03 02 05 a0
          ...0...U........
*Aug 28 10:50:06.607: 000000d0: 30 1d 06 03 55 1d 0e 04  16 04 14 d1 45 fd a7 c9
          0...U.......E...
*Aug 28 10:50:06.607: 000000e0: 65 d2 d3 28 8c ae 02 b4  de c4 26 1b f8 69 b6 30
          e..(......&..i.0
*Aug 28 10:50:06.607: 000000f0: 1f 06 03 55 1d 23 04 18  30 16 80 14 d0 c5 22 26
          ...U.#..0....."&
*Aug 28 10:50:06.607: 00000100: ab 4f 46 60 ec ae 05 91  c7 dc 5a d1 b0 47 f7 6c
          .OF`......Z..G.l
*Aug 28 10:50:06.607: 00000110: 30 3f 06 03 55 1d 1f 04  38 30 36 30 34 a0 32 a0
          0?..U...80604.2.
*Aug 28 10:50:06.607: 00000120: 30 86 2e 68 74 74 70 3a  2f 2f 77 77 77 2e 63 69
          0..http://www.ci
*Aug 28 10:50:06.607: 00000130: 73 63 6f 2e 63 6f 6d 2f  73 65 63 75 72 69 74 79
          sco.com/security
*Aug 28 10:50:06.607: 00000140: 2f 70 6b 69 2f 63 72 6c  2f 63 6d 63 61 2e 63 72
          /pki/crl/cmca.cr
*Aug 28 10:50:06.607: 00000150: 6c 30 4c 06 08 2b 06 01  05 05 07 01 01 04 40 30
          l0L..+........@0
*Aug 28 10:50:06.607: 00000160: 3e 30 3c 06 08 2b 06 01  05 05 07 30 02 86 30 68
          >0<..+.....0..0h
*Aug 28 10:50:06.607: 00000170: 74 74 70 3a 2f 2f 77 77  77 2e 63 69 73 63 6f 2e
```

(continues)

Example 4-1   *DTLS Debugs Taken on a Controller (continued)*

```
ttp://www.cisco.
*Aug 28 10:50:06.607: 00000180: 63 6f 6d 2f 73 65 63 75   72 69 74 79 2f 70 6b 69
com/security/pki
*Aug 28 10:50:06.607: 00000190: 2f 63 65 72 74 73 2f 63   6d 63 61 2e 63 65 72 30
/certs/cmca.cer0
*Aug 28 10:50:06.607: 000001a0: 3f 06 09 2b 06 01 04 01   82 37 14 02 04 32 1e 30
?..+.....7...2.0
*Aug 28 10:50:06.607: 000001b0: 00 49 00 50 00 53 00 45   00 43 00 49 00 6e 00 74
.I.P.S.E.C.I.n.t
*Aug 28 10:50:06.607: 000001c0: 00 65 00 72 00 6d 00 65   00 64 00 69 00 61 00 74
.e.r.m.e.d.i.a.t
*Aug 28 10:50:06.607: 000001d0: 00 65 00 4f 00 66 00 66   00 6c 00 69 00 6e 00 65
.e.O.f.f.l.i.n.e
*Aug 28 10:50:06.607: 000001e0: 30 0d 06 09 2a 86 48 86   f7 0d 01 01 05 05 00 03
0...*.H.........
*Aug 28 10:50:06.607: 000001f0: 82 01 01 00 3b 63 6e 94   90 b6 e5 f1 1e f3 f9 19
....;cn.........
*Aug 28 10:50:06.607: 00000200: c7 80 6d 25 7d 26 42 57   27 1d 63 ba e4 52 38 fe
..m%}&BW'.c..R8.
*Aug 28 10:50:06.607: 00000210: c9 0b 19 84 cc 36 55 dd   e7 93 dd 4c 14 30 07 d2
.....6U....L.0..
*Aug 28 10:50:06.607: openssl_dtls_send: Sending 318 bytes
*Aug 28 10:50:06.607: 00000000: 16 fe ff 00 00 00 00 00   00 00 04 00 d4 0b 00 04
...............
*Aug 28 10:50:06.607: 00000010: 83 00 02 00 03 af 00 00   c8 09 08 62 d7 04 c9 7e
...........b...~
*Aug 28 10:50:06.607: 00000020: cb 7c 56 46 08 ba 9e 87   7b e5 22 81 4c 7e e6 2a
.¦VF....{.".L~.*
*Aug 28 10:50:06.607: 00000030: 0c 17 0b ce 54 17 b8 48   31 ed dd 72 d2 ac 68 d2
....T..H1..r..h.
*Aug 28 10:50:06.607: 00000040: ed ad 8f 81 61 50 c3 ae   c0 7d 93 17 f6 05 98 02
....aP...}......
*Aug 28 10:50:06.607: 00000050: a3 c0 20 00 47 96 90 74   92 f2 b5 2b d0 e0 87 3d
....G..t...+...=
*Aug 28 10:50:06.607: 00000060: ba c9 28 9e d1 4f ce 59   d2 47 b1 ce 33 fd ef 6e
..(..O.Y.G..3..n
*Aug 28 10:50:06.607: 00000070: d7 0a ed 5d 71 b2 da 9d   84 2a c5 c2 f9 1f c0 74
...]q....*.....t
*Aug 28 10:50:06.607: 00000080: b6 3d b8 70 a7 26 da e9   f5 e7 3a ef 88 09 93 db
.=.p.&....:.....
*Aug 28 10:50:06.607: 00000090: f8 dd dd 34 6c c1 71 9a   ec da e4 25 42 7d 71 a6
...4l.q....%B}q.
*Aug 28 10:50:06.607: 000000a0: 5f 70 18 53 e8 72 06 e9   df 4c 13 3a a4 8b e6 ad
_p.S.r...L.:....
```

```
*Aug 28 10:50:06.607: 000000b0: 13 3d 7a 7b e9 be 96 22   e6 b4 81 d6 03 07 72 cb
  .=z{...".......r.
*Aug 28 10:50:06.607: 000000c0: 5d 1f fd 01 b3 ba 91 21   fb d5 b8 e5 15 e5 09 7f
  ]......!.........
*Aug 28 10:50:06.607: 000000d0: f5 62 44 1f 7c 81 7d 59   f3 7f b9 75 cd 6f 24 dc
  .bD.¦.}Y...u.o$.
*Aug 28 10:50:06.607: 000000e0: 2b 16 fe ff 00 00 00 00   00 00 00 05 00 18 0b 00
  +...............
*Aug 28 10:50:06.607: 000000f0: 04 83 00 02 00 04 77 00   00 0c 84 5b aa 06 b1 28
  ......w....[...(
*Aug 28 10:50:06.607: 00000100: 75 c6 58 0d 32 88 16 fe   ff 00 00 00 00 00 00 00
  u.X.2...........
*Aug 28 10:50:06.607: 00000110: 06 00 12 0d 00 00 06 00   03 00 00 00 00 00 06 03
  ................
*Aug 28 10:50:06.607: 00000120: 01 02 40 00 00 16 fe ff   00 00 00 00 00 00 00 07
  ..@.............
*Aug 28 10:50:06.607: 00000130: 00 0c 0e 00 00 00 00 04   00 00 00 00 00 00
  ..............
*Aug 28 10:50:06.607: openssl_dtls_send: No data to send
*Aug 28 10:50:06.625: openssl_dtls_process_packet: Callled...
  for connection 0x1791b964
*Aug 28 10:50:06.625: local_openssl_dtls_record_inspect:
  record=Handshake epoch=0 seq=2
*Aug 28 10:50:06.625: local_openssl_dtls_record_inspect:
  msg=Certificate len=1146 seq=2 frag_off=0 frag_len=519
*Aug 28 10:50:06.625: openssl_shim_info_callback: SSL state = 0x2181;
  where = 0x2002; ret = 0xffffffff
*Aug 28 10:50:06.625: openssl_dtls_process_packet: Handshake in progress...
*Aug 28 10:50:06.625: openssl_dtls_send: No data to send
*Aug 28 10:50:06.625: openssl_dtls_process_packet: Callled...
  for connection 0x1791b964
*Aug 28 10:50:06.625: local_openssl_dtls_record_inspect:
  record=Handshake epoch=0 seq=3
*Aug 28 10:50:06.625: local_openssl_dtls_record_inspect:
  msg=Certificate len=1146 seq=2 frag_off=519 frag_len=519 *Aug 28 10:50:06.625:
  openssl_shim_info_callback: SSL state = 0x2181; where = 0x2002; ret = 0xffffffff
*Aug 28 10:50:06.625: openssl_dtls_process_packet: Handshake in progress...
*Aug 28 10:50:06.625: openssl_dtls_send: No data to send
*Aug 28 10:50:06.625: openssl_dtls_process_packet: Callled...
  for connection 0x1791b964
*Aug 28 10:50:06.625: local_openssl_dtls_record_inspect:
  record=Handshake epoch=0 seq=4
```

(continues)

Example 4-1 *DTLS Debugs Taken on a Controller (continued)*

```
*Aug 28 10:50:06.625: local_openssl_dtls_record_inspect:
  msg=Certificate len=1146 seq=2 frag_off=1038 frag_len=108 *Aug 28 10:50:06.636:
  openssl_shim_cert_verify_callback: Certificate verification - passed!
*Aug 28 10:50:06.636: openssl_shim_info_callback: SSL state = 0x2181;
  where = 0x2001; ret = 0x1
*Aug 28 10:50:06.636: openssl_shim_info_callback: SSL state = 0x2190;
  where = 0x2002; ret = 0xffffffff *Aug 28 10:50:06.636:
openssl_dtls_process_packet: Handshake in  progress...
*Aug 28 10:50:06.636: openssl_dtls_send: No data to send
*Aug 28 10:50:07.068: openssl_dtls_process_packet: Callled...
  for connection 0x1791b964
*Aug 28 10:50:07.068: local_openssl_dtls_record_inspect:
  record=Handshake epoch=0 seq=5
*Aug 28 10:50:07.068: local_openssl_dtls_record_inspect:
  msg=ClientKeyExchange len=258 seq=3 frag_off=0 frag_len=258
  *Aug 28 10:50:07.172: openssl_shim_info_callback: SSL state = 0x2190;
  where = 0x2001; ret = 0x1
*Aug 28 10:50:07.172: openssl_shim_info_callback: SSL state = 0x21a0
  ; where = 0x2002; ret = 0xffffffff
*Aug 28 10:50:07.172: openssl_dtls_process_packet: Handshake in progress...
*Aug 28 10:50:07.172: openssl_dtls_send: No data to send
*Aug 28 10:50:07.172: openssl_dtls_process_packet: Callled...
  for connection 0x1791b964
*Aug 28 10:50:07.172: local_openssl_dtls_record_inspect:
  record=Handshake epoch=0 seq=6
*Aug 28 10:50:07.172: local_openssl_dtls_record_inspect:
  msg=CertificateVerify len=258 seq=4 frag_off=0 frag_len=258
*Aug 28 10:50:07.172: local_openssl_dtls_record_inspect:
  record-ChangeCipherSpec epoch=0 seq=7
*Aug 28 10:50:07.172: local_openssl_dtls_record_inspect:
  record=Handshake epoch=1 seq=0
*Aug 28 10:50:07.172: local_openssl_dtls_record_inspect:
  msg=Unknown or Encrypted
*Aug 28 10:50:07.175: openssl_shim_info_callback: SSL state = 0x21a0;
  where = 0x2001; ret = 0x1
*Aug 28 10:50:07.175: openssl_shim_info_callback: SSL state = 0x21c0;
  where = 0x2001; ret = 0x1
*Aug 28 10:50:07.175: openssl_shim_info_callback: SSL state = 0x21d0;
  where = 0x2001; ret = 0x1
*Aug 28 10:50:07.175: openssl_shim_info_callback: SSL state = 0x21e0;
  where = 0x2001; ret = 0x1
*Aug 28 10:50:07.175: openssl_shim_info_callback: SSL state = 0x2100;
  where = 0x2001; ret = 0x1
*Aug 28 10:50:07.175: openssl_shim_info_callback: SSL state = 0x3;
```

```
   where = 0x20; ret = 0x1
*Aug 28 10:50:07.176: openssl_shim_info_callback: SSL state = 0x3;
   where = 0x2002; ret = 0x1
*Aug 28 10:50:07.176: openssl_dtls_process_packet: Connection established!
*Aug 28 10:50:07.176: openssl_dtls_mtu_update: Called...
*Aug 28 10:50:07.176: openssl_dtls_mtu_update: Setting DTLS MTU for link to
   peer 192.168.1.23:41148
```

Join/Config/Run

After the successful DTLS session establishment, the join and configuration requests/responses follow. Because after every ChangeCipherSpec in DTLS the session uses previous negotiated encryption, you only see "DTLS application data" in a sniffer trace, which makes all the following packets such as Join or Configure packets invisible. Also, refer to Figure 4-6, which shows the sniffer trace from a complete CAPWAP session establishment. Starting at frame 62, you only see DTLS Application-Data.

To troubleshoot what is going on inside the DTLS application data tunnel, you have to run debugs on the controller or on the AP. Example 4-2 shows the debug output taken on an AP. From there you see the join request and response and how the AP does an image and configuration verification to make sure it is running the same version of code that resides on the controller and has the most up-to-date configuration.

Example 4-2   *Access Point debug capwap client packet Output*

```
SE.AP-01-1240#debug capwap client detail
CAPWAP Client DETAIL display debugging is on
SE.AP-01-1240#debug capwap client event
CAPWAP Client EVENT display debugging is on
SE.AP-01-1240#debug capwap client packet
CAPWAP Client Packet display debugging is on


*Mar  1 00:00:21.101: %DHCP-6-ADDRESS_ASSIGN: Interface FastEthernet0 assigned
   DHCP address 10.0.102.113, mask 255.255.255.0, hostname SE.AP-01-1240
*Mar  1 00:00:21.101: %CAPWAP-3-EVENTLOG: ADDING IP 10.0.102.113, 255.255.255.0
   resolvemethod  A, ip_dhcp_addr 1
*Mar  1 00:00:29.546: %CAPWAP-3-EVENTLOG: Starting Discovery.
*Mar  1 00:00:29.546: %CAPWAP-3-EVENTLOG: CAPWAP State: Discovery.
*Mar  1 00:00:29.547: %CAPWAP-3-ERRORLOG: Not sending discovery request AP does
   not have an Ip !!
*Mar  1 00:00:29.591: %CAPWAP-3-EVENTLOG: CAPWAP State: Init.
*Mar  1 00:00:29.591: %CAPWAP-3-EVENTLOG: CAPWAP State: Discovery.
*Mar  1 00:00:29.595: %CAPWAP-3-EVENTLOG: CAPWAP State: Init.
*Mar  1 00:00:29.595: %CAPWAP-3-EVENTLOG: CAPWAP State: Discovery.
*Mar  1 00:00:30.087: Logging LWAPP message to 255.255.255.255.
```

(continues)

Example 4-2   *Access Point debug capwap client packet Output (continued)*

```
*Mar  1 00:00:30.133: %SYS-6-LOGGINGHOST_STARTSTOP: Logging to host
  255.255.255.255 started - CLI initiated
*Mar  1 00:00:33.326: %CDP_PD-4-POWER_OK: Full power - NEGOTIATED inline
  power source
*Mar  1 00:00:33.327: %CAPWAP-3-EVENTLOG: Discarding msg type 9 in
  CAPWAP state: 2.
*Mar  1 00:00:33.328: %CAPWAP-3-EVENTLOG: Send channel power message sent to
  0:0:0:0

*Mar  1 00:00:33.365: %CAPWAP-3-EVENTLOG: CAPWAP state not up. Abort sending
  channel and power levels info.0:0:0:0

*Mar  1 00:00:33.367: %CAPWAP-3-EVENTLOG: Discarding msg type 9 in
  CAPWAP state: 2.
*Mar  1 00:00:33.367: %CAPWAP-3-EVENTLOG: Send channel power message sent to
  0:0:0:0

*Mar  1 00:00:33.367: %LINK-3-UPDOWN: Interface Dot11Radio1, changed state to up
*Mar  1 00:00:33.405: %CAPWAP-3-EVENTLOG: CAPWAP state not up. Abort sending
  channel and power levels info.0:0:0:0

*Mar  1 00:00:33.406: %LINK-3-UPDOWN: Interface Dot11Radio0, changed state to up
*Mar  1 00:00:34.327: %LINEPROTO-5-UPDOWN: Line protocol on Interface
  Dot11Radio1, changed state to up
*Mar  1 00:00:34.368: %LINEPROTO-5-UPDOWN: Line protocol on Interface
  Dot11Radio0, changed state to up
*Mar  1 00:00:39.595:   capwapHandleDiscoveryTimer Expired

Translating "CISCO-CAPWAP-CONTROLLER"...domain server (144.254.10.123)

Translating "CISCO-LWAPP-CONTROLLER"...domain server (144.254.10.123)

*Mar  1 00:00:39.595: %CAPWAP-3-EVENTLOG: Could not discover any MWAR.
*Mar  1 00:00:39.595: %CAPWAP-3-EVENTLOG: Starting Discovery.
*Mar  1 00:00:39.595: %CAPWAP-3-EVENTLOG: CAPWAP State: Discovery.
*Mar  1 00:00:40.595: %CAPWAP-3-EVENTLOG: Controller address 10.0.102.254
  obtained through DHCP
*Mar  1 00:00:40.595: %CAPWAP-3-ERRORLOG: Did not get log server settings
  from DHCP.
*Mar  1 00:00:40.629: %CAPWAP-3-ERRORLOG: Could Not resolve
  CISCO-CAPWAP-CONTROLLER
*Mar  1 00:00:40.659: %CAPWAP-3-ERRORLOG: Could Not resolve
  CISCO-LWAPP-CONTROLLER
```

```
*Mar  1 00:00:40.660: CAPWAP Control mesg Sent to 10.0.102.254, Port 5246
*Mar  1 00:00:40.660:           Msg Type   : CAPWAP_DISCOVERY_REQUEST
*Mar  1 00:00:40.660:           Msg Length : 29
*Mar  1 00:00:40.660:           Msg SeqNum : 0
*Mar  1 00:00:41.660: %CAPWAP-3-EVENTLOG: Discovery Request sent to
  10.0.102.254 with discovery type set to 1
*Mar  1 00:00:41.660: CAPWAP Control mesg Sent to 10.0.102.254, Port 5246
*Mar  1 00:00:41.661:           Msg Type   : CAPWAP_DISCOVERY_REQUEST
*Mar  1 00:00:41.661:           Msg Length : 29
*Mar  1 00:00:41.661:           Msg SeqNum : 0
*Mar  1 00:00:41.661: %CAPWAP-3-EVENTLOG: Discovery Request sent to
  10.0.102.254 with discovery type set to 2
*Mar  1 00:00:41.662: CAPWAP Control mesg Sent to 10.0.108.254, Port 5246
*Mar  1 00:00:41.662:           Msg Type   : CAPWAP_DISCOVERY_REQUEST
*Mar  1 00:00:41.662:           Msg Length : 29
*Mar  1 00:00:41.662:           Msg SeqNum : 0
*Mar  1 00:00:41.662: %CAPWAP-3-EVENTLOG: Discovery Request sent to
  10.0.108.254 with discovery type set to 5
*Mar  1 00:00:41.663: CAPWAP Control mesg Sent to 10.66.210.2, Port 5246
*Mar  1 00:00:41.663:           Msg Type   : CAPWAP_DISCOVERY_REQUEST
*Mar  1 00:00:41.663:           Msg Length : 29
*Mar  1 00:00:41.663:           Msg SeqNum : 0
*Mar  1 00:00:41.663: %CAPWAP-3-EVENTLOG: Discovery Request sent to
  10.66.210.2 with discovery type set to 5
*Mar  1 00:00:41.664: CAPWAP Control mesg Sent to 10.0.107.254, Port 5246
*Mar  1 00:00:41.664:           Msg Type   : CAPWAP_DISCOVERY_REQUEST
*Mar  1 00:00:41.664:           Msg Length : 29
*Mar  1 00:00:41.664:           Msg SeqNum : 0
*Mar  1 00:00:41.664: %CAPWAP-3-EVENTLOG: Discovery Request sent to
  10.0.107.254 with discovery type set to 5
*Mar  1 00:00:41.664: CAPWAP Control mesg Sent to 255.255.255.255, Port 5246
*Mar  1 00:00:41.665:           Msg Type   : CAPWAP_DISCOVERY_REQUEST
*Mar  1 00:00:41.665:           Msg Length : 29
*Mar  1 00:00:41.665:           Msg SeqNum : 0
*Mar  1 00:00:41.665: %CAPWAP-3-EVENTLOG: Discovery Request sent to
  255.255.255.255 with discovery type set to 0
*Mar  1 00:00:41.666: CAPWAP Control mesg Recd from 10.0.102.254, Port 5246
*Mar  1 00:00:41.666:           HLEN 2,   Radio ID 0,    WBID 1
*Mar  1 00:00:41.666:           Msg Type   : CAPWAP_DISCOVERY_RESPONSE
*Mar  1 00:00:41.667:           Msg Length : 126
*Mar  1 00:00:41.667:           Msg SeqNum : 0
*Mar  1 00:00:41.667: %CAPWAP-3-EVENTLOG: Discovery Response from
  10.0.102.254wtpDecodeDiscovery Response numOfCapwapDiscoveryResp = 0
```

(continues)

Example 4-2   *Access Point debug capwap client packet Output (continued)*

```
*Mar  1 00:00:41.667: CAPWAP_DETAIL: Vendor specific payload validated.
*Mar  1 00:00:41.667: CAPWAP_DETAIL: Vendor specific payload validated.
*Mar  1 00:00:41.667: CAPWAP Control mesg Recd from 10.0.102.254, Port 5246
*Mar  1 00:00:41.667:          HLEN 2,   Radio ID 0,   WBID 1
*Mar  1 00:00:41.667:          Msg Type   : CAPWAP_DISCOVERY_RESPONSE
*Mar  1 00:00:41.668:          Msg Length : 126
*Mar  1 00:00:41.668:          Msg SeqNum : 0
*Mar  1 00:00:41.668: %CAPWAP-3-EVENTLOG: Discovery Response from
   10.0.102.254wtpDecodeDiscovery Response numOfCapwapDiscoveryResp = 1


*Mar  1 00:00:41.668: CAPWAP_DETAIL: Vendor specific payload validated.
*Mar  1 00:00:41.668: CAPWAP_DETAIL: Vendor specific payload validated.
*Mar  1 00:00:41.668: CAPWAP Control mesg Recd from 10.0.102.254, Port 5246
*Mar  1 00:00:41.668:          HLEN 2,   Radio ID 0,   WBID 1
*Mar  1 00:00:41.668:          Msg Type   : CAPWAP_DISCOVERY_RESPONSE
*Mar  1 00:00:41.668:          Msg Length : 126
*Mar  1 00:00:41.669:          Msg SeqNum : 0
*Mar  1 00:00:41.669: %CAPWAP-3-EVENTLOG: Discovery Response from
   10.0.102.254wtpDecodeDiscovery Response numOfCapwapDiscoveryResp = 2


*Mar  1 00:00:41.669: CAPWAP_DETAIL: Vendor specific payload validated.
*Mar  1 00:00:41.669: CAPWAP_DETAIL: Vendor specific payload validated.
*Mar  1 00:00:51.665:   capwapHandleDiscoveryTimer Expired

*Mar  1 00:00:51.665: %CAPWAP-3-EVENTLOG: Selected MWAR 'Chtac-WIR-WLC02'
 (index 0).
*Mar  1 00:00:51.665: %CAPWAP-3-EVENTLOG: Selected MWAR 'Chtac-WIR-WLC02'
 (index 0).
*Mar  1 00:00:51.665: %CAPWAP-3-EVENTLOG: Ap mgr count=1
*Mar  1 00:00:51.665: %CAPWAP-3-ERRORLOG: Go join a capwap controller
*Mar  1 00:00:51.666: %CAPWAP-3-EVENTLOG: Choosing AP Mgr with index 0,
 IP = 0xA0066FD , load = 7..
*Mar  1 00:00:51.666: %CAPWAP-3-EVENTLOG: Synchronizing time with AC time.
*Aug 20 15:47:20.000: %CAPWAP-3-EVENTLOG: Setting time to 15:47:20
 UTC Aug 20 2009
*Aug 20 15:47:20.000: %CAPWAP-5-DTLSREQSEND: DTLS connection request
   sent peer_ip: 10.0.102.253 peer_port: 5246
*Aug 20 15:47:21.000: %CAPWAP-3-EVENTLOG: CAPWAP State: DTLS Setup.
*Aug 20 15:47:22.417: CAPWAP_DETAIL: Dtls Event = 39 Capwap State = 3.
*Aug 20 15:47:22.417: %CAPWAP-5-DTLSREQSUCC: DTLS connection created
   successfully peer_ip: 10.0.102.253 peer_port: 5246
! At this stage, the DTLS session has been successfully established
! and the CAPWAP state changes to Join followed by the configuration.
```

```
*Aug 20 15:47:22.417: %CAPWAP-3-EVENTLOG: Dtls Session Established with the
   AC 10.0.102.253,port= 5246
*Aug 20 15:47:22.418: %CAPWAP-3-EVENTLOG: CAPWAP State: Join.
*Aug 20 15:47:22.418: %CAPWAP-3-EVENTLOG: Join request: version=84062720
*Aug 20 15:47:22.418: %CAPWAP-3-EVENTLOG: WTP descriptor: version=84062720
*Aug 20 15:47:22.418: %CAPWAP-3-EVENTLOG: Join request: hasMaximum
   Message Payload
*Aug 20 15:47:22.418: %CAPWAP-3-EVENTLOG: Sending Join Request Path
   MTU payload, Length 1376

*Aug 20 15:47:22.420: %CAPWAP-5-SENDJOIN: sending Join Request to 10.0.102.253
*Aug 20 15:47:22.420: %CAPWAP-5-CHANGED: CAPWAP changed state to JOIN
*Aug 20 15:47:22.426: CAPWAP Control mesg Recd from 10.0.102.253, Port 5246
*Aug 20 15:47:22.426:              HLEN 2,   Radio ID 0,   WBID 1
*Aug 20 15:47:22.426:              Msg Type   : CAPWAP_JOIN_RESPONSE
*Aug 20 15:47:22.426:              Msg Length : 1384
*Aug 20 15:47:22.426:              Msg SeqNum : 0
*Aug 20 15:47:22.426: %CAPWAP-3-EVENTLOG: Join Response from 10.0.102.253
*Aug 20 15:47:22.427: CAPWAP_DETAIL: Vendor specific payload validated.
*Aug 20 15:47:22.427: %CAPWAP-3-EVENTLOG: PTMU : Setting MTU to : 1485

*Aug 20 15:47:22.431: %CAPWAP-3-EVENTLOG: CAPWAP State: Configure.
*Aug 20 15:47:22.431: %CAPWAP-3-EVENTLOG: CAPWAP State: Image Data.
*Aug 20 15:47:22.448: %CAPWAP-3-EVENTLOG: CAPWAP State: Configure.
*Aug 20 15:47:22.476: %CAPWAP-3-EVENTLOG: reboot reason flag 4
*Aug 20 15:47:22.520: CAPWAP Control mesg Sent to 10.0.102.253, Port 5246
*Aug 20 15:47:22.520:              Msg Type   : CAPWAP_CONFIGURATION_STATUS
*Aug 20 15:47:22.520:              Msg Length : 1749
*Aug 20 15:47:22.521:              Msg SeqNum : 1
*Aug 20 15:47:22.522: %CAPWAP-3-EVENTLOG: Configuration Status sent to
   10.0.102.253
*Aug 20 15:47:22.522: %CAPWAP-5-CHANGED: CAPWAP changed state to CFG
*Aug 20 15:47:22.523: %CAPWAP-3-EVENTLOG: Current image is good.
   Connecting to the controller.
*Aug 20 15:47:22.567: CAPWAP Control mesg Recd from 10.0.102.253, Port 5246
*Aug 20 15:47:22.567:              HLEN 2,   Radio ID 0,   WBID 1
*Aug 20 15:47:22.567:              Msg Type   :
   CAPWAP_CONFIGURATION_STATUS_RESPONSE
*Aug 20 15:47:22.568:              Msg Length : 984
*Aug 20 15:47:22.568:              Msg SeqNum : 1
*Aug 20 15:47:22.568: %CAPWAP-3-EVENTLOG: Configuration Status Response from
   10.0.102.253
*Aug 20 15:47:22.612: CAPWAP_DETAIL: Vendor specific payload validated.
*Aug 20 15:47:22.612: CAPWAP_DETAIL: Vendor specific payload validated.
```

(continues)

Example 4-2   *Access Point debug capwap client packet Output (continued)*

```
*Aug 20 15:47:22.612: CAPWAP_DETAIL: Vendor specific payload validated.
*Aug 20 15:47:22.612: CAPWAP_DETAIL: Vendor specific payload validated.
*Aug 20 15:47:22.612: CAPWAP_DETAIL: Vendor specific payload validated.
*Aug 20 15:47:22.621: %CAPWAP-3-EVENTLOG: CAPWAP state not up.
  Abort sending channel and power levels info.10:0:102:253

*Aug 20 15:47:22.621: CAPWAP_DETAIL: Vendor specific payload validated.
*Aug 20 15:47:22.629: %CAPWAP-3-EVENTLOG: CAPWAP state not up.
  Abort sending channel and power levels info.10:0:102:253

*Aug 20 15:47:22.629: CAPWAP_DETAIL: Vendor specific payload validated.
*Aug 20 15:47:22.630: CAPWAP_DETAIL: Vendor specific payload validated.
*Aug 20 15:47:22.630: CAPWAP_DETAIL: Vendor specific payload validated.
*Aug 20 15:47:22.631: CAPWAP_DETAIL: Vendor specific payload validated.
*Aug 20 15:47:22.631: CAPWAP_DETAIL: Vendor specific payload validated.
*Aug 20 15:47:22.631: CAPWAP_DETAIL: Vendor specific payload validated.
*Aug 20 15:47:22.631: CAPWAP_DETAIL: Vendor specific payload validated.
*Aug 20 15:47:22.631: CAPWAP_DETAIL: Vendor specific payload validated.
*Aug 20 15:47:22.631: CAPWAP_DETAIL: Vendor specific payload validated.
*Aug 20 15:47:22.631: CAPWAP_DETAIL: Vendor specific payload validated.
*Aug 20 15:47:22.632: CAPWAP_DETAIL: Vendor specific payload validated.
*Aug 20 15:47:22.632: CAPWAP_DETAIL: Vendor specific payload validated.
*Aug 20 15:47:22.632: CAPWAP_DETAIL: Vendor specific payload validated.
*Aug 20 15:47:22.632: %LINK-5-CHANGED: Interface Dot11Radio0,
  changed state to administratively down
*Aug 20 15:47:22.639: %CAPWAP-3-EVENTLOG: CAPWAP state not up.
  Abort sending channel and power levels info.10:0:102:253

*Aug 20 15:47:22.640: CAPWAP_DETAIL: Vendor specific payload validated.
*Aug 20 15:47:22.647: %CAPWAP-3-EVENTLOG: CAPWAP state not up.
  Abort sending channel and power levels info.10:0:102:253

*Aug 20 15:47:22.647: CAPWAP_DETAIL: Vendor specific payload validated.
*Aug 20 15:47:22.647: CAPWAP_DETAIL: Vendor specific payload validated.
*Aug 20 15:47:22.648: CAPWAP_DETAIL: Vendor specific payload validated.
*Aug 20 15:47:22.649: CAPWAP_DETAIL: Vendor specific payload validated.
*Aug 20 15:47:22.649: CAPWAP_DETAIL: Vendor specific payload validated.
*Aug 20 15:47:22.649: CAPWAP_DETAIL: Vendor specific payload validated.
*Aug 20 15:47:22.649: CAPWAP_DETAIL: Vendor specific payload validated.
*Aug 20 15:47:22.649: CAPWAP_DETAIL: Vendor specific payload validated.
*Aug 20 15:47:22.649: CAPWAP_DETAIL: Vendor specific payload validated.
*Aug 20 15:47:22.649: %CAPWAP-5-CHANGED: CAPWAP changed state to UP
*Aug 20 15:47:22.650: CAPWAP_DETAIL: Vendor specific payload validated.
```

```
*Aug 20 15:47:22.650: CAPWAP_DETAIL: Vendor specific payload validated.
*Aug 20 15:47:22.650: CAPWAP_DETAIL: Vendor specific payload validated.
*Aug 20 15:47:22.650: CAPWAP_DETAIL: Vendor specific payload validated.
*Aug 20 15:47:22.650: CAPWAP_DETAIL: Vendor specific payload validated.
*Aug 20 15:47:22.650: CAPWAP_DETAIL: Vendor specific payload validated.
*Aug 20 15:47:22.651: %LINK-5-CHANGED: Interface Dot11Radio1,
  changed state to administratively down
*Aug 20 15:47:22.652: CAPWAP_DETAIL: Result Code message element len = 15.
*Aug 20 15:47:22.652: CAPWAP_DETAIL: encodeLen = 15 len = 8.
*Aug 20 15:47:22.652: CAPWAP Control mesg Sent to 10.0.102.253, Port 5246
*Aug 20 15:47:22.652:             Msg Type   : CAPWAP_CHANGE_STATE_EVENT_REQUEST
*Aug 20 15:47:22.652:             Msg Length : 15
*Aug 20 15:47:22.652:             Msg SeqNum : 2
*Aug 20 15:47:22.654: CAPWAP_DETAIL: Vendor specific payload validated.
*Aug 20 15:47:22.654: CAPWAP_DETAIL: Vendor specific payload validated.
*Aug 20 15:47:22.654: CAPWAP_DETAIL: Vendor specific payload validated.
*Aug 20 15:47:22.654: CAPWAP_DETAIL: Vendor specific payload validated.
*Aug 20 15:47:22.654: CAPWAP_DETAIL: Result Code message element len = 15.
*Aug 20 15:47:22.654: CAPWAP_DETAIL: encodeLen = 15 len = 8.
*Aug 20 15:47:22.655: CAPWAP_DETAIL: Result Code message element len = 15.
*Aug 20 15:47:22.655: CAPWAP_DETAIL: encodeLen - 15 len = 8.
*Aug 20 15:47:22.655: %CAPWAP-3-EVENTLOG: CAPWAP State: Run.
*Aug 20 15:47:22.655: %CAPWAP-5-JOINEDCONTROLLER:
  AP has joined controller Chtac-WIR-WLC02
*Aug 20 15:47:22.655: %CAPWAP-3-EVENTLOG: Configuration update for
  LinkAuditPayload  sent to10:0:102:253

*Aug 20 15:47:22.701: CAPWAP Control mesg Recd from 10.0.102.253, Port 5246
*Aug 20 15:47:22.701:             HLEN 2,   Radio ID 0,   WBID 1
*Aug 20 15:47:22.702:             Msg Type   : CAPWAP_CONFIGURATION_UPDATE_REQUEST
*Aug 20 15:47:22.702:             Msg Length : 556
*Aug 20 15:47:22.702:             Msg SeqNum : 1
*Aug 20 15:47:22.702: %CAPWAP-3-EVENTLOG: Configuration update request from
  10.0.102.253
*Aug 20 15:47:22.702: CAPWAP_DETAIL: Vendor specific payload validated.
*Aug 20 15:47:22.702: CAPWAP_DETAIL: Vendor specific payload validated.
*Aug 20 15:47:22.702: CAPWAP_DETAIL: Vendor specific payload validated.
*Aug 20 15:47:22.702: CAPWAP_DETAIL: Vendor specific payload validated.
*Aug 20 15:47:22.703: CAPWAP_DETAIL: Result code message element len = 8.
*Aug 20 15:47:22.703: CAPWAP Control mesg Sent to 10.0.102.253, Port 5246
*Aug 20 15:47:22.703:             Msg Type   :
  CAPWAP_CONFIGURATION_UPDATE_RESPONSE
*Aug 20 15:47:22.703:             Msg Length : 8
*Aug 20 15:47:22.703:             Msg SeqNum : 1
```

(continues)

Example 4-2   *Access Point debug capwap client packet Output (continued)*

```
*Aug 20 15:47:22.703: %CAPWAP-3-EVENTLOG: Configuration update response sent to
  10.0.102.253
*Aug 20 15:47:22.704: CAPWAP Control mesg Recd from 10.0.102.253, Port 5246
*Aug 20 15:47:22.704:            HLEN 2,   Radio ID 0,    WBID 1
*Aug 20 15:47:22.704:          Msg Type  : CAPWAP_CHANGE_STATE_EVENT_RESPONSE
*Aug 20 15:47:22.705:          Msg Length : 0
*Aug 20 15:47:22.705:          Msg SeqNum : 2
*Aug 20 15:47:22.705: CAPWAP Control mesg Sent to 10.0.102.253, Port 5246
*Aug 20 15:47:22.705:          Msg Type  : CAPWAP_CHANGE_STATE_EVENT_REQUEST
*Aug 20 15:47:22.705:          Msg Length : 15
*Aug 20 15:47:22.705:          Msg SeqNum : 3
*Aug 20 15:47:22.706: %CAPWAP-3-EVENTLOG: Change State Event Response from
  10.0.102.253
*Aug 20 15:47:22.706: CAPWAP Control mesg Recd from 10.0.102.253, Port 5246
*Aug 20 15:47:22.707:            HLEN 2,   Radio ID 0,    WBID 1
*Aug 20 15:47:22.707:          Msg Type  : CAPWAP_CONFIGURATION_UPDATE_REQUEST
*Aug 20 15:47:22.707:          Msg Length : 492
*Aug 20 15:47:22.707:          Msg SeqNum : 2
*Aug 20 15:47:22.707: %CAPWAP-3-EVENTLOG: Configuration update request from
  10.0.102.253
*Aug 20 15:47:22.707: CAPWAP_DETAIL: Vendor specific payload validated.
*Aug 20 15:47:22.707: CAPWAP_DETAIL: Vendor specific payload validated.
*Aug 20 15:47:22.707: CAPWAP_DETAIL: Vendor specific payload validated.
*Aug 20 15:47:22.708: CAPWAP_DETAIL: Vendor specific payload validated.
*Aug 20 15:47:22.708: CAPWAP_DETAIL: Result code message element len = 8.
*Aug 20 15:47:22.708: CAPWAP Control mesg Sent to 10.0.102.253, Port 5246
*Aug 20 15:47:22.708:          Msg Type  :
  CAPWAP_CONFIGURATION_UPDATE_RESPONSE
*Aug 20 15:47:22.708:          Msg Length : 8
*Aug 20 15:47:22.708:          Msg SeqNum : 2
*Aug 20 15:47:22.709: %CAPWAP-3-EVENTLOG: Configuration update response sent to
  10.0.102.253
*Aug 20 15:47:22.709: CAPWAP Control mesg Recd from 10.0.102.253, Port 5246
*Aug 20 15:47:22.709:            HLEN 2,   Radio ID 0,    WBID 1
*Aug 20 15:47:22.709:          Msg Type  : CAPWAP_CHANGE_STATE_EVENT_RESPONSE
*Aug 20 15:47:22.709:          Msg Length : 0
*Aug 20 15:47:22.710:          Msg SeqNum : 3
*Aug 20 15:47:22.710: CAPWAP Control mesg Sent to 10.0.102.253, Port 5246
*Aug 20 15:47:22.710:          Msg Type  : CAPWAP_CHANGE_STATE_EVENT_REQUEST
*Aug 20 15:47:22.710:          Msg Length : 15
*Aug 20 15:47:22.710:          Msg SeqNum : 4
*Aug 20 15:47:22.710: %CAPWAP-3-EVENTLOG: Change State Event Response from
  10.0.102.253
*Aug 20 15:47:22.711: CAPWAP Control mesg Recd from 10.0.102.253, Port 5246
```

```
*Aug 20 15:47:22.711:            HLEN 2,   Radio ID 0,    WBID 1
*Aug 20 15:47:22.711:            Msg Type   : CAPWAP_CONFIGURATION_UPDATE_REQUEST
*Aug 20 15:47:22.712:            Msg Length : 428
*Aug 20 15:47:22.712:            Msg SeqNum : 3
*Aug 20 15:47:22.712: %CAPWAP-3-EVENTLOG: Configuration update request from
  10.0.102.253
*Aug 20 15:47:22.712: CAPWAP_DETAIL: Vendor specific payload validated.
*Aug 20 15:47:22.712: CAPWAP_DETAIL: Vendor specific payload validated.
*Aug 20 15:47:22.712: CAPWAP_DETAIL: Vendor specific payload validated.
*Aug 20 15:47:22.712: CAPWAP_DETAIL: Vendor specific payload validated.
*Aug 20 15:47:22.712: CAPWAP_DETAIL: Result code message element len = 8.
*Aug 20 15:47:22.713: CAPWAP Control mesg Sent to 10.0.102.253, Port 5246
*Aug 20 15:47:22.713:            Msg Type   :
  CAPWAP_CONFIGURATION_UPDATE_RESPONSE
*Aug 20 15:47:22.713:            Msg Length : 8
*Aug 20 15:47:22.713:            Msg SeqNum : 3
*Aug 20 15:47:22.713: %CAPWAP-3-EVENTLOG: Configuration update response sent to
  10.0.102.253
*Aug 20 15:47:22.732: %CAPWAP-3-EVENTLOG: Configuration update response sent to
  10.0.102.253
*Aug 20 15:47:23.631: %LINEPROTO-5-UPDOWN: Line protocol on
  Interface Dot11Radio0, changed state to down
*Aug 20 15:47:23.650: %LINEPROTO-5-UPDOWN: Line protocol on Interface
  Dot11Radio1, changed state to down
*Aug 20 15:47:52.655: %CAPWAP-3-EVENTLOG: Echo Interval Expired.
*Aug 20 15:47:52.655: CAPWAP Control mesg Sent to 10.0.102.253, Port 5246
*Aug 20 15:47:52.655:            Msg Type   : CAPWAP_ECHO_REQUEST
*Aug 20 15:47:52.655:            Msg Length : 0
*Aug 20 15:47:52.655:            Msg SeqNum : 7
*Aug 20 15:47:52.656: %CAPWAP-3-EVENTLOG: Echo Request sent to 10.0.102.253
*Aug 20 15:47:52.657: CAPWAP Control mesg Recd from 10.0.102.253, Port 5246
*Aug 20 15:47:52.658:            HLEN 2,   Radio ID 0,    WBID 1
*Aug 20 15:47:52.658:            Msg Type   : CAPWAP_ECHO_RESPONSE
*Aug 20 15:47:52.658:            Msg Length : 0
*Aug 20 15:47:52.658:            Msg SeqNum : 7
*Aug 20 15:47:52.658: %CAPWAP-3-EVENTLOG: Echo Response from 10.0.102.253
```

The final state that you want all APs to be in is Run and after the AP passes the configuration and version validation, it moves the AP state into the Run state so it can start servicing clients.

Troubleshooting CAPWAP Session Establishment/AP Discovery and Join

Usually, in failures in which the DTLS is never established, you have to identify at what step the process is failing. Once again, you usually have to defer to a packet trace to determine that. You have to look at two different views:

■ At the WLC port

■ At the switch port the AP is plugged into

In most cases, something happens between these two segments; however, you must understand that these points in the network are crucial. Technically, these are the starting and finishing points.

To get a good grasp on troubleshooting the issue, you must comprehend and understand the CAPWAP join process. On paper it is pretty straightforward, but you can take another look at it from a different angle. Looking at the process from a debug output perspective might be a better approach. This approach might also help solidify the foundation of what you have already learned. The commented output in Example 4-3 is with CAPWAP and DTLS debugs enabled at the same time. To read the debugs and explanations that follow, please refer to the CAPWAP packet flow in Figure 4-4.

Example 4-3 *CAPWAP and DLTS Debugs on the Controller*

```
(Cisco Controller) >show debug

Debug Flags Enabled:
  capwap detail enabled.
  capwap events enabled.
  capwap state enabled.
  dtls event enabled.
  dtls trace enabled.
  dtls packet enabled.
  lwapp detail enabled.


*51.790: Received CAPWAP_MESSAGE
*51.790: CAPWAP Control Msg Received from 10.0.102.117:4309
*51.790: 00:1e:79:d4:f3:90 packet received of length 53 from 10.0.102.117:4309
*51.790: 00:1e:79:d4:f3:90 Msg Type = 1 Capwap state = 0

! Here you see that Discovery Request from the AP with the AP address
! 10.0.102.117 reached the controller. If this is not happening at all,
! there is no need to troubleshoot further on the controller: Accessing the
! AP via CLI and capturing a sniffer trace on the switch port the AP is plugged
! into will be the next step. Here, you see that the AP sends the
```

```
! discovery request successfully and the controller is responding with a
! discovery response.

*51.790: 00:1e:79:d4:f3:90 Discovery Request from 10.0.102.117:4309
*51.790: 00:1e:79:d4:f3:90 msgEleLength = 1 msgEleType = 20
*51.790: 00:1e:79:d4:f3:90 Total msgEleLen = 24
*51.790: 00:1e:79:d4:f3:90 msgEleLength = 1 msgEleType = 41
*51.790: 00:1e:79:d4:f3:90 Total msgEleLen = 19
*51.790: 00:1e:79:d4:f3:90 msgEleLength = 1 msgEleType = 44
*51.790: 00:1e:79:d4:f3:90 Total msgEleLen = 14
*51.790: 00:1e:79:d4:f3:90 msgEleLength = 10 msgEleType = 37
*51.790: 00:1e:79:d4:f3:90 Vendor specific payload from AP   00:1E:79:D4:F3:90
  validated
*51.790: 00:1e:79:d4:f3:90 Total msgEleLen = 0
*51.790: 1. 0 0
*51.790: 2. 232 3
*51.790: 3. 0 0
*51.790: 4. 50 0


*51.790: 00:1e:79:d4:f3:90 Discovery resp: AC Descriptor message element
  len = 40
*51.790: acName = Chtac-WIR-WLC02
*51.790: 00:1e:79:d4:f3:90 Discovery resp:AC Name message element length = 59
*51.790: 00:1e:79:d4:f3:90 Discovery resp: WTP Radio Information msg length = 68
*51.790: 00:1e:79:d4:f3:90 Discovery resp: CAPWAP Control IPV4 Address len = 78
*51.790: 00:1e:79:d4:f3:90 Discovery resp: CAPWAP Control IPV6 Address len = 100
*51.790: 00:1e:79:d4:f3:90 Discovery resp: Mwar type payload len = 111
*51.790: 00:1e:79:d4:f3:90 Discovery resp: Time sync payload len = 126
*51.790: 00:1e:79:d4:f3:90 Discovery Response sent to 10.0.102.117:4309


*51.790: 00:1e:79:d4:f3:90 WTP already released

! Upon receiving the discovery response, the AP starts establishing the
! DTLS session by sending a ClientHello, whereas from the logs you see
! that now the DTLS handshake started Handshake in progress...

*02.790: Received CAPWAP_MESSAGE
*02.790: CAPWAP Control Msg Received from 10.0.102.117:4309
*02.790: dtls_conn_hash_search: Connection not found in hash table - Table empty
*02.790: DTLS connection not found, creating new connection for 10:0:102:117
  (4309) 10:0:102:253 (5246)
*02.790: dtls_secret_pki_init: Called...
*02.861: dtls_secret_pki_add_idcert: Called...
*02.861: acDtlsCallback: Certificate installed for PKI based authentication.
```

(continues)

Example 4-3 *CAPWAP and DLTS Debugs on the Controller (continued)*

```
*02.861: openssl_dtls_process_packet: Called... for connection 0x1797ebc4
*02.861: local_openssl_dtls_record_inspect: record=Handshake epoch=0 seq=0
*02.861: local_openssl_dtls_record_inspect:    msg=ClientHello len=44 seq=0
  frag_off=0 frag_len=44
*02.862: openssl_shim_cookie_generate_callback: Called...
*02.862: openssl_shim_info_callback: SSL state = 0x2113; where = 0x2001;
*02.862: openssl_dtls_process_packet: Handshake in progress...
*02.862: openssl_dtls_send: Sending 60 bytes
*02.862: 00000000: 16 fe ff 00 00 00 00 00  00 00 00 00 2f 03 00 00   ...........
*02.862: openssl_dtls_send: No data to send

*02.863: Received CAPWAP_MESSAGE
*02.863: CAPWAP Control Msg Received from 10.0.102.117:4309
*02.863: openssl_dtls_process_packet: Called... for connection 0x1797ebc4
*02.864: local_openssl_dtls_record_inspect: record=Handshake epoch=0 seq=1
*02.864: local_openssl_dtls_record_inspect:    msg=ClientHello len=76 seq=1
        frag_off=0 frag_len=76
*02.864: openssl_shim_cookie_verify_callback: Called...

! The second "ClientHello" sent by the AP contains the previous sent
! cookie, which now is verified by the controller "cookie_verify_callback."
! If this is successful, the Server Hello and certificate exchange take place.
! You see this on the size of the huge packet-hex-dumps (omitted in the example)
! as well in the debugs showing msg=Certificate.

*02.864: openssl_shim_info_callback: SSL state = 0x2111; where = 0x2001;
*02.864: openssl_dtls_process_packet: Handshake in progress...*02.864:
  openssl_dtls_send: Sending 544 bytes
*02.865: 00000000: 16 fe ff 00 00 00 00 00  00 00 01 00 52 02 00 00   ...........
*02.865: 00000010: 46 00 01 00 00 00 00 00  46 fe ff 4a 8e 6f aa 02   F.......F..
*02.865: 00000020: ad af fd e2 42 12 3e 56  68 4d e1 40 db ca f7 55   ....B.>VhM.
*02.865: 00000030: 36 e9 aa 36 6e 91 70 8d  a8 dd 3c 20 69 da 55 6b   6..6n.p...<
*02.865: 00000040: 46 b9 a2 b4 fd fb 16 1c  ea fd e9 f5 e6 77 6f d6   F..........
*02.865: 00000050: 69 68 d7 e

! Parts of DTLS hex dump output omitted

  06 00 12 0d 00 00 06 00   ...........
*02.868: 00000110: 03 00 00 00 00 00 06 03  01 02 40 00 00 16 fe ff   ..........
*02.868: 00000120: 00 00 00 00 00 00 00 07  00 0c 0e 00 00 00 00 04   ...........
*02.868: 00000130: 00 00 00 00 00 00                                 ......
*02.869: openssl_dtls_send: No data to send

*02.923: Received CAPWAP_MESSAGE
```

```
*02.923: CAPWAP Control Msg Received from 10.0.102.117:4309
*02.923: openssl_dtls_process_packet: Called... for connection 0x1797ebc4
*02.923: local_openssl_dtls_record_inspect: record=Handshake epoch=0 seq=2
*02.923: local_openssl_dtls_record_inspect:   msg=Certificate len=1146 seq=2
  frag_off=0 frag_len=519
*02.923: openssl_shim_info_callback: SSL state = 0x2181; where = 0x2002;
*02.923: openssl_dtls_process_packet: Handshake in progress...
*02.923: openssl_dtls_send: No data to send

*02.923: Received CAPWAP_MESSAGE
*02.923: CAPWAP Control Msg Received from 10.0.102.117:4309
*02.923: openssl_dtls_process_packet: Called... for connection 0x1797ebc4
*02.923: local_openssl_dtls_record_inspect: record=Handshake epoch=0 seq=3
*02.923: local_openssl_dtls_record_inspect:   msg=Certificate len=1140 seq=2
  frag_off=519 frag_len=519
*02.923: openssl_shim_info_callback: SSL state = 0x2181; where = 0x2002;
*02.923: openssl_dtls_process_packet: Handshake in progress...
*02.923: openssl_dtls_send: No data to send
*02.924: Received CAPWAP_MESSAGE

*02.924: CAPWAP Control Msg Received from 10.0.102.117:4309
*02.924: openssl_dtls_process_packet: Called... for connection 0x1797ebc4
*02.924: local_openssl_dtls_record_inspect: record=Handshake epoch=0 seq=4
*02.924: local_openssl_dtls_record_inspect:   msg=Certificate len=1146 seq=2
  frag_off=1038 frag_len=108
*02.934: openssl_shim_cert_verify_callback: Certificate verification - passed!
*02.934: openssl_shim_info_callback: SSL state = 0x2181; where = 0x2001;
*02.934: openssl_shim_info_callback: SSL state = 0x2190; where = 0x2002;
*02.934: openssl_dtls_process_packet: Handshake in progress...
*02.935: openssl_dtls_send: No data to send
*04.097: Received CAPWAP_MESSAGE

*04.097: CAPWAP Control Msg Received from 10.0.102.117:4309
*04.097: openssl_dtls_process_packet: Called... for connection 0x1797ebc4
*04.097: local_openssl_dtls_record_inspect: record=Handshake epoch=0 seq=5
*04.097: local_openssl_dtls_record_inspect:   msg=ClientKeyExchange len=258
  seq=3 frag_off=0 frag_len=258
*04.200: openssl_shim_info_callback: SSL state = 0x2190; where = 0x2001;
*04.200: openssl_shim_info_callback: SSL state = 0x21a0; where = 0x2002;
*04.200: openssl_dtls_process_packet: Handshake in progress...
*04.200: openssl_dtls_send: No data to send

*04.200: Received CAPWAP_MESSAGE
*04.200: CAPWAP Control Msg Received from 10.0.102.117:4309
```

(continues)

Example 4-3 *CAPWAP and DLTS Debugs on the Controller (continued)*

```
*04.200: openssl_dtls_process_packet: Called... for connection 0x1797ebc4
*04.201: local_openssl_dtls_record_inspect: record=Handshake epoch=0 seq=6
*04.201: local_openssl_dtls_record_inspect:   msg=CertificateVerify len=258
  seq=4 frag_off=0 frag_len=258
*04.201: local_openssl_dtls_record_inspect: record=ChangeCipherSpec epoch=0
  seq=7
*04.201: local_openssl_dtls_record_inspect: record=Handshake epoch=1 seq=0
*04.201: local_openssl_dtls_record_inspect:   msg=Unknown or Encrypted
*04.204: openssl_shim_info_callback: SSL state = 0x21a0; where = 0x2001;
*04.204: openssl_dtls_process_packet: Connection established!
*04.204: DTLS connection established
*04.204: openssl_dtls_mtu_update: Called...
*04.204: openssl_dtls_mtu_update: Setting DTLS MTU for link to peer
  10.0.102.117:4309

*04.204: openssl_dtls_send: Sending 91 bytes
*04.204: 00000000: 14 fe ff 00 00 00 00 00  00 00 08 00 01 01 16 fe  ...........
*04.204: 00000010: ff 00 01 00

! Parts of DTLS hex dump output omitted

                                               0a 6b 31 ad 97 ce
.o......g..
*04.204: 00000050: 36 4d 86 c3 1f 08 d5 c1  4c 73 6e              6M......Lsn
*04.204: openssl_dtls_send: No data to send
*04.205: Received CAPWAP_MESSAGE

*04.205: CAPWAP DTLS session established msg

! Once you see "DTLS connection established" in the logs, you know that
! the handshake and therefore also the certificate validations were successful.
! In case of failure, it makes sense to capture a sniffer trace from the DTLS
! handshake because this allows you to find more details about the exchanged
! certificates. In the debug, you see following the certificate exchange
! "DTLS connection established" and know, therefore, that there is no need
! to dig further into certificate details.

! From this point on, the CAPWAP session will be encrypted (DTLS application data),
! so a sniffer trace is not providing further information apart from packets
! being exchanged. But from the debugs you see that the AP proceeds with the
! join request and that the controller is sending the join response with
! all detailed information.

*04.205: DTLS Session established server (10.0.102.253:5246), client
```

```
    (10.0.102.117:4309)
*04.205: Starting wait join timer for DTLS connection 0x1797ebc4!, AP:
   10.0.102.117:4309


*04.209: Received CAPWAP_MESSAGE
*04.209: CAPWAP Control Msg Received from 10.0.102.117:4309
*04.209: openssl_dtls_process_packet: Called... for connection 0x1797ebc4
*04.209: local_openssl_dtls_record_inspect: record=ApplicationData epoch=1 seq=1
*04.209: openssl_dtls_process_packet:  1400 bytes decrypted
*04.209: openssl_dtls_send: No data to send
*04.209: 00:1e:79:d4:f3:90 packet received of length 1400 from 10.0.102.117:4309
*04.209: 00:1e:79:d4:f3:90 Msg Type = 3 Capwap state = 0
*04.209: 00:1e:79:d4:f3:90 Join Request from 10.0.102.117:4309
*04.209: 00:1e:79:d4:f3:90 Total msgEleLen = 1348
*04.210: 00:1e:79:d4:f3:90 Created AP 00:1e:79:d4:f3:90
*04.210: 00:1e:79:d4:f3:90 Join timer: Found DTLS session for 10.0.102.117:4309
*04.210: 00:1e:79:d4:f3:90 Join Request: Total msgEleLen = 1348
*04.210: 00:1e:79:d4:f3:90 Join Request: Total msgEleLen = 0
*04.210: DTL Adding AP 0 - 10.0.102.117
*04.211: Join Version: = 84062720


*04.211: Join resp: Result Code message element len = 8
*04.211: 1. 0 0
*04.211: 2. 232 3
*04.211: 3. 1 0
*04.211: 4. 50 0
*04.211: Join resp: AC Descriptor message element len = 48
*04.211: acName = Chtac-WIR-WLC02
*04.211: Join resp: AC Name message element len = 67
*04.211: Join resp: WTP Radio Information message element len = 76
*04.211: Join resp: CAPWAP Control IPV4 Address len = 86
*04.211: Join resp: CAPWAP Maximum Msg element len = 92
*04.211: 00:1e:79:d4:f3:90 Sending encrypted packet to AP 10:0:102:117 (4309)


*04.211: openssl_dtls_encrypt_and_send: Called...
*04.211: openssl_dtls_send: Sending 1453 bytes
*04.215: 00000000: 17 fe ff 00 01 00 00 00  00 00 01 05 a0 04 c6 83   ...........
*04.215: 00000010: 22 e9 9d f3 ff aa f5 0c


! Parts of DTLS hex dump output omitted


                                        5f ed 97 92 54 de e5 94
R..!...._..
*04.216: 000005a0: f0 d7 d4 82 30 ed 1f 76  73 0b 4e fc 84         ....0..vs.N
```

(continues)

Example 4-3   *CAPWAP and DLTS Debugs on the Controller (continued)*

```
*04.216: openssl_dtls_send: No data to send
*04.216:

! Upon a successful join request/response sequence, the CAPWAP state changes to
! configure "CAPWAP State: Configure" followed by several configuration exchanges.
! In case of a different AP image, the AP would download the image from the
! controller and reboot. In the debug example, the image running on the AP
! was already the same, so the AP moves into the run state:
! "CAPWAP State: Run". The CAPWAP session is successfully established.


*04.216: CAPWAP State: Configure

*04.216: 00:1e:79:d4:f3:90 capwap_ac_platform.c:1179 - Operation State 0 ===> 4
*04.235: 00:1e:79:d4:f3:90 Sending LWAPP Event Reg to
  'asTrackSigDisableAllEvent+168' for AP 00:1e:79:d4:f3:90(1)
*04.236: 00:1e:79:d4:f3:90 WTP already released
*04.236: 00:1e:79:d4:f3:90 Register LWAPP event for AP 00:1e:79:d4:f3:90 slot 0
*04.236: Received SPAM_NOTIFY_LCB_CONFIGURED_MSG
*04.237: 00:1e:79:d4:f3:90 Register LWAPP event for AP 00:1e:79:d4:f3:90 slot 1
*04.237: Received SPAM_NOTIFY_LCB_CONFIGURED_MSG
*04.312: Received CAPWAP_MESSAGE

*04.312: CAPWAP Control Msg Received from 10.0.102.117:4309
*04.312: openssl_dtls_process_packet: Called... for connection 0x1797ebc4
*04.312: local_openssl_dtls_record_inspect: record=ApplicationData epoch=1 seq=2
*04.312: openssl_dtls_process_packet:  1352 bytes decrypted
*04.312: openssl_dtls_send: No data to send
*04.312: Received CAPWAP_MESSAGE


*04.313: openssl_dtls_process_packet: Called... for connection 0x1797ebc4
*04.313: local_openssl_dtls_record_inspect: record=ApplicationData epoch=1 seq=3
*04.313: openssl_dtls_process_packet:  429 bytes decrypted
*04.313: openssl_dtls_send: No data to send
*04.313: 00:1e:79:d4:f3:90 packet received of length 1773 from 10.0.102.117:4309

*04.313: 00:1e:79:d4:f3:90 Msg Type = 5 Capwap state = 8
*04.313: 00:1e:79:d4:f3:90 Configuration Status from 10.0.102.117:4309


*04.314: 00:1e:79:d4:f3:90 Config status: Total msgEleLen = 172

! Parts of Config Message Elements omitted
```

```
*04.314: 00:1e:79:d4:f3:90 Config req: msgEleLength = 19 msgEleType = 37
*04.314: 00:1e:79:d4:f3:90 Updating IP info for AP 00:1e:79:d4:f3:90 —
  static 0, 10.0.102.117/255.255.255.0, gtw 10.0.102.1
*04.314: 00:1e:79:d4:f3:90 Updating IP 10.0.102.117 ===> 10.0.102.117 for
  AP 00:1e:79:d4:f3:90
*04.314: 00:1e:79:d4:f3:90 Setting MTU to 1485
*04.315: 00:1e:79:d4:f3:90 Config status: Total msgEleLen = 0
*04.315: Config resp: AC IPv4 List message element len = 8
*04.315: 00:1e:79:d4:f3:90 Config resp: AC IPv6 List message element len = 12
*04.315: 00:1e:79:d4:f3:90 Config resp: CAPWAP Timers message element len = 18
*04.315: 00:1e:79:d4:f3:90 Config resp: Radio Administrative State message
  element for slot 0, length = 30.
*04.315: 00:1e:79:d4:f3:90 Config resp: Radio Administrative State message
  element for slot 1, length = 36.
*04.315: 00:1e:79:d4:f3:90 Config resp: Decryption Error Report Period message
  element len = 50
*04.315: 00:1e:79:d4:f3:90 Config resp: Idle Timeout message element len = 58
*04.315: 00:1e:79:d4:f3:90 Config resp: WTP Fallback message element len = 63
*04.357: 00:1e:79:d4:f3:90 Config resp: Vendor specific message element
  len = 984
*04.357: 00:1e:79:d4:f3:90 Sending encrypted packet to AP 10:0:102:117 (4309)

*04.357: openssl_dtls_encrypt_and_send: Called...
*04.357: openssl_dtls_send: Sending 1053 bytes
*04.359: 00000000: 17 fe ff 00 01 00 00 00  00 00 02 04 10 a9 21 8d   ...........
*04.359: 00000010: 16 b1 5f 33 1f b7 69 7d  0e c2 02 93 b0 42 76 87   .._3..i}...
*04.359: 00000020: 79 36 ad aa b0 03 90 ca

! Parts of DTLS hex dump output omitted

                                         85 78 88 4f bf c3 60 99
&E.6.....x.
*04.360: 00000260: 72 58 a3 22 38 2e 6d 7b  df 0a c7 70 65 25 fc 14   rX."8.m{...
*04.360: 00000270: 27 ed 6e c1 59 a1 0c 78  b7 33 31 0c 08            '.n.Y..x.31
*04.360: openssl_dtls_send: No data to send
*04.360: 00:1e:79:d4:f3:90 Configuration update request for configuring
  association limit params sent to 10.0.102.117:4309

*04.361: 00:1e:79:d4:f3:90 Releasing WTP

*04.440: Received CAPWAP_MESSAGE
*04.440: CAPWAP Control Msg Received from 10.0.102.117:4309
*04.440: openssl_dtls_process_packet: Called... for connection 0x1797ebc4
*04.440: local_openssl_dtls_record_inspect: record=ApplicationData epoch=1 seq=4
```

(continues)

Example 4-3   *CAPWAP and DLTS Debugs on the Controller (continued)*

```
*04.440: openssl_dtls_process_packet:  39 bytes decrypted
*04.440: openssl_dtls_send: No data to send
*04.440: 00:1e:79:d4:f3:90 packet received of length 39 from 10.0.102.117:4309
*04.440: 00:1e:79:d4:f3:90 Msg Type = 11 Capwap state = 8
*04.440: 00:1e:79:d4:f3:90 Change State Event Request from 10.0.102.117:4309
*04.440: 00:1e:79:d4:f3:90 Change state: Total msgEleLen = 15
*04.440: 00:1e:79:d4:f3:90 Change state: msgEleLength = 3 msgEleType = 32
*04.450: 00:1e:79:d4:f3:90 Change state: msgEleLength = 4 msgEleType = 33
*04.450: 00:1e:79:d4:f3:90 Change state: Total msgEleLen = 0


*04.450: 00:1e:79:d4:f3:90 Sending encrypted packet to AP 10:0:102:117 (4309)


*04.450: openssl_dtls_encrypt_and_send: Called...
*04.451: openssl_dtls_send: Sending 77 bytes
*04.451: 00000000: 17 fe ff 00 01 00 00 00  00 00 04 00 40 f1 33 6c  ...........
*04.451: 00000010: fe 37 27 cf b5 4f 62 0e


! Parts of DTLS hex dump output omitted


                                             37 05 d2 b6 35 ed a4 f9
..{.}.._7..
*04.451: 00000040: b5 78 91 a9 67 1c 83 5a  7d 6a 7e 0a 11            .x..g..Z}j~
*04.451: openssl_dtls_send: No data to send
*04.451: CAPWAP State: Run


*04.451: 00:1e:79:d4:f3:90 Change State Event Response sent to 10.0.102.117:4309
```

CAPWAP Communication: Control and Data Encryption

After the DTLS session is established, CAPWAP control traffic is encrypted and CAPWAP data traffic can be encrypted.

For troubleshooting reasons, it is possible to disable CAPWAP control traffic. Whether the CAPWAP control traffic is encrypted or not is controlled via the CAPWAP preamble. The CAPWAP preamble is common to all CAPWAP transport headers and is used to identify the header type that immediately follows. If the CAPWAP preamble type is equal to 0, the CAPWAP header immediately follows, which means that the packet is not encrypted. If the CAPWAP preamble type is equal to 1, a CAPWAP DTLS header immediately follows, which means that the packet is encrypted. Figure 4-10 and Figure 4-11 highlight this CAPWAP preamble type field.

Enabling or disabling CAPWAP-Control Packet encryption needs to be done on the control using the **test capwap encr** *APNAME* **disable** command and on the AP using **test capwap dtls ctrl disable**.

Type = 0 followed by cleartext data

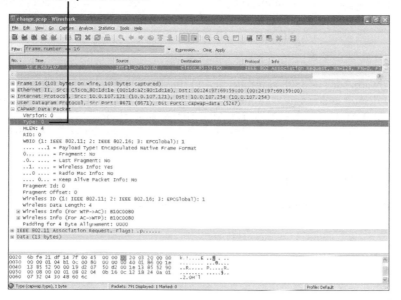

Figure 4-10   *CAPWAP Preamble Field–Cleartext Data*

Type = 1 followed by encrypted DTLS data

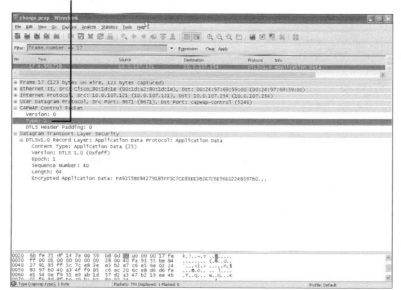

Figure 4-11   *CAPWAP Preamble Field–Encrypted Data*

> **Note**   Those **test** commands are for troubleshooting purposes only and are not persistent; upon reloading the AP or the controller, CAPWAP control packets become encrypted again.

As mentioned earlier, CAPWAP-Data encryption is optional and only supported on specific hardware, such as 5508 controller and 1130 APs. CAPWAP-Data encryption is disabled by default and can be configured per AP. Example 4-4 shows how to configure and verify CAPWAP-Data encryption. The AP with the name **chtac-LAP1130-04** has CAPWAP-Data encryption disabled, and the AP with the name **chtac-LAP1130-03** is configured to encrypt CAPWAP-Data.

Example 4-4   *CAPWAP Data Encryption*

```
(Cisco Controller) >config ap link-encryption  enable chtac-LAP1130-03

(Cisco Controller) >show dtls connections

       AP Name            Local Port         Peer IP          Ciphersuite
   ----------------    -------------    ---------------    ------------------------------
   chtac-LAP1130-04       CAPWAP_Ctrl    10.0.107.114      TLS_RSA_WITH_AES_128_CBC_SHA
   chtac-LAP1130-03       CAPWAP_Ctrl    10.0.107.123      TLS_RSA_WITH_AES_128_CBC_SHA
   chtac-LAP1130-03       CAPWAP_Data    10.0.107.123      TLS_RSA_WITH_AES_128_CBC_SHA

(Cisco Controller) >show ap link-encryption all

                   Encryption   Dnstream   Upstream   Last
AP Name            State        Count      Count      Update
----------------   ---------    ---------  ---------  --------
chtac-LAP1130-04   Dis          0          0          9:16
chtac-LAP1130-03   En           0          0          Never
```

CAPWAP Communication: Sequence Numbers and Retransmissions

The CAPWAP protocol operates as a reliable transport. For each request message, a response message is defined, which acknowledges receipt of the request message. In addition, the control header Sequence Number field is used, which is an identifier value used to match request and response packets. When a CAPWAP packet with a Request Message Type Value is received, the value of the Sequence Number field is copied into the corresponding response message.

Response messages are not explicitly acknowledged; therefore, if a response message is not received, the original request message is retransmitted until "MaxRetransmit" has been reached. After this level has been reached, the link layer considers the peer dead and the AP goes to CAPWAP State DTLS Teardown, which means that the AP needs to reestablish the DTLS session from the beginning. Also refer to the CAPWAP protocol state machine, shown in Figure 4-5.

The CAPWAP data channel uses a Keep-Alive packet to bind the CAPWAP control channel with the data channel and to maintain freshness of the data channel, ensuring that the channel is still functioning.

The CAPWAP data channel Keep-Alive packet is transmitted by the AP when the DataChannelKeepAlive timer expires. (The default is 30 seconds.)

The AP retransmits the CAPWAP data channel Keep-Alive packet in the same manner as the CAPWAP control messages. If the DataChannelDeadInterval timer expires, the AP tears down the control DTLS session and the data DTLS session if one existed.

CAPWAP Fragmentation and Path MTU Discovery

Taking into account that CAPWAP is "tunneling" IP data traffic from wireless clients and that CAPWAP runs over WAN links (Hybrid Remote Edge Access Point [H-REAP] setups), it is important for troubleshooting to understand the fragmentation behavior as well as the Path MTU Discovery mechanism from CAPWAP. The following sections provide an overview of how this works. For a more detailed explanation, refer to the CAPWAP and DTLS RFCs, as outlined in Figure 4-1.

CAPWAP-Control Packets Fragmentation

DTLS handshake messages can be quite large (in theory up to $2^{24} - 1$ bytes, but in practice many kilobytes). By contrast, UDP datagrams are often limited to less than 1500 bytes if fragmentation is not desired. Therefore, DTLS provides a mechanism for fragmenting a handshake message over numerous records. That is why you see the certificate exchanges divided into several frames. This is, for example, visible in Figure 4-5, described as **Certificate (fragment)** in frame 54 and onward.

CAPWAP-Data Packets Fragmentation

Like all tunnel protocols, CAPWAP adds overhead to data it is transporting, which might cause fragmentation. Although IP provides fragmentation and reassembly services, the CAPWAP protocol also provides such services. Environments in which the CAPWAP protocol is used involve firewall, NAT, and "middlebox" devices, which tend to drop IP fragments to minimize possible DoS attacks. By providing fragmentation and reassembly at the application layer, any fragmentation required due to the tunneling component of the CAPWAP protocol becomes transparent to these intermediate devices.

CAPWAP–MTU DISCOVERY and TCP-MSS Adjustment

To fix the fragmentation issue by the root, CAPWAP implementations perform MTU Discovery, which can avoid the need for fragmentation of CAPWAP packets. Initial path MTU discovery is done during the JOIN message (Path MTU discovery). After the AP is in the RUN state, you can adjust it (Dynamic Path MTU Discovery).

CAPWAP–P-MTU DISCOVERY

The initial path MTU discovery is done during the JOIN messages. The conditions are as follows:

Step 1.   Join message will be sent from the AP to the controller by padding the message to 1485 bytes with a Don't Fragment (DF) bit set.

Step 2.   If the controller receives the message, it returns a join response padded up to 1485 bytes, and the AP updates its MTU size to 1485.

Step 3.   If the join request with padded bytes of 1485 does not reach the controller, the AP times out after 3 seconds and sends a new join request without padding (MTU size 576).

Therefore, the AP will join the controller with an MTU size of either 1485 or 576 bytes; it can be changed only after the AP is in its run state (Dynamic Path MTU Discovery).

CAPWAP–Dynamic P-MTU Discovery

The dynamic Path-MTU is done as per RFC 1191:

Step 1.   The AP sends CAPWAP (control and data) packets with the DF bit set.

Step 2.   If the MTU has changed, the router sends an Internet Control Message Protocol (ICMP) error to the AP to fragment the packet.

Step 3.   The AP immediately changes the MTU size to 576 bytes.

Step 4.   The AP looks for next-hop MTU information in the ICMP error message and sends a P-MTU discovery packet. If the controller receives it, the AP uses it for all the future communications with the controller.

Step 5.   If the ICMP error message does not have a next-hop MTU value, the AP starts from the lowest MTU (576) and increases every 30 seconds in steps of (576, 1006, 1492, 1500).

Notice MTU changes in the following output from the controller debugs:

```
openssl_dtls_mtu_update: Setting DTLS MTU for link to peer  192.168.1.23:41148
```

TCP-MSS Adjustment Feature

Because fragmentation and reassembly in the middle of the data transport can slow the performance, the best solution is to prevent large packets already at the application layer.

The TCP-MSS-Adjustment feature modifies the maximum segment size (MSS) for TCP SYN packets traveling through the network and prohibits the application from sending packets that are too large. It can be enabled globally or configured per AP.

802.11 Bindings and Payloads

As you learned at the beginning of this chapter, the CAPWAP protocol does not include specific wireless technologies; instead, it relies on a binding specification to extend the technology to a particular wireless technology. Those binding specifications for the IEEE 802.11 wireless protocol are defined in RFC 5416.

CAPWAP-Data Binding and Payloads

To differentiate which protocol is transported by CAPWAP-Data, the CAPWAP Header requires all CAPWAP binding specifications to have a Wireless Binding Identifier (WBID) assigned. The IEEE 802.11 binding uses the value 1. If CAPWAP-Data encryption is not enabled, you can read this value directly from a sniffer trace. Figure 4-12 highlights the WBID in the packet. After the WBID there is some wireless information that follows and then you see the transported 802.11 frame itself.

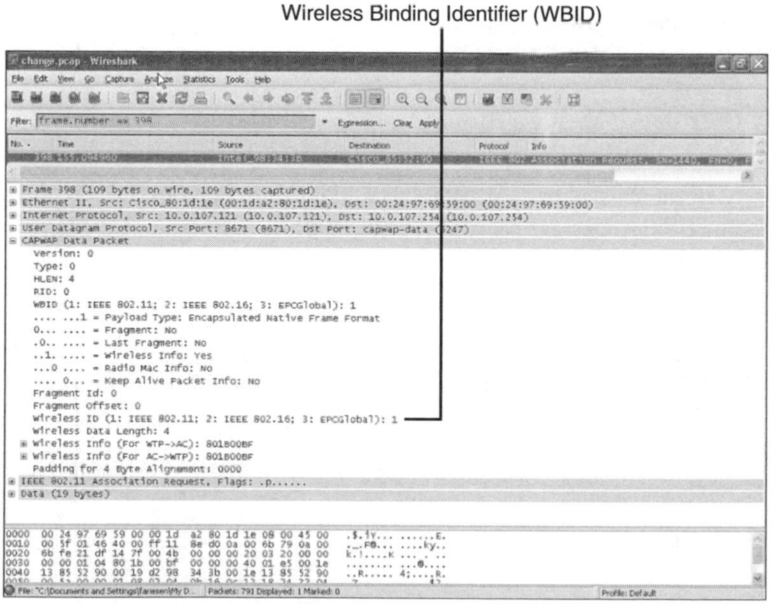

Figure 4-12   *Wireless Binding Identifier (WBID)*

CAPWAP-Control Binding and Payloads

Depending on the control message type, both CAPWAP and LWAPP control messages contain zero or more LWAPP/CAPWAP Protocol message elements. Figure 4-13 (CAPWAP) and Figure 4-14 (LWAPP) show the corresponding control message format. The message elements are highlighted in **bold**. Message elements are used to carry information needed in control messages.

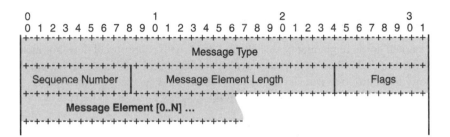

Figure 4-13 *CAPWAP Control Message Format*

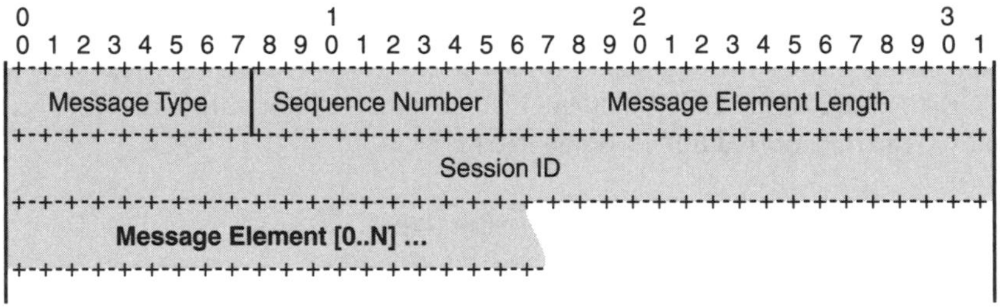

Figure 4-14 *LWAPP Control Message Format*

Every message element (carried by CAPWAP or LWAPP Controller messages) is identified by the Type Value field. A message element uses the type, length, value (TLV) format shown in Figure 4-15.

Figure 4-15 *TLV Format*

Note Table B-1 in Appendix B, "LWAPP and CAPWAP Payloads," outlines all CAPWAP/LWAPP message elements.

Table B-2 details the payloads (every message element) sent in LWAPP control messages and the corresponding ones that will be sent in CAPWAP control messages.

When debugging CAPWAP packets on the controller or capturing CAPWAP packets with the latest CAPWAP dissector, you will find all those elements in the CAPWAP control messages.

LWAPP and CAPWAP Vendor-Specific Payloads

CAPWAP uses almost identical message elements to LWAPP. If no corresponding CAPWAP element exists, such as Radio Resource Management (RRM), the Cisco Unified Wireless Solution transports LWAPP message elements within the CAPWAP vendor-specific elements and maintains all functionality.

The Vendor-Specific Payload message element (Type 37) uses the format shown in Figure 4-16.

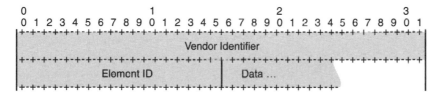

Figure 4-16   *CAPWAP Vendor-Specific Payload Message Element*

Therefore, the complete LWAPP/Cisco vendor-specific message element appears in a trace, as shown in Figure 4-17, using the Cisco OID (Vendor ID) 0x00-40-96-00.

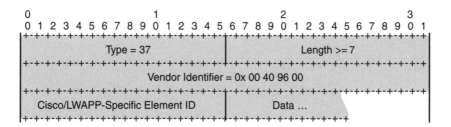

Figure 4-17   *Cisco's/LWAPP-Specific Payload Message Element*

Summary

CAPWAP is a standard, interoperable protocol that enables an access controller (AC; WLC) to manage a collection of WTPs; APs). CAPWAP is based on LWAPP, which is the protocol used in the controllers and APs. One essential reason for moving to CAPWAP is to standardize. As a standard, CAPWAP will enable interoperability of Cisco controllers with third-party APs. A second critical reason is because CAPWAP enables management of radio-frequency identification, RFID, readers (and in the future other devices via sensor gateways). To summarize, the following are the major benefits:

- Support for Path-MTU discovery

- Fragmentation/reassembly using the CAPWAP protocol

- Supported legacy as well as next-generation WLC platforms (such as the 5500s)

- Uses DTLS for Control and Data Channel encryption between AP and WLC

With the introduction of CAPWAP, there are no new command-line interface (CLI) commands other than the debugging ones. The goal here is to help you understand the troubleshooting process utilizing CAPWAP and offer the most versatile, scalable, and powerful product that the market has seen. CAPWAP is simply the next step in making this transition happen.

Chapter 5

Network Design Considerations

The Cisco Unified Wireless Network (CUWN) solution provides significant flexibility for network design and redundancy. Although the physical location of controllers and access points (APs) has some best practices depending on the actual network design, for the most part you can install a controller anywhere on your network and have the APs register to it and start serving wireless clients.

Controller Placement

Before you decide where to locate a controller, you need to decide what model of controller you are going to use. Each controller model has its place within the network. The smaller 2100 series and Network Module–based controllers are usually implemented in small networks or remote locations where you are placing only a few APs and expect few clients. For a large campus deployment where you need hundreds of APs and expect thousands of clients, however, the Wireless Integrated Service Module (WiSM) is a much better solution than installing several smaller-capacity controllers.

To provide wireless redundancy, you can configure multiple controllers to be backups for each other. Unlike other Cisco devices that exchange heartbeats with their redundant device to determine if the primary failed, the APs are configured with primary, secondary, and tertiary controllers. The APs currently exchange heartbeats with the controller they are registered with; should the heartbeats fail, they acknowledge that the controller is down and then try to move to an alternative controller that has been configured or discovered by other means. (Refer to Chapter 3, "Introduction to LWAPP," for a detailed explanation of the discovery and join process.) Starting in code Release 5.0 and higher, you can configure global primary and secondary backup controllers that apply to all the APs that are registered to a controller. If no secondary or tertiary controllers are defined for an AP and their current controller fails, the AP tries to join the global primary backup controller. Cisco refers to this as *high availability* in later code releases. Chapter 9, "Mobility," covers configuring and troubleshooting high availability on the controllers/APs in more detail.

Using high availability provides network resiliency in the case of hardware or network failure; you should take this into account when determining where to locate your controllers in the network. You can use three backup configurations:

■ With an N+1 scenario, you have two controllers, and all the APs are joined to one of them. Should that controller fail, the APs are configured to move to the backup controller.

■ When you have APs joined to both controllers and the APs have the other controller as their backup, this is known as N+N. Should one controller fail, the APs on that controller move to the second controller. Usually the redundant controllers are on the same physical network, if not the same management VLAN on the network.

■ An N+N+1 configuration has three controllers. Two of the controllers back up each other, and the third controller backs up the two primary controllers. The +1 controller might be at the network core while the N+N controllers are installed at the access or distribution layer.

Many other combinations exist for configuring the controllers and APs for redundancy. You can configure a primary, secondary, and tertiary controller as well as a global primary and secondary backup starting in code Release 5.0. Chapter 9 discusses AP failover in detail.

> Note   Regardless of the failover scenario you decide to deploy, make sure that the backup controllers have the capacity to accept any and all APs from a failed controller. If you have two 4402-12s with ten APs on each and one of them fails, eight APs will be stranded with no controller to join.

Although restrictions do not limit the model of controller you should use, the type of redundancy you want (if any), or where in the network you decide to install them, the sections that follow cover some design considerations/suggestions that might aid in your decision.

Access Layer Deployments

The access layer of your network is where client devices access the network. It is also where the majority of the network resources the clients would need access to would reside. In wireless terms, the WLAN would be the access layer.

You can install your controller(s) at the access layer, or wiring closet, of your network. In most cases, you would use the integrated 3750G model in this scenario, but you could use the 4400 series just as easily.

Deploying your controllers at the access layer of the network keeps the access traffic of the wireless clients at the access layer. If you choose the 3750G model, you can take advantage of a lower cost controller, with Layer 3 uplink redundancy at the network edge, as well as the Power over Ethernet (PoE) features of the switch to power your APs. You can also set up N+N redundancy within the switch stack.

Having your controllers at the access layer might introduce some inter-controller roaming challenges. Should the wireless clients be able to roam between APs joined to controllers in different access layers of the network, you might be able to introduce Layer 3 roaming events and client traffic routing events that you need to consider. Chapter 9 details the traffic flow and network best practices for Layer 3 roaming.

Distribution Layer Deployments

The distribution layer of your network is where access layer traffic is aggregated and network policies are enforced. This makes the distribution layer a great place to install your controllers. You can easily implement controller redundancy and AP load-balancing with controllers deployed at the distribution layer. Although WiSMs are usually the controller model deployed in this scenario, the 4400 and 3750G series work just as well.

When you place controllers at the distribution layer, you effectively collapse the access layer into the distribution layer of the network. You should consider what access layer switching features you will need at the distribution layer switches so they can be applied to the incoming and outgoing WLAN traffic from the controller.

Service Block Deployments

Service blocks are groups of service modules in a Catalyst 6500 series switch. A single 6500 switch could hold a Firewall Service Module (FWSM), several WiSM blades, an Intrusion Detection System (IDS) Module, a Network Analysis Module (NAM), as well as high-speed switching modules such as a WS-X6548 line cards.

Like distribution layer deployments, service block deployments usually incorporate one or more WiSMs, but you can also use 4400 series controllers here. These deployments usually lead to highly efficient inter-controller mobility and simplified network management. For large campuses, there is also an incremental economy of scale as the size of the network grows.

You would normally install a service block in a data center where you have redundant power, routing, and switching to prevent a network down situation in the event of a device failure. Also, data centers are usually manned by skilled IT professionals.

Data centers are usually located across the network core, so bandwidth and latency are important factors for you to consider.

In large networks, you can install service blocks in a redundant arm off the distribution layer switches. This design is valuable when core bandwidth is at a premium, such as when there are several large distributed campuses connected via a metropolitan-area network (MAN).

WAN Considerations

Depending on your network topology, you might have offices or remote networks that are connected to the core network across a WAN. The WAN link could be a dedicated T1 line or Multiprotocol Label Switching (MPLS) network connection.

The type of WAN connection you have plays a part in your decision of where to place your controllers. If you have only a low-bandwidth link such as a T1 line, you might consider placing a 2106 or Network Module Controller (NMC) at the site or perhaps using the APs in Hybrid Remote Edge Access Point (H-REAP) mode. (Chapter 13, "H-REAP," discusses H-REAP deployments.) An AP operating in H-REAP mode only sends LWAPP/CAPWAP control traffic across the WAN link and bridges client data traffic directly to the local switch. Otherwise, a client that is trying to access a local resource, such as a printer, eats up the WAN bandwidth with the data packets going back to the controller and then returning across the WAN to reach the local resource. If you have a high-speed connection like MPLS or dedicated OC3, you could probably get away with the APs not using H-REAP mode at the remote location and have them register to your controller at the network core in Local mode. Placing a controller locally or using H-REAP helps you conserve bandwidth and provides wireless access in the event of a WAN failure.

Another WAN consideration is network delay. If your WAN link experiences significant delay and your APs are not in H-REAP mode, wireless client access to network resources could be sluggish or time out altogether. This would not be the case if the AP directly bridged the client data traffic to the local network switch. If the round-trip ping times from the remote network to where the controller will be installed are greater than 300 ms, you are better off using standalone APs or installing a small controller. The controller and H-REAP APs can handle only a 300 ms delay.

AP Placement

The results of your wireless survey determine where to locate your APs on the campus, buildings, and floors. The survey tells you how many APs you need and what power levels provide the best coverage. Every wireless installation is unique, and what looks good to the human eye on a map might not be the best layout for the wireless solution.

The APs would be connected to your access layer switches in a management or other isolated VLAN to keep the APs from having to process unnecessary packets.

Another consideration is how to deploy the APs per controller on the network if you will have more than one. A common deployment is known as a salt-and-pepper or checkerboard deployment. With salt-and-pepper, the idea is that you have every other AP on the floor joined to a different controller, as shown in Figure 5-1. This physical deployment provides dynamic traffic load-balancing between the controllers and radio frequency (RF) resiliency. In the case of a single controller failure, only half of the APs on a particular floor would be lost; the remaining APs could still service the wireless clients.

Although salt-and-pepper sounds like a good idea in theory, it does have several drawbacks. With every other AP joined to a different controller, the number of inter-controller roaming events increases many-fold. As illustrated in Figure 5-1, almost every time a client roams, it roams to an AP joined to the other controller. Even though inter-controller roaming is highly optimized when you configure it correctly (see Chapter 9), intracontroller roaming is more efficient. The aggressive load-balancing feature of the controller, if enabled, works on a per-controller basis, so a salt-and-pepper deployment would essentially defeat the feature. Troubleshooting client issues also becomes more difficult because it adds a layer of complexity.

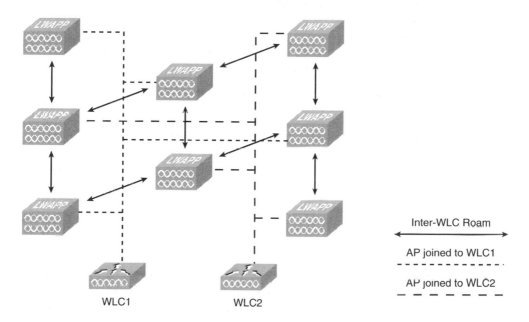

Figure 5-1   *Salt-and-Pepper Deployment*

Client traffic patterns become unpredictable, which makes troubleshooting more difficult. Regardless of how the APs are dispersed across controllers in your network, should one controller fail, all clients associated to APs on the failed controller are disconnected. A salt-and-pepper design does not overcome this fundamental aspect of the CUWN, so you gain no high availability. Cisco does not recommend a salt-and-pepper deployment because, in addition to the reasons already stated, a failure in this scenario will result in the Radio Resource Management (RRM) feature performing harsh adjustments with the loss of the surrounding APs. Because the radios adjust power and channel, even though half of the APs did not drop, the clients will still be affected until the system settles under the new RF conditions. When the situation is cleared, the process will start again as the missing APs come back online.

A better solution is to separate the APs between the controllers into logical coverage areas such as by floor. In this case, should you have a controller or network failure that takes down one controller, you would only lose wireless on a particular floor(s) until the APs were able to join their secondary or backup controller (see Chapter 9).

Dense AP Deployment Considerations

Not every wireless deployment consists of placing APs on a floor to provide coverage to a dispersed number of clients. Conference rooms and convention centers pose a unique problem in that you have a concentrated client base in a confined space. Your AP placement and channel design must take this into account because here, even more than usual, the drawbacks of a half-duplex medium such as wireless are highlighted.

In the 2.4-GHz band, you have only three nonoverlapping channels: 1, 6, and 11. This limitation creates unique design constraints for a dense deployment because you need to mitigate co-channel interference while still providing adequate coverage for the users. As the number of clients increases, the majority of the co-channel interference will be caused by the clients sending and receiving packets on the same channel.

Although you can have up to 254 clients associated with a single AP (128 per radio if AP has both b/g and a radio), because wireless is half-duplex, a single 802.11b client can only realize about 5.6 Mbps throughput at best. For 802.11g or 802.11a only, a client can realize only around 28 Mbps. If you are mixing 802.11b and 802.11g clients, the 802.11g clients are forced to use protection mechanisms that essentially cut the throughput in half. You also need to consider the type of client traffic you are expecting. The situation is much different for clients just surfing the web as opposed to 200 clients trying to download MP3 files at the same time. Cisco recommends designing the network for no more than 40–50 users per AP in an auditorium-like environment. You can place the APs as close as to within 6 feet of each other. APs on the same channel should be as far apart from each other as you can manage.

To help mitigate co-channel interference and improve performance, you would ideally disable all the data rates below 12 Mbps. The majority of wireless clients these days are 802.11g compliant, and the newest are usually 802.11a compliant as well. Disabling the lower data rates prevents 802.11b clients from connecting and causes the 802.11g clients to initiate the protection mechanisms. The protection mechanisms cause the 802.11g clients to send Request To Send (RTS) and Clear To Send (CTS) messages so the 802.11b clients know if the channel is in use. The clients send RTS/CTS frames at the slowest supported rate in addition to the beacon frames. The additional traffic at the slowest rate further degrades the efficiency of the channel. If you know you will have 802.11b clients, only enable the 11-Mbps data rate and set it to Mandatory/Basic.

Disabling the lower data rates also means that you have less cell coverage by each AP, so co-channel overlap is reduced. In addition, it means that the radios use the channel less for beaconing. An AP radio can send more than 5 times the number of 100-byte beacons at 11 Mbps than it can at 1 Mbps. Table 5-1 shows the comparison of data rates and beacon size and how long the radio occupies the channel in microseconds to send it.

Note   The values listed in Table 5-1 are for the beacon only. The PHY header is an additional 100 microseconds. Because of this, when you have multiple WLANs, the transmission time is multiplied. Therefore, if you have four WLANs, it increases the transmission time by a factor of four.

Table 5-1 *Beacon Transmission Times (Microseconds) Versus Data Rate*

802.11b	Beacon Size				
	100	200	250	300	350
Data Rate (Mbps)					
1	896	1696	2096	2496	2896
2	496	896	1096	1296	1496
5.5	241	387	460	532	605
11	169	241	278	314	351
802.11a/g/n	Beacon Size				
	100	200	250	300	350
Data Rate (Mbps)					
6	153	287	353	420	487
12	87	153	187	220	253
24	53	87	103	120	137
54	35	50	57	64	72
130	26	32	35	38	42
300	23	25	27	28	29

Having higher data rates means the radio uses the channel less often and decreases the cell size. In most cases, this improves client roaming.

When designing a dense AP deployment, Cisco recommends using the 5-GHz band. Unlike the 2.4-GHz range where you are limited to only three nonoverlapping channels, the 5-GHz band has 21 nonoverlapping channels. Having more channels to use can mean that no two APs have to use the same channel, which greatly reduces co-channel interference. If you needed to place more than 21 APs, you could really increase the physical distance between APs on the same channel.

Most new wireless supplicants that support the 5-GHz band try to associate using a 5-GHz channel first and only try using b/g if all the 5-GHz channels fail. If the client supports this feature, it helps keep 802.11a capable clients from using the 802.11g channels and helps minimize channel usage on channels 1, 6, and 11.

Note An upcoming controller code release allows the APs to aid in steering wireless clients that are 802.11a capable toward the 5-GHz radio.

If you know you will only have 802.11a clients or you want to prevent any non-802.11a clients from associating to a particular WLAN, you can always use the Radio Policy feature and limit the WLAN to 5 GHz. You can also use this feature to limit a WLAN to just 802.11g, 802.11a/g, or 802.11b/g clients. Figure 5-2 shows the Radio Policy limiting the WLAN to 802.11a.

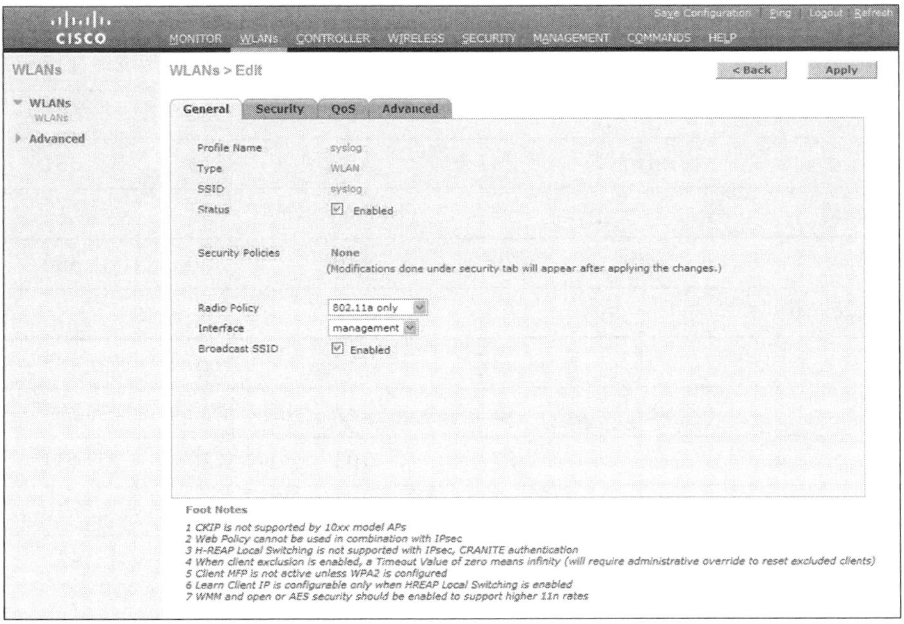

Figure 5-2   *WLAN Radio Policy Feature*

When designing an 802.11a network, you need to be aware that the controller automatically enables Dynamic Frequency Selection (DFS) on 15 channels (52-140). If an AP detects radar on the channel it is currently using, it scans for a new channel and waits 60 seconds to make sure no radar is on that channel before it starts using it. An AP does not try to use the previous channel again for 30 minutes. Even if you hard-code the AP channel and do not use Auto-RF, the AP must change channels when radar is detected. This is a key point when designing the network. If you have a sparse AP deployment and an AP detects radar and changes channels, your clients may not have another AP they can roam to. If not, the client experiences a significant loss of service until the original AP selects another channel and stars servicing those clients again.

802.11n

Another design consideration is the new 802.11n Standard Client devices that support 802.11n can achieve data rates up to 144 Mbps on the 2.4-GHz band and 300 Mbps on the 5-GHz band. Cisco currently offers two AP models that support 802.11n: the 1140 and 1250 series APs. The coverage of these APs is almost identical to the non-802.11n APs such as the 1242 AP. This means transitioning from legacy deployments should be fairly painless based on RF coverage. As with any wireless deployment, however, you should perform a site survey to determine proper AP density and placement. Designing an 802.11n network is similar to designing a legacy wireless network, but you need to take other considerations into account.

If you want to provide the highest N data rates, you have to use channel bonding. With channel bonding, you aggregate two channels to get increased bandwidth. Bonding two channels means you cut the number of non-overlapping channels to one for 2.4 GHz and nine for 5 GHz. Cisco only recommends using channel bonding on the 5-GHz band because you essentially wreck the 2.4-GHz band if you use channel bonding.

Another issue is power. To fully realize the 802.11n rates, the APs require a little more power than standard APs. A 1250 series AP requires 18.5W, and the 1140 series needs 12.95W. Regular 802.3af PoE switches can provide a maximum of 15.4W, so if you are planning to use 1250 series APs, the switch would not be able to fully power the unit. You need to use a local power supply or a power injector to fully power the AP. This can affect the physical placement of your APs.

The physical port speed of your switch is another factor. Although the 802.11n APs support 10/100/1000 Mbps, you can create a bottleneck at the switch port if you connect the AP to a 10- or 100-Mbps port. This logic also applies to the 2100 series controllers. The network ports on those controllers are only 10/100. You can imagine the bottleneck of a 2125 with 25 1250 series APs and hundreds of 802.11n clients all trying to pass traffic through a 100-Mbps port.

Just as 802.11g uses protection mechanisms to allow for backward compatibility with older clients, 802.11n uses protection to allow for non-11n clients to associate and use the wireless medium. Also just like 802.11g, the coexistence with legacy clients lowers the performance of the 802.11n network compared to an 11n-only network. Despite the resulting lower throughput, the overall throughput is much higher than the older standards.

Finally, in addition to channel bonding, a controller needs to have the correct configuration to support 802.11n clients. The 802.11n mode must be enabled, as illustrated in Figure 5-3.

Also, the WLAN that the 802.11n clients use must have the correct security and quality of service (QoS) enabled. The 802.11n Standard requires either no security or WPA2 with Advanced Encryption Standard (AES) encryption. It also requires that Wi-Fi Multimedia (WMM) be allowed or required. (Chapter 11, "Wireless Voice," discusses WMM in greater detail.) If you have legacy clients that cannot use WPA2/AES, you need to plan accordingly and either create a separate WLAN for those clients or perhaps even remove those clients from the network.

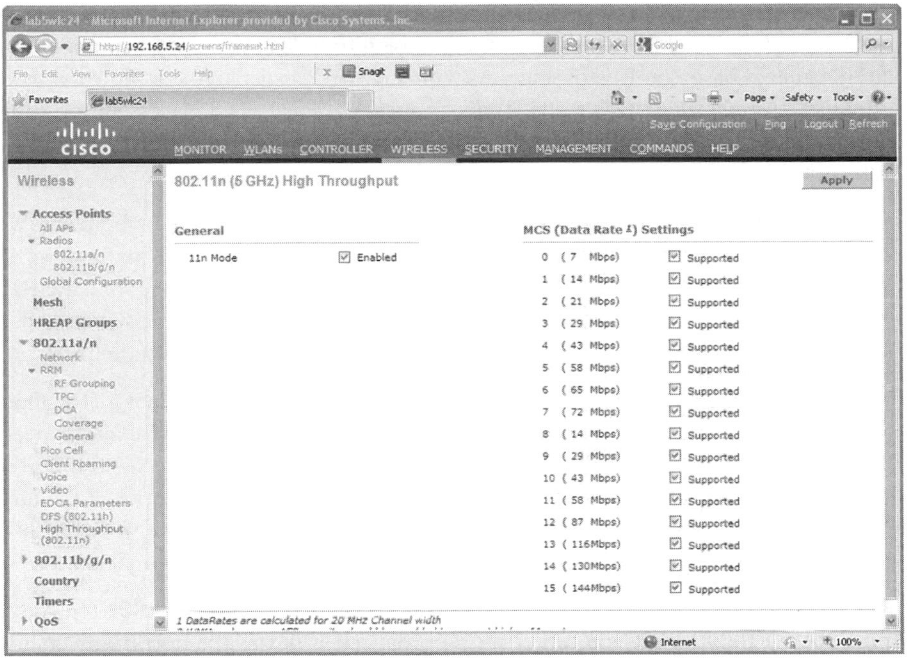

Figure 5-3 *Enabling 802.11n Mode*

Location Design Considerations

The Cisco Wireless Location Appliance and the new, more powerful Mobility Services Engine (MSE) aggregate client information from the APs on the controllers to track locations of wireless devices. A single Location Appliance can track up to 2500 individual devices, including legitimate wireless clients, rogue clients, rogue APs, and radio frequency identification (RFID) tags. The 3350 MSE can track up to 18,000 devices, 3,000 Monitor Mode APs, and its Mobile Intelligent Roaming software supports up to 2,000 registered devices simultaneously. Although the Location Appliance and MSE are outside the scope of this book, it is important to understand the design considerations that a location-based deployment requires.

Cisco advertises accuracy within 30 feet (10 m) 90 percent of the time when using the Location Appliance. The more APs that hear a wireless device, the better the location accuracy is going to be. You want to ensure that no fewer than three APs, and preferably four or five, provide coverage to every area where device location is required.

Make sure these two important guidelines are adhered to, listed in order of priority:

1. Access points should surround the desired location.

2. One access point should be placed roughly every 50 to 70 linear feet (about 17 to 20 meters). This translates into one access point every 2500 to 5000 square feet (about 230 to 450 square meters).

You should place APs around the periphery of the environment to help locate devices close to outside walls. Staggering APs within the interior as well as the periphery greatly improve location accuracy, as illustrated in Figure 5-4.

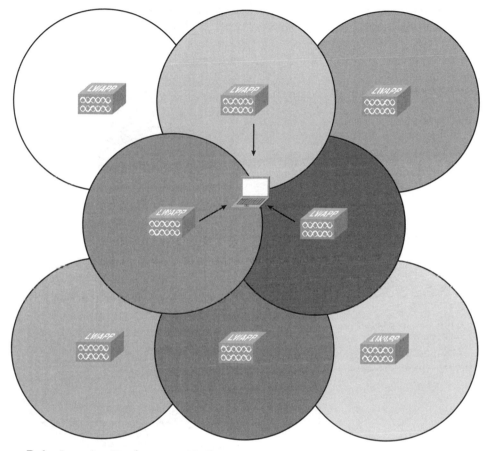

Figure 5-4   *Location Deployment AP Placement*

In Figure 5-4, three APs hear the client, which aids in triangulating the client and provides much more accurate location results.

Using directional antennas on the APs along the walls also helps by keeping the wireless signal within the building.

Note   Devices must be detected at signals greater than –75 dBm for the controllers to forward information to the location appliance or MSE. No fewer than three access points should be able to detect any device at signals below –75 dBm.

As you already know, dense deployments pose unique design and RF considerations. Should you have both voice and data clients, a dense deployment of APs can actually hinder the voice clients because the phones hear too many APs and are not able to make good roaming decisions. To have a deployment that satisfies the requirements for good location accuracy and allows your wireless phones to operate optimally, you can place APs in Monitor mode throughout the network, as illustrated in Figure 5-5.

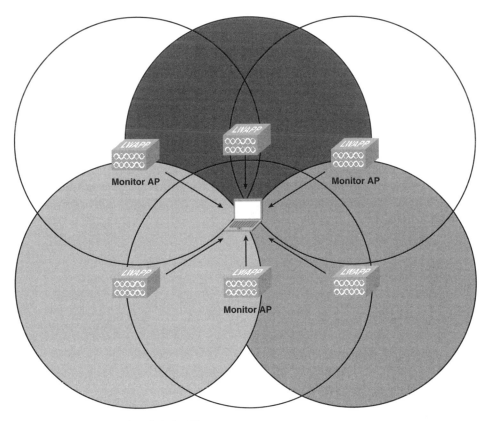

Figure 5-5   *Using Monitor Mode APs*

In Figure 5-5, the client device is heard by all six APs, but it can only associate with the non-Monitor Mode APs. An AP in Monitor Mode does not service wireless clients (clear RF circles); therefore, it is not considered when a client is roaming or trying to associate with a WLAN. Monitor APs act as dedicated sensors for the location-based services (LBS), such as rogue AP detection and IDS. When the APs are in Monitor Mode, they can only receive; therefore, they cannot service clients or attach to suspected rogue APs they detect. A Monitor AP scans through every configured channel once every 12 seconds.

With this design, you have a high AP density, which is good for location services, but because only half of the APs actually service wireless clients, the density is not too high for a voice deployment.

Perhaps the worst possible AP placement for location is if the APs are in a straight line, as illustrated in Figure 5-6.

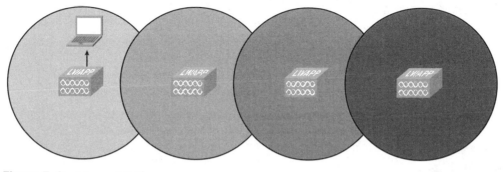

Figure 5-6   *Linear AP Placement*

Although the AP placement in Figure 5-6 provides plenty of wireless coverage, the location algorithm suffers dramatically because a single AP hears the client device. If two APs hear the client, the location algorithms have no way of telling whether the devices are above or below the AP.

Summary

When designing your wireless controller installation, you need to understand all the different factors that affect the performance of the system. You need to understand the different controller models and their features to make sure they meet your design goals. You also need to understand the physical placement of the controller and the APs within the network and how that affects traffic flow between the APs and the controller. Are you planning for a conference that services thousands of clients or just provides wireless access for a remote office with five employees? You also need to consider the network itself; what type of bandwidth do you have at your disposal, and is there an inherent delay that might warrant placing a controller locally at a particular site, using H-REAP, or simply installing a standalone AP(s)? Understanding the capabilities of your wireless clients allows you to design your network to best service those clients. Putting all of that together aids you in designing a stable and usable wireless infrastructure.

Chapter 6

Understanding the Troubleshooting Tools

The purpose of this chapter is to educate you about the options and possibilities for troubleshooting wired and wireless issues within your deployments. This also makes it easier for you to formulate a troubleshooting plan. It might even provide seasoned engineers with new options in troubleshooting their everday issues in a fresh manner.

Troubleshooting on the WLC

The Wireless LAN Controller (WLC) has some diagnostic logs and tools built in it that can assist us when a potential problem arises. However, these tools alone are not comprehensive enough in most cases to fully troubleshoot many issues. In fact, the controllers do not contain nearly the amount or the caliber of information and logs that a typical IOS device contains. The controller does have features and other tools that do not exist on typical IOS devices that can make up for the differences, which this chapter covers in detail.

Debugging

Debugging is one of the most common and usually initial forms of troubleshooting any network problem. Because the WLC products were acquired through a company acquisition, they obviously had a debugging system that was different from typical IOS debug commands. One of the challenges is getting used to a new list of debugs. For a comprehensive list of debugs, see Appendix A, "Debugging Commands." Another key piece of information to be aware of is that debugs may change from one version to the next or when new features are added. For instance, one of the more useful debugs created in the newer 6.0 version of code is the new memory debugs that help detect a memory leak that can be initiated and applied to the WLC or the access point (AP) in question. Consider the following example of a WLC debug set:

■ **config memory monitor errors {enable | disable}:** Enables or disables monitoring for memory errors and leaks. Your changes are not saved across reboots. After the controller reboots, it uses the default setting for this feature. The default value is disabled.

■ **config memory monitor leaks** *low_thresh high_thresh*: Configures the controller to perform an auto-leak analysis between two memory thresholds (in kilobytes) if you suspect that a memory leak has occurred.

If the free memory is lower than the *low_thresh* threshold, the system crashes, generating a crash file.

The default value for this parameter is 10,000 kilobytes, and you cannot set it below this value. Set the *high_thresh* threshold to the current free memory level or higher so that the system enters auto-leak-analysis mode. After the free memory reaches a level lower than the specified *high_thresh* threshold, the process of tracking and freeing memory allocation begins. As a result, the **debug memory events enable** command shows all allocations and frees, and the **show memory monitor detail** command starts to detect any suspected memory leaks. The default value for this parameter is 30,000 kilobytes.

■ **show memory monitor:** Displays a summary of any discovered memory issues. Information similar to the following appears:

```
Memory Leak Monitor Status:

low_threshold(10000), high_threshold(30000), current status(disabled)


-----------------------------------------

Memory Error Monitor Status:

Crash-on-error flag currently set to (disabled)

No memory error detected.
```

■ **show memory monitor detail:** Displays details of any memory leaks or corruption. Information similar to the following appears:

```
Memory error detected. Details:

-----------------------------------------

- Corruption detected at pmalloc entry address: (0x179a7ec0)

- Corrupt entry:headerMagic(0xdeadf00d),trailer(0xabcd),poison(0xreadceef),

entrysize(128),bytes(100),thread(Unknown task name, task id = (332096592)),

file(pmalloc.c),line(1736),time(1027)

Previous 1K memory dump from error location.

-----------------------------------------

(179a7ac0): 00000000 00000000 00000000 ceeff00d readf00d 00000080 00000000
00000000
```

```
(179a7ae0):  17958b20 00000000 1175608c 00000078 00000000 readceef 179a7afc
00000001

(179a7b00):  00000003 00000006 00000001 00000004 00000001 00000009 00000009
0000020d

(179a7b20):  00000001 00000002 00000002 00000001 00000004 00000000 00000000
5d7b9aba

(179a7b40):  cbddf004 192f465e 7791acc8 e5032242 5365788c a1b7cee6 00000000
00000000

(179a7b60):  00000000 00000000 00000000 00000000 00000000 ceeff00d readf00d
00000080

(179a7b80):  00000000 00000000 17958dc0 00000000 1175608c 00000078 00000000
readceef

(179a7ba0):  179a7ba4 00000001 00000003 00000006 00000001 00000004 00000001
00003763

(179a7bc0):  00000002 00000002 00000010 00000001 00000002 00000000 0000001e
00000013

(179a7be0):  0000001a 00000089 00000000 00000000 000000d8 00000000 00000000
17222194

(179a7c00):  1722246c 1722246c 00000000 00000000 00000000 00000000 00000000
ceeff00d

(179a7c20):  readf00d 00000080 00000000 00000000 179a7b78 00000000 1175608c
00000078
```

As far as the controller is concerned, the majority of the debugging will be done on this device. However, debugging on the AP is common also. It is best to be familiar with both devices. Debugging on the AP is called *remote debugging* and must be enabled because it is disabled by default. To enable the controller to send **debug** commands to an AP converted to lightweight mode, enter the following command:

```
debug ap {enable ¦ disable ¦ command cmd} Cisco_AP
```

When this command is enabled, the controller sends debug commands to the AP as character strings. You can send any **debug** command supported by Cisco Aironet APs that run Cisco IOS software in lightweight mode. See Appendix A for a more detailed list. To disable debugging on the AP, use the **no debug all** command.

Consider the following similar memory debugs that you can run on the AP side. If a memory leak occurs, enter the following command to enable debugging of errors or events during memory allocation:

```
debug memory {errors ¦ events} {enable ¦ disable}
```

Additional commands to display AP information useful for debugging are as follows:

- **show memory debug leaks**
- **show buffers leak**
- **show buffers address** *DataArea* Example: **35DC7F4**
- **show buffers input-interface G0 dump**
- **show interfaces g0**
- **show buffers all dump**
- **show memory processor dead**

Please referece Appendix A for a list of complete debugging commands for the IOS to Lightweight Access Point Protocol (LWAPP) or Control and Provisioning of Wireless Access Points (CAPWAP) device. One rule of thumb to go by is that typically all the IOS commands are still available and will work, especially the **show** and **debug** commands. The list to be aware of is the current one that contains LWAPP/CAPWAP debugs. This is a small list, so you can see the difference between these APs and the 1000 series.

Other notable commands are as follows:

- **show cap client rcb:** Displays AP config
- **show cap reap:** Displays Remote-Edge AP (REAP) info
- **show cap reap association:** Displays REAP association
- **show debug:** Displays currently enabled debugs
- **test capwap restart:** Restarts the AP, similar to rebooting
- **debug dtls events:** Enables Datagram Transport Layer Security (DTLS) events debugging
- **debug dtls error:** Enables DTLS error debugging
- **show capwap client rcb:** Displays CAPWAP client config
- **debug capwap client events:** Debugs CAPWAP client events
- **debug capwap client error:** Debugs CAPWAP client errors
- **debug dtls client event:** Debugs DTLS client events
- **debug dtls client error:** Debugs DTLS client errors

A command is also available to enable remote debugging on the older 1000 series APs. This is used only in rare cases but is worth mentioning in the event it is needed. To enable or disable remote debugging of a Cisco 1000 series lightweight AP or to remotely execute a command on a Cisco 1000 series lightweight AP, use the same command as mentioned earlier. However, in earlier versions, you have to use the **config ap remote-debug** command:

```
config ap remote-debug {enable ¦ disable ¦ exc-command cmd} Cisco_AP
```

The following are a few commands used by the 1000 series APs. (For a complete list, please consult Appendix A.)

- **help:** Displays CLI command list

- **ping:** Ping

- **reboot:** Reboots AP

- **timeofday:** Displays current time of day

- **version:** Displays software version

- **get config:** Displays current AP configuration

- **get ipaddr:** Displays IP address

- **get ipmask:** Displays IP subnet mask

- **get key:** Displays encryption key

- **get keyentrymethod:** Displays encyrption key entry method

- **get keysource:** Displays source of encryption keys

- **get login:** Displays login user name

- **get nameaddr:** Displays IP address of name server

- **get power:** Displays transmit power setting

- **get radiusname:** Displays RADIUS server name or IP address

- **set antenna:** Sets antenna

- **set authentication:** Sets authentication type

- **set autochannelselect:** Sets auto-channel selection

- **set beaconinterval:** Modifies beacon interval

- **set cfpperiod:** Sets contention-free period interval

- **set cfpmaxduration:** Sets contention-free period max duration

- **set cfpstatus:** Sets contention-free period status

- **set channel:** Sets radio channel

- **set cipher:** Sets cipher

- **set encryption:** Sets encryption mode

- **set factorydefault:** Restores to default factory settings

- **set fragmentthreshold:** Sets fragment threshold

- **set frequency:** Sets radio frequency (MHz)

- **set gateway:** Sets gateway IP address

- **set groupkeyupdate:** Sets group key update interval (in seconds)

Various debugging tools are available depending on the vendor of the device. For wireless, there are controller, AP, client, RADIUS, and even switch debugs. As you can see, almost every hop in a Cisco deployment has a debug point. Debugging is discussed in more depth in each chapter when referring to the type of service or technology being discussed.

Advanced Debugging

One of the downfalls of the WLC is that it does not contain many of the IOS tools commonly found on Cisco routers and switches. For instance, you cannot look at the packet detail on a WLC without obtaining a packet trace. However, you can look at the raw data that hits the CPU on the controller. Starting from code Version 4.2, a new command exists to assist you in doing so. This is the debug packet command. What exactly does it do? It captures all the packets or the ones you specify that hit the CPU. That is critical to remember, because if your issue is in reference to traffic that does not interface with the CPU, this command will do you no good. The command is **debug packet logging enable all** *number_of_packets*; if you just press Enter, the default is 25. The output of this command is a raw text dump of all packets that transverse the CPU. The command allows you to specify a hex output as well. Example 6-1 shows the output.

Example 6-1 *Debug Packet Logging Example*

```
(Cisco Controller) >debug packet logging ?
acl             Filter displayed packets.
disable         Disables debug.
enable          Enables debug.
format          Configures the format for debug output.
(Cisco Controller) >debug packet logging enable
(Cisco Controller) >
rx len=161, encap=dot11-probe, port=1
0000 00 24 97 69 51 00 00 1F CA 2A 0B ac 08 00 45 00 .$.iQ...J*.,..E.
0010 00 AD 99 C1 40 00 FF 11 5E 02 C0 a8 01 25 C0 A8 .-.A@...^.@(.%
0020 01 06 A0 BD 14 7F 00 99 00 00 01 00 00 00 17 FE ...=..........~
0030 FF 00 01 00 00 00 00 92 AE 00 80 9e 19 67 0F 39 .............g.9
0040 3A D8 F6 9E 0E E0 A7 23 72 64 5A 01 20 03 20 00 :Xv..`'#rdZ.....
0050 00 00 00 01 04 AE 1B 00 A9 00 00 00 40 0B A9 00 ........)...(@.).
0060 1F 9E 8D 85 F0 00 13 E8 DC F9 57 00 1F 9E 8D 85 ....p..h\yW....
0070 F0 80 EF 00 00 01 08 02 04 0B 16 0c 12 18 24 32 p.o..........$2
0080 04 30 48 60 6C 2D 1A 3C 08 17 FF ff 00 00 00 00 .0H`l-.<........
0090 00 00 00 00 00 00 00 00 00 00 00 00 00 00 00 00 ................
00A0 00                                              .
rx len=136, encap=dot11-probe, port=1
```

```
0000 00 24 97 69 51 00 00 1F CA 2A 0B ac 08 00 45 00  .$.iQ...J*.,..E.
0010 00 9D 99 C2 40 00 FF 11 5E 11 C0 a8 01 25 C0 A8  ...B@...^.@(.%
0020 01 06 A0 BD 14 7F 00 89 00 00 01 00 00 00 17 FE  ...=...........~
0030 FF 00 01 00 00 00 00 92 AF 00 70 41 21 BA B4 E9  ......../.pA!:4i
0040 1F 2D 2A 0A 39 9B 31 E1 AB FF AD 01 20 43 20 00  .-*.9.1a+.-..C..
0050 00 00 00 01 04 AB 11 00 B0 00 00 00 40 A1 3A 00  .....+..0....
0060 1F 9E 8D 85 F0 00 18 DE 9D 17 1B 00 1F 9E 8D 85  ....p..^........
0070 F0 70 68 00 00 01 08 02 04 0B 16 0c 12 18 24 0A  pph...........$.
0080 01 07 32 04 30 48 60 6C                          ..2.0H`l
rx len=133, encap=dot11-probe, port-1
0000 00 24 97 69 51 00 00 1F CA 2A 0B ac 08 00 45 00  .$.iQ...J*.,..E.
0010 00 8D 99 C3 40 00 FF 11 5E 20 C0 a8 01 25 C0 A8  ...C@...^.@(.%
0020 01 06 A0 BD 14 7F 00 79 00 00 01 00 00 00 17 FE  ...=...y.......~
0030 FF 00 01 00 00 00 00 92 B0 00 60 98 A6 ED 06 C6  ........0.`.&m.F
0040 98 37 63 13 2D B7 03 68 BA C2 CB 01 20 03 20 00  .7c.-7.h:BK.....
0050 00 00 00 01 04 A9 18 00 AE 00 00 00 40 0B D8 00  .....)......@.X.
0060 1F 9E 8D 85 F0 00 40 96 A0 7C 7C 00 1F 9E 8D 85  ....p.@..||.....
0070 F0 50 0D 00 00 01 08 82 84 8B 96 0c 18 30 48 32  pP...........0H2
0080 04 12 24 60 6C                                   ..$`l
rx len=133, encap=dot11-probe, port=1
```

You might be thinking, "What can I do with this data?" If you take the output and save it to a text file, you can convert it to a capture file and actually view it as a wired trace. All you need is a coversion utility, which most packet capture software bundles contain. For example, Wireshark has a text2pcap program that converts the text to a pcap file that Wireshark can then read. Example 6-2 gives you an idea of how to do this.

Example 6-2   *Converting Packet Debugs to Wired Traces*

```
C:\PROGRA~1\Wireshark>text2pcap raw-text-dump.txt wlc-viewable.pcap
Input from: raw-text-dump
Output to: wlc-viewable.pcap
Wrote packet of 161 bytes at 0
Wrote packet of 136 bytes at 161
Wrote packet of 133 bytes at 297
! Output omitted for brevity
Wrote packet of 136 bytes at 10063
Wrote packet of 133 bytes at 10199
Read 75 potential packets, wrote 75 packets

C:\PROGRA~1\Wireshark>
```

You can then view the file using Wireshark or your favorite packet viewing program. The command also allows you to create access control lists (ACL) and apply them if you happen to be looking for specific traffic types. The result is a built-in packet capture that allows you to view packets hitting the CPU of the controller. This is great for client-related issues, AP join issues, and so on.

This debug facility enables you to display all packets going to and from the controller CPU. By default, all packets received by the debug facility are displayed, but you can enable it for either received or transmitted packets or both. You can use ACLs to filter packets before they are displayed so you are not looking at so much data. Packets not passing the ACLs are discarded without being displayed. Each ACL includes an action (permit, deny, or disable) and one or more fields that can match the packet. The debug facility provides ACLs that operate at the following levels and on the following values:

- Driver ACL

  Network processing unit (NPU) encapsulation type

  Port

- Ethernet header ACL

  Destination address

  Source address

  Ethernet type

  VLAN ID

- IP header ACL

  Source address

  Destination address

  Protocol

  Source port (if applicable)

  Destination port (if applicable)

- Ethernet over IP (EoIP) payload Ethernet header ACL

  Destination address

  Source address

  Ethernet type

  VLAN ID

- EoIP payload IP header ACL

  Source address

  Destination address

  Protocol

Source port (if applicable)

Destination port (if applicable)

- CAPWAP payload 802.11 header ACL

Destination address

Source address

Basic service set identifier (BSSID)

Subnetwork Access Protocol (SNAP) header type

- CAPWAP payload IP header ACL

Source address

Destination address

Protocol

Source port (if applicable)

Destination port (if applicable)

The first ACL that matches the packet is the one that is selected. You can identify multiple ACLs as each level. If you run into a scenario in which no packets are enabled, you can troubleshoot to determine why packets might not be displayed:

```
debug packet error {enable | disable}
```

You can also use the typical **show debug packet** command to see what debug is actually enabled as well as demonstrated in Example 6-3.

Example 6-3 *show debug packet Command Output*

```
Status....................................... disabled
Number of packets to display.................... 25
Bytes/packet to display......................... 0
Packet display format........................... text2pcap
Driver ACL:
  [1]: disabled
  [2]: disabled
  [3]: disabled
  [4]: disabled
  [5]: disabled
  [6]: disabled
Ethernet ACL:
  [1]: disabled
  [2]: disabled
  [3]: disabled
  [4]: disabled
```

(continues)

Example 6-3 *show debug packet Command Output (continued)*

```
  [5]: disabled
  [6]: disabled
IP ACL:
  [1]: disabled
  [2]: disabled
  [3]: disabled
  [4]: disabled
  [5]: disabled
  [6]: disabled
EoIP-Ethernet ACL:
  [1]: disabled
  [2]: disabled
  [3]: disabled
  [4]: disabled
  [5]: disabled
  [6]: disabled
EoIP-IP ACL:
  [1]: disabled
  [2]: disabled
  [3]: disabled
  [4]: disabled
  [5]: disabled
  [6]: disabled
LWAPP-Dot11 ACL:
  [1]: disabled
  [2]: disabled
  [3]: disabled
  [4]: disabled
  [5]: disabled
  [6]: disabled
LWAPP-IP ACL:
  [1]: disabled
  [2]: disabled
  [3]: disabled
  [4]: disabled
  [5]: disabled
  [6]: disabled
```

Another advanced tool is the wireless sniffing mode of an AP. The controller enables you to configure an AP as a network "sniffer," which captures and forwards all the packets on a particular channel to a remote machine that runs packet analyzer software. These packets contain elements such as timestamps, signal strength, packet size, and additional information. Sniffers allow you to monitor and record network activity and to detect problems.

You can view additional information on how to set this up and configure it in any of the controller configuration guides.

mping and eping

Controllers in a mobility list communicate with each other by controlling information over a well-known User Datagram Protocol (UDP) port and exchanging data traffic through an EoIP tunnel. Because UDP and EoIP are not reliable transport mechanisms, a mobility control packet or data packet is not guaranteed to be delivered to a mobility peer. Mobility packets might become lost in transit due to a firewall filtering the UDP port or EoIP packets or due to routing issues. Controller software Release 4.0 or later enables you to test the mobility communication environment by performing mobility ping tests. Because the WLCs communicate using ports 16666 and Protocol 97 to establish and maintain roaming and anchoring sessions, these must be open for these transaction types to occur. One of the difficulties is the lack of an easy way, other than a trace, to validate the flow of these traffic types. You can use mping and eping to validate. mping actually runs a ping over UDP port 16666 using the management interfaces. This tells you whether the network path is allowing this traffic type through. The other is eping, which ensures that you are allowing protocol 97 throughout the network path using the management interfaces. These tests are good for validating the condition or current state of a mobility member. If you navigate to the page on any WLC of any mobility member, you will see one of the reported conditions:

- **UP:** The controller is reachable and able to pass data.

- **CNTRL_PATH_DOWN:** The mpings failed. The controller cannot be reached through the control path and is considered failed.

- **DATA_PATH_DOWN:** The epings failed. The controller cannot be reached and is considered failed.

- **CNTRL_DATA_PATH_DOWN:** Both the mpings and epings failed. The controller cannot be reached and is considered failed.

Note   These ping tests are not Internet Control Message Protocol (ICMP) based. The term *ping* indicates an echo request and an echo reply message.

You can determine a failed mobility member by looking at the status field. In any event, eping and mping help you conclude what traffic type might be failing from one controller to the next.

Message Log

The message log on the controller is important. It usually goes hand in hand with the **show run-config** command. If anyone asks for your configuration for troubleshooting purposes, including **show msglog**, which is the message log, it can sometimes be helpful. Different levels exist, and you want to make sure you have the log set so that it will pick up any important information. The lowest (most verbose) level is recommended. The **config msglog level** command shown in Example 6-4 shows how to configure the reported levels of issues to the WLC. It is best practice to select the most verbose level during troubleshooting. It pays off if you do run into a particular situation or you are proactively reviewing levels for potential issues. Another command, **show running-config**, contains different information and is not as comprehensive as **show run-config**. It is vital not to confuse these two commands when someone asks for the **show run**. People refer to the **show run-config** command whenever this question is asked.

Example 6-4 *Configuring the Reported Levels of Issues to the WLC*

```
(Cisco Controller) >config msglog level ?

critical      Critical hardware or software Failure.
error         Non-Critical software error.
warning       Unexpected software events.
verbose       Significant system events.
```

In many circumstances, if you are running into problems, the message log tells you what exactly the issue is. Example 6-5 is a sample msglog.

Example 6-5 *Displaying a Message Log*

```
(Cisco Controller) >show msglog

Message Log Severity Level ..................... ERROR
*May 03 09:34:23.892: %INIT-0-LICENSED_EXIT_NORMAL: bootos.c:3128 License daemon
exited normally with code 0.
*May 03 08:41:14.361: %DATAPLANE-3-DP_MSG: broffu_fp_dapi_cmd.c:1757
DP04:cmdAddTun4:1752 failed to create ifIndex 1026 tunType 1
*May 03 08:41:13.843: %RRM-3-RRM_LOGMSG: rrmChanUtils.c:292 RRM LOG: Airewave
Director: Could not find valid channel lists for 802.11bg
*May 03 08:40:52.373: %SIM-3-PORT_UP: sim.c:9207 Physical port 1 is up!.
*May 03 08:40:41.836: %SYSTEM-3-FILE_READ_FAIL: nvstore.c:422 Failed to read con-
figuration file 'cliWebInitParms.cfg'
*May 03 08:40:41.836: %CNFGR-3-INV_COMP_ID: cnfgr.c:2078 Invalid Component Id :
Unrecognized (81) in cfgConfiguratorInit.
*May 03 08:40:41.780: %SYSTEM-3-FILE_READ_FAIL: nvstore.c:422 Failed to read con-
figuration file 'rfidInitParms.cfg'
*May 03 08:40:41.766: %SYSTEM-3-FILE_READ_FAIL: nvstore.c:422 Failed to read con-
figuration file 'dhcpParms.cfg'
```

```
*May 03 08:40:41.752: %SYSTEM-3-FILE_READ_FAIL: nvstore.c:422 Failed to read con-
figuration file 'bcastInitParms.cfg'

*May 03 08:40:41.691: %SYSTEM-3-FILE_READ_FAIL: nvstore.c:422 Failed to read con-
figuration file 'rrmInitParms.cfg'

*May 03 08:40:41.536: %SYSTEM-3-FILE_READ_FAIL: nvstore.c:422 Failed to read con-
figuration file 'apfInitParms.cfg'

*May 03 08:40:41.431: %MM-3-MEMBER_ADD_FAILED: mm_dir.c:860 Could not add
Mobility Member. Reason: IP already assigned, Member-Count:1,MAC:
00:00:00:00:00:00, IP: 0.0.0.0

*May 03 08:40:41.226: %SYSTEM-3-FILE_READ_FAIL: nvstore.c:422 Failed to read con-
figuration file 'mmInitParms.cfg'

*May 03 08:40:41.216: %SYSTEM-3-FILE_READ_FAIL: nvstore.c:422 Failed to read con-
figuration file 'aaaapiInitParms.cfg'

*May 03 08:40:41.214: %SYSTEM-3-FILE_READ_FAIL: nvstore.c:422 Failed to read con-
figuration file 'pemInitParms.cfg'

*May 03 08:40:41.098: %SYSTEM-3-FILE_READ_FAIL: nvstore.c:422 Failed to read con-
figuration file 'dot1xInitParms.cfg'

*May 03 08:40:39.938: %SSHPM-3-FREAD_FAILED: sshpmlscscep.c:1268 Error reading
file /mnt/application/lscca_pem.crt

*May 03 08:40:19.781: %SYSTEM-3-FILE_READ_FAIL: nvstore.c:422 Failed to read con-
figuration file 'sshpmInitParms.cfg'

*May 03 08:40:19.774: %CNFGR-3-INV_COMP_ID: cnfgr.c:2078 Invalid Component Id :
Unrecognized (36) in cfgConfiguratorInit.

*May 03 08:40:19.678: %SYSTEM-3-FILE_READ_FAIL: nvstore.c:422 Failed to read con-
figuration file 'capwapInitParms.cfg'

—More— or (q)uit
```

This log file can be quite important. As mentioned before, including it along with the **show run-config** configuration file can prove helpful. You can never have too much information.

Trap Log

The trap log is similar to the message log except that it is broader in scope. It carries status messages along with other device updates. This is another great log to refer to but can be quite cumbersome due to everything that is reporting to it, as Example 6-6 demonstrates. It can give you a general idea of what is happening prior to, during, or after a network failure. These are the SNMP notifications.

Example 6-6 *Displaying the Trap Log*

```
(Cisco Controller) >show traplog

Number of Traps Since Last Reset ............ 120
Number of Traps Since Log Last Displayed .... 120


Log System Time                  Trap
```

(continues)

Example 6-6 *Displaying the Trap Log (continued)*

```
─·─ ─ ─ ─ ─ ─ ─ ─ ─ ─ ─   ─ ─ ─ ─ ─ ─ ─ ─ ─ ─ ─ ─ ─ ─ ─ ─ ─ ─ ─ ─ ─ ─·

  0 Sun May  3 11:51:12 2009 Rogue AP : 00:18:74:48:33:7b  removed from Base R
                             adio MAC : 00:1f:9e:8d:85:f0 Interface no:1(802.1
                             1a)
  1 Sun May  3 11:50:06 2009 Rogue AP : 00:18:74:48:7a:11 detected on Base Rad
                             io MAC : 00:1f:9e:8d:85:f0  Interface no:0(802.11
                             b/g) with RSSI: -90 and SNR: 11 and Classificatio
                             n: unclassified
  2 Sun May  3 11:50:06 2009 Rogue AP : 00:19:07:06:88:d0 detected on Base Rad
                             io MAC : 00:1f:9e:8d:85:f0  Interface no:0(802.11
                             b/g) with RSSI: -92 and SNR: 9 and Classification
                             : unclassified
  3 Sun May  3 11:47:05 2009 Rogue AP : 00:1e:13:06:e7:80 detected on Base Rad
                             io MAC : 00:1f:9e:8d:85:f0  Interface no:0(802.11
                             b/g) with RSSI: -92 and SNR: 11 and Classificatio
                             n: unclassified


Would you like to display more entries? (y/n) y




Log System Time            Trap
─·─ ─ ─ ─ ─ ─ ─ ─ ─ ─ ─   ─ ─ ─ ─ ─ ─ ─ ─ ─ ─ ─ ─ ─ ─ ─ ─ ─ ─ ─ ─ ─·

  4 Sun May  3 11:45:20 2009 Rogue AP : 00:1d:70:d2:bc:e0  removed from Base R
                             adio MAC : 00:1f:9e:8d:85:f0 Interface no:0(802.1
                             1n24)
  5 Sun May  3 11:44:06 2009 Rogue AP : 00:18:74:48:7a:14 detected on Base Rad
                             io MAC : 00:1f:9e:8d:85:f0  Interface no:0(802.11
                             b/g) with RSSI: -91 and SNR: 8 and Classification
                             : unclassified
  6 Sun May  3 11:42:20 2009 Rogue AP : 00:18:74:48:7a:12  removed from Base R
                             adio MAC : 00:1f:9e:8d:85:f0 Interface no:0(802.1
                             1b/g)
  7 Sun May  3 11:39:20 2009 Rogue AP : 00:1e:13:06:e7:80  removed from Base R
                             adio MAC : 00:1f:9e:8d:85:f0 Interface no:0(802.1
                             1b/g)
  8 Sun May  3 11:30:20 2009 Rogue AP : 00:18:74:48:7a:11  removed from Base R
                             adio MAC : 00:1f:9e:8d:85:f0 Interface no:0(802.1
                             1b/g)


Would you like to display more entries? (y/n) y
```

Statistics

As far as statistics go, these are not as heavily utilized as those on a router or a switch interface. As newer versions come out, vast improvements and new additions are being made to this area. You can find all these categories under the MONITOR tab and under Statistics on the left menu.

Controller Statistics

The controller statistics include a nice summary of all types of traffic that have transversed the controller. As you can see in Figure 6-1, the Controller Statistics screen also contains VLAN information, which is very useful.

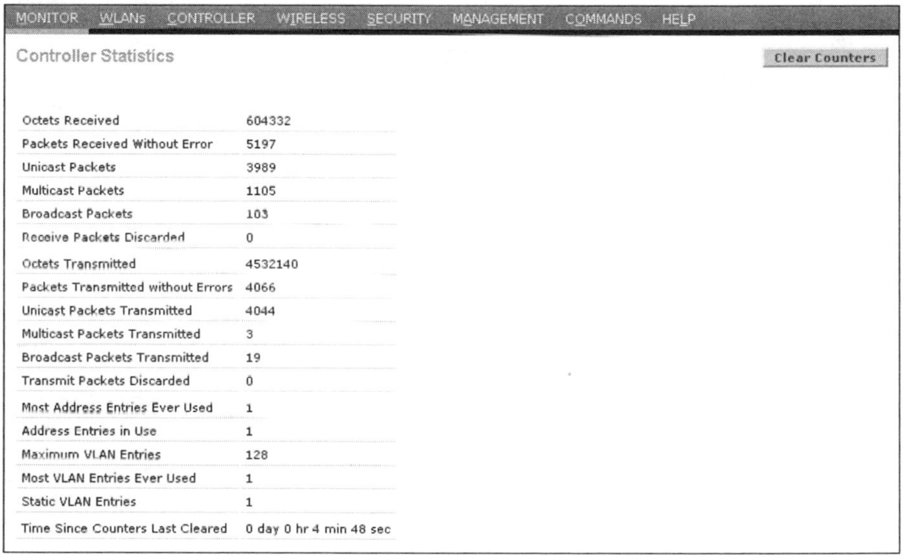

Figure 6-1 *Controller Statistics*

This page helps you learn how heavy of a network load this controller is dealing with. Although this screen is informative, it is not the most useful regarding troubleshooting.

AP Statistics

One of the most useful statistics page is the ap join stats page. These statistics were added in WLC Version 6.0, so they are not available in earlier versions. After you select the AP statistics, you will see a list of the APs. To see single AP statistics, click on the MAC address of the corresponding AP you want to see, as illustrated in Figure 6-2.

After you select the AP you want to view, it displays general AP information, discovery, and join phase statistics. See Figure 6-3.

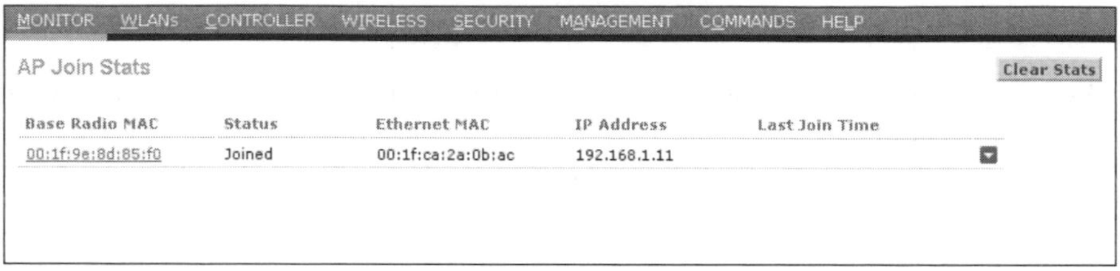

Figure 6-2 *AP Statistics*

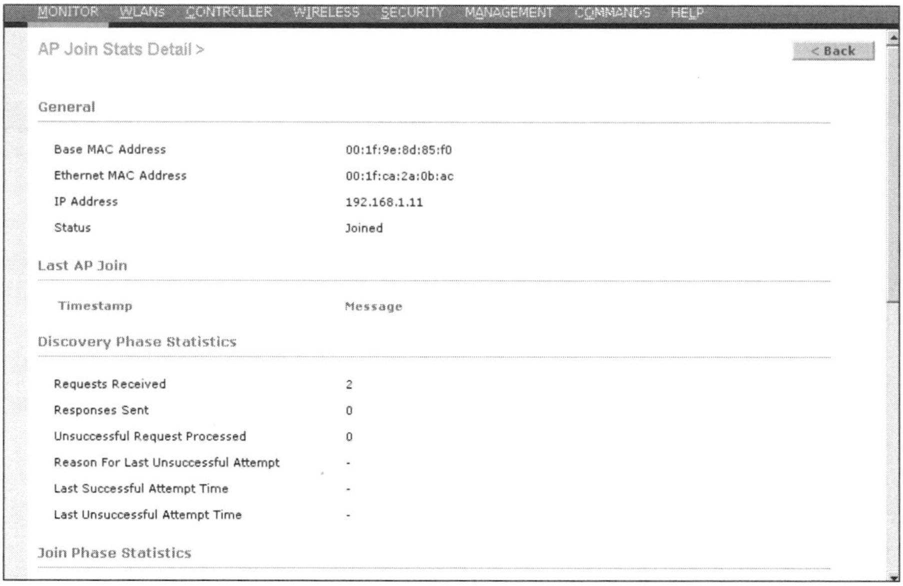

Figure 6-3 *Detailed AP Statistics*

The Detailed AP Statistics screen is probably the most useful screen as far as troubleshooting. It alerts you to whether there is a problem with the AP and the frequency. Although the other statistics screens are also very informative, this screen can actually assist you in pinpointing a particular discovery or join issue. With the time stamps on the page, it also indicates when to potentially anticipate the next failure.

The Last Error Summary, as seen in Figure 6-4, is an informative log that lists the AP error events. Once again, this is a key area to determine if an existing issue is present.

The configuration statistics are another key area in the AP stats that are commonly referred to.

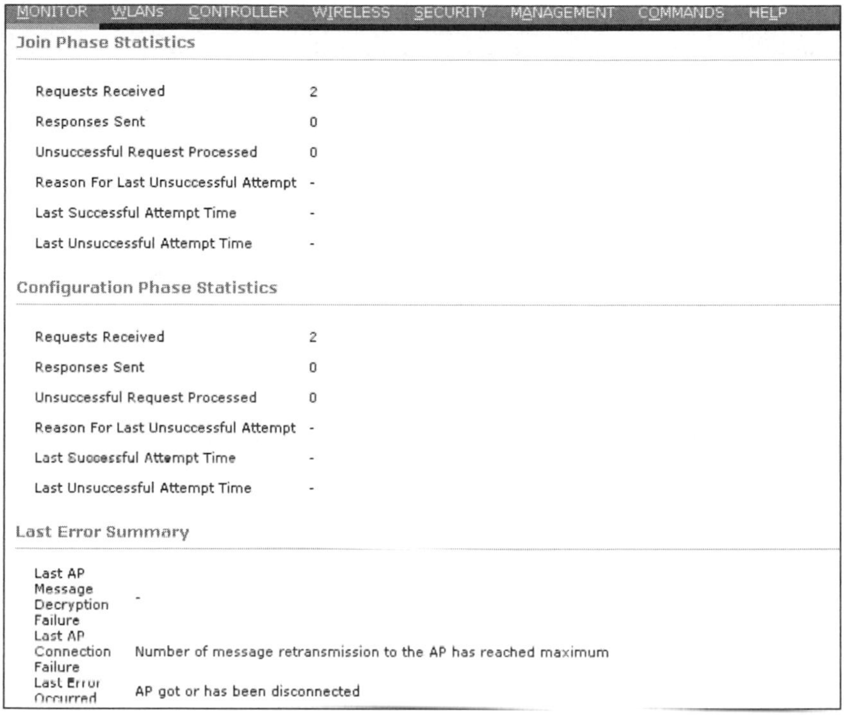

Figure 6-4 *Last Error Summary*

RADIUS Server Statistics

The RADIUS Server Statistics page is another informative page to notify you of a failed link or RADIUS server. The statistics on this page can indicate whether aggressive RADIUS-failover would be an issue. To configure the controller to mark a RADIUS server as down (not responding) after the server does not reply to three consecutive clients, use the **config radius aggressive-failover disabled** command.

Port Statistics

The port statistics on the controller refer to the physical links that are connected to the switch. On integrated controller modules, the port statistics are still there and referenced. These statistics are pretty straightforward and can easily point out any physical layer issues. Other than that, these statistics are not highly utilized. The port statistics are definitely worth a look in the event of trouble, but you should not spend much time on them. Refer to Figure 6-5 for common output on the port statistics.

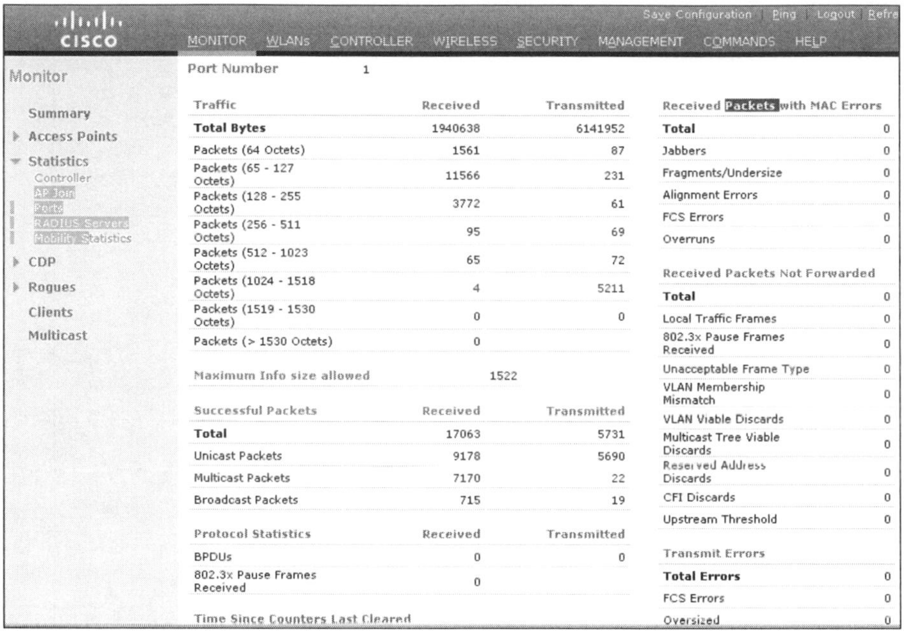

Figure 6-5 *Controller Port Statistics*

Mobility Statistics

The mobility statistics, along with the client statistics, can troubleshoot roaming, anchoring, and even association problems. The key element to remember prior to digging deeper here is to validate that each controller is a mobility member for the other and that the MAC addresses are correct in the mobility member page for each controller. The virtual interface address must also be the same for controllers to communicate mobility messages and events. The first glance at the mobility statistics, as seen in Figure 6-6, should not be all zeros across all stats. This controller is not communicating a single packet at the mobility level, which is a problem.

For review, whenever you are troubleshooting a mobility issue, the following are the first items to review:

■   Mobility members for each WLC, which should be the same on all WLCs for identifying all members

■   MAC address for each WLC, which should also be the same on all WLCs for each member entry

■   Mobility group, which should be listed for each WLC

■   Virtual interface address, which is the same for all WLCs

■   Mobility statistics, which show traffic

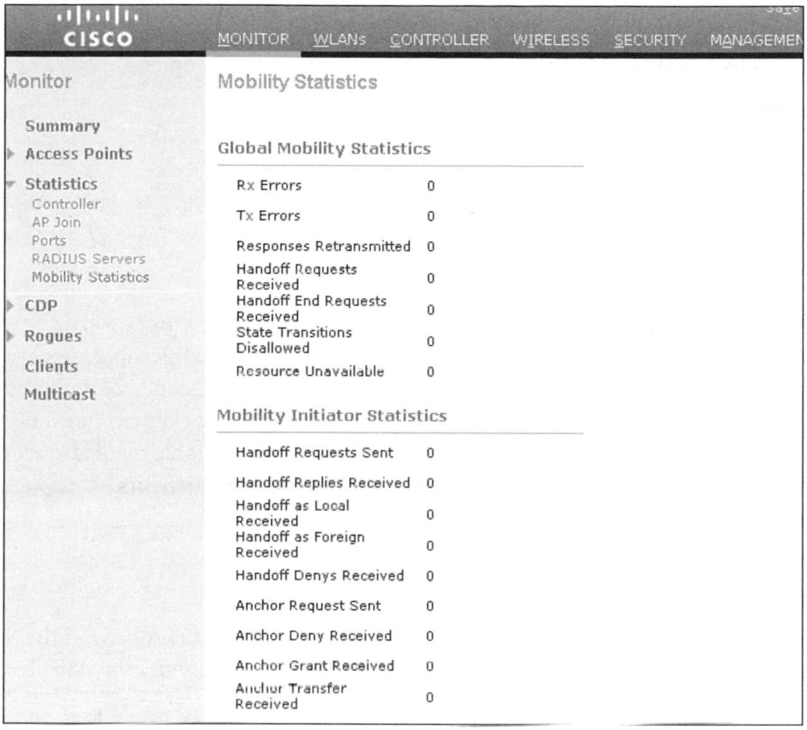

Figure 6-6 *Mobility Statistics*

Packet Captures

A packet capture tool (also known as a packet analyzer, protocol analyzer, Ethernet sniffer, or just sniffer) is hardware or software that captures and logs network traffic at a point in the network. The packet capture breaks down network traffic to individual packets and decodes them to the appropriate RFC or specification.

Spanning a port on a switch is common for obtaining a packet capture. You can find additional information at http://tinyurl.com/5bs385. Another method is using the wireless sniffer mode of an AP to obtain a wireless trace. More information can be found on that in any of the Controller Configuration Guides.

When debugs cannot provide the level of diagnostics you need to solve a problem, the next step is usually a packet capture. As mentioned, this provides a packet-by-packet view at the network traffic. A packet capture is usually used in conjunction with a debug to accurately depict what is occuring. The following are some common uses of a packet capture:

■ Isolate network problems

■ Monitor network traffic

- Provide network reporting statistics

- Filter desired network traffic

- Prevent network intrusion

- Provide security

- Debug network protocols

- Debug client/server communications

Many free packet captures are available on the Internet for everyday use. Make sure you are familiar with your analyzer software or hardware. If you are troubleshooting network issues often, it is just a matter of time before you will need the assistance of a packet capture. Most people have a difficult time reading or understanding packet captures. It is highly recommended that you spend some time becoming comfortable reading traces. Doing so will help your troubleshooting skills and will yeild great benefits.

WLC Config Analyzer

Another tool developed by a Cisco Wireless Engineer, Javier Contreras Albesa, is the WLC Config Analyzer. It is located at the Cisco Support Wiki at http://tinyurl.com/45jvph.

The goal of this tool was to save as much time as possible while processing long and related WLC config files. You can use this tool to detect basic configuration errors. The WLC Config Analyzer has a database of more than 100 checks (small expert system), with rules to validate issues that have generated Technical Assistance Center (TAC) cases in the past. You can disable or adjust all rules to evaluate the environment. Some of the features are as follows:

- Quick summary of a group of WLCs

- Analysis of the radio frequency (RF) relationships between APs

- Relationship summary between APs: which AP can see neighbor APs() and at what level for a given AP (Seeme)

- Text file with sh run-config output from one or more controllers (up to 24 in a single file)

- Assumption that all WLCs in the config file belong to the same mobility group

- Simple implementation; nothing fancy to store the processed results

- Ability to work offline on controller configurations.

- Audit voice settings

- Offsite RF analysis tools

Remember that this is *not* management software, but a post-deployment support tool. It is also not a TAC supported tool. Support is on best effort at wlc-conf-app-dev @cisco.com.

Software Bug Toolkit

Whenever software is created, human error is possible. The result of this error is software bugs. These bugs can be critical in any deployment, and it is key that you know as much as possible so you can compensate and adjust accordingly to avoid any service impact or degeneration.

The software bug toolkit is an online source that contains the most current and comprehensive software bug information available on all Cisco operating systems. It is a great tool for any customer regardless of size. The Software Bug ToolKit is located at http://www.cisco.com/cgi-bin/Support/Bugtool/launch_bugtool.pl. When you are aware of potential software bugs, you are in a much better state to make better decisions. Partners whose job is maintaining customer networks and customers themselves can troubleshoot problems more quickly. They can also plan and formulate future upgrades with this added information.

Features and benefits:

■ Having a web-based tool provides access to the most up-to-date known bugs in Cisco IOS Software, Cisco Catalyst OS software, and most other Cisco software.

■ You have access to more bug data, including those of low severity.

■ Comprehensive alerts and notifications are available, with real-time updates.

■ Search accuracy is improved, using new bug data sources within Cisco.

■ Filtering capabilities are better, so you can narrow the search for specific bugs. This capability allows frequent offering of specific resolutions to the problem.

■ You can scan bug details to quickly preview search results.

■ You can export data to a spreadsheet for offline analysis.

■ Search results have sortable columns.

■ Feedback mechanisms are enhanced. Action-directed reports are an example.

■ Partners can troubleshoot issues associated with known bugs and determine the appropriate corrective action.

■ Partners can retain and satisfy customers by improving network uptime and reducing the risks associated with software upgrades.

■ Partners can be proactive in tracking bugs that can affect the network of each customer.

- Troubleshooting is quicker. You can pinpoint probable bugs faster and, in many cases, provide proven workaround solutions.

- Partners have the flexibility they need to analyze bug data.

- Partners and customers can quickly report any problems or concerns about Bug Toolkit.

- Partners and customers can rate the overall quality of a bug and provide feedback about a specific bug.

Every engineer needs to make it common practice when running into a particular problem to always consult the bug toolkit. Nothing is more frustrating than troubleshooting a problem only to find out it is a software defect. By checking the bug toolkit, you can save hours and many resources. In addition, the bug toolkit usually includes workarounds. Even if the customer is in a situation to identify a bug with no fix at this point in time, the toolkit might offer a work-around until a fix becomes available. The time spent investigating possible bugs will pay for itself ten times over in the long run.

Summary

This chapter taught you new avenues to pursue to solve or diagnose whatever issue you might be facing. When Cisco acquired Airespace, the product did not have the same caliber of troubleshooting venues as a typical IOS device. As the product evolves, newer features are established to identify ways of solving problems. Hopefully, this chapter has armed you with additional facets to help complete any picture that needs to be developed.

Chapter 7

Deploying and Configuring the Wireless LAN Controller

A distribution system port connects the controller to a neighbor switch and serves as the data path between these two devices. This chapter discusses a few common methods on the models that have these options.

Cisco 4402 controllers have two Gigabit Ethernet distribution system ports, each of which is capable of managing up to 48 access points (AP). The Cisco 4404 controllers have four Gigabit Ethernet distribution system ports, each of which is capable of managing up to 48 APs per port. The 4404-25, 4404-50, and 4404-100 models allow a total of 25, 50, or 100 APs to join the controller. The Gigabit Ethernet ports on the 4402 and 4404 controllers accept these SX/LC/T small form-factor plug-in (SFP) modules:

- 1000BASE-SX SFP modules, which provide a 1000-Mbps wired connection to a network through an 850nM (SX) fiber-optic link using an LC physical connector

- 1000BASE-LX SFP modules, which provide a 1000-Mbps wired connection to a network through a 1300nM (LX/LH) fiber-optic link using an LC physical connector

- 1000BASE-T SFP modules, which provide a 1000-Mbps wired connection to a network through a copper link using an RJ-45 physical connector

The Cisco 5508 controllers have eight Gigabit Ethernet distribution system ports through which the controller can manage multiple APs. The 5508-12, 5508-25, 5508-50, 5508-100, and 5508-250 models allow for 12, 25, 50, 100, or 250 APs to join the controller. Cisco 5508 controllers have no restrictions on the number of APs per port. However, Cisco recommends using link aggregation (LAG) or configuring dynamic AP-Manager interfaces on each Gigabit Ethernet port to automatically balance the load. If more than 100 APs are connected to the 5500 series controller, make sure that more than one Gigabit Ethernet interface is connected to the upstream switch. The Gigabit Ethernet ports on the 5508 controllers accept these SX/LC/T small form-factor plug-in (SFP) modules:

■ 1000BASE-SX SFP modules, which provide a 1000-Mbps wired connection to a network through an 850nM (SX) fiber-optic link using an LC physical connector

■ 1000BASE-LX SFP modules, which provide a 1000-Mbps wired connection to a network through a 1300nM (LX/LH) fiber-optic link using an LC physical connector

■ 1000BASE-T SFP modules, which provide a 1000-Mbps wired connection to a network through a copper link using an RJ-45 physical connector

The Cisco Catalyst 6500 Series Switch Wireless Integrated Services Module (WiSM) and the Cisco 7600 Series Router WiSM have eight internal Gigabit Ethernet distribution system ports (ports 1 through 8) that connect the switch or router and the integrated controller. These internal ports are located on the backplane of the switch or router and are not visible on the front panel. Through these ports, the controller can support up to 300 APs.

The controller network module within the Cisco 28/37/38xx Series WiSM can support up to 6, 8, 12, or 25 APs (and up to 256, 256, 350, or 350 clients, respectively), depending on the version of the network module. The network module supports these APs through a Fast Ethernet distribution system port (on the NM-AIR-WLC6-K9 6-access-point version) or a Gigabit Ethernet distribution system port (on the 8-, 12-, and 25-access-point versions and on the NME-AIR-WLC6-K9 6-access-point version) that connects the router and the integrated controller. This port is located on the router backplane and is not visible on the front panel. The Fast Ethernet port operates at speeds up to 100 Mbps, and the Gigabit Ethernet port operates at speeds up to 1 Gbps.

The Catalyst 3750G integrated Wireless LAN Controller (WLC) switch has two internal Gigabit Ethernet distribution system ports (ports 27 and 28) that connect the switch and the integrated controller. These internal ports are located on the switch backplane and are not visible on the front panel. Each port is capable of managing up to 48 APs. However, Cisco recommends no more than 25 APs per port due to bandwidth constraints. The -S25 and -S50 models allow a total of 25 or 50 APs to join the controller.

Each distribution system port is, by default, an 802.1Q VLAN trunk port. The VLAN trunking characteristics of the port are not configurable. Some controllers support LAG, which bundles all the distribution system ports of the controller into a single 802.3ad port channel. Cisco 4400 series controllers support LAG in software Releases 3.2 and later; Cisco 5500 series controllers support LAG in software Releases 6.0 and later; and LAG is enabled automatically on the controllers within the Cisco WiSM and the Catalyst 3750G integrated WLC switch.

Connecting the WLC to the Switch

Regardless of operating mode, all controllers use the network as an 802.11 distribution system. Regardless of the Ethernet port type or speed, each controller monitors and communicates with its related controllers across the network. Two common methods are typically used when connecting the WLCs that have multiple ports to the neighboring switch. One method is with multiple independent links managed on their own, and the other method is similar to a port channel setup or LAG. LAG came out after the original idea of creating an additional AP-Manager on a port to manage additional APs.

Multiple AP-Manager Support

If you are not using LAG, how do you utilize the other ports to support additional APs? You have to create additional AP-Manager interfaces to manage the ports so they are able to handle WLC-to-AP communications. After you do this, APs can start using these ports to join the WLC. One of the key elements to remember is that this was only intended to be used with the Cisco 4400 series standalone controllers. You will not have this option for any of the integrated WLCs because they will only use a LAG setup. Refer to Figure 7-1 for a multiple AP-Manager setup. In this setup, both AP-Managers have been enabled for AP support. If this were a 4404 and two ports were configured as such and the other two ports were active then you would have support for additional APs, and two redundancy ports.

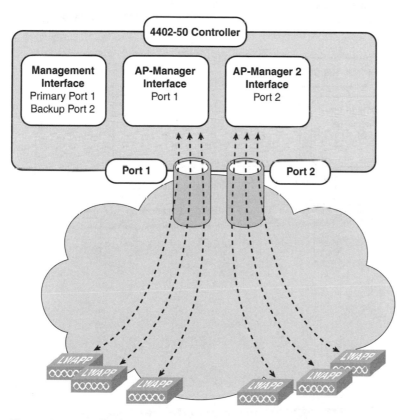

Figure 7-1 *Multiple AP-Manager Setup: Two AP-Managers*

For best housekeeping, configure the ports in sequential order such that AP-Manager interface 2 is on port 2, AP-Manager interface 3 is on port 3, and AP-Manager interface 4 is on port 4. Another common question that comes into play here is this: Do the

AP-Managers need to be in the same VLAN? The answer is no. The AP-Manager inter-faces need not be on the same VLAN as the other AP-Managers or the Management interface. However, from a management and troubleshooting perspective, it is highly rec-ommended that you configure all AP-Manager interfaces on the same VLAN or IP subnet.

Note You must assign an AP-Manager interface to each port on the controller.

Another key question is this: How do the AP-Managers work, and where do they fit into the normal AP join process? Before an AP joins a controller, it sends out a discovery request. From the discovery response that it receives, the number of AP-Manager inter-faces available and the capacity of each manager is relayed to the AP in the discovery response. Unless another form of load balancing exists, the AP joins the AP-Manager with the lowest capacity. The result is a round robin load-balancing effect. Another important fact to remember about AP-Managers is that for each AP-Manager port created, you lose a port for redundancy. Refer to Figure 7-2; when we refer to losing a port for redundancy. We are referring to port redundancy, not port redundancy, for AP support.

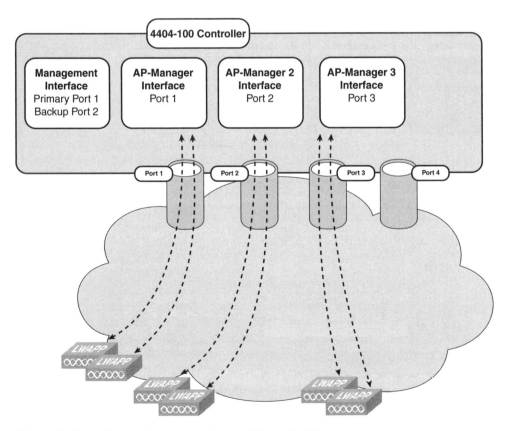

Figure 7-2 *Multiple AP-Manager Setup: Three AP Managers*

Note   APs may not be distributed completely evenly across all the AP-Manager interfaces, but a certain level of load balancing occurs.

If you consider a scenario in which a WLC has all its ports assigned as AP-Managers, for a total of 100 APs (see Figure 7-3), how would this affect the AP failover and port failover? One key concept in this design is that it has the advantage of load-balancing all 100 APs evenly across all four AP-Manager interfaces. If one of the AP-Manager interfaces fails, all the APs connected to the controller would be evenly distributed among the three available AP-Manager interfaces. For example, if AP-Manager interface 2 fails, the remaining AP-Manager interfaces (1, 3, and 4) would each manage approximately 33 APs.

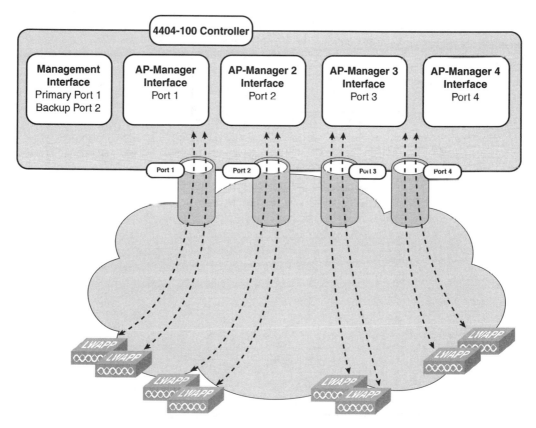

Figure 7-3   *Multiple AP-Manager Setup: Four AP Managers*

A key element to remember is that for every port that is physically connected and turned on, there must be an AP-Manager for each port. Having two AP-Managers for the 4402 or four for the 4404 is mandatory if all ports are to be used.

LAG

LAG is a partial implementation of the 802.3ad port aggregation standard. It bundles all the ports of the controller into a single 802.3ad port channel. The controller manages redundancy and load balancing of all the APs across the ports. See Figure 7-4 for an example of LAG implemented in a network. LAG does make managing your WLC a little easier. It reduces the number of IP addresses needed, and APs have a faster convergence time than if all four ports were up and connected. In addition, you do not need to configure primary and secondary ports for each interface. If a link fails, service is not interrupted. In the case of having all four ports up individually, an interruption of service would occur for APs using the failed link. The APs in this case would have to register again with the WLC. In the case of LAG, this would not occur.

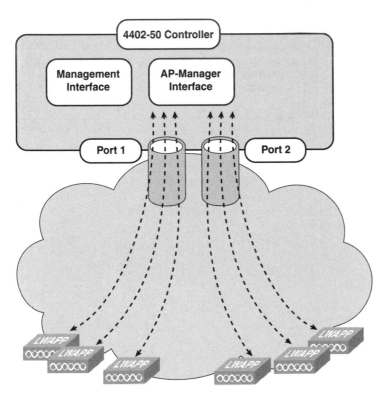

Figure 7-4   *A Typical LAG Setup*

LAG was introduced in the WLC in Version 3.2. LAG is the only method of communication with the WiSM and the Foxhound 3750G. These are the 6500 and 3750 integrated WLC switches. If you are using a non-LAG setup, each port on the controller ideally supports up to 48 APs. You can configure LAG on a WLC and only enable one port but have 100 APs joined to the WLC. Although this is not preferred, it is possible. With LAG enabled, the WLC supports up to 50 APs on its logical port. A 4402 supports 50 APs, whereas the 4404 supports 100 APs on its logical port. A WiSM has two WLCs per blade. The WiSM supports 150 APs on the logical port for a total of 300 on the blade.

Note   You can bundle all four ports on a 4404 controller (or two on a 4402 controller) into a single link.

When configuring bundled ports on the controller, you might want to consider terminating on two switch modules within a modular switch such as the Catalyst 6500; however, Cisco does not recommend connecting the LAG ports of a 4400 controller to multiple Catalyst 6500 or 3750G switches.

Terminating on two different modules within a single Catalyst 6500 switch provides redundancy and ensures that connectivity between the switch and the controller is maintained when one module fails. A 4402-50 controller is connected to two Gigabit modules (slots 2 and 3) within the Catalyst 6500. Port 1 of the controller is connected to Gigabit interface 3/1, and port 2 of the controller is connected to Gigabit interface 2/1 on the Catalyst 6500. Both switch ports are assigned to the same channel group.

When installing your WLC, if you plan to use load balancing, one of the key items to remember is that the controllers do their own form of load balancing, internally, for their APs. Other than that, they have no other form of port load balancing like your typical switches do. In addition, they do not use a mechanism for channel negotiation between the controller and the switch, such as Link Aggregation Control Protocol (LACP) or Cisco proprietary Port Aggregation Protocol (PAgP). Therefore, when you are configuring your EtherChannel on your switch, the mode is simply ON; it is nothing else. Configuring an option other than ON results in odd behavior. The WLC does not support LACP or Cisco PAgP. The load-balancing method configured on the Catalyst switch must be one that terminates all IP datagram fragments on a single controller port. Not following this recommendation can result in problems with AP registration and association. It is recommended that you specify *src-dest-ip* by using the following command:

```
port-channel load-balance src_dest_ip
```

If you are using a third-party switch and you are unable to configure the recommended load-balancing method, try disabling LAG. The only good way to still run LAG is to only enable one port so each packet has only one path for the source and destination.

Refer to the following LAG guidelines when installing your WLC. The LAG guidelines are as follows:

■   You cannot configure the ports of the controller into separate LAG groups. Only one LAG group is supported per controller. Therefore, you can connect a controller in LAG mode to only one neighbor device.

Note   The two internal Gigabit ports on the controller within the Catalyst 3750G integrated WLC switch are always assigned to the same LAG group.

- When you enable LAG or change the LAG configuration, you must immediately reboot the controller.

- When you enable LAG, you can configure only one AP-Manager interface because only one logical port is needed. LAG removes the requirement for supporting multiple AP-Manager interfaces.

- When you enable LAG, all dynamic AP-Manager interfaces and untagged interfaces are deleted, and all WLANs are disabled and mapped to the management interface. Also, the management, static AP-Manager, and VLAN-tagged dynamic interfaces are moved to the LAG port.

- Multiple untagged interfaces to the same port are not allowed.

- When you enable LAG, you cannot create interfaces with a primary port other than 29.

- When you enable LAG, all ports participate in LAG by default. Therefore, you must configure LAG for all the connected ports in the neighbor switch.

- When you enable LAG, port mirroring is not supported.

- When you enable LAG, if any single link goes down, traffic migrates to the other links.

- When you enable LAG, only one functional physical port is needed for the controller to pass client traffic.

- When you enable LAG, APs remain connected to the switch, and data service for users continues uninterrupted.

- When you enable LAG, you eliminate the need to configure primary and secondary ports for each interface.

- When you enable LAG, the controller sends packets out on the same port on which it received them. If a Control and Provisioning of Wireless Access Points (CAPWAP) packet from an AP enters the controller on physical port 1, the controller removes the CAPWAP wrapper, processes the packet, and forwards it to the network on physical port 1. This might not be the case if you disable LAG.

- When you disable LAG, the management, static AP-Manager, and dynamic interfaces are moved to port 1.

- When you disable LAG, you must configure primary and secondary ports for all interfaces.

- When you disable LAG, you must assign an AP-Manager interface to each port on the controller if you have multiple ports connected.

Note   Depending on the platform, LAG is enabled or disabled by default and is the only option on the WiSM controller and the controller in the Catalyst 3750G-integrated WLC switch.

In summary, LAG can simplify life and is usually the preferred method of connecting for a few reasons. On the WiSM and the Catalyst 3750G, LAG is enabled by default and is the only option, similar to Layer 3 Lightweight Access Point Protocol (LWAPP) transport mode. LAG only operates in Layer 3 LWAPP transport mode. One of the benefits is that only one interface, AP-Manager, is needed to manage the ports. The purpose of having multiple links is additional bandwidth for connecting additional APs. If LAG was not used, you would have to create an AP-Manager for each interface you brought online. For instance, if your WLC had three out of the four gigabit links active, you would have three AP-Manager interfaces, one for each port.

Layer 2 and Layer 3 LWAPP Transport Modes of Operation

LWAPP communication between the AP and the WLC can be in native, Layer 2 Ethernet frames. This is known as Layer 2 LWAPP mode. Although defined in the RFC draft, Layer 2 LWAPP mode is considered deprecated in Cisco implementation. Layer 2 LWAPP mode is described in this section for completeness, but the rest of this deployment guide assumes the controller is operating in Layer 3 LWAPP mode.

As you can see from Figure 7-5, the LWAPP control and data messages are encapsulated in Ethernet frames using Ethertype 0xBBBB. In Layer 2 LWAPP mode, although the APs might get an IP address via Dynamic Host Configuration Protocol (DHCP), all LWAPP communications between the AP and WLC are in Ethernet encapsulated frames, not IP packets. The APs must be on the same Ethernet network as the WLC. For this reason, Layer 2 LWAPP mode might not be suitable for scalability purposes in most deployments.

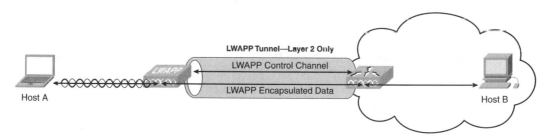

Figure 7-5 *LWAPP Layer 2 Mode*

Furthermore, Layer 2 mode is supported only by the Cisco 410x and 440x series of WLCs and the Cisco 1000 series APs. Layer 2 LWAPP is not supported by lightweight Cisco Aironet 1200, 1252, 1130AG, or 1240AG APs, or the Cisco 2006, WiSM, or Wireless LAN Controller Module (WLCM) series WLCs.

Consider the scenario in Figure 7-5, where Host A is a wireless LAN (WLAN) client communicating with the wired device, Host B. The LWAPP control Messages, including the LWAPP header with the C-Bit set to 1, and the control message elements are Ethernet encapsulated in a frame that traverses the local network. The MAC addresses in the Ethernet MAC header are the AP Ethernet MAC address and the WLC MAC address.

The source and destination MAC addresses depend on the direction of the frame. An LWAPP control frame sent from the AP to the WLC uses the AP Ethernet MAC address as the source address and the WLC MAC address as the destination address. An LWAPP control frame sent from the WLC to the AP uses the WLC MAC address as the source address and the AP MAC address as the destination address.

Data packets between WLAN clients and other hosts are typically IP packets.

When Host A sends a packet to Host B, the following sequence occurs:

Step 1.   An IP packet is transmitted by Host A over the 802.11 radio frequency (RF) interface after being encapsulated in an 802.11 frame with the MAC address of Host A as the source address and the radio interface MAC address of the AP as the destination address.

Step 2.   At the AP, the AP adds an LWAPP header to the frame with the C-Bit set to 0 and then encapsulates the LWAPP header and 802.11 frame into an Ethernet frame. This Ethernet frame uses the AP Ethernet MAC address as the source MAC address and the WLC MAC address as the destination MAC address.

Step 3.   At the WLC, the Ethernet and LWAPP headers are removed and the original 802.11 frame is processed.

Step 4.   After processing the 802.11 MAC header, the WLC extracts the payload (the IP packet), encapsulates it into an Ethernet frame, and then forwards the frame onto the appropriate wired network, typically adding an 802.1Q VLAN tag.

Step 5.   The packet then travels through the wired switching and routing infrastructure to Host B.

When Host B sends an IP packet to Host A, the following sequence occurs:

Step 1.   The packet is carried from Host B over the wired switching and routing network to the WLC, where an Ethernet frame arrives with the MAC address of Host A as the destination MAC address. The IP packet from Host B is encapsulated inside this Ethernet frame.

Step 2.   The WLC takes the entire Ethernet frame, adds the LWAPP header with the C-Bit set to 0, and then encapsulates the combined frame inside an LWAPP Ethernet frame. This LWAPP Ethernet frame uses the WLC MAC address as the source MAC address and the AP Ethernet MAC address as the destination MAC address. This frame is sent over the switched network to the AP.

Step 3.   At the AP, the Ethernet and LWAPP headers are removed and processed.

Step 4.   The payload (the IP packet) is then encapsulated in an 802.11 MAC frame and transmitted over the air by the AP to Host A.

You will read about the LWAPP discovery and join process in more detail later, but for now understand that a mechanism is included to determine if the path between the AP and WLC supports jumbo frames. If jumbo frames are not supported, a maximum transmission unit (MTU) of 1500 bytes is assumed. Both the AP and WLC handle fragmentation and reassembly of LWAPP-encapsulated packets. The architecture currently supports reassembly of a maximum of two LWAPP fragments, but it is highly unlikely that there will ever be more than two fragments with Layer 2 LWAPP.

LWAPP control messages are encrypted using the industry standard AES-CCM encryption method. The shared encryption key is derived and exchanged when the AP joins the WLC. The payloads of encapsulated LWAPP data messages are not specially encrypted. A trusted Ethernet-wired network is assumed and standard best practices for protecting Ethernet networks should be followed. Standards-based wireless Layer 2 encryption is handled at the AP.

Because the WLC is the point of ingress/egress for WLAN traffic on that IP network, the IP address of WLAN clients such as Host A comes from the pool of addresses on the network upstream of the WLC. This might not necessarily be the same network as the APs downstream from the WLC. For example, suppose that the packets bridged to and from the WLC are on the upstream side on network 192.168.1.0/24 and that the network between the WLC and AP is 192.168.2.0/24. The IP address of Host A is on the 192.168.1.0/24 network. The address of the WLAN client can be either statically assigned or dynamically assigned via DHCP.

LWAPP Layer 3 Transport Mode

Layer 3 LWAPP control and data messages are transported over the IP network in User Datagram Protocol (UDP) packets. This transport architecture is inherently more flexible and scalable than Layer 2 LWAPP and is the generally preferred solution. Layer 3 LWAPP is supported on all Cisco WLC platforms and lightweight APs (LAP). Figure 7-6 illustrates the topology for the discussion of Layer 3 LWAPP.

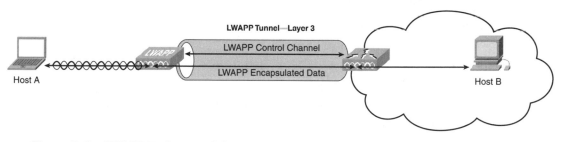

Figure 7-6 *LWAPP Packet Breakdown*

In this scenario, the LWAPP control and data messages are encapsulated in UDP packets that are carried over the IP network. The only requirement is established IP connectivity between the APs and the WLC. The LWAPP tunnel uses the IP address of the AP and the AP Manager interface IP address of the WLC as endpoints.. On the AP side, both LWAPP control and data messages use an ephemeral port that is derived from a hash of the AP MAC address as the UDP port. On the WLC side, LWAPP data messages always use UDP port 12222. On the WLC side, LWAPP control messages always use UDP port 12223.

The mechanics and sequencing of Layer 3 LWAPP are similar to Layer 2 LWAPP except that the packets are carried in UDP packets instead of being encapsulated in Ethernet frames. Figure 7-3 shows how LWAPP control messages, including the LWAPP header with the C-Bit set to 1, and the LWAPP control message elements are transported in UDP packets encapsulated in IP.

In Figure 7-6, Host A is a WLAN client communicating with the wired device, Host B. When Host A sends a data packet to Host B, the following sequence occurs:

Step 1.   The packet is transmitted by Host A over the 802.11 RF interface. This packet is encapsulated in an 802.11 frame with the MAC address of Host A as the source address and the radio interface MAC address of the AP as the destination address.

Step 2.   At the AP, the AP adds an LWAPP header to the frame with the C-Bit set to 0 and then encapsulates the LWAPP header and 802.11 frame into a UDP packet that is transmitted over IP. The source IP address is the IP address of the AP, and the destination IP address is the AP Manager address of the WLC. The source UDP port is the ephemeral port based on a hash of the AP MAC address. The destination UDP port is 12222.

Step 3.   The IP packet is encapsulated in Ethernet as it leaves the AP and transported by the switching and routed network to the WLC.

Step 4.   At the WLC, the Ethernet, IP, UDP, and LWAPP headers are removed from the original 802.11 frame.

Step 5.   After processing the 802.11 MAC header, the WLC extracts the payload (the IP packet from Host A), encapsulates it into an Ethernet frame, and then forwards the frame onto the appropriate wired network, typically adding an 802.1Q VLAN tag.

Step 6.   The packet is then transmitted by the wired switching and routing infrastructure to Host B.

When Host B sends an IP packet to Host A, the process is essentially reversed.

Step 1.   The packet is delivered by the wired switching and routing network to the WLC, where an Ethernet frame arrives with the MAC address of Host A as the destination MAC address.

Step 2.   The WLC removes the Ethernet header and extracts the payload (the IP packet destined for Host A).

Step 3.   The original IP packet from Host A is encapsulated with an LWAPP header, with the C-Bit set to 0, and then transported in a UDP packet to the AP over the IP network. The packet uses the WLC AP Manager IP address as the source IP address and the AP IP address as the destination address. The source UDP port is 12222, and the destination UDP port is the ephemeral port derived from the AP MAC address hash.

Step 4.   This packet is carried over the switching and routing network to the AP.

Step 5.   The AP removes the Ethernet, IP, UDP and LWAPP headers and extracts the payload, which is then encapsulated in an 802.11 frame and delivered to Host A over the RF network.

Layer 3 LWAPP assumes a 1500-byte MTU. Both the AP and WLC handle fragmentation and reassembly of LWAPP-encapsulated packets based on the 1500-byte MTU assumption. The architecture currently supports reassembly of a maximum of two LWAPP fragments.

LWAPP control messages are encrypted using the industry standard AES-CCM encryption method. The shared encryption key is derived and exchanged when the AP joins the WLC. The payloads of encapsulated LWAPP data messages are not specially encrypted. A trusted wired network is assumed and standard best practices for protecting networks should be followed. Standards-based wireless Layer 2 encryption is handled at the AP.

Because the WLC is the point of ingress/egress for WLAN traffic on that IP network, the IP address of WLAN clients such as Host A comes from the pool of addresses on the network upstream of the WLC. This might not necessarily be the same network as the APs downstream from the WLC. For example, if the packets bridged to and from the WLC are on the upstream side on network 192.168.1.0/24, and the network between the WLC and AP is 192.168.2.0/24, the IP address of Host A will be on the 192.168.1.0/24 network. The address of the WLAN client can be either statically assigned or dynamically assigned through DHCP.

Some of the WLCs can operate in both Layer 2 and Layer 3 LWAPP transport mode. Layer 2 is old and is typically rarely used. (Please refer to Figure 7-5, which shows LWAPP Layer 2 mode.) Layer 2 support has been removed from newer versions of code because of its limitations. The WiSM, 3750 Foxhound, 2006, 2106, and Network Module Controller (NMC) are some of the WLCs that operate only in Layer 3 LWAPP transport mode. One of the major differences is that in Layer 2, the packets are encapsulated in Ethernet frames using Ethertype 0xBBBB, whereas in Layer 3 they are encapsulated in UDP packets. In the case of Layer 3, all the LWAPP control and data messages are transported over the IP network in UDP packets.

As far as configurations regarding LAG, you will have two setups for the controller and two for the switch.

```
interface GigabitEthernet interface id
    switchport
    channel-group id mode on
    no shutdown
```

Configure the port channel on the neighbor switch as follows:

```
interface port-channel id
    switchport
    switchport trunk encapsulation dot1q
    switchport trunk native vlan native vlan id
    switchport trunk allowed vlan allowed vlans
    switchport mode trunk
    no shutdown
```

The controller will be much easier as you only configure LAG on or off. Depending on the mode you choose, other configurations will be necessary.

Interfaces on the WLC

The WLC has multiple interfaces. This will be different from the newer-generation WLCs where only one IP address exists for the entire box. Before discussing this further, it is important to explore how the controller communicates using a handful of different interfaces. This can help you to understand how the controller communicates to the APs and general traffic flow.

Refer to Figure 7-7 to get an understanding of the relationships between the interfaces, WLANs, and ports. This can assist you in understanding overall flow.

As the current WLC design now stands, 440x and WiSM, you usually have a minimum of three interfaces and in most cases many more:

- Management interface
- AP-Manager interface
- Dynamic interfaces
- Virtual interface
- Service port

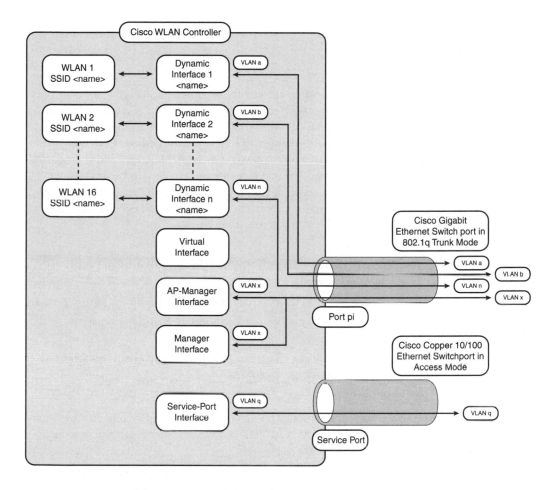

Figure 7-7   *Relationship Between WLANs, Interfaces, and Physical Ports*

The management interface represents the entire unit on the network. This is the only interface on the controller that reliably responds to pings when the controller is up and operational. It is the interface that the network admin uses to manage the box via Telnet, Secure Shell (SSH), web–HTTP, HTTPS, and so on. For CAPWAP, starting with code revision 5.2.x and later, the controller requires one management interface to control all controller communications and one AP-Manager interface to control all controller-to-AP communications, regardless of the number of ports.

> **Note**   If the service port is in use, the management interface must be on a different super-net from the service-port interface.

The AP-Manager interface handles all controller-to-AP communications. If the controller is not using LAG, it has an AP-Manager for each physical port that is enabled. The reason for additional ports is for additional AP support. Because the port is going to handling AP communications, it needs an AP-Manager to handle the traffic flow. Each AP-Manager has a unique address. Cisco recommends that the AP-Manager and management interface reside on the same subnet. The interfaces are not required to be on the same subnet, but that is highly recommended. If they are in different subnets, you must make sure that the APs have IP connectivity to both the management and AP-Manager inter-faces and allow CAPWAP/LWAPP to transverse these links.

> **Note**   If LAG is enabled, only one AP-Manager interface can exist. But when LAG is dis-abled, you must assign an AP-Manager interface to each port on the controller.
>
> If only one distribution system port can be used, you should use distribution system port 1.
>
> Port redundancy for the AP-Manager interface is not supported. You cannot map the AP-Manager interface to a backup port.
>
> Refer to the "Multiple AP-Manager Support" section earlier in this chapter for information on creating and using multiple AP-Manager interfaces.

The AP-Manager interface communicates through any distribution system port by listen-ing across the Layer 3 network for AP CAPWAP or LWAPP join messages to associate and communicate with as many LAPs as possible.

Dynamic interfaces, also known as VLAN interfaces, are created by users and designed to be analogous to VLANs for WLAN clients. A controller can support up to 512 dynamic interfaces (VLANs). Each dynamic interface is individually configured and allows separate communication streams to exist on any or all of the distribution sys-tem ports of a controller. Each dynamic interface controls VLAN and other communica-tions between controllers and all other network devices, and each acts as a DHCP relay for wireless clients associated to WLANs mapped to the interface. You can assign dynamic interfaces to distribution system ports, WLANs, the Layer 2 management inter-face, and the Layer 3 AP Manager interface, and you can map the dynamic interface to a backup port. You can configure zero, one, or multiple dynamic interfaces on a distribu-tion system port. However, all dynamic interfaces must be on a different VLAN and IP subnet from all other interfaces configured on the port. If the port is untagged, all dynamic interfaces must be on a different IP subnet from any other interface configured on the port.

Note   Configuring a dynamic interface with a secondary subnet is not supported. Cisco recommends using tagged VLANs for dynamic interfaces.

This configuration enables you to manage the controller directly or through a dedicated operating system network, such as 10.1.2.x, which can ensure service access during network downtime. The service port can obtain an IP address using DHCP, or it can be assigned a static IP address, but a default gateway cannot be assigned to the service-port interface. Static routes can be defined through the controller for remote network access to the service port.

Note   Only Cisco 4400 series controllers have a service-port interface.

You must configure an IP address on the service-port interface of both Cisco WiSM controllers; otherwise, the neighbor switch cannot check the status of each controller.

The virtual interface actually has a variety of tasks. The important fact to remember about this interface is that it is used only in communications within the controller and encapsulated in LWAPP/CAPWAP tunnel for client traffic in certain scenarios. It never appears as the source or destination address of a packet that goes out a distribution system port and onto a switched network. For the WLC and mobility functions to operate correctly, the virtual interface IP address must be set to a unique value, and no other device in the network realm can have the same IP address. The virtual IP address for the interface cannot exist, nor should it ever, in a routing table in the network. The only stipulation is that it cannot be the value of 0.0.0.0. This interface is not designed to respond to pings. In addition, the virtual interface must be configured with an unassigned and unused gateway IP address, which is why many network administrators use 1.1.1.1.

The virtual interface is never mapped to a backup port. The main roles of the virtual interface are to act as a DHCP server placeholder for the wireless clients that obtain their IP address from a DHCP server and to serve as the redirect address for the web authentication login page. The virtual interface is used for few tasks, such as to support mobility management, DHCP relay, and embedded Layer 3 security such as guest web authentication, and to maintains the Domain Name System (DNS) gateway host name used by Layer 3 security and mobility managers to verify the source of certificates when Layer 3 web authorization is used. All WLCs within the same mobility group should have the same virtual address for WLC communication to occur.

DHCP Proxy Vs. DHCP Bridging

One of the biggest questions that is asked is how does the controller handle DHCP, in earlier versions, and what is the difference between DHCP proxy and bridging in the newer versions. WLC supports two modes of DHCP operations in case an external DHCP server is used, DHCP proxy mode and DHCP bridging mode. The DHCP proxy mode serves as a DHCP helper function to achieve better security and control over DHCP transaction between the DHCP server and the wireless clients. DHCP bridging mode provides an option to make controller's role in DHCP transaction entirely transparent to the wireless clients. The DHCP proxy is not a DHCP relay agent as specified in DHCP relay RFCs . It is essentially a helper function that utilizes some relay functionality to direct and transform DHCP transactions between the server and the client. It is not designed to be compliant with the DHCP relay RFCs.

Table 7-1 *Proxy Mode and Bridging Mode in Comparison*

Handling Client DHCP	DHCP Proxy Mode	DHCP Bridging Mode
Modify giaddr	Yes	No
Modify siaddr	Yes	No
Modify Packet Content	Yes	No
Redundant offers not forwarded	Yes	No
Option 82 Support	Yes	No
BOOTP support	No	Server
Per WLAN configurable	Yes	No
RFC Non-compliant	Proxy and relay agent are not exactly the same concept. But DHCP bridging mode is recommended for full RFC compliance.	No

DHCP Proxy Mode

The DHCP proxy is not ideal for all network environments. The controller modifies and relays all DHCP transactions to provide helper function and address certain security issues. The controller's virtual IP address is normally used as the source IP address of all DHCP transactions to the client. As a result, the real DHCP server IP address is not exposed in the air. This approach was adopted from the early days of the product to help address certain security concerns on open university campus who were among our first Beta customers. University campus usually have open WLAN deployed. Exposing real DHCP server IP would cause security issues. The virtual IP is displayed in dcbug output for DHCP transactions on the controller.

DHCP proxy mode operation maintains the same behavior for both symmetric and asymmetric mobility protocols. When multiple offers are coming from external DHCP servers, the DHCP proxy will always select the first one that comes in and set the ip address of the server in the client data structure. As a result, all following transactions, renews will go through the same server, until a transaction fails after retries. Then the proxy will likely to select a different server for the client. The DHCP renew will go through the DHCP proxy in DHCP proxy mode. This is how the designed proxy behavior is used to serve license requests in different scenarios:

Handling of packets for local mode clients:

- DHCP Discover

    - *giaddr* is initialized to *Wlan IP*.

    - The Discover is unicast from *Wlan IP* to each of the DHCP servers that are configured on the interface (or the WLAN).

- DHCP Offer

    - The first Offer received is processed and sent to the client. All subsequent offers are dropped by the proxy.

    - *giaddr* is set to INADDR_ANY.

    - The DHCP server identifier (Option 54) is set to *Virt IP*. As a result, the client believes this to be the IP address of its DHCP server.

    - The Offer is unicast from *Virt IP* to the client (*yiaddr*).

- DHCP Request

    - *giaddr* is initialized to *Wlan IP*.

    - The Request is unicast from *Wlan IP* to the appropriate DHCP server (the server that returned the first Offer to the client).

- DHCP Ack

    - *giaddr* is set to INADDR_ANY.

    - The DHCP server identifier (Option 54) is set to *Virt IP*.

    - The ACK is unicast from *Virt IP* to the client (*yiaddr*).

Handling of packets for foreign clients:

- DHCP Discover

    - *giaddr* is initialized to be *Mgmt IP*.

    - The Discover is unicast from *Mgmt IP* to the management IP address of the anchor controller.

- DHCP Offer

    - Validation is done to make sure the Offer was received from the Anchor.

    - *giaddr* is set to INADDR_ANY.

    - The DHCP server identifier (Option 54) is set to *Virt IP*. As a result, the client believes this to be the IP address of its DHCP server.

    - The Offer is unicast from *Virt IP* to the client (*yiaddr*).

- DHCP Request

  - *giaddr* is initialized to be *Mgmt IP*.

  - The Request is unicast from *Mgmt IP* to the management IP address of the anchor controller.

- DHCP Ack (Same behavior as local mode)

  - *giaddr* is set to INADDR_ANY.

  - The DHCP server identifier (Option 54) is set to *Virt IP*.

  - The ACK is unicast from *Virt IP* to the client (*yiaddr*).

Handling of packets for anchor clients:

- DHCP Discover (Same behavior as local mode)

  - *giaddr* is initialized to be *Wlan IP*.

  - The Discover is unicast from *Wlan IP* to each of the DHCP servers that are configured on the interface (or the WLAN).

- DHCP Offer

  - The first Offer received is processed and sent to the client. All subsequent offers are dropped by the proxy.

  - *giaddr* is initialized to INADDR_ANY.

  - *siaddr* is initialized to INADDR_ANY.

  - The Offer is unicast from *Wlan IP* to the management IP address of the foreign controller.

- DHCP Request (Same behavior as local mode).

  - *giaddr* is initialized to *Wlan IP*.

  - The Request is unicast from *Wlan IP* to the appropriate DHCP server (the server that returned the first Offer to the client).

- DHCP Ack

  - *giaddr* is initialized to INADDR_ANY.

  - The Ack is unicast from *Wlan IP* to the management IP address of the foreign controller.

Handling of packets for export-foreign clients:

In this case, DHCP packets are EoIP tunneled directly from the export-foreign to the export-anchor. The packets are never processed by the DHCP proxy.

Handling of packets for export-anchor clients:

> In this case, the proxy handles packets for a client just as if the client were a local mode client. However, when sending packets to the client it performs EoIP encapsulation (rather than 802.11 encapsulation).

DHCP Bridging Mode

The DHCP bridging feature is designed to make controller's role in the DHCP transaction entirely transparent to the client. With the exception of 802.11 to Ethernet II conversion, packets from the client are bridged unmodified from the LWAPP tunnel to the client's VLAN (or EoIP tunnel in the L3 roaming case). Similarly, with the exception of Ethernet II to 802.11 conversion, packets to the client are bridged unmodified from the client's VLAN (or EoIP tunnel in the L3 roaming case) to the LWAPP tunnel.

When the DHCP Proxy is disabled and the system is performing Bridging, packets are passed to/from the client unmodified. The only packet transformations performed by the DHCP proxy are encapsulation/decapsulation (e.g., 802.11 to Ethernet II or EoIP tunneling). All packets between controllers (anchor/foreign, export anchor/export foreign) are EoIP tunneled to preserve L2 information. For both the anchor and foreign case, the DHCP Proxy, when performing EoIP encapsulation, sets bit 1 of the EoIP header flags field. This indicates to the fast path on the receiving end of the tunnel that the encapsulated packet is DHCP and needs to be sent to the control path.

Overview and Configuration

If the APs reside in a different subnet than the WLC, you must implement one of these methods to allow WLC discovery:

- Use DHCP with Option 43.

- Use DNS entry CISCO-LWAPP-CONTROLLER.localdomain to resolve the management IP address of the WLC.

- Prime the AP.

The Cisco 1000 Series APs use a string format for DHCP Option 43, whereas the Aironet APs use the type, length, value (TLV) format for DHCP Option 43. DHCP servers must be programmed to return the option based on the AP DHCP Vendor Class Identifier (VCI) string (DHCP Option 60). Table 7-2 lists the VCI strings for Cisco APs that can operate in lightweight mode. See Chapter 3, "Introduction to LWAPP," for additional information on Options 43 and 60.

The format of the TLV block is as follows:

- **Type:** 0xf1 (decimal 241)

- **Length:** Number of controller IP addresses * 4

- **Value:** List of WLC management interfaces

Table 7-2 *VCI Strings for Cisco APs Operating in Lightweight Mode*

AP	Vendor Class Identifier
Cisco Aironet 1000 Series	Airespace.AP1200
Cisco Aironet 1100 Series	Cisco AP c1100
Cisco Aironet 1130 Series	Cisco AP c1130
Cisco Aironet 1200 Series	Cisco AP c1200
Cisco Aironet 1240 Series	Cisco AP c1240
Cisco Aironet 1250 Series	Cisco AP c1250
Cisco Aironet 1300 Series	Cisco AP c1300
Cisco Aironet 1500 Series	Cisco AP c1500[1] Cisco AP.OAP1500[2] Cisco AP.LAP1505[3] Cisco AP.LAP1510[4] Airespace.AP1200[5]
Cisco 3201 LAP	Cisco AP C3201 WMIC

[1]*Any 1500 Series AP running 4.1 software*

[2]*1500 OAP AP running 4.0 software*

[3]*1505 Model AP running 4.0 software*

[4]*1510 Model AP running 4.0 software*

[5]*Any 1500 Series AP running 3.2 software*

You can configure DHCP servers to return WLC IP addresses in vendor-specific Option 43 in the DHCP offer to Cisco LAPs. When the AP gets an IP address through DHCP, the AP looks for WLC IP addresses in the Option 43 field in the DHCP offer. The AP sends a unicast LWAPP discovery message to each of the WLCs that are listed in DHCP Option 43. WLCs that receive the LWAPP discovery request messages unicast an LWAPP discovery response to the AP. The AP attempts to resolve the DNS name CISCO-LWAPP-CONTROLLER.localdomain. When the AP is able to resolve this name to one or more IP addresses, the AP sends a unicast LWAPP discovery message to the resolved IP addresses. Each of the WLCs that receives the LWAPP discovery request message replies with a unicast LWAPP discovery response to the AP.

The first thing you need to do is get to an AP registered with the controller. To do that you much accomplish the following steps:

Step 1.   Have a DHCP server present so that the APs can acquire a network address.

Step 2.   Configure the WLC for basic operation.

Note   Option 43 is used if the APs reside in a different subnet.

Step 3.   Configure the switch for the WLC.

Step 4.   Configure the switch for the APs.

Step 5.   Register the LAPs to the WLCs.

Step 6.   Configure mobility groups for the WLCs. Multiple mobility groups are typically used with a multiple controller set up to identify roaming boundaries.

Note   Use the Command Lookup tool with a valid CCO account on Cisco.com to obtain
more information on the commands used in this section. The Command Lookup tool is
located at http://www.cisco.com/cgi-bin/Support/Cmdlookup/home.pl.

When the controller is installed for the first time, the switches and other network devices
must use a specific configuration. With that being said, look at the network diagram in
Figure 7-8 to see the natural flow of the VLANs and how they are carried on the WLC
and vice versa.

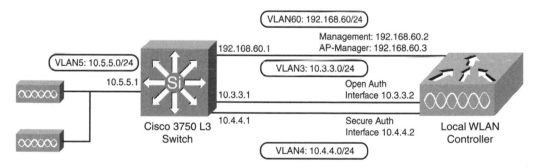

Figure 7-8   *Network Diagram*

Now is a good opportunity to look at configuring the controller for the first time.
When the controller boots at factory defaults, the bootup script runs the configuration
wizard, which prompts the installer for initial configuration settings. This procedure
describes how to use the configuration wizard on the command-line interface (CLI) to
enter initial configuration settings. Any time you are adding input into the wizard, if
the user presses the hyphen (-) key, the wizard backs up to the previous configuration
statement. That way if the user makes an error, it is possible to always go back after
pressing the Enter key.

> **Note**   Be sure that you understand how to configure an external DHCP server and DNS.

Complete these steps to configure the WLC for basic operation:

Step 1.   Connect your computer to the WLC with a DB-9 null modem serial cable.

Step 2.   Open a terminal emulator session with these settings:

- 9600 baud
- 8 data bits
- 1 stop bit
- No parity
- No hardware flow control

Step 3.   At the prompt, log in to the CLI. The default username is **admin**, and the default password is **admin**.

Step 4.   If necessary, enter **reset system** to reboot the unit and start the wizard.

Step 5.   At the first wizard prompt, enter a system name. The system name can include up to 32 printable ASCII characters.

Step 6.   Enter an administrator username and password. The username and password can include up to 24 printable ASCII characters.

Step 7.   Enter the service-port interface IP configuration protocol, either **none** or **DHCP**. Enter **none** if you do not want to use the service port or if you want to assign a static IP address to the service port.

Step 8.   If you entered **none** in Step 7 and need to enter a static IP address for the service port, enter the service-port interface IP address and netmask for the next two prompts. If you do not want to use the service port, enter **0.0.0.0** for the IP address and netmask.

Step 9.   Enter values for these options:

- Management interface IP address.
- Netmask.
- Default router IP address.
- Optional VLAN identifier. You can use a valid VLAN identifier or 0 for untagged.

> **Note**   When the management interface on the controller is configured as part of the native VLAN on the switchport to which it connects, the controller should *not* tag the frames. Therefore, you must set the VLAN to be 0 on the controller.

Step 10. Enter the network interface (Distribution System) physical port number. For the WLC, the possible ports are 1 through 4 for a front-panel Gigabit Ethernet port.

Step 11. Enter the IP address of the default DHCP server that supplies IP addresses to clients, the management interface, and the service-port interface, if you use one.

Step 12. Enter the LWAPP transport mode, either **LAYER2** or **LAYER3**.

Note   If you configure the WLC 4402/4404/41xx via wizard and select AP transport mode **LAYER2**, the wizard does not ask the details of AP Manager.

Step 13. Enter the virtual gateway IP address. This address can be any fictitious, unassigned IP address, such as 1.1.1.1, for the Layer 3 Security and Mobility managers to use.

Note   Usually the virtual gateway IP address that is used is a private address. This should not be a routed interface anywhere in the network!

Step 14. Enter the Cisco WLAN Solution Mobility Group/RF Group name.

Step 15. Enter the WLAN 1 service set identifier (SSID) or network name. This identifier is the default SSID that LAPs use to associate to a WLC.

Step 16. Allow or disallow static IP addresses for clients. Enter **yes** to allow clients to supply their own IP addresses. Enter **no** to require clients to request an IP address from a DHCP server.

Step 17. If you need to configure a RADIUS server on the WLC, enter **yes** and enter this information:

- RADIUS server IP address

- Communication port

- Shared secret

   If you do not need to configure a RADIUS server or you want to configure the server later, enter **no**.

Step 18. Enter a country code for the unit.

Step 19. Enter **help** to see a list of the supported countries.

Step 20. Enable and disable support for IEEE 802.11b, IEEE 802.11a, and IEEE 802.11g.

Step 21. Enable or disable Radio Resource Management (RRM) (auto RF).

Example 7-1 shows the Configuration Wizard tool along with the questions it displays during the initial startup.

Example 7-1 *WLC 4402—Configuration Wizard*

```
Welcome to the Cisco Wizard Configuration Tool
Use the '-' character to backup
System Name [Cisco_43:eb:22]: c4402
Enter Administrative User Name (24 characters max): admin
Enter Administrative Password (24 characters max): *****
Service Interface IP Address Configuration [none][DHCP]: none
Enable Link Aggregation (LAG) [yes][NO]: No
Management Interface IP Address: 192.168.60.2
Management Interface Netmask: 255.255.255.0
Management Interface Default Router: 192.168.60.1
Management Interface VLAN Identifier (0 = untagged): 60
Management Interface Port Num [1 to 2]: 1
Management Interface DHCP Server IP Address: 192.168.60.25
AP Transport Mode [layer2][LAYER3]: LAYER3
AP Manager Interface IP Address: 192.168.60.3
AP-Manager is on Management subnet, using same values
AP Manager Interface DHCP Server (192.168.50.3): 192.168.60.25
Virtual Gateway IP Address: 1.1.1.1
Mobility/RF Group Name: RFgroupname
Network Name (SSID): SSID
Allow Static IP Addresses [YES][no]: yes
Configure a RADIUS Server now? [YES][no]: no
Enter Country Code (enter 'help' for a list of countries) [US]: US
Enable 802.11b Network [YES][no]: yes
Enable 802.11a Network [YES][no]: yes
Enable 802.11g Network [YES][no]: yes
Enable Auto-RF [YES][no]: yes
```

Note The management interface on the WLC is the only consistently pingable interface from outside of the WLC unless under a significant load. Internet Control Message Protocol (ICMP) is not 100 percent reliable. Dynamic interfaces are reachable too, if mgmt-via-dynamic is enabled. Therefore, it is an expected behavior if you are not able to ping the AP manager interface from outside of the WLC.

You must configure the AP manager interface for the APs to associate with the WLC.

Configure the Switch for the WLC

Example 7-2 employs a Catalyst 3750 switch that uses only one port. The example tags the AP-Manager and management interfaces and places these interfaces on VLAN 60. The switch port is configured as an IEEE 802.1Q trunk and only the appropriate VLANs, which are VLANs 2 through 4 and 60 in this case, are allowed on the trunk. The management and AP-Manager VLAN (VLAN 60) is tagged and is not configured as the native VLAN of the trunk. When the example configures those interfaces on the WLC, the interfaces are assigned a VLAN identifier.

Example 7-2 *802.1Q Switch Port Configuration*

```
Switch(config-if)# interface GigabitEthernet1/0/1
Switch(config-if)# description Trunk Port to Cisco WLC
Switch(config-if)# switchport trunk encapsulation dot1q
Switch(config-if)# switchport trunk allowed vlan 2-4,60
Switch(config-if)# switchport mode trunk
Switch(config-if)# no shutdown
```

Notice that this example configures the neighbor switch port in a way that only allows relevant VLANs on the 802.1Q trunk. All other VLANs are pruned. This type of configuration is not necessary, but it is a deployment best practice. When you prune irrelevant VLANs, the WLC only processes relevant frames, which optimizes performance. Now that you have the controller and the switch configured for interaction with the WLC, you can configure the switch so it can talk with the APs. The switch setup is completely different from the autonomous AP in the way it is configured for access ports. An exception exists, which you will see firsthand when you get into configuring Hybrid Remote Edge Access Point (H-REAP). However, at this point, you are looking at a standard installation. Example 7-3 shows the VLAN interface configuration from the Catalyst 3750.

Example 7-3 *Switch Interface VLAN Configuration*

```
Switch(config-if)# interface VLAN5
Switch(config-if)# description AP VLAN
Switch(config-if)# ip address 10.5.5.1 255.255.255.0
```

Note   The interface VLAN does not always have to have an IP address.

Although the Cisco WLCs can connect to 802.1Q trunks, Cisco LAPs do not understand VLAN tagging and should only be connected to the access ports of the neighbor switch. The exception to this is when the APs are configured in H-REAP mode, where the APs are connected and configured as trunks to the switch. Cisco-IOS refers to the native VLAN with a tag of 0. The typical WLC naming convention does not use the wording "native" but rather the wording "default" VLAN. The word "default" indicates a tagging value of 0 in the WLC world.

Example 7-4 shows the switch port configuration from the Catalyst 3750.

Example 7-4 *Gigabit Switch Port Configuration*

```
Switch(config-if)# interface GigabitEthernet1/0/22
Switch(config-if)# description Access Port Connection to Cisco Lightweight AP
Switch(config-if)# switchport access vlan 5
Switch(config-if)# switchport mode access
Switch(config-if)# no shutdown
```

The infrastructure is now ready for connection to the APs. The time it takes for the AP to register with the controller depends on a number of factors. Overall, it does not take a long time for the registration process to occur. The controller is limited to a specific number of APs it can pass the configuration/software to at the same time. This does vary depending on code version.

After configuring everything, you can validate that it is working correctly using either the controller GUI or the CLI. After the APs register with the controller, you can view them under the **Wireless** tab at the top of the user interface of the controller (see Figure 7-9).

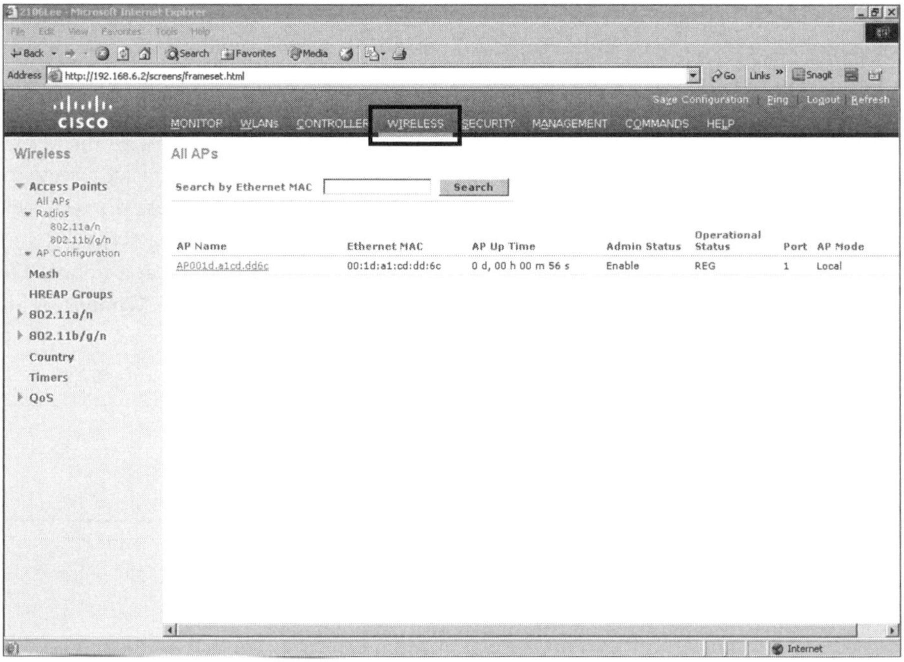

Figure 7-9 *Web GUI Screen of Registered APs*

On the CLI, you can use the **show ap summary** command to verify that the APs are registered with the WLC, as demonstrated in Example 7-5.

Example 7-5   *Using the CLI to Verify AP Registration with the WLC*

```
(Cisco Controller) >show ap summary

AP Name          Slots  AP Model   Ethernet MAC       Location         Port
-------.         --.    ----.      --------.          --------         --

ap:64:a3:a0      2      AP1010     00:0b:85:64:a3:a0  default_location 1

(Cisco Controller) >
```

On the WLC CLI, you can also use the **show client summary** command to see the clients
that are registered with the WLC, as demonstrated in Example 7-6.

Example 7-6   *Displaying Clients Registered with the WLC*

```
(Cisco Controller) >show client summary

Number of Clients................................ 1

MAC Address        AP Name       Status      WLAN  Auth  Protocol  Port
--------.          ------.       ------.     --    --    ----      --

00:40:96:a1:45:42  ap:64:a3:a0   Associated  4     Yes   802.11a   1

(Cisco Controller) >
```

Troubleshooting WLC Issues

How would you begin to troubleshoot an AP that does not register with a WLC issue?
You can start by using one of the most basic but important debug commands: **debug
lwapp events enable**.

Note   If you are enabling large amounts of debugs or global debugs—debugs that apply
to all devices—the console can become unresponsive because of the vast output and
results in the buffering filling up. In circumstances like this, it is best to define a syslog
server to output the debugs—available in Version 5.2. For any version prior to that and as
another alternative, it is best to filter the debugs with a MAC address—**debug mac addr
00:00:00:00:00:00**—and then enter your remaining debugs.

The **debug lwapp events enable** WLC command output in Example 7-7 shows that the
LAP is registered to the WLC.

Example 7-7   *Sample Output from debug lwapp events enable*

```
(Cisco Controller) >debug lwapp events enable
Tue Apr 11 13:38:47 2006: Received LWAPP DISCOVERY REQUEST from AP
    00:0b:85:64:a3:a0 to ff:ff:ff:ff:ff:ff on port '1'
Tue Apr 11 13:38:47 2006: Successful transmission of LWAPP Discovery-Response
    to AP 00:0b:85:64:a3:a0 on Port 1
Tue Apr 11 13:38:58 2006: Received LWAPP JOIN REQUEST from AP
    00:0b:85:64:a3:a0 to 00:0b:85:33:a8:a0 on port '1'
Tue Apr 11 13:38:58 2006: LWAPP Join-Request MTU path from AP 00:0b:85:64:a3:a0
    is 1500, remote debug mode is 0
Tue Apr 11 13:38:58 2006: Successfully added NPU Entry for AP
    00:0b:85:64:a3:a0 (index 48) Switch IP: 192.168.60.2, Switch Port: 12223,
    intIfNum 1, vlanId 60 AP IP: 10.5.5.10, AP Port: 19002, next hop MAC:
    00:0b:85:64:a3:a0
Tue Apr 11 13:38:58 2006: Successfully transmission of LWAPP Join-Reply to AP
    00:0b:85:64:a3:a0
Tue Apr 11 13:38:58 2006: Register LWAPP event for AP
    00:0b:85:64:a3:a0 slot 0
Tue Apr 11 13:38:58 2006: Register LWAPP event for AP 00:0b:85:64:a3:a0 slot 1
Tue Apr 11 13:39:00 2006: Received LWAPP CONFIGURE REQUEST from AP
    00:0b:85:64:a3:a0 to 00:0b:85:33:a8:a0
Tue Apr 11 13:39:00 2006: Updating IP info for AP 00:0b:85:64:a3:a0 —
    static 0, 10.5.5.10/255.255.255.0, gtw 192.168.60.1
Tue Apr 11 13:39:00 2006: Updating IP 10.5.5.10 ===> 10.5.5.10 for AP
    00:0b:85:64:a3:a0
Tue Apr 11 13:39:00 2006: spamVerifyRegDomain RegDomain set for slot 0 code 0
    regstring -A regDfromCb -A
Tue Apr 11 13:39:00 2006: spamVerifyRegDomain RegDomain set for slot 1 code 0
    regstring -A regDfromCb -A
Tue Apr 11 13:39:00 2006: spamEncodeDomainSecretPayload:Send domain secret
    Mobility Group<6f,39,74,cd,7e,a4,81,86,ca,32,8c,06,d3,ff,ec,6d,95,10,99,dd>
    to AP 00:0b:85:64:a3:a0
Tue Apr 11 13:39:00 2006: Successfully transmission of LWAPP
    Config-Message to AP 00:0b:85:64:a3:a0
Tue Apr 11 13:39:00 2006: Running spamEncodeCreateVapPayload for SSID 'SSID'
Tue Apr 11 13:39:00 2006: AP 00:0b:85:64:a3:a0 associated. Last AP failure was
    due to Configuration changes, reason:  operator changed 11g mode
Tue Apr 11 13:39:00 2006: Received LWAPP CHANGE_STATE_EVENT from AP
    00:0b:85:64:a3:a0
! For State Changes refer to Figure 3-4 in chapter 3.
Tue Apr 11 13:39:00 2006: Successfully transmission of LWAPP Change-State-Event
    Response to AP 00:0b:85:64:a3:a0
Tue Apr 11 13:39:00 2006: Received LWAPP Up event for AP 00:0b:85:64:a3:a0 slot 0!
Tue Apr 11 13:39:00 2006: Received LWAPP CONFIGURE COMMAND RES from AP
    00:0b:85:64:a3:a0
```

```
Tue Apr 11 13:39:00 2006: Received LWAPP CHANGE_STATE_EVENT from AP
    00:0b:85:64:a3:a0
Tue Apr 11 13:39:00 2006: Successfully transmission of LWAPP Change-State-Event
    Response to AP 00:0b:85:64:a3:a0
Tue Apr 11 13:39:00 2006: Received LWAPP Up event for AP
    00:0b:85:64:a3:a0 slot 1!
```

The output in Example 7-8 shows these useful WLC **debug** commands in action:

- **debug pem state enable:** Displays the access policy manager state machine debug options

- **debug pem events enable:** Displays policy manager events

- **debug dhcp message enable:** Shows the debug of DHCP messages that are exchanged to and from the DHCP server

- **debug dhcp packet enable:** Shows the debug of DHCP packet details that are sent to and from the DHCP server

Example 7-8 *Debug PEM and DHCP Debug Output*

```
Tue Apr 11 14:30:49 2006: Applied policy for mobile 00:40:96:a1:45:42
Tue Apr 11 14:30:49 2006: STA [00:40:96:a1:45:42, 192.168.1.41] Replacing Fast
    Path rule type = Airespace AP Client  on AP 00:0B:85:64:A3:A0, slot 0
    InHandle = 0x00000000, OutHandle = 0x00000000  ACL Id = 255, Jumbo Frames
                = NO, interface = 1  802.1P = 0, DSCP = 0, T
Tue Apr 11 14:30:49 2006: Successfully plumbed mobile rule for mobile
    00:40:96:a1:45:42 (ACL ID 255)
 Tue Apr 11 14:30:49 2006: Plumbed mobile LWAPP rule on AP 00:0b:85:64:a3:a0
    for mobile 00:40:96:a1:45:42
 Tue Apr 11 14:30:53 2006: DHCP proxy received packet, src: 0.0.0.0,
    len = 320
Tue Apr 11 14:30:53 2006: dhcpProxy: Received packet: Client 00:40:96:a1:45:42
    DHCP Op: BOOTREQUEST(1), IP len: 320, switchport: 1, encap: 0xec03
Tue Apr 11 14:30:53 2006: dhcpProxy(): dhcp request, client:
    00:40:96:a1:45:42: dhcp op: 1, port: 1, encap 0xec03, old mscb
    port number: 1
Tue Apr 11 14:30:53 2006: dhcp option len, including the magic cookie = 84
Tue Apr 11 14:30:53 2006: dhcp option: received DHCP REQUEST msg
Tue Apr 11 14:30:53 2006: dhcp option: skipping option 61, len 7
Tue Apr 11 14:30:53 2006: dhcp option: requested ip = 192.168.1.41
Tue Apr 11 14:30:53 2006: dhcp option: skipping option 12, len 15
Tue Apr 11 14:30:53 2006: dhcp option: skipping option 81, len 19
Tue Apr 11 14:30:53 2006: dhcp option: vendor class id = MSFT 5.0 (len 8)
Tue Apr 11 14:30:53 2006: dhcp option: skipping option 55, len 11
Tue Apr 11 14:30:53 2006: dhcpParseOptions: options end, len 84, actual 84
```

(continues)

Example 7-8   *Debug PEM and DHCP Debug Output (continued)*

```
Tue Apr 11 14:30:53 2006: mscb->dhcpServer: 192.168.60.2, mscb->dhcpNetmask:
    255.255.255.0,mscb->dhcpGateway: 192.168.60.1, mscb->dhcpRelay:
    192.168.60.2 VLAN: 60
Tue Apr 11 14:30:53 2006: Local Address: 192.168.60.2, DHCP Server:
    192.168.60.2, Gateway Addr: 192.168.60.2, VLAN: 60, port: 1
Tue Apr 11 14:30:53 2006: DHCP Message Type received: DHCP REQUEST msg
Tue Apr 11 14:30:53 2006:    op: BOOTREQUEST, htype: Ethernet, hlen: 6, hops: 1
Tue Apr 11 14:30:53 2006:    xid: 3371152053, secs: 0, flags: 0
Tue Apr 11 14:30:53 2006:    chaddr: 00:40:96:a1:45:42
Tue Apr 11 14:30:53 2006:    ciaddr: 0.0.0.0,  yiaddr: 0.0.0.0
Tue Apr 11 14:30:53 2006:    siaddr: 0.0.0.0,  giaddr: 192.168.60.2
Tue Apr 11 14:30:53 2006: Forwarding DHCP packet locally (348 octets) from
    192.168.60.2 to 192.168.60.2
Tue Apr 11 14:30:53 2006: Received 348 byte dhcp packet from 0x0201a8c0
    192.168.60.2:68
Tue Apr 11 14:30:53 2006: DHCP packet: 192.168.60.2 -> 192.168.60.2 using
    scope "InternalScope"
Tue Apr 11 14:30:53 2006: received REQUEST
Tue Apr 11 14:30:53 2006: Checking node 192.168.1.41  Allocated 1144765719,
    Expires 1144852119 (now: 1144765853)
Tue Apr 11 14:30:53 2006: adding option 0x35
Tue Apr 11 14:30:53 2006: adding option 0x36
Tue Apr 11 14:30:53 2006: adding option 0x33
Tue Apr 11 14:30:53 2006: adding option 0x03
Tue Apr 11 14:30:53 2006: adding option 0x01
Tue Apr 11 14:30:53 2006: dhcpd: Sending DHCP packet (giaddr:192.168.60.2)to
192.168.60.2:67  from 192.168.60.2:1067
Tue Apr 11 14:30:53 2006: sendto (548 bytes) returned 548
Tue Apr 11 14:30:53 2006: DHCP proxy received packet, src: 192.168.60.2,
    len = 548
Tue Apr 11 14:30:53 2006: dhcpProxy: Received packet: Client 00:40:96:a1:45:42
    DHCP Op: BOOTREPLY(2), IP len: 548, switchport: 0, encap: 0x0
Tue Apr 11 14:30:53 2006: dhcp option len, including the magic cookie = 312
Tue Apr 11 14:30:53 2006: dhcp option: received DHCP ACK msg
Tue Apr 11 14:30:53 2006: dhcp option: server id = 192.168.60.2
Tue Apr 11 14:30:53 2006: dhcp option: lease time (seconds) = 86400
Tue Apr 11 14:30:53 2006: dhcp option: gateway = 192.168.60.1
Tue Apr 11 14:30:53 2006: dhcp option: netmask = 255.255.255.0
Tue Apr 11 14:30:53 2006: dhcpParseOptions: options end, len 312, actual 64
Tue Apr 11 14:30:53 2006: DHCP Reply to AP client: 00:40:96:a1:45:42,
    frame len 412, switchport 1
Tue Apr 11 14:30:53 2006: DHCP Message Type received: DHCP ACK msg
```

```
Tue Apr 11 14:30:53 2006:    op: BOOTREPLY, htype: Ethernet, hlen: 6, hops: 0
Tue Apr 11 14:30:53 2006:    xid: 3371152053, secs: 0, flags: 0
Tue Apr 11 14:30:53 2006:    chaddr: 00:40:96:a1:45:42
Tue Apr 11 14:30:53 2006:    ciaddr: 0.0.0.0,  yiaddr: 192.168.1.41
Tue Apr 11 14:30:53 2006:    siaddr: 0.0.0.0,  giaddr: 0.0.0.0
Tue Apr 11 14:30:53 2006:    server id: 1.1.1.1  rcvd server id: 192.168.60.2
```

In addition to the aforementioned debug commands, you can use the following debug commands to troubleshoot your configuration:

- **debug lwapp errors enable:** Shows output of the debug of LWAPP errors

- **debug pm pki enable:** Shows the debug of certificate messages that are passed between the AP and the WLC

One of the major issues to notice is that the controller does not defend the AP-Manager address. If an IP address is duplicated, it can take some time to resolve because of the way the controller handles the issue—or does not handle, in this case. This problem manifests itself in some odd circumstances. On the positive side, this issue has been resolved but still exists in older code versions. This issue is a result of bug CSCsg75863.

If the user accidentally injects a device on the subnet that uses the AP-Manager IP address of the controller, the Address Resolution Protocol (ARP) cache on the default gateway router is refreshed with the wrong MAC address. When this occurs, the APs can no longer reach the controller and drop into their discovery phase to look for a controller. The APs send discovery requests, and the controller responds with discovery replies, but the join requests never reach the AP-Manager interface of the controller because of the bad ARP entry on the gateway router. After the default 4-hour ARP refresh interval, the APs join the controller if the device is removed.

A workaround for this issue is to configure the static ARP entries on the gateway router of the controller for these IP addresses:

- **Management IP address:** Customers gain access to the graphical user interface (GUI) from another subnet, and the controller receives the AP discovery requests.

- **AP-Manager IP address:** APs join the controller from another subnet.

- **Every Dynamic interface IP address:** Packets from other subnets reach the dynamic interface of the controller.

DHCP packets transmit from the interface of the wireless client. Telnet or SSH to the gateway address of the controller, and use the **arp** *ip address hhhh.hhhh.hhhh* command to add the ARP entries. Use the **ping** command on the default router of the controller to the different addresses to refresh the ARP cache on the router. To discover the MAC addresses, use the **show arp | include** *ip address* command.

Summary

Once again, understanding the architecture of the product and how it works plays a key role in allowing you to design the best topology for your network and troubleshoot it. Keeping abreast on the changes of the product as new controllers are introduced is also important. (An example would be the new 5508 that no longer has an AP-Manager interface.) That knowledge can change your understanding of how the system works and the way you intend to troubleshoot it. As the product grows and changes are made to improve the overall system, you are forced to educate yourself. Knowing the product prior to any implementations makes the understanding of why those changes were made much easier to understand. Nevertheless, keeping up with the product and understanding its benefits always places you in the best position even if your objective is for designing or troubleshooting an issue.

Chapter 8

Access Point Registration

Access point (AP) registration consists of a discovery and join process. Registration is the first step in getting your wireless network up and running. If you understand how the discovery and join process works, your job will be much easier when you have to troubleshoot it. One of the major selling points of the AP and Controller design product is its scalability. You can take an AP out of the box and literally plug it into any port on your network and the AP will join the controller. This only happens if you have everything configured correctly. The point is that the port that you plug the AP into might be thousands of miles of away from the controller that it is supposed to join. What does this mean in terms of troubleshooting? It is vital that you understand the discovery process because there could be multiple networks—large complex networks at that.

The world of wireless just became much more complex because of the Lightweight Access Point Protocol (LWAPP) and Control and Provisioning of Wireless Access Points (CAPWAP) protocols. Scalability has a price.

The introduction of CAPWAP in Version 5.2 added another way for the AP to join the WLC. This is not a big issue, but it does complicate the process because it is now necessary to talk about both discovery and join processes for LWAPP and CAPWAP.

AP Discovery and Join Process

AP registration is really two parts: the discovery and join phases, as seen in Figure 8-1. The discovery is just that—the AP discovering and validating that it is indeed talking to a controller. The join process is essentially the AP joining the Wireless LAN Controller (WLC) and the building of the encrypted tunnel between the AP-Manager and the AP. The discovery and join process do differ between LWAPP and CAPWAP. This chapter takes a look at LWAPP first.

Note   The Cisco 5508 wireless controller does not require AP-Manager interfaces. The Management interface in a Cisco 5508 controller can act like a dynamic AP-Manager interface.

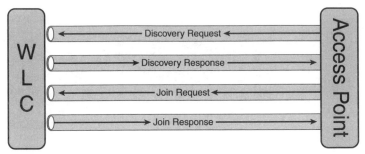

Figure 8-1 *Discovery and Join Process*

This is where the management and AP-Manager functions come into play. Each interface plays a role in this procedure. The management interface handles the discovery, whereas the AP-Manager handles the join, as seen in Figure 8-2.

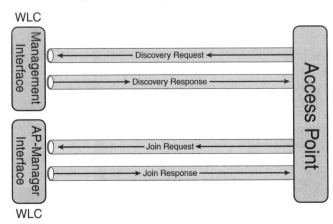

Figure 8-2 *Discovery, Join Packets, and Interface Handling (Excluding 5500 Series)*

An exception to this exists, and that exception applies to the WLC 5500 series because this platform has no AP-Manager. The management interface handles both functions on the 5500 series platform, as seen in Figure 8-3.

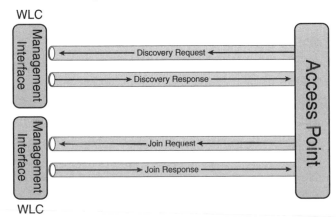

Figure 8-3 *Discovery, Join Packets, and Interface Handling for 5500 Series*

Cisco APs use a process called discovery to join a WLC. Both of the wireless devices use LWAPP to communicate with each other. The LWAPP APs and the WLC are known for their scalability. Regardless of the physical or logical location in the network, they can be plugged in anywhere. A new AP, right from the box, can be plugged in anywhere regardless of the subnet. After it is plugged in, it finds the WLC. The AP then receives the WLC version of code and configuration. After this is sent to the AP, it is ready to start serving clients.

Lightweight access points (LAP) are "zero-touch" deployed. The steps in this process are as follows:

Step 1.   LWAPP begins with a WLC discovery and join phase. The APs send LWAPP discovery request messages to WLCs.

Step 2.   Any WLC receiving the LWAPP discovery request responds with an LWAPP discovery response message.

Step 3.   From the LWAPP, the AP proceeds to step discovery responses received. Then an AP selects a WLC to join.

Step 4.   The AP sends an LWAPP join request to the WLC, expecting an LWAPP join response.

Step 5.   The WLC validates the AP and then sends an LWAPP join response to the AP. The AP validates the WLC to complete the discovery and join process. The validation on both the AP and WLC is a mutual authentication mechanism. An encryption key derivation process is subsequently initiated. The encryption key secures future LWAPP messages.

The first problem, though, is how to determine where to send the LWAPP discovery request messages. The Cisco implementation defines an AP controller hunting process and discovery algorithm. The AP builds a list of WLCs using the search and discovery process, and then it selects a controller to join from the list.

The search process is as follows:

Step 1.   The AP issues a Dynamic Host Configuration Protocol (DHCP) discover request to get an IP address, unless it has previously had a static IP address configured.

Step 2.   If the AP supports Layer 2 LWAPP mode, it broadcasts an LWAPP discovery message in a Layer 2 LWAPP frame. Any WLC connected to the network that is configured to operate in Layer 2 LWAPP mode responds with a Layer 2 LWAPP discovery response. If Layer 2 LWAPP mode is not supported by the AP or the AP fails to receive an LWAPP discovery response to the Layer 2 LWAPP discovery message broadcast, the AP proceeds to Step 3.

Step 3.   If Step 1 fails or if the AP does not support Layer 2 LWAPP mode, attempt a Layer 3 LWAPP WLC discovery.

Step 4.   If Step 3 fails, reset and return to Step 1.

The controller search process repeats until at least one WLC is found and joined.

Figure 8-4 illustrates the process using a flowchart for a different perspective.

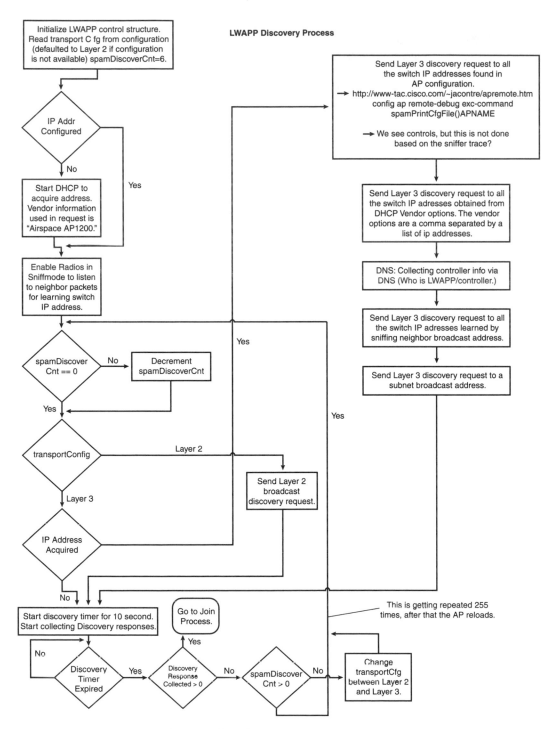

Figure 8-4 *Discovery and Join Packet Flow*

Troubleshooting Network Connectivity and AP Registration

The following section can help you troubleshoot connectivity issues between the AP and the WLC. In most cases, registration and join issues can be resolved with debugs and analysis of configurations. In other situations a wireless trace is needed—sometimes concurrent. This also includes the use of wireless sniffers.

Verifying VLAN Configuration

The configuration of the interface on a switch that connects to a WLC is usually always configured as a trunk port. The switchport interfaces for an AP are set up as access ports. In some situations the AP switch interface is configured as a trunk port. These configuration setups include Hybrid Remote Edge Access Point (H-REAP) deployments. Another situation is when the AP is configured as a rogue detector. This chapter notes these configurations when discussing the AP roles and H-REAP configurations.

The following example uses a Catalyst 3750 switch utilizing only one port. The example tags the AP-Manager and management interfaces and places them on VLAN 60. The switch port is configured as an IEEE 802.1Q trunk; only the appropriate VLANs, which are VLANs 2 through 4 and 60 in this case, are allowed on the trunk. The management and AP-Manager VLAN (VLAN 60) is tagged and is not configured as the native VLAN of the trunk. The management and AP-Manager interfaces do not have to be configured as tagged interfaces; however, they are configured that way here so you understand how to do this in case you decide to configure it this way. Therefore, when the example configures those interfaces on the WLC, the interfaces are assigned a VLAN identifier. As a quick note, Portfast trunk/edge are preferred for WLC ports.

Example 8-1 shows the 802.1Q switch port configuration.

Example 8-1 *Switch Port Configuration That Connects to a WLC*

```
interface GigabitEthernet1/0/1
description Trunk Port to Cisco WLC
switchport trunk encapsulation dot1q
switchport trunk allowed vlan 2-4,60
switchport mode trunk
no shutdown
```

Note   When you connect the WLC Gigabit port, make sure it is connected to the switch Gigabit port only. If you connect the WLC Gigabit Ethernet to the Switch FastEthernet port, it will not work.

Notice that this configuration example configures the neighbor switch port in a way that only allows relevant VLANs on the 802.1Q trunk. All other VLANs are pruned. This type of configuration is not necessary, but it is a deployment best practice. When you prune irrelevant VLANs, the WLC only processes relevant frames, which optimizes performance.

The APs are connected to access ports of the switch. Consider another example on how to configure an AP connection on the switch. Example 8-2 shows the VLAN interface configuration from the Catalyst 3750.

Example 8-2   *Switchport Configuration of Switch Connection to AP*

```
interface VLAN5
description AP VLAN
ip address 10.5.5.1 255.255.255.0
```

Whereas the Cisco WLCs always connect to 802.1Q trunks, in most cases, Cisco APs should be configured on access ports because trunking is not enabled on the APs.

Example 8-3 shows the switch port configuration from the Catalyst 3750.

Example 8-3   *Switchport Configuration of Switch Connection to AP*

```
interface GigabitEthernet1/0/22
description Access Port Connection to Cisco Lightweight AP
switchport access vlan 5
switchport mode access
no shutdown
```

The infrastructure is now ready for connection to the APs.

Verifying IP Addressing Information

After the APs register with the controller, you can view them under wireless at the top of the user interface of the controller.

On the command-line interface (CLI), you can use the **show ap summary** command to verify that the APs are registered with the WLC, as shown in Example 8-4.

Example 8-4   *Registered AP Summary*

```
((Cisco Controller) >show ap summary
AP Name         Slots  AP Model   Ethernet MAC       Location        Port
-------------.  --.   ----.      ----------.        -------   --

ap:64:a3:a0     2      AP1010     00:0b:85:64:a3:a0 default_location  1

(Cisco Controller) >
```

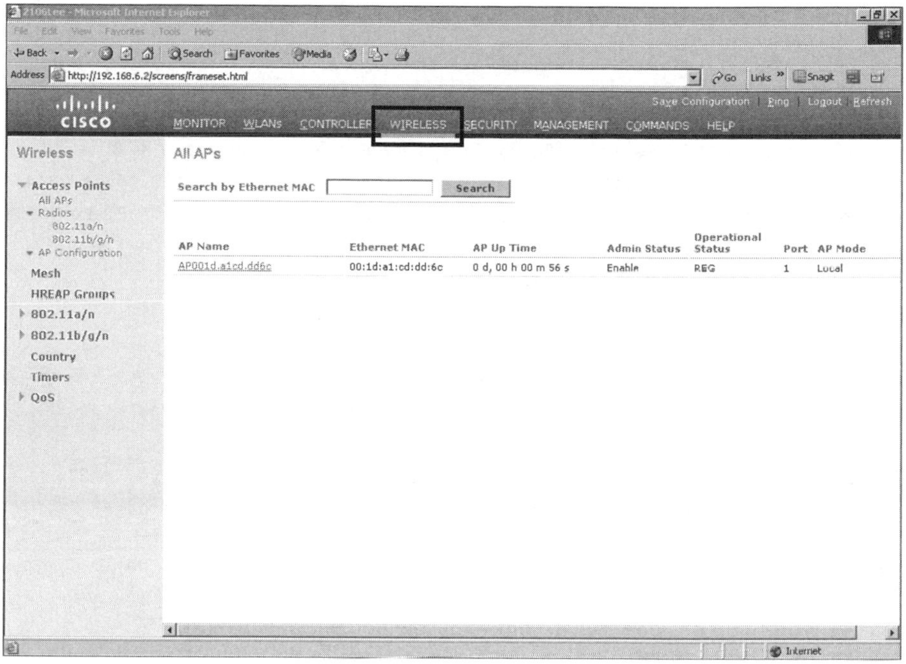

Figure 8-5 *GUI Screenshot of Registered APs*

Understanding the AP Discovery and AP Join Process

In a CAPWAP environment, a LAP discovers a controller by using CAPWAP discovery mechanisms and then sends the controller a CAPWAP join request. The controller sends the AP a CAPWAP join response, allowing the AP to join the controller. When the AP joins the controller, the controller manages its configuration, firmware, control transactions, and data transactions. Upgrade and downgrade paths from LWAPP to CAPWAP or from CAPWAP to LWAPP are supported. An AP with an LWAPP image starts the discovery process in LWAPP. If it finds an LWAPP controller, it starts the LWAPP discovery process to join the controller.

Whether LWAPP discovery can even be tried really depends on the version of code. In other cases, both discovery messages should be tried, and then the join phase determines the WLC to join.

Example 8-5 shows a successful AP join debug that is using CAPWAP as the communication protocol between the AP and the WLC.

Example 8-5 *Debug Output of an AP Join*

```
*Aug 28 10:36:33.175: Received a message from AP of length 95 on interface = 1
 *Aug 28 10:36:33.176: Received CAPWAP_MESSAGE
 *Aug 28 10:36:33.176: CAPWAP Control Msg Received from 192.168.1.23:41148
```

(continues)

Example 8-5   *Debug Output of an AP Join (continued)*

```
 *Aug 28 10:36:33.176: length = 4, packet received from 0:1f:9e:8d:85:f0
 *Aug 28 10:36:33.176: 00:1f:9e:8d:85:f0 packet received of length 53 from
192.168.1.23:41148
 *Aug 28 10:36:33.176: 00:1f:9e:8d:85:f0 Msg Type = 1 Capwap state = 0
 *Aug 28 10:36:33.176: 00:1f:9e:8d:85:f0 Discovery Request from 192.168.1.23:41148
 *Aug 28 10:36:33.176: 00:1f:9e:8d:85:f0 Discovery request: Total msgEleLen = 29
 *Aug 28 10:36:33.176: 00:1f:9e:8d:85:f0 msgEleLength = 1 msgEleType = 20
 *Aug 28 10:36:33.176: Discovery Type = Unknown
 *Aug 28 10:36:33.176: 00:1f:9e:8d:85:f0 Total msgEleLen = 24
 *Aug 28 10:36:33.176: 00:1f:9e:8d:85:f0 msgEleLength = 1 msgEleType = 41
 *Aug 28 10:36:33.176: 00:1f:9e:8d:85:f0 Total msgEleLen = 19
 *Aug 28 10:36:33.176: 00:1f:9e:8d:85:f0 msgEleLength = 1 msgEleType = 44
 *Aug 28 10:36:33.176: 00:1f:9e:8d:85:f0 Total msgEleLen = 14
 *Aug 28 10:36:33.176: 00:1f:9e:8d:85:f0 msgEleLength = 10 msgEleType = 37
 *Aug 28 10:36:33.176: 00:1f:9e:8d:85:f0 Vendor specific payload from AP
00:1F:9E:8D:85:F0 validated
 *Aug 28 10:36:33.176: 00:1f:9e:8d:85:f0 Discovery request: Vendor payload type =
401, length = 10
 *Aug 28 10:36:33.176: Board data options: apType 0, joinPriority 1
 *Aug 28 10:36:33.176: 00:1f:9e:8d:85:f0 Total msgEleLen = 0
 *Aug 28 10:36:33.176: 1. 0 0
 *Aug 28 10:36:33.176: 2. 232 3
 *Aug 28 10:36:33.176: 3. 0 0
 *Aug 28 10:36:33.176: 4. 50 0
 *Aug 28 10:36:33.176: msgLength = 36
 *Aug 28 10:36:33.176: 00:1f:9e:8d:85:f0 Discovery resp: AC Descriptor message
element len = 40
 *Aug 28 10:36:33.176: acName = MLG-4402
 *Aug 28 10:36:33.176: 00:1f:9e:8d:85:f0 Discovery resp:AC Name message element
length = 52
 *Aug 28 10:36:33.176: CAPWAP_DOT11_MSGELE_WTP_RADIO_INFORMATION supported radio
types 0
 *Aug 28 10:36:33.176: 00:1f:9e:8d:85:f0 Discovery resp: WTP Radio Information msg
length = 61
 *Aug 28 10:36:33.176: 00:1f:9e:8d:85:f0 Discovery resp: CAPWAP Control IPV4
Address len = 71
 *Aug 28 10:36:33.176: 00:1f:9e:8d:85:f0 Discovery resp: CAPWAP Control IPV6
Address len = 93
 *Aug 28 10:36:33.176: 00:1f:9e:8d:85:f0 Discovery resp: Mwar type payload len =
104
 *Aug 20 10:36:33.176: Send AP Timesync of 1219919793 source MANUAL
 *Aug 28 10:36:33.176: 00:1f:9e:8d:85:f0 Discovery resp: Time sync payload len = 119
 *Aug 28 10:36:33.176: 00:1f:9e:8d:85:f0 encodeLen = 119 len = 16
 *Aug 28 10:36:33.176: 00:1f:9e:8d:85:f0 Discovery Response sent to
192.168.1.23:41148
 *Aug 28 10:36:33.176: 00:1f:9e:8d:85:f0 WTP already released
*Aug 28 10:36:44.174: Received a message from AP of length 115 on interface = 1
```

```
 *Aug 28 10:36:44.174: Received CAPWAP_MESSAGE
 *Aug 28 10:36:44.174: CAPWAP Control Msg Received from 192.168.1.23:41148
 *Aug 28 10:36:44.174: DTLS Connection not found for 192:168:1:23:41148
 *Aug 28 10:36:44.174: DTLS connection not found, creating new connection for
192:168:1:23 (41148) 192:168:1:3 (5246)
 *Aug 28 10:36:44.246: record_consumed or success *Aug 28 10:36:44.248: Received a
message from AP of length 147 on interface = 1
 *Aug 28 10:36:44.248: Received CAPWAP_MESSAGE
 *Aug 28 10:36:44.248: CAPWAP Control Msg Received from 192.168.1.23:41148
 *Aug 28 10:36:44.250: record_consumed or success *Aug 28 10:36:44.266: Received a
message from AP of length 590 on interface = 1
 *Aug 28 10:36:44.266: Received CAPWAP_MESSAGE
 *Aug 28 10:36:44.266: CAPWAP Control Msg Received from 192.168.1.23:41148
 *Aug 28 10:36:44.266: record_consumed or success *Aug 28 10:36:44.266: Received a
message from AP of length 590 on interface = 1
 *Aug 28 10:36:44.266: Received CAPWAP_MESSAGE
 *Aug 28 10:36:44.266: CAPWAP Control Msg Received from 192.168.1.23:41148
 *Aug 28 10:36:44.267: record_consumed or success *Aug 28 10:36:44.267: Received a
message from AP of length 179 on interface = 1
 *Aug 28 10:36:44.267: Received CAPWAP_MESSAGE
 *Aug 28 10:36:44.267: CAPWAP Control Msg Received from 192.168.1.23:41148
 *Aug 28 10:36:44.278: record_consumed or success *Aug 28 10:36:44.710: Received
a message from AP of length 329 on interface = 1
 *Aug 28 10:36:44.710: Received CAPWAP_MESSAGE
 *Aug 28 10:36:44.711: CAPWAP Control Msg Received from 192.168.1.23:41148
 *Aug 28 10:36:44.814: record_consumed or success *Aug 28 10:36:44.814: Received a
message from AP of length 420 on interface = 1
 *Aug 28 10:36:44.814: Received CAPWAP_MESSAGE
 *Aug 28 10:36:44.814: CAPWAP Control Msg Received from 192.168.1.23:41148
 *Aug 28 10:36:44.817: DTLS connection established *Aug 28 10:36:44.817:
record_consumed or success *Aug 28 10:36:44.817: Received CAPWAP_MESSAGE
 *Aug 28 10:36:44.817: CAPWAP DTLS session established msg
 *Aug 28 10:36:44.818: dtls connection = 0x1791b964
 *Aug 28 10:36:44.818: Starting wait join timer for DTLS connection 0x1791b964!,
AP: 192.168.1.23:41148
 *Aug 28 10:36:44.820: Received a message from AP of length 1499 on interface = 1
 *Aug 28 10:36:44.820: Received CAPWAP_MESSAGE
 *Aug 28 10:36:44.820: CAPWAP Control Msg Received from 192.168.1.23:41148
 *Aug 28 10:36:44.821: length = 4, packet received from 0:1f:9e:8d:85:f0
 *Aug 28 10:36:44.821: 00:1f:9e:8d:85:f0 packet received of length 1400 from
192.168.1.23:41148
 *Aug 28 10:36:44.821: 00:1f:9e:8d:85:f0 Msg Type = 3 Capwap state = 0
 *Aug 28 10:36:44.821: 00:1f:9e:8d:85:f0 Join Request from 192.168.1.23:41148
 *Aug 28 10:36:44.821: 00:1f:9e:8d:85:f0 Total msgEleLen = 1368
 *Aug 28 10:36:44.821: 00:1f:9e:8d:85:f0 msgEleLength = 16 msgEleType = 28
 *Aug 28 10:36:44.821: 00:1f:9e:8d:85:f0 Total msgEleLen = 1348
 *Aug 28 10:36:44.821: 00:1f:9e:8d:85:f0 msgEleLength = 65 msgEleType = 38
```

(continues)

Example 8-5   *Debug Output of an AP Join (continued)*

```
 *Aug 28 10:36:44.821: 00:1f:9e:8d:85:f0 Total msgEleLen = 1279
 *Aug 28 10:36:44.821: 00:1f:9e:8d:85:f0 msgEleLength = 40 msgEleType = 39
 *Aug 28 10:36:44.821: 00:1f:9e:8d:85:f0 Total msgEleLen = 1235
 *Aug 28 10:36:44.821: 00:1f:9e:8d:85:f0 msgEleLength = 16 msgEleType = 45
 *Aug 28 10:36:44.821: 00:1f:9e:8d:85:f0 Total msgEleLen = 1215
 *Aug 28 10:36:44.821: 00:1f:9e:8d:85:f0 msgEleLength = 4 msgEleType = 35
 *Aug 28 10:36:44.821: 00:1f:9e:8d:85:f0 Total msgEleLen = 1207
 *Aug 28 10:36:44.821: 00:1f:9e:8d:85:f0 msgEleLength = 1 msgEleType = 41
 *Aug 28 10:36:44.821: 00:1f:9e:8d:85:f0 Total msgEleLen = 1202
 *Aug 28 10:36:44.821: 00:1f:9e:8d:85:f0 msgEleLength = 1 msgEleType = 44
 *Aug 28 10:36:44.821: 00:1f:9e:8d:85:f0 Total msgEleLen = 1197
 *Aug 28 10:36:44.821: 00:1f:9e:8d:85:f0 msgEleLength = 4 msgEleType = 42
 *Aug 28 10:36:44.821: 00:1f:9e:8d:85:f0 Total msgEleLen = 1189
 *Aug 28 10:36:44.821: 00:1f:9e:8d:85:f0 msgEleLength = 5 msgEleType = 1048
 *Aug 28 10:36:44.821: 00:1f:9e:8d:85:f0 Total msgEleLen = 1180
 *Aug 28 10:36:44.821: 00:1f:9e:8d:85:f0 msgEleLength = 5 msgEleType = 1048
 *Aug 28 10:36:44.821: 00:1f:9e:8d:85:f0 Total msgEleLen = 1171
 *Aug 28 10:36:44.821: 00:1f:9e:8d:85:f0 msgEleLength = 2 msgEleType = 29
 *Aug 28 10:36:44.821: 00:1f:9e:8d:85:f0 Total msgEleLen = 1165
 *Aug 28 10:36:44.821: 00:1f:9e:8d:85:f0 msgEleLength = 13 msgEleType = 37
 *Aug 28 10:36:44.821: 00:1f:9e:8d:85:f0 Vendor specific payload from AP
00:1F:9E:8D:85:F0 validated
 *Aug 28 10:36:44.821: 00:1f:9e:8d:85:f0 Vendor payload type = 2, length = 13
 *Aug 28 10:36:44.821: 00:1f:9e:8d:85:f0 Total msgEleLen = 1148
 *Aug 28 10:36:44.821: 00:1f:9e:8d:85:f0 msgEleLength = 10 msgEleType = 37
 *Aug 28 10:36:44.821: 00:1f:9e:8d:85:f0 Vendor specific payload from AP
00:1F:9E:8D:85:F0 validated
 *Aug 28 10:36:44.821: 00:1f:9e:8d:85:f0 Vendor payload type = 401, length = 10
 *Aug 28 10:36:44.822: 00:1f:9e:8d:85:f0 Created AP 00:1f:9e:8d:85:f0
*Aug 28 10:36:44.822: 00:1f:9e:8d:85:f0 Join timer: Found DTLS session for
192.168.1.23:41148
 *Aug 28 10:36:44.822: 00:1f:9e:8d:85:f0 Join Request: Total msgEleLen = 1368
 *Aug 28 10:36:44.822: 00:1f:9e:8d:85:f0 Join Request: msgEleLength = 16
msgEleType = 28
 *Aug 28 10:36:44.822: 00:1f:9e:8d:85:f0 Join Request: Total msgEleLen = 1348
 *Aug 28 10:36:44.822: 00:1f:9e:8d:85:f0 Join Request: msgEleLength = 65
msgEleType = 38
 *Aug 28 10:36:44.822: 00:1f:9e:8d:85:f0 WTP_MODEL_NUMBER: apModel AIR-AP1252AG-A-
K9   , length 20
 *Aug 28 10:36:44.822: 00:1f:9e:8d:05:f0 WTP_SERIAL_NUMBER: apSerialNum
FCW1213Z01T, length 11
 *Aug 28 10:36:44.822: BOARD DATA card id is 0x0
 *Aug 28 10:36:44.822: 00:1f:9e:8d:85:f0 Join Request: Total msgEleLen = 1279
 *Aug 28 10:36:44.822: 00:1f:9e:8d:85:f0 Join Request: msgEleLength = 40
msgEleType = 39
 *Aug 28 10:36:44.822: 00:1f:9e:8d:85:f0 Join Request: Total msgEleLen = 1235
```

```
  *Aug 28 10:36:44.822: 00:1f:9e:8d:85:f0 Join Request: msgEleLength = 16
msgEleType = 45
  *Aug 28 10:36:44.822: 00:1f:9e:8d:85:f0 Join Request: Total msgEleLen = 1215
  *Aug 28 10:36:44.822: 00:1f:9e:8d:85:f0 Join Request: msgEleLength = 4
msgEleType = 35
  *Aug 28 10:36:44.822: 00:1f:9e:8d:85:f0 SESSION_ID - -1263901711
  *Aug 28 10:36:44.822: 00:1f:9e:8d:85:f0 Join Request: Total msgEleLen = 1207
  *Aug 28 10:36:44.822: 00:1f:9e:8d:85:f0 Join Request: msgEleLength = 1
msgEleType = 41
  *Aug 28 10:36:44.822: 00:1f:9e:8d:85:f0 Join Request: Total msgEleLen = 1202
  *Aug 28 10:36:44.822: 00:1f:9e:8d:85:f0 Join Request: msgEleLength = 1
msgEleType = 44
  *Aug 28 10:36:44.822: 00:1f:9e:8d:85:f0 Join Request: Total msgEleLen = 1197
  *Aug 28 10:36:44.822: 00:1f:9e:8d:85:f0 Join Request: msgEleLength = 4
msgEleType = 42
  *Aug 28 10:36:44.822: 00:1f:9e:8d:85:f0 Join Request: Total msgEleLen = 1189
  *Aug 28 10:36:44.822: 00:1f:9e:8d:85:f0 Join Request: msgEleLength = 5
msgEleType = 1048
  *Aug 28 10:36:44.822: RADIO_INFO Supported radios 1
  *Aug 28 10:36:44.822: 00:1f:9e:8d:85:f0 Join Request: Total msgEleLen = 1180
  *Aug 28 10:36:44.822: 00:1f:9e:8d:85:f0 Join Request: msgEleLength = 5
msgEleType = 1048
  *Aug 28 10:36:44.822: RADIO_INFO Supported radios 2
  *Aug 28 10:36:44.822: 00:1f:9e:8d:85:f0 Join Request: Total msgEleLen = 1171
  *Aug 28 10:36:44.822: 00:1f:9e:8d:85:f0 Join Request: msgEleLength = 2
msgEleType = 29
  *Aug 28 10:36:44.822: 00:1f:9e:8d:85:f0 Maximum Message Size - 14000
  *Aug 28 10:36:44.822: 00:1f:9e:8d:85:f0 Join Request: Total msgEleLen = 1165
  *Aug 28 10:36:44.822: 00:1f:9e:8d:85:f0 Join Request: msgEleLength = 13
msgEleType = 37
  *Aug 28 10:36:44.822: 00:1f:9e:8d:85:f0 Vendor specific payload from AP
00:1F:9E:8D:85:F0 validated
  *Aug 28 10:36:44.822: 00:1f:9e:8d:85:f0 Join request: Vendor payload type = 2,
length = 13
  *Aug 28 10:36:44.822: mwarType is 0
  *Aug 28 10:36:44.822: 00:1f:9e:8d:85:f0 Join Request: Total msgEleLen = 1148
  *Aug 28 10:36:44.822: 00:1f:9e:8d:85:f0 Join Request: msgEleLength = 10
msgEleType = 37
  *Aug 28 10:36:44.822: 00:1f:9e:8d:85:f0 Vendor specific payload from AP
00:1F:9E:8D:85:F0 validated
  *Aug 28 10:36:44.822: 00:1f:9e:8d:85:f0 Join request: Vendor payload type = 401,
length = 10
  *Aug 28 10:36:44.822: Board data options: apType 0, joinPriority 1
  *Aug 28 10:36:44.822: 00:1f:9e:8d:85:f0 Join Request: Total msgEleLen = 1134
  *Aug 28 10:36:44.822: 00:1f:9e:8d:85:f0 Join Request: msgEleLength = 19
msgEleType = 37
  *Aug 28 10:36:44.822: 00:1f:9e:8d:85:f0 Vendor specific payload from AP
00:1F:9E:8D:85:F0 validated
```

(continues)

Example 8-5   *Debug Output of an AP Join (continued)*

```
 *Aug 28 10:36:44.822: 00:1f:9e:8d:85:f0 Join request: Vendor payload type = 123,
length = 19
 *Aug 28 10:36:44.822: 00:1f:9e:8d:85:f0 Join Request: Total msgEleLen = 1111
 *Aug 28 10:36:44.822: 00:1f:9e:8d:85:f0 Join Request: msgEleLength = 1107
msgEleType = 37
 *Aug 28 10:36:44.822: 00:1f:9e:8d:85:f0 Vendor specific payload from AP
00:1F:9E:8D:85:F0 validated
 *Aug 28 10:36:44.822: 00:1f:9e:8d:85:f0 Join request: Vendor payload type = 104,
length = 1107
 *Aug 28 10:36:44.822: 00:1f:9e:8d:85:f0 Join Request: Total msgEleLen = 0
 *Aug 28 10:36:44.822: DTL Adding AP 0 - 192.168.1.23 *
Aug 28 10:36:44.825: Join Version: = 84041472
 *Aug 28 10:36:44.825: RESULT_CODE: 0
 *Aug 28 10:36:44.825: Join resp: Result Code message element len = 8
 *Aug 28 10:36:44.825: 1. 0 0
 *Aug 28 10:36:44.825: 2. 232 3
 *Aug 28 10:36:44.825: 3. 1 0
 *Aug 28 10:36:44.825: 4. 50 0
 *Aug 28 10:36:44.825: msgLength = 36
 *Aug 28 10:36:44.825: Join resp: AC Descriptor message element len = 48
 *Aug 28 10:36:44.825: acName = MLG-4402
 *Aug 28 10:36:44.825: Join resp: AC Name message element len = 60
 *Aug 28 10:36:44.825: CAPWAP_DOT11_MSGELE_WTP_RADIO_INFORMATION supported radio
types 7
 *Aug 28 10:36:44.825: Join resp: WTP Radio Information message element len = 69
 *Aug 28 10:36:44.825: Join resp: CAPWAP Control IPV4 Address len = 79
 *Aug 28 10:36:44.825: Join resp: CAPWAP Maximum Msg element len = 85
 *Aug 28 10:36:44.825: 00:1f:9e:8d:85:f0 encodeLen = 1384 len = 8
 *Aug 28 10:36:44.825: 00:1f:9e:8d:85:f0 Sending encrypted packet to AP
192:168:1:23 (41148)
 *Aug 28 10:36:44.825:  *Aug 28 10:36:44.825: CAPWAP State: Configure
 *Aug 28 10:36:44.825: 00:1f:9e:8d:85:f0 CAPWAP_ac_platform.c:1179 - Operation
State 0 ===> 4
*Aug 28 10:36:44.832: 00:1f:9e:8d:85:f0 Sending LWAPP Event Reg to
'mfpApCanValidate+108' for AP 00:1f:9e:8d:85:f0(0) *Aug 28 10:36:44.834:
00:1f:9e:8d:85:f0 Sending LWAPP Event Reg to 'l2roamNotifyClientAssociation+236'
for AP 00:1f:9e:8d:85:f0(0)
*Aug 28 10:36:44.836: 00:1f:9e:8d:85:f0 Sending LWAPP Event Reg to
'apfPrintApGroups+464' for AP 00:1f:9e:8d:85:f0(0) *Aug 28 10:36:44.838:
00:1f:9e:8d:85:f0 Sending LWAPP Event Reg to
'apfSpamSendAAAFileDbBlackListTable+328' for AP 00:1f:9e:8d:85:f0(0)
*Aug 28 10:36:44.839: 00:1f:9e:8d:85:f0 Sending LWAPP Event Reg to
'rrmGetChannelOverlapList+288' for AP 00:1f:9e:8d:85:f0(0)
*Aug 28 10:36:44.841: 00:1f:9e:8d:85:f0 Sending LWAPP Event Reg to
'asTrackSigDisableAllEvent+168' for AP 00:1f:9e:8d:85:f0(0)
*Aug 28 10:36:44.843: 00:1f:9e:8d:85:f0 Sending LWAPP Event Reg to
'mfpApCanValidate+108' for AP 00:1f:9e:8d:85:f0(1) *Aug 28 10:36:44.845:
```

```
00:1f:9e:8d:85:f0 Sending LWAPP Event Reg to 'l2roamNotifyClientAssociation+236'
for AP 00:1f:9e:8d:85:f0(1)

*Aug 28 10:36:44.846: 00:1f:9e:8d:85:f0 Sending LWAPP Event Reg to
'apfPrintApGroups+464' for AP 00:1f:9e:8d:85:f0(1) *Aug 28 10:36:44.848:
00:1f:9e:8d:85:f0 Sending LWAPP Event Reg to
'apfSpamSendAAAFileDbBlackListTable+328' for AP 00:1f:9e:8d:85:f0(1)

*Aug 28 10:36:44.849: 00:1f:9e:8d:85:f0 Sending LWAPP Event Reg to
'rrmGetChannelOverlapList+288' for AP 00:1f:9e:8d:85:f0(1)

*Aug 28 10:36:44.851: 00:1f:9e:8d:85:f0 Sending LWAPP Event Reg to
'asTrackSigDisableAllEvent+168' for AP 00:1f:9e:8d:85:f0(1)

*Aug 28 10:36:44.851: 00:1f:9e:8d:85:f0 WTP already released

*Aug 28 10:36:44.852: 00:1f:9e:8d:85:f0 Register LWAPP event for AP
00:1f:9e:8d:85:f0 slot 0

*Aug 28 10:36:44.852: Received SPAM_NOTIFY_LCB_CONFIGURED_MSG

 *Aug 28 10:36:44.852: 00:1f:9e:8d:85:f0 Register LWAPP event for AP
00:1f:9e:8d:85:f0 slot 1

*Aug 28 10:36:44.853: Received SPAM_NOTIFY_LCB_CONFIGURED_MSG

 *Aug 28 10:36:44.904: Received a message from AP of length 1451 on interface = 1

 *Aug 28 10:36:44.904: Received CAPWAP_MESSAGE

 *Aug 28 10:36:44.904: CAPWAP Control Msg Received from 192.168.1.23:41148

 *Aug 28 10:36:44.904: IP = 192:168:1.23 Port = 41148 Frag Id = 41146 offset = 0
last bit = 0 index = 186 total len = 1352 CAPWAPlen = 1352 fragCount = 0

*Aug 28 10:36:44.904: 00:1f:ca:2a:0b:ac No fragment found

*Aug 28 10:36:44.904: 00:1f:ca:2a:0b:ac No fragment found

*Aug 28 10:36:44.904: 00:1f:ca:2a:0b:ac No fragment found

*Aug 28 10:36:44.904: 00:1f:ca:2a:0b:ac No fragment found

*Aug 28 10:36:44.904: Received a message from AP of length 683 on interface = 1

 *Aug 28 10:36:44.904: Received CAPWAP_MESSAGE

 *Aug 28 10:36:44.904: CAPWAP Control Msg Received from 192.168.1.23:41148

 *Aug 28 10:36:44.905: IP - 192:168:1:23 Port = 41148 Frag Id = 41146 offset =
167 last bit = 1 index = 186 total len = 586 CAPWAPlen = 586 fragCount = 1

*Aug 28 10:36:44.905: Incoming offset = 167 offset 2 = 0

 *Aug 28 10:36:44.905: Available index = 186 i = 0 j = 1 data = 0x364eaa7c

 *Aug 28 10:36:44.905: Added to list j = 1 count = 2

*Aug 28 10:36:44.905: 00:1f:ca:2a:0b:ac zeroth fragment: offset = 0 total len =
1352 header len = 4

 *Aug 28 10:36:44.905: 00:1f:ca:2a:0b:ac Other fragment: header len = 2, offset =
167 last bit = 1 data = 0x364eaa7c

 *Aug 28 10:36:44.905: Last Fragment

*Aug 28 10:36:44.905: length = 4, packet received from 0:1f:9e:8d:85:f0

 *Aug 28 10:36:44.905: 00:1f:9e:8d:85:f0 packet received of length 1930 from
192.168.1.23:41148

 *Aug 28 10:36:44.905: 00:1f:9e:8d:85:f0 Msg Type = 5 Capwap state = 8

 *Aug 28 10:36:44.905: 00:1f:9e:8d:85:f0 Configuration Status from
192.168.1.23:41148
```

What does an LWAPP-to-CAPWAP AP conversion look like? Refer to Figures 8-6 through 8-8 for a detailed view of the registration and join process.

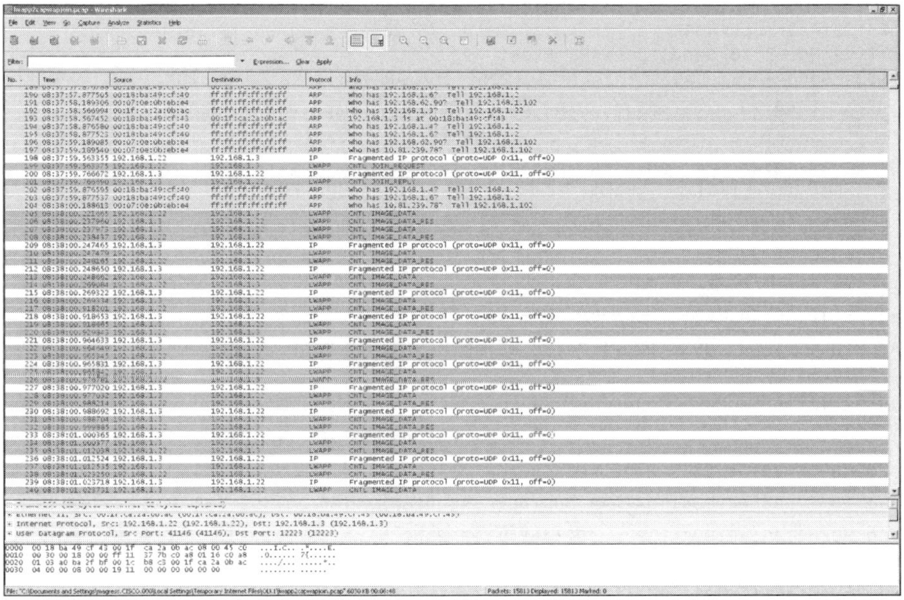

Figure 8-6   *Join Request*

After the AP joins using LWAPP and downloads the new CAPWAP image, it reboots and restarts the registration process, this time using Datagram Transport Layer Security (DTLS) as the encryption scheme and CAPWAP as the protocol (see Figure 8-7).

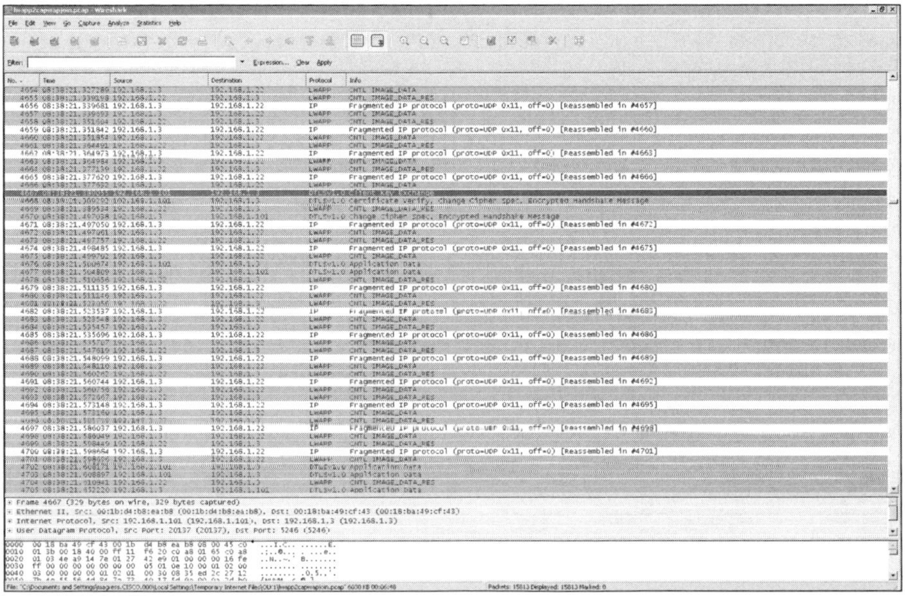

Figure 8-7   *Key Exchange*

In Figure 8-8, you can see a straight AP join using CAPWAP.

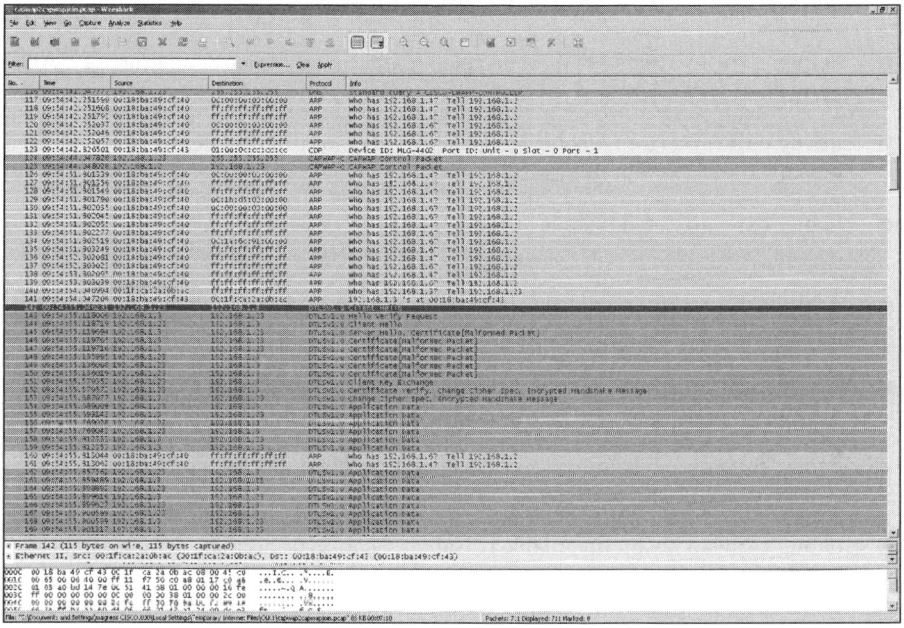

Figure 8-8 *Debug Output of AP Join Using CAPWAP*

Troubleshooting the AP Discovery and AP Join Process

Many people cringe when faced with the complicated task of troubleshooting. The debugs might look like another language, but the key here is to practice. The more you practice, the easier the debugs are to perform and read. If you break down the debugs that are available to you, you will have the following commands. The most important item to remember is that CAPWAP and LWAPP have different debugs.

Use these commands to obtain LWAPP debug information:

■ **debug LWAPP events enable:** Provides debug information on LWAPP events

■ **debug LWAPP error enable:** Provides debug information on LWAPP errors

■ **debug pem state enable:** Provides debug information on the policy manager state machine

■ **debug pem events enable:** Provides debug information on policy manager events

■ **debug dhcp packet enable:** Provides debug information on DHCP packets

- **debug dhcp message enable:** Provides debug information on DHCP error messages

Use these CLI commands to obtain CAPWAP debug information:

- **debug capwap events** {**enable** | **disable**}: Enables or disables debugging of CAPWAP events

- **debug capwap errors** {**enable** | **disable**}: Enables or disables debugging of CAPWAP errors

- **debug capwap detail** {**enable** | **disable**}: Enables or disables debugging of CAPWAP details

- **debug capwap info** {**enable** | **disable**}: Enables or disables debugging of CAPWAP information

- **debug capwap packet** {**enable** | **disable**}: Enables or disables debugging of CAPWAP packets

- **debug capwap payload** {**enable** | **disable**}: Enables or disables debugging of CAPWAP payloads

- **debug capwap hexdump** {**enable** | **disable**}: Enables or disables debugging of the CAPWAP hexadecimal dump

All CAPWAP control packets except discovery request and response are encrypted, so an ethereal trace does not give details such as, "Join request was sent but not received by the controller." For debugging, disabling encryption is supported, in which case understanding the CAPWAP message type is possible.

New debugs are available on AP and controller:

- **debug capwap ?** (on controller)
- **debug capwap client ?** (on AP)

At the time of this writing, you need additional ethereal executables to be installed to look at CAPWAP packets.

Along with the troubleshooting process and each situation you are faced with, it is common to prefer some results of certain debugs over others. The best idea is to create a template and note the debugs for the given scenario.

Debug for AP not registering with controller (Basic):

```
debug mac addr AP-MAC-address xx:xx:xx:xx:xx:xx
debug lwapp events enable
debug pm pki enable
```

Debug for AP not registering with controller (Advanced):

```
debug mac addr AP-MAC-address xx:xx:xx:xx:xx:xx
debug lwapp events enable
debug dhcp message enable
debug dhcp packet enable
debug pm pki enable
```

Debugs to run on converted APs (AP not registering with controller):

```
debug lwapp client event
debug lwapp client error
debug lwapp client packet
```

The **debug lwapp events enable** WLC command output in Example 8-6 shows that the LAP is registered to the WLC.

Example 8-6 *debug lwapp events enable Output*

```
(Cisco Controller) >debug lwapp events enable
Tue Apr 11 13:38:47 2006: Received LWAPP DISCOVERY REQUEST from AP
    00:0b:85:64:a3:a0 to ff:ff:ff:ff:ff:ff on port '1'
Tue Apr 11 13:38:47 2006: Successful transmission of LWAPP Discovery-Response
    to AP 00:0b:85:64:a3:a0 on Port 1
Tue Apr 11 13:38:58 2006: Received LWAPP JOIN REQUEST from AP
    00:0b:85:64:a3:a0 to 00:0b:85:33:a8:a0 on port '1'
Tue Apr 11 13:38:58 2006: LWAPP Join-Request MTU path from AP 00:0b:85:64:a3:a0
    is 1500, remote debug mode is 0
Tue Apr 11 13:38:58 2006: Successfully added NPU Entry for AP
    00:0b:85:64:a3:a0 (index 48) Switch IP: 192.168.60.2, Switch Port: 12223,
    intIfNum 1, vlanId 60 AP IP: 10.5.5.10, AP Port: 19002, next hop MAC:
    00:0b:85:64:a3:a0
Tue Apr 11 13:38:58 2006: Successful transmission of LWAPP Join-Reply to AP
    00:0b:85:64:a3:a0
Tue Apr 11 13:38:58 2006: Register LWAPP event for AP
    00:0b:85:64:a3:a0 slot 0
Tue Apr 11 13:38:58 2006: Register LWAPP event for AP 00:0b:85:64:a3:a0 slot 1
Tue Apr 11 13:39:00 2006: Received LWAPP CONFIGURE REQUEST from AP
    00:0b:85:64:a3:a0 to 00:0b:85:33:a8:a0
Tue Apr 11 13:39:00 2006: Updating IP info for AP 00:0b:85:64:a3:a0 —
    static 0, 10.5.5.10/255.255.255.0, gtw 192.168.60.1
Tue Apr 11 13:39:00 2006: Updating IP 10.5.5.10 ===> 10.5.5.10 for AP
    00:0b:85:64:a3:a0
Tue Apr 11 13:39:00 2006: spamVerifyRegDomain RegDomain set for slot 0 code 0
    regstring -A regDfromCb -A
Tue Apr 11 13:39:00 2006: spamVerifyRegDomain RegDomain set for slot 1 code 0
```

(continues)

Example 8-6 *debug lwapp events enable Output (continued)*

```
      regstring -A regDfromCb -A
Tue Apr 11 13:39:00 2006: spamEncodeDomainSecretPayload:Send domain secret
      Mobility Group<6f,39,74,cd,7e,a4,81,86,ca,32,8c,06,d3,ff,ec,6d,95,10,99,dd>
      to AP 00:0b:85:64:a3:a0
Tue Apr 11 13:39:00 2006: Successful transmission of LWAPP
      Config-Message to AP 00:0b:85:64:a3:a0
Tue Apr 11 13:39:00 2006: Running spamEncodeCreateVapPayload for SSID 'SSID'
Tue Apr 11 13:39:00 2006: AP 00:0b:85:64:a3:a0 associated. Last AP failure was
      due to Configuration changes, reason:  operator changed 11g mode
Tue Apr 11 13:39:00 2006: Received LWAPP CHANGE_STATE_EVENT from AP
      00:0b:85:64:a3:a0
Tue Apr 11 13:39:00 2006: Successful transmission of LWAPP Change-State-Event
      Response to AP 00:0b:85:64:a3:a0
Tue Apr 11 13:39:00 2006: Received LWAPP Up event for AP 00:0b:85:64:a3:a0 slot 0!
Tue Apr 11 13:39:00 2006: Received LWAPP CONFIGURE COMMAND RES from AP
      00:0b:85:64:a3:a0
Tue Apr 11 13:39:00 2006: Received LWAPP CHANGE_STATE_EVENT from AP
      00:0b:85:64:a3:a0
Tue Apr 11 13:39:00 2006: Successful transmission of LWAPP Change-State-Event
      Response to AP 00:0b:85:64:a3:a0
Tue Apr 11 13:39:00 2006: Received LWAPP Up event for AP
      00:0b:85:64:a3:a0 slot 1!
```

What do you do if the WLC never receives a join request? Because you know the AP generates the join request, you should start there.

This is going to be a case where you need to utilize a packet capture tool such as Wireshark. What you are looking for is the AP sending the join request and placing it on the wire. After you verify that, you need to pick another point within its path and revalidate the presence of the join request packet. Follow it all the way to the WLC if possible. If you do determine that the join request is making it to the WLC, you have to determine what the controller is doing with the packet. In most cases, this step is not needed, but it is covered here to round your troubleshooting experience. The **debug IP packet** output shows all packets that hit the CPU.

You can get pretty creative with this command because you can configure access control lists (ACLs) and apply them to the command to customize your output. In large traffic scenarios, this is actually a mandatory step. If you fail to do so, the output simply fills the buffer and renders the keyboard useless until it finishes with the output—if it finishes.

The output in Example 8-7 shows these useful WLC **debug** commands:

■ **debug pem state enable:** Configures the access policy manager debug options

■ **debug dhcp message enable:** Shows the debug of DHCP messages that are exchanged to and from the DHCP server

■ **debug dhcp packet enable:** Shows the debug of DHCP packet details that are sent to and from the DHCP server

Example 8-7 *Multiple Debug Output*

```
Tue Apr 11 14:30:49 2006: Applied policy for mobile 00:40:96:a1:45:42
Tue Apr 11 14:30:49 2006: STA [00:40:96:a1:45:42, 192.168.1.41] Replacing Fast
    Path rule type = Airespace AP Client  on AP 00:0B:85:64:A3:A0, slot 0
    InHandle = 0x00000000, OutHandle = 0x00000000  ACL Id = 255, Jumbo Frames
                 = NO, interface = 1  802.1P = 0, DSCP = 0, T
Tue Apr 11 14:30:49 2006: Successfully plumbed mobile rule for mobile
    00:40:96:a1:45:42 (ACL ID 255)
Tue Apr 11 14:30:49 2006: Plumbed mobile LWAPP rule on AP 00:0b:85:64:a3:a0
    for mobile 00:40:96:a1:45:42
Tue Apr 11 14:30:53 2006: DHCP proxy received packet, src: 0.0.0.0,
    len = 320
Tue Apr 11 14:30:53 2006: dhcpProxy: Received packet: Client 00:40:96:a1:45:42
    DHCP Op: BOOTREQUEST(1), IP len: 320, switchport: 1, encap: 0xec03
Tue Apr 11 14:30:53 2006: dhcpProxy(): dhcp request, client:
    00:40:96:a1:45:42: dhcp op: 1, port: 1, encap 0xec03, old mscb
    port number: 1
Tue Apr 11 14:30:53 2006: dhcp option len, including the magic cookie = 84
Tue Apr 11 14:30:53 2006: dhcp option: received DHCP REQUEST msg
Tue Apr 11 14:30:53 2006: dhcp option: skipping option 61, len 7
Tue Apr 11 14:30:53 2006: dhcp option: requested ip = 192.168.1.41
Tue Apr 11 14:30:53 2006: dhcp option: skipping option 12, len 15
Tue Apr 11 14:30:53 2006: dhcp option: skipping option 81, len 19
Tue Apr 11 14:30:53 2006: dhcp option: vendor class id = MSFT 5.0 (len 8)
Tue Apr 11 14:30:53 2006: dhcp option: skipping option 55, len 11
Tue Apr 11 14:30:53 2006: dhcpParseOptions: options end, len 84, actual 84
Tue Apr 11 14:30:53 2006: mscb->dhcpServer: 192.168.60.2, mscb->dhcpNetmask:
    255.255.255.0,mscb->dhcpGateway: 192.168.60.1, mscb->dhcpRelay:
    192.168.60.2 VLAN: 60
Tue Apr 11 14:30:53 2006: Local Address: 192.168.60.2, DHCP Server:
    192.168.60.2, Gateway Addr: 192.168.60.2, VLAN: 60, port: 1
Tue Apr 11 14:30:53 2006: DHCP Message Type received: DHCP REQUEST msg
Tue Apr 11 14:30:53 2006:    op: BOOTREQUEST, htype: Ethernet, hlen: 6, hops: 1
Tue Apr 11 14:30:53 2006:    xid: 3371152053, secs: 0, flags: 0
Tue Apr 11 14:30:53 2006:    chaddr: 00:40:96:a1:45:42
Tue Apr 11 14:30:53 2006:    ciaddr: 0.0.0.0,   yiaddr: 0.0.0.0
Tue Apr 11 14:30:53 2006:    siaddr: 0.0.0.0,   giaddr: 192.168.60.2
Tue Apr 11 14:30:53 2006: Forwarding DHCP packet locally (348 octets) from
    192.168.60.2 to 192.168.60.2
Tue Apr 11 14:30:53 2006: Received 348 byte dhcp packet from 0x0201a8c0
```

(continues)

Example 8-7 *Multiple Debug Output (continued)*

```
     192.168.60.2:68
Tue Apr 11 14:30:53 2006: DHCP packet: 192.168.60.2 -> 192.168.60.2 using
     scope "InternalScope"
Tue Apr 11 14:30:53 2006: received REQUEST
Tue Apr 11 14:30:53 2006: Checking node 192.168.1.41  Allocated 1144765719,
     Expires 1144852119 (now: 1144765853)
Tue Apr 11 14:30:53 2006: adding option 0x35
Tue Apr 11 14:30:53 2006: adding option 0x36
Tue Apr 11 14:30:53 2006: adding option 0x33
Tue Apr 11 14:30:53 2006: adding option 0x03
Tue Apr 11 14:30:53 2006: adding option 0x01
Tue Apr 11 14:30:53 2006: dhcpd: Sending DHCP packet (giaddr:192.168.60.2)to
192.168.60.2:67  from 192.168.60.2:1067
Tue Apr 11 14:30:53 2006: sendto (548 bytes) returned 548
Tue Apr 11 14:30:53 2006: DHCP proxy received packet, src: 192.168.60.2,
     len = 548
Tue Apr 11 14:30:53 2006: dhcpProxy: Received packet: Client 00:40:96:a1:45:42
     DHCP Op: BOOTREPLY(2), IP len: 548, switchport: 0, encap: 0x0
Tue Apr 11 14:30:53 2006: dhcp option len, including the magic cookie = 312
Tue Apr 11 14:30:53 2006: dhcp option: received DHCP ACK msg
Tue Apr 11 14:30:53 2006: dhcp option: server id = 192.168.60.2
Tue Apr 11 14:30:53 2006: dhcp option: lease time (seconds) = 86400
Tue Apr 11 14:30:53 2006: dhcp option: gateway = 192.168.60.1
Tue Apr 11 14:30:53 2006: dhcp option: netmask = 255.255.255.0
Tue Apr 11 14:30:53 2006: dhcpParseOptions: options end, len 312, actual 64
Tue Apr 11 14:30:53 2006: DHCP Reply to AP client: 00:40:96:a1:45:42,
     frame len 412, switchport 1
Tue Apr 11 14:30:53 2006: DHCP Message Type received: DHCP ACK msg
Tue Apr 11 14:30:53 2006:    op: BOOTREPLY, htype: Ethernet, hlen: 6, hops: 0
Tue Apr 11 14:30:53 2006:    xid: 3371152053, secs: 0, flags: 0
Tue Apr 11 14:30:53 2006:    chaddr: 00:40:96:a1:45:42
Tue Apr 11 14:30:53 2006:    ciaddr: 0.0.0.0,  yiaddr: 192.168.1.41
Tue Apr 11 14:30:53 2006:    siaddr: 0.0.0.0,  giaddr: 0.0.0.0
Tue Apr 11 14:30:53 2006:    server id: 1.1.1.1  rcvd server id: 192.168.60.2
```

You can use these additional **debug** commands to troubleshoot your configuration:

- **debug lwapp errors enable:** Shows output of the debug of LWAPP errors.

- **debug pm pki enable:** Shows the debug of certificate messages that are passed between the AP and the WLC. This debug is excellent when troubleshooting join issues with any converted APs that utilize self-signed certificates (SSC). All APs manufactured after approximately March 2007 have manufactured installed certificates and do not need entries into the controller for the AP to join. The debug indicates whether the AP is using an SSC. Also, if you see a hash key in the output, you can rest assured that you are dealing with an SSC.

WLC Config Analyzer

The WLC Analyzer application works with the output **show run-config** from any WLC. You can either have several controllers from the same mobility group in a single file or load one by one.

To load a file, select **File > Open** or click the folder icon on the left of the application.

The program presents several audit checks. Each one of them uses a different set of validations depending on the devices present in your network. Some general checks are always done (interfaces, mobility, RF, AP checks, and so on), as illustrated in Figure 8-9.

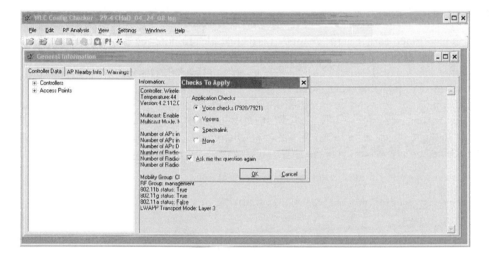

Figure 8-9   *WLC Config Analyzer*

After the audit check has been selected, the program shows a File Open dialog to select the file. The default location is the root system disk, which can be changed in the Settings > Application Settings menu. The application is useful when troubleshooting RRM issues because it breaks down the neighboring AP information in an easy-to-read format. If you look at **show run-config**, the majority of the output is the AP neighboring information and cannot be viewed on one screen.

AP Debugs

Step 1.   To initiate a remote debug of the AP, enter this command:

```
debug ap enable Cisco_AP
```

Step 2.   To see all the multicast group IDs (MGID) on the AP and the number of clients per wireless LAN (WLAN), enter this command:

```
debug ap command "show capwap mcast mgid all" Cisco_AP
```

Step 3.   To see all the clients per MGID on the AP and the number of clients per WLAN, enter this command:

```
debug ap command "show capwap mcast mgid id mgid_value" Cisco_AP
```

Debug Template

As mentioned earlier in the chapter, it is a great idea to note the debugs you use in a given scenario. Create a list while you troubleshoot different scenarios. Some people prefer other debugs or deem that certain debugs are not needed. This chapter purposefully included all possible debugs that are going to yield the most output. The list is a good starting point and can be modified when you troubleshoot different issues. Remember that this chapter shows only a few of the debugs for AP registration. For the complete list of debugs, please refer to Appendix A, "Debugging Commands." Also, the remote AP debugs are important; you can find a full list of those in Appendix A as well.

It is always a good idea to get the show run and logs:

```
show run-config (not the running-config)
show msglog
show traplog
```

Debug for AP not registering with controller (Basic):

```
debug mac addr <AP-MAC-address xx:xx:xx:xx:xx:xx>
debug lwapp events enable
debug pm pki enable
```

Debug for AP not registering with controller (Advanced):

```
debug mac addr AP-MAC-address xx:xx:xx:xx:xx:xx
debug lwapp events enable
debug dhcp message enable (Depending if we have reached DHCP stage)
debug dhcp packet enable (Depending if we have reached DHCP stage)
debug pm pki enable
```

Debugs to run on IOS-based (non-1000 series) APs (AP not registering with controller):

```
debug lwapp client event
```

```
debug lwapp client error
debug lwapp client packet
```

As mentioned earlier, debugging does not have to be a horrible task. The more you use the debug features, the better you will become at reading debug output. Unfortunately, this is not a Cisco IOS platform, so the debugging is different. Because the controller does not have the best debugs, you have to get used to reading packet captures. This will become a natural part of your troubleshooting with the controller. Deployments can get complicated; despite this, you must remember the basics. If you remember how the protocols work, you can verify each step and troubleshoot accordingly.

Summary

Troubleshooting AP join events can be easy or difficult depending on the topology of your network. However, if you stick with the basics and understand the events that need to occur, you will always be on track. For instance, if you are running **debug lwapp events** on the WLC but see no output, you know the AP discovery request is not making it to the WLC. Is the AP in the same subnet of the WLC? If so, you need to validate it is getting an IP address. You can do this by logging into the AP and checking the interface assignments, checking the leases on your DHCP server, or with a packet capture and looking at the packets coming from the AP. If the AP is in a different subnet, you must ensure the same events take place if the AP was in the same subnet, as mentioned earlier. You can then take it a step further and determine what discovery mechanism you are using and validating that the AP is obtaining that correctly. The best way to determine that is with a packet capture and verifying that you are seeing a unicast User Datagram Protocol (UDP) discovery request to the management IP address of the WLC from the AP. If you are not seeing that, you know you have an incorrect discover mechanism in place that is not working.

No matter what the issue is, if you remember the basics and how the LWAPP and CAPWAP protocols work, you know where to take your next troubleshooting step. If you do not understand the registration process, reread the section again until registration is as easy as your ABCs. This will make you an excellent troubleshooter and prepare you for any issue that might come your way. Do not second-guess yourself along the way. Make sure you validate each point of the process using your troubleshooting tools.

Chapter 9

Mobility

A mobility event occurs if a client roams between access points (AP) or between controllers. If the wireless LAN (WLAN) is secured, 802.1x or Wi-Fi Protected Access (WPA), the client must reauthenticate to comply with the 802.11i IEEE standard. You want this process to have low latency and appear as transparent to the user as possible while still maintaining security. If this process happens fast enough, it is considered a seamless roaming event.

Controller mobility addresses two key issues:

- After the introduction of 802.1x-key-handshakes and 802.1x/ EAP authentication on top of the legacy 802.11 protocol, it is mandatory to recheck the client credentials when the client changes its basic service set identifier (BSSID)—roaming from one AP to another with the same WLAN/service set identifier (SSID). This might cause long traffic interruptions while roaming when using secure authentication methods such as Extensible Authentication Protocol Transport Layer Security (EAP-TLS), which exchanges up to 20 packets during an authentication.

- 802.11 is a link-layer protocol; therefore, it does not address roaming between two broadcast domains (Layer 3 networks/subnets).

Cisco Unified Mobility addresses both these issues in single controller and multiple controller scenarios. The controller acts as central "authenticator" and handles all the 802.1x frames. After the authentication has completed, the controller forwards the needed encryption material to the AP. Based on the Lightweight Access Point Protocol (LWAPP)/Control and Provisioning of Wireless Access Points (CAPWAP) architecture, all client traffic is centrally tunneled to the controller. This fundamental feature allows all registered APs to service every client VLAN even if the APs are in different subnets/VLANs (intra-controller roaming). This is something that is not possible in a standalone solution. In addition to tunneling client traffic between the AP and the controller, mobility allows for tunneling client traffic between controllers. This is necessary if the management interfaces of the controller happen to be in a separate subnet/Layer 3 network (inter-controller roaming) from one another.

When the client associates with an AP, the controller creates a client entry in its database. This entry includes the WLAN, security context, quality of service (QoS), IP, and MAC address of the client, the associated AP, and the LWAPP/CAPWAP tunnel where the client traffic is sourced and destined.

Client Roaming/Mobility Events

As wireless clients move between APs on the same controller and APs join to different controllers within the network, four different types of roaming events can take place:

- Intra-controller

- Inter-controller

- Inter-subnet/Layer 3 mobility event

- Auto-anchor mobility

Each type of roam results in a different behavior on the controller(s). The following sections describe the different roaming and mobility types in detail.

Intra-Controller Roaming

If a client roams between APs on the same controller, it is called an intra-controller mobility event. Intra-controller roaming is the most simplistic in that all the controller needs to do is update the database with the AP association and establish new security contexts if necessary. Basically, the Layer 3–related mobility is handled by the controller, and the link layer mobility is handled by the AP. As the client roams, the controller updates the client state. The client traffic then flows through the new AP LWAPP/CAPWAP tunnel to the controller and out on the network. Figure 9-1 illustrates an intra-controller roam.

Inter-Controller Roaming

Inter-controller roaming occurs when a client roams between two APs registered to two different controllers, where each controller has an interface in the client subnet. When a client roams between controllers on the same subnet, the controllers exchange mobility messages, and the client database entry is transferred from the original controller to the new controller. Client traffic then flows through the new controller on to the network just like it did on the original controller. Figure 9-2 illustrates an inter-controller roam on the same subnet.

Inter-Subnet Roaming/Layer 3 Mobility Events

If the client roams between APs registered to different controllers and the client WLAN on the two controllers is on different subnets, then an inter-subnet roam, or Layer 3 mobility event, takes place. For example, if a client is on WLAN-X on Controller-1 using

VLANx and the client roams to WLAN-X on Controller-2, but WLAN-X on controller-2 is using VLANy, then an inter-subnet roam for that client occurs.

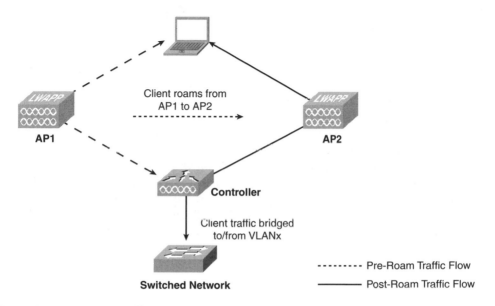

Figure 9-1 *Intra-Controller Roam*

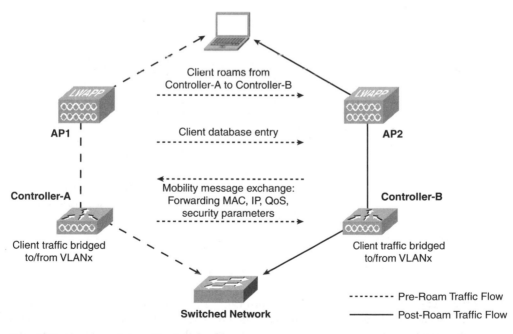

Figure 9-2 *Inter-Controller Roam*

> **Note**   It is important to remember that a Layer 3 mobility event occurs only when the interface assigned to the WLAN between the controllers is not the same. Whether or not the management interfaces of each controller are in the same subnet has no bearing on a client Layer 3 roaming event.

When the client roams between them, the controllers still exchange mobility messages, but they handle the client database entry in a completely different manner. The original controller marks the client entry as Anchor, whereas the new controller marks the client entry as Foreign. The two controllers are now referred to as anchor and foreign, respectively. The client has no knowledge of this and retains its original IP address on the new controller. Traffic flow to and from the client on the network becomes asymmetrical. Traffic from the client is bridged directly to the wired network by the foreign controller. The foreign controller spoofs the IP and MAC address of the client. Traffic from the wired network to the client, however, is received by the original controller and sent to the new controller through an Ethernet over IP (EtherIP) tunnel to the new controller. The new controller then passes that traffic to the client. Figure 9-3 illustrates asymmetrical mobility tunneling.

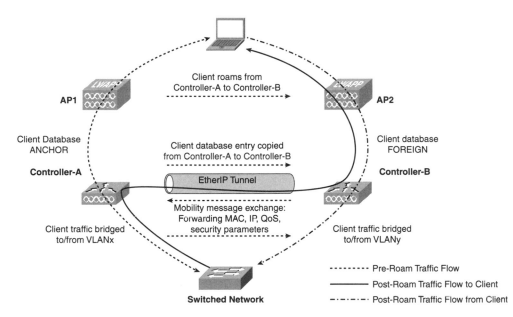

Figure 9-3   *Inter-Subnet Roam/Asymmetric Tunneling*

If the client roams back to the original controller, the Anchor and Foreign markings are removed and the client database entry is deleted from the foreign controller. If the client should roam to a different foreign controller, the original anchor controller is maintained, and the foreign client entry is transferred to the new foreign controller.

Asymmetrical tunneling can cause client issues if firewalls or an upstream router has reverse path filtering (RPF) enabled. RPF prevents multicast forwarding loops and prevents IP address spoofing in unicast routing. Because the client maintains its IP address from the WLAN subnet on the anchor controller, the downstream (to the client) network path is not the same as the upstream (from the client) network path, and RPF blocks it. Asymmetric tunneling can also cause jitter for voice clients if the network delay between the network upstream and downstream paths is different. Starting in code Release 4.1.171.0, Cisco added the symmetric mobility tunneling feature to alleviate the limitations of asymmetric mobility tunneling. Figure 9-4 shows where to enable symmetric mobility tunneling from the controller GUI. After enabling this feature, you must reboot the controller for it to take effect.

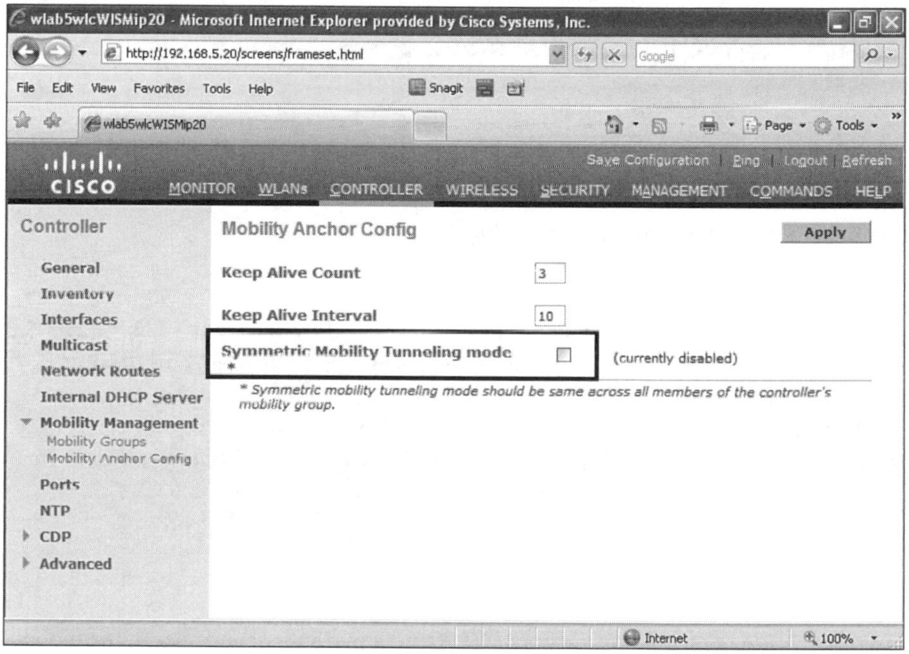

Figure 9-4 *Enabling Symmetric Mobility Tunneling*

When using symmetric mobility tunneling, RPF does not come into consideration because the client traffic path has the same ingress and egress point on the network. Figure 9-5 illustrates the symmetric mobility tunneling flow.

If you decide to use symmetric mobility tunneling, you should configure it on every controller in the mobility group. Symmetric mobility tunneling is the same tunneling scheme that is used in auto-anchoring. Auto-anchoring is covered in the next section. Starting in code Release 5.2, asymmetric tunneling is deprecated.

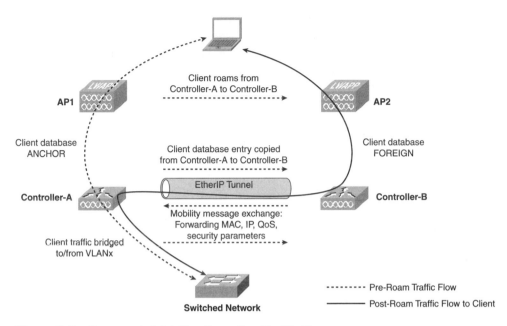

Figure 9-5   *Symmetric Mobility Tunneling Traffic Flow*

Tip   If symmetric mobility tunneling is not enabled on the controllers when a Layer 3 mobility event with AP Groups takes place, the client might not be able to pass traffic properly because the data is sent on an incorrect VLAN. You must enable symmetric mobility tunneling if the AP Group VLAN interface on the foreign controller is using a different VLAN interface than the anchor controller. See the AP Groups section of this chapter for more information on AP Groups.

Auto-Anchor Mobility

Auto-anchoring is when you anchor a WLAN to a particular controller in the mobility domain or group. Auto-anchoring can be used for load balancing and security. You can force clients to be on a particular controller/subnet regardless of the controller they access the wireless network from. Perhaps the most common use for auto-anchor is with guest networking. See Chapter 14, "Guest Networking," for more information.

With auto-anchor, regardless of which controller's APs a client associates with, the client traffic is anchored to this one controller. Auto-anchoring is basically symmetric tunneling using a fixed anchor. Unlike the behavior with normal client roaming events, the anchor controller designated when configuring auto-anchor can never change. When a client first associates with a controller on an anchored WLAN, a Local Session entry is created for the client. The controller sends out a Mobile Announce message to the mobility group. When that message is not answered, the Foreign controller contacts the configured anchor controller and creates a foreign session for the client in its database. The anchor controller then creates an Anchor session for the client.

All traffic to and from the client associated with an anchored WLAN passes through the anchor controller. This is known as a bidirectional tunnel because the foreign controller encapsulates the client packets in EtherIP and sends them to the anchor. The anchor de-encapsulates the packets and delivers them to the wired network. Packets destined for the client are encapsulated in the EtherIP tunnel by the anchor and sent to the foreign controller. The foreign controller de-encapsulates the packets and forwards them to the client. Figure 9-6 illustrates the symmetric traffic flow with auto-anchoring.

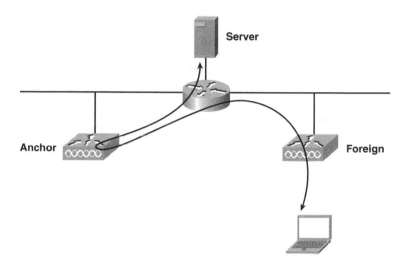

Figure 9-6 *Auto-Anchoring Symmetric Tunnel*

AP Groups

When you create a WLAN on the controller, you have to assign an interface to that WLAN for the client traffic to use. Imagine that you have a 4404 series controller with 100 registered APs and 25 clients per AP on the same WLAN. You now have 2500 clients on the same subnet. The initial goal of AP Groups was to separate the clients for a single WLAN into different subnets to decrease the size of the broadcast domain for that WLAN. The AP Group feature on the controllers allows you to use the same SSID but override the interface configured on the WLAN. In addition to decreasing the size of the broadcast domain for a single WLAN, there are many reasons why you might want to use the same SSID but have the clients on different subnets. There could be geographical reasons or a lack of enough IP addresses for a given subnet. Clients that are roaming between APs in different AP Groups on the same controller are not required to change VLANs because of intra-controller roaming.

A perfect example of when to use AP Groups would be a campus with three separate buildings, each on their own subnet, VLAN 10, 20, and 30 respectively, and a single controller. You would not want to have three separate SSIDs for each building because the clients would have to have three separate profiles to connect to the wireless network depending on which building they happened to be in. With AP Groups configured, the clients would need to have only a single wireless profile set up. The controller could have three AP Groups configured, each one using the correct dynamic interface for the subnet for the particular building, and the APs in those buildings would be members of their respective AP Group. So when a client in building Two, for example, connects to the SSID Corporate just like a user in building One, because the AP Group overrides the interface configured on the WLAN; the client in building Two is on VLAN 20, whereas the client in building One is on VLAN 10. The same goes for a client in building Three. That client would be on VLAN 30.

When a client first associates to an AP on a controller, the controller applies the AP Group VLAN override policy as configured for that WLAN. When the client roams to another AP on the same controller, the AP Group policy for that AP is reapplied. During a single session, a client does not change VLANs when it roams among APs on a single controller. This allows for seamless roaming. When a client roams across APs associated to different controllers, however, the process follows the normal roaming process.

In the 5.2 release of code, the AP Group feature has changed dramatically. The new AP Group feature not only allows you to override the interface for a WLAN, it also allows you to determine what WLANs the APs in a particular AP Group will service. In previous versions of code, a separate feature known as WLAN override allowed you to configure what WLANs an AP would service. By default, an AP will service all the WLANs configured on the controller. For more information on WLAN override and the new AP Group feature, visit Cisco.com.

Troubleshooting AP Groups

To troubleshoot client mobility, you use the same debugs covered under "Troubleshooting Mobility," later in this chapter. The most common mistake, however, when trying to use AP Groups is not enabling the feature. On the AP Groups configuration page, there is a small check box to enable the feature. Figure 9-7 shows the AP Groups check box on a 4.2 controller. This must be selected and applied. You can configure all the AP Groups you like and assign APs to those groups, but if this check box is overlooked, nothing works as expected.

You can also verify that AP Groups is enabled via the command-line interface (CLI) using the following commands:

In code prior to the 4.1.181.0 release, the command is

```
show location summary
```

In code after the 4.1.181.0 release, the command is

```
show wlan apgroups
```

In Example 9-1, you can see the output of **show wlan apgroups** from a 4.2 controller.

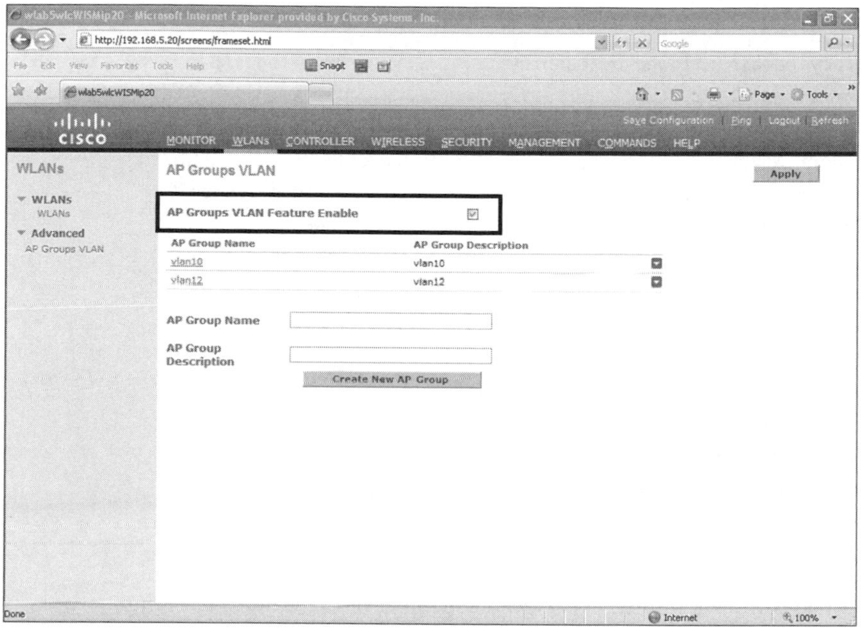

Figure 9-7 *Enabling AP Groups*

Example 9-1 *show wlan apgroups Command Output*

```
(Cisco Controller) >show wlan apgroups


Status......................................... disabled


Site Name...................................... vlan20
Site Description............................... vlan 20
```

In this output you can see that an AP Group is configured, but the actual AP Group feature is disabled. With this configuration, AP Groups will fail.

You will also want to make sure that your APs are in the correct AP Group. You assign APs to an AP Group under the AP Configuration Advanced tab. You can verify the configuration with **show ap config general** *ap-name*. Example 9-2 shows the output of this command.

Example 9-2 *show ap config general Command Output*

```
(Cisco Controller) >show ap config general 1242


Cisco AP Identifier............................ 3
Cisco AP Name.................................. 1242
Country code................................... US  - United States
```

(continues)

Example 9-2   *show ap config general Command Output (continued)*

```
Regulatory Domain allowed by Country............. 802.11bg:-AB    802.11a:-AB
AP Country code................................. US  - United States
AP Regulatory Domain............................ 802.11bg:-A     802.11a:-A
Switch Port Number ............................. 1
MAC Address..................................... 00:1d:a1:cd:dd:6c
IP Address Configuration........................ DHCP
IP Address...................................... 192.168.6.18
IP NetMask...................................... 255.255.255.0
Gateway IP Addr................................. 192.168.6.1
Telnet State.................................... Enabled
Ssh State....................................... Disabled
Cisco AP Location............................... default location
Cisco AP Group Name............................. vlan20
Primary Cisco Switch Name....................... Cisco_50:a8:c0
Primary Cisco Switch IP Address................. 192.168.6.2
```

Here you can see that the AP is indeed a member of the vlan20 AP Group.

Mobility Groups

A *mobility group* is a collection of controllers that share RF, client, and AP information. Mobility has two categories: mobility domains (or lists) and mobility groups. If controllers are in the same mobility domain, they are present in the mobility configuration lists of the others, and the controllers listed recognize and communicate with one another. Controllers do not recognize or communicate with other controllers unless they are present in the mobility list. The lack of inter-controller communication in this scenario allows you to limit client roaming on the network by using different mobility group names on your controllers. You can assign mobility by floor, buildings, or campus if you choose. This does not, however, stop a client from roaming between APs joined to controllers with different mobility group names in the list.

The group names constrain the distribution of the security context of a client. It also constrains AP failover between controllers. Client security context updates are sent only to controllers with the same mobility group name as the controller sending the update. This behavior changes in the 5.1 code release and is discussed further a little later in this section. The same goes for AP lists. An AP will not move to a controller that is not in the same mobility group as its current controller if that controller fails.

Figure 9-8 shows the GUI output of a controller mobility configuration.

As you can see, this controller has three controllers in its mobility group, wireless-west, and one controller with a mobility group name of dmz in its mobility list.

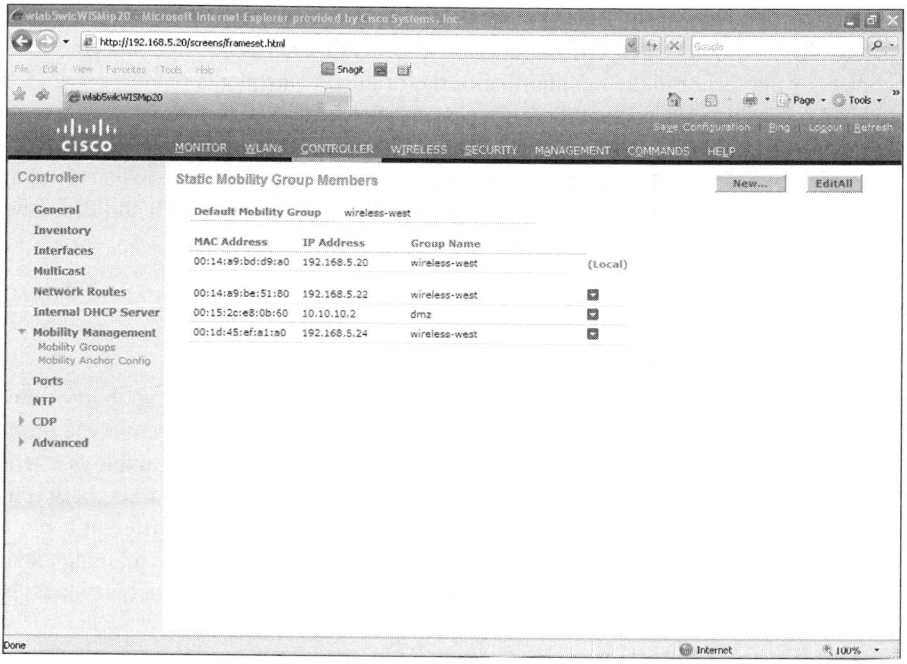

Figure 9-8 *Mobility Configuration*

Note Remember that, although the RF Group and the mobility group name on a controller are usually the same, they are completely independent functions and not required to be the same. You can change the RF Group and mobility group name for a controller any time after the initial configuration is complete. For more information on RF Groups, please see Chapter 12, "Radio Resource Management."

Controller code Release 5.1 or later supports three mobility groups with up to 24 controllers in a single group for a total of 72 controllers in the mobility list. Prior to controller code Release 5.1, only 48 controllers were allowed in the mobility list.

The number of APs in a single mobility group depends on the model of controllers in that mobility group.

For example, a single Wireless Integrated Service Module (WiSM) controller supports up to 150 APs for a total of 300 APs per WiSM blade. Therefore, if you have 12 WiSMs, or 24 controllers total, the maximum number of APs in that mobility group would be 3600.

Note Starting in code Release 4.2, you can configure APs with controllers outside the mobility group of the controller they are joined to. This feature is covered later in the chapter under "AP Mobility."

Controller code Release 5.1 or later allows for seamless roaming across multiple mobility groups in the mobility list of the controller. If a client roams to an AP connected to a controller that is not in the mobility list of the original controller, a seamless roam is not possible. During the inter-mobility group roam, the client is fully authenticated and maintains its current IP address. The controllers initiate a foreign/anchor relationship and EtherIP tunnel for the Layer 3 roaming event just like a regular intra-mobility group roam. If, however, you are using Cisco Centralized Key Management (CCKM) and Proactive Key Caching (PKC), only intra-mobility group roaming is supported.

Mobility Messaging

Controllers use mobility messages to hand off client state and set up a mobility tunnel session among group members for a mobile client. The Mobility Protocol is the protocol that controllers use for this message exchange. The Mobility Protocol employs a series of announcements, handoffs, and session termination messages as clients roam between controllers in the mobility group. The following sections discuss the different types of mobility messages, the mobility role of the controller in relation to the roaming client, Mobility Handoff types, mobility packet format, error recovery, and mobility messaging enhancements.

Mobility Message Types

Controllers in the same mobility group exchange a multitude of different messages to allow a wireless client to roam properly between them.

The 11 different mobility messages are as follows:

- **Controller Announce:** Sent every 20 seconds as long as the controller is operational and carries no status information.

- **Mobile Announce:** Sent when a client first associates with a controller. The controller sends up to four mobile announce messages. The message can be sent as either a unicast to each controller in the group or a multicast (multicast messaging is covered later under the "Mobility Messaging Enhancements in 5.0" section) to the mobility group multicast IP. As long as no Mobile Handoff message is received, the controller creates a Local client session. If the client was previously associated with another controller in the mobility group, that controller sends a Mobile Handoff to the new controller. Only a controller with a Local or Foreign client session can send a Mobile Handoff. A controller with an Anchor client session never answers the Mobile Announce message.

  The Mobile Announce contains sufficient information to allow a local or foreign controller receiving the packet to determine the type of connection to which the client will transition on the new controller and the type of mobility transfer that will be necessary.

- **Mobile Handoff:** Sent when a mobile client session is either transferred or a new foreign client session is established. It is always sent in response to a Mobile Announce and is always a unicast message.

- **Mobile Anchor Request:** Sent by the new foreign controller to the anchor controller when it receives a handoff from another foreign controller. It notifies the anchor that the new foreign controller is ready to take over from the old foreign controller.

- **Mobile Anchor Grant:** Sent by the anchor controller to the new foreign controller in response to a Mobile Anchor Request. It is only sent in response to an Anchor Request.

- **Mobile Anchor Transfer Request:** Sent by the old foreign controller to the anchor controller when it sends a handoff to the new foreign or local controller. It notifies the anchor that the new controller is ready to take over.

- **Mobile Anchor Transfer ACK:** Sent by the anchor controller to the old foreign controller in response to a Mobile Anchor Transfer Request. It is only sent in response to an Anchor Transfer Request. It closes the client session on the old foreign controller.

- **Mobile Handoff End:** Sent by either the anchor or foreign controller to its respective peer to inform the peer that the client session is being terminated.

- **Mobile Handoff End ACK:** Sent in response to a Mobile Handoff End.

- **Anchor Export Request:** Sent when a mobile client first associates with a controller, the controller has not received a handoff in response to the mobile announcement, and the WLAN is configured for Auto-Anchor. It is sent as a unicast message to a single controller configured as an Export Anchor for that WLAN.

- **Anchor Export ACK:** Sent in response to an Anchor Export Request. It is always a unicast message sent to the controller that sent the Anchor Export Request.

Mobility Role of the Controller to the Client

Any device on an IP network has an IP point of presence. The IP point of presence for a device is its IP and MAC address. Knowing the IP point of presence for a device is the way the network knows where to send traffic destined for that particular device. When using WLAN Controllers (WLC), the controller provides the client IP point of presence. Depending on the mobility role of a controller for a particular client, the controller with the AP that the client is actually joined to might not provide the IP point of presence for the client.

Controllers can play one of the following five roles to the client during client mobility session:

- **Local:** The controller provides both AP association and IP point of presence.

- **Anchor:** The controller provides the IP point of presence only and is always paired with a foreign controller. This is seen with asymmetric tunneling. Packets for the client are forwarded via an EtherIP encapsulated tunnel to the foreign controller for delivery to the client. The anchor controller provides proxy Address Resolution Protocol (ARP) for the client and is the relay to the Dynamic Host Configuration Protocol (DHCP) server for the client. DHCP reply is relayed back to the foreign controller outside the mobility tunnel.

- **Foreign:** The controller provides the AP association only and is always paired with an anchor controller. This is seen with asymmetrical tunneling. Packets from the client are forwarded directly to the network except for ARP and DHCP requests. ARP requests are forwarded to the anchor controller via a mobility tunnel (EtherIP). DHCP requests are proxied by the foreign controller to the anchor (outside mobility tunnel) and then proxied by the anchor to the DHCP server.

- **Export Anchor:** The controller provides the IP point of presence only and is always paired with an export foreign controller. This is seen with symmetric mobility tunneling and auto-anchoring. Packets for the client are forwarded via a mobility tunnel (EtherIP) to the foreign controller for delivery to the client. The anchor controller provides proxy ARP for the client and is the relay to the DHCP server for the client. DHCP packets for the client are forwarded directly to the client via mobility tunnel (EtherIP) to the Export Foreign controller rather than by relay outside mobility tunnel.

- **Export Foreign:** The controller provides the AP association only and is always paired with an export anchor controller. This is seen with symmetric mobility tunneling and auto-anchoring. Packets from the client are forwarded via mobility tunnel (EtherIP) to the anchor controller, where they are de-encapsulated and delivered directly to the network. All packets, including ARP and DHCP packets, are sent within the mobility tunnel.

As you can see, there is a distinct difference between an anchor/foreign and an export anchor/foreign scenario. The anchor/foreign session uses asymmetric tunneling. Because the traffic path for the client is asymmetrical in an anchor-foreign connection, any Layer 3 service provided to the client, such as IPsec virtual private network (VPN), Layer 2 Tunneling Protocol (L2TP) VPN, and DHCP, cannot be processed on the anchor controller. The service session information must be extracted from the local or foreign controller and included as part of the handoff. As mentioned before, asymmetric tunneling is inefficient, can cause network routing problems, and is deprecated in code Release 5.2. The sections that follow assume that symmetric mobility tunneling is configured.

Mobility Handoff Types

Handoffs occur only between controllers in the same mobility group. A Mobile Handoff is sent when a mobile client session is either transferred or a new foreign client session is established. It is always sent in response to a Mobile Announce.

The mobile client connection to the network can take two forms:

■ A Local connection, where the client IP point of presence on the wired LAN (the subnet containing the client IP address) and the AP to which the client is associated are both directly accessible through a single controller.

■ An Export Anchor-Export Foreign (symmetric mobility) connection, where the client IP point of presence is accessible through one controller (the Anchor) and the AP to which the client is associated is accessible through another controller.

Mobility Handoffs come in six types:

■ Local to Local

■ Local to Foreign

■ Foreign to Local (1)

■ Foreign to Local (2)

■ Foreign to Foreign

■ Auto-Anchor

The sections that follow describe each handoff type in greater detail.

Local to Local

Local-to-Local Handoff occurs when the client performs a Layer 2 roam between two controllers and requires only two packets. Figure 9-9 illustrates a Local-to-Local Handoff.

As shown in Figure 9-9, when the client roams to an AP on WLC1, WLC1 sends a Mobile Announce to the mobility group members. WLC1 responds with a Mobile Handoff, and the client database entry is moved from WLC1 to WLC2. WLC1 no longer has the client database entry. WLC2 becomes the IP point of presence for the client.

Local to Foreign

A Local-to-Foreign Handoff occurs when the client performs a Layer 3 (inter-controller inter-subnet) roam and requires only two packets. Figure 9-10 illustrates a Local-to-Foreign Handoff.

As seen in Figure 9-10, in a Local-to-Foreign Handoff, when the client roams from WLC1 to WLC2, WLC2 sends a Mobile Announce, and WLC1 responds with a Mobile Handoff. The client database entry is copied from WLC1 to WLC2. WLC1 marks the client entry as Export Anchor, and WLC2 marks the client entry as Export Foreign. The IP point of presence for the client remains WLC1.

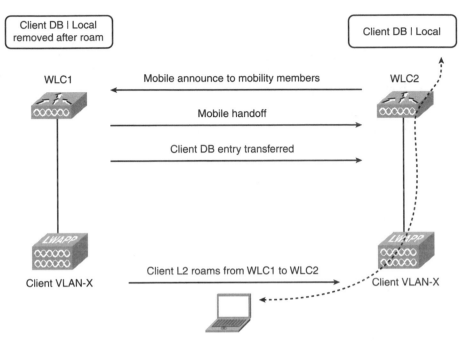

Figure 9-9   *Local-to-Local Handoff*

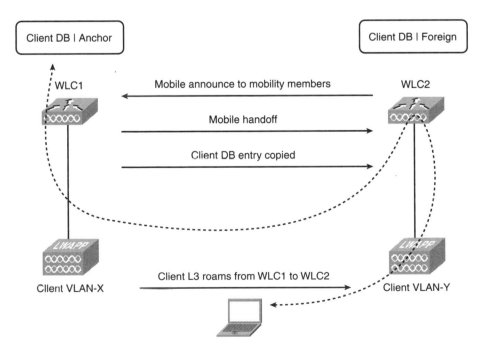

Figure 9-10   *Local-to-Foreign Handoff*

Foreign to Local (1)

A Foreign-to-Local (1) Handoff is the opposite of the Local-to-Foreign Handoff and again requires only two packets. The client is roaming from the foreign controller back to the anchor controller it came from. Figure 9-11 illustrates a Foreign-to-Local (1) Handoff.

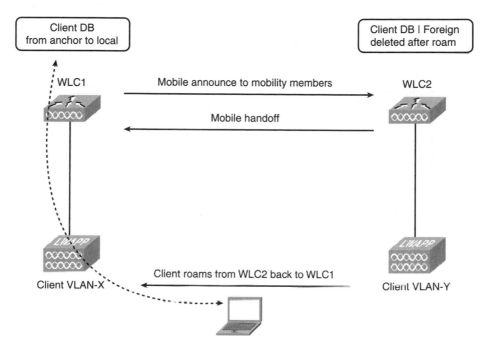

Figure 9-11 *Foreign to Local (1)*

Figure 9-11 shows that when the client roams back to WLC1, WLC1 sends out a Mobile Announce, and WLC2 responds with a Mobile Handoff. WLC1 knows it used to have a Local entry for that client and removes the Export Anchor designation from the client entry and once again marks it as Local. WLC2 deletes the database entry for the client. WLC1 remains the IP point of presence for the client.

Foreign to Local (2)

With a Foreign-to-Local (2) Handoff, three controllers are involved and four packets are needed. The client roams from the foreign controller to a third controller whose WLAN is in the same subnet as the anchor controller. Figure 9-12 illustrates a Foreign-to-Local (2) Handoff.

As shown in Figure 9-12, when the client roams to WLC3, WLC3 sends out a Mobile Announce, and WLC2 responds with a Mobile Handoff. The client database information is extracted from WLC2 by WLC3. WLC2 sends a Mobility Handoff End, and WLC1 responds with a Mobility Handoff End ACK. WLC1 and WLC2 delete the client data-base entry, and WLC3 marks the client entry as Local because its WLAN is in the same subnet as the client IP and becomes the IP point of presence for the client.

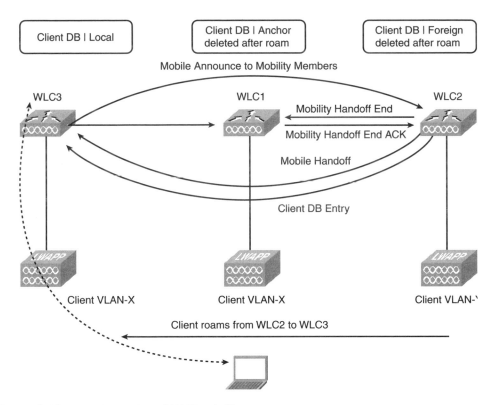

Figure 9-12   *Foreign-to-Local (2) Handoff*

Foreign to Foreign

Foreign-to-Foreign Handoffs involve three controllers and require six packets to complete the transaction. The client data path is set up after the first three packets are processed. This is the most complicated handoff transaction. A Foreign-to-Foreign Handoff occurs whenever the client has already established an Export Anchor-Export Foreign connection and the new controller to which the client has associated does not share a common sub-net assignment with the anchor controller for the WLAN in which the client is roaming, as seen in Figure 9-13.

As shown in Figure 9-13, when the client roams to WLC3, WLC3 sends out a Mobile Announce to the mobility members. WLC2 responds with a Mobile Handoff, and all client entry information is extracted from WLC2 and transferred to WLC3. After send-ing the Mobile Handoff, WLC2 sends an Anchor Xfer message to the WLC1, at which time WLC1 responds with an Anchor Xfer ACK and sets up the new client forwarding path. WLC2 then deletes the client session. WLC3 sends an Anchor Req message to

WLC1, and WLC1 responds with an Anchor Grant message. The IP point of presence for the client remains with WLC1.

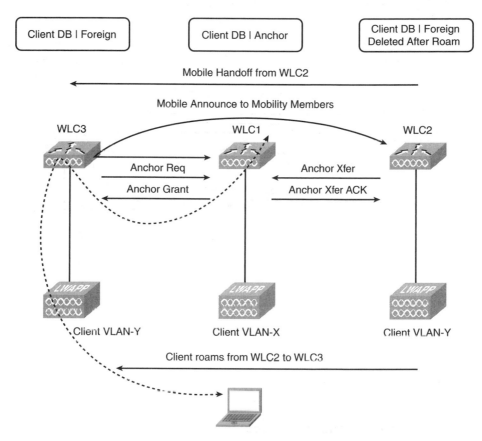

Figure 9-13 *Foreign-to-Foreign Handoff*

Auto-Anchor Transfer

If a WLAN is configured for auto-anchoring, the setup of the client upon entering the network is different from normal. When the client associates, the controller sends out Mobile Announce messages (as seen in Figure 9-14) to the mobility members like normal just in case the client is roaming from another controller. A mobility auto-anchor controller never responds to a Mobile Announce message.

After WLC2 sends the fourth Mobile Announce and does not receive a Mobile Handoff from any other controllers in the mobility group, instead of creating a Local entry for the client, WLC2 sends an Export Anchor Request to WLC1, which is configured as the auto-anchor for the client WLAN. The anchor controller responds with an Export Anchor ACK. The client database entry is copied to the anchor controller. WLC1 marks the client entry with Export Foreign, and WLC1 marks the entry as Export Anchor. WLC1 is the IP point of presence for the client. With the auto-anchoring scenario, you have a fixed anchor controller for the client WLAN that will never change. The client will have an IP address in the same VLAN as the anchored WLAN interface on WLC1.

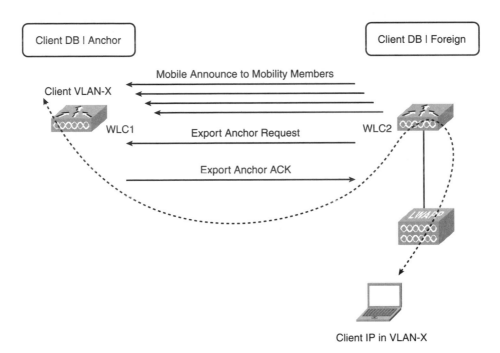

Figure 9-14 *Auto-Anchor Transfer*

Mobility Session Termination Message

A Mobility Session termination will be sent only when the controllers need to end an Export Foreign-Export Anchor relationship. The session termination may be initiated by either the foreign or anchor controller and requires only two packets. The termination might be required because of a client disconnect, timeout, or for administrative purposes. The client session will be deleted on both the foreign and anchor controller. Figure 9-15 illustrates Mobility Session termination.

In this example, the WLC2 (foreign) initiated the session termination to the WLC1 (anchor).

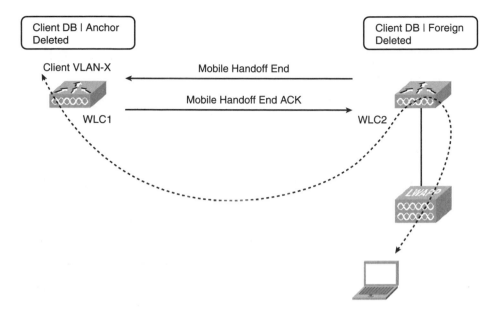

Figure 9-15 *Mobility Session Termination*

Mobility Packet Format

The mobility packet is a User Datagram Protocol (UDP) packet sent and received using port 16666. Because UDP is an unreliable delivery mechanism, any packet that requires a response retries up to four times at one-second intervals.

The mobility packet consists of a mobility packet header, which is required for all packets, followed by one or more Type, Length, Value (TLV) payloads carrying specific client or session data.

Mobility Packet Header

The Mobility Packet Header is part of every mobility packet. It is always the first record in the mobility packet. The header is fixed format and may be followed by one or more payloads, defined next, depending on the packet type and subtype.

Figure 9-16 shows the Mobility Packet Header, the fields for which are explained in the list that follows.

- **Packet Type:** 1 octet. This can be thought of as a command code; it defines the overall purpose of the packet. See the previous subsection.

- **Packet Subtype:** 1 octet. This is a 1-byte status field that is specific to the packet type. It is typically used as an OK/error code field in ACK messages.

- **Protocol Version:** 1 octet.

- **Flags:** 1 octet. Reserved, always 0.

- **Length:** 2 octets. Length of the header + payloads in octets. The length may include padding.

- **Sequence Number:** 2 octets. Monotonically increasing value used to detect retransmissions.

- **Exchange ID:** 4 octets. Session ID used to bind request and answer packets. The Exchange ID plus the querying controller IP guarantee a unique session value.

- **Controller UID:** 4 octets. UID portion (3 octets) of the controller MAC; leftmost octet is always 0.

- **Controller OUI:** 4 octets. OUI portion (3 octets) of the controller MAC; leftmost octet is always 0.

- **Mobility Group Identifier:** 16 octets. MD5 hash of the Mobility Group name. Mobility messages from groups other than the assigned Mobility Group name are ignored.

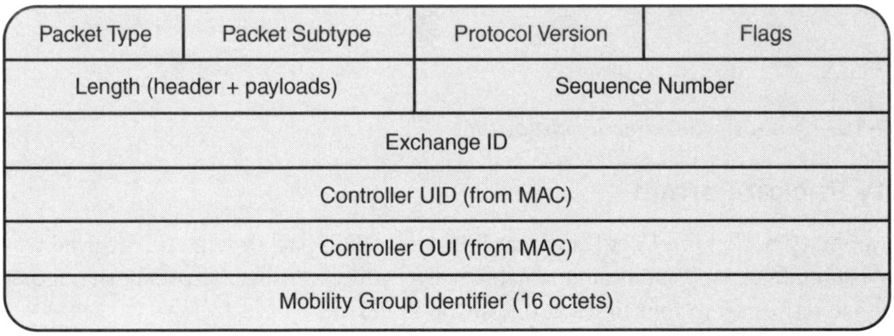

Packet Type	Packet Subtype	Protocol Version	Flags
Length (header + payloads)		Sequence Number	
Exchange ID			
Controller UID (from MAC)			
Controller OUI (from MAC)			
Mobility Group Identifier (16 octets)			

Figure 9-16 *Mobility Packet Header*

Mobility Packet Payloads

All Mobility Packet payloads follow a Type, Length, Value (TLV) format. The TLV header has the following format:

- **Type:** 1 octet. The payload type.

- **Version:** 1 octet. The version of the payload format. Currently, all Mobility payloads use Version 1.

- **Length:** 2 octets. The length of the entire payload, including the TLV header.

The payloads can occur in any order following the packet header except for the Packet End payload. The Packet End payload, if included in the packet, must be the last payload in the packet.

Seven payload types exist

- Client: Identifies a client.

- **DHCP:** Transfers a client IP address.

- **Authentication:** Username for client.

- **PEM policy:** All information to restore PEM state.

- **IPSec:** Transfers the Internet Key Exchange (IKE) Security Association (SA) and the HiFN Contexts specific to the client VPN session.

- **Anchor:** Information to transfer an anchor session.

- **Payload End:** The Packet End payload is necessary only if the length in the packet header includes padding beyond the last payload. Payload processing stops when the Packet End payload is encountered.

The packet payloads are hard-coded into the controller code so that when a controller receives a mobility packet, it knows how to decode it.

Error Recovery

In most cases, the mobility protocol is designed to fail in favor of client connectivity. If Layer 3 session information cannot be extracted or if the handoff cannot be completed, generally the response of the mobility group is to delete any existing client session information. This allows the client to start over with a new Local connection. Although the client may lose its existing network sessions and obtain a new IP address, it is not denied connectivity to the network.

Client Collision

Connection to the network in 802.11 is client initiated and, due to lost packets, a client might appear to associate with multiple controllers simultaneously. This condition is detected by the receipt of a Mobile Announce packet from another controller while waiting for a Mobile Handoff. In this case, if a Mobile Handoff is not received, the client is deauthenticated, the client session is deleted, and the client must either try again or complete the connection attempt on the other controller.

In the case of controller failure, no state information is retained among the mobility group or active status updates to allow recovery. Some failure recovery is built into the protocol handling.

Foreign Controller Failure

If a foreign controller fails, any clients associated to that controller attempt to associate elsewhere. If the anchor controller receives a Mobile Announce and does not receive an Anchor Transfer (Xfer) or Anchor Request (Req) within 10 seconds of the last Mobile Announce retry, it deletes the client and attempts to terminate the session with the foreign controller.

Anchor Controller Failure

Before code Release 4.1, there was no mechanism for a foreign controller to know if its anchor controller was down. If an anchor controller failed, you had to manually delete it on the foreign controller; if the clients reassociated with a new controller, the failure of the Anchor Xfer would delete the client session from the old foreign, and the failure of the Anchor Req would cause the client to transition to a Local session on the new controller. With 4.1 and higher code, the controllers regularly exchange mpings and epings to quickly detect a mobility group member failure. Now if an anchor is lost, the foreign controller disassociates all the clients tunneled to that particular anchor so it can reassociate and be tunneled to a working anchor if one exists.

Mobility Messaging Enhancements in 5.0

With code Release 5.0 or later, Cisco has added two mobility messaging improvements.

The first improvement is that a controller sends Mobile Announce messages to all the controllers in its mobility group first; then it sends those announcements to other controllers in the mobility list. Before this enhancement, the controller sent the messages to all controllers in the mobility list regardless of the configured mobility group. If the controller needs to retry the announcement, it includes the other controllers in the list. This reduces the number of messages a controller needs to send and receive.

The second improvement is multicasting the Mobile Announce messages instead of unicasting them. Most messages, such as Mobile Announce, PMK Updates, AP List Updates, and IDS Shun, are meant for all members in the group. This means that a controller has to replicate a single message for every controller in the group. In code Release 5.0 or later, you can configure the controllers to multicast the Mobile Announce messages. With multicast enabled, the controller has to send only a single copy of the message to the multicast group that contains all the controllers in the mobility group. Using multicast is a much more efficient delivery method. Cisco recommends that it be enabled on all mobility group members to gain the maximum benefits.

> **Tip**   If a firewall exists in the network path between controllers, it is important to remember that multicast needs to be allowed on the firewall for the controller multicast group IP.

Configuring Mobility Groups

To add an entry to a controller mobility configuration using the GUI, go to **CONTROLLER > Mobility Management > Mobility Groups**, as shown in Figure 9-17, and click on **New**. Here you enter the MAC address and IP address of the controller management interface you are adding along with the mobility group name of that controller.

If you are adding several controllers, you can choose **Edit All**, as shown in Figure 9-18, instead of **New** and paste in the MAC address, IP, and group name of all the controllers at once.

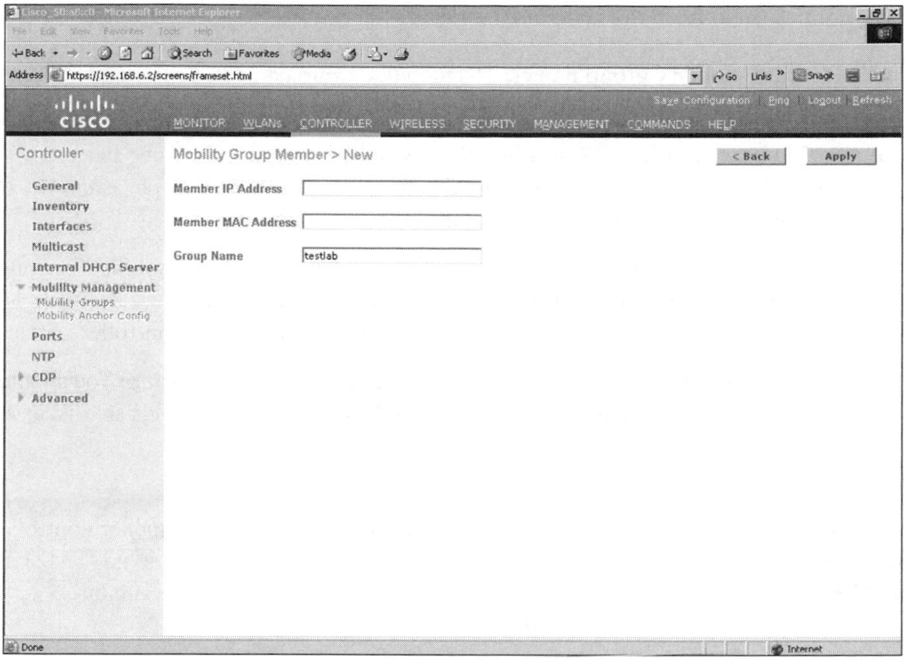

Figure 9-17   *Mobility Group Configuration*

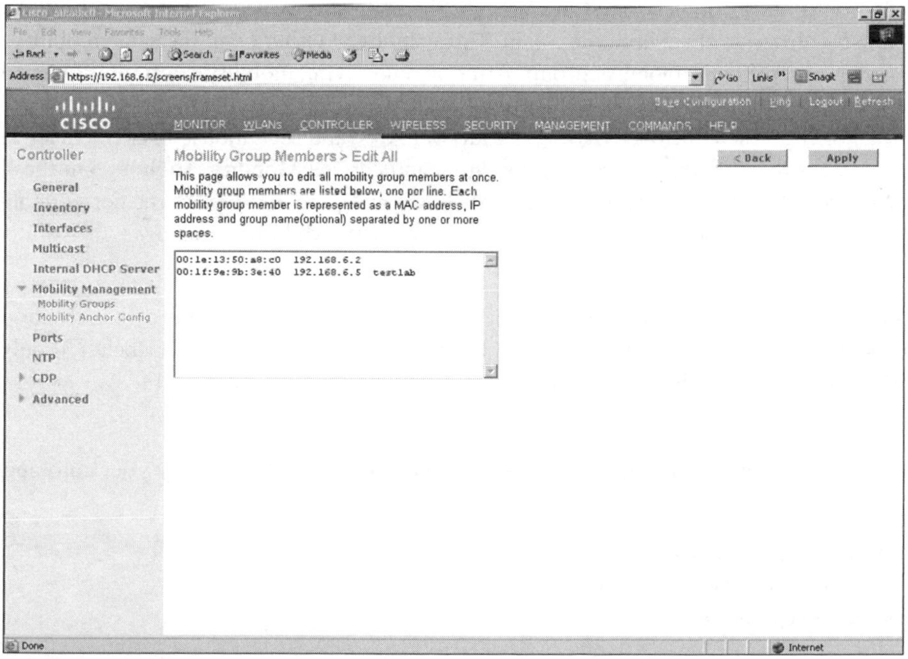

Figure 9-18   *Mobility Group Edit All*

For controllers to be in the same mobility group, they need to meet the following criteria:

- **Identical mobility group names:** The mobility group name is case sensitive. A mobility group name of WLC is not the same as wlc from the controller perspective.

- **Same virtual interface IP address:** If the virtual IPs are not the same between the controllers, the handoff of the client database entry will not take place and the client will be disconnected for a short period.

- **Same version of code:** This is true for supporting normal client mobility. Starting with the 5.2 release, a 5.2 or 6.0 controller supports auto-anchoring (discussed later in the chapter) with 4.2 and higher code running on the anchor controller.

- **Network connectivity between the controller in the mobility group:** You should be able to mping and eping between the controllers. These special pings are discussed later in the chapter.

Note   With controller Release 5.2, mobility is supported between auto-anchor controllers running 4.2 or higher code. This means the controller in the demilitarized zone (DMZ) could be running 5.0 code while the controllers that are anchored to it are running 5.2 code. See Chapter 14 more information on guest networking.

Configuring Auto-Anchoring

To configure auto-anchoring for a WLAN, the controller you want to use as the anchor must be listed in the mobility domain. The anchor can either be in the same mobility group or a different mobility group. After the underlying mobility configuration is complete, you configure the WLAN mobility anchor. To configure the WLAN mobility anchor from the controller GUI, you go to **WLANs**, and then mouse over the drop-down arrow for the WLAN you want to configure and choose **Mobility Anchors**. On the Mobility Anchors configuration page, as shown in Figure 9-19, select the correct controller from the drop-down menu and click on **Create Mobility Anchor**.

Note   When you are configuring auto-anchor, the WLAN of the anchor controller should be anchored only to itself. The WLAN of the foreign controller should be anchored only to the anchor(s) controller. This concept is discussed in detail in Chapter 14.

You can use the following commands from the controller CLI to verify your auto-anchor configuration:

```
show mobility anchor
show mobility achor wlan wlan_id
show wlan wlan_id
```

The output of **show mobility anchor** displays the global anchoring configuration for the entire controller, as demonstrated in Example 9-3.

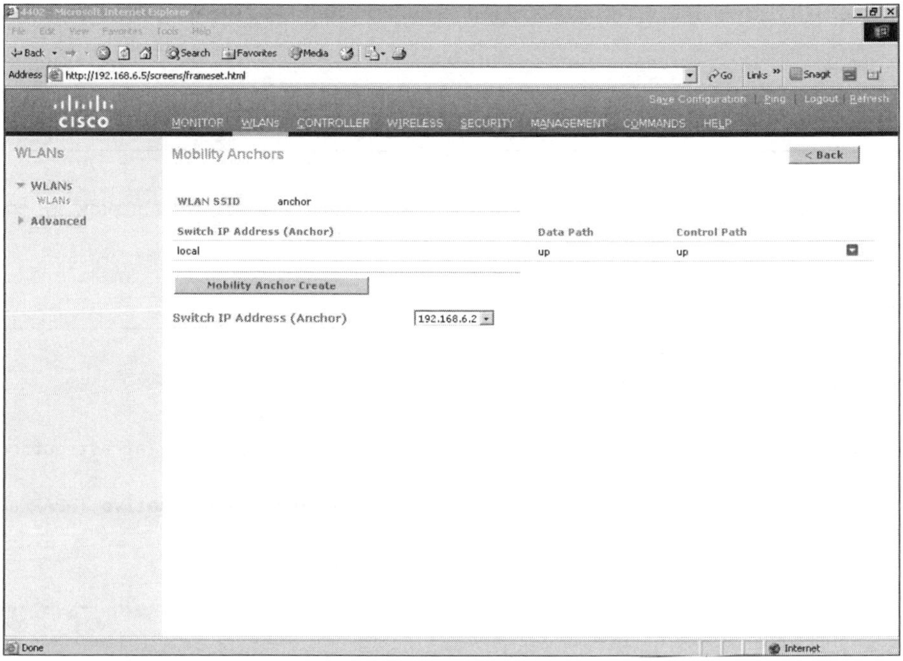

Figure 9-19   *WLAN Mobility Anchor Configuration*

Example 9-3   *show mobility anchor Command Output*

```
(Cisco Controller) >show mobility anchor


Mobility Anchor Export List

  WLAN ID     IP Address        Status
  -------     ---------------   -------
  3           192.168.6.5       Up


  GLAN ID     IP Address        Status
  -------     ---------------   -------
```

If you only want to check the auto-anchoring configuration for a specific WLAN, use
show mobility anchor wlan *wlan_id*, as shown in Example 9-4.

Example 9-4   *show mobility anchor wlan wlan_ID Command Output*

```
(Cisco Controller) >show mobility anchor wlan 3
Mobility Anchor Export List
```

(continues)

Example 9-4 *show mobility anchor wlan wlan_ID Command Output (continued)*

```
WLAN ID     IP Address           Status
-------     ---------------      -------
3           192.168.6.5          Up
```

The output of **show wlan,** as shown in Example 9-5, also displays the auto-anchor configuration.

Example 9-5 *show wlan Command Output*

```
(Cisco Controller)>show wlan 3
Output omitted for brevity
    H-REAP Local Switching....................... Disabled
    Infrastructure MFP protection................ Enabled (Global Infrastructure
MFP Disabled)
    Client MFP................................... Optional but inactive (WPA2 not
configured)
    Tkip MIC Countermeasure Hold-down Timer....... 60

Mobility Anchor List
WLAN ID     IP Address           Status
-------     ---------------      -------
3           192.168.6.5          Up
```

In the output of all three **show** commands in Examples 9-3 through 9-5, you can verify the IP address of the anchor controller as well as its status.

Determining Controllers to Add to a Mobility Group

The general rule of thumb for determining what controllers on your network should be in the same mobility group is quite simple. If a wireless client can roam between the APs joined to those controllers without dropping its wireless connection, those controllers should be in the same mobility group. If two controllers and their APs are located across the country from one another, you would probably not want them to be in the same mobility group.

Secure Mobility

With the default configuration, mobility packets are sent using UDP port 16666. This means that the mobility packets are not encrypted and anyone with a wired sniffer can view the packet contents. If you had mobility traffic traversing an unsecured network, you might want to enable secure mobility on the controllers to encrypt that data. Secure mobility uses UDP port 16667.

To enable secure mobility, enter the following commands from the controller CLI:

```
config mobility secure-mode enable
config certificate compatibility on
```

After entering those two commands, you need to reboot the controller. Secure mobility, if used, must be configured on all controllers in the mobility group. Secure mobility to nonsecure mobility is not supported.

> **Tip**   Secure mobility never really worked that well. Although the commands still exist in the controller CLI code up to 5.2, the feature is deprecated in the 6.0 release and is no longer supported.

Troubleshooting Mobility

For mobility to be established between a set of controllers, the controllers need to be able to communicate with one another across the network. This not only means that you should be able to ICMP ping between them (assuming network access control lists [ACLS], firewall, and so on allow ICMP ping on the network), but UDP port 16666 and protocol 97 communication exists as well. A successful ICMP ping between controllers does not mean that mobility will work.

When controllers are mobility group members, the data (16666) and control (protocol 97) paths between the controllers show as Up in the output of **show mobility summary**, as demonstrated in Example 9-6.

Example 9-6   *Displaying Data/Control Path Status Between Mobility Group Controllers*

```
(WLC1) >show mobility summary
Symmetric Mobility Tunneling (current) .......... Disabled
Symmetric Mobility Tunneling (after reboot) ..... Disabled
Mobility Protocol  Port.......................... 16666
Mobility Security Mode........................... Disabled
Default Mobility Domain.......................... wireless-west
Mobility Keepalive interval...................... 10
Mobility Keepalive count......................... 3
Mobility Group members configured................ 4
Controllers configured in the Mobility Group
  MAC Address        IP Address       Group Name        Status
  00:14:a9:bd:d9:a0    192.168.5.20      wireless-west     Up
  00:14:a9:be:51:80    192.168.5.22      wireless-west     Up
  00:1d:45:ef:a1:a0    192.168.5.24      wireless-west     Up
```

If either the control or the data path is down, you know you have a potential misconfiguration or network issue. You can verify the data and control paths using mping and eping respectively from the controller CLI. Mping sends mobility echo packets on UDP port 16666, and eping sends EtherIP echo packets using protocol 97.

Perhaps the biggest network issue with mobility occurs when a firewall is present between the controllers. This is a common setup when using guest networking (see Chapter 14). If the firewall rules are incorrect, mobility cannot be established.

Until the release of the 4.2 code, mobility was not supported when using Network Address Translation (NAT). In the older codes, the IP address from the source controller was validated with the source IP address of the IP header in the packet. Because the IP address in the header would change if NAT was taking place, mobility would fail. With the 4.2 code and higher, the controllers now validate the source MAC address from the sending controller, which allows mobility to work with NAT.

When setting up mobility with NAT, ensure that you use the IP address from the NAT device as opposed to the IP address of the controllers management interface.

Note Port Address Translation (PAT) is not supported on any code release.

To debug mobility on the controllers, use the following commands:

- **debug dot11 mobile enable:** Use this command to configure the debug of 802.11 mobile events.

- **debug mobility handoff enable:** Debugs Mobility Handoff packets. Here you will see the client database entries being moved between controllers.

- **debug mobility director enable:** Debugs mobility errors.

- **Debug mobility keepalive enable:** Debugs EtherIP and mobility UDP echoes.

- **debug pem {packet | events} enable:** Use this command to configure the access policy manager debug options. This shows the state of the client (such as START, DHCP_REQ, RUN, and so on).

  Enter **packet** to configure the debug of policy manager events.

  Enter **events** to configure the debug of policy manager State Machine.

Example 9-7 demonstrates sample output from **debug mobility keepalive enable** showing sent and received echo packets as well as a down mobility member.

Example 9-7 *debug mobility keepalive enable Command Output*

```
(testWLC) >Sun Mar  1 14:25:47 2009: EOIP Keepalive received from: 192.
168.120.100
Sun Mar  1 14:25:47 2009:   version : 02, opcode : ETHOIP_OP_REQ sequence no. 492
23 peerStatus: 0
Sun Mar  1 14:25:47 2009: EOIP Keepalive sent to: 192.168.120.100
Sun Mar  1 14:25:47 2009:   version : 02, opcode : ETHOIP_OP_RESP sequence no. 49
223 peerStatus: 0
Sun Mar  1 14:25:52 2009: EOIP Keepalive sent to: 192.168.5.26
```

```
Sun Mar  1 14:25:52 2009:  version : 02, opcode : ETHOIP_OP_REQ sequence no.
812273 peerStatus: 0
Sun Mar  1 14:25:52 2009: EOIP Keepalive sent to: 192.168.5.26
Sun Mar  1 14:25:52 2009:  version : 01, opcode : ETHOIP_OP_REQ sequence no.
812274 peerStatus: 0
Sun Mar  1 14:25:52 2009: UDP Keepalive sent to ::
Sun Mar  1 14:25:52 2009:   192.168.5.26, port 16666
Sun Mar  1 14:25:52 2009:   type: 20(MobilityPingRequest)  subtype: 0  version: 1
xid: 144839  seq: 2094  len 36 flags 0
Sun Mar  1 14:25:52 2009:   group id: 30a33488 9524b58e 4a4d006c fcebcee8
Sun Mar  1 14:25:52 2009: Mobility Member 192.168.5.26 detected DOWN status 3,
cleaning up client entries.
```

The configured mobility keepalive interval is the interval the controllers will send the
EtherIP (eping) packets. The mping packets are sent at 3 times the keepalive interval. So
for the default setting of 10 seconds, an mping is sent every 30 seconds.

It is also important to note that although you can initiate an eping or mping from any
controller to any other controller in the mobility group using the CLI, a controller will
send keepalives to some and receive them from others. The controller will send keepalives
to any controller in its mobility group that has a higher MAC address than itself and
receive keepalives from controllers that have lower MAC addresses.

Example 9-8 shows sample output of **debug client** and **debug mobility handoff** for a
client with a MAC address 00:40:96:a1:4a:f6 that is performing an inter-subnet roam
between two controllers.

Example 9-8   *debug Output Showing an Inter-Subnet Roaming Event*

```
! Original controller that the client is roaming from:
!Here we see the Mobile Announce from the controller the client is roaming to:

(Cisco Controller) >Mon Mar 23 08:15:51 2009: Mobility packet received from:
Mon Mar 23 08:15:51 2009:   192.168.6.5, port 16666
Mon Mar 23 08:15:51 2009:   type: 3(MobileAnnounce)  subtype: 0  version: 1  xid:
5  seq: 17  len 116 flags 0
Mon Mar 23 08:15:51 2009:   group id: dd6bc6e0 18d902a7 d3d26a44 650a60dc
Mon Mar 23 08:15:51 2009:   mobile MAC: 00:40:96:a1:4a:f6, IP: 0.0.0.0, instance: 0
Mon Mar 23 08:15:51 2009:   VLAN IP: 192.168.6.5, netmask: 255.255.255.0
Mon Mar 23 08:15:51 2009: Switch IP: 192.168.6.5
Mon Mar 23 08:15:51 2009: 00:40:96:a1:4a:f6 Handoff as Local, Client IP:
192.168.20.20 Anchor IP: 192.168.6.2
Mon Mar 23 08:15:51 2009: Anchor Mac : 00.1e.13.50.a8.c0
```

(continues)

Example 9-8   *debug Output Showing an Inter-Subnet Roaming Event (continued)*

```
!Here the controller responds with the Mobile Handoff:

Mon Mar 23 08:15:51 2009: Mobility packet sent to:
Mon Mar 23 08:15:51 2009:    192.168.6.5, port 16666
Mon Mar 23 08:15:51 2009:    type: 5(MobileHandoff)  subtype: 0  version: 1  xid:
5  seq: 184  len 556 flags 0
Mon Mar 23 08:15:51 2009:    group id: dd6bc6e0 18d902a7 d3d26a44 650a60dc
Mon Mar 23 08:15:51 2009:    mobile MAC: 00:40:96:a1:4a:f6, IP: 192.168.20.20,
instance: 1
Mon Mar 23 08:15:51 2009:    VLAN IP: 192.168.20.2, netmask: 255.255.255.0
Mon Mar 23 08:15:51 2009: 00:40:96:a1:4a:f6 192.168.20.20 RUN (20) State Update
from Mobility-Complete to Mobility-Incomplete
Mon Mar 23 08:15:51 2009: 00:40:96:a1:4a:f6 192.168.20.20 RUN (20) Setting handles
to 0x00000000
Mon Mar 23 08:15:51 2009: 00:40:96:a1:4a:f6 192.168.20.20 RUN (20) Deleted mobile
LWAPP rule on AP [00:1c:b1:07:fa:20]
Mon Mar 23 08:15:51 2009: 00:40:96:a1:4a:f6 Updated location for station old AP
00:00:00:00:00:00-0, new AP 00:00:00:00:00:00-0
!The controller marks the client entry as Anchor:
Mon Mar 23 08:15:51 2009: 00:40:96:a1:4a:f6 192.168.20.20 RUN (20) mobility role
update request from Local to Anchor
  Peer = 192.168.6.5, Old Anchor = 192.168.6.2, New Anchor = 192.168.6.2
Mon Mar 23 08:15:51 2009: 00:40:96:a1:4a:f6 Stopping deletion of Mobile Station:
(callerId: 42)
Mon Mar 23 08:15:51 2009: 00:40:96:a1:4a:f6 192.168.20.20 RUN (20) State Update
from Mobility-Incomplete to Mobility-Complete, mobility role=Anchor
Mon Mar 23 08:15:51 2009: 00:40:96:a1:4a:f6 192.168.20.20 RUN (20) Change state to
RUN (20) last state RUN (20)
! This is the controller the client roams to:
!Client roams to AP on the controller:
Mon Mar 23 08:34:24 2009: 00:40:96:a1:4a:f6 Adding mobile on LWAPP AP
00:1e:13:06:f6:50(1)
Mon Mar 23 08:34:24 2009: 00:40:96:a1:4a:f6 Scheduling deletion of Mobile Station:
(callerId: 23) in 5 seconds
!output omitted for brevity
Mon Mar 23 08:34:26 2009: 00:40:96:a1:4a:f6 0.0.0.0 8021X_REQD (3) Change state to
L2AUTHCOMPLETE (4) last state L2AUTHCOMPLETE (4)
Mon Mar 23 08:34:26 2009: 00:40:96:a1:4a:f6 Mobility query, PEM State: L2AUTHCOM-
PLETE
!Controller sends Mobile Announce
Mon Mar 23 08:34:26 2009: Mobility packet sent to:
Mon Mar 23 08:34:26 2009:    192.168.6.2, port 16666
Mon Mar 23 08:34:26 2009:    type: 3(MobileAnnounce)  subtype: 0  version: 1  xid:
5  seq: 17  len 116 flags 0
Mon Mar 23 08:34:26 2009:    group id: dd6bc6e0 18d902a7 d3d26a44 650a60dc
Mon Mar 23 08:34:26 2009:    mobile MAC: 00:40:96:a1:4a:f6, IP: 0.0.0.0, instance: 0
Mon Mar 23 08:34:26 2009:    VLAN IP: 192.168.6.5, netmask: 255.255.255.0
```

```
!Original controller responds with Mobile Handoff:
Mon Mar 23 08:34:26 2009: Mobility packet received from:
Mon Mar 23 08:34:26 2009:    192.168.6.2, port 16666
Mon Mar 23 08:34:26 2009:    type: 5(MobileHandoff)  subtype: 0  version: 1  xid:
5  seq: 184   len 556 flags 0
Mon Mar 23 08:34:26 2009:    group id: dd6bc6e0 18d902a7 d3d26a44 650a60dc
Mon Mar 23 08:34:26 2009:    mobile MAC: 00:40:96:a1:4a:f6, IP: 192.168.20.20,
instance: 1
Mon Mar 23 08:34:26 2009:    VLAN IP: 192.168.20.2, netmask: 255.255.255.0
Mon Mar 23 08:34:26 2009: Switch IP: 192.168.6.2
Mon Mar 23 08:34:26 2009: 00:40:96:a1:4a:f6 Mobility handoff for client:
  Ip: 192.168.20.20
  Anchor IP: 192.168.6.2, Peer IP: 192.168.6.2
Mon Mar 23 08:34:26 2009: 00:40:96:a1:4a:f6    DHCP Relay: 192.168.20.2   DHCP
Server: 192.168.1.10
  Lease: 1800 secs Expires 1713 secs
Mon Mar 23 08:34:26 2009: 00:40:96:a1:4a:f6 192.168.20.20 DHCP_REQD (7) Change
state to RUN (20) last state RUN (20)
Mon Mar 23 08:34:26 2009: 00:40:96:a1:4a:f6 192.168.20.20 RUN (20) Reached PLUMB-
FASTPATH: from line 4717
Mon Mar 23 08:34:26 2009: 00:40:96:a1:4a:f6 192.168.20.20 RUN (20) Change state to
RUN (20) last state RUN (20)
!Client maintains original IP address:
Mon Mar 23 08:34:26 2009: 00:40:96:a1:4a:f6 Assigning Address 192.168.20.20 to
mobile
Mon Mar 23 08:34:26 2009: 00:40:96:a1:4a:f6 Handoff confirm: Pre Handoff PEM
State: RUN
Mon Mar 23 08:34:26 2009: 00:40:96:a1:4a:f6    DHCP Relay: 192.168.20.2   DHCP
Server: 192.168.1.10
  Lease: 1800 sec Expires 1713
Mon Mar 23 08:34:26 2009: 00:40:96:a1:4a:f6 Username entry () created for mobile
Mon Mar 23 08:34:26 2009: 00:40:96:a1:4a:f6    Pem State update: RUN(20), VAP
Security mask 40004040,   IPsec len: 0, ACL Name: 'allowall'
Mon Mar 23 08:34:26 2009: 00:40:96:a1:4a:f6 Applying post-handoff policy for sta-
tion 00:40:96:a1:4a:f6 - valid mask 0x0
Mon Mar 23 08:34:26 2009: 00:40:96:a1:4a:f6    QOS Level: -1, DSCP: -1, dot1p: -1,
   Data Avg: -1, realtime Avg: -1, Data Burst -1, Realtime Burst -1
Mon Mar 23 08:34:26 2009: 00:40:96:a1:4a:f6    Session: -1, User session: -1,
User elapsed -1
   Interface: N/A ACL: N/A
!Client enters the RUN state on new controller:
Mon Mar 23 08:34:26 2009: 00:40:96:a1:4a:f6 192.168.20.20 RUN (20) Change state to
RUN (20) last state RUN (20)
Mon Mar 23 08:34:26 2009: 00:40:96:a1:4a:f6 Scheduling deletion of Mobile Station:
(callerId: 55) in 1800 seconds
!New controller marks client entry as Foreign
Mon Mar 23 08:34:26 2009: 00:40:96:a1:4a:f6 192.168.20.20 RUN (20) mobility role
update request from Unassociated to Foreign
```

(continues)

Example 9-8 *debug Output Showing an Inter-Subnet Roaming Event (continued)*

```
 Peer = 192.168.6.2, Old Anchor = 192.168.6.2, New Anchor = 192.168.6.2
Mon Mar 23 08:34:26 2009: 00:40:96:a1:4a:f6 192.168.20.20 RUN (20) State Update
from Mobility-Incomplete to Mobility-Complete, mobility role=Foreign
```

In these two debugs you can clearly see the controllers exchange the mobility messages, client security, DHCP, and so on and update their databases for the client with Anchor and Foreign flags. Also notice that the client keeps the same IP address even though the VLANs between the WLANs on the controllers are different.

The output of **show client detail** from each controller shows the anchor and mobility roles. See Example 9-9.

Example 9-9 *show client detail Command Output*

```
! Anchor controller:
(WLC1) >show client detail 00:40:96:a1:4a:f6
Client MAC Address............................... 00:40:96:a1:4a:f6
Client Username ................................. N/A
AP MAC Address................................... 00:00:00:00:00:00
Client State..................................... Associated
Wireless LAN Id.................................. 1
BSSID............................................ 00:00:00:00:00:00
Connected For ................................... 124 secs
Channel.......................................... N/A
IP Address....................................... 192.168.20.20
!Output omitted for brevity
Supported Rates.................................. 6.0,9.0,12.0,18.0,24.0,36.0,
................................................. 48.0,54.0
Mobility State................................... Anchor
Mobility Foreign IP Address...................... 192.168.6.5
Mobility Move Count.............................. 1
Security Policy Completed........................ Yes
Policy   Manager State........................... RUN
Policy Manager Rule Created...................... Yes
Policy Type...................................... WPA2
Authentication Key Management.................... PSK
Encryption Cipher................................ CCMP (AES)
Management Frame Protection...................... No
EAP Type......................................... Unknown
Interface........................................ vlan20
VLAN............................................. 20
! Foreign controller:
(WLC2) >show client detail 00:40:96:a1:4a:f6
Client MAC Address............................... 00:40:96:a1:4a:f6
Client Username ................................. N/A
```

```
AP MAC Address................................... 00:1e:13:06:f6:50
Client State..................................... Associated
Wireless LAN Id.................................. 3
BSSID............................................ 00:1e:13:06:f6:5d
Connected For ................................... 42 secs
Channel.......................................... 36
IP Address....................................... 192.168.20.20
!Output omitted for brevity
Supported Rates.................................. 6.0,9.0,12.0,18.0,24.0,36.0,
................................................ 48.0,54.0
Mobility State................................... Foreign
Mobility Anchor IP Address....................... 192.168.6.2
Mobility Move Count.............................. 2
Security Policy Completed........................ Yes
Policy Manager State............................. RUN
Policy Manager Rule Created...................... Yes
NPU Fast Fast Notified........................... Yes
Policy Type...................................... WPA2
Authentication Key Management.................... PSK
Encryption Cipher................................ CCMP (AES)
Management Frame Protection...................... No
EAP Type......................................... Unknown
Interface........................................ management
VLAN............................................. 0
```

You can also view mobility statistics from either the graphical user interface (GUI) or the CLI. You can view three types of mobility group statistics from the controller GUI:

■ **Global statistics:** Affect all mobility transactions

■ **Mobility initiator statistics:** Generated by the controller initiating a mobility event

■ **Mobility responder statistics:** Generated by the controller responding to a mobility event

To view this from the controller GUI, go to **MONITOR > Statistics > Mobility Statistics**. From the CLI, use the following command:

```
show mobility statistics
```

Table 9-1 describes each mobility statistic.

As you can see, the statistics page provides thorough information about the mobility state of the controller. Should you want to clear the current mobility statistics, select **Clear Stats.**

Table 9-1 *Mobility Statistics*

Parameter	Description
Global Mobility Statistics	
Rx Errors	Generic protocol packet receive errors, such as packet too short or format incorrect.
Tx Errors	Generic protocol packet transmit errors, such as packet transmission fail.
Responses Retransmitted	The mobility protocol uses UDP, and it resends requests several times if it does not receive a response. Because of network or processing delays, the responder may receive one or more retry requests after it initially responds to a request. This field shows a count of the response resends.
Handoff End Requests Received	The total number of handoff requests received, ignored, or responded to.
State Transitions Disallowed	The policy enforcement module (PEM) has denied a client state transition, usually resulting in the handoff being aborted.
Resource Unavailable	A necessary resource, such as a buffer, was unavailable, resulting in the handoff being aborted.
Mobility Initiator Statistics	
Handoff Requests Sent	The number of clients that have associated to the controller and have been announced to the mobility group.
Handoff Replies Received	The number of handoff replies that have been received in response to the requests sent.
Handoff as Local Received	The number of handoffs in which the entire client session has been transferred.
Handoff as Foreign Received	The number of handoffs in which the client session was anchored elsewhere.
Handoff Denys Received	The number of handoffs that were denied.

Table 9-1 *Mobility Statistics*

Parameter	Description
Global Mobility Statistics	
Anchor Request Sent	The number of anchor requests that were sent for a three-party (foreign-to-foreign) handoff. The handoff was received from another foreign controller, and the new controller is requesting the anchor to move the client.
Anchor Deny Received	The number of anchor requests that were denied by the current anchor.
Anchor Grant Received	The number of anchor requests that were approved by the current anchor.
Anchor Transfer Received	The number of anchor requests that closed the session on the current anchor and transferred the anchor back to the requestor.
Mobility Responder Statistics	
Handoff Requests Ignored	The number of handoff requests or client announcements that were ignored because the controller had no knowledge of that client.
Ping Pong Handoff Requests Dropped	The number of handoff requests that were denied because the handoff period was too short (3 seconds).
Handoff Requests Dropped	The number of handoff requests that were dropped due to either an incomplete knowledge of the client or a problem with the packet.
Handoff Requests Denied	The number of handoff requests that were denied.
Client Handoff as Local	The number of handoff responses sent while the client is in the local role.
Client Handoff as Foreign	The number of handoff responses sent while the client is in the foreign role.

(continues)

Table 9-1   *Mobility Statistics (continued)*

Parameter	Description
Global Mobility Statistics	
Anchor Requests Received	The number of anchor requests received.
Anchor Requests Denied	The number of anchor requests denied.
Anchor Requests Granted	The number of anchor requests granted.
Anchor Transferred	The number of anchors transferred because the client has moved from a foreign controller to a controller on the same subnet as the current anchor.

PMKID Caching

If a client is using WPA2 or CCKM, the controller issues the client a Pairwise Master Key ID (PMKID) when the client first associates, as demonstrated in Example 9-10.

Example 9-10   *PMKID Caching*

```
Wed May 27 23:50:21 2009: 00:00:f0:05:c4:03 Association received from
mobile on AP 00:13:5f:57:43:60
Wed May 27 23:50:21 2009: 00:00:f0:05:c4:03 Processing RSN IE type 48,
length 20 for mobile 00:00:f0:05:c4:03
Wed May 27 23:50:21 2009: 00:00:f0:05:c4:03 Received RSN IE with 0 PMKIDs
from mobile 00:00:f0:05:c4:03


!Because there is no PMKID, the controller creates one and sends it to the client:

Wed May 27 23:50:24 2009: 00:00:f0:05:c4:03 Creating a PKC PMKID Cache
entry for station 00:00:f0:05:c4:03 (RSN 2)
Wed May 27 23:50:24 2009: 00:00:f0:05:c4:03 Adding BSSID 00:13:5f:57:43:62
to PMKID cache for station 00:00:f0:05:c4:03
Wed May 27 23:50:24 2009: New PMKID: (16)
Wed May 27 23:50:24 2009:      [0000] 6f 95 b2 2b 93 65 cf be 8b 8d ff ac
d6 ac 0e 0d
Wed May 27 23:50:24 2009: Including PMKID in M1  (16)
Wed May 27 23:50:24 2009:      [0000] 6f 95 b2 2b 93 65 cf be 8b 8d ff ac
d6 ac 0e 0d
```

When the client roams to another AP, it can send this PMIKD in the reassociation request to the AP. The controller takes this value and compares it to its internal PMIKID database. If it finds a match and the PMKID is still valid, the client does not have to perform a full reauthentication during the roaming event. The benefit of PMKID caching is that the time it takes to roam when a client is using 802.1x authentication is greatly reduced. This is an ideal situation for voice clients. You certainly do not want a full 802.1x reauthentication to take place while a phone conversation is in progress.

If you are experiencing an issue where your WPA2 or CCKM clients are performing a full 802.1x reauthentication, you can use **debug client** to see if the client is passing the correct PMKID and if the controller is able to validate it.

A key concept is *sticky PMKID caching* versus *opportunistic or proactive PMKID caching*. With sticky PMKID caching, the client receives and stores a different PMIKID for every AP it associates with. The APs also maintain a database of the PMKID issued to the client. When the AP roams back to an AP it was associated with before, it sends the corresponding PMKID for that particular AP. With opportunistic PMKID caching, however, the client and AP/controller maintain a single PMKID. The same PMKID is used for every reassociation regardless of the AP it associates with. The controller supports only opportunistic PMKID caching, so a client trying to do sticky caching will always perform a full reauthentication.

Example 9-11 is partial output of **debug client** for a client performing sticky PMKID caching and therefore having to perform a full reauthentication every time it roams between APs on the same controller.

Example 9-11 *Sticky PMKID Caching*

```
!Initial association, no PMKID as expected:

Wed May 27 23:50:21 2009: 00:00:f0:05:c4:03 Association received from
mobile on AP 00:13:5f:57:43:60
Wed May 27 23:50:21 2009: 00:00:f0:05:c4:03 Processing RSN IE type 48,
length 20 for mobile 00:00:f0:05:c4:03
Wed May 27 23:50:21 2009: 00:00:f0:05:c4:03 Received RSN IE with 0
PMKIDs from mobile 00:00:f0:05:c4:03

!Since no PMKID, the controller creates one and sends it to the client:

Wed May 27 23:50:24 2009: 00:00:f0:05:c4:03 Creating a PKC PMKID Cache
entry for station 00:00:f0:05:c4:03 (RSN 2)
Wed May 27 23:50:24 2009: 00:00:f0:05:c4:03 Adding BSSID
00:13:5f:57:43:62 to PMKID cache for station 00:00:f0:05:c4:03
Wed May 27 23:50:24 2009: New PMKID: (16)
Wed May 27 23:50:24 2009:      [0000] 6f 95 b2 2b 93 65 cf be 8b 8d ff
ac d6 ac 0e 0d
Wed May 27 23:50:24 2009: Including PMKID in M1   (16)
Wed May 27 23:50:24 2009:      [0000] 6f 95 b2 2b 93 65 cf be 8b 8d ff
```

(continues)

Example 9-11   *Sticky PMKID Caching (continued)*

```
ac d6 ac 0e 0d
!Then when the client roams to a new AP, since it is sticky and has no
PMKID for that AP, the client does not send the PMKID it just got from
the WLC:

Wed May 27 23:52:58 2009: 00:00:f0:05:c4:03 Reassociation received from
mobile on AP 00:0e:d7:d1:e0:e0
Wed May 27 23:52:58 2009: 00:00:f0:05:c4:03 Processing RSN IE type 48,
length 20 for mobile 00:00:f0:05:c4:03
Wed May 27 23:52:58 2009: 00:00:f0:05:c4:03 Received RSN IE with 0
PMKIDs from mobile 00:00:f0:05:c4:03

!The controller creates and sends a new PMKID and the cycle continues with
each new AP:

Wed May 27 23:53:29 2009: 00:00:f0:05:c4:03 Reassociation received from
mobile on AP 00:0f:23:21:05:f0
Wed May 27 23:53:29 2009: 00:00:f0:05:c4:03 Processing RSN IE type 48,
length 20 for mobile 00:00:f0:05:c4:03
Wed May 27 23:53:29 2009: 00:00:f0:05:c4:03 Received RSN IE with 0
PMKIDs from mobile 00:00:f0:05:c4:03

!You can see this over and over until the client roams back to an AP it
was previously associated with. Here you see the client did send the PMKID with
the reassociation request because it was associated to AP with the mac ending in
e0:e0 before:

Wed May 27 23:54:09 2009: 00:00:f0:05:c4:03 Reassociation received from
mobile on AP 00:0e:d7:d1:e0:e0
Wed May 27 23:54:09 2009: 00:00:f0:05:c4:03 Processing RSN IE type 48,
length 38 for mobile 00:00:f0:05:c4:03
Wed May 27 23:54:09 2009: 00:00:f0:05:c4:03 Received RSN IE with 1
PMKIDs from mobile 00:00:f0:05:c4:03
Wed May 27 23:54:09 2009: Received PMKID:   (16)
Wed May 27 23:54:09 2009:      [0000] 00 29 f1 c5 0d 18 fa 94 27 8d 2e
35 6b d1 ee 01

!The WLC only supports opportunistic PMKID caching and only has the PMKID from
when the client was associated to AP ending in
05:f0. Because of this, the WLC is not able to validate the PMKID from the
client even though at one point, it was a valid PMKID value:

Wed May 27 23:54:09 2009: 00:00:f0:05:c4:03 Reassociation received from
mobile on AP 00:0e:d7:d1:e0:e0
Wed May 27 23:54:09 2009: 00:00:f0:05:c4:03 Processing RSN IE type 48,
```

```
length 38 for mobile 00:00:f0:05:c4:03
Wed May 27 23:54:09 2009: 00:00:f0:05:c4:03 Received RSN IE with 1
PMKIDs from mobile 00:00:f0:05:c4:03
Wed May 27 23:54:09 2009: Received PMKID:  (16)
Wed May 27 23:54:09 2009:     [0000] 00 29 f1 c5 0d 18 fa 94 27 8d 2e
35 6b d1 ee 01
Wed May 27 23:54:09 2009: 00:00:f0:05:c4:03 No valid PMKID found in the
cache for mobile 00:00:f0:05:c4:03
Wed May 27 23:54:09 2009: 00:00:f0:05:c4:03 Unable to compute a valid
PMKID from dot1x PMK cache for mobile 00:00:f0:05:c4:03
```

The problem in Example 9-11 is that the controller maintains only a single PMKID and therefore cannot validate the PMKID from the client because it only has the value from the last AP the client was associated with. Because no valid PMKID is found, the client is forced to go through a full 802.1x authentication.

AP Mobility

Although Chapter 8, "Access Point Registration," covers the majority of the following section, it is important to understand how AP mobility and AP registration work.

When an AP is fully joined to a controller, the AP learns of all the controllers configured in the mobility group. Should the controller that an AP is currently registered with go down, the AP will send discoveries to any and all controllers in the mobility group. Assuming one of the controllers has the capacity to accept the AP, the AP should join the least loaded controller it can find. If many controllers are in the mobility group, it can be difficult to determine what controller the APs will join should their current controller fail.

Primary, Secondary, and Tertiary Controllers

If you want to have more control over how the APs move between controllers on your network, you can configure the APs with primary, secondary, and tertiary controller names. Figure 9-20 shows this configuration for APs joined to a controller running version 4.2.176.0.

With the controller name configured on the APs, the APs always try to register to the primary controller first. Should the primary controller go down, the AP tries to register with the secondary controller, and then the third should the AP not be able to join the secondary controller. If the AP is not able to join any of the configured controllers, it tries to join any controller with the Master Controller setting configured, or if no Master Controller, then the least loaded controller in the mobility group.

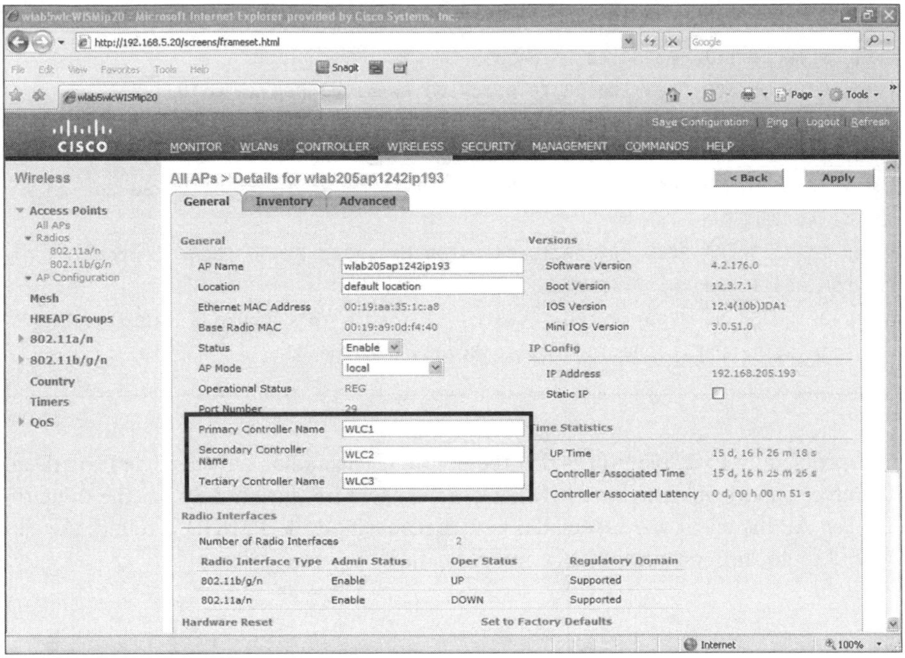

Figure 9-20 *AP Primary, Secondary, Tertiary Controller Configuration*

In 3.0 code and higher, should you want to set a global primary backup and secondary global backup controller for all the APs joined to a particular controller, use the following commands:

```
config ap primary-base controller_name Cisco_AP [controller_ip_address]
config ap secondary-base controller_name Cisco_AP [controller_ip_address]
config ap tertiary-base controller_name Cisco_AP [controller_ip_address]
```

Should you want to set a global primary backup and or secondary backup controller for all the APs joined to a particular controller, use the following commands:

```
config advanced backup-controller primary backup_controller_name
backup_controller_ip_address
config advanced backup-controller secondary backup_controller_name
backup_controller_ip_address
```

When using both the local (primary, secondary, tertiary) and global backup configurations, the locally configured settings take precedence in the event of a controller failure. If an AP is not able to join any of the locally configured controllers, it then tries to join the global backup controller(s).

With the 5.1 code release and higher, these configuration options were moved to the GUI as well. Figure 9-21 shows the High Availability tab for an individual AP. Figure 9-22 shows the global primary backup and secondary backup controller configuration.

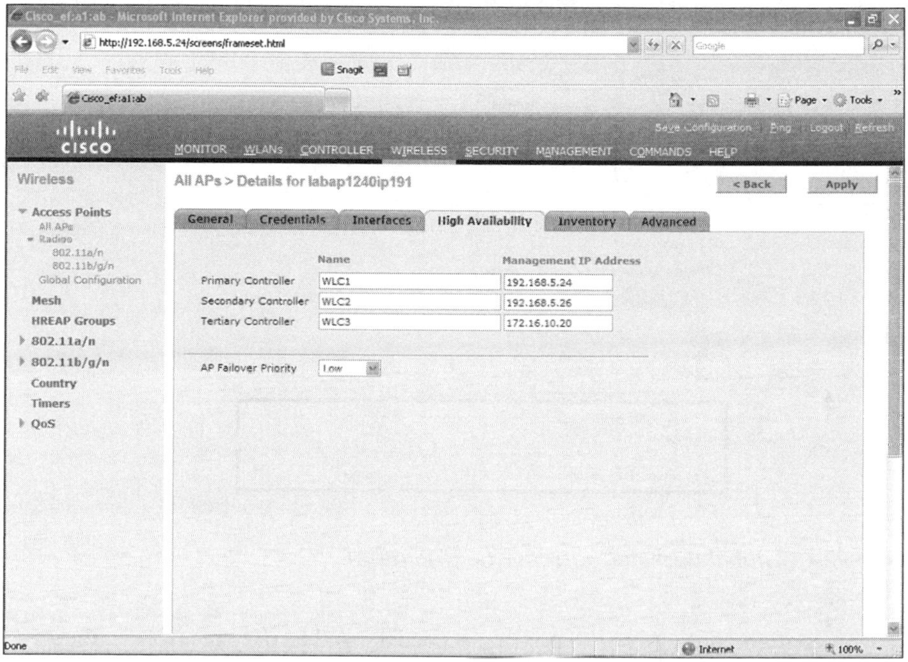

Figure 9-21   *AP High Availability Configuration*

> **Tip**   Should you configure the global primary and backup controllers for the APs but fail to set a primary, secondary, or tertiary controller for the individual APs, there is nothing to dictate what controller the APs will join should they not be able to join either of those two controllers. This can create havoc on the network because the APs could be bouncing between controllers for various reasons, different code versions, different configurations, and so on, and it may take some time for the APs to settle in the event of a controller failure.

AP Load Balancing

As mentioned earlier, unless you specify what controllers you want your APs to be registered to, the APs will join the least loaded controller in the mobility group. If, for example, you have two controllers, WLC1 and WLC2, on the network with no APs joined and you start adding APs, the first AP has an equal chance of joining either controller. If it happens to join WLC1, the next AP should join WLC2. Then the third AP should join WLC1, and so on until all the APs have joined a controller and the distribution of APs between the two controllers should be roughly 50-50.

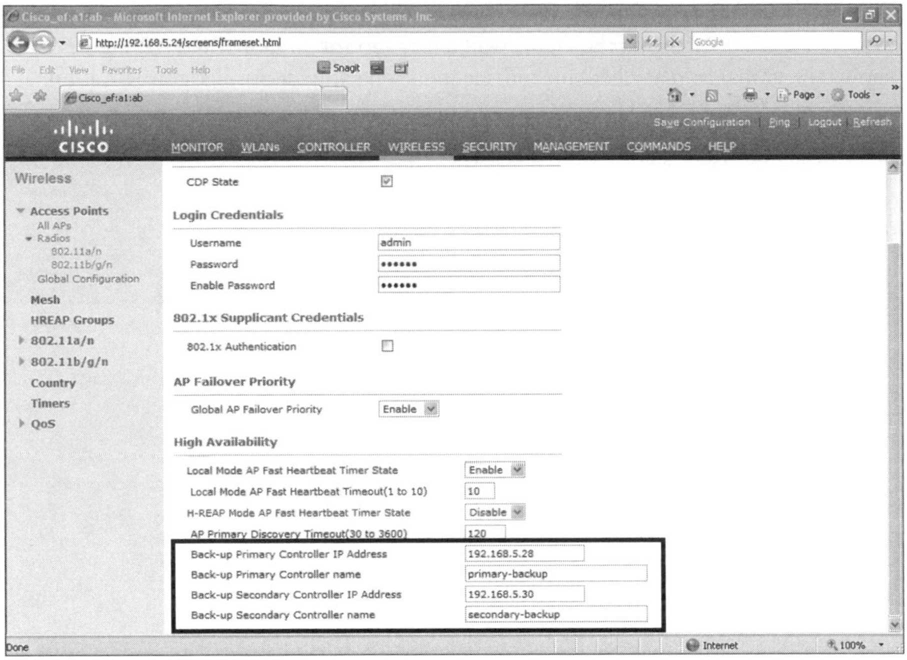

Figure 9-22   *Global Backup Controller Configuration*

If you configured the APs with primary, secondary, and tertiary controllers, the APs should always try to join the primary controller first. This way, you can dictate which APs are joined to which controller in the ratio you decide. You might want to have all the APs on a single controller and have the second controller purely as a backup in the event of a failure. This type of configuration is referred to as an N+1. If you have some APs on one controller and some on another and each controller is the backup for the other, this is known as an N+N. Lastly, you could have an N+N+1 configuration in which two controllers back up each other and the third controller serves as the backup for the first two.

AP Failover

After the primary controller that an AP is joined to fails, or the AP loses communication, the AP should move to the configured secondary, tertiary global backup, or if neither is configured, any controller in the mobility group that will accept it.

When an AP moves off the primary controller, it joins another controller and stays registered to that controller until the primary controller comes back online. The AP continues to send primary discovery requests every 30 seconds to the configured primary controller. In newer codes, you can configure the primary discovery interval between 30 and 3600 seconds. Figure 9-23 is a packet showing the primary discovery requests from an AP that is joined to its secondary controller running 4.2 code.

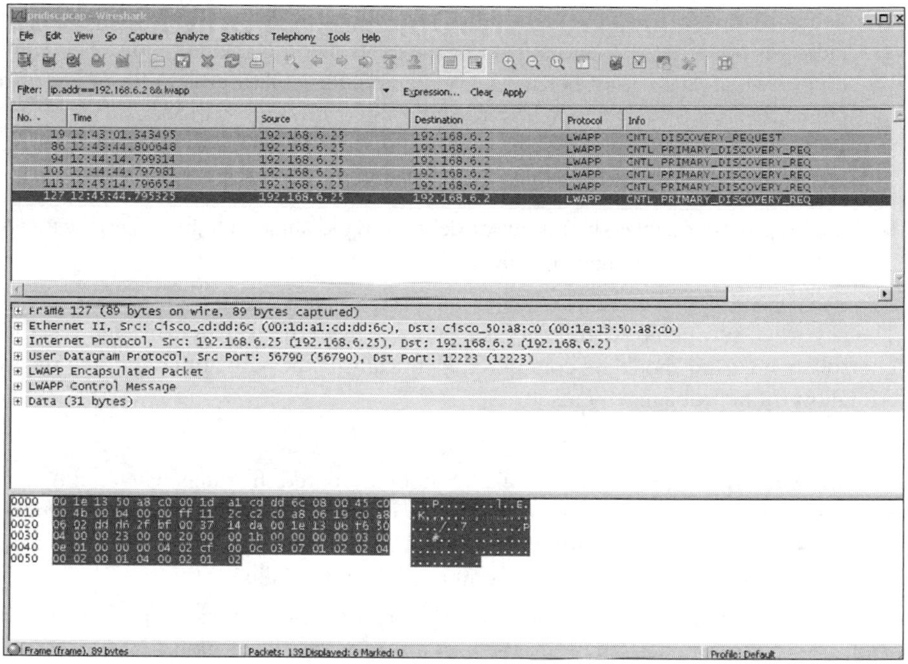

Figure 9-23 *LWAPP Primary Discovery Requests*

As soon as the primary controller responds, the AP tries to rejoin it. During the join process to the primary controller, the AP disconnects from the secondary controller. Should the primary controller not be able to accept the AP, the AP rejoins the secondary (if it can) and the cycle repeats. In this scenario, you now have a flapping AP on the network.

Troubleshooting AP Mobility

If the controller fails and the APs do not move to the controllers you expect, you can use several tools to determine the root cause.

The best debugs you can run on the controllers are the same debugs you can use to troubleshoot initial AP join problems:

■ **debug {lwapp/capwap} events enable:** The output from **debug {lwapp/capwap} events** tells you if the APs are talking to the controllers you expect them to and sending join requests. If you see no output from this, the AP is not talking to the controller. If you see discoveries but no joins, you might have a duplicate IP address for the AP-Manager interface on the secondary controller or a firewall or ACL might be blocking UDP port 12223/5246.

■ **debug {lwapp/capwap packet} enable:** The output of **debug {lwapp/capwap} packet** indicates how the AP found out about the controller it is trying to join. This can be crucial when APs are not behaving as expected. Possibilities might be an out-of-date Domain Name System (DNS) host record for cisco-lwapp-controller, an incorrect DHCP option 43, or over-the-air provisioning (OTAP) messages from other APs informing your APs of controllers you never intended.

■ **debug pm pki enable:** The output of **debug pm pki** shines a light on certificate issue, between the APs and the controllers.

The key when setting up AP mobility is that, aside from the system name and IPs, the controllers involved should be configured identically. If they are not configured the same, AP failover/join problems can result.

> **Tip**   If the 802.11g mode on the controllers is not configured the same, when the APs move between them, they have to reboot to either enable or disable the 802.11g radio. If your high availability is not configured correctly, the APs can bounce around the network and may take some time to settle in the event of a controller failure.
>
> For example, if you only have the global backup server configured on a controller and that controller fails, the APs try to move to the backup controller. If the global backup server has 802.11g enabled while the original controller has it disabled, the APs reboot to change that setting. If the APs do not have a primary, secondary, or tertiary controller set, the APs might try to join any controller on the network after that reboot.

If the LWAPP/CAPWAP debugs do not help you determine the root cause of the issue, you need to get wired packet captures to tell what is taking place on the network and if the packets from the AP are making it to the controller or being sent to the correct device.

If you have console access to one of the APs that is not moving between controllers as expected, you can get some valuable information there as well. The higher the code running on the AP, the more informative the console output will be.

Another common issue is that the APs move to the backup or secondary controller and then do not move back to the configured primary controller when that controller is back on the network. When this happens, ensure that AP fallback is enabled under **CONTROLLER > General**. If that setting is disabled, the APs remain on the backup controller until you manually reboot them.

AP fallback is enabled by default on the controllers and can be verified in the controller GUI under **CONTROLLER > General > AP Fallback**. Figure 9-24 shows AP fallback enabled on the controller.

Always double-check your AP Policies under **SECURITY > AAA > AP Policies** on the controller you expect the APs to move to in the event of a primary controller failure. A configuration discrepancy here can cause frustrating AP join issues because these settings affect AP trying to join the controller.

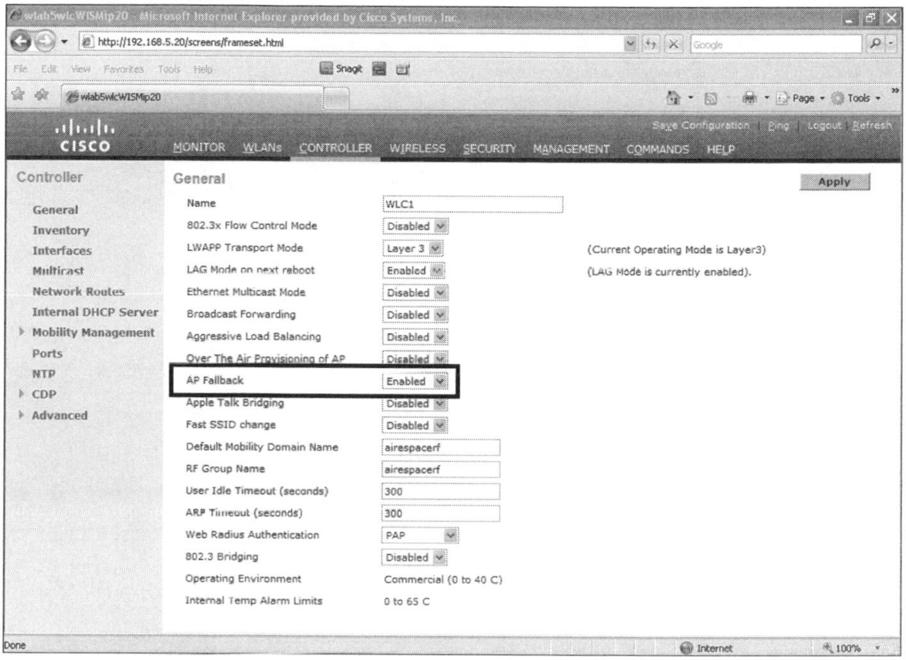

Figure 9-24 *AP Fallback*

If, for example, you have Authorize APs Against AAA disabled, but it becomes enabled, the existing APs joined to the controller will be fine, but any new APs that try to join will be rejected unless the configured RADIUS server has an entry for that AP. Another example is if the APs happen to be converted from autonomous and have self-signed certificates (SSCs). In this case the secondary or backup controller must have the SSCs and MAC address of the APs listed, as well as Accept SSCs enabled, for the APs to join.

Summary

Controller mobility allows for seamless roaming of a wireless client between APs joined to a single controller or APs joined to separate controllers. Seamless client roaming is possible because the controller serves as a centralized authenticator and services all configured WLANs regardless of the AP broadcast domain. Added controllers to mobility groups facilitate seamless roaming between APs that are joined to different controllers. The benefits of mobility are only realized when coverage is overlapping between the APs on the different controllers. As the controller code has advanced, so has the mobility feature set. Controller code Release 4.1 introduced symmetric mobility tunneling and auto-anchor N+1 redundancy/mobility failover using eping and mping to determine if a mobility member was down. Code Release 4.2 added NAT mobility support, whereas Release 5.0 introduced mobility multicast messaging. Code Release 5.1 added support for seamless inter-mobility group roaming. Starting in code Release 5.2, auto-anchoring is supported with controllers running 4.2 and higher code (for example 4.2 to 6.0). In all, controller mobility allows for a fast and secure wireless roaming experience for the user.

Chapter 10

Troubleshooting Client-Related Issues

Wireless client vendors are numerous. Each vendor interprets and implements the wireless fidelity (Wi-Fi) standards differently. As long as the standards are adhered to, however, different client vendor wireless clients should be able to associate and authenticate to the wireless infrastructure of any other vendor. With this in mind, you might notice that some clients work better than others. You can also have situations in which two clients using the same model of wireless adapter behave differently.

When a client issue occurs, the first thing you should do is gather as much information about the problem as you can. You need to know if the problem is every type of wireless client in the network or if it is isolated to a particular type of client such as a handheld scanner, personal desktop assistant (PDA), tablet PC, or a particular brand of laptop. If a single device has a problem, it might just be that one device is defective and your wireless network is fine. Another key piece of information is determining if the problem is widespread, if it happens only in certain areas of a building, or at certain times of the day. Knowing this information can help you narrow down the root cause because the issue might not have anything to do with the client, controller, or access point (AP). It might simply be that a piece of equipment in that area turns on and causes a lot of non-802.11 interference and the wireless clients suffer.

This chapter discusses general client information, client associations, debugs on the client, use of wireless and wired sniffer traces, local AP debugs, and interpretation of the output of **debug client** on the controller command-line interface (CLI).

General Client Information

When troubleshooting client-related issues, it is important to know what type of wireless adapter is installed in the client device. You need to know the vendor, model, driver version, supplicant (the software that controls the wireless connection), and feature sets available for that card. All this information plays a major role in how the client card functions.

Client adapters can be out of date. If the particular card is old enough, the vendor might not even support it anymore. It is important to know if the client device is using the latest, or in some cases the last, firmware drivers. Older firmware might have bugs that prevent the card from performing certain functions correctly or have other limitations that the latest driver release resolves. New drivers might also enhance roaming behavior. According to the 802.11 standard, roaming is purely a client decision. The client decides with which AP it will try to associate. Whenever you have a client issue, check the driver date and see if the vendor has a newer release. You might have a client running drivers released five or six years ago. By simply upgrading the firmware for the client card, you could resolve your issue.

The capability and hardware limitations of the client adapter are important. Is the adapter 802.11b, 802.11g, 802.11a, or 802.11n capable? First-generation wireless cards have several limitations in modern wireless networks. When these cards were released, only 802.11b-capable wireless networks existed and used simplistic (by today's standards) wireless encryption methods such as Wired Equivalent Privacy (WEP). As wireless security has progressed, wireless protocols and encryption methods have become more robust. There is Wireless Protected Access (WPA) using Temporal Key Integrity Protocol (TKIP) encryption and WPA2 with Advanced Encryption Standard (AES) encryption. A client adapter that can use TKIP might not be able to use AES because AES requires certain hardware. Most modern wireless cards do support AES, so this is only an example.

You also need to know the capability of the client supplicant that controls the wireless connection. Examples of supplicants include Intel PROSet, Lenovo (IBM) ThinkVantage, Cisco Aironet Desktop Utility (ADU), Cisco Secure Services Client (CSSC), and Microsoft (MS) Windows Wireless Zero Configuration (WZC). Older or out-of-date supplicants might not support the more advanced security methods. The supplicant might support WPA but not WPA2 or the security method you want to use. You might want to use more advanced Enterprise security that incorporates 802.1x and various Extensible Authentication Protocol (EAP) methods, such as Protected Extensible Authentication Protocol (PEAP) or Extensible Authentication Protocol-Transport Layer Security (EAP-TLS). The supplicant might also have a known bug such as the one with WZC and PEAP on Windows XP Service Pack (SP) 2 clients outlined in MS knowledge base article KB885453. You need to install the provided hotfix or SP3 to resolve that client issue.

The key point from all of this is that you must know if the client adapter and supplicant are capable of performing the action you want it to do.

Client Association Packet Flow

When a wireless client and an AP communicate, they exchange several wireless frames. Wireless frames come in three main categories:

- **Management frames:** Used to manage the wireless connection between the AP and the client device. Table 10-1 describes the different types of management frames.

- **Control frames:** Acknowledgements, Request to Send (RTS), Clear to Send (CTS), Power Save.

- **Data frames:** Contain data.

For the purpose of troubleshooting wireless client issues (the majority of the time), the problem lies somewhere in the management frames. Naturally, you can have issues such as missed acknowledgments (ACKs) or dropped packets with control and data frames, and you need to be aware of that, but the focus here is on the management frames.

Table 10-1 *Wireless Management Frames*

Management Frame	Description
Beacon	Sent by the AP on a specified interval. Provides WLAN information such as SSID, supported data rates, and security parameters.
Probe request	Active client searching for a particular SSID. Can also be a generic probe request (not specifying a SSID[1]) just to see who is out there.
Probe response	Sent by the AP in response to a client probe request. Contains similar information to the beacon.
Authentication request	Sent by the client when it wants to authenticate to a WLAN[2].
Authentication response	Sent by the AP in response to a client authentication request.
Association request	After authentication, sent by a client to associate to the WLAN.
Association response	Sent by the AP in response to a client association request.
Reassociation request	Used when the client is roaming within the same ESS[3].
Reassociation response	Sent by AP in response to a client reassociation request.
Deauthentication	Sent by either the AP or the client to terminate an authentication relationship.
Disassociation	Sent by either the AP or the client to terminate an association relationship.
Announcement traffic indication message (ATIM)	Seen in IBSS[4] wireless networks because no central AP exists to buffer data.

[1]SSID = service set identifier

[2]WLAN = wireless LAN

[3]ESS = Extended Service Set

[4]IBSS = Independent Basic Service Set

A wireless client can be either passive or active scanning. A passive wireless client waits and listens for beacons, which are sent out periodically from an AP. The client does this to determine if it can connect to the service set identifier (SSID) serviced by that AP. An active client knows what SSID it wants to connect to based on the configured wireless profile. It can also send a generic probe request to see what APs are there and what networks they are advertising.

During a successful connection, the wireless client and AP exchange the frames as shown in Figure 10-1. In this example, the client with MAC address 00:40:96:A1:4A:F6 is connecting to a WPA2-PSK WLAN. When you are analyzing a wireless packet capture, this process is what you will be looking into. You will want to know if a step is missing or where it stops and why.

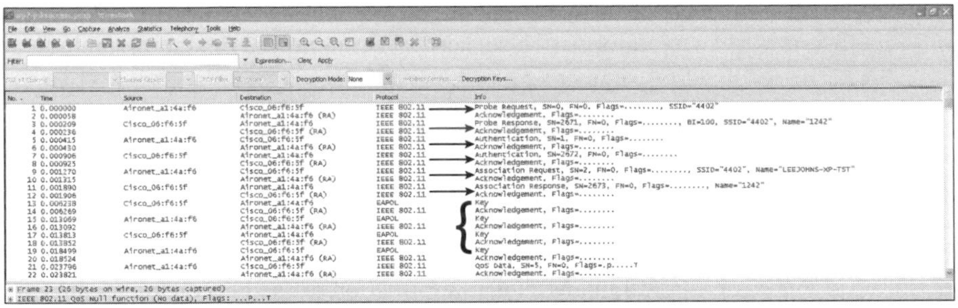

Figure 10-1 *Wireless Management Frame Exchange*

In Figure 10-1, the following occurs:

Step 1.   The actively scanning client sends a probe request, Packet 1, saying it wants to connect to a particular SSID called 4402.

Step 2.   Upon receiving a probe request, the AP in turn sends a probe response seen in Packet 3. The main difference between a beacon and probe response from the AP is that the AP sends a probe response only after receiving a probe request from a potential client device. Pay attention to things like the SSID name and whether it is correct, supported data rates, which of those rates are mandatory on both the client and AP, and whether they match.

Step 3.   After the beacon and probe process, the client knows the capabilities of the AP/SSID and can try to connect by sending an authentication request as seen in Packet 5.

Step 4.   The AP responds with an authentication response seen in Packet 7. What you are looking for is whether an authentication response exists and, if so, whether and why it is successful or not.

Step 5.   When the client has successfully completed authentication, it sends an association request as seen in Packet 9.

Step 6.   The AP responds, Packet 12, with an association response.

Step 7.   After the association response, if any keys need to be exchanged (Packets 13, 15, 17, 19), that takes place as well.

Step 8.   After all of that completes successfully, the client is fully associated to the WLAN.

A client sends reassociation requests when it roams between APs in the same ESS. The AP replies with a reassociation response. Depending on the type of authentication method in use, the client might not have to go through a full reauthentication process. An example is if Cisco Centralized Key Management (CCKM) was used for key management. On this same topic, if you are seeing full 802.1x authentications, keep in mind that the controller supports only opportunistic Pairwise Master Key ID (PMKID) caching; if the client is using sticky PMKID caching, you will always see a full authentication when a client roams between APs. See Chapter 9, "Mobility," for more information on PMKID caching.

The AP or the client can send deauthentication and disassociation frames to terminate the wireless connection. Either frame contains a reason code indicating why the connection was terminated. Table 10-2 lists the 802.11 reason codes and explanations.

Table 10-2   *802.11 Reason Codes*

Reason Code	Explanation
0	Reserved
1	Unspecified reason
2	Previous authentication no longer valid
3	Deauthenticated because sending station is leaving (or has left) IBSS or ESS
4	Disassociated due to inactivity
5	Disassociated because the AP is unable to handle all currently associated stations
6	Class 2 frame received from nonauthenticated station
7	Class 3 frame received from nonassociated station
8	Disassociated because sending station is leaving (or has left) IBSS
9	Station requesting (re)association is not authenticated with responding station

Other reason codes exist for 802.11i and 802.11h and can be found on the Internet.

Figure 10-2 and Figure 10-3 show some of the management frame interactions for clients failing to successfully connect to a wireless network.

Figure 10-2 shows a failed association attempt by the client using a static WEP key.

In this case, the client has the correct SSID and supported data rates, but the client is trying to connect using WEP encryption instead of WPA2, which is configured on the WLAN. The association response from the AP shows that the association failed.

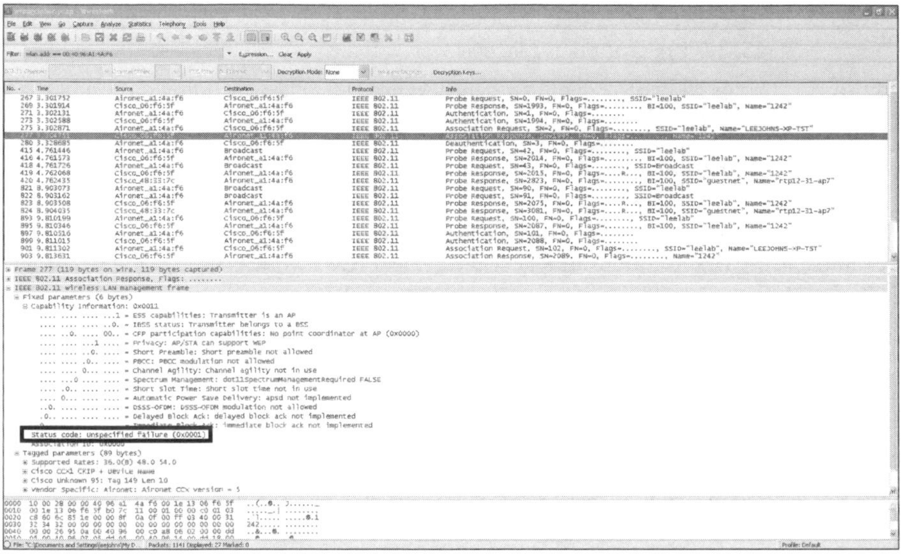

Figure 10-2   *Authentication Request and Response with Incorrect Encryption*

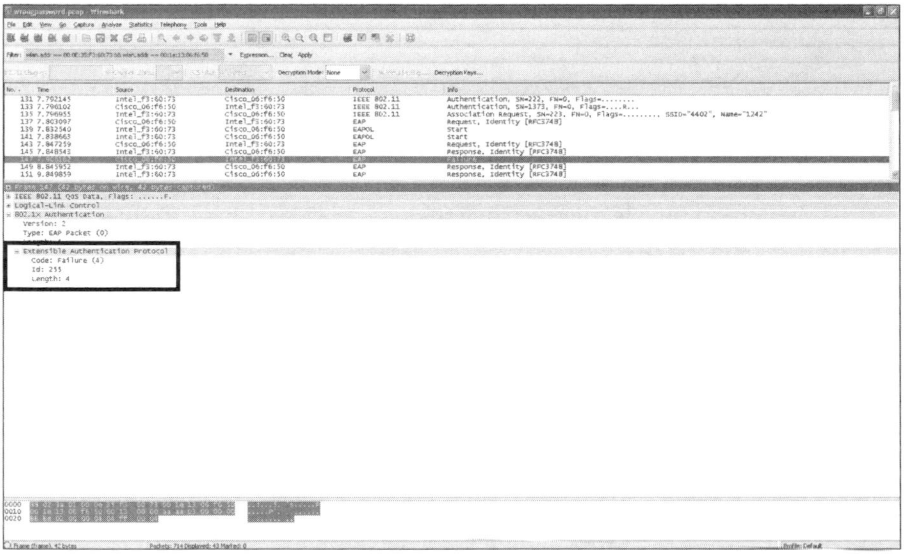

Figure 10-3   *Authentication Request and Response with Incorrect Password*

In the exchange shown in Figure 10-3, the client is using 802.1x for key management and PEAP authentication.

In this case, everything between the client and the AP is correct, but the client fails to authenticate because the client password is incorrect and the controller received an Access-Reject from the RADIUS server so you see an EAP failure in the trace.

Note   It is important to understand that when using EAP authentications methods, unless you are using local EAP on the controller, the controller itself is the authenticator. The RADIUS server is the authentication server, and the client is the supplicant. The authenticator simply passes RADIUS packets between the supplicant and authentication server. If you were having problems authenticating with PEAP, for example, and using Cisco ACS for the RADIUS server, you might see failed authentication attempts in the ACS logs, such as "EAP-TLS or PEAP authentication failed during SSL handshake." This has nothing to do with the wireless controller; rather, it indicates a missing or expired certificate on the RADIUS server.

Client Utilities and Logging

Most wireless client adapter software comes with some form of troubleshooting utility or logging feature. The robustness of the troubleshooting utility can vary greatly. You might only be able to mouse over the wireless connection icon to see if the client is connected, determine what the IP address is, and observe the signal strength, or there may be special troubleshooting options. Figure 10-4 shows the two troubleshooting tools available with the Intel PROSet Wireless software.

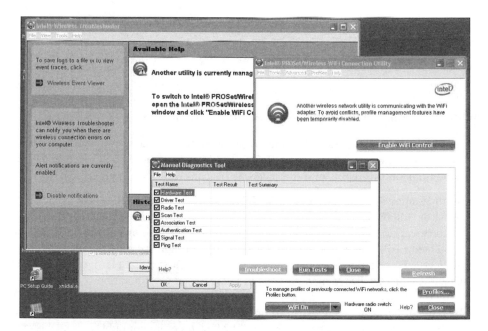

Figure 10-4   *Intel PROSet Troubleshooting Tools*

You can use the client tools to determine if the client has a misconfiguration or authentication issue or if it is trying to connect to a network that you did not intend.

For Cisco client adapters, such as the CB21AG or PI21AG, and supplicant software, such as the ADU, you can click the Diagnostics tab to see Adapter Information and Advanced Statistics, and you can run Client and Network tests. Figure 10-5 shows the ADU diagnostic window with the Advanced Statistics page.

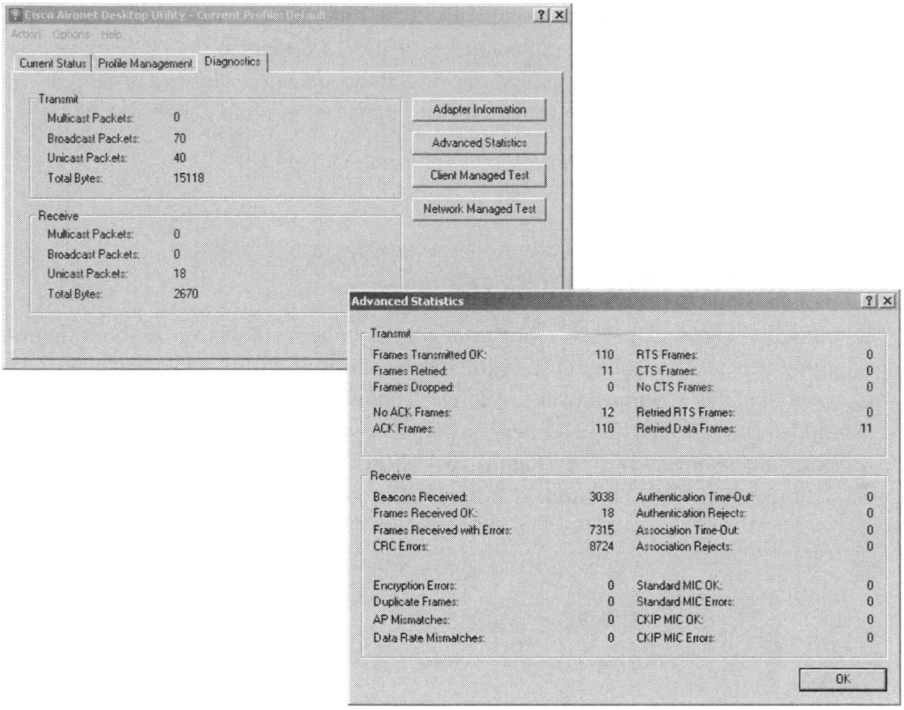

Figure 10-5   *Cisco ADU Diagnostics and Advanced Statistics*

As you can see from Figure 10-5, the Advanced Statistics page shows you Transmit and Receive statistics. Here you can see if the client has experienced association or authentication timeouts or rejects or if it is receiving beacons, CRC errors, and so on.

With Windows Vista, you can use the Windows Event Log Server to generate logs when using the following EAP methods: Cisco's Lightweight EAP (LEAP), Extensible Authentication Protocol-Flexible Authentication via Secure Tunneling (EAP-FAST), or Protected EAP-Generic Token Card (PEAP-GTC). For more information on using the Windows Event Logs for debugging, see the "Cisco Aironet 802.11a/b/g Wireless LAN Client Adapters (CB21AG and PI21AG) Installation and Configuration Guide for Windows Vista" at Cisco.com. It is also possible to enable low-level debugs for the CB21 by editing the Windows registry. Editing the registry can be dangerous, and the edits to enable the low-level client debugs for the CB21 adapters are not publicly available.

The latest client supplicant for Cisco is the Secure Service Client (SSC). Unlike the ADU software, SSC is vendor card independent and can be used with any wireless or wired adapter. You can use SSC to view the current connection status of your wireless connection. The connection status window, as shown in Figure 10-6, shows you the connections settings, security settings, and wireless settings for the connection.

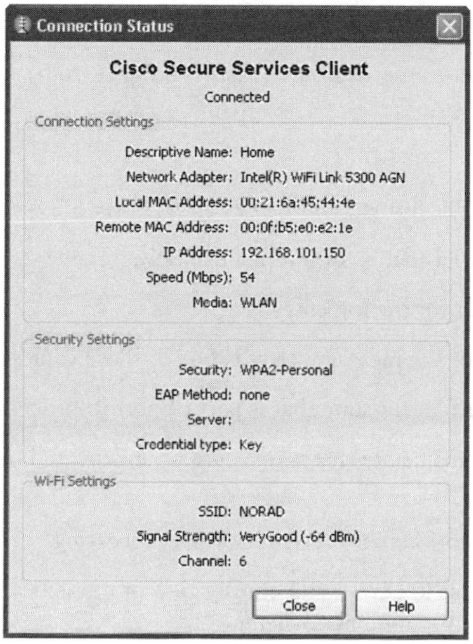

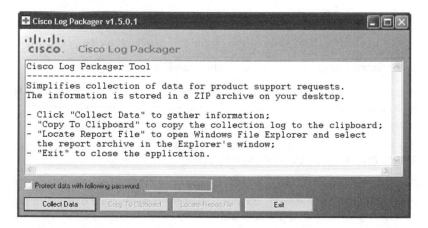

Figure 10-6   *SSC Connection Status Window*

The SCC includes the diagnostic utility called Log Packager. Figure 10-7 shows the Log Packager window.

Figure 10-7   *Log Packager*

The utility provides the current SSC status, interface and driver details, *Federal Information Processing Standards* (FIPS) status, and WLAN information (SSIDs detected, association status, and so on).

Every log entry has the following format:

```
<date & time> [process] <log Message id> <log message class> <context IDs>
<grammatical log message>
```

where:

- <date & time> is the date and time in this format: *mm/dd/yyyy HH:mm:SS.sss*

- [process] is the internal process identifier that is for internal use only.

- <log message id> is the unique number for the log entry.

- <log message class> is the class type of log message; class is one of these values:

  I: Informational. This value indicates a client state that is part of normal processing.

  W: Warning. This value indicates a client state that is insecure or unexpected but still allows processing.

  E: Error. This value indicates an exception that prevents normal processing.

- <context IDs> define the context of this log event and convey zero or more identifiers in this format: <code><unique string/number>, where:

  <code> is a two-letter code that indicates the class of the term:

  AD: Adapter identifier. The adapter MAC address in hexadecimal.

  AC: Access identifier. The MAC basic service set identifier (BSSID) for the access device.

  MT: Media type. Either Ethernet or Wi-Fi.

  CN: Connection identifier. An integer that identifies the connection.

  PR: Profile identifier. The name of the profile truncated to 16 characters.

  <unique string/number> is a string or number that is guaranteed to be unique.

- <grammatical log message> is a sentence that describes the event. The log message might contain a value (<value>) that is a placeholder for a variable to be placed in the message.

AP Debugs and Show Commands

Although you usually run debug and show commands from the wireless controller CLI, in some instances running these directly on the AP that the client is associating with is necessary. There might actually be a problem with the AP radio; perhaps it stops beaconing as addressed by Cisco bug ID CSCsr09415. In this case, the controller showed no signs of a problem with the AP radio. After issuing a **show controller** on the AP, however, it became clear that the AP had stopped beacons and probes even though the radio was up.

Another example of when you might need to run debugs directly on the AP is if you are troubleshooting a client problem with an H-REAP mode AP that is in standalone mode. H-REAP is covered in Chapter 13, "H-REAP."

You can access the AP CLI in a few different ways:

■ Use the AP console if feasible.

■ Enable debugging on the AP from the controller CLI using **debug ap enable** *<AP_Name>*. After debugging is enabled on the AP, you can run standard autonomous AP commands on the AP from the controller CLI using **debug ap command** "*<command>*" *<AP_Name>*. Enabling AP debugging and then performing a **show controllers** is shown in Example 10-1.

■ Enable remote telnet on the AP from the controller CLI using **config ap telnet enable** *AP_name*. After turning on Telnet, you can session to the AP via its IP and run the necessary debugs. The **debug dot11** options are shown in Example 10-2.

Example 10-1   *show controller Command Output*

```
(Cisco Controller) >debug ap enable 1242
(Cisco Controller) >debug ap command "show controllers" 1242
(Cisco Controller) >Mon Aug 17 14:39:50 2009: 1242:
Mon Aug 17 14:39:50 2009: 1242: !
Mon Aug 17 14:39:50 2009: 1242: interface Dot11Radio0
Mon Aug 17 14:39:50 2009: 1242: Radio AIR-AP1242GA, Base Address 001e.1306.f650,
BBlock version 0.00, Software version 6.20.11
Mon Aug 17 14:39:50 2009: 1242: Serial number: GAM11403917
Mon Aug 17 14:39:50 2009: 1242: Number of supported simultaneous BSSID on
Dot11Radio0: 16
Mon Aug 17 14:39:50 2009: 1242: Carrier Set: Americas (US) (-A)
Mon Aug 17 14:39:50 2009: 1242: Uniform Spreading Required: No
Mon Aug 17 14:39:50 2009: 1242: Configured Frequency: 2437 MHz   Channel 6
Mon Aug 17 14:39:50 2009: 1242: Allowed Frequencies: 2412(1) 2417(2) 2422(3)
2427(4) 2432(5) 2437(6) 2442(7) 2447(8) 2452(9) 2457(10) 2462(11)
Mon Aug 17 14:39:50 2009: 1242: Listen Frequencies: 2412(1) 2417(2) 2422(3)
2427(4) 2432(5) 2437(6) 2442(7) 2447(8) 2452(9) 2457(10) 2462(11) 2467(12)
2472(13) 2484(14)
Mon Aug 17 14:39:50 2009: 1242: Beacon Flags: 0; Beacons are disabled; Probes
are disabled
!the rest of the output is omitted for brevity
```

The output of **show controllers** in Example 10-1 allows you to see information such as the base radio MAC address, the regulatory domain, the current channel, and whether beacons and probes are enabled. In this case the 802.11b/g network on the controller is disabled so the beacons and probes on the b/g radio on the AP are disabled.

Example 10-2   *Local AP Debugs*

```
Switch#192.168.6.55
Trying 192.168.6.55 ... Open
User Access Verification
Password:
1242>en
Password:
1242#debug dot11 ?
  Dot11Radio         IEEE 802.11 WLAN
  aaa                Authentication, Authorization, and Accounting
  amacdbg            AMAC Debugger Server
  arp-cache          ARP Cache
  cac                Admission Control
  drv-intf           dot11 driver interface
  events             IEEE 802.11 events
  forwarding         802.11 AP forwarding
  ip                 IP Protocols
  l2roam             L2Roam E2E
  lbs                802.11 Location Based Management
  leap-dot1x         802.1X LEAP debugging
  mfp                Management Frame Protection
  mgmt               802.11 Management
  network-map        Network Map
  packets            IEEE 802.11 packets
  policing           Traffic policing
  rx-filter          802.11 driver rx filter
  rxprobe            RX Probe Debug
  station            Debug station connection failures
  supp-sm-dot1x      802.1X supplicant state machine debugging
  syslog             Turn Off Dot11 syslog msgs
  tsm                Traffic Stream Metrics
  virtual-interface  802.11 virtual interface
  wpa-cckm-km-dot1x  WPA/WPA-PSK/CCKM supplicant key management debugging
```

Note   Remember to use **term mon** when running debugs on the AP from a Telnet session.

You can use these commands to debug radio management on the AP, local client authentication issues when in H-REAP standalone mode, client connection failures, and so on. For more information on the individual debugs, see Appendix A, "Debugging Commands."

> **Note**   Remember to turn off debugging on the AP when you are finished using **undebug all**.

Wireless and Wired Sniffer Traces

Wired sniffer traces are usually pretty easy to obtain and can provide you with a wealth of information when troubleshooting a client-related issue. You can configure a monitor session for the switch port of an AP or the port-channel to the controller. A wired capture shows you if the client traffic is leaving the AP, going through the LWAPP/CAPWAP tunnel of the controller, or if the controller properly decapsulates the packet and then properly bridges it to the switched network. In turn, you verify that the return traffic is flowing as expected. You might need to SPAN the AP switch port or the port-channel for the controller or both. Despite all the information you can get from a wired packet capture, with the clients being wireless, it does not capture the entire story.

As discussed earlier in the "Client Association Packet Flow" section of this chapter, you might have to get a wireless sniffer trace to determine what is taking place in the air between the AP and the client when a problem occurs. You need to analyze the packet exchange and determine if there is a problem with the beacons, probes, authentication, association, and so on. If the problem occurs while roaming, you need to perform concurrent wireless traces on two or more channels as the client moves between APs. Also keep in mind that you want to run the wireless sniffer from a device that is not the problem device. If the client has an issue, running the sniffer from the problem client might mask the root cause. If the device is a phone or PDA, you cannot run a sniffer program on it anyway. By using a separate device, you know if the AP or client ignored an ACK, failed to send a packet, or just stopped responding.

Applications might run slowly, time out, fail to connect to a server or, if you are using wireless voice, suffer in terms of call quality. If a wireless client authenticates and associates fine but then has problems accessing the Internet, using email, or failing in terms of multicast applications, you might not be able to conclusively determine where the problem lies from a wired or wireless sniffer capture alone. For example, if a wireless client is not receiving expected traffic from the wired network, was the missing data lost at the controller, dropped by the AP, or never sent from the source device in the first place? In these situations, you have to get concurrent wired and wireless sniffer captures to determine where in the network path the problem exists.

If the situation arises when you need to get concurrent wireless and wired captures (as well as concurrent debugs from the controller CLI), time is of the essence. Every device that is used to gather information needs to be time synced. Ideally, every device will be using the same Network Time Protocol (NTP) server. If the concurrent captures are not time synced, it might be impossible to correlate the wireless to wired packets and determine where the problem lies.

Besides the packet times, you can use packet sequence numbers to help sync up the captures. If you know exactly what you are looking for, such as the start of an HTTP session, you can find that instance in one trace and then find the same instance in the other trace. Then if there happens to be a time offset, you might still be able to follow the packets from one trace to the other.

Debug Client

The command **debug client** *mac_address* is a macro that enables nine debug commands, plus a filter on the MAC address provided, so only messages that contain the specified MAC address are shown. The nine debug commands show the most important details on client association and authentication. The filter helps when multiple wireless clients are present. Examples include situations such as when too much output is generated or the controller CLI is overloaded when debugging is enabled without the filter.

The information collected covers important details about client association and authentication (with two exceptions mentioned later in this chapter). Make sure to run these debugs via a Telnet or Secure Shell (SSH) session over a fast network link to the CLI of the controller. Even with a serial connection baud rate of 115K, the output might come too quickly and overflow the console buffer. It is good practice to log the terminal session to a file using Putty or some other terminal program that allows you to log your sessions. Doing so makes it easy to go back and analyze the debug output.

The commands that are enabled are shown in Example 10-3.

Example 10-3   *show debug Command Output*

```
(Cisco Controller) >show debug

MAC address ............................. 00:21:6A:45:44:4E00:21:6A:45:44:4E

Debug Flags Enabled:
  dhcp packet enabled.
  dot11 mobile enabled.
  dot11 state enabled.
  dot1x events enabled.
  dot1x states enabled.
  pem events enabled.
  pem state enabled.
CCKM client debug enabled
```

These commands cover the 802.11 client state machine, 802.1x authentication, policy enforcement module (PEM), and address negotiation (Dynamic Host Configuration Protocol, or DHCP).

> **Note**   CCKM client debug was added to debug client in code Release 5.0. In 4.2 and lower code releases, debug client will only enable the original eight debugs.

Debug Client Variations

For most scenarios, the **debug client** *mac_address* command is enough to get the needed information. However, the following are two important situations in which additional debugging is needed:

■ Mobility (client roaming between controllers)

■ EAP Authentication Troubleshooting

Mobility

In this situation, mobility debugs need to be enabled after the **debug client** *mac_address* command has been introduced to gain additional information on the mobility protocol interaction between controllers.

> **Note**   Mobility debugging is covered in depth in Chapter 9.

To enable mobility debugs, use **debug client** *mac_address*, and then use the **debug mobility handoff enable** command, as shown in Example 10-4.

Example 10-4   *show debug with Mobility debug Command Output*

```
(Cisco Controller) >debug client 00:21:6A:45:44:4E00:21:6A:45:44:4E
 (Cisco Controller) >debug mobility handoff enable

(Cisco Controller) >show debug

MAC address ............................... 00:21:6A:45:44:4E00:21:6A:45:44:4E

Debug Flags Enabled:
  dhcp packet enabled.
  dot11 mobile enabled.
  dot11 state enabled
  dot1x events enabled.
  dot1x states enabled.
  mobility handoff enabled.
  pem events enabled.
  pem state enabled.
```

Authentication, Authorization, and Accounting (AAA) Troubleshooting

To troubleshoot the interaction between the controller and the authentication server (external RADIUS or internal EAP server), use the command **debug aaa all enable**, which shows the required details. This command should be used after the **debug client** *mac_address* command and can be combined with other debug commands as needed (for example, **debug mobility handoff enable**). See Example 10-5.

Example 10-5   *show debug with AAA debug Command Output*

```
(Cisco Controller) >debug client 00:21:6A:45:44:4E00:21:6A:45:44:4E
(Cisco Controller) >debug aaa all enable
(Cisco Controller) >show debug
MAC address ............................. 00:21:6A:45:44:4E00:21:6A:45:44:4E
Debug Flags Enabled:
  aaa detail enabled.
  aaa events enabled.
  aaa packet enabled.
  aaa packet enabled.
  aaa ldap enabled.
  aaa local-auth db enabled.
  aaa local-auth eap framework errors enabled.
  aaa local-auth eap framework events enabled.
  aaa local-auth eap framework packets enabled.
  aaa local-auth eap framework state machine enabled.
  aaa local-auth eap method errors enabled.
  aaa local-auth eap method events enabled.
  aaa local-auth eap method packets enabled.
  aaa local-auth eap method state machine enabled.
  aaa local-auth shim enabled.
  aaa tacacs enabled.
  dhcp packet enabled.
  dot11 mobile enabled.
  dot11 state enabled
  dot1x events enabled
  dot1x states enabled.
  mobility handoff enabled.
  pem events enabled.
  pem state enabled.
```

> **Note**   Not all **AAA** debugs are filtered on the client address you specify with **debug client,** so the output can get quite verbose if the controller has many clients.

Client Connection

For the purposes of this chapter, client connection is the process for a wireless client to pass through these steps:

Step 1.   802.11 Section

Probing to find a valid AP to associate

802.11 authentication: Can be Open (null) or Shared. Normally, Open is selected.

Association: Requesting data services to the AP

Step 2.   L2 Policies Section

None; PSK or EAP authentication takes place depending on configuration.

Key negotiation, if an encryption method is selected

Step 3.   L3 Policies Section

Address learning

Web authentication, if selected

> **Note**   These steps represent a subset or summary of the full process. This example describes a simplified scenario that covers 802.11 and Layer 2 policies and uses WPA-PSK, plus address learning. No external AAA or Layer 3 policies for authentication are used.

Controller Processes

In each section, the controller uses separated processes to keep track of the state of the client at each moment. The processes interact between them to ensure that the client is added to the connection table (per the security policies configured). To help you understand the client connection steps to the controller, following is a short summary of the most relevant processes:

■   **PEM:** Controls the client state and forces it through each of the security policies on the WLAN configuration

■   **Access point functions (APF):** Basically, the 802.11 state machine

- **Dot1x:** Implements the state machine for 802.1x, PSK authentication, and key handling for the wireless clients

- **Mobility:** Tracks interaction with other controllers on the same mobility group

- **Data transformational (DTL):** Sits between the software components and the network hardware acceleration (NPU); controls the ARP information

The PEM, APF, and Dot1x processes are discussed in detail in the following sections. Mobility is covered in detail in Chapter 9 and will not be covered here. Discussion on DTL is outside the scope of this book.

PEM

Based on the WLAN configuration, the client passes through a series of steps. PEM ensures this is done for it to comply with the required Layer 2 and Layer 3 security policies.

Following is a subset of the PEM states relevant for the analysis of a client debug:

- **START:** Initial status for new client entry.

- **AUTHCHECK:** WLAN has an Layer 2 authentication policy to enforce.

- **8021X_REQD:** Client must complete 802.1x authentication.

- **L2AUTHCOMPLETE:** Client has successfully finished the Layer 2 policy. The process can now proceed to Layer 3 policies (address learning, web authentication, and so on). Controller sends the mobility announcement to learn Layer 3 information from other controllers if this is a roaming client in the same mobility group.

- **WEP_REQD:** Client must complete WEP authentication.

- **DHCP_REQD:** Controller needs to learn the Layer 3 address from the client. If static IP addresses are allowed, any IP packet, DHCP request or renew, or information learned from other controllers in the mobility group is used. If DHCP Required is marked on the WLAN, only DHCP or mobility information are used.

- **WEBAUTH_REQD:** Client must complete web authentication (Layer 3 policy).

- **RUN:** Client has successfully completed the required Layer 2 and Layer 3 policies and can now transmit traffic to the network.

Figure 10-8 shows a simplified PEM state machine with the client transitions until it reaches the RUN state. When in the RUN state, the client can now send traffic to the network.

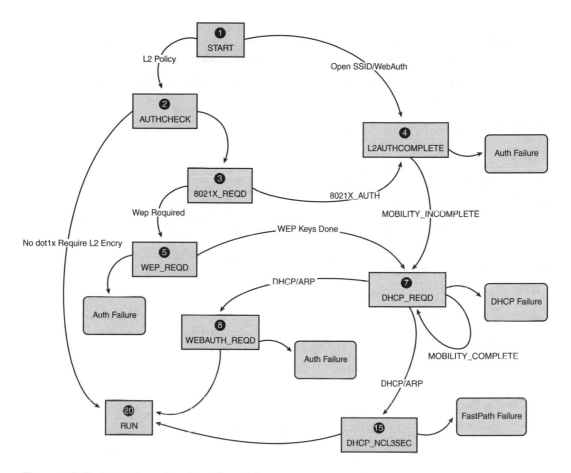

Figure 10-8   *PEM State Machine Transitions*

> **Note**   Figure 10-8 does not cover all possible transitions and states. Some intermediate steps have been removed for clarity.

Client Traffic Forwarding

Between the **START** state and the final **RUN** state, the client traffic is not forwarded to the network but is passed to the main CPU on the controller for analysis. The information that is forwarded depends on the state and the policies in place; for example, if 802.1x is enabled, EAP over LAN (EAPOL) traffic is forwarded to the CPU. If web authentication is used, HTTP and Domain Name System (DNS) are allowed to do the web redirection and obtain client authentication credentials. See Chapter 14, "Guest Networking," for more information on web authentication.

When the client reaches the **RUN** state, the client information is sent to the NPU to enable FastPath switching, which does line-rate forwarding of the user traffic to the client VLAN and frees the central CPU of user data forwarding tasks.

The traffic that is forwarded depends on the client type that is applied to the NPU. Table 10-3 describes the most relevant types.

Table 10-3   *Common Client Types*

Type	Description
1	Normal client traffic forwarding.
9	IP learning state. One packet from this client is sent to CPU to learn the IP address used.
2	ACL pass-through. Used when the WLAN has an ACL configured to inform the NPU of what client traffic should be allowed or denied.

APF

This process handles the state of the client through the 802.11 state machine and MAC address authentication via the AAA server. It also interacts with mobility code to validate the different roaming scenarios. This chapter does not cover the mobility details or its states.

Table 10-4 shows the more relevant client states that are entered during a client association to the controller.

Figure 10-9 represents a state machine transition and shows only the most relevant states and transitions.

Table 10-4 *Client States*

Name	Description
Idle	New client or temporary state on some situations.
AAA Pending	Client waiting for MAC address authentication.
Authenticated	Open authentication successful or intermediate state in some situations.
Associated	Association response from AP has been sent. 802.11 association is completed.
Disassociated	Client sent disassociation/deauthentication or association timer expired.
To Delete	Client marked to be deleted (normally after exclusion timer expired).
Probe	Probe request received for new client.
Excluded/Blacklisted	Client has been marked as excluded. Normally related to WPS policies.
Invalid	Error on client state.

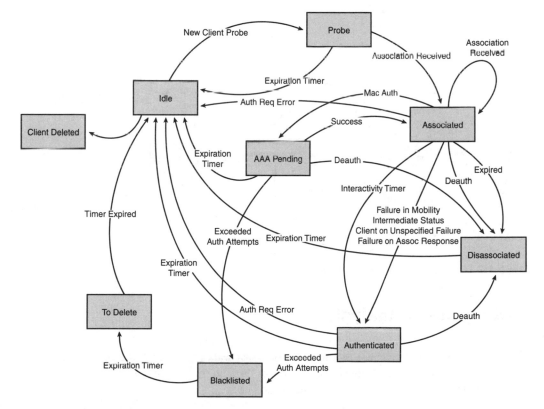

Figure 10-9 *Client States and Transitions*

802.1x Authentication (Dot1x)

The Dot1x process is responsible for 802.1x authentication and key management for the client. This means that, even on WLANs that do not have an EAP policy requiring 802.1x, Dot1x participates to handle the key creation and negotiation with the client and for the cached key handling (PMK or CCKM).

Figure 10-10 shows the full 802.1x transitions for the state machines.

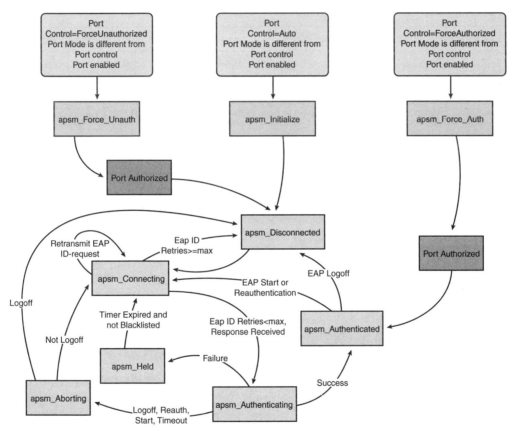

Figure 10-10 *State Machine 802.1x Transitions*

Debug Client Analysis

In order to help you understand the flow of the client debug output, Example 10-6 provides a sample **debug client** output with notes that walk you through the client process. Be sure to take notice of how the client moves through the various stages of the client state machine from Figure 10-10 on the controller.

Example 10-6 *debug client Analysis*

```
(Cisco Controller)>debug client 00:1b:77:42:07:69
APF Process
Wed Oct 31 10:46:13 2007: 00:1b:77:42:07:69 Adding mobile on LWAPP AP
    00:17:df:ab:76:f0(0)

!--- A new station is received. After validating type, it is added to the
!--- AP that received it. This can happen both on processing association
!--- request or probe requests. The client is Idle in the APF state machine shown.


Wed Oct 31 10:46:13 2007: 00:1b:77:42:07:69 Scheduling deletion of Mobile
    Station:  (callerId: 23) in 5 seconds

!--- Sets an expiration timer for this entry in case it does not progress
!--- beyond probe status. 5 Seconds corresponds to Probe Timeout. This message
!--- might appear with other time values because, during client processing,
!--- other functions might set different timeouts depending on state.


Wed Oct 31 10:46:13 2007: 00:1b:77:42:07:69 apfProcessProbeReq
    (apf_80211.c:4057) Changing state for mobile 00:1b:77:42:07:69 on AP
    00:17:df:ab:76:f0 from Idle to Probe

!--- APF state machine for the client is updated to Probe.


Wed Oct 31 10:46:13 2007: 00:1b:77:42:07:69 Scheduling deletion of Mobile
    Station:  (callerId: 24) in 5 seconds

!--- New Probe request update sent AP about client. IMPORTANT:
!--- APs do not forward all probe requests to the controller; they
!--- summarize per time interval (by default 500 msec). This information is
!--- used later by location and load-balancing processes.


Wed Oct 31 10:46:14 2007: 00:1b:77:42:07:69 Scheduling deletion of Mobile
    Station:  (callerId: 24) in 5 seconds

!--- New Probe request update sent AP about client.


Wed Oct 31 10:46:14 2007: 00:1b:77:42:07:69 Scheduling deletion of Mobile
    Station:  (callerId: 24) in 5 seconds
```

(continues)

Example 10-6   *debug client Analysis (continued)*

```
!--- New Probe request update sent AP about client.


Wed Oct 31 10:46:15 2007: 00:1b:77:42:07:69 Scheduling deletion of Mobile
    Station:  (callerId: 24) in 5 seconds

!--- New Probe request update sent AP about client.


Wed Oct 31 10:46:15 2007: 00:1b:77:42:07:69 Association received from
    mobile on AP 00:17:df:ab:76:f0

!--- AP reports an association request from the client.
!--- When the process reaches this point, the client is not excluded and not
!--- in mobility intermediate state


Wed Oct 31 10:46:15 2007: 00:1b:77:42:07:69 STA - rates (8): 140 18 152
    36 176 72 96 108 0 0 0 0 0 0 0 0

!--- Controller saves the client supported rates into its connection table.
!--- Units are values of 500 kbps, basic (mandatory) rates have the MSB set.
!--- The above would be 6 Mbps basic, 9, 12 basic, 18, 24 basic, 36, 48, 54.
!--- The MSB adds 128. So for 6 Mbps it would be 12 + 128 = 140.



Wed Oct 31 10:46:15 2007: 00:1b:77:42:07:69 Processing WPA IE type 221,
    length 24 for mobile 00:1b:77:42:07:69

!--- Controller validates the 802.11i security information element.

PEM Process
Wed Oct 31 10:46:15 2007: 00:1b:77:42:07:69 0.0.0.0 START (0) Deleted mobile
    LWAPP rule on AP [00:17:df:ab:76:f0]

!--- As the client requests new association, APF requests to PEM to delete the
!--- client state and remove any traffic forwarding rules that it could have.

APF Process
Wed Oct 31 10:46:15 2007: 00:1b:77:42:07:69 Updated location for station old
    AP 00:00:00:00:00:00-0, new AP 00:17:df:ab:76:f0-1

!--- APF updates where this client is located. For example, this client is
!--- a new addition; therefore, no value exists for the old location.
```

```
!---Client is in START of the state machine shown in Figure 10-10.


Wed Oct 31 10:46:15 2007: 00:1b:77:42:07:69 0.0.0.0 START (0) Initializing
    policy


!--- PEM notifies that this is a new user. Security policies are checked
!--- for enforcement.


PEM Process
Wed Oct 31 10:46:15 2007: 00:1b:77:42:07:69 0.0.0.0 START (0) Change state
    to AUTHCHECK (2) last state AUTHCHECK (2)


!--- PEM marks as authentication check needed.
!---Client enters the AUTHCHECK state shown in Figure 10-10



Wed Oct 31 10:46:15 2007: 00:1b:77:42:07:69 0.0.0.0 AUTHCHECK (2) Change
    state to 8021X_REQD (3) last state 8021X_REQD


!--- After the WLAN configuration is checked, the client will need either
!—- 802.1x or PSK authentication.
!---Client moves to 802.1X_REQD in Figure 10-10.



Wed Oct 31 10:46:15 2007: 00:1b:77:42:07:69 0.0.0.0 8021X_REQD (3) Plumbed
    mobile LWAPP rule on AP 00:17:df:ab:76:f0


!--- PEM notifies the LWAPP component to add the new client on the AP with
!--- a list of negotiated capabilities, rates, Qos, etc.


APF Process
Wed Oct 31 10:46:15 2007: 00:1b:77:42:07:69 apfPemAddUser2 (apf_policy.c:209)
    Changing state for mobile 00:1b:77:42:07:69 on AP 00:17:df:ab:76:f0 from
    Probe to Associated


!--- APF notifies that the client has been moved successfully into the
Associated state



Wed Oct 31 10:46:15 2007: 00:1b:77:42:07:69 Stopping deletion of Mobile
    Station: (callerId: 48)


!--- The expiration timer for client is removed, as now the session timeout
!--- is taking place. This is also part of the above notification
```

(continues)

Example 10-6   *debug client Analysis (continued)*

```
!--- (internal code callerId: 48).


Wed Oct 31 10:46:15 2007: 00:1b:77:42:07:69 Sending Assoc Response to
     station on BSSID 00:17:df:ab:76:f0 (status 0)

!--- APF builds and sends the association response to client.


Wed Oct 31 10:46:15 2007: 00:1b:77:42:07:69 apfProcessAssocReq
     (apf_80211.c:3838) Changing state for mobile 00:1b:77:42:07:69 on AP
     00:17:df:ab:76:f0 from Associated to Associated

!--- The association response was sent successfully; now APF keeps the
!--- client in Associated state and sets the association timestamp on this point.

Dot1x Process
Wed Oct 31 10:46:15 2007: 00:1b:77:42:07:69 Creating a new PMK Cache Entry
     for station 00:1b:77:42:07:69 (RSN 0)

!--- APF calls Dot1x to allocate a new PMK cached entry for the client.
!--- RSN is disabled (zero value).


Wed Oct 31 10:46:15 2007: 00:1b:77:42:07:69 Initiating WPA PSK to mobile
     00:1b:77:42:07:69

!--- Dot1x signals a new WPA or WPA2 PSK exchange with mobile.


Wed Oct 31 10:46:15 2007: 00:1b:77:42:07:69 dot1x - moving mobile
     00:1b:77:42:07:69 into
     Force Auth state

!--- As no EAPOL authentication takes place, the client port is marked as
!--- Forced_Auth. Dot1x performs key negotiation with PSK clients only.


Wed Oct 31 10:46:15 2007: 00:1b:77:42:07:69 Skipping EAP-Success to mobile
     00:1b:77:42:07:69

!--- For PSK, CCKM, or RSN, the EAP success is not sent to client, because there
!--- was no EAPOL authentication taking place.
```

```
Wed Oct 31 10:46:15 2007: 00:1b:77:42:07:69 Sending EAPOL-Key Message to
    mobile
    00:1b:77:42:07:69

    state INITPMK (message 1), replay counter 00.00.00.00.00.00.00.00

!--- Dot1x starts the exchange to arrive into PTK. PMK is known, as this
!--- is PSK auth. First message is ANonce.


Wed Oct 31 10:46:15 2007: 00:1b:77:42:07:69 Received EAPOL-Key from mobile
    00:1b:77:42:07:69

!--- Message received from client.


Wed Oct 31 10:46:15 2007: 00:1b:77:42:07:69 Received EAPOL-key in PKT_START
    state (message 2) from mobile 00:1b:77:42:07:69

!--- This signals the start of the validation of the second message
!    from client (SNonce+MIC). No errors are shown, so process continues.
!--- Potential errors at this point could be: deflection attack (ACK bit
!--- not set on key), MIC errors, invalid key type, invalid key length, etc.


Wed Oct 31 10:46:15 2007: 00:1b:77:42:07:69 Stopping retransmission timer
    for mobile 00:1b:77:42:07:69

!--- Dot1x got an answer for message 1, so retransmission timeout is stopped.


Wed Oct 31 10:46:15 2007: 00:1b:77:42:07:69 Sending EAPOL-Key Message to
    mobile 00:1b:77:42:07:69

    state PTKINITNEGOTIATING (message 3), replay counter
    00.00.00.00.00.00.00.01

!--- Derive PTK; send GTK + MIC.


Wed Oct 31 10:46:15 2007: 00:1b:77:42:07:69 Received EAPOL-Key from mobile
    00:1b:77:42:07:69
```

(continues)

Example 10-6 *debug client Analysis (continued)*

```
!--- Message received from client.


Wed Oct 31 10:46:15 2007: 00:1b:77:42:07:69 Received EAPOL-key in
    PTKINITNEGOTIATING state (message 4) from mobile 00:1b:77:42:07:69

!--- This signals the start of validation of message 4 (MIC), which
!--- means client installed the keys. Potential errors after this message
!--- are MIC validation errors, invalid key types, etc.

PEM Process
Wed Oct 31 10:46:15 2007: 00:1b:77:42:07:69 0.0.0.0 8021X_REQD (3) Change
    state to L2AUTHCOMPLETE (4) last state L2AUTHCOMPLETE (4)

!--- PEM receives notification and signals the state machine to change to L2
!--- authentication completed.
!---Client moves into L2AUTHCOMPLETE in state machine


Wed Oct 31 10:46:15 2007: 00:1b:77:42:07:69 0.0.0.0 L2AUTHCOMPLETE (4)
    Plumbed mobile LWAPP rule on AP 00:17:df:ab:76:f0

!--- PEM pushes client status and keys to AP through LWAPP component.


Wed Oct 31 10:46:15 2007: 00:1b:77:42:07:69 0.0.0.0 L2AUTHCOMPLETE (4)
    Change state to DHCP_REQD (7) last state DHCP_REQD (7)

!--- PEM sets the client on address learning status.
!---Client is now in DHCP_REQD in the state machine.


Wed Oct 31 10:46:15 2007: 00:1b:77:42:07:69 0.0.0.0 DHCP_REQD (7)
    pemAdvanceState2 4238, Adding TMP rule

!--- PEM signals NPU to allow DHCP/ARP traffic to be inspected by controller
!--- for the address learning.


Wed Oct 31 10:46:15 2007: 00:1b:77:42:07:69 0.0.0.0 DHCP_REQD (7)
    Adding Fast Path rule

  type = Airespace AP - Learn IP address
```

```
   on AP 00:17:df:ab:76:f0, slot 1, interface = 1, QOS = 0

   ACL Id = 255, Jumbo Frames = NO, 802.1P = 0, DSCP = 0, TokenID = 5006

!--- Entry is built for client and prepared to be forwarded to NPU.
!--- Type is 9 (see the table in the "Client Traffic Forwarding" section of
!--- this chapter) to allow controller to learn the IP address.


Wed Oct 31 10:46:19 2007: 00:1b:77:42:07:69 0.0.0.0 DHCP_REQD (7)
     Successfully plumbed mobile rule (ACL ID 255)

!--- A new rule is successfully sent to internal queue to add the client
!--- to the NPU.

Dot1x Process
Wed Oct 31 10:46:19 2007: 00:1b:77:42:07:69 Stopping retransmission timer
     for mobile 00:1b:77:42:07:69

!--- Dot1x received message from client.


Wed Oct 31 10:46:19 2007: 00:1b:77:42:07:69 Sending EAPOL-Key Message to
     mobile 00:1b:77:42:07:69

   state PTKINITDONE (message 5 - group), replay counter
     00.00.00.00.00.00.00.02

!--- Group key update prepared for client.

PEM Process
Wed Oct 31 10:46:19 2007: 00:1b:77:42:07:69 0.0.0.0 Added NPU entry of type 9

!--- NPU reports that entry of type 9 is added (learning address state).
!--- See the table in the "Client Traffic Forwarding" section of this document.


Wed Oct 31 10:46:19 2007: 00:1b:77:42:07:69 Sent an XID frame

!--- No address known yet, so the controller sends only XID frame
!--- (destination broadcast, source client address, control 0xAF).

Dot1x Process
Wed Oct 31 10:46:19 2007: 00:1b:77:42:07:69 Sent EAPOL-Key M5 for mobile
```

(continues)

Example 10-6   *debug client Analysis (continued)*

```
    00:1b:77:42:07:69

!--- Key update sent.


Wed Oct 31 10:46:19 2007: 00:1b:77:42:07:69 Received EAPOL-Key from mobile
    00:1b:77:42:07:69

!--- Key received.


Wed Oct 31 10:46:19 2007: 00:1b:77:42:07:69 Received EAPOL-key in
    REKEYNEGOTIATING state (message 6) from mobile 00:1b:77:42:07:69

!--- Successfully received group key update.


Wed Oct 31 10:46:19 2007: 00:1b:77:42:07:69 Stopping retransmission timer
    for mobile 00:1b:77:42:07:69

!--- Group key timeout is removed.

DHCP Process
Wed Oct 31 10:46:19 2007: 00:1b:77:42:07:69 DHCP received op BOOTREQUEST
    (1) (len 308, port 1, encap 0xec03)

!--- First DHCP message received from client.


Wed Oct 31 10:46:19 2007: 00:1b:77:42:07:69 DHCP dropping packet due to
    ongoing mobility handshake exchange, (siaddr 0.0.0.0,  mobility
    state = 'apfMsMmQueryRequested'

!---Controller drops the first DHCP packet because it is still waiting to hear
from other mobility group members to see if this client might have roamed.

PEM Process
Wed Oct 31 10:46:19 2007: 00:1b:77:42:07:69 0.0.0.0 DHCP_REQD (7) mobility
    role update request from Unassociated to Local

  Peer = 0.0.0.0, Old Anchor = 0.0.0.0, New Anchor = 192.168.100.11

!--- NPU is notified that this controller is the local anchor, so to
!--- terminate any previous mobility tunnel. Because this is a new client,
```

```
!--- old address is empty.


Wed Oct 31 10:46:19 2007: 00:1b:77:42:07:69 0.0.0.0 DHCP_REQD (7) State
    Update from Mobility-Incomplete to Mobility-Complete, mobility
    role=Local

!--- Role change was successful.


Wed Oct 31 10:46:19 2007: 00:1b:77:42:07:69 0.0.0.0 DHCP_REQD (7)
    pemAdvanceState2 3934, Adding TMP rule

!--- Adding temporary rule to NPU for address learning now with new mobility
!--- role as local controller.


Wed Oct 31 10:46:19 2007: 00:1b:77:42:07:69 0.0.0.0 DHCP_REQD (7)
    Replacing Fast Path rule

  type = Airespace AP - Learn IP address

  on AP 00:17:df:ab:76:f0, slot 1, interface = 1, QOS = 0

  ACL Id = 255, Jumbo Frames = NO, 802.1P = 0, DSCP - 0, TokenID = 5006

!--- Entry is built.


Wed Oct 31 10:46:19 2007: 00:1b:77:42:07:69 0.0.0.0 DHCP_REQD (7)
    Successfully plumbed mobile rule (ACL ID 255)

!--- A new rule is successfully sent to internal queue to add the
!--- client to the NPU.


Wed Oct 31 10:46:19 2007: 00:1b:77:42:07:69 0.0.0.0 Added NPU entry of type 9

!--- Client is on address learning state; see the table in the
!--- "Client Traffic Forwarding" section of this chapter. Now mobility
!--- has finished.


Wed Oct 31 10:46:19 2007: 00:1b:77:42:07:69 Sent an XID frame
```

(continues)

Example 10-6   *debug client Analysis (continued)*

```
!--- No address known yet, so controller sends only XID frame (destination
!--- broadcast, source client address, control 0xAF).

DHCP Process
Wed Oct 31 10:46:21 2007: 00:1b:77:42:07:69 DHCP received op BOOTREQUEST
    (1) (len 308, port 1, encap 0xec03)

!--- DHCP request from client.


Wed Oct 31 10:46:21 2007: 00:1b:77:42:07:69 DHCP selecting relay 1 -
    control block settings:

                    dhcpServer: 0.0.0.0, dhcpNetmask: 0.0.0.0,

                    dhcpGateway: 0.0.0.0, dhcpRelay: 0.0.0.0  VLAN: 0

!--- Based on the WLAN configuration, the controller selects the identity to
!--- use to relay the DHCP messages.


Wed Oct 31 10:46:21 2007: 00:1b:77:42:07:69 DHCP selected relay 1 -
    192.168.100.254 (local address 192.168.100.11, gateway 192.168.100.254,
    VLAN 100, port 1)

!--- Interface selected.


Wed Oct 31 10:46:21 2007: 00:1b:77:42:07:69 DHCP
    transmitting DHCP DISCOVER (1)

Wed Oct 31 10:46:21 2007: 00:1b:77:42:07:69 DHCP
    op: BOOTREQUEST, htype: Ethernet, hlen: 6, hops: 1

Wed Oct 31 10:46:21 2007: 00:1b:77:42:07:69 DHCP
    xid: 0xd3d3b6e9 (3553867497), secs: 1024, flags: 0

Wed Oct 31 10:46:21 2007: 00:1b:77:42:07:69 DHCP
    chaddr: 00:1b:77:42:07:69

Wed Oct 31 10:46:21 2007: 00:1b:77:42:07:69 DHCP
    ciaddr: 0.0.0.0,  yiaddr: 0.0.0.0
```

```
Wed Oct 31 10:46:21 2007: 00:1b:77:42:07:69 DHCP
    siaddr: 0.0.0.0,  giaddr: 192.168.100.11

!--- Debug parsing of the frame sent. The most important fields are included.


Wed Oct 31 10:46:21 2007: 00:1b:77:42:07:69 DHCP sending REQUEST to
    192.168.100.254 (len 350, port 1, vlan 100)


!--- DHCP request forwarded.


Wed Oct 31 10:46:21 2007: 00:1b:77:42:07:69 DHCP selecting relay 2 -
    control block settings:

                        dhcpServer: 0.0.0.0, dhcpNetmask: 0.0.0.0,

                        dhcpGateway: 0.0.0.0, dhcpRelay: 192.168.100.11  VLAN: 100

Wed Oct 31 10:46:21 2007: 00:1b:77:42:07:69 DHCP selected relay 2 ? NONE

!--- No secondary server configured, so no additional DHCP requests are
!--- prepared (configuration dependant).


Wed Oct 31 10:46:21 2007: 00:1b:77:42:07:69 DHCP received op BOOTREPLY (2)
    (len 308, port 1, encap 0xec00)

Wed Oct 31 10:46:21 2007: 00:1b:77:42:07:69 DHCP setting server from OFFER
    (server 192.168.100.254, yiaddr 192.168.100.105)

!--- DHCP received for a known server. Controller discards any offer not on
!--- the DHCP server list for the WLAN/Interface.


Wed Oct 31 10:46:21 2007: 00:1b:77:42:07:69 DHCP sending REPLY to STA
    (len 416, port 1, vlan 100)

!--- After building the DHCP reply for client, it is sent to AP for forwarding.


Wed Oct 31 10:46:21 2007: 00:1b:77:42:07:69 DHCP transmitting DHCP OFFER (2)
```

(continues)

Example 10-6   *debug client Analysis (continued)*

```
Wed Oct 31 10:46:21 2007: 00:1b:77:42:07:69 DHCP
    op: BOOTREPLY, htype: Ethernet, hlen: 6, hops: 0

Wed Oct 31 10:46:21 2007: 00:1b:77:42:07:69 DHCP
    xid: 0xd3d3b6e9 (3553867497), secs: 0, flags: 0

Wed Oct 31 10:46:21 2007: 00:1b:77:42:07:69 DHCP
    chaddr: 00:1b:77:42:07:69

Wed Oct 31 10:46:21 2007: 00:1b:77:42:07:69 DHCP
    ciaddr: 0.0.0.0,  yiaddr: 192.168.100.105

Wed Oct 31 10:46:21 2007: 00:1b:77:42:07:69 DHCP
    siaddr: 0.0.0.0,  giaddr: 0.0.0.0

Wed Oct 31 10:46:21 2007: 00:1b:77:42:07:69 DHCP
    server id: 1.1.1.1  rcvd server id: 192.168.100.254


!--- Debug parsing of the frame sent. The most important fields are included.


Wed Oct 31 10:46:21 2007: 00:1b:77:42:07:69 DHCP received op BOOTREQUEST (1)
    (len 316, port 1, encap 0xec03)

!--- Client answers


Wed Oct 31 10:46:25 2007: 00:1b:77:42:07:69 DHCP selecting relay 1 -
    control block settings:

                    dhcpServer: 192.168.100.254, dhcpNetmask: 0.0.0.0,

                    dhcpGateway: 0.0.0.0, dhcpRelay: 192.168.100.11  VLAN: 100

Wed Oct 31 10:46:25 2007: 00:1b:77:42:07:69 DHCP selected relay 1 -
    192.168.100.254 (local address 192.168.100.11, gateway 192.168.100.254,
    VLAN 100, port 1)

!--- DHCP relay selected per WLAN config


Wed Oct 31 10:46:25 2007: 00:1b:77:42:07:69 DHCP transmitting DHCP REQUEST (3)
```

```
Wed Oct 31 10:46:25 2007: 00:1b:77:42:07:69 DHCP
    op: BOOTREQUEST, htype: Ethernet, hlen: 6, hops: 1

Wed Oct 31 10:46:25 2007: 00:1b:77:42:07:69 DHCP
    xid: 0xd3d3b6e9 (3553867497), secs: 1024, flags: 0

Wed Oct 31 10:46:25 2007: 00:1b:77:42:07:69 DHCP
    chaddr: 00:1b:77:42:07:69

Wed Oct 31 10:46:25 2007: 00:1b:77:42:07:69 DHCP
    ciaddr: 0.0.0.0,  yiaddr: 0.0.0.0

Wed Oct 31 10:46:25 2007: 00:1b:77:42:07:69 DHCP
    siaddr: 0.0.0.0,  giaddr: 192.168.100.11

Wed Oct 31 10:46:25 2007: 00:1b:77:42:07:69 DHCP
    requested ip: 192.168.100.105

Wed Oct 31 10:46:25 2007: 00:1b:77:42:07:69 DHCP
    server id: 192.168.100.254  rcvd server id: 1.1.1.1

!--- Debug parsing of the frame sent. The most important fields are included.


Wed Oct 31 10:46:25 2007: 00:1b:77:42:07:69 DHCP sending REQUEST to
    192.168.100.254 (len 358, port 1, vlan 100)

!--- Request sent to server.


Wed Oct 31 10:46:25 2007: 00:1b:77:42:07:69 DHCP selecting relay 2 -
    control block settings:

                      dhcpServer: 192.168.100.254, dhcpNetmask: 0.0.0.0,

                      dhcpGateway: 0.0.0.0, dhcpRelay: 192.168.100.11  VLAN: 100

Wed Oct 31 10:46:25 2007: 00:1b:77:42:07:69 DHCP selected relay 2 ? NONE

!--- No other DHCP server configured.


Wed Oct 31 10:46:25 2007: 00:1b:77:42:07:69 DHCP received op BOOTREPLY
    (2) (len 308, port 1, encap 0xec00)
```

(continues)

Example 10-6   *debug client Analysis (continued)*

```
!--- Server sends a DHCP reply, most probably an ACK (see below).

PEM Process
Wed Oct 31 10:46:25 2007: 00:1b:77:42:07:69 192.168.100.105 DHCP_REQD
    (7) Change state to RUN (20) last state RUN (20)

!--- DHCP negotiation successful, address is now known, and client
!--- is moved to RUN status in the state machine.


Wed Oct 31 10:46:25 2007: 00:1b:77:42:07:69 192.168.100.105 RUN (20)
    Reached PLUMBFASTPATH: from line 4699

!--- No Layer 3 security; client entry is sent to NPU.


Wed Oct 31 10:46:25 2007: 00:1b:77:42:07:69 192.168.100.105 RUN (20)
    Replacing Fast Path rule

  type = Airespace AP Client

  on AP 00:17:df:ab:76:f0, slot 1, interface = 1, QOS = 0

  ACL Id = 255, Jumbo Frames = NO, 802.1P = 0, DSCP = 0, TokenID = 5006

Wed Oct 31 10:46:25 2007: 00:1b:77:42:07:69 192.168.100.105 RUN (20)
    Successfully plumbed mobile rule (ACL ID 255)

DHCP Process
Wed Oct 31 10:46:25 2007: 00:1b:77:42:07:69 Assigning Address
    192.168.100.105 to mobile

Wed Oct 31 10:46:25 2007: 00:1b:77:42:07:69 DHCP sending REPLY to STA
    (len 416, port 1, vlan 100)

Wed Oct 31 10:46:25 2007: 00:1b:77:42:07:69 DHCP transmitting DHCP ACK (5)

Wed Oct 31 10:46:25 2007: 00:1b:77:42:07:69 DHCP
    op: BOOTREPLY, htype: Ethernet, hlen: 6, hops: 0

Wed Oct 31 10:46:25 2007: 00:1b:77:42:07:69 DHCP
    xid: 0xd3d3b6e9 (3553867497), secs: 0, flags: 0
```

```
Wed Oct 31 10:46:25 2007: 00:1b:77:42:07:69 DHCP
    chaddr: 00:1b:77:42:07:69

Wed Oct 31 10:46:25 2007: 00:1b:77:42:07:69 DHCP
    ciaddr: 0.0.0.0,  yiaddr: 192.168.100.105

Wed Oct 31 10:46:25 2007: 00:1b:77:42:07:69 DHCP
    siaddr: 0.0.0.0,  giaddr: 0.0.0.0

Wed Oct 31 10:46:25 2007: 00:1b:77:42:07:69 DHCP
    server id: 1.1.1.1  rcvd server id: 192.168.100.254

PEM Process
Wed Oct 31 10:46:25 2007: 00:1b:77:42:07:69 192.168.100.105 Added NPU
    entry of type 1


!--- Client is now successfully associated to controller.
!--- Type is 1; see the table in the Client Traffic Forwarding
!--- section of this chapter.


Wed Oct 31 10:46:25 2007: 00:1b:77:42:07:69 Sending a gratuitous ARP for
    192.168.100.105, VLAN Id 100

!--- As address is known, gratuitous ARP is sent to notify.
```

Troubleshooting Examples

The following sections show examples of common client related problems. Each section outlines what the problem is and how to interpret the debug output in each situation to reach that determination. Keep in mind that there are many reasons why a client might fail to associate to a WLAN and that these are only a few examples, not a comprehensive list.

Wrong Client Cipher Configuration

Example 10-7 shows a client with different capabilities to the AP. The client is probing for the SSID, but because the probe request shows some parameters not supported, the client never proceeds to authentication/association phases. In particular, the problem introduced was a mismatch between the client using WPA and the AP advertising only WPA2 support.

Example 10-7   *Wrong Cipher Configuration*

```
Wed Oct 31 10:51:37 2007: 00:1b:77:42:07:69 Scheduling deletion of Mobile
    Station:  (callerId: 23) in 5 seconds
Wed Oct 31 10:51:37 2007: 00:1b:77:42:07:69 apfProcessProbeReq
    (apf_80211.c:4057) Changing state for mobile 00:1b:77:42:07:69 on AP
    00:1c:b0:ea:5f:c0 from Idle to Probe

!--- Controller adds the new client, moving into probing status

Wed Oct 31 10:51:37 2007: 00:1b:77:42:07:69 Scheduling deletion of Mobile
    Station:  (callerId: 24) in 5 seconds
Wed Oct 31 10:51:38 2007: 00:1b:77:42:07:69 Scheduling deletion of Mobile
    Station:  (callerId: 24) in 5 seconds
Wed Oct 31 10:51:38 2007: 00:1b:77:42:07:69 Scheduling deletion of Mobile
    Station:  (callerId: 24) in 5 seconds

!--- AP is reporting probe activity every 500 ms as configured



Wed Oct 31 10:51:41 2007: 00:1b:77:42:07:69 Scheduling deletion of Mobile
    Station:  (callerId: 24) in 5 seconds
Wed Oct 31 10:51:41 2007: 00:1b:77:42:07:69 Scheduling deletion of Mobile
    Station:  (callerId: 24) in 5 seconds
Wed Oct 31 10:51:41 2007: 00:1b:77:42:07:69 Scheduling deletion of Mobile
    Station:  (callerId: 24) in 5 seconds
Wed Oct 31 10:51:41 2007: 00:1b:77:42:07:69 Scheduling deletion of Mobile
    Station:  (callerId: 24) in 5 seconds
Wed Oct 31 10:51:44 2007: 00:1b:77:42:07:69 Scheduling deletion of Mobile
    Station:  (callerId: 24) in 5 seconds
Wed Oct 31 10:51:44 2007: 00:1b:77:42:07:69 Scheduling deletion of Mobile
    Station:  (callerId: 24) in 5 seconds
Wed Oct 31 10:51:44 2007: 00:1b:77:42:07:69 Scheduling deletion of Mobile
    Station:  (callerId: 24) in 5 seconds
Wed Oct 31 10:51:44 2007: 00:1b:77:42:07:69 Scheduling deletion of Mobile
    Station:  (callerId: 24) in 5 seconds
Wed Oct 31 10:51:49 2007: 00:1b:77:42:07:69 apfMsExpireCallback (apf_ms.c:433)
    Expiring Mobile!
Wed Oct 31 10:51:49 2007: 00:1b:77:42:07:69 0.0.0.0 START (0) Deleted mobile
    LWAPP rule on AP [00:1c:b0:ea:5f:c0]
Wed Oct 31 10:51:49 2007: 00:1b:77:42:07:69 Deleting mobile on AP
    00:1c:b0:ea:5f:c0(0)

!--- After 5 seconds of inactivity, client is deleted, never moved into
!--- authentication or association phases.
```

Wrong Preshared Key

Example 10-8 shows a client trying to authenticate by WPA-PSK to the infrastructure but failing due to mismatch of the preshared key between the client and controller, resulting in the eventual exclusion of the client.

Example 10-8   *Wrong Preshared Key*

```
Wed Oct 31 10:55:55 2007: 00:1b:77:42:07:69 Adding mobile on LWAPP AP
    00:1c:b0:ea:5f:c0(0)
Wed Oct 31 10:55:55 2007: 00:1b:77:42:07:69 Scheduling deletion of Mobile
    Station:  (callerId: 23) in 5 seconds
Wed Oct 31 10:55:55 2007: 00:1b:77:42:07:69 apfProcessProbeReq (apf_80211.c:
    4057) Changing state for mobile 00:1b:77:42:07:69 on AP 00:1c:b0:ea:5f:c0
    from Idle to Probe
Wed Oct 31 10:55:55 2007: 00:1b:77:42:07:69 Scheduling deletion of Mobile
    Station:  (callerId: 24) in 5 seconds
Wed Oct 31 10:55:55 2007: 00:1b:77:42:07:69 Association received from mobile
    on AP 00:1c:b0:ea:5f:c0
Wed Oct 31 10:55:55 2007: 00:1b:77:42:07:69 STA - rates (8): 130 132 139 150
    12 18 24 36 0 0 0 0 0 0 0 0
Wed Oct 31 10:55:55 2007: 00:1b:77:42:07:69 STA - rates (12): 130 132 139 150
    12 18 24 36 48 72 96 108 0 0 0 0
Wed Oct 31 10:55:55 2007: 00:1b:77:42:07:69 Processing WPA IE type 221,
    length 24 for mobile 00:1b:77:42:07:69
Wed Oct 31 10:55:55 2007: 00:1b:77:42:07:69 0.0.0.0 START (0)
    Initializing policy
Wed Oct 31 10:55:55 2007: 00:1b:77:42:07:69 0.0.0.0 START (0) Change state to
    AUTHCHECK (2) last state AUTHCHECK (2)
Wed Oct 31 10:55:55 2007: 00:1b:77:42:07:69 0.0.0.0 AUTHCHECK (2) Change
    state to 8021X_REQD (3) last state 8021X_REQD (3)
Wed Oct 31 10:55:55 2007: 00:1b:77:42:07:69 0.0.0.0 8021X_REQD (3) Plumbed
    mobile LWAPP rule on AP 00:1c:b0:ea:5f:c0
Wed Oct 31 10:55:55 2007: 00:1b:77:42:07:69 apfPemAddUser2 (apf_policy.c:209)
    Changing state for mobile 00:1b:77:42:07:69 on AP 00:1c:b0:ea:5f:c0 from
    Probe to Associated
Wed Oct 31 10:55:55 2007: 00:1b:77:42:07:69 Stopping deletion of Mobile
    Station: (callerId: 48)
Wed Oct 31 10:55:55 2007: 00:1b:77:42:07:69 Sending Assoc Response to station
    on BSSID 00:1c:b0:ea:5f:c0 (status 0)
Wed Oct 31 10:55:55 2007: 00:1b:77:42:07:69 apfProcessAssocReq (apf_80211.c:
    3838) Changing state for mobile 00:1b:77:42:07:69 on AP 00:1c:b0:ea:5f:c0
    from Associated to Associated
Wed Oct 31 10:55:55 2007: 00:1b:77:42:07:69 Creating a new PMK Cache Entry
    for station 00:1b:77:42:07:69 (RSN 0)
```

(continues)

Example 10-8 *Wrong Preshared Key (continued)*

```
Wed Oct 31 10:55:55 2007: 00:1b:77:42:07:69 Initiating WPA PSK to mobile
    00:1b:77:42:07:69
Wed Oct 31 10:55:55 2007: 00:1b:77:42:07:69 dot1x - moving mobile
    00:1b:77:42:07:69 into Force Auth state
Wed Oct 31 10:55:55 2007: 00:1b:77:42:07:69 Skipping EAP-Success to mobile
    00:1b:77:42:07:69
Wed Oct 31 10:55:55 2007: 00:1b:77:42:07:69 Sending EAPOL-Key Message to
    mobile 00:1b:77:42:07:69
state INITPMK (message 1), replay counter 00.00.00.00.00.00.00.00
Wed Oct 31 10:55:55 2007: 00:1b:77:42:07:69 Received EAPOL-Key from mobile
    00:1b:77:42:07:69
Wed Oct 31 10:55:55 2007: 00:1b:77:42:07:69 Received EAPOL-key in PKT_START
    state (message 2) from mobile 00:1b:77:42:07:69
Wed Oct 31 10:55:55 2007: 00:1b:77:42:07:69 Received EAPOL-key M2 with
    invalid MIC from mobile 00:1b:77:42:07:69
Wed Oct 31 10:55:56 2007: 00:1b:77:42:07:69 802.1x 'timeoutEvt' Timer expired
    for station 00:1b:77:42:07:69
Wed Oct 31 10:55:56 2007: 00:1b:77:42:07:69 Retransmit 1 of EAPOL-Key M1
    (length 99) for mobile 00:1b:77:42:07:69
Wed Oct 31 10:55:56 2007: 00:1b:77:42:07:69 Received EAPOL-Key from mobile
    00:1b:77:42:07:69
Wed Oct 31 10:55:56 2007: 00:1b:77:42:07:69 Received EAPOL-key in PKT_START
    state (message 2) from mobile 00:1b:77:42:07:69
Wed Oct 31 10:55:56 2007: 00:1b:77:42:07:69 Received EAPOL-key M2 with invalid
    MIC from mobile 00:1b:77:42:07:69


!--- MIC error due to wrong preshared key


Wed Oct 31 10:55:57 2007: 00:1b:77:42:07:69 802.1x 'timeoutEvt' Timer expired
    for station 00:1b:77:42:07:69
Wed Oct 31 10:55:57 2007: 00:1b:77:42:07:69 Retransmit 2 of EAPOL-Key M1
    (length 99) for mobile 00:1b:77:42:07:69
Wed Oct 31 10:55:57 2007: 00:1b:77:42:07:69 Received EAPOL-Key from mobile
    00:1b:77:42:07:69
Wed Oct 31 10:55:57 2007: 00:1b:77:42:07:69 Received EAPOL-key in PKT_START
    state (message 2) from mobile 00:1b:77:42:07:69
Wed Oct 31 10:55:57 2007: 00:1b:77:42:07:69 Received EAPOL-key M2 with invalid
    MIC from mobile 00:1b:77:42:07:69
Wed Oct 31 10:55:58 2007: 00:1b:77:42:07:69 802.1x 'timeoutEvt' Timer expired
    for station 00:1b:77:42:07:69
Wed Oct 31 10:55:58 2007: 00:1b:77:42:07:69 Retransmit failure for EAPOL-Key
    M1 to mobile 00:1b:77:42:07:69, retransmit count 3, mscb deauth count 0
Wed Oct 31 10:55:58 2007: 00:1b:77:42:07:69 Sent Deauthenticate to mobile on
```

```
     BSSID 00:1c:b0:ea:5f:c0 slot 0(caller 1x_ptsm.c:462)

!--- Client is deauthenticated after three retries



!--- The process is repeated three times, until client is blacklisted


Wed Oct 31 10:56:10 2007: 00:1b:77:42:07:69 Blacklisting (if enabled) mobile
    00:1b:77:42:07:69
Wed Oct 31 10:56:10 2007: 00:1b:77:42:07:69 apfBlacklistMobileStationEntry2
    (apf_ms.c:3560) Changing state for mobile 00:1b:77:42:07:69 on AP
    00:1c:b0:ea:5f:c0 from Associated to Exclusion-list (1)
Wed Oct 31 10:56:10 2007: 00:1b:77:42:07:69 Scheduling deletion of Mobile
    Station:  (callerId: 44) in 10 seconds
Wed Oct 31 10:56:10 2007: 00:1b:77:42:07:69 0.0.0.0 8021X_REQD (3) Change
    state to START (0) last state 8021X_REQD (3)
Wed Oct 31 10:56:10 2007: 00:1b:77:42:07:69 0.0.0.0 START (0) Reached FAILURE:
    from line 3522
Wed Oct 31 10:56:10 2007: 00:1b:77:42:07:69 Scheduling deletion of Mobile
    Station:  (callerId: 9) in 10 seconds
```

Incorrect User Credentials with EAP

Example 10-9 shows an 802.1x EAP authentication with RADIUS failing because the client credentials are incorrect.

Example 10-9   *RADIUS Access-Reject*

```
(Cisco Controller) >debug client 00:0E:35:F3:60:73
Mon Aug 17 16:20:17 2009: 00:0e:35:f3:60:73 Adding mobile on LWAPP AP
00:1e:13:06:f6:50(0)
Mon Aug 17 16:20:17 2009: 00:0e:35:f3:60:73 Scheduling deletion of Mobile Station:
(callerId: 23) in 5 seconds
Mon Aug 17 16:20:17 2009: 00:0e:35:f3:60:73 apfProcessProbeReq (apf_80211.c:4142)
Changing state for mobile 00:0e:35:f3:60:73 on AP 00:1e:13:06:f6:50 from Idle to
Probe
Mon Aug 17 16:20:17 2009: 00:0e:35:f3:60:73 Scheduling deletion of Mobile Station:
(callerId: 24) in 5 seconds
Mon Aug 17 16:20:17 2009: 00:0e:35:f3:60:73 Association received from mobile on AP
00:1e:13:06:f6:50
Mon Aug 17 16:20:17 2009: 00:0e:35:f3:60:73 STA - rates (8): 130 132 139 12 18
150 24 36 0 0 0 0 0 0 0 0
Mon Aug 17 16:20:17 2009: 00:0e:35:f3:60:73 STA - rates (12): 130 132 139 12 18
150 24 36 48 72 96 108 0 0 0 0
```

(continues)

Example 10-9 *RADIUS Access-Reject (continued)*

```
!—-Because this is a new association, there is no PMKID from the client. You
will also notice that the RSN IE is type 48, indicating that it is WPA2.

Mon Aug 17 16:20:17 2009: 00:0e:35:f3:60:73 Processing RSN IE type 48, length 20
for mobile 00:0e:35:f3:60:73
Mon Aug 17 16:20:17 2009: 00:0e:35:f3:60:73 Received RSN IE with 0 PMKIDs from
mobile 00:0e:35:f3:60:73
Mon Aug 17 16:20:17 2009: 00:0e:35:f3:60:73 0.0.0.0 START (0) Initializing policy
Mon Aug 17 16:20:17 2009: 00:0e:35:f3:60:73 0.0.0.0 START (0) Change state to
AUTHCHECK (2) last state AUTHCHECK (2)
Mon Aug 17 16:20:17 2009: 00:0e:35:f3:60:73 0.0.0.0 AUTHCHECK (2) Change state to
8021X_REQD (3) last state 8021X_REQD (3)
Mon Aug 17 16:20:17 2009: 00:0e:35:f3:60:73 0.0.0.0 8021X_REQD (3) Plumbed mobile
LWAPP rule on AP 00:1e:13:06:f6:50
Mon Aug 17 16:20:17 2009: 00:0e:35:f3:60:73 apfPemAddUser2 (apf_policy.c:212)
Changing state for mobile 00:0e:35:f3:60:73 on AP 00:1e:13:06:f6:50 from Probe to
Associated
Mon Aug 17 16:20:17 2009: 00:0e:35:f3:60:73 Stopping deletion of Mobile Station:
(callerId: 48)
Mon Aug 17 16:20:17 2009: 00:0e:35:f3:60:73 Sending Assoc Response to station on
BSSID 00:1e:13:06:f6:50 (status 0)
Mon Aug 17 16:20:17 2009: 00:0e:35:f3:60:73 apfProcessAssocReq (apf_80211.c:3888)
Changing state for mobile 00:0e:35:f3:60:73 on AP 00:1e:13:06:f6:50 from
Associated to Associated
Mon Aug 17 16:20:17 2009: 00:0e:35:f3:60:73 Station 00:0e:35:f3:60:73 setting
dot1x reauth timeout = 1800
Mon Aug 17 16:20:17 2009: 00:0e:35:f3:60:73 dot1x - moving mobile
00:0e:35:f3:60:73 into Connecting state

!—-802.1x process begins, and the controller sends the EAP identity request to
the client.

Mon Aug 17 16:20:17 2009: 00:0e:35:f3:60:73 Sending EAP-Request/Identity to mobile
00:0e:35:f3:60:73 (EAP Id 1)
Mon Aug 17 16:20:17 2009: 00:0e:35:f3:60:73 Received EAPOL EAPPKT from mobile
00:0e:35:f3:60:73
Mon Aug 17 16:20:17 2009: 00:0e:35:f3:60:73 Username entry (LEEJOHNS-XP-
TST\Administrator) created for mobile
Mon Aug 17 16:20:17 2009: 00:0e:35:f3:60:73 Received Identity Response (count=1)
from mobile 00:0e:35:f3:60:73
Mon Aug 17 16:20:17 2009: 00:0e:35:f3:60:73 EAP State update from Connecting to
Authenticating for mobile 00:0e:35:f3:60:73
Mon Aug 17 16:20:17 2009: 00:0e:35:f3:60:73 dot1x - moving mobile
00:0e:35:f3:60:73 into Authenticating state
Mon Aug 17 16:20:17 2009: 00:0e:35:f3:60:73 Entering Backend Auth Response state
for mobile 00:0e:35:f3:60:73

!—-RADIUS server returns an Access-Reject because the client user credentials are
incorrect.
```

```
!—-Controller passes EAP-failure to the client.

Mon Aug 17 16:20:27 2009: 00:0e:35:f3:60:73 Processing Access-Reject for mobile
00:0e:35:f3:60:73
Mon Aug 17 16:20:27 2009: 00:0e:35:f3:60:73 Sending EAP-Failure to mobile
00:0e:35:f3:60:73 (EAP Id -1)
Mon Aug 17 16:20:27 2009: 00:0e:35:f3:60:73 Entering Backend Auth Failure state
(id=-1) for mobile 00:0e:35:f3:60:73
```

Summary

When you are troubleshooting client-related problems, it is important to understand the type of client involved and whether the issue is widespread or localized to a particular group of clients or location. After you gather general information about the issue, use debug client on the controller CLI for a problem client. Should that not allow you to determine the root cause of the problem, continue to add the other methods to gain more information. Use the client debugs or troubleshooting utilities, and then move on to sniffer traces to verify the debugs. If you do not have a wireless sniffer, use a wired sniffer to verify that the client traffic is entering and leaving the controller as expected. Should adding wired sniffer traces fail to shed light on the issue, capture a wireless trace. When gathering concurrent information from different sources, remember that all the devices should be NTP time synced. Also remember that it might be necessary to run debugs on the AP to get to the bottom of the issue.

Chapter 11

Wireless Voice

Wireless voice can be a great asset to any wireless network. Mobile users such as doctors, nurses, warehouse associates, sales floor staff, and call center personnel are no longer tied to a desk where they can miss important, perhaps life saving, phone calls. The Cisco Unified Wireless Networking (CUWN) solution provides a robust wireless infrastructure for voice applications.

Cisco currently offers two wireless phone models: the 7921 and 7925. The 7920 model was the first Cisco wireless phone and is still found in the field, but it is End-of-Life and reached End-of-Support in June 2009. The 7920 is an 802.11b-only device and does not have the security protocol support of the newer models. This book does not cover the 7920.

The controllers also support any wireless voice device of a vendor as long as it adheres to the wireless standards. Some examples of third-party wireless devices are Vocera badges and SpectraLink wireless phones.

Prerequisites for Voice Deployments

Although you might be able to get away with simply placing access points (AP) in the network based on what looks good on a floor map for a data-only deployment, voice is a radio frequency (RF)-sensitive, throughput demanding, and latency-unforgiving application. If a data client has to retransmit a packet, odds are the end user will never notice. That is not so for voice. Lost packets, delayed packets, coverage gaps, and incorrect AP power and channel assignments will wreck a wireless voice implementation. The end user on a voice call will definitely notice if part of the conversation is lost.

Note   It is highly recommended that you take advantage of the 802.11a capability of the 7921 and 7925 phones and conduct the site survey accordingly. In most cases, the 802.11b/g network is already saturated, which is detrimental to a voice deployment. This is especially true if you are planning to use the coexistence feature of the 7925.

The one prerequisite you must have completed is a site survey for voice. You must use a Cisco certified partner that has advanced wireless LAN (WLAN) specialization. Walking around with a laptop using a Cisco CB21 card with the site survey tool is not going to be sufficient. In fact, you are not even supposed to be able to purchase a 792x phone without a professional site survey. You must use nonoverlapping channels and allow at least 20 percent overlap with adjacent channels when deploying phones in the environment. Figure 11-1 shows a 20 percent cell overlap.

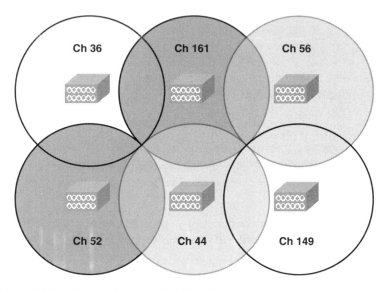

Figure 11-1   *Twenty Percent Cell Overlap*

For acceptable voice quality, the phones should always have a signal of −67 dBm or higher when using 2.4 or 5 GHz. You should also ensure that the packet error rate (PER) is no higher than 1 percent. You also want to maintain a minimum signal-to-noise ratio (SNR) of 25 dB.

You should design the voice deployment for a data rate of 24 Mbps. You can enable the higher data rates if you desire.

Cisco recommends that you set the minimum data rate on the 802.11 networks to 11 Mbps or 12 Mbps for 2.4 GHz as long as the other wireless clients can support it. For the 802.11a network, the minimum data rate should be 12 Mbps, and only 12 Mbps should be set to mandatory.

Other prerequisites you want to keep in mind are having the correct CallManager and controller code to support the phones. All the wireless controller and AP models support the 792x phones. Table 11-1 shows the supported versions of CallManager and controller for the 792x phones.

Table 11-1   *792x CallManager and Controller Versions*

Phone Model	CallManager	CallManager Express	Wireless Controller
7921	4.1 and later*	4.1 and later (minimum of 12.4[15]T7)	4.0.217.0, 5.1 or higher-recommended
7925	4.1 and later*	4.1 and later (minimum of 12.4[15]T7)	4.0.217.0, 5.1 or higher-recommended

*CallManager requires a device package or service release update to enable support for the 7921 and 7925 phones. You can find these packages at http://www.cisco.com/kobayashi/sw_center/swvoice.shtml.

You also want to make sure that your wired network quality of service (QoS) is properly configured for a voice deployment. QoS is covered later in this chapter in the "QoS" section.

Tip   It is usually a best practice to make sure that the phones are running the latest firmware. Unlike some devices, the latest firmware for the phones is usually the best and can clear up many intermittent issues.

Remember to separate voice, data, and management VLANs. Doing so isolates the different types of traffic and allows you greater control over that traffic. You would never want to have your data and voice clients sharing a service set identifier (SSID)/VLAN.

Phone Features

The 792x family of wireless phones provides a myriad of protocol and security support configurations.

Supported Protocols, Specifications, and Certifications

The Cisco 792x wireless phones support the following protocols:

- 802.11a/b/g.
- Skinny Client Control Protocol (SCCP).
- Real Time Protocol (RTP).
- G.711u-law, G.711a-law, G.729a, G.729ab, G.722, and iLBC.

- Real Time Control Protocol (RTCP).

- Cisco Discovery Protocol (CDP).

- Syslog.

- Cisco Compatible Extension (CCX) v4.

- Wi-Fi Multimedia (WMM) and Traffic Specification (TSPEC).

- Unscheduled Auto Power Save Delivery (U-APSD) and Power Save Poll (PS-POLL).

- Bluetooth 2.0—7925 only.

- IP54 rated—Protects from dust, being splashed by liquid, and moisture. 7925 only.

Security

The 792x phones support an array of wireless authentication types, key-management types, and encryption methods.

The supported authentications are as follows:

- Extensible Authentication Protocol-Flexible Authentication via Secure Tunneling (EAP-FAST)

- Extensible Authentication Protocol Transport Layer Security (EAP-TLS)

- Protected Extensible Authentication Protocol (PEAP)

- Lightweight access point (LEAP)

- Open and Shared Key

The support key-managements are as follows:

- Cisco Centralized Key Management (CCKM)

- 802.11i 802.1x authentication

- 802.11i Pre-Shared Key (PSK)

The supported encryptions are as follows:

- Advanced Encryption Standard (AES)

- Temporal Key Integrity Protocol (TKIP)/Message Integrity Check (MIC)

- WEP—40 and 128 bit

The 792x phones support the following voice security methods:

- Certificates

- Image authentication

- Device authentication

- File authentication

- Signaling authentication

- Secure Cisco Unified SRST

- Media encryption using Secure Real-time Transport Protocol (SRTP)

- Signaling encryption (Transport Layer Security [TLS])

- Certificate authority proxy function (CAPF)

- Secure profiles

- Encrypted configuration files

- Settings access (can limit user access to configuration menus)

- Locked network profiles

- Administrator password

Coexistence

Coexistence refers to using the Bluetooth feature of the 7925 along with 802.11b/g radio simultaneously. Because both Bluetooth and 802.11b/g utilize the 2.4GHz spectrum, you have deployment considerations and limitations:

- **Capacity:** Up to two bidirectional RTP streams per AP/channel are supported.

- **Battery Life:** There can be up to 50 percent reduction of battery life when on a call and using coexistence.

- **Multicast audio:** Multicast audio from Push To Talk (PTT), Music on Hold (MMOH), and other applications are not supported when using coexistence.

- **Data Rate Configuration:** It is advised to only enable 802.11g Orthogonal frequency-division multiplexing (OFDM) data rates (that is, > 12 Mbps) to prevent engaging in Clear To Send (CTS) for 802.11g protection, which can impact voice quality.

QoS

QoS is the capability of a network to provide differentiated service to selected network traffic over various network technologies. Configuring QoS does not increase the bandwidth of your network. It merely gives you more control over how the bandwidth you have is allocated to different devices on the network. Make sure you understand your traffic, the protocols involved, and the sensitivity of the application to network delays.

Latency, Jitter, and Loss

The quality of a network transmission is a result of three things:

- Latency
- Jitter
- Loss

Latency is how long it takes for a packet to be received by the endpoint after it is sent from the source. Latency is also referred to as *delay*. Asymmetrical tunneling after a Layer 3 roaming event between controllers can introduce delay. Again, symmetrical mobility tunneling is the recommended configuration. See Chapter 9, "Mobility," for more information on symmetrical versus asymmetrical tunneling.

Delay can be broken into two parts:

- **Fixed delay:** The time it takes to encode and decode the packets and the time it takes for the packet to traverse the network.
- **Variable delay:** Caused by network conditions. If the network is highly utilized at certain times of the day, the variable delay would be higher at those times than others.

Jitter is the value that results from the difference in end-to-end latency between packets. If a packet takes 50 ms to traverse the network and the next packet takes 100 ms, you have a jitter value of 50 ms.

Loss is simply the ratio of packets that are successfully received by the endpoint to those that were sent by the transmitter.

Correct Packet Marking

You need to be familiar with three types of packet classifications:

- AVVID 802.1p User Priorities (UP)
- AVVID IP Differentiated Services Code Point (DSCP)
- IEEE 802.11e UP

Depending on the traffic flow of a packet, these classifications are used to properly classify, or mark, that traffic on the network. There are two key concepts to understanding the traffic flow and the way the packets are marked:

- With Layer 3, both wired and wireless traffic trust Architecture for Voice, Video, and Integrated Data (AVVID) IP DSCP end to end.
- With Layer 2, wired uses AVVID 802.1p UP markings, and wireless uses IEEE 802.11e UP.

Because wired and wireless are using different Layer 2 classifications to mark the packets, the AP must convert between AVVID 802.1p UP and IEEE 802.11e UP. Table 11-2 shows the QoS conversion table that allows the AP to convert between the different classifications.

Table 11-2   *Access Point QoS Translation Values*

QoS Baseline IEEE 802.1 UP-Based Traffic Type	AVVID IP DSCP	AVVID IEEE 802.1p UP	IEEE 802.11e UP
Network control	—	7	—
Inter-network control (LWAPP[1] control, IEEE 802.11 management)	48	6	7
Voice	46 (EF[2])	5	6
Video	34 (AF41)	4	5
Voice Control	26 (AF31) 25(CS3)	3	4
Background (gold)	18 (AF21)	2	2
Background (gold)	20 (AF22)	2	2
Background (gold)	22 (AF23)	2	2
Background (silver)	10 (AF11)	1	1
Background (silver)	12 (AF12)	1	1
Background (silver)	14 (AF13)	1	1
Best Effort	0 (BE)	0	0, 3
Background	2	0	1
Background	4	0	1
Background	6	0	1

[1]LWAPP = Lightweight Access Point Protocol

[2]EF = Expedited Forwarding

Figure 11-2 shows an example of voice packet markings and necessary conversions.

As you can see in Figure 11-2, the Layer 3 AVVID IP DCSP packet marking for the Voice Control packet remains the same between the wired and wireless medium. The Layer 2 markings, however, are different, and the AP has to convert between the wireless 802.11e UP value of 6 and the wired AVVID 802.1p UP value of 5.

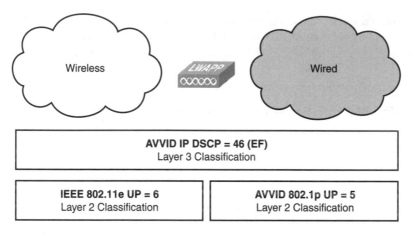

Figure 11-2 *Sample QoS Packet Markings and Conversion*

In an LWAPP/Control and Provisioning of Wireless Access Points (CAPWAP) deployment, the AP and the controller exchange LWAPP/CAPWAP control and LWAPP/CAPWAP data packets. For LWAPP/CAPWAP control packets, QoS is simple in that the AP always sends control packets with an AVVID IP DSCP tag of 46 in the LWAPP/CAPWAP header. The controller also sets the AVVID IP DSCP tag to 46 for control packets to the AP. If the interface is tagged—that is, the controller network port on the switch is a trunked interface—it also sets the AVVID 802.1p UP to 7.

For LWAPP/CAPWAP data packets, the AP must convert the QoS markings as traffic is sent to and from the wireless clients. If a mistake is made here, it is important to realize that the mistake only affects wireless QoS because the AVVID IP DSCP tag of the payload is never altered. Figure 11-3 outlines the QoS tagging conversions for wireless-to-wired and wired-to-wireless traffic.

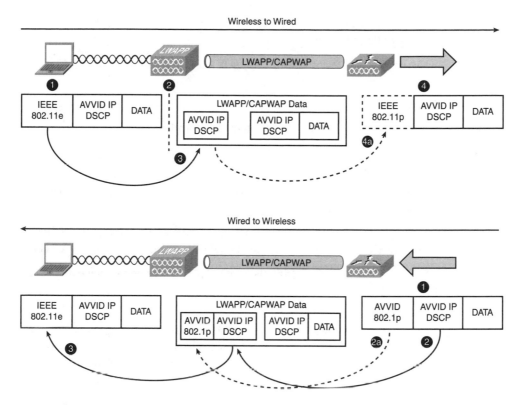

Figure 11-3 *Traffic Flow QoS Classification Mappings*

In Figure 11-3 the following occurs:

Wireless to Wired:

Step 1.   The wireless client sends a packet that contains Layer 2 IEEE 802.11e, Layer 3 AVVID IP UP, and data.

Step 2.   When the packet reaches the AP, because an AP never sends tagged packets, the 802.11e UP information is stripped without changing the original AVVID IP DSCP or data.

Step 3.   The AP encapsulates the packet and uses the QoS conversion table (Table 11-2) to convert the IEEE 802.11e UP value from the packet to get the AVVID IP DSCP tag to correctly mark the LWAPP/CAPWAP header.

Step 4.   The packet reaches the controller and the controller de-encapsulates the packet, removing the LWAPP/CAPWAP header and bridging the "naked" packet onto the wired network.

Step 4a.   If the packet is sent out of the controller on a tagged interface, the controller uses the QoS conversion table to properly map the AVVID IP DSCP marking

from the LWAPP/CAPWAP header of the packet to the correct Layer 2
AVVID 802.1p UP tag.

Notice that the AVVID IP DSCP from the client never changed throughout the whole
process.

Wired to Wireless:

Step 1.   A packet destined for the client enters the controller.

Step 2.   The controller copies the AVVID IP DSCP marking from the incoming packet
to use on the LWAPP/CAPWAP packet header.

Step 2a. If the packet arrives at the controller on a tagged interface, the controller also
copies the AVVID 802.1p UP tag.

Step 3.   The AP strips the LWAPP/CAPWAP header and uses the AVVID IP DSCP tag
to correctly map the IEEE 802.11e tag before sending the packet to the client.

Again, the AVVID IP DSCP marking from the original packet was never changed
throughout the whole process.

Note   With controller code Release 5.1, Cisco introduced Traffic Classification (TCLAS)
to ensure that voice streams are properly classified. Because LWAPP/CAPWAP data packets always use the same ports, 12222 and 5247 respectively, and the AP uses the outside
QoS marking to determine which queue the packets should be placed in, using port-based
QoS policies is inadequate. With TCLAS, even if the LWAPP/CAPWAP AVVID IP DSCP
markings are incorrect, the traffic is tagged correctly.

Upstream and Downstream QoS

When discussing QoS, it is important to understand the terminology and direction of
the traffic flow to and from the AP and the controller. You have both upstream and
downstream QoS:

- **Radio downstream:** Traffic leaving the AP and traveling to the WLAN clients.

- **Radio upstream:** Traffic leaving the WLAN clients and traveling to the AP.
  Enhanced Distributed Channel Access (EDCA) rules provide upstream QoS settings
  for WLAN clients.

- **Network downstream:** Traffic leaving the controller traveling to the AP. QoS can be
  applied at this point to prioritize and rate-limit LWAPP/CAPWAP traffic to the AP.
  Configuration of Ethernet downstream QoS is not covered in this book.

- **Network upstream:** Traffic leaving the AP, traveling to the controller. The AP marks
  the traffic according to the value set by the wireless client using the IEEE 802.11c UP
  to AVVID IP DSCP conversion table.

Figure 11-4 outlines the QoS traffic flow concepts.

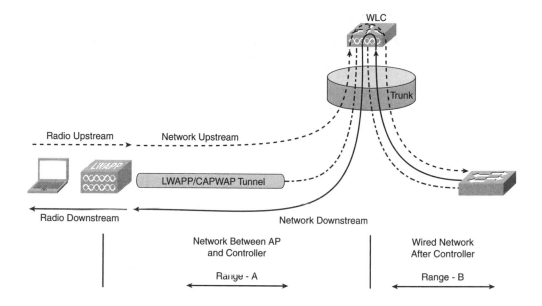

Figure 11-4 *QoS Traffic Flow*

In Figure 11-4, the diagram is broken into two separate ranges: A and B. Range A specifies the network between the AP and the controller (the LWAPP/CAPWAP tunnel). Range B refers to the wired network after the controller. Keep these range designations in mind as you read through the rest of the chapter because this concept will come up again.

Wi-Fi Multimedia

WMM is a certification that applies to both clients and APs. The features are taken from the 802.11e draft.

Using the eight IEEE-developed 802.1p QoS classifications, WMM maps the classifications into four access categories. The four access categories are mapped to the WMM queues required by a WMM certified device. Table 11-3 outlines the 802.1p to WMM mappings.

Each of the four WMM queues competes for the wireless bandwidth available on the channel. WMM uses Enhanced Distributed Coordination Function (EDCF) for handling the queue traffic. If more than one frame from different access categories collides internally, the frame with the higher priority is sent. The lower-priority frame adjusts its back-off parameters as though it had collided with a frame external to the queuing mechanism.

WMM prioritization helps minimize delays in wireless networks for time-sensitive applications such as voice and video. WMM is the default EDCA parameter set on the controller.

Table 11-3   *802.1p WMM Mappings*

Priority	802.1P Priority	Access Category	WMM Queue
Lowest	1	AC_BK	Background
	2		
	0	AC_BE	Best Effort
	3		
	4	AC_VI	Video
	5		
	6	AC_VO	Voice
Highest	7		

TSPEC

TSPEC allows an 802.11 wireless client to signal its traffic requirements to the AP. The client includes the TSPEC in the add traffic stream (ADDTS). The TSPEC from the client includes requirements for data rate, packet size, number of streams, and more. The 802.11e standard specifies TSPEC to provide the management link between higher QoS protocols and the channel access functions. Channel access functions are defined by the EDCA mechanism. TSPEC allows the AP to control access bandwidth to avoid traffic congestion. To enable TSPEC on the controller, you enable Call Admission Control (CAC).

ADDTS

The ADDTS function is how a WLAN client (STA) performs an admission request to an AP. Signaling its TSPEC request to the AP, an admission request is in one of two forms:

- **ADDTS action frame:** This happens when a client originates a phone call associated to the AP. The ADDTS contains TSPEC and might contain a traffic stream rate set (TSRS) information element (IE) (Cisco Compatible Extensions v4 clients). A Cisco wireless phone actually performs two ADDTS because the codec used in the call is not known before the RTP stream is established.

- **Association and reassociation message:** The association message might contain one or more TSPECs and one TSRS IE if the STA wants to establish the traffic stream as part of the association. The reassociation message might contain one or more TSPECs and one TSRS IE if an STA roams to another AP.

The ADDTS contains the TSPEC element that describes the traffic request. Apart from key data describing the traffic requirements, such as data rates and frame sizes, the TSPEC element tells the AP the minimum physical rate (PHY) that the client device will use. This allows the calculation of how much time that station can consume in sending and receiving in this TSPEC, thereby allowing the AP to calculate whether it has the resources to meet the TSPEC. TSPEC admission control is used by the WLAN client (target clients are Voice over IP [VoIP] handsets) when a call is initiated and during a roam request. During a roam, the TSPEC request is appended to the reassociation request.

When the traffic stream finishes, the STA must send a Delete Traffic Stream (DELTS) to release the CAC resources used for that stream.

QoS and H-REAP

When using voice on a Hybrid Remote Edge Access Point (H-REAP) AP, the traffic flow may change depending on the configuration. For WLANs that have data traffic forwarded to the WLC (that is, for centrally switched WLANs with WMM traffic), the behavior is the same as local mode APs. For WLANs that are locally switched, however, a different approach is taken. The AP marks the dot1p value in the dot1q VLAN tag for upstream traffic. This occurs only on tagged VLANs—that is, not native VLANs.

For downstream traffic, the H-REAP AP uses the incoming dot1q tag from the Ethernet side to queue and mark the WMM values on the radio of the locally switched VLAN.

The WLAN QoS profile is applied both for upstream and downstream packets. For downstream, if an IEEE 802.1P value that is higher than the default WLAN value is received, the default WLAN value is used. For upstream, if the client sends a WMM value that is higher than the default WLAN value, the default WLAN value is used. For non-WMM traffic, there is no class of service (CoS) marking on the client frames from the AP.

Configuration

To have a successful voice deployment with 792x phones, not only do you need a professional site survey, you also need to make sure that the controller and the switched network are properly configured for voice.

Controller

The controller has several settings for a proper voice configuration:

- Set the WLAN QoS policy to Platinum.

- The Platinum QoS profile should be set for 802.1p with a tag of 6.

- WMM must be enabled to use U-APSD.

- A Delivery Traffic Indication Message (DTIM) of 2 is recommended.

- A Beacon Interval of 100 is recommended.

- Dynamic Host Configuration Protocol (DHCP) address assignment should not be required.

- Aggressive Load Balancing should be disabled.

- ARP Unicast should be disabled; this was deprecated in 5.1 code and is disabled by default on older codes.

- Peer-to-Peer Blocking (P2P Blocking) Public Secure Packet Forwarding (PSPF) should be disabled.

- Client Management Frame Protection (MFP) should be disabled or optional.

- Symmetric Tunneling should be enabled if the network is configured for Layer 3 mobility.

- If you are using 2.4 GHz, enable short preambles if no legacy clients will be using the network.

- CCKM is recommended when using 802.1x authentication.

- Enable CAC.

You should treat voice packets with the highest priority. When you configure the voice WLAN on the controller, make sure that the QoS is configured for Platinum and WMM is set to Allowed or Required (see Figure 11-5).

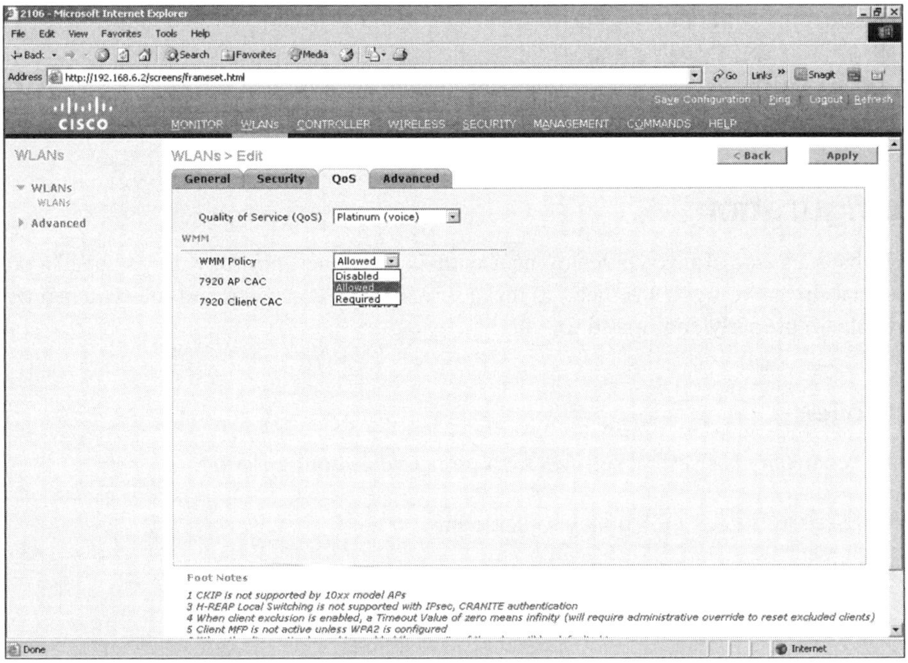

Figure 11-5   *WLAN QoS Configuration*

Under the Advanced tab for the WLAN, make sure that DHCP Addr. Assignment is disabled. The short time it takes for a phone to go through a DHCP request when it roams from one AP to another is more than enough to cause audio problems. Make sure that P2P

Blocking is disabled. If it is enabled, wireless-to-wireless phone calls can fail. You should disable or set Management Frame Protection to optional. DTIM is no longer a global 802.11 setting and is now WLAN specific. A DTIM of 2 is recommended for optimal battery life. Figure 11-6 shows the Advanced tab for a voice WLAN.

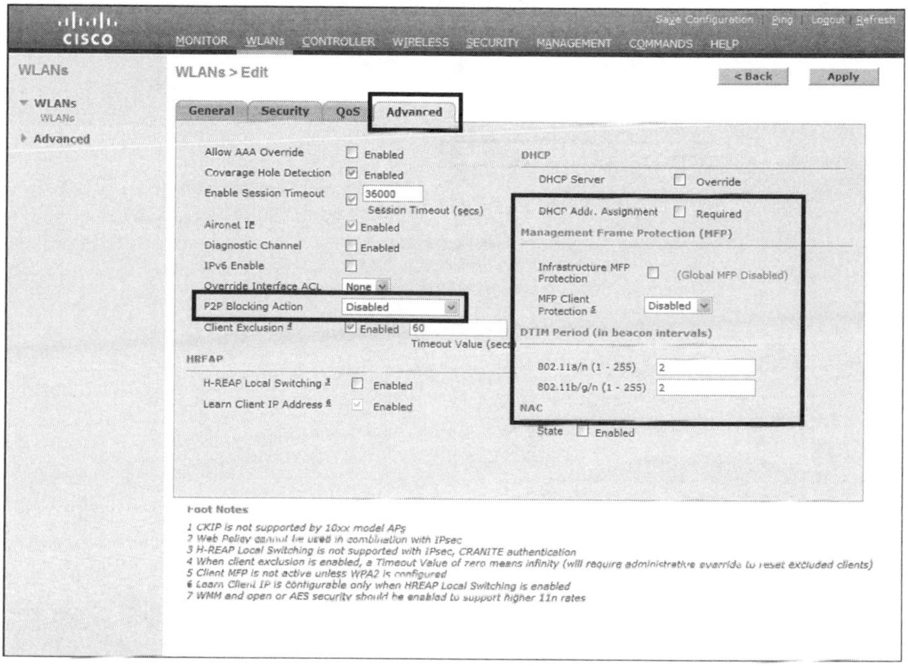

Figure 11-6   *WLAN Advanced Configuration*

For client MFP to function, the clients must be CCXv5 compliant and using WPA2 with either TKIP or AES. Because the 792x phones are only CCXv4, they will not be able to connect to a WLAN requiring MFP.

Aggressive load balancing is a controller feature that tries to redistribute clients more evenly between APs to prevent an excessive load on one AP while another AP has only a few clients associated. Although in theory this sounds like a great feature, the controller ignores association requests for clients when an AP is overloaded to see if they will associate with another AP. Should this take place during a voice call, you can imagine that the voice quality would suffer. You want to make sure that the Aggressive load balancing option is disabled (default) on the controller (see Figure 11-7). AP-assisted roaming and CAC function to help a 792x connect to the proper APs.

To ensure proper DCSP mappings for QoS take place, you should configure the Platinum profile for 802.1p with a tag of 6 for the Wired QoS Protocol. Remember that everything on the controller is from a wireless point of view, IEEE 802.11e. Figure 11-8 shows the proper configuration for the QoS profile.

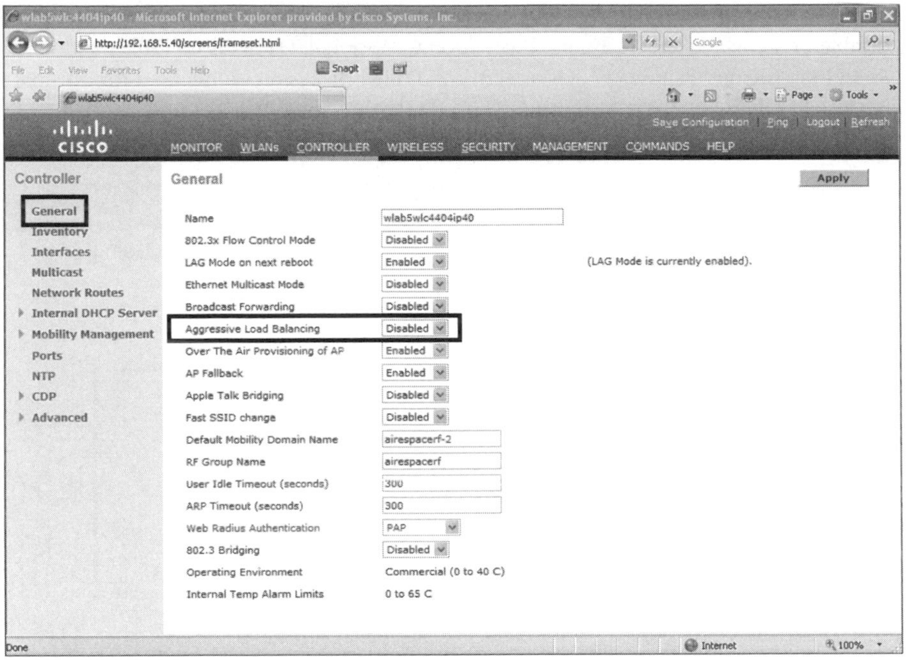

Figure 11-7   *Disable Aggressive Load Balancing*

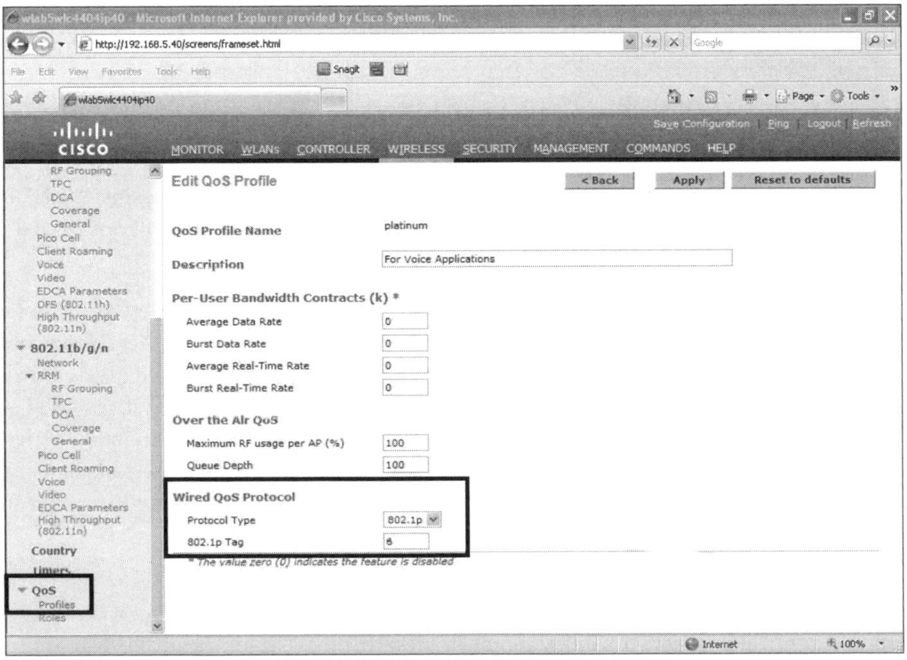

Figure 11-8   *Platinum QoS Configuration*

Enabling symmetric mobility tunneling, introduced in code Release 4.1, allows for better inter-controller roaming. Starting in code Release 5.2, symmetric mobility tunneling is the default and asymmetric tunneling is deprecated. See Chapter 9 for more information on mobility. Figure 11-9 shows symmetric mobility enabled on a controller running 5.2 code.

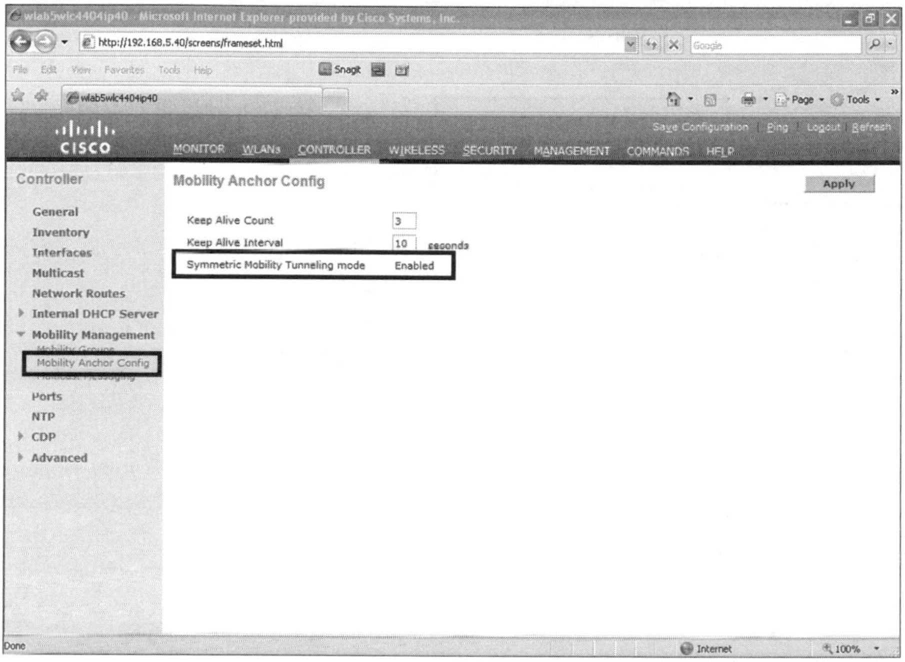

Figure 11-9   *Enabling Symmetric Mobility Tunneling*

If you are planning to use the wireless phones on the 2.4 GHz band, you will want to enable short preambles under the 802.11b/g/n network configuration (see Figure 11-10). Short Premable is enabled by default.

With Short Preamble enabled, the 802.11g clients do not have to send Request To Send (RTS)/CTS messages before sending traffic. This improves voice quality. Keep in mind that enabling short preambles can disrupt 802.11b clients. Figure 11-10 also shows the Beacon interval set to 100. In older code, you would also see the DTIM period here, but in newer code, DTIM is a WLAN-specific configuration (refer to Figure 11-6).

To use TSPEC, CAC must be enabled for the wireless network. The default bandwidth percentages are sufficient for the majority of installations. By default, the maximum setting is 75 percent, with 6 percent of the 75 percent reserved for roaming clients. To account for non-TSPEC clients or other energy that might be on the channel and used by the AP, enable load-based CAC. Figure 11-11 shows the CAC configuration for the 802.11a network.

With Expedited Bandwidth enabled, CCXv5 clients are able to use TSPEC to indicate to the controller that a call is urgent. An example would be an e911 call. As long as the controller can facilitate the urgent call without disrupting the quality of existing calls, it will do so.

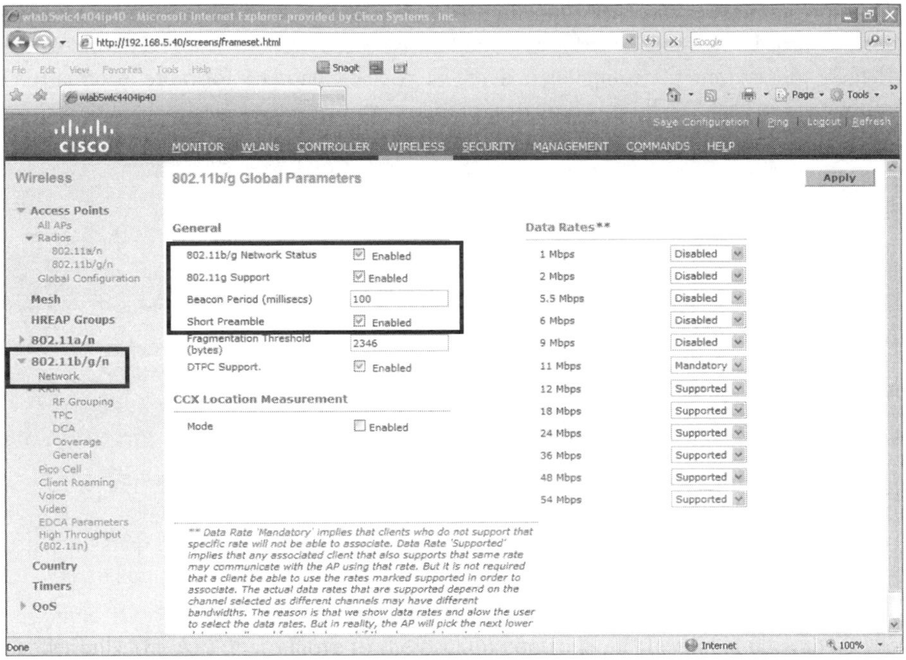

Figure 11-10 *Enabling Short Preamble*

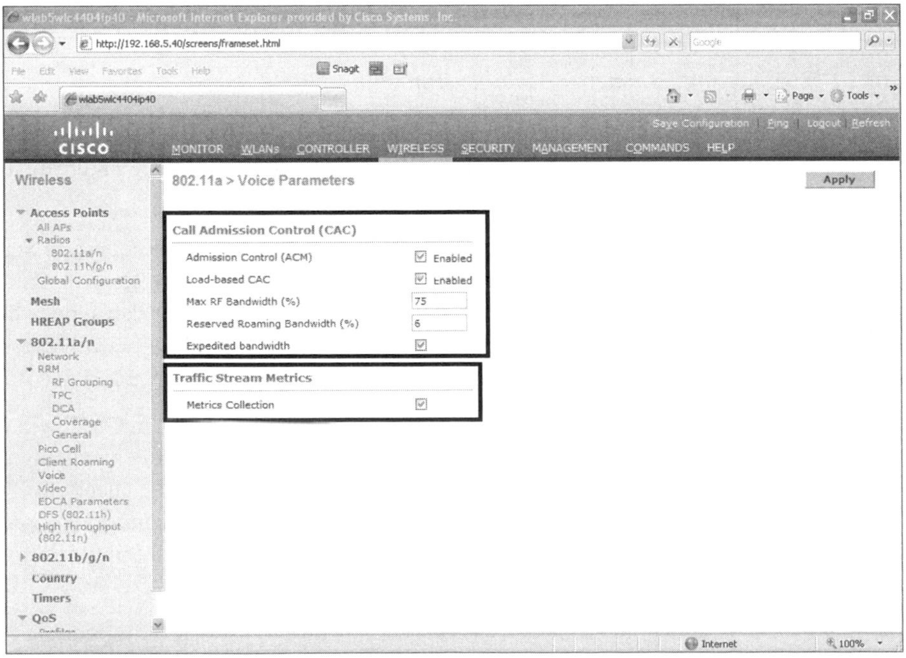

Figure 11-11 *CAC*

Enabling Traffic Stream Metrics (TSM) collection allows you to view the call statistics. You can enable TSM in the same area as CAL in the controller GUI (see Figure 11-11).

If you plan to use 802.1x authentication, LEAP, PEAP, and EAP-FAST for the voice WLAN security, Cisco recommends that you use CCKM for the key management (see Figure 11-12).

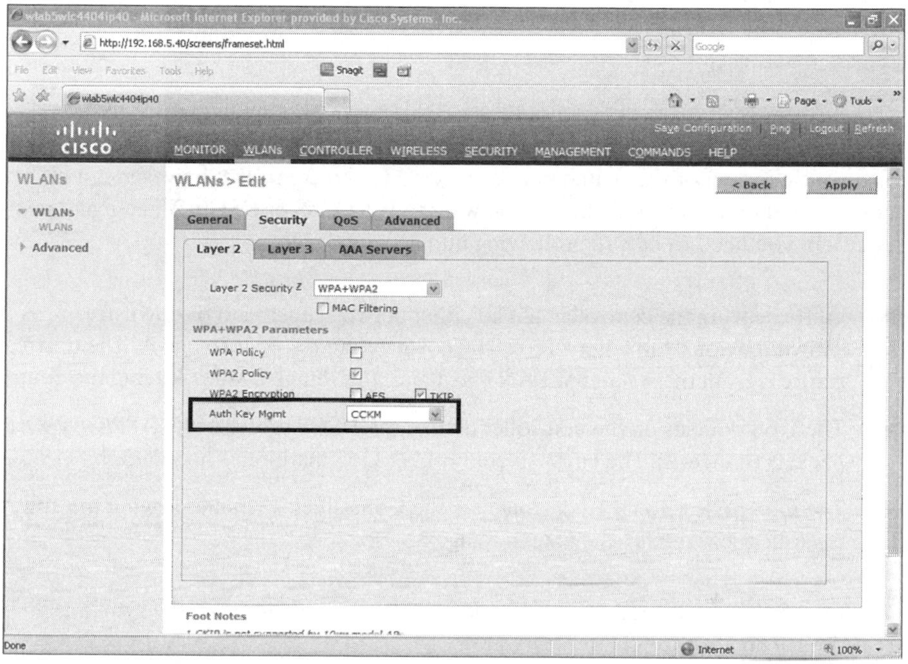

Figure 11-12   *CCKM for Key Management*

During a roaming event, the full reauthentication required by 802.1x can introduce some delay, which might adversely affect voice quality. With centralized key management available with CCKM, however, key exchanges do not occur during a client reassociation, so a roaming event experiences less delay. Currently, the Cisco wireless phones cannot use CCKM with AES encryption, so you need to use TKIP instead.

Switch Ports

For the switch port connected to the AP, make sure you are trusting DSCP. The LWAPP/CAPWAP frames generated by the AP have no CoS marking. The controller configuration determines the DSCP marking of the encapsulated packet between the WLC and AP, and you want to ensure that the switch handles the packet correctly.

If, for example, you are deploying your AP in VLAN 100 on a 3750 access switch, the port would have the configuration shown in Example 11-1.

Example 11-1 *Switch Port QoS Configuration*

```
mls qos
!
interface GigabitEthernet1/0/1
 switchport access vlan 100
 switchport mode access
 mls qos trust dscp
 spanning-tree portfast
```

The configuration of the switch port connected to the controller, however, is a bit more complicated. You have to decide if you want to trust CoS or DSCP. When making your decision, you need to take the following into account:

- Traffic leaving the controller can be either network upstream or downstream, as shown previously in Figure 11-4. The downstream traffic is Range A. The upstream traffic is from the AP and WLAN client and is in Range B when leaving the controller.

- The QoS policies on the controller dictate the DSCP values of LWAPP/CAPWAP packets (Range A). The encapsulated packet QoS marking is not altered.

- The QoS policies on the controller set the CoS values of frames leaving the controller regardless of whether they are in Range A or B.

With the following interface configuration shown in Example 11-2, the switch is going to trust DSCP and not CoS.

Example 11-2 *show interface Command Output Trust DSCP*

```
interface GigabitEthernet1/0/13
 switchport trunk encapsulation dot1q
 switchport trunk allowed vlan 11-13,60,61
 switchport mode trunk
 mls qos trust dscp
```

WLAN Profile on the Phone

To configure the WLAN profiles on the phone, go to **Settings > Network Profiles** and select the profile you want to configure. From here you can set the profile name and configure the WLAN settings. The WLAN setting includes the SSID, security method, and any usernames and passwords that might be required. To unlock the Network Profile menu, use the key sequence **#.

You can also configure the phone using the Universal Serial Bus (USB) connection to access the web configuration pages. The default username and password to access the phone web page is "admin" and "Cisco", respectively. Figure 11-13 shows the WLAN configuration for a 7925 phone.

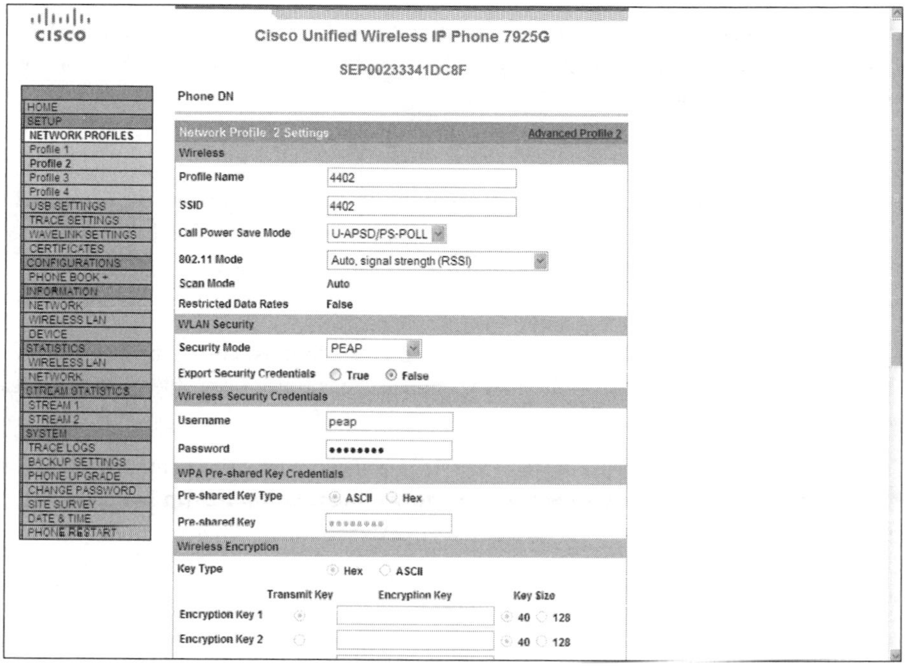

Figure 11-13   *7925 Web Page Configuration*

You have to install the USB adapter software on your machine to access the phone web pages. The USB software is found on the Cisco website at http://www.cisco.com/pcgi-bin/tablebuild.pl/ip-7900ser-crypto.

You also can make configuration changes to the phones using CallManager, but that is outside the scope of this book.

Troubleshooting 792x Voice Quality Issues

Wireless voice applications are much less forgiving than data applications. Where data will retransmit a packet that is not acknowledged and the end user is none the wiser, a voice end user will certainly hear a delay or lost or choppy audio.

The controller, Wireless Control System (WCS), and third-party spectrum analysis tools can provide you with information to locate the source or sources of poor audio.

Basic Troubleshooting/Connectivity

You can resolve the majority of wireless voice issues simply by verifying the configuration of the controller and network connectivity. Verify that the phone is registered to CallManager and whether you can ping the phone from the network.

Note   Pings should only be used to verify network connectivity, not latency. If a 792x phone is not on an active call, ping times can be as high as 2000 ms even if the Call Power Save Mode is set to None.

Tip   To quickly analyze a controller configuration for voice, you can use the Cisco WLC Configuration Analyzer with the voice checks enabled. You can download this tool at http://supportwiki.cisco.com/wiki/index.php/WLC_Config_Analyzer.

Also check the firmware build running on the phones. In most cases, the latest firmware build available for the phone is the best version and has fixes for problems found in earlier releases.

From the phone graphical user interface (GUI), you can check the firmware release running on the phone by going to **Settings > Model Information > App Load ID**. Here you should see the build such as CP7921G-1.3.2.LOADS. Should you see a build such as CP7921G-MFG-D.1LOADS, the phone is running a manufacturing build, and you should upgrade the phone to an official release.

If the problem is association or authentication, verify that the phone has the correct SSID and authentication configured. SSIDs are case sensitive. If the WLAN is using an SSID of "Voice" and the phone has the SSID configured as "voice," the phone will fail to associate.

Tip   It is easy to add an unintentional space after entering the SSID, username, or password when configuring the phones using the phone keypad. Be mindful of this when configuring the phone settings.

The 792x phones by default require that the 12 Mb data rate be enabled. If you disable the 12 Mb data rate on the controller and do not change the phone settings, you will not be able to make calls.

Use the site survey tool built into the phone to see the channel, Received Single Strength Indicator (RSSI), and Channel Utilization of the AP the phone is associated with. Remember that the phone should always see at least one AP at −67 dBm or greater.

The output of **debug client** taken from the controller command-line interface (CLI) provides insight into why the phone is failing authentication. Example 11-3 is partial output from **debug client** showing a 7925 trying to authenticate using PEAP.

Example 11-3   *debug client with 7925 Using PEAP*

```
(Cisco Controller)>debug client 00:23:33:41:dc:8f
!output omitted for brevity
(Cisco Controller) >Mon Aug 10 14:34:33 2009: 00:23:33:41:dc:8f 802.1x
'timeoutEvt' Timer expired for station 00:23:33:41:dc:8f
```

```
Mon Aug 10 14:34:33 2009: 00:23:33:41:dc:8f Retransmit 9 of EAP-Request (length
84) for mobile 00:23:33:41:dc:8f
Mon Aug 10 14:34:34 2009: 00:23:33:41:dc:8f 802.1x 'timeoutEvt' Timer expired for
station 00:23:33:41:dc:8f
Mon Aug 10 14:34:34 2009: 00:23:33:41:dc:8f Retransmit 10 of EAP-Request (length
84) for mobile 00:23:33:41:dc:8f
Mon Aug 10 14:34:35 2009: 00:23:33:41:dc:8f 802.1x 'timeoutEvt' Timer expired for
station 00:23:33:41:dc:8f
Mon Aug 10 14:34:35 2009: 00:23:33:41:dc:8f Retransmit 11 of EAP-Request (length
84) for mobile 00:23:33:41:dc:8f
Mon Aug 10 14:34:36 2009: 00:23:33:41:dc:8f 802.1x 'timeoutEvt' Timer expired for
station 00:23:33:41:dc:8f
Mon Aug 10 14:34:36 2009: 00:23:33:41:dc:8f Retransmit 12 of EAP-Request (length
84) for mobile 00:23:33:41:dc:8f
```

In this debug you see 802.1x timeout events for the phone. This means that the controller has forwarded a request from the RADIUS server to the phone and the phone is not responding quickly enough. When you are using EAP methods to authenticate the phones, it takes more processing power and the phones are just not fast enough, so the controller times them out. To prevent this, you can increase the advanced EAP request timeout values to provide the slower clients more time to respond.

To increase the EAP timeout values on the controller, use the controller CLI:

```
config advanced eap identity-request-timeout 20
oonfig advanced eap request-timeout 20
save config
```

Caution Although you can adjust the retry values as well, increasing the retries can disrupt the network, so use caution when doing so.

You can see the current timer settings using **show advanced eap** from the CLI, as shown in Example 11-4.

Example 11-4 *show advanced eap Command Output*

```
(Cisco Controller) >show advanced eap

EAP-Identity-Request Timeout (seconds)........... 1
EAP-Identity-Request Max Retries................. 2
EAP Key-Index for Dynamic WEP.................... 0
EAP Max-Login Ignore Identity Response........... enable
EAP-Request Timeout (seconds).................... 1
EAP-Request Max Retries.......................... 2
EAPOL-Key Timeout (seconds)...................... 1
EAPOL-Key Max Retries............................ 2
```

As you can see here, the EAP identity and request timeouts are only 1 second by default. This is not nearly enough time for a wireless phone to process a certificate or Protected Access Credential (PAC) file.

> **Note**   In older code, the EAP timers were aggressive. Starting in code Release 5.2, these timers now default to 30 seconds. That should be more than enough time for most clients.

Keep in mind that if you are using CCKM, you will want to use TKIP and not AES encryption because the 792x phones cannot use CCKM with AES. If you are using TKIP, you will want to disable the TKIP hold-down timer for MIC errors. The TKIP counter-measure is triggered when an AP detects two MIC errors within 60 seconds. When the countermeasure takes place, all TKIP clients are deauthenticated, and no TKIP clients can connect for the duration of the hold-off period. By default, the TKIP countermeasures are enabled with a hold-off period of 60 seconds.

You can disable the TKIP countermeasure from the controller CLI using the following commands:

```
config wlan disable wlan-id
config wlan security tkip hold-down seconds wlan-id
config wlan enable wlan-id
```

If just a single phone seems to be having issues but the rest of the deployed units do not, you can try resetting the problem phone to factory default and reconfiguring it.

To reset a 792x to factory default using the phone keypad, go to **Settings > Phone Settings**. While on the Phone Settings main page, enter ****2**. You then see a message on the screen stating, "Start factory reset now?" Choose **Yes** to reset the phone.

Choppy/Lost Audio

Choppy or lost audio sounds like a robotic voice to the listener. If packets are lost, the phone tries to retransmit four times but then stops and you lose audio. Lost packets can be caused by RF conditions or incorrect QoS configuration on the wire, the controller, or the voice device.

Even if you have a single phone, the channel utilization can be quite high because of other devices. Non-802.11 devices such as microwaves or cordless phones, other legitimate wireless devices like laptops, general background noise, and so on all contribute to channel utilization. High-channel utilization can prohibit the phone and AP from hearing each other. For example, if you are using a phone near a working microwave that is poorly shielded, the entire 2.4 spectrum can be affected and severely degrade voice quality. Figure 11-14 shows the effect of a microwave on the 2.4-GHz band.

As you can see, all channels in the 2.4 band show extremely high utilization while the microwave is running.

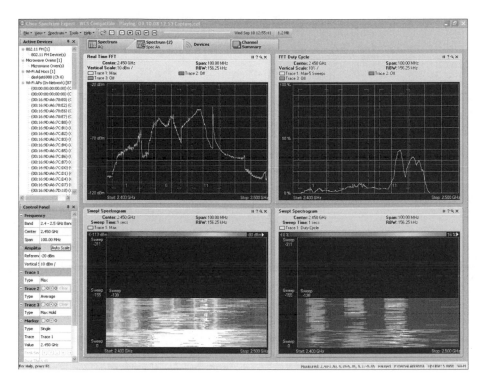

Figure 11-14   *Effect of a Microwave in the 2.4-GHz Band*

If you have never had a professional site survey conducted, you might have an AP density issue. Not only could the wireless deployment not be dense enough, it could be too dense. Although you want to have 20 percent cell overlap to ensure proper roaming with the phones, if the APs are too dense, the phones will have too many roaming options. High AP density can cause the phones to constantly roam between several APs, resulting in lost ACKs and contributing to choppy audio.

If you have not correctly configured QoS end to end on the wired network and the controller is not running 5.1 code with TCLAS enabled, you might have incorrect forwarding of the voice packets, increasing delay. If the voice application is not correctly marking packets leaving the device, the wired network will not correctly prioritize them.

Figure 11-15 shows a wireless packet from a third-party wireless phone using PTT. Looking at the DSCP marking, you can see that the phone is not marking the packets with EF.

Figure 11-16 shows that the LWAPP packet does have a DSCP marking of EF because the WLAN QoS setting is Platinum, but the encapsulated packet from the phone shows a DSCP marking of unknown.

When the controller bridges the PTT packet to the switch (Figure 11-17), the packet has a default DSCP marking, and the switch will not expedite the forwarding of this packet. This scenario can result in choppy or lost audio.

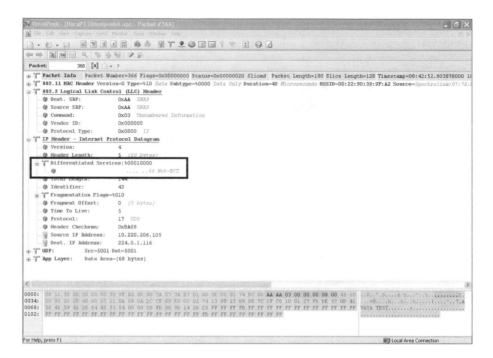

Figure 11-15 *PTT Packet from Third-Party Phone Not Setting EF Bit*

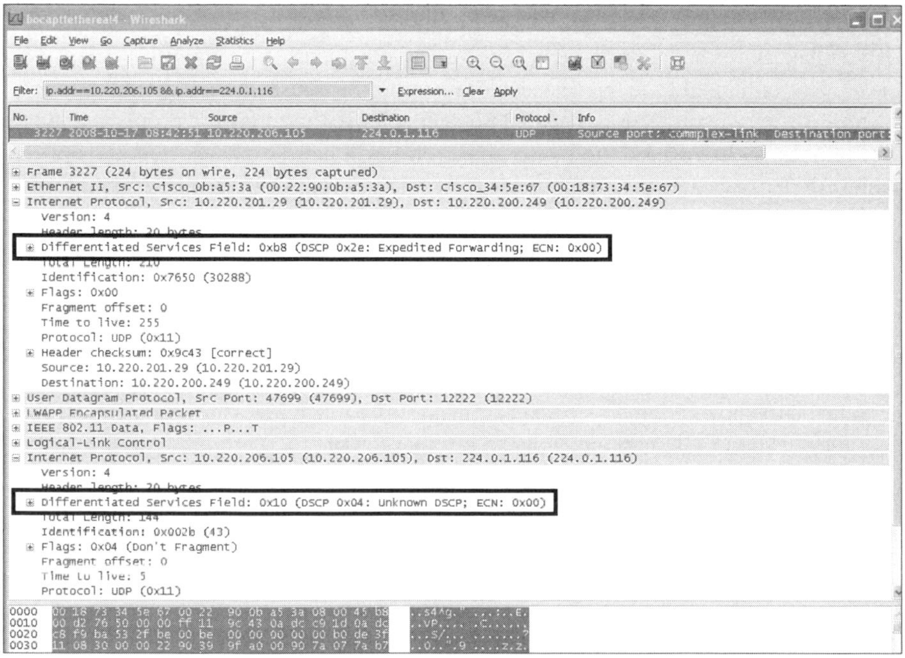

Figure 11-16 *LWAPP Encapsulated PTT Packet From Third-Party Phone*

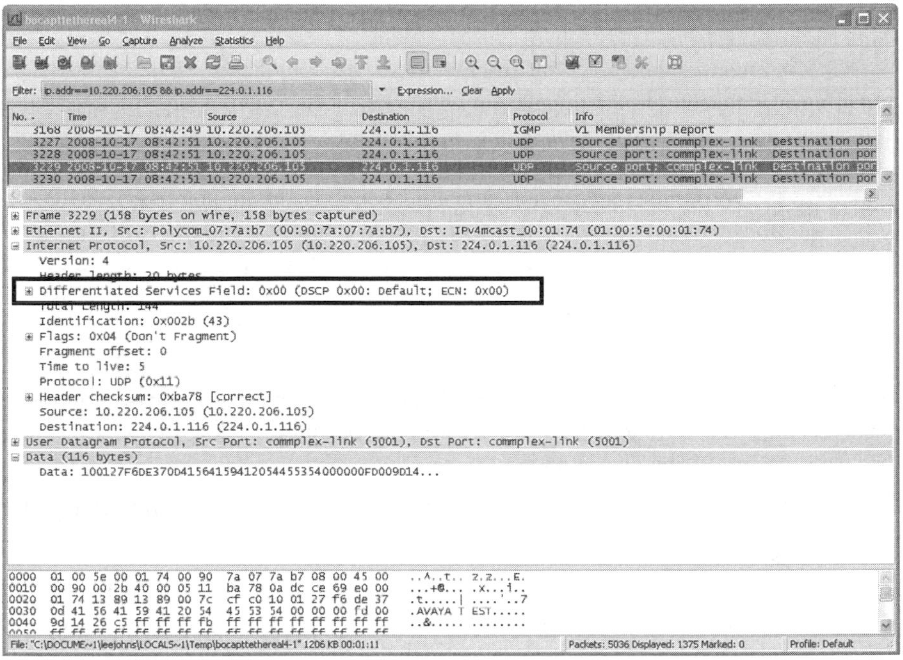

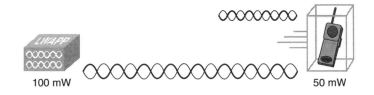

Figure 11-17   *Third-Party Phone PTT Packet on the Switched Network*

One-Way Voice

When a user experiences one-way audio, the usual culprit is a large power discrepancy between the AP the phone (see Figure 11-18).

Figure 11-18   *AP and Phone Power*

If the AP is blasting at 100 mW and the phone is at a maximum power of 50 mW (2.4 GHz) or 40 mW (5 GHz), the phone can hear the AP, but the AP cannot hear the phone. This results in one-way audio.

Ideally, you would have Dynamic Transmit Power Control (DTPC) enabled on the controller so that the phone auto-adjusts its power accordingly. The power setting on the APs and the power settings on the phones do not match exactly. If an AP has set its power level to 25 mW on the 5-GHz band, for example, the phone has to adjust its power to 32 mW. Table 11-4 shows the different transmit power levels for the phones.

Table 11-4 *792x Transmit Power Levels*

802.11b CCK	802.11g OFDM	802.11a OFDM
50 mW (17 dBm)	40 mW (16 dBm)	40 mW (16 dBm)
20 mW (13 dBm)	32 mW (15 dBm)	32 mW (15 dBm)
8 mW (9 dBm)	20 mW (13 dBm)	20 mW (13 dBm)
3.2 mW (5 dBm)	8 mW (9 dBm)	8 mW (9 dBm)
1 mW (0 dBm)	3.2 mW (5 dBm)	3.2 mW (5 dBm)
	1 mW (0 dBm)	1 mW (0 dBm)

With DTPC, if Client Transmit Power is set in the AP, the phone automatically uses the same client power setting. If the AP is set for the maximum setting, the AP uses the Transmit Power setting on the phone.

You can also experience one-way audio if a firewall or any Network Address Translation (NAT) is in the path of the RTP packets.

If your controller is running 5.0 or lower code, check to make sure that ARP unicast is disabled using **show network summary** from the controller CLI, as shown in Example 11-5.

Example 11-5 *show network summary Command Output*

```
(Cisco Controller) >show network summary

RF-Network Name............................. airespacerf
Web Mode.................................... Enable
Secure Web Mode............................. Enable
Secure Web Mode Cipher-Option High.......... Disable
Secure Shell (ssh).......................... Enable
Telnet...................................... Enable
Ethernet Multicast Mode..................... Disable    Mode: Ucast
Ethernet Broadcast Mode..................... Disable
IGMP snooping............................... Disabled
IGMP timeout................................ 60 seconds
User Idle Timeout........................... 300 seconds
ARP Idle Timeout............................ 300 seconds
ARP Unicast Mode............................ Disabled
Cisco AP Default Master..................... Disable
Mgmt Via Wireless Interface................. Disable
```

Should ARP unicast be enabled, you can disable it using the following CLI command:

```
config network arpunicast disable
```

If ARP unicast is enabled, the controller responds to an ARP query on behalf of the client instead of unicasting the request directly to the target host. This behavior can cause one-way audio with voice clients.

Starting in the 5.1 code release, this command is deprecated. Furthermore, the proxy ARP nature of the controller cannot be modified and is always turned off.

Network Busy

When you try to place a call, the phone might display a message indicating that the network is busy. Network Busy messages are generated by two conditions:

■ Physical settings.

■ CAC is enabled, but no bandwidth is available.

By default, the 792x phones use 12 Mb as the PHY rate in the TSPEC. If the 12 Mb data rate is disabled and CAC is enabled on the controller, the phone cannot place a call. A mismatch here between the phone and controller configuration results in an ADDTS refusal or timeout. You can change the PHY rate on the phone, but Cisco does not recommend it. The controller/AP only supports PHY rates of 6, 11, 12, and 24 with CAC enabled. Although higher PHY rates are possible, no gain in the number of simultaneous voice calls or voice quality occurs with data rates higher than 24 Mbps.

> **Note**   With the 1.3.3 firmware release, the phones are able to rate-shift to the next highest supported PHY rate. For example, if you had 12 Mbps disabled but 24 Mbps was enabled, the phone would still be able to place a call. Another example would be if you had only 802.11b radios; at that point, the phone could use 11 Mbps because that is the next highest supported PHY rate available. This feature is nice because you do not have to reconfigure every 792x phone if the 12MBps data rate is not available.

If the WLAN is not able to allocate enough bandwidth for the phone to complete the call, you receive a Network Busy message. To see the CAC information when a client is having issues, use **debug cac all enable** from the controller CLI. When you use the "all" parameter, you are enabling both **cac events** and **cac packets**.

In Example 11-6, you can see that the phone is not able to place a call because of an invalid TSPEC parameter on the controller. You can also see a PHY rate of 12 Mb.

Example 11-6   *debug cac all enable Output*

```
(Cisco Controller) >debug cac all enable
(Cisco Controller) >Wed Oct 24 07:19:04 2007: 00:1b:d4:58:e4:d6 ADD TS from mobile
00:1b:d4:58:e4:d6 on AP 00:1c:57:e2:31:60 slotId 1 up = 6, tid = 6, upsd = 1,
mediumTime = 1056, TSRSIE No
Wed Oct 24 07:19:04 2007: 00:1b:d4:58:e4:d6 up=6 tsid=6 direc=3
```

(continues)

Example 11-6   *debug cac all enable Output (continued)*

```
                                                            NomMsduSize=200

                                                            MaxMsduSize=200

MinServIntvl=0

MaxServIntvl=0

InactIntval=0
MinDataRate=80000
MeanDataRate=80000
PeakDataRate=80000
MinPhyRate=12000000

                                                            SBA=0x2999

MediumTime=1056
Wed Oct 24 07:19:04 2007: Max stream Size is 0
Wed Oct 24 07:19:04 2007: 00:1b:d4:58:e4:d6 TSPEC from mobile 00:1b:d4:58:e4:d6
(up = 6), Invalid TSPEC parameters.
Wed Oct 24 07:19:04 2007: 00:1b:d4:58:e4:d6 Sending Failed ADD TS resp to mobile
00:1b:d4:58:e4:d6 on AP 00:1c:57:e2:31:60 slotId 1
```

The max stream size on the controller should not be 0. You can correct an issue such as this using the following command from the controller CLI:

```
config 802.11a cac voice stream-size <stream-size> max-streams <max-streams>
```

The stream size can be between 84000 and 92100, and the max-streams can be 1 to 5.

The **cac voice stream-size** command dictates the TSPEC size and the number of streams per call. This is a per-call setting that does not limit the number of calls per AP.

You can see the configured CAC for a particular 802.11 network on the controller using **show 802.11** from the controller CLI, as shown in Example 11-7.

Example 11-7   *show dot11 Command Output*

```
(wlab5wlcWISMip22) >show 802.11a

802.11a Network................................. Enabled

*****output omitted*****

Call Admission Control (CAC) configuration
   Voice AC - Admission control (ACM)........... Enabled
   Voice max RF bandwidth....................... 75
```

```
Voice reserved roaming bandwidth.............. 6
Voice load-based CAC mode.................... Enabled
Voice tspec inactivity timeout............... Disabled
Voice tspec inactivity timeout............... Disabled
Video AC - Admission control (ACM)........... Disabled
Voice Stream-Size............................ 84000
Voice Max-Streams............................ 2
Video max RF bandwidth....................... Infinite
Video reserved roaming bandwidth............. 0
```

The default Voice Stream-Size is 84000, and the default Max-Streams is set to 2. This means that the controller will accept a TSPEC from a phone that has up to 2 phone calls (RTP streams), and each call will have a mean data rate of 84000 Kbps or less.

Poor Audio When Roaming

If voice quality deteriorates while roaming, verify the following:

■ Check the RSSI on the destination AP to see if the signal strength is adequate. The next AP should have an RSSI value of −67 dBm or greater.

■ Check the site survey to determine if the channel overlap is adequate for the phone and the AP to hand off the call to the next AP before the signal is lost from the previous AP.

■ Check to see if noise or interference in the coverage area is too great.

■ Check that SNR levels are 25 db or higher for acceptable voice quality.

■ Verify that DHCP Required is disabled on the voice WLAN. The DHCP process causes delay and degrades the quality of the call.

■ Symmetric mobility tunneling should be enabled. Asymmetrical tunneling can cause jitter. See Chapter 9 for more information.

■ If performing inter-controller roaming, check that the controllers involved are mobility members of each other.

■ If you are using 802.1x, it is recommended that you use CCKM because 802.1x requires full reauthentication, which can introduce delay.

■ Use **debug client**, **debug mobility handoff**, and **debug aaa all** to see if mobility or authentication is an issue when the client roams.

Multicast Applications Fail

Features like PTT and MOH are multicast applications. The controllers have three multicast modes:

- **Multicast-Disabled:** Multicast is off; default setting.

- **Multicast-Unicast:** The controller replicates any multicast packets and sends them as unicasts to all registered APs.

- **Multicast-Multicast:** The controller sends multicast traffic to a configured AP multicast group IP.

With the controller set to Multicast-Unicast mode, the controller replicates the multicast packet for every AP joined to it. This is extremely inefficient because all clients, whether they are part of the multicast group or not, receive the multicast traffic. Considering the overhead associated with this, Cisco does not recommend using Multicast-Unicast.

When using Multicast-Multicast on a controller-based wireless infrastructure, you must have multicast routing enabled on your wired network and multicast enabled on the controller.

The **ip multicast-routing** command should be enabled on all routers within your network between the controller(s) and their respective APs.

```
Router(config)#ip multicast-routing
```

Protocol Independent Multicast (PIM) must be enabled on the following VLANs on your network:

- **Controller Management VLAN:** The VLAN the controller's management interface resides in

- **AP VLAN:** The VLAN the APs have their IP address in

- **Client VLAN:** The VLAN the clients have their IP address in

Multicast routing needs to be enabled on the management interface VLAN of the controller because the controller uses that interface to send and receive multicast traffic. The APs are members of the multicast group you configure on the controller, so you need PIM on that VLAN. Again, the AP VLAN is the VLAN the APs have their IP address in. Lastly, the client VLAN needs to have PIM enabled so the clients can join their desired multicast group.

Enabling PIM allows Internet Group Management Protocol (IGMP) routing on the interface. The PIM mode determines how the router populates the multicast routing table. Using sparse-dense-mode is the easiest configuration because it does not require that you designate a rendezvous point (RP).

```
Router(config-if)#ip pim sparse-dense-mode
```

Make sure no network ACLs are blocking multicast traffic to or from these VLANs.

Also ensure that you have configured multicast on the controller. You configure the multicast mode you want to use and if using Multicast-Multicast, configure the IP address the APs will use for their multicast group.

Figure 11-19 shows a controller with Multicast-Multicast enabled.

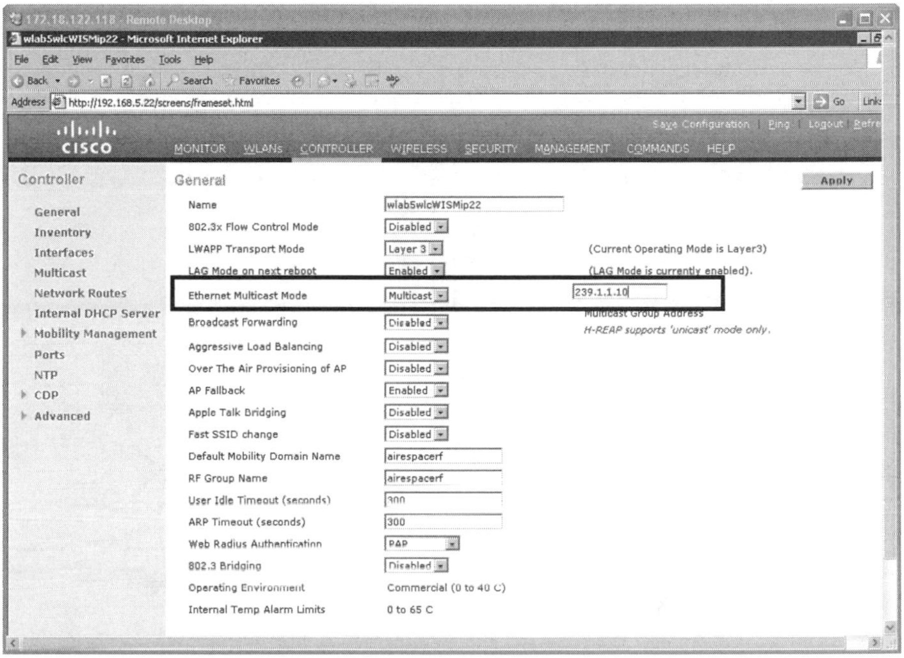

Figure 11-19 *Enabling Multicast*

You should use a multicast address in the IANA administratively reserved private multicast domain range of 239.0.0.0-239.255.255.255. Do not use IPs in the 239.0.0.x and 239.128.0.x address range. Choosing an address outside these ranges prevents overlap with local MAC addresses and prevents multicast floods on the network.

Multicast-Multicast mode is true multicast. With Multicast-Multicast mode enabled, the controller encapsulates the received multicast packet using LWAPP/CAPWAP and forwards the packet to the multicast group address you configured. The controller always uses the management interface for sending multicast packets. Access points in the configured multicast group receive the packet and check to see if it has any clients that are a member of that multicast group. If so, the AP broadcasts the multicast traffic on the client basic service set identifier (BSSID). From the AP perspective, the multicast appears to be a broadcast to all clients within the same Basic Service Set (BSS).

Controller Multicast Delivery Evolution

Before the 3.2 release code, the controllers were capable only of Multicast-Unicast delivery. With the 3.2 release, Cisco introduced the Multicast-Multicast delivery method. This feature made multicast delivery to wireless clients much more efficient because packet replication only had to occur at a point in the network where it was necessary. Figure 11-20 illustrates the Multicast-Multicast traffic flow.

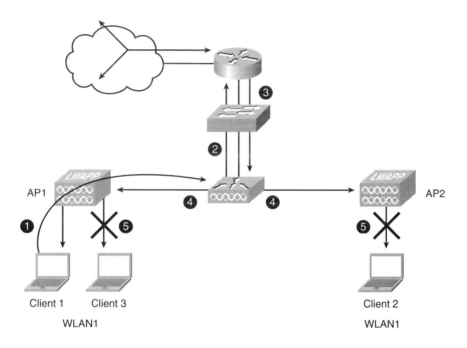

Figure 11-20 *Multicast Traffic Flow*

From Figure 11-20, you can see several steps in how the client IGMP join and multicast delivery takes place:

Step 1.   Client 1 is associated to AP1 on WLAN1 and sends an IGMP join request that goes through the AP to the controller in the LWAPP/CAPWAP tunnel.

Step 2.   The controller forwards the client join on the client VLAN through the upstream switch to the PIM-enabled router. The PIM router adds the IP address of Client 1 to the appropriate IGMP group address.

Step 3.   The PIM-enabled router forwards the multicast packets destined for the IGMP group of Client 1 to the controller.

Step 4.   The controller then forwards the packets to the AP multicast group address. Every AP receives the multicast traffic.

Step 5.   If the AP is servicing WLAN1 and has any clients on that WLAN, it broadcasts the traffic on the appropriate BSSID regardless of whether any of those clients are actually members of the multicast group. Client 2 and Client 3 still receive the traffic but ignore it because they are not members of the IGMP group of Client 1.

When a wireless client wants to leave an IGMP group in pre-4.2 code, it sends an IGMP Leave. The controller bridges it through the upstream switch to the PIM-enabled router, and the router removes Client 1 from the IGMP group.

In code releases before 4.0.206.0, if multicast was enabled in any way, broadcast forwarding was also enabled. If IGMP snooping was enabled on the wired network, this could disrupt wireless multicast delivery. In 4.0.206.0 and higher, broadcast forwarding is no longer enabled by default.

Note   The multicast traffic is sent at the highest basic data rate enabled on the AP, so ensure that only the lowest enabled rate is configured as the only basic rate.

Starting in code release 4.2 or later, Cisco introduced IGMP snooping on the controller to better direct multicast packets. With IGMP enabled (Figure 11-21), the controller gathers IGMP reports from the clients, processes them, and creates unique multicast group IDs (MGIDs) from the IGMP reports.

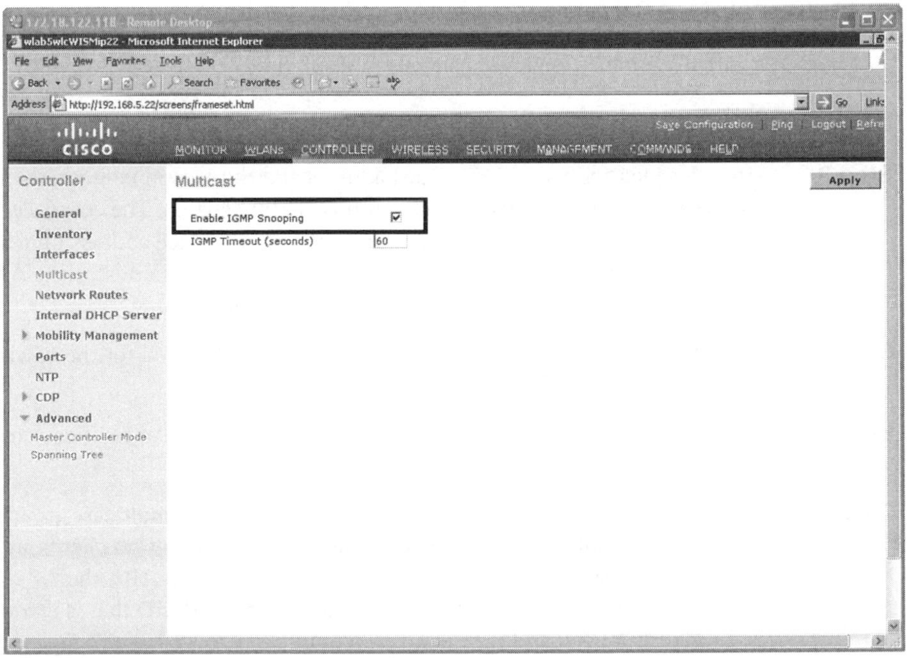

Figure 11-21   *Enabling IGMP Snooping*

Figure 11-22 illustrates the post 4.2 code release multicast delivery with IGMP snooping enabled on the controller.

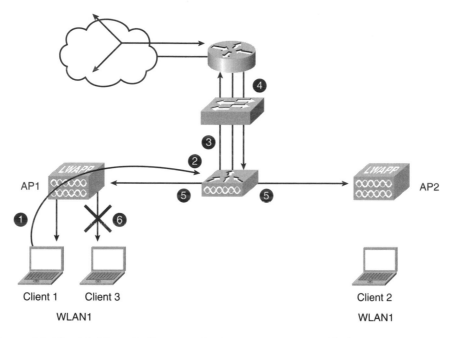

Figure 11-22   *Multicast Delivery with IGMP Snooping Enabled*

Step 1.   Client 1 sends an IGMP join request through the AP to the controller.

Step 2.   The controller creates a unique MGID for the client.

Step 3.   After checking the Layer 3 multicast address and the VLAN number, the controller sends the IGMP reports to the infrastructure switch. The controller sends these reports with the source address as the interface address on which it received the reports from the clients. The controller then updates the AP MGID table on the AP with the client MAC address.

Step 4.   The PIM-enabled router forwards multicast packets destined for the IGMP group of Client 1 to the controller.

Step 5.   When the controller receives multicast traffic for a particular multicast group, it forwards it to all the APs.

Step 6.   If the AP has active clients listening or subscribed to that multicast group, it broadcasts the multicast traffic on that particular WLAN. If no clients are subscribed or listening on that particular WLAN like with AP2, the AP drops the multicast traffic. IP packets are forwarded with an MGID that is unique for an ingress VLAN and the destination multicast group. Layer 2 multicast packets are forwarded with an MGID that is unique for the ingress interface.

Unlike previous releases, in 4.2 and higher code, when a client sends an IGMP Leave, the controller does not bridge it to the network. It simply intercepts it and removes the client from the MGID table. The network PIM-enabled router eventually times out the client and removes it from the IGMP group.

When troubleshooting multicast issues, you need to keep in mind the limitations of using multicast with a controller-based wireless infrastructure:

- 2100 series controllers do not support Multicast-Unicast.

- 2100 series controller with directly connected APs do not support Multicast-Multicast.

- An LWAPP controller drops multicast packets using UDP ports 12222, 12223, and 12224. Make sure your multicast applications do not use these ports.

- A CAPWAP controller drops multicast packets using UDP ports 5246 and 5247. Make sure your multicast applications do not use these ports.

- APs in monitor mode, sniffer mode, or rogue detector mode do not join the AP multicast group address.

- Multicast is not supported with AP groups until code Release 5.0. If you are using AP groups with 4.2 and higher code, make sure IGMP snooping is enabled on the controller to prevent clients from missing multicast traffic when roaming between APs in different AP groups.

- IGMP snooping is not supported on 2100 or Network Module series controllers.

- Multicast traffic is transmitted at 6 Mbps in an 802.11a network. Therefore, if several clients attempt to transmit at 1.5 Mbps, packet loss can occur and break the multicast session.

- Do not use the 239.0.0.X address range or the 239.128.0.X address range. Addresses in these ranges overlap with the link local MAC addresses and flood out all switch ports, even with IGMP snooping turned on.

- Controllers do not support multicast across intersubnet mobility events, such as guest tunneling, site-specific VLANs, or an interface override that uses RADIUS. The multicast mode does work in these subnet mobility events when you disable the Layer 2 IGMP snooping/Cisco Group Management Protocol (CGMP) features on the wired LAN.

- Controllers running code Release 4.2 or later do support multicast mode with interface overrides that use RADIUS (but only when IGMP snooping is enabled) and with site-specific VLANs (AP group VLANs).

Enabling Trace Logs on the 792x

You can enable trace logs on the 792x phones. Viewing the logs can help pinpoint where an issue lies if you are having problems with the phone.

You can enable logging on the following phone modules:

- **Kernel:** Operating system data

- **Wireless LAN Driver:** Channel scanning, roaming, authentication data

- **Wireless LAN Manager:** WLAN management, QoS

- **Configuration:** Phone configuration data

- **Call Control:** Cisco Unified CallManager data

- **Network Services:** DHCP, TFTP, CDP data

- **Security Subsystem:** Application-level security data

- **User Interface:** Keystrokes, softkeys, Modem Management Interface (MMI) data

- **Audio System:** RTP, SRTP, RTCP, Digital Signal Processor (DSP) data

- **System:** Firmware, upgrade data

- **Bluetooth:** Bluetooth data; 7925s only

To access the trace log setup on the phone, use the phone web GUI. Figure 11-23 shows the trace log configuration page from a 7925.

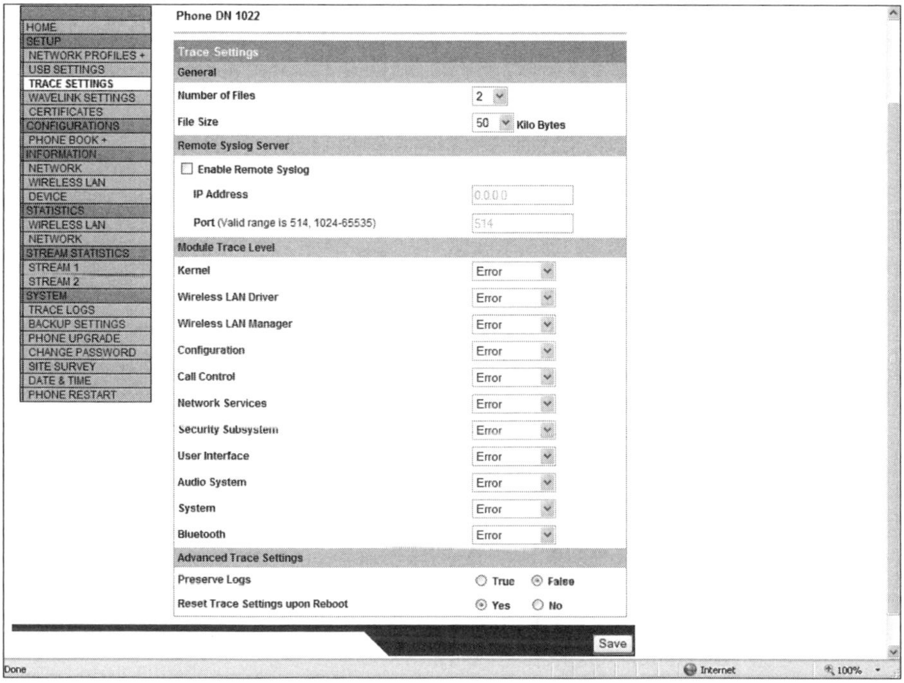

Figure 11-23 *7925 Trace Log Settings*

From this page, you can set up the syslog server information, define how many trace log files to keep and if the phone should keep the logs permanently, and set the level of logging for each module.

You can either download the logs directly from the phone or have the phone send that information to a syslog server.

Example 11-8 is sample output from a 7921 with the Kernel and WLAN Driver modules set to Debug. From this output you can see that this environment has poor coverage and does not meet the RF requirements for using the phones. This in turn results in poor audio quality.

Example 11-8 *WLAN Module Debug Level Trace Log from 7921*

```
! You can see that the RSSI levels are not at the required -67 dBm or better.
! The phone is currently associated to an AP with an RSSI of -75 dBm. Below you
! see that the first candidate AP the phone sees with its scan has an RSSI
! of -71 dBm, which is better but is still less than the requirement of -67 dBm.

Jun 29 16:02:39 10.35.137.142 SEP0021A0B3A06D-kernel: WLAN_DRVR: 2403.668708: Curr
BSS: 00:21:1b:ea:1d:1e
Jun 29 16:02:39 10.35.137.142 SEP0021A0B3A06D-kernel: WLAN_DRVR: 2403.673655:
Channel: 149, av RSSI: -75 dBm, AAC = 22361, ACM = 1, hostName = LeeLab-ap2
Jun 29 16:02:39 10.35.137.142 SEP0021A0B3A06D-kernel: WLAN_DRVR: 2403.682776:
***Neigh entries = 9
Jun 29 16:02:39 10.35.137.142 SEP0021A0B3A06D-kernel: WLAN_DRVR: 2403.687090:
BSSID #0: 00:1e:4a:e0:23:ce
Jun 29 16:02:39 10.35.137.142 SEP0021A0B3A06D-kernel: WLAN_DRVR: 2403.692096:
Channel: 153, avg RSSI: -71 dBm, track fail: 2, AAC = 23437, ACM = 1, hostName =
LeeLab-ap3
Jun 29 16:02:39 10.35.137.142 SEP0021A0B3A06D-kernel: WLAN_DRVR: 2403.702745:
BSSID #1: 00:1e:4a:e0:0d:cc
Jun 29 16:02:39 10.35.137.142 SEP0021A0B3A06D-kernel: WLAN_DRVR: 2403.707755:
Channel: 60, avg RSSI: -77 dBm, track fail: 0, AAC = 22361, ACM = 1, hostName =
LeeLab-ap4
Jun 29 16:02:39 10.35.137.142 SEP0021A0B3A06D-kernel: WLAN_DRVR: 2403.718374:
BSSID #2: 00:1f:6d:b9:f5:4e
Jun 29 16:02:39 10.35.137.142 SEP0021A0B3A06D-kernel: WLAN_DRVR: 2403.723430:
Channel: 153, avg RSSI: -79 dBm, track fail: 0, AAC = 23437, ACM = 1, hostName =
LeeLab-ap5
Jun 29 16:02:39 10.35.137.142 SEP0021A0B3A06D-kernel: WLAN_DRVR: 2403.734098:
BSSID #3: 00:1e:4a:df:e3:4e
Jun 29 16:02:39 10.35.137.142 SEP0021A0B3A06D-kernel: WLAN_DRVR: 2403.739107:
Channel: 60, avg RSSI: -79 dBm, track fail: 0, AAC = 23437, ACM = 1, hostName =
LeeLab-ap6
Jun 29 16:02:39 10.35.137.142 SEP0021A0B3A06D-kernel: WLAN_DRVR: 2403.749614:
BSSID #4: 00:1e:4a:8f:eb:ae
Jun 29 16:02:39 10.35.137.142 SEP0021A0B3A06D-kernel: WLAN_DRVR: 2403.754654:
Channel: 60, avg RSSI: -81 dBm, track fail: 0, AAC = 23437, ACM = 1, hostName =
LeeLab-ap7
Jun 29 16:02:39 10.35.137.142 SEP0021A0B3A06D-kernel: WLAN_DRVR: 2403.765320:
BSSID #5: 00:1e:4a:e0:0c:6e
```

(continues)

Example 11-8 *WLAN Module Debug Level Trace Log from 7921 (continued)*

```
Jun 29 16:02:39 10.35.137.142 SEP0021A0B3A06D-kernel: WLAN_DRVR: 2403.770330:
Channel: 60, avg RSSI: -82 dBm, track fail: 1, AAC = 23437, ACM = 1, hostName =
LeeLab-ap8
Jun 29 16:02:39 10.35.137.142 SEP0021A0B3A06D-kernel: WLAN_DRVR: 2403.780851:
BSSID #6: 00:1e:4a:df:e1:fe
Jun 29 16:02:39 10.35.137.142 SEP0021A0B3A06D-kernel: WLAN_DRVR: 2403.785862:
Channel: 52, avg RSSI: -88 dBm, track fail: 2, AAC = 23437, ACM = 1, hostName =
LeeLab-ap9
Jun 29 16:02:39 10.35.137.142 SEP0021A0B3A06D-kernel: WLAN_DRVR: 2403.796478:
BSSID #7: 00:1e:4a:df:e9:0e
Jun 29 16:02:39 10.35.137.142 SEP0021A0B3A06D-kernel: WLAN_DRVR: 2403.801483:
Channel: 153, avg RSSI: -93 dBm, track fail: 0, AAC = 23437, ACM = 1, hostName =
LeeLab-ap10
Jun 29 16:02:39 10.35.137.142 SEP0021A0B3A06D-kernel: WLAN_DRVR: 2403.812585:
BSSID #8: 00:23:ab:26:28:5e
Jun 29 16:02:39 10.35.137.142 SEP0021A0B3A06D-kernel: WLAN_DRVR: 2403.817594:
Channel: 52, avg RSSI: -97 dBm, track fail: 0, AAC = 23437, ACM = 1, hostName =
LeeLab-ap11
Jun 29 16:02:39 10.35.137.142 SEP0021A0B3A06D-kernel: WLAN_DRVR: 2403.828156:
***End of List

! Even though there is another AP with a better RSSI, for the phone to make the
! roaming decision, a difference in RSSI of at least 5 dBm is required.
! So in this case, the phone does not roam.

Jun 29 16:02:39 10.35.137.142 SEP0021A0B3A06D-kernel: WLAN_DRVR: 2403.831944: Cont
scan complete, Curr AP RSSI = -75 => DiffThr = 5

!The phone then scans again.

Jun 29 16:02:40 10.35.137.142 SEP0021A0B3A06D-kernel: WLAN_DRVR: 2404.360721:
ScanMgr Perform Cont Scan
Jun 29 16:02:40 10.35.137.142 SEP0021A0B3A06D-kernel: WLAN_DRVR: 2404.365532: Num
chans in A list = 6, Period is 750
Jun 29 16:02:40 10.35.137.142 SEP0021A0B3A06D-kernel: WLAN_DRVR: 2404.371457:
CounterN 1 ¦ PeriodN 3 ¦ CounterO 13 ¦ PeriodO 31
Jun 29 16:02:40 10.35.137.142 SEP0021A0B3A06D-kernel: WLAN_DRVR: 2404.378313: Next
list is A.
Jun 29 16:02:40 10.35.137.142 SEP0021A0B3A06D-kernel: WLAN_DRVR: 2404.382230:
Scanning channel 52, 1 times, type: active  triggered, UP - 6, AC3Admitted = 1,
SlicedScan = N
Jun 29 16:02:40 10.35.137.142 SEP0021A0B3A06D-kernel: WLAN_DRVR: 2404.393256:
Total number of channels in scan command = 1
Jun 29 16:02:40 10.35.137.142 SEP0021A0D3A06D-kernel: WLAN_DRVR: 2404.434261: Scan
CB received frame.
Jun 29 16:02:40 10.35.137.142 SEP0021A0B3A06D-kernel: WLAN_DRVR: 2404.447596: No
probe response from AP in channel 52, updating RSSI Value from -88 to -91
Jun 29 16:02:40 10.35.137.142 SEP0021A0B3A06D-kernel: WLAN_DRVR: 2404.456996: No
probe response from AP in channel 52, updating RSSI Value from -97 to -97
```

```
Jun 29 16:02:40 10.35.137.142 SEP0021A0B3A06D-kernel: WLAN_DRVR: 2404.466490: Curr
BSS: 00:21:1b:ea:1d:1e

Jun 29 16:02:40 10.35.137.142 SEP0021A0B3A06D-kernel: WLAN_DRVR: 2404.471369:
Channel: 149, av RSSI: -77 dBm, AAC = 22361, ACM = 1, hostName = LeeLab-ap1

Jun 29 16:02:40 10.35.137.142 SEP0021A0B3A06D-kernel: WLAN_DRVR: 2404.480497:
***Neigh entries = 10

Jun 29 16:02:40 10.35.137.142 SEP0021A0B3A06D-kernel: WLAN_DRVR: 2404.484935:
BSSID #0: 00:1e:4a:e0:23:ce

Jun 29 16:02:40 10.35.137.142 SEP0021A0B3A06D-kernel: WLAN_DRVR: 2404.489954:
Channel: 153, avg RSSI: -71 dBm, track fail: 2, AAC = 23437, ACM = 1, hostName =
LeeLab-ap3

Jun 29 16:02:40 10.35.137.142 SEP0021A0B3A06D-kernel: WLAN_DRVR: 2404.500647:
BSSID #1: 00:1e:4a:df:ca:ee

Jun 29 16:02:40 10.35.137.142 SEP0021A0B3A06D-kernel: WLAN_DRVR: 2404.505673:
Channel: 52, avg RSSI: -71 dBm, track fail: 0, AAC = 23437, ACM = 1, hostName =
LeeLab-ap13

Jun 29 16:02:40 10.35.137.142 SEP0021A0B3A06D-kernel: WLAN_DRVR: 2404.516242:
BSSID #2: 00:1e:4a:e0:0d:ee

Jun 29 16:02:40 10.35.137.142 SEP0021A0B3A06D-kernel: WLAN_DRVR: 2404.521275:
Channel: 60, avg RSSI: -77 dBm, track fail: 0, AAC = 22361, ACM = 1, hostName =
LeeLab-ap4

Jun 29 16:02:40 10.35.137.142 SEP0021A0B3A06D-kernel: WLAN_DRVR: 2404.531856:
BSSID #3: 00:1f:6d:b9:f5:4e

Jun 29 16:02:40 10.35.137.142 SEP0021A0B3A06D-kernel: WLAN_DRVR: 2404.536864:
Channel: 153, avg RSSI: -79 dBm, track fail: 0, AAC = 23437, ACM = 1, hostName =
LeeLab-ap5

Jun 29 16:02:40 10.35.137.142 SEP0021A0B3A06D-kernel: WLAN_DRVR: 2404.547465:
BSSID #4: 00:1e:4a:df:e3:4e

Jun 29 16:02:40 10.35.137.142 SEP0021A0B3A06D-kernel: WLAN_DRVR: 2404.552479:
Channel: 60, avg RSSI: -79 dBm, track fail: 0, AAC = 23437, ACM = 1, hostName =
LeeLab-ap6

Jun 29 16:02:40 10.35.137.142 SEP0021A0B3A06D-kernel: WLAN_DRVR: 2404.562932:
BSSID #5: 00:1e:4a:8f:eb:ae

Jun 29 16:02:40 10.35.137.142 SEP0021A0B3A06D-kernel: WLAN_DRVR: 2404.567945:
Channel: 60, avg RSSI: -81 dBm, track fail: 1, AAC = 23437, ACM = 1, hostName =
LeeLab-ap7

Jun 29 16:02:40 10.35.137.142 SEP0021A0B3A06D-kernel: WLAN_DRVR: 2404.578580:
BSSID #6: 00:1e:4a:e0:0c:6e

Jun 29 16:02:40 10.35.137.142 SEP0021A0B3A06D-kernel: WLAN_DRVR: 2404.583594:
Channel: 60, avg RSSI: -82 dBm, track fail: 3, AAC = 23437, ACM = 1, hostName =
LeeLab-ap8

Jun 29 16:02:40 10.35.137.142 SEP0021A0B3A06D-kernel: WLAN_DRVR: 2404.594049:
BSSID #7: 00:1e:4a:df:e1:fe

Jun 29 16:02:40 10.35.137.142 SEP0021A0B3A06D-kernel: WLAN_DRVR: 2404.599062:
Channel: 52, avg RSSI: -91 dBm, track fail: 0, AAC = 23437, ACM = 1, hostName =
LeeLab-ap9

Jun 29 16:02:40 10.35.137.142 SEP0021A0B3A06D-kernel: WLAN_DRVR: 2404.609697:
BSSID #8: 00:1e:4a:df:e9:0e

Jun 29 16:02:40 10.35.137.142 SEP0021A0B3A06D-kernel: WLAN_DRVR: 2404.614714:
Channel: 153, avg RSSI: -93 dBm, track fail: 1, AAC = 23437, ACM = 1, hostName =
LeeLab-ap10
```

(continues)

Example 11-8 *WLAN Module Debug Level Trace Log from 7921 (continued)*

```
Jun 29 16:02:40 10.35.137.142 SEP0021A0B3A06D-kernel: WLAN_DRVR: 2404.625810: BSSID
#9: 00:23:ab:26:28:5e
Jun 29 16:02:40 10.35.137.142 SEP0021A0B3A06D-kernel: WLAN_DRVR: 2404.630815:
Channel: 52, avg RSSI: -97 dBm, track fail: 0, AAC = 23437, ACM = 1, hostName =
LeeLab-ap11
Jun 29 16:02:41 10.35.137.142 SEP0021A0B3A06D-kernel: WLAN_DRVR: 2404.641362:
***End of List

!After this scan, the current AP RSSI is -77 dBm. The RSSI of a potential
! candidate AP is -71 dBm. The differential of 5 dBm is now met and the phone
! attempts to roam to 00:1e:4a:e0:23:ce on channel 153 from 00:21:1b:ea:1d:1e
! from channel 149.


Jun 29 16:02:41 10.35.137.142 SEP0021A0B3A06D-kernel: WLAN_DRVR: 2404.645140: Cont
scan complete, Curr AP RSSI = -77 => DiffThr = 5
Jun 29 16:02:41 10.35.137.142 SEP0021A0B3A06D-kernel: WLAN_DRVR: 2404.652377: RSSI
diff condition met: QBSSCACThr = 70, b5GHz - 1, bQBSSCACThrOK = 1, bRSSIDiff = 1,
bRSSIDiffQSS = 0
Jun 29 16:02:41 10.35.137.142 SEP0021A0B3A06D-kernel: WLAN_DRVR: 2404.664139:
Calling InvokeRoamingTrigger, trigger = 4
Jun 29 16:02:41 10.35.137.142 SEP0021A0B3A06D-kernel: WLAN_DRVR: 2404.670355:
roamingMngr_triggerRoamingCb, higher trigger = 4
Jun 29 16:02:41 10.35.137.142 SEP0021A0B3A06D-kernel: WLAN_DRVR: 2404.677217: Roam
trigger = ROAMING_TRIGGER_RSSIDIFF
Jun 29 16:02:41 10.35.137.142 SEP0021A0B3A06D-kernel: WLAN_DRVR: 2404.683229:
smSelection invokedRoaming Mngr BSS list, num of candidates = 10
Jun 29 16:02:41 10.35.137.142 SEP0021A0B3A06D-kernel: WLAN_DRVR: 2404.691477:
Candidate 0, BSSID=00:1e:4a:e0:23:ce, RSSI =-71


!output omitted for brevity


Jun 29 16:02:41 10.35.137.142 SEP0021A0B3A06D-kernel: WLAN_DRVR: 2404.793134:
Current BSSID = 00:21:1b:ea:1d:1e
Jun 29 16:02:41 10.35.137.142 SEP0021A0B3A06D-kernel: , requestType = 2
Jun 29 16:02:41 10.35.137.142 SEP0021A0B3A06D-kernel: WLAN_DRVR: 2404.806391:
Candidate BSSID = 00:1e:4a:e0:23:ce
Jun 29 16:02:41 10.35.137.142 SEP0021A0B3A06D-kernel: TIWLAN: 749729.144: CCX_MAN-
AGER      ,^IERROR:      ccxMngr_parseCcxVer, supported version: 5
Jun 29 16:02:41 10.35.137.142 SEP0021A0B3A06D-kernel:
Jun 29 16:02:41 10.35.137.142 SEP0021A0B3A06D-kernel:   Auth Succ Event from
Driver to another BSSID.
Jun 29 16:02:41 10.35.137.142 SEP0021A0B3A06D-kernel: WLAN_DRVR: 2404.907103:
Assoc/Reassoc status code =  0, connStatus = 3
Jun 29 16:02:41 10.35.137.142 SEP0021A0B3A06D-kernel: WLAN_DRVR: 2404.913754:
connStatus: HANDOVER SUCCESSFUL


!output omitted for brevity
```

```
Jun 29 16:02:41 10.35.137.142 SEP0021A0B3A06D-kernel: WLAN_DRVR: 2405.011953:
Roamed successfully to candidate with index=0, new BSSID is 00:1e:4a:e0:23:ce.
Jun 29 16:02:41 10.35.137.142 SEP0021A0B3A06D-kernel: WLAN_DRVR: 2405.021528:
Reassociated with status code = 0.
Jun 29 16:02:41 10.35.137.142 SEP0021A0B3A06D-kernel: WLAN_DRVR: 2405.027021:
Moving old channel 149 to A List
Jun 29 16:02:41 10.35.137.142 SEP0021A0B3A06D-kernel: WLAN_DRVR: 2405.032357:
Channel list does not need update.
Jun 29 16:02:41 10.35.137.142 SEP0021A0B3A06D-kernel: WLAN_DRVR: 2405.037844:
Handover Done
Jun 29 16:02:41 10.35.137.142 SEP0021A0B3A06D-kernel: WLAN_DRVR: 2405.041412:
Invoking RemoveBSSListEntry
Jun 29 16:02:41 10.35.137.142 SEP0021A0B3A06D-kernel: WLAN_DRVR: 2405.046274:
Removing entry 0 of 10
Jun 29 16:02:41 10.35.137.142 SEP0021A0B3A06D-kernel: TIWLAN: 749729.360: --------
--------------------------------
Jun 29 16:02:41 10.35.137.142 SEP0021A0B3A06D-kernel: TIWLAN: 749729.360: --
NEW CONNECTION
Jun 29 16:02:41 10.35.137.142 SEP0021A0B3A06D-kernel: TIWLAN: 749729.360: --------
--------------------------------
Jun 29 16:02:41 10.35.137.142 SEP0021A0B3A06D-kernel: TIWLAN: 749729.360: --
SSID = LeeLAB
Jun 29 16:02:41 10.35.137.142 SEP0021A0B3A06D-kernel: TIWLAN: 749729.360: -- BSSID
= 00-1E-4A-E0-23-CE

! Here you can see that the 7921 loses connection to the current AP (BSS Loss)
! and a roam is triggered.


Jun 29 16:02:42 10.35.137.142 SEP0021A0B3A06D-kernel: WLAN_DRVR: 2405.961529: Cont
scan complete, Curr AP RSSI = -81 => DiffThr = 5
Jun 29 16:02:42 10.35.137.142 SEP0021A0B3A06D-kernel: WLAN_DRVR: 2405.968792: RSSI
diff condition met: QBSSCACThr = 70, b5GHz = 1, bQBSSCACThrOK = 1, bRSSIDiff = 1,
bRSSIDiffQSS = 0
Jun 29 16:02:42 10.35.137.142 SEP0021A0B3A06D-kernel: WLAN_DRVR: 2405.980635:
Calling InvokeRoamingTrigger, trigger = 4
Jun 29 16:02:42 10.35.137.142 SEP0021A0B3A06D-kernel: WLAN_DRVR: 2405.986861:
roamingMngr_triggerRoamingCb, higher trigger = 4
Jun 29 16:02:42 10.35.137.142 SEP0021A0B3A06D-kernel: WLAN_DRVR: 2405.993767:
roamingMngr_triggerRoamingCb, trigger = 4 Ignored!!,deltaTs=1317,
lowPassFilterRoamingAttempt=5000
Jun 29 16:02:42 10.35.137.142 SEP0021A0B3A06D-kernel: WLAN_DRVR: 2406.016487: Roam
trigger = ROAMING_TRIGGER_BSS_LOSS

!The phone then tries to roam to 00:1e:4a:df:ca:ee, which has a signal of -71 dBm.


Jun 29 16:02:42 10.35.137.142 SEP0021A0B3A06D-kernel: WLAN_DRVR: 2406.302372:
Candidate BSSID = 00:1e:4a:df:ca:ee
Jun 29 16:02:42 10.35.137.142 SEP0021A0B3A06D-kernel: WLAN_DRVR: 2406.329079:
ScanMgr Perform Cont Scan
```

(continues)

Example 11-8 *WLAN Module Debug Level Trace Log from 7921 (continued)*

```
Jun 29 16:02:42 10.35.137.142 SEP0021A0B3A06D-kernel: WLAN_DRVR: 2406.333861: Num
chans in A list = 6, Period is 750

Jun 29 16:02:42 10.35.137.142 SEP0021A0B3A06D-kernel: WLAN_DRVR: 2406.339748:
CounterN 0 ¦ PeriodN 3 ¦ CounterO 15 ¦ PeriodO 31

Jun 29 16:02:42 10.35.137.142 SEP0021A0B3A06D-kernel: WLAN_DRVR: 2406.346592: Next
list is A.

Jun 29 16:02:42 10.35.137.142 SEP0021A0B3A06D-kernel: WLAN_DRVR: 2406.350443:
Scanning channel 56, 1 times, type: active  triggered, UP = 6, AC3Admitted = 1,
SlicedScan = N

Jun 29 16:02:42 10.35.137.142 SEP0021A0B3A06D-kernel: WLAN_DRVR: 2406.361459:
Total number of channels in scan command = 1

Jun 29 16:02:42 10.35.137.142 SEP0021A0B3A06D-kernel: WLAN_DRVR: 2406.367924:
Failed to start tracking continuous scan, return code 3.

Jun 29 16:02:42 10.35.137.142 SEP0021A0B3A06D-kernel: TIWLAN: 749730.710: CCX_MAN-
AGER      ,^IERROR:       ccxMngr_parseCcxVer, supported version: 5

Jun 29 16:02:42 10.35.137.142 SEP0021A0B3A06D-kernel:

Jun 29 16:02:42 10.35.137.142 SEP0021A0B3A06D-kernel:    Auth Succ Event from
Driver to another BSSID.

Jun 29 16:02:42 10.35.137.142 SEP0021A0B3A06D-kernel: WLAN_DRVR: 2406.474143:
Assoc/Reassoc status code =  0, connStatus = 3

Jun 29 16:02:42 10.35.137.142 SEP0021A0B3A06D-kernel: WLAN_DRVR: 2406.480806:
connStatus: HANDOVER SUCCESSFUL


! ouput omitted for brevity


Jun 29 16:02:42 10.35.137.142 SEP0021A0B3A06D-kernel: WLAN_DRVR: 2406.560914:
Successful roam due to trigger ROAMING_TRIGGER_BSS_LOSS


Jun 29 16:02:42 10.35.137.142 SEP0021A0B3A06D-kernel: WLAN_DRVR: 2406.568416:
Admission is currently required

Jun 29 16:02:42 10.35.137.142 SEP0021A0B3A06D-kernel: WLAN_DRVR: 2406.573643:
Setting AC3 to admitted status.

Jun 29 16:02:42 10.35.137.142 SEP0021A0B3A06D-kernel: WLAN_DRVR: 2406.578975:
Roamed successfully to candidate with index=0, new BSSID is 00:1e:4a:df:ca:ee.

Jun 29 16:02:43 10.35.137.142 SEP0021A0B3A06D-kernel: TIWLAN: 749730.927: --------
----------------------------------

Jun 29 16:02:43 10.35.137.142 SEP0021A0B3A06D-kernel: TIWLAN: 749730.927: --
NEW CONNECTION          --

Jun 29 16:02:43 10.35.137.142 SEP0021A0B3A06D-kernel: TIWLAN: 749730.927: --------
----------------------------------

Jun 29 16:02:43 10.35.137.142 SEP0021A0B3A06D-kernel: TIWLAN: 749730.927: SSID  =
LeeLAB Jun 29 16:02:43 10.35.137.142 SEP0021A0B3A06D-kernel: TIWLAN: 749730.927:
— BSSID = 00-1E-4A-DF-CA-EE


!As you can see above, it takes 1.567 seconds between the connection to
! 00:1e:4a:e0:23:ce > BSS Loss > roam to 00:1e:4a:df:ca:ee. There is a
! 596 ms delta between the BSS Loss and the roam to 00:1e:4a:df:ca:ee.
! This will definitely be an audible gap.
```

> **Note**   The RSSI differential value needed to trigger a roaming event depends on the current RSSI of the AP the phone is associated with. The better the RSSI, the greater the differential value will be.

> **Note**   After the phone is registered to CallManager, the configuration of the phone from the GUI may be disabled. To re-enable it, find the phone in CallManager, set Web Access rights to Full, update the phone, and reboot it.

Troubleshooting and Monitoring Tools

Many different tools are available to help configure, monitor, and troubleshoot your voice deployments.

Wireless Controller

Along with client debug information, the controller can provide voice statistics for the clients as long as you have enabled the Traffic Stream Metrics (TSM) collection (see Figure 11-10) under CAC. The TSM for the client displays packet delay and packet loss. Figure 11-24 shows the TSM for a 7921.

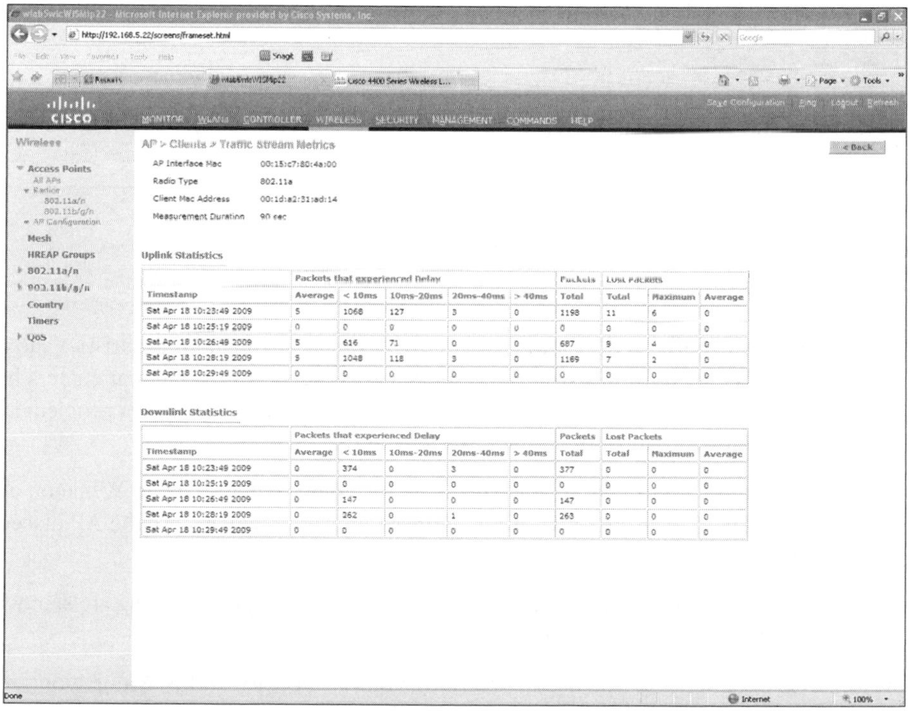

Figure 11-24   *Traffic Stream Metrics*

Packet loss and delay are key components of voice quality. The TSM output provides insight into what the caller is experiencing.

You can also view radio statistics for a particular AP. The radio statistics show how busy the channel is, interference levels, load, radar, and other information. Figure 11-25 shows the radio statistics for the 802.11a radio of a 1242 AP.

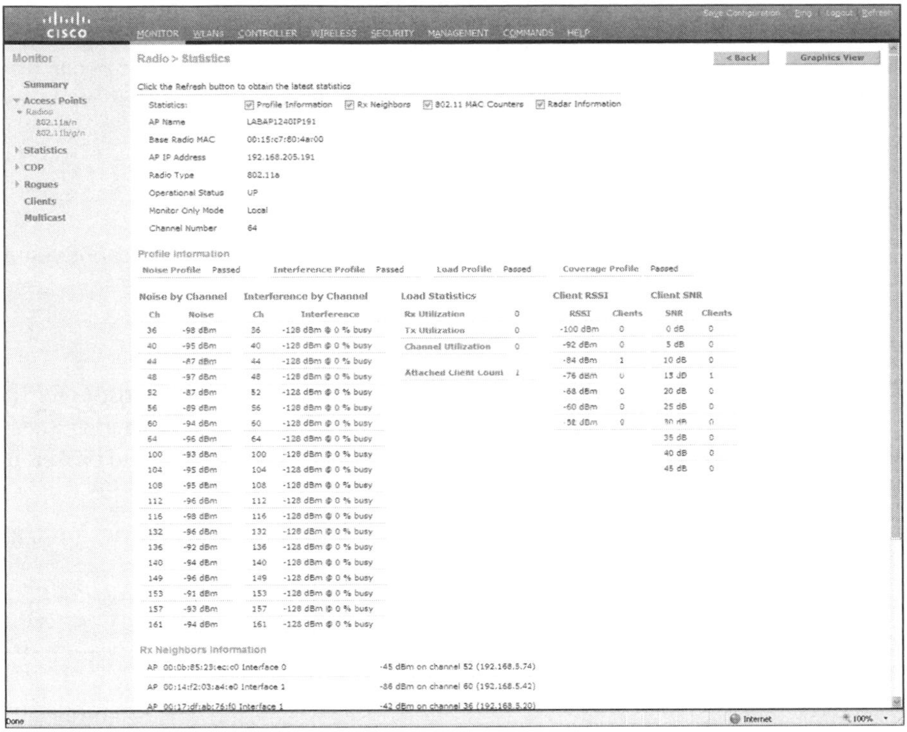

Figure 11-25   *AP 802.11a Radio Statistics*

WCS

WCS provides a centralized location for you to view and aggregate the statistics shown by the controller(s). You can also use the WCS reports to view how key parameters have changed over time. This information allows you to determine if you have a problem area on a floor, an area of that floor, a single AP, and so on.

You can use WCS to inspect the voice readiness of your AP deployment. While on a map, you can select Inspect VoWLAN Readiness, and WCS will access the AP placement for a particular floor and show you the results (see Figure 11-26).

The output of the voice readiness report shows you a color map indicating areas in which there is good coverage for voice, marginal coverage, and poor coverage.

With WCS code Release 5.0, WCS also allows you to run voice audits against your controllers for key voice configurations such as QoS settings, CCKM with 802.1x, and so on. Figure 11-27 shows a WCS voice audit against a single controller.

This output shows you what WLANs or configurations do not comply with the recommended best practices for configuring a controller for a voice deployment.

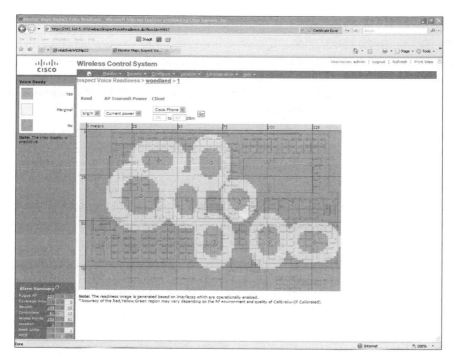

Figure 11-26   *WCS Voice Readiness*

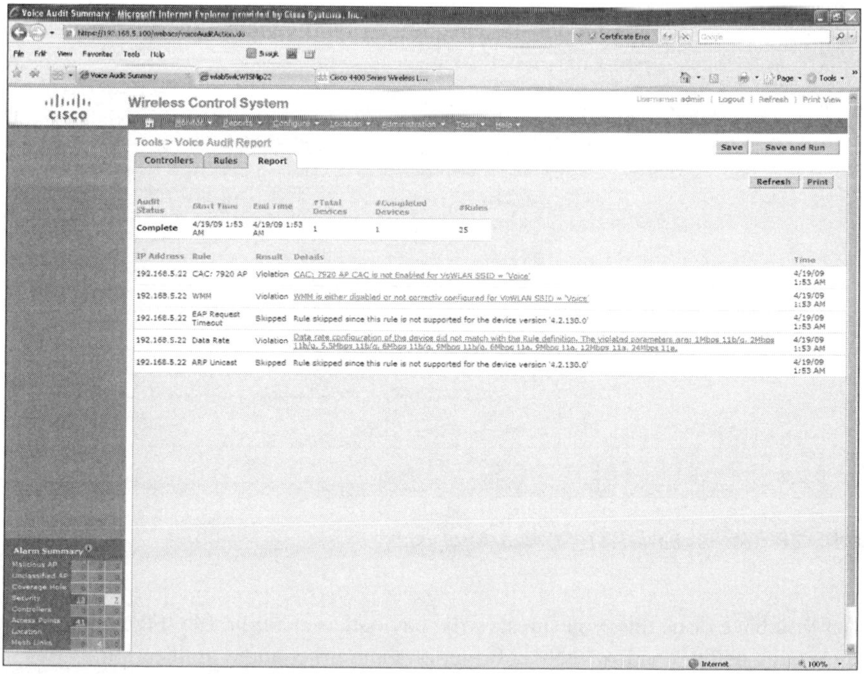

Figure 11-27   *WCS Voice Audit*

Packet Capture Software

Packet captures are an invaluable tool when troubleshooting wireless networks. In fact, sometimes only a packet capture tells you the root cause for a problem. Using packet captures can tell you if QoS markings are being preserved as the traffic traverses the wireless and wired network (as seen in Figures 11-15 through 11-17), if retransmissions are excessive, or if a device is not responding as it should.

Many free packet capture programs are available, such as Wireshark, which replaces the older Ethereal software. This program is great for captures and allows you to perform lots of packet analysis. Using Wireshark, you can actually take a wired packet capture of an RTP voice stream and create an audio file to hear the voice call.

To do this, open the capture and filter it on the RTP protocol. From here, select one of the packets in the stream and go to **Statistics > RTP > Stream Analysis** (see Figure 11-28). Newer versions of Wireshark have a Telephony tab you can use instead of Statistics.

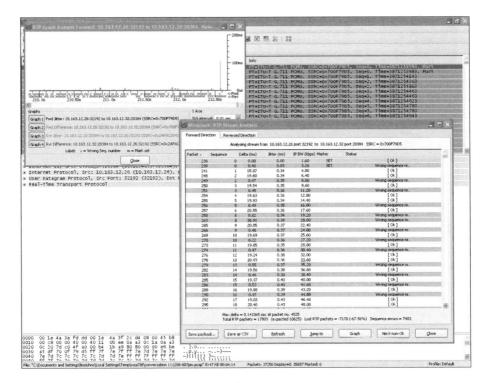

Figure 11-28 *Wireshark RTP Stream Analysis*

After you have done this, you can save the payload as an audio file (Figure 11-29) and play it back using Windows Media Player or some other audio application.

When you play the audio file back, you can listen for jitter, delay, or lost audio in the call.

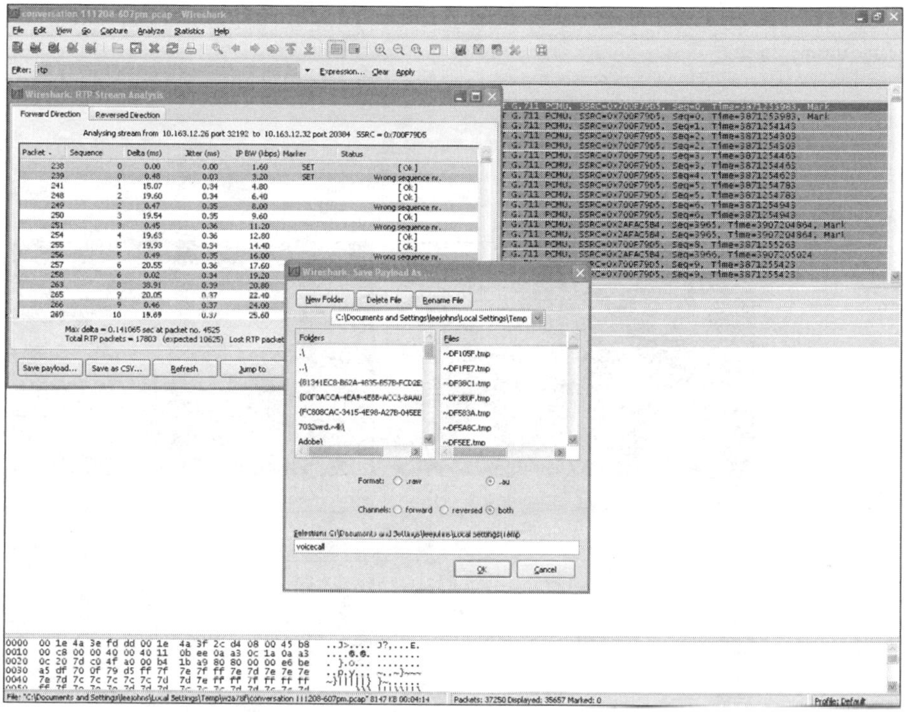

Figure 11-29 *Using Wireshark to Create an Audio File*

Spectrum Analysis Tools

Spectrum analysis tools allow you to see the RF environment. Although the RRM features of the controller do their best to avoid co-channel and non-802.11 interface, you cannot identify the sources of the interference. Spectrum analysis tools can detect Bluetooth devices, wireless video, ad-hoc devices such as wireless printers, and so on. All these products contribute to the energy on wireless channels and can adversely affect your voice deployment.

Perhaps the two most common spectrum analysis tools are Cisco Spectrum Expert and Airmagnet Spectrum Analyzer. These products allow you to detect and identify the devices in the RF environment. Because the 2.4- and 5-GHz bands are unlicensed frequencies, anyone can install and power up a wireless device. This means that two legitimate businesses can inadvertently disrupt the wireless network of the other simply by providing a Wi-Fi hotspot or installing a wireless video surveillance system.

Figure 11-30 shows a Cisco Spectrum Expert analysis detecting DECT cordless phones in the 2.4-GHz band.

DECT cordless phones are frequency-hopping devices that operate in the 2.4-GHz band. Because they are frequency-hopping devices, they affect all channels. You would not want to have DECT phones in your wireless voice RF space. Without a spectrum analysis, you would never know these devices were present unless you happened to notice someone using them.

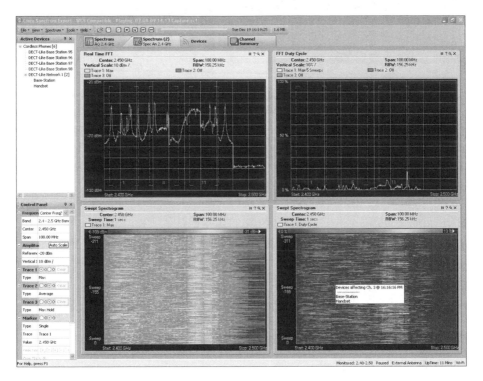

Figure 11-30 *Spectrum Expert DECT Phone Analysis*

SpectraLink and Vocera Deployments

SpectraLink and Vocera devices are fairly common in wireless networks today. The basic controller configuration and troubleshooting methods for these devices are the same as for the Cisco phones. Each device, however, has a certain set of configuration best practices that you need to consider.

SpectraLink

SpectraLink offers several Wi-Fi certified Wi-Fi voice devices that function in the 802.11a/b/g bands. Polycom, Inc. acquired SpectraLink in 2007, but the SpectraLink brand name remains with models such as the Polycom SpectraLink 8030.

SpectraLink phones use proprietary protocols for communication in a SpectraLink VoWLAN infrastructure. SpectraLink Voice Priority (SVP) and SpectraLink Radio Protocol (SRP) provide the inter-device communication. The SpectraLink phones do not support DTPC or other CCX features, so they are not able to take advantage of the benefits those protocols provide. The phones also do not support Quality-of-Service Basic Service Set (QBSS) or CAC, so it is possible to overload a particular channel an AP is using and create call quality or capacity issues. SpectraLink offers several SVP servers with capacity ranges from 10, 20, or 80 simultaneous calls per server.

When configuring the controller for a SpectraLink phone deployment, keep these guidelines in mind:

- SpectraLink recommends cell coverage of –70 dBm, but to support 11 Mbps, the cell coverage needs to be –60 dBm.

- SpectraLink phones support static WEP, WPA-PSK, WPA2-PSK, WPA2 Enterprise, PEAP, EAP-FAST, Opportunistic Key Caching, and CCKM.

- SpectraLink recommends 10 to 12 calls per AP. This number drops to 6 when using PTT.

- Controller QoS profiles are separate from and have no bearing on the SVP server QoS options.

- SpectraLink does not support DTPC, so you should set the phone transmit power to match the maximum power setting of the APs.

SpectraLink recommends the following controller configuration:

- Use LWAPP transport mode Layer 3.
- Use Multicast-Multicast.
- Use a beacon period of 100.
- Set the DTIM to 2.
- If only 802.11g clients exist, enable Short Preamble.
- Set the WLAN QoS to Platinum.
- Disable WMM on the WLAN.
- Configure the EDCA Parameter Set for the 802.11 network for SpectraLink Voice Priority (see Figure 11-31).

You can also configure SpectraLink Voice Priority from the controller CLI:

```
config advanced 802.11[a¦b] edca-parameters svp-voice
```

Note   You must disable the 802.11 network before you can change the EDCA parameter set.

You can verify that the EDCA parameters are enabled on the APs by enabling remote debugging for the AP and checking on the controller configuration using the following commands from the controller CLI:

```
debug ap enable ap name
debug ap command "show controller [d0¦d1]" ap name
```

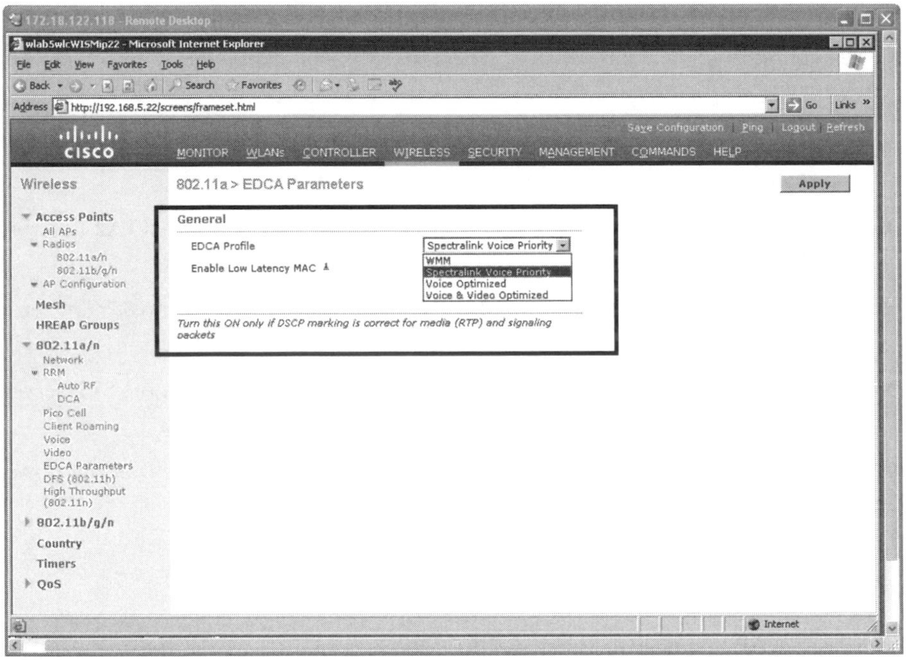

Figure 11-31   *Enabling SpectraLink Voice Priority*

If EDCA Parameter Set is enabled for svp-voice and no CAC is enabled, you should see the following in the put of **show controller**:

```
Back: cw-min 4 cw-max 10 fixed-slot 7 admission-control Off txop 0
Best: cw-min 4 cw-max 6 fixed-slot 3 admission-control Off txop 0
Video: cw-min 3 cw-max 4 fixed-slot 3 admission-control Off txop 3008
Voice: cw-min 0 cw-max 3 fixed-slot 2 admission-control Off txop 1504
```

For more information on SpectraLink best practices, see the SpectraLink Phone Design and Deployment Guide at http://tinyurl.com/y3kx6z.

You can also reference the design guides for the particular SpectraLink phone you plan to deploy at the Polycom.com website at http://tinyurl.com/nzzapt.

Vocera Deployments

Vocera manufactures lightweight, wearable, hands-free wireless voice badges that operate in the 802.11b/g bands. The hands-free nature of the product allows the user more freedom. A user can simply ask to "Call Nurse Campbell," and the system will call the badge of Nurse Campbell. You can also page a group of badges at once using multicast. The back of the units have a high-contrast Organic Light-Emitting Diode (OLED) display that allows the user to receive text messages and alerts. Vocera even offers a telephony option that allows users to receive phone calls on their badge.

The first Vocera badge release was the B1000 model. Vocera has since replaced the B1000 with the B2000. The B2000 has several radio enhancements that make it more robust than the B1000. If you plan to deploy a Vocera badge system, you will definitely want to use the B2000 model.

Vocera badges support Open, PSK, PEAP v0 MSCHAP v2, EAP-FAST with CCKM, and LEAP authentication with WEP 64, WEP 128, TKIP, and AES encryption.

The Vocera badge utilizes both unicast and multicast packet delivery to provide several key features. Here are four of the essential features that rely on proper packet delivery. Also provided is a basic understanding of how each feature uses the underlying network for delivery and functionality.

- **Badge-to-Badge Communications:** When one Vocera user calls another, the badge first contacts the Vocera server, which looks up the IP address of the badge of the callee and contacts the badge user to ask the user if she can take a call. If the callee accepts the call, the Vocera server notifies the calling badge of the IP address of the callee badge to set up direct communication between the badges with no further server intervention. All communication with the Vocera server uses the G.711 codec, and all badge-to-badge communication uses a Vocera proprietary codec.

- **Badge Telephony Communication:** When a Vocera Telephony server is installed and set up with a connection to a private branch exchange (PBX), a user is able to call internal extensions off the PBX or outside telephone lines. Vocera allows users to make calls by either saying the numbers (five, six, three, two) or by creating an address book entry in the Vocera database for the person or function at that number (for example, pharmacy, home, pizza). The Vocera server determines the number that is being called, either by intercepting the numbers in the extension or by looking up the name in the database and selecting the number. The Vocera server then passes that information to the Vocera Telephony server, which connects to the PBX and generates the appropriate telephony signaling (for example, DTMF). All communication between the badge and Vocera server and Vocera server and Vocera telephony server uses the G.711 codec over unicast UDP.

- **Vocera Broadcast:** A Vocera Badge user can call and communicate with a group of Vocera badge wearers at the same time by using the Broadcast command. When a user broadcasts to a group, their badges sends the command to the Vocera server, which then looks up the members of a group, determines which members of the group are active, assigns a multicast address to use for this broadcast session, and sends a message to each active user's badge instructing it to join the multicast group with the assigned multicast address.

- **Badge Location Function:** The Vocera server keeps track of the AP to which each active badge is associated as each badge sends a 30-second keepalive to the server with the associated BSSID. This allows the Vocera system to roughly estimate the location of a badge user. This function has a relatively low degree of accuracy because a badge might not be associated to the AP it is closest to.

Vocera recommends the following controller deployment configurations:

- Use Multicast-Multicast.

- Configure an unused multicast group address such as 239.0.0.255.

- Disable Aggressive Load Balancing.

- Set all badge WLANs to the same broadcast domain across the entire network.

- Set the DTIM to 1.

- Disable Short Preamble.

- Disable DTPC.

- Use a high WLAN session timeout (that is, shift hours).

- Set the WLAN QoS to Platinum.

- Broadcast the SSID.

- Enable all data rates.

- Disable WLAN client exclusions.

- Use controller code 4.1.185.0 or higher.

- If using RRM, AP density should be great enough that no AP has a power setting higher than 3.

- Disable DHCP required on the WLAN.

- Use symmetric Mobility Tunneling.

- WMM should be optional or disabled.

- ARP unicast should be disabled (disabled by default and deprecated in 5.1 code).

- RSSI of −65 dBm or better.

- SNR of 25 db.

Table 11-5   *Key Vocera Functions and Controller Recommendations*

	Single Controller	Inter-Controller L2 Roam	Inter-Controller L3 Roaming
Badge to Badge	No special requirements	No special requirements	No special requirements
Badge to Phone	No special requirements	No special requirements	No special requirements
Badge to Broadcast	Enable multicast on the controller	Disable IGMP snooping or use 4.0.206.0 or higher	Use 4.0.206.0 or higher
Badge Location	No special requirements	No special requirements	No special requirements

For Vocera administrative, user, and deployment guides, refer to the Vocera product documentation at http://www.vocera.com/documentation/default.aspx.

Summary

To have a quality wireless voice deployment, you need to make sure that you have had a professional wireless survey conducted by a Cisco partner that specializes in voice installations. AP placement, the configuration of the controller and WLANs, as well as the wired network need to be set up properly to adhere to voice installation best practices. Failing to do so will result in poor voice quality. Should you have problems with your voice deployment, you can use many tools and debugs to determine the issue. Considering that wireless phones are nothing more than a wireless client, the information in Chapter 10, "Troubleshooting Client-Related Issues," is essentially a prerequisite to troubleshooting wireless voice problems.

Chapter 12

Radio Resource Management

The 2.4-GHz and 5-GHz bands used for wireless are not regulated by communications commissions such as the FCC or European Regulators Group (ERG). Because the spectrum is not regulated, anyone can install and power on a wireless device that operates on those channels without checking with their neighbor across the street or even the FCC. This can pose various problems for any wireless network because the radio frequency (RF) environment is going to be dynamic, and a site survey conducted before you install your wireless network might not be valid three months down the road.

To help combat the ever-changing nature of wireless, the Cisco Unified Wireless Network (CUWN) solution uses Radio Resource Management (RRM) to continuously monitor the RF environment. The controller uses the information from the access points (AP) and makes any changes to AP channels and power levels to try to mitigate such things as non-802.11 signal (noise), interference from other 802.11 devices, coverage gaps, and co-channel interference caused by the network.

How RRM Works

The RRM feature, also known as Auto-RF, uses the RF information gathered by the APs to make decisions on whether channel assignment or power levels need to be adjusted. Just because the RF environment has changed does not necessarily mean that the controller will change.

Before covering the intricacies of the RRM algorithm and RF grouping, following is a high-level overview of the basic workflow involved:

Step 1. The controllers and their APs use the configured RF group name to determine if other APs they hear are part of their RF group.

Step 2. The APs use neighbor messages (sent every 60 seconds) that are authenticated by other APs that hear them. The neighbor messages include information about the AP, the controller, and the configured RF group name.

Step 3. The APs that hear the neighbor message of another AP authenticate that message using the RF group name and pass it to their respective controller.

Step 4. The controllers use this information to determine what other controllers should be in their RF group, then form logical groups to share the RF information from their respective APs, and elect an RF group leader.

Step 5. The RF group leader runs the RRM algorithm against the RF information from all the APs in the RF group. Depending on the outcome, a power level or channel change for an AP or group of APs might take place.

You need to remember several important points when dealing with RRM:

■ The controllers elect the RF group leader.

■ The RF group leader is responsible for dynamic channel assignment (DCA) and transmit power control (TPC).

■ An individual controller handles coverage hole detection and correction.

■ RF groups and mobility groups are independent functions.

Note RRM (and RF grouping) is a separate function from inter-controller mobility (and mobility grouping). The only similarity is the use of a common ASCII string assigned to both group names during the initial controller configuration wizard. This is done for a simplified setup process and can be changed later.

■ In large deployments, it is normal to have multiple logical RF groups. The APs have to hear one another to form the RF group; so if you have multiple buildings across a large campus, the APs in one building will not hear the APs in another, and if they do not sh are a common controller, they will not combine into one RF group.

■ Prior to the 4.1 release, the transmit power threshold was a hard-coded setting of −65 dB, but after significant testing, it was realized that this was not the optimal setting for most deployments. The setting is now configurable, and the default and recommended setting is −70 dB. This means that for optimal performance, each AP should be heard by at least three other APs at −70 dB or greater.

Although the TPC threshold setting is adjustable, it is the setting Cisco recommends for most deployments unless a significant amount of testing and calibration has been done to suggest otherwise.

■ RF grouping is per radio. The RF group leader for the 802.11b/g network might not be the same RF group leader for the 802.11a network.

■ With code Release 4.2.99 or higher, RRM supports up to 20 controllers and 1000 APs in a single RF group.

■ RF fluctuations can cause the RF group leader to change.

- By default, the RF group leader polls the other controllers in the RF group for AP statistics and neighbor messages.

- The transmit power threshold setting should be the same between all controllers in the same RF group, because you do not want an entire network to start fluctuating because of a group leader change.

- Starting with code Release 4.1.185.0 and higher, the default configuration for RRM is optimal for most deployments.

Because RRM allows the controller to constantly monitor the RF environment, the system is self-healing in the event of the loss of AP from the network. The surrounding APs compensate by increasing their power and changing channels if necessary to try to fill the gap left by the failed AP.

RF Grouping

RF groups are groups of controllers that share the same RF group name and whose APs can hear the neighbor messages of each other. It is possible to have two controllers with the same RF group name but not be in the same RF group because their APs cannot hear each other.

The APs send the neighbor messages every 60 seconds at maximum power, at the lowest data rate, and on all serviced channels to the multicast address of 01:0B:85:00:00:00, as illustrated in Figure 12-1. When an AP receives a neighbor message, it forwards that frame to its controller and the controller verifies the embedded hash in the frame to see if it came from an AP in the same RF group.

The neighbor message contains the following information:

- **Radio Identifier:** If the AP had multiple radios, this field identifies the radio used to transmit the message.

- **Group ID:** The 16-bit value and controller MAC address.

- **WLC IP Address:** RF group leader's management IP address.

- **AP Channel:** The native channel that the AP uses to service clients.

- **Neighbor Message Channel:** The channel the message is sent on.

- **Power:** The power level at which the message is transmitted.

- **Antenna Pattern:** The antenna pattern currently in use.

If the AP receives a neighbor message that it cannot decode or it never receives a neighbor message from an AP, that AP is considered a rogue AP.

When controllers learn of another controller from the AP neighbor messages, they communicate directly with one another to form a system-wide RF group. After the system-wide RF group is formed, the controllers elect an RF group leader.

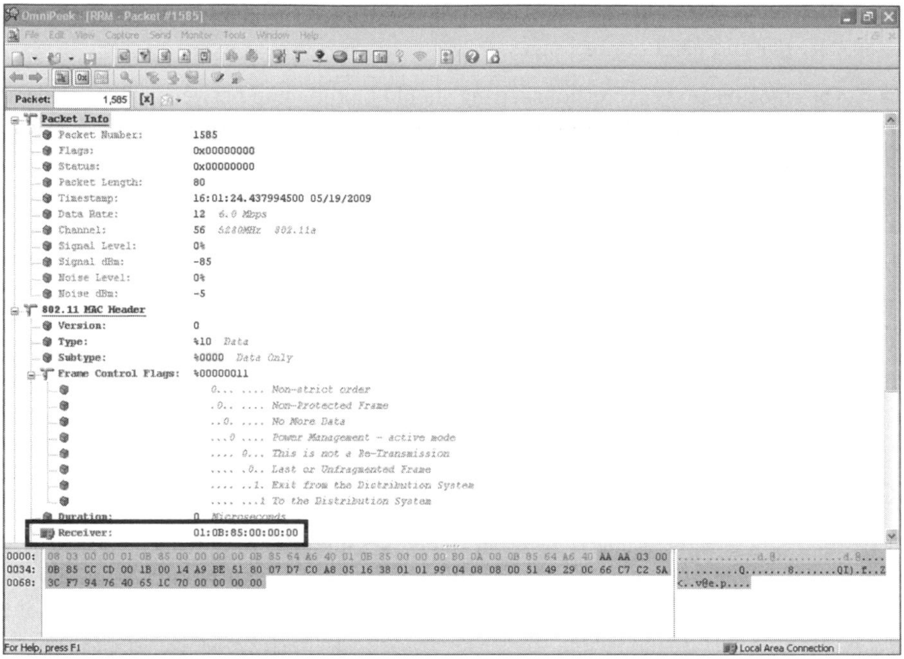

Figure 12-1 *AP Neighbor Message*

The group leader is the controller with the highest group leader priority. The group leader priority is based on the group identifier (group ID) information element (IE) contained in the AP neighbor messages. Every controller maintains a 16-bit counter that starts at 0 and increments following events like adding or leaving an RF group or the controller being rebooted. This counter value and the MAC address of the controller make up the group ID IE. Every controller in the RF group selects one controller, or itself, that has the highest group ID value and compares this to the selected controller from the other controllers in the group. The single controller with the highest group ID is elected the RF group leader.

If the RF group leader goes offline, the entire RF group breaks up and the RF grouping process and election of an RF group leader starts over.

For an RF group to form, it takes only one AP on one controller to hear another AP on a different controller. Figures 12-2 through 12-4 shows some examples of how different RF groups can form.

In Figure 12-2, you have three APs joined to a single controller, but only two of those three APs hear each other. In this situation, you have a single RF group and two RF subgroups.

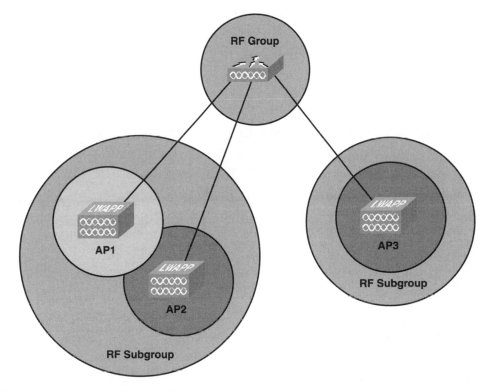

Figure 12-2   *AP RF Groups*

Figure 12-3 shows a single RF group with two controllers. Notice how AP1 on Controller 2 is part of the RF subgroup with the APs on Controller 1. AP2 on Controller 2 is in its own RF subgroup because it is not heard by any other APs on the network.

Figure 12-4 shows two distinct RF groups. Controller 3 has a different RF group name than Controllers 1 and 2, and they do not form an RF group.

If the APs on one controller will not be able to hear the APs on another controller, it is not practical to configure the controllers with the same RF group name. To prevent flapping, APs only add a neighbor AP to the neighbor list if that AP is heard at −80 dBm or greater. It is only removed from the neighbor list if the received signal strength indication, RSSI, drops below −85 dBm.

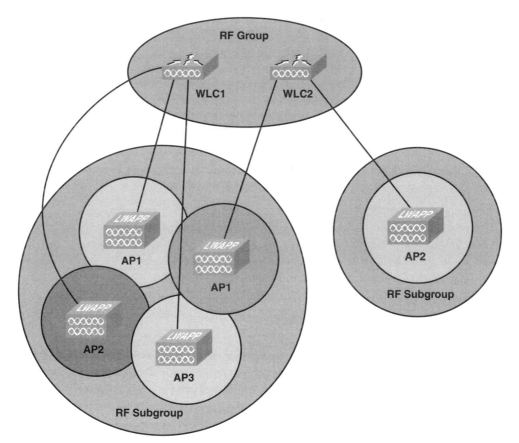

Figure 12-3 *AP RF Group with Two WLCs*

RF Group Leader Election

Initially, every controller assumes that it is the RF group leader for its configured RF group. It creates its unique group ID and adds itself to the group. After this, the controller sends a HELLO packet to all the controllers it knows about every 10 seconds.

In addition to the HELLO message, the controller collects neighbor messages from its APs. When all the connected APs have sent the neighbor packets they accumulated or a timeout is reached, the controller uses this information to determine if another controller has a higher group ID. If that is the case, the controller joins the RF group and becomes a GROUPIE. After a controller finds another controller with a group ID larger than itself, it triggers a 60-second timer to make sure the current leader is still active. If the GROUPIE controller does not receive a HELLO response within the allotted time, the controller considers the RF group leader down and the election process starts again.

Before any RRM grouping features can function, the RRM subsystem has to initialize. When the system initializes, it creates an RRM manager for each 802.11 network. This means that a separate manager exists for the 2.4-GHz and 5-GHz bands. That is why you can have different RF group leaders for the 802.11b/g and 802.11a networks. The initialization process also creates a grouping task.

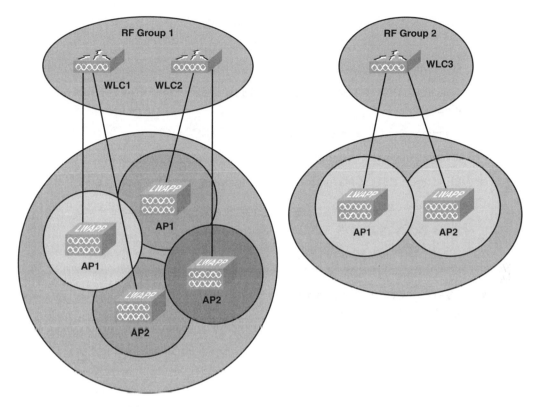

Figure 12-4   *Multiple AP RF Groups*

The grouping task creates four timers:

- **HELLO_TIMER:** 10 seconds
- **CALC_TIMER:** 10 seconds
- **PREP_TIMER:** 12 * 2 seconds
- **TRANSMISSION_TIMER:** 1 second

The RRM state machine uses these timers to handle the different RRM states of the controller.

The state machine of the RRM manager handles the various states of the leader and determines when to run the RRM algorithms. Currently, a controller can be in eight states:

- **UNDEFINED:** Used before the RRM state machine is initialized.
- **RESET:** In this state, the controller creates its default group, group ID, and adds itself to the group. The controller then enters the LEADER_IDLE state.

- **LEADER_IDLE:** Several things happen in this state:

  The HELLO_TIMER and CALC_TIMER start.

  When the CALC_TIMER expires, enter LEADER_PREP state.

  When the HELLO_TIMER expires, send a HELLO message to all controllers in the RF group.

  If a join request is received, check and send an ACK/NACK.

  If client data is received, process it.

- **LEADER_PREP:** While in this state, the controller performs these steps:

  Starts the PREP_TIMER.

  Starts TRANSMISSION_TIMER and starts polling.

  When PREP_TIMER is finished and all the switches are updated, goes to the LEADER_COMP state.

- **LEADER_COMP:** The different controller group IDs are compared. After that calculation is complete, moves to the **LEADER_ASSIGN** state.

- **LEADER_ASSIGN:** If another controller has a higher group ID, enter **JOIN_WAIT** state. Otherwise, the controller assumes it is group leader and goes into the **LEADER_IDLE** state.

- **JOIN_WAIT:** The controller sends a join message to the RF group leader from the **LEADER_ASSIGN** state and waits for a response. When a response is received, it moves to GROUPIE state. If the controller does not receive a join response from the RF group leader, it assumes it is the leader and moves to the LEADER_IDLE state.

- **GROUPIE:** While the controller is in this state, it believes there is another controller with a higher group ID than itself. It remains in this state until the grouping algorithm runs again.

Note   You cannot manually set an RF group leader at this point. That would actually be a desirable feature because the RF group leader is responsible for performing the majority of the RRM calculations, and you would ideally want the least-loaded controller to be the leader. The phrase *least loaded* refers to the AP load. All hardware platforms are fully capable of performing this function under a full load. The idea is to optimize for top network performance.

Dynamic Channel Assignment

DCA is handled by the RF group leader for a particular RF group. As you saw in Figures 12-2 through 12-4, you can have RF subgroups. DCA runs separately for each RF subgroup that might exist.

The DCA algorithm takes the following information into account:

- **Load measurement:** Every AP measures the percentage of total time occupied by transmitting or receiving 802.11 frames.

- **Noise:** APs calculate noise values on every serviced channel.

- **Interference:** APs report on the percentage of the medium taken up by interfering 802.11 transmissions. (This can be from overlapping signals from foreign APs as well as non-neighbors).

- **Signal strength:** Every AP listens for neighbor messages on all serviced channels and records the RSSI values at which these messages are heard. This AP signal strength information is the most important metric considered in the DCA calculation of channel energy.

Based on these metrics, if the worst performing AP will benefit by at least 5 dB or more, a channel change will take place. The decision to change the channel of an AP is also weighted to prevent a mass change within the RF group. You would not want to have a single AP change channel and have that change result in 20 other APs having to change their channel. The controller also takes into account how heavily an AP is used. A less utilized AP is more likely to have a channel change instead of a heavily used neighbor. This helps mitigate client disassociations during a DCA event because a radio channel change disconnects all associated clients.

When an AP first boots up out the box, it transmits on channel 1 on the 802.11b/g radio and channel 36 for the 802.11a radio. The channels change according to any DCA adjustments if necessary. If a reboot occurs, the APs remain on the same channel they were using before the reboot until a DCA event occurs. If an AP is on channel 149 and reboots, it will continue to use channel 149 when it comes back up.

Systemic Problems

One of the issues with DCA is that the channel plan adjustments are driven by a single radio. In the worst case, administrators can see radio channel changes throughout the entire wireless LAN (WLAN). The source of this issue is when one of the radios that initiates these changes is misinformed or not in a position to intelligently make this decision. The result is multiple radios making bad judgments as well. In addition, it prevents the radios that can make positive changes from making them because they are making adjustments from a poor radio leader.

Another major issue is when too many radios change channels during a single update. When this occurs, you throw too many changes in the RF network at once, so you might miss the best channel adjustments across multiple radios. This can obviously result in instability for wireless users because too many radios are changing transmission channels at once. Also, each radio affects the channel cost metrics for each of its neighboring radios, better known as RF neighbors. Versions 6.x and later plan to add cost-based build metrics into the search algorithm that would penalize a tentative channel plan if the plan includes too many radio changes during the same DCA iteration.

RF environments can pose many challenges. Every deployment usually has a particular area that is susceptible to bad RF interference, co-channel interference, or simply poor RF. Unfortunately, the radios that are located in these areas might never be able to improve enough to offer the most optimal wireless coverage. Radios in these circumstances start making decisions for other radios that do not have the same environmental challenges, which is referred to as *pinning*. The result of pinning is that the worst cost metric radio prevents other radios from moving to more favorable channels. The bad apples inhibit channel plan changes that could improve channel assignments to other radios.

As mentioned, constant changes go into each major WLC revision that improve RRM. The purpose of this section was to inform you of potential negative scenarios that exist. By the time this book is published, code should already be available to address these major concerns. Another important factor to remember is that you might never run into these issues, and even if you do, you can mitigate them from happening by making intelligent decisions within your deployment. Always remember that RRM is not a substitute for a good site survey.

TPC

Controllers use the TPC algorithm to determine whether the power of an AP needs to be adjusted down. Reducing the power of an AP helps mitigate co-channel interference with another AP on the same channel in close proximity. This is especially beneficial on the 802.11b/g network because you only have three nonoverlapping channels you can use.

The TPC algorithm runs every 10 minutes. Like DCA, the RF group leaders runs TPC on a per-radio, per-AP basis. Therefore, a power adjustment on 802.11b/g has no bearing on the 802.11a power level settings for the same AP.

Note   TPC only adjusts radio power levels down. An AP out of the box always transmits at the maximum power until a TPC event lowers the power setting. Like DCA, when AP reboots, it uses the previous power level setting before it rebooted.

The more APs that hear each other at −70 dBm or greater, the better the TPC algorithm functions. As stated earlier, the minimum requirement for TPC is that a single AP needs to be heard by at least three other APs at −70 dBm or greater. Therefore, you must have at least four APs total. The logic behind the lowering of the power levels is that the third loudest neighbor is heard at −70 dBm or lower after the change.

TPC uses the following criteria to determine if a power level change is necessary:

Step 1. Are three neighbors at –70 dBm or greater?

Step 2. If Step 1 is satisfied, determine the transmit power using the following equation:

Tx_Max for given AP + (Tx power control threshold – RSSI of third highest neighbor above the threshold)

Step 3. Is the value from Step 2 with the current Tx power level? Verify whether it exceeds the TPC hysteresis.

If the value is 6 dB or greater, the controller lowers the power of the AP by one power level.

If the value is 3 dB, the AP increases its power. A power increase is almost always the result of not having a third neighbor (no third neighbor or the third neighbor was lost). Power increases are handled by the coverage hole detection system, as discussed in the section that follows.

For example, assume that you have four APs operating in the 5-GHz band in close proximity to one another. The maximum power level would be 17 dBm (50 mW). Your controller is running 4.2 with a transmit power level threshold of –70 dBm. The AP in question hears the third loudest neighbor at –60 dBm. When you put this information into the preceding equation, you get a value of 7 dBm:

$$17(\text{Tx\_Max}) + (-70 - (-60)) = 7$$

Because this value is greater than 6 dBm, the controller lowers the power level by one (3 dBm) to 14 dBm. Provided everything remains the same between now and the next polling interval, the power level remains at 14 dBm.

It is important to remember that decreases in AP radio power levels are gradual, whereas increases can take place immediately. Therefore, if you change the RRM configuration settings, do not expect to start seeing the APs changing channels and adjusting their power as soon as you click Apply.

Coverage Hole Detection

The controller uses the quality of client signal levels reported by the APs to determine if the power level of that AP needs to be increased. Coverage hole detection is controller independent, so the RF group leader is not involved in those calculations. The controller knows how many clients are associated with a particular AP and what the signal-to-noise ratio (SNR) values are for each client.

If a client SNR drops below the configured threshold value on the controller, the AP increases its power level to try to compensate for the client. The SNR threshold is based on the transmit power of the AP and the coverage profile settings on the controller.

The controller uses the following equation for detecting a coverage hole:

Client SNR Cutoff Value (|dB|) = [AP Transmit Power (dBm) – Constant (17 dBm) – Coverage Profile (dB)]

Depending on the number of clients that are at or below this value for longer than 60 seconds, coverage hole correction might be triggered, and the AP could increase its power level to try to remove the SNR violation.

For example, if a client has an SNR of 15, the AP is at power level 2 (17 dB, 50 mW) on the 802.11b radio, and the controller coverage profile is at the default of 12, will the radio need to power up?

If you put the values into the coverage hole detection equation, you can determine the answer to that question:

Client SNR Cutoff = 17 (AP transmit power) – 17 (Constant) – 12 (Coverage threshold)= |–12 dB|

The client SNR of 15 dB is above the SNR cutoff value, so the AP does not increase its power in this situation.

> **Note**   If the AP is already at power level 1, it cannot increase the power any further, and clients at the edge of the cell coverage suffer a performance hit or disassociate altogether if the signal gets weak enough.

Aside from a real coverage hole, a client with a poor roaming logic might not roam to another AP as expected and be "sticky." A sticky client can remain associated with an AP until the SNR is very low and triggers a false coverage hole detection.

The coverage hole algorithm also allows the network to heal itself if an AP fails. When a neighbor AP is lost, it increases the power of nearby APs as needed to compensate. Again, the increase in power for an AP is a gradual process, increasing the power one level at a time.

Enhancements to RRM

As the controller code has advanced, RRM has evolved with it. RRM is much more configurable than in older versions. The algorithms used to take into account a lot more information than in previous versions, such as high ceilings for warehouse environments. Also, they are more granular to allow an experienced wireless administrator to tweak the RF environment. The release of 4.1.185.0 saw the biggest changes in RRM behavior and each subsequent release.

Following are a few examples of how RRM has improved:

- **DCA Anchor Time:** Introduced in 4.1.185.0. Allows you to configure the start of the 10-minute DCA interval in start-up mode. Start-up mode is the time in which DCS operates every 10 minutes for the first 10 iterations using a High Sensitivity level of 5 dB. This helps the network stabilize quickly.

- **DCA Interval:** The elapsed time between DCA calculations. This value used to be fixed.

- **DCA Sensitivity:** Three configurable levels are now available for the sensitivity of the DCA algorithm to RF changes.

- **Tx Power Threshold:** Changed from −65 dB to −70 dB. The overall enhancements to RRM in 4.1.185.0 code resulted in the old default of −65 dB to be too hot for most indoor deployments. The new setting of −70 dB results in better cell overlap for most deployments out of the box.

- **Better Simple Network Management Protocol (SNMP) traps:** RRM-generated SNMP traps are more descriptive. They indicate why an AP changed channel and what the metrics were before and after the change.

- **Tx-Power-Up Control:** To mitigate drastic power fluctuations during a coverage hole event, an AP only adjusts its power up one level at a time. This keeps the APs from running too hot and increasing co-channel interference.

- **In code Release 5.0 and higher, the RRM graphical user interface (GUI) configuration is split into five separate GUI pages:** RF Grouping, TPC, DCA, Coverage, and General. The separation allows for ease of use.

- **CLI versus GUI operations:** Commands for configuring the interval, anchor time, and channel sensitivity level for DCA that used to be CLI only have been moved to the GUI starting in Release 5.1.

- **In 5.1, the On Demand option for DCA (see the "Configuring RRM" section that follows) is renamed to Freeze:** Freeze better describes the actual function of the feature, which is to cause the controller to evaluate and update the channel assignment for all joined APs if necessary, but only when you click **Invoke Channel Update Now**.

- **Up until code Release 5.1, DCA was not supported when using channel bonding (40-MHz wide channels) for 802.11n:** You were responsible for statically configuring the AP channels. This could be a tedious task when dealing with a large deployment. This feature is available only on the 5-GHz radio.

- **Starting in code Release 5.2, coverage hole detection is no longer a global setting and can be enabled or disabled on a per-WLAN basis:** Coverage hole detection is enabled by default on the WLAN. One of the reasons you might want to disable this is because if you know a device is going to roam, it is advised that you enable the wireless on the device so that it can assist in finding coverage holes. Conversely, if several devices are stationary and have wireless as a backup, it would be advisable to disable this because you know the devices are not going to move and will not be able to provide intelligent information to help the coverage hole detection algorithm with its calculations. In all actuality, it would be wasting cycles on devices such as these.

Configuring RRM

For the majority of wireless deployments, you would not need to configure anything other than the RF group name you wanted your controllers to use (Figure 12-5). The default settings for RRM are optimal for most installations, and you should not adjust them unless you suspect a problem. Adjusting some of the timers too high can result in the RRM algorithms running algorithms with stale RF environment information.

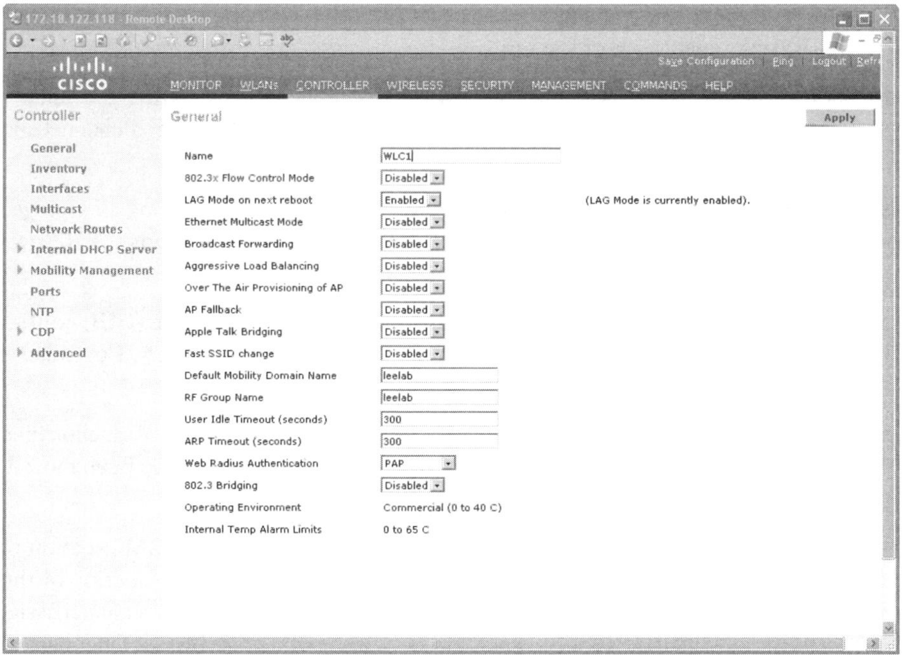

Figure 12-5 *RF Group Name*

When you want to view or edit the RRM configuration, use the controller GUI and go to WIRELESS and then RRM under either the 802.11b/g/n or 802.11a/n network.

Here you can view the RF group information:

- **Group Mode:** This setting is enabled by default, and the MAC address of the other RF group members is listed under RF group members. Should you disable this setting, the controller will not form an RF group with any controllers and will make any RF changes itself.

- **Group Update Interval:** This displays the group update interval. In early code, it cannot be changed. The default interval is 10 minutes.

- **Group Leader:** Displays the MAC address of the RF group leader. Remember that the group leader can be different for the 802.11a and 802.11b/g networks.

- **Is This Controller a Group Leader:** If the particular controller you are viewing is the group leader, it will say "Yes." If "No", the group leader's MAC address is listed under the Group Leader section.

- **Last Group Update:** Indicates the elapsed time since the last 10-minute update interval ran. It does not, however, indicate the time elapsed since the last RRM change.

Figure 12-6 shows the RF group information for a 5.2 controller.

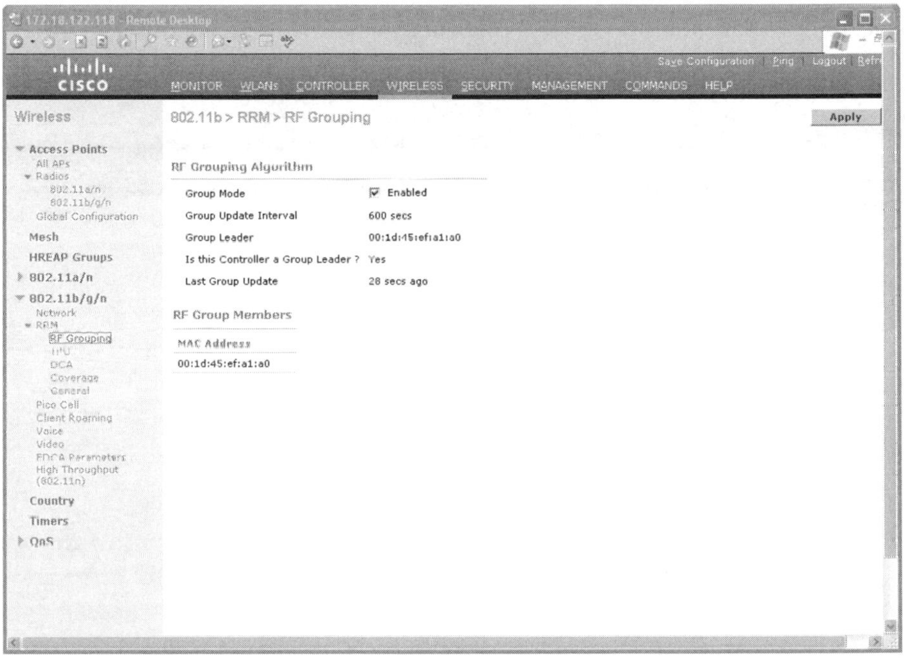

Figure 12-6   *RF Group Name*

From this output, you can see that this particular controller is the only one in; therefore, it is the leader for its RF group.

Dynamic Channel Assignment

You can configure DCA in three ways:

- **Automatic:** The default DCA setting. The DCA algorithm runs every 10 minutes by default and makes any changes as necessary. You can change this setting to run the algorithm every 24 hours with several time intervals in between. Starting in code

Release 5.1, you can also configure an anchor time. This value determines when the DCA algorithm will start. The values range from 0 to 23 and correspond to the hours of day from 12:00 a.m. to 11:00 p.m.

■ **Freeze (On Demand):** With the setting of On Demand, no RF changes are made until you click Invoke Channel Update Now. The important thing to remember here is that the update does not run immediately. It runs at the next 10-minute interval.

■ **Off:** If you set DCA to Off, all DCA functions are disabled. You are responsible for statically configuring all the AP channels. An important note to remember here is that when this setting is set to Off, all radios are reset to their default power and channel levels.

Figure 12-7 shows the 802.11a DCA configuration page for a 5.2 controller.

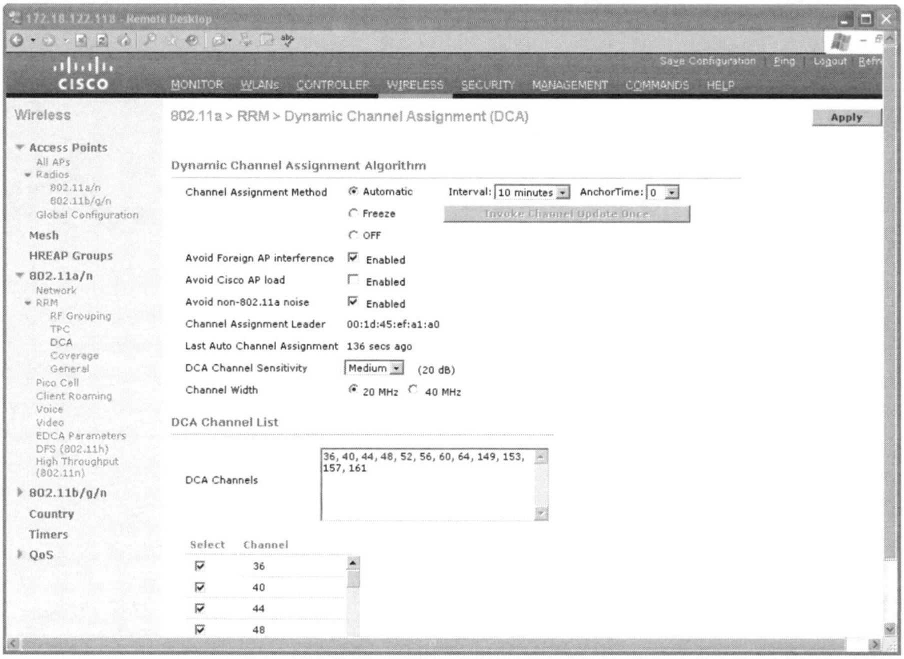

Figure 12-7   *DCA Configuration*

Under the DCA configuration page, you can also configure the following:

■ **Avoid Foreign AP Interference:** Enabled by default. When enabled, the co-channel interference metric is included in the DCA calculations.

■ **Avoid Cisco AP Load:** Disabled by default. When enabled, the client load on an AP is taken into consideration before making a channel change. AP utilization is dynamic, and you might not want it included in the RRM calculations.

■ **Avoid non-802.11a/b Noise:** Enabled by default. The non-802.11 noise level of an AP is taken into consideration by the DCA algorithm.

This page shows you that Signal Strength Contribution is enabled (nonconfigurable setting), who the channel assignment leader is, and the last time the DCA algorithm ran.

You can also adjust the DCA Sensitivity Level. You can choose from three levels:

■ Low

■ Medium

■ High

The default setting for the DCA Sensitivity Level is Medium. When you change this setting, it adjusts how sensitive the DCA algorithm is to environmental changes such as signal, load, noise, and interference. Low means it is not particularly sensitive, and High means it is very sensitive to RF changes.

The values listed in Table 12-1 indicate the improvement in decibels that needs to take place for a channel change to occur.

Table 12-1   *Change in Decibels Required for Channel Change*

Sensitivity Level	2.4 GHz	5 GHz
Low	30 dB	35 dB
Medium	15 dB	20 dB
High	5 dB	5 dB

With the DCA Sensitivity Level set to High, because only a 5-dB improvement is required, the system would be very sensitive to an RF change.

As you can see in Figure 12-6, starting in code Release 5.1 and higher, you can use DCA with 802.11n. Before the 5.1 code release, DCA was not supported with channel bonding, and you had to set the channels manually.

At the bottom of Figure 12-7, you can see the DCA channel list and where you can either add or remove the channels you want the APs to be able to use.

Transmit Power Control (TPC)

Prior to code Release 4.1.185.0, the default TPC defaulted to –65 dB. Although this setting was fine for the majority of deployments on older code, the overall RRM enhancements introduced with the 4.1.185.0 code meant that –65 dB could be too "hot." Cisco adjusted the algorithm to function optimally at a setting of –70 dB. If you are upgrading your controller from a release prior to 4.1.185.0 to 4.1.185.0 or higher, verify that TPC is set to –70 dB. You verify this setting either through the GUI from the TPC setting page (Figure 12-8) or by using the following command from the controller CLI:

```
show advanced [802.11b ¦ 802.11a] txpower
```

Should the setting not be a –70 dB, you can correct using the following CLI command:

```
config advanced [802.11b ¦ 802.11a] tx-power-control-thresh -70
```

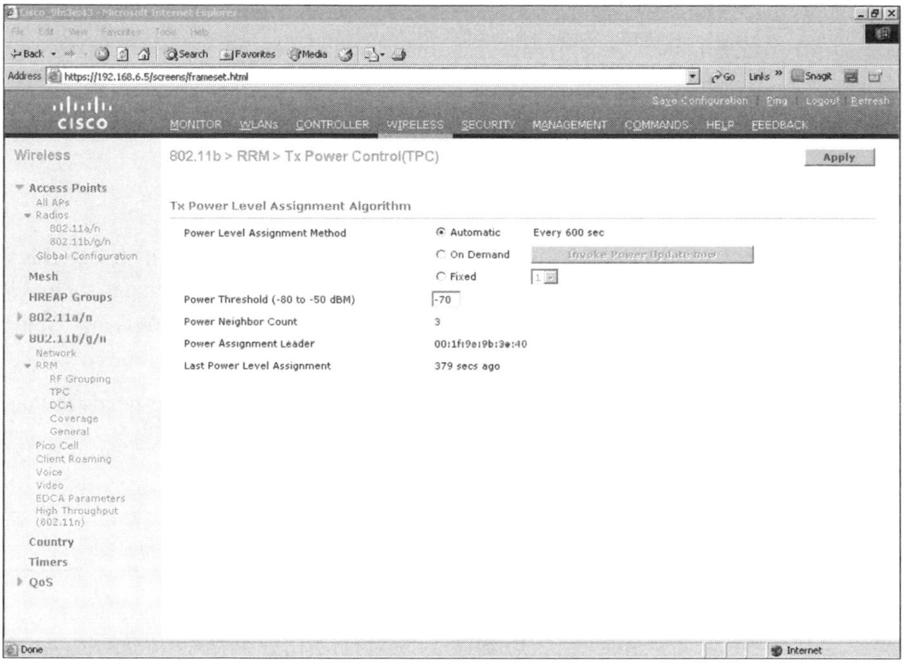

Figure 12-8   *TPC Configuration*

Like DCA, TPC has three modes of operation:

■ **Automatic:** The Automatic setting is the default. When enabled, the TPC algorithm runs every 10 minutes and makes any necessary adjustments.

■ **On Demand:** With TPC set to On Demand, the controller still periodically updates the channel information but does not make changes until you click Invoke Power Update Now. Just like Freeze with DCA, no changes occur until the next 10-minute interval.

■ **Fixed:** Setting TPC to Fixed turns the feature off. The controller does not evaluate or make any changes to the AP transmit power levels.

The TPC page also shows the following nonconfigurable transmit power level parameter settings:

■ **Power Threshold:** Shows the current Transmit Power Threshold setting.

■ **Power Neighbor Count:** Shows the minimum number of neighbor APs for TPC to run effectively. The setting is 3 and cannot be changed.

- **Power Assignment Leader:** Shows the MAC address of the RF group leader. The RF group leader is responsible for any power changes.

- **Last TPC Iteration:** Shows the elapsed time since the last time the TPC algorithm ran.

Coverage

Under the Coverage page for RRM, as shown in Figure 12-9, you can configure the minimum RSSI for both data and voice clients. In older codes, you simply set the RSSI for a client, and voice and data packets were not distinguished. This value is used in the coverage algorithm to calculate whether a coverage hole alarm should be triggered.

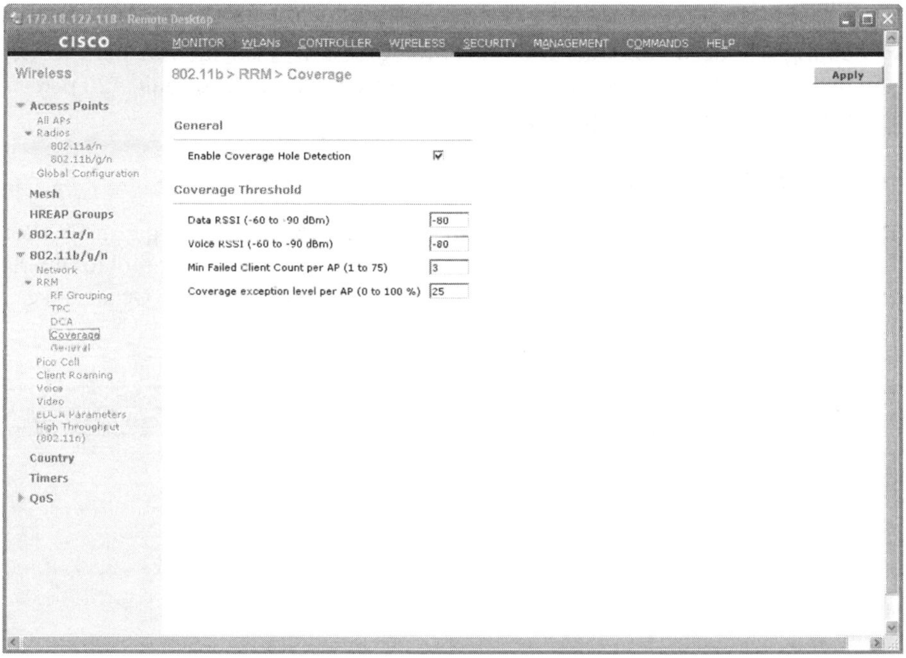

Figure 12-9 *RRM Coverage*

You can also configure the minimum number of failed clients (from 1 to 75) that the AP should detect before triggering the alarm. If you have sticky clients, you might want to increase this value from the default of 3 so you are not constantly bombarded with false alarms.

Last is the coverage exception level per AP setting. This setting is the percentage of clients on an AP with poor signal strength that cannot roam to another AP. The maximum setting is 25 percent.

Should the number and percentage of failed packets exceed the values configured for Failed Packet Count and Failed Packet Percentage (configurable through the controller CLI) for 5 seconds, the client is considered to be in a prealarm condition. The controller uses this information to distinguish between real and false coverage holes. A coverage hole is detected if both the number and percentage of failed clients meet or exceed the values entered in the Min Failed Client Count per AP and Coverage Exception Level per AP fields over a 90-second period. The controller determines if the coverage hole can be corrected and, if appropriate, mitigates the coverage hole by increasing the transmit power level for that specific AP.

The Failed Packet Count and Failed Packet Percentage used in determining a coverage hole are CLI-only commands:

■ **config advanced {802.11a | 802.11b} coverage {data | voice} packet-count** *packets*: Sets the minimum failure count threshold for uplink data or voice packets. The default value is 10 packets, with a range of 1 to 255.

■ **config advanced {802.11a | 802.11b} coverage {data | voice} fail-rate** *percent*: Sets the failure rate threshold for uplink data or voice packets. The default is 20 percent, with a range of 1 to 100 percent.

Profiles and Monitor Intervals

The Profile Threshold configuration determines the thresholds that trigger an SNMP trap alarm to Wireless Control System (WCS) or another SNMP monitoring tool for interference, client load, noise, and channel utilization. Figure 12-10 shows the General page for configuring these settings.

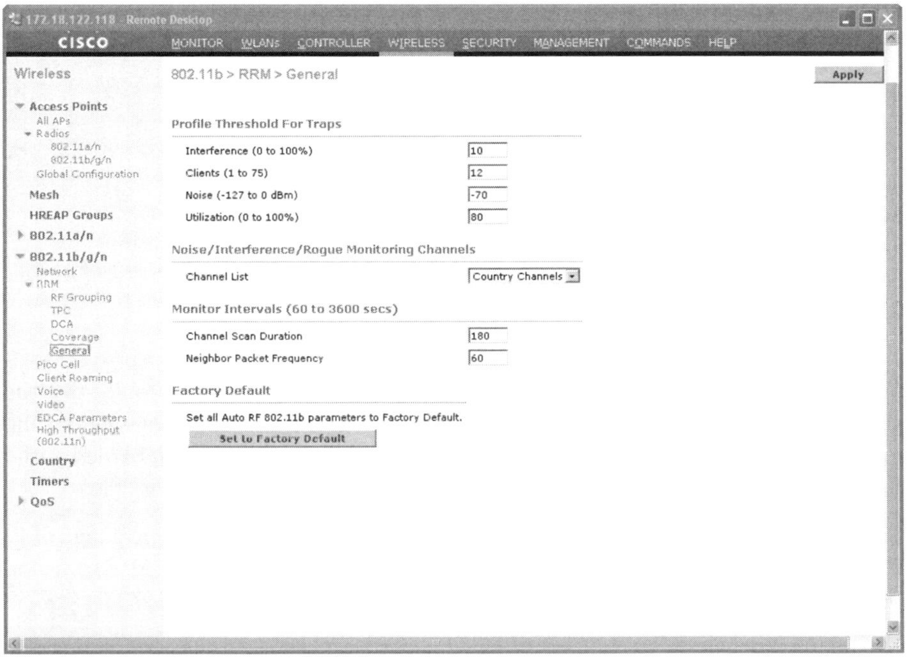

Figure 12-10 *RRM General Page*

The General page also allows you to configure the monitor intervals for RRM. All Lightweight Access Point Protocol (LWAPP)/Control and Provisioning of Wireless Access Points (CAPWAP)-based APs periodically go off-channel to record RRM measurements. The off-channel scanning takes approximately 50 ms and is transparent to any associated clients.

The *channel scan duration* is the interval (valid range of 60 to 3600 seconds) that the AP has to scan all the channels. On the 2.5-GHZ band in the United States, for example, with the default interval of 180 seconds, the AP goes off-channel roughly every 16 seconds to scan all 11 channels: 180/11 = ~16.

The *neighbor packet frequency* is how often the APs exchange neighbor messages. The default setting is 60 seconds. The APs also use the neighbor messages to maintain the neighbor list. In code prior to 4.1.185.0, neighbor APs were removed from the list after 20 minutes. In later code, an AP must not receive neighbor messages from its neighbor for an hour before that neighbor is removed from the neighbor list. This change makes the system less aggressive and allows for short outages.

Note   Changing the monitor intervals to a setting that is greater than the DCA and TPC intervals can result in stale RF information being used in the RRM calculations.

If you need to reset the profile and monitor configurations to factory default, you can click **Set to Factory Default**. This is a useful option if you had made changes in the past and want to get the settings back to their original state.

Note   You must disable the 802.11 network before you can reset these parameters to their default settings.

Overriding Global RRM

Should you desire to set the channel and power level manually for an AP or group of APs, you can override the global RRM settings.

Figure 12-11 shows the 802.11a radio configuration page for an AP.

Here you can statically assign power and channel to the radio and override the global.

By clicking on the Performance Profile button and then disabling the option Profile Parameters Globally Controlled, as shown in Figure 12-12, you can adjust the AP profile settings to fine-tune them as you want.

You might have an AP in a particular area where you know you will have a higher client load or known interference and increase those profile settings to prevent alarms from being triggered.

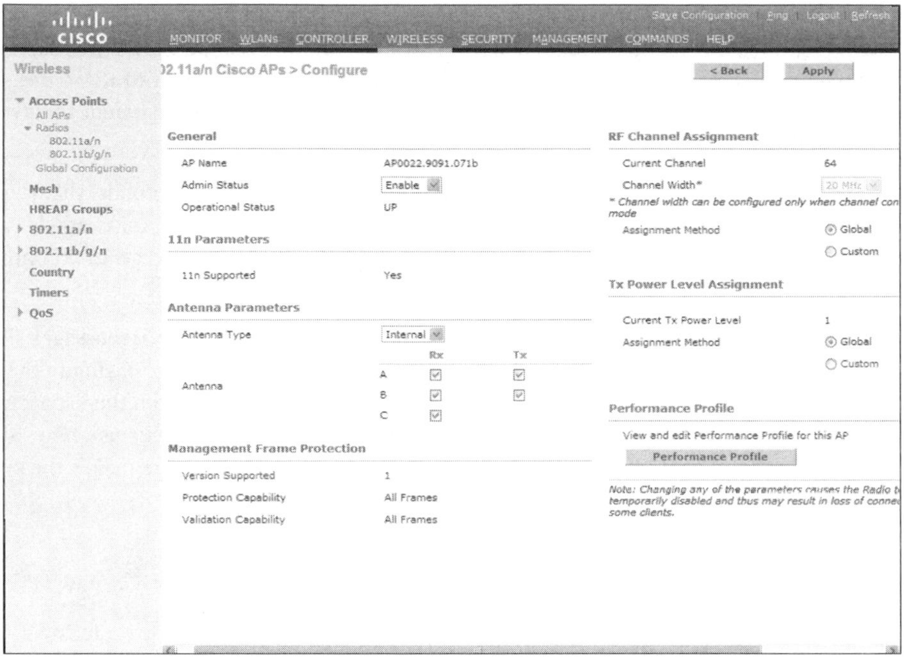

Figure 12-11 *Radio Configuration Page*

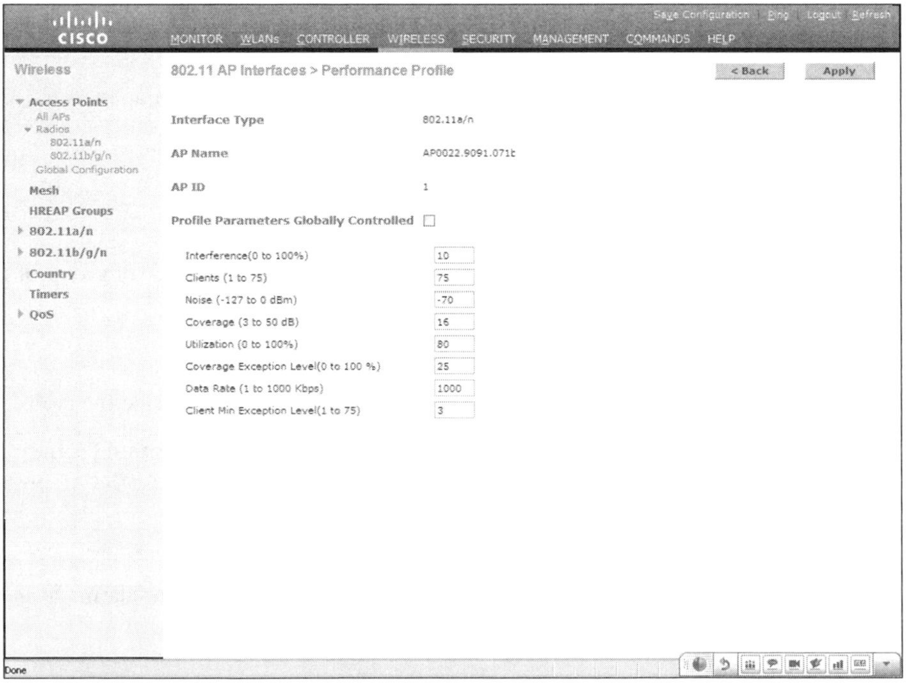

Figure 12-12 *Adjusting AP Profile Settings*

Troubleshooting RRM

If you believe you are having excessive RRM functions or RRM is not functioning properly, you have several ways of investigating the problem:

- Enable SNMP traps for RRM. These traps should be on by default.

- Use **show** commands to verify the configuration and see RRM information.

- Debug RRM.

SNMP Traps

The RRM SNMP traps generate trap messages for the following:

- Load profile

- Noise profile

- Interference profile

- Coverage profile

- Channel update

- Transmit power update

Figure 12-13 shows the Auto RF tab for SNMP traps on a 5.2 controller.

When an RRM event occurs that meets the necessary criteria to generate an SNMP trap, you see messages in the controller trap logs. If you are sending the traps to an SNMP trap receiver such as WCS, you might see alarms in WCS or even have notifications sent to your email account or pager to notify you of the event.

Following are some sample traplog outputs from a controller showing various RRM events:

- Interference:

  ```
  Tue May 19 13:17:33 2009 Interference Profile Failed for Base Radio MAC:
  00:1e:13:06:f6:50 and slotNo: 0

  Tue May 19 13:35:33 2009 Interference Profile Updated to Pass for Base Radio
  MAC: 00:1e:13:06:f6:50 and slotNo: 0
  ```

  In this case, you can see that the interference profile failed for the 802.11b/g radio for the AP with MAC address 00:1e:13:06:f6:50. A short time later, the interference disappears or is dropped below the configured threshold, and the controller generates a trap indicating that the interference profile has passed.

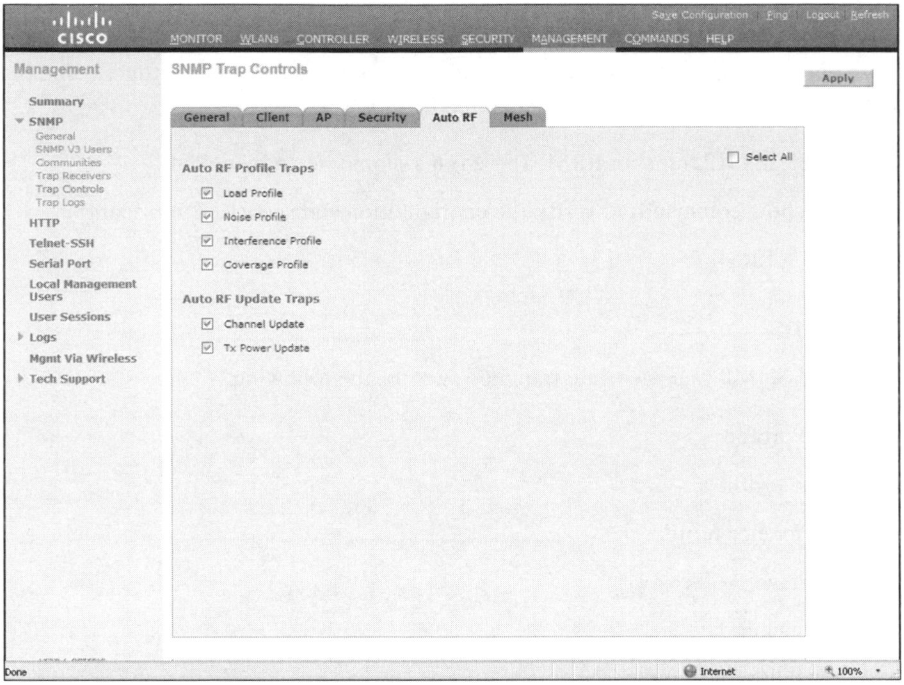

Figure 12-13 *Auto RF SNMP Trap Controls*

■ **Channel update:**

```
Channel changed for Base Radio MAC: 00:17:df:a7:c7:40 on 802.11b/g radio.
Old Channel: 6. New
```

```
Channel: 11. Why: Interference. Energy before/after change: -74/-81. Noise
before/after change:
```

```
-80/-82. Interference before/after change: -75/-86.
```

This information not only tells you that the AP has changed channels, but why. The root cause for this channel change is interference. When the AP changes from channel 6 to channel 11, the interference drops 11 dB.

```
Channel changed for Base Radio MAC: 00:1d:46:24:43:a0 on 802.11a radio. Old
Channel: 52. New
Channel: 44. Why: Radar. Energy before/after change: 0/0. Noise before/after
change: 0/0.
Interference before/after change: 0/0.
```

```
Tue Feb 10 11:05:14 2009—Radar signals have been detected on channel 52 by
802.11a radio with
MAC: 00:1d:46:24:43:a0 and slot 1
```

In this case, the channel change was the direct result of a DFS event. The AP detected radar on channel 52, so it had to change to a different channel. The AP picked channel 44 because it was an available channel and no radar was detected after a 60-second scan.

- **Coverage hole:**

  ```
  Coverage Hole Detected for AP 1242 whose Base Radio MAC is
  00:1e:13:06:f6:50. Number of Failing Clients 1
  ```

  In this case, the controller generated a coverage hole trap because a client fell below the configured SNR cutoff value.

- **Transmit power:**

  ```
  RF Manager updated TxPower for Base Radio MAC: 00:1f:26:28:d3:f0 and slotNo:
  0. New Tx Power is: 2
  ```

This output indicates that the AP changed the power level of its 802.11b/g radio to 2.

show Commands

You can see the current RRM configuration on the controller as well as current RRM information by AP using the following **show** commands:

```
show advanced [802.11a | 802.11b] txpower
show advanced [802.11a | 802.11b] channel
show ap auto-rf [802.11a | 802.11b] AP_name
```

As demonstrated in Example 12-1, the **show advanced [802.11a | 802.11b] txpower** command displays the current transmit power configuration as well as the MAC address of the current group leader.

Example 12-1 *Displaying Group Leader Transmit Power Configuration and MAC Address Information*

```
(Cisco Controller) >show advanced 802.11a txpower
Automatic Transmit Power Assignment
  Transmit Power Assignment Mode................ AUTO
  Transmit Power Update Interval................ 600 seconds
  Transmit Power Threshold...................... -70 dBm
  Transmit Power Neighbor Count................. 3 APs
  Transmit Power Update Contribution............ SNI.
  Transmit Power Assignment Leader.............. 00:1f:9e:9b:3e:40
  Last Run...................................... 290 seconds ago
```

This particular controller is set to the txpower default settings, and the MAC address of the group leader is 00:1f:9e:9b:3e:40. You can tell that this controller is the group leader because it shows the TPC algorithm last ran 290 seconds ago. Only the RF group leader would show a value for **Last Run.**

As demonstrated in Example 12-2, the output of **show advanced [802.11a | 802.11b} channel** command shows the current RRM channel information and configuration.

Example 12-2 *Displaying RRM Channel and Configuration Information*

```
(Cisco Controller) >show advanced 802.11a channel
Automatic Channel Assignment
  Channel Assignment Mode........................ AUTO
  Channel Update Interval........................ 600 seconds [startup]
  Anchor time (Hour of the day)................. 0
  Channel Update Contribution................... SNI.
  Channel Assignment Leader..................... 00:1f:9e:9b:3e:40
  Last Run...................................... 319 seconds ago
  DCA Sensitivity Level......................... STARTUP (5 dB)
  DCA 802.11n Channel Width..................... 20 MHz
  Channel Energy Levels
    Minimum..................................... -86 dBm
    Average..................................... -86 dBm
    Maximum..................................... -86 dBm
  Channel Dwell Times
    Minimum..................................... 0 days, 01 h 15 m 23 s
    Average..................................... 0 days, 01 h 23 m 38 s
    Maximum..................................... 0 days, 01 h 31 m 53 s
  802.11a 5 GHz Auto-RF Channel List
    Allowed Channel List........................ 36,40,44,48,52,56,60,64,149,
                                                 153,157,161
    Unused Channel List......................... 100,104,108,112,116,132,136,
                                                 140,165
  802.11a 4.9 GHz Auto-RF Channel List
    Allowed Channel List........................ 20,26
    Unused Channel List......................... 1,2,3,4,5,6,7,8,9,10,11,12,
                                                 13,14,15,16,17,18,19,21,22,
                                                 23,24,25
  DCA Outdoor AP option......................... Disabled
```

Here you can see the dwell times on the controller for how long APs retain their channel settings between DCA changes. Like the **txpower** command, you can also see the current DCA Channel group leader. Again, this particular controller is the group leader because you see a Last Run interval. This output also shows the current channel list that the DCA algorithm can use. This controller is using the default 12 channels for the 802.11a band.

Example 12-3 shows output from the **show auto-rf 802.11a** command for a 1242 AP from the controller CLI. From this output you can see interference, load, and coverage profile information, radar events, AP neighbor information, the current power level and channel information, as well as client information.

Example 12-3   *show ap auto-rf Output*

```
(Cisco Controller) >show ap auto-rf 802.11a 1242
Number Of Slots.................................. 2
AP Name.......................................... 1242
MAC Address...................................... 00:1d:a1:cd:dd:6c
  Slot ID........................................ 1
  Radio Type..................................... RADIO_TYPE_80211a
  Sub-band Type.................................. All
  Noise Information
    Noise Profile................................ PASSED
    Channel 36................................... -96 dBm
    Channel 40................................... -98 dBm
    Channel 44................................... -98 dBm
    Channel 48................................... -97 dBm
    Channel 52................................... -96 dBm
    Channel 56................................... -100 dBm
    Channel 60................................... -94 dBm
    Channel 64................................... -98 dBm
    Channel 100.................................. -96 dBm
    Channel 104.................................. -98 dBm
    Channel 108.................................. -97 dBm
    Channel 112.................................. -97 dBm
    Channel 116.................................. -97 dBm
    Channel 132.................................. -97 dBm
    Channel 136.................................. -96 dBm
    Channel 140.................................. -96 dBm
    Channel 149.................................. -96 dBm
    Channel 153.................................. -96 dBm
    Channel 157.................................. -97 dBm
    Channel 161.................................. -97 dBm
  Interference Information
    Interference Profile......................... PASSED
    Channel 36................................... -128 dBm @   0 % busy
    Channel 40................................... -128 dBm @   0 % busy
    Channel 44................................... -128 dBm @   0 % busy
    Channel 48................................... -128 dBm @   0 % busy
    Channel 52................................... -128 dBm @   0 % busy
    Channel 56................................... -128 dBm @   0 % busy
    Channel 60................................... -128 dBm @   0 % busy
```

(continues)

Example 12-3 *show ap auto-rf Output (continued)*

```
    Channel 64.................................. -128 dBm @  0 % busy
    Channel 100................................. -128 dBm @  0 % busy
    Channel 104................................. -128 dBm @  0 % busy
    Channel 108................................. -128 dBm @  0 % busy
    Channel 112................................. -128 dBm @  0 % busy
    Channel 116................................. -128 dBm @  0 % busy
    Channel 132................................. -128 dBm @  0 % busy
    Channel 136................................. -128 dBm @  0 % busy
    Channel 140................................. -128 dBm @  0 % busy
    Channel 149................................. -128 dBm @  0 % busy
    Channel 153................................. -128 dBm @  0 % busy
    Channel 157................................. -128 dBm @  0 % busy
    Channel 161................................. -128 dBm @  0 % busy
    Rogue Histogram (20/40_ABOVE/40_BELOW)
    ...........................................
    Channel 36................................. 4/ 2/ 0
    Channel 40................................. 0/ 0/ 0
    Channel 44................................. 2/ 0/ 0
    Channel 48................................. 3/ 0/ 0
    Channel 52................................. 1/ 0/ 0
    Channel 56................................. 2/ 0/ 0
    Channel 60................................. 1/ 0/ 0
    Channel 64................................. 1/ 0/ 0
    Channel 100................................ 0/ 0/ 0
    Channel 104................................ 0/ 0/ 0
    Channel 108................................ 0/ 0/ 0
    Channel 112................................ 0/ 0/ 0
    Channel 116................................ 0/ 0/ 0
    Channel 132................................ 0/ 0/ 0
    Channel 136................................ 0/ 0/ 0
    Channel 140................................ 0/ 0/ 0
    Channel 149................................ 1/ 0/ 0
    Channel 153................................ 2/ 0/ 1
    Channel 157................................ 1/ 0/ 0
    Channel 161................................ 5/ 0/ 0
Load Information
    Load Profile............................... PASSED
    Receive Utilization........................ 0 %
    Transmit Utilization....................... 0 %
    Channel Utilization........................ 3 %
    Attached Clients........................... 0 clients
Coverage Information
    Coverage Profile........................... PASSED
    Failed Clients............................. 0 clients
```

```
Client Signal Strengths
  RSSI -100 dbm.............................. 0 clients

  RSSI  -92 dbm.............................. 0 clients

  RSSI  -84 dbm.............................. 0 clients

  RSSI  -76 dbm.............................. 0 clients

  RSSI  -68 dbm.............................. 0 clients

  RSSI  -60 dbm.............................. 0 clients

  RSSI  -52 dbm.............................. 0 clients

Client Signal To Noise Ratios

  SNR    0 dB............................... 0 clients

  SNR    5 dB............................... 0 clients

  SNR   10 dB............................... 0 clients

  SNR   15 dB............................... 0 clients

  SNR   20 dB............................... 0 clients

  SNR   25 dB............................... 0 clients

  SNR   30 dB............................... 0 clients

  SNR   35 dB............................... 0 clients

  SNR   40 dB............................... 0 clients

  SNR   45 dB............................... 0 clients
Nearby APs
  AP 00:17:df:a7:c7:40 slot 1................. -78 dBm on 153 (192.168.6.5)
  AP 00:1c:b1:07:fa:20 slot 1................. -59 dBm on  56 (192.168.6.5)
Radar Information

Channel Assignment Information

  Current Channel Average Energy.............. unknown
```

(continues)

Example 12-3 *show ap auto-rf Output (continued)*

```
      Previous Channel Average Energy.............. unknown
      Channel Change Count......................... 0
      Last Channel Change Time..................... Tue May 19 12:12:01 2009
      Recommended Best Channel..................... 36
   RF Parameter Recommendations
      Power Level.................................. 6
      RTS/CTS Threshold............................ 2347
      Fragmentation Threshold...................... 2346
      Antenna Pattern............................. 0
```

From this output, you can tell the following:

■   The AP interference, load, and coverage profiles are all passed.

■   The current channel utilization is 3 percent.

■   No clients are associated with this AP.

■   From the Nearby APs section, the AP does not meet the minimum requirements for RRM to function properly because only two neighbor APs now exist. Remember that RRM requires four APs at minimum.

■   The AP radio channel has never changed.

■   The recommended best channel is the default power on channel 36 because no RRM events have triggered a channel change.

■   No radar events exist.

Debugs

To debug RRM, use the debug **airewave-director** command as demonstrated in Example 12-4.

Example 12-4 *Debug Options for Airewave Director*

```
(Cisco Controller) >debug airewave-director ?
all             Configures debug of all Airewave Director logs
channel         Configures debug of Airewave Director channel assignment protocol
error           Configures debug of Airewave Director error logs
detail          Configures debug of Airewave Director detail logs
group           Configures debug of Airewave Director grouping protocol
manager         Configures debug of Airewave Director manager
message         Configures debug of Airewave Director messages
packet          Configures debug of Airewave Director packets
power           Configures debug of Airewave Director power assignment protocol
radar           Configures debug of Airewave Director radar detection/avoidance
protocol
```

```
plm              Configures debug of CCX S60 Power Measurement Loss messages
rf-change        Configures logging of Airewave Director rf changes
profile          Configures logging of Airewave Director profile events
```

Enabling the **all** keyword invokes all the RRM debugs listed in the output from Example 12-4. The output of **debug airewave-director all** can be quite verbose. The more APs on the WLC, the more output it yields. If you have a heavily loaded WLC, you can imagine that the logs would be filled pretty quickly, so you will more than likely want to log it to a file for analysis.

This chapter focuses on the power, channel, detail, and manager debug outputs from the RF group leader.

debug airewave-director power Command

The output in Example 12-5 shows the TPC algorithm running for both the 802.11a radios.

Example 12-5   *debug airewave-director power Output*

```
(Cisco Controller) >debug airewave-director power enable
*May 19 16:50:14.287: Airewave Director: Computing power control assignment on
802.11a
*May 19 16:50:14.287: Airewave Director: Preparing for power control assignment
on 802.11a
*May 19 16:50:14.287: Airewave Director: AP 00:17:95:81:A9:F0(1) has nearby neigh-
bor 00:1E:13:06:F6:50(1) (RSSI -74) — adjusting power to 21
*May 19 16:50:14.287: Airewave Director: AP 00:1C:B1:07:FA:20(1) has nearby neigh
bor 00:1E:13:06:F6:50(1) (RSSI -56) — adjusting power to 3
*May 19 16:50:14.287: Airewave Director: AP 00:1F:13:06:F6:50(1) has nearby neigh-
bor 00:17:95:81:A9:F0(1) (RSSI -71) — adjusting power to 18
*May 19 16:50:14.287: Airewave Director: AP 00:17:DF:A7:C7:40(1) has nearby neigh-
bor 00:1E:13:06:F6:50(1) (RSSI -83) — adjusting power to 30
*May 19 16:50:16.128: Airewave Director: Set raw transmit power on 802.11a AP
00:17:95:81:A9:F0(1) to (  14 dBm, level  3)
*May 19 16:50:16.128: Airewave Director: Set adjusted transmit power on 802.11a AP
00:17:95:81:A9:F0(1) to (  14 dBm, level  3)
*May 19 16:50:16.128: Airewave Director: Set raw transmit power on 802.11a AP
00:1C:B1:07:FA:20(1) to (   5 dBm, level  6)
*May 19 16:50:16.128: Airewave Director: Set adjusted transmit power on 802.11a AP
00:1C:B1:07:FA:20(1) to (   5 dBm, level  6)
*May 19 16:50:16.129: Airewave Director: Set raw transmit power on 802.11a AP
00:1E:13:06:F6:50(1) to (  14 dBm, level  3)
*May 19 16:50:16.129: Airewave Director: Set adjusted transmit power on 802.11a AP
00:1E:13:06:F6:50(1) to (  14 dBm, level  3)
*May 19 16:50:16.129: Airewave Director: Set raw transmit power on 802.11a AP
00:17:DF:A7:C7:40(1) to (  20 dBm, level  1)
*May 19 16:50:16.129: Airewave Director: Set adjusted transmit power on 802.11a AP
00:17:DF:A7:C7:40(1) to (  20 dBm, level  1)
```

For this particular AP, you can see TPC start and comparing the power levels of the four APs that are currently joined to the controller. In this case, the APs did not adjust their power levels.

If one of the four APs is shut down, however, the configuration does not meet the requirements for RRM. The lack of APs results in the remaining APs immediately adjusting their power to level 1:

```
*May 19 18:00:52.667: Airewave Director: Computing power control assignment on
802.11a
*May 19 18:00:52.667: Airewave Director: Preparing for power control assignment
on 802.11a
*May 19 18:00:54.521: Airewave Director: Set raw transmit power on 802.11a AP
00:17:95:81:A9:F0(1) to (  17 dBm, level          1)
*May 19 18:00:54.522: Airewave Director: Set adjusted transmit power on 802.11a
AP 00:17:95:81:A9:F0(1) to (  17 dBm, l         evel  1)
*May 19 18:00:54.522: Airewave Director: Set raw transmit power on 802.11a AP
00:1E:13:06:F6:50(1) to (  17 dBm, level          1)
*May 19 18:00:54.523: Airewave Director: Set adjusted transmit power on 802.11a
AP 00:1E:13:06:F6:50(1) to (  17 dBm, l         evel  1)
*May 19 18:00:54.523: Airewave Director: Set raw transmit power on 802.11a AP
00:17:DF:A7:C7:40(1) to (  20 dBm, level          1)
*May 19 18:00:54.524: Airewave Director: Set adjusted transmit power on 802.11a
AP 00:17:DF:A7:C7:40(1) to (  20 dBm, l         evel  1)
```

The following takes a deeper look at the Airewave Director so you can see the coverage hole feature in action. Here, in the following example, you can see the coverage hole algorithm working:

802.11a:

```
Airewave Director: Coverage Hole Check on 802.11a AP 00:1E:13:06:F6:50(1)
Airewave Director: Found 0 failed clients on 802.11a AP 00:1E:13:06:F6:50(1))
Airewave Director: Found 0 clients close to coverage edge on 802.11a AP
00:1E:13:06:F6:50(1)
```

802.11b/g:

```
Airewave Director: Coverage Hole Check on 802.11bg AP 00:1E:13:06:F6:50 (0)
Airewave Director: Found 0 failed clients on 802.11bg AP 00:1E:13:06:F6:50 (0)
Airewave Director: Found 0 clients close to coverage edge on 802.11bg
AP 00:1E:13:06:F6:50 (0)
Airewave Director: Last power increase 183 seconds ago on 802.11bg
AP 00:1E:13:06:F6:50 (0)
```

As you can see, no failed clients exist on either radio or clients that are in danger of triggering a coverage hole event.

Note   You must run **debug airewave-director power** from the controller where the AP you are interested in is joined to see the coverage hole corrections for that AP.

debug airewave-director channel Command Output

You will see four phases when the DCA algorithm runs, as outlined in Examples 12-6 through 12-9.

Example 12-6   *Phase 1: The Controller Collects and Records the Current Statistics to Run Through the DCA Algorithm*

```
*May 19 17:30:36.162: Airewave Director: Computing channel assignment for 802.11a
*May 19 17:30:36.183: Airewave Director: Checking quality of current assignment
for 802.11a
*May 19 17:30:36.185: Airewave Director: 802.11a AP 00:17:95:81:A9:F0(1) ch 161
(before -81.72, after -128.00)
*May 19 17:30:36.185: Airewave Director:         00:17:95:81:A9:F0(1)( 20,
128.00)( 26, 128.00)( 36, -59.48)( 40, -66.68)
*May 19 17:30:36.185: Airewave Director:         00:17:95:81:A9:F0(1)( 44, -
66.87)( 48, -63.35)( 52, -45.88)( 56, -25.91)
*May 19 17:30:36.185: Airewave Director:         00:17:95:81:A9:F0(1)( 60, -
45.88)( 64, -63.37)(149, -48.93)(153, -59.27)
*May 19 17:30:36.185: Airewave Director:         00:17:95:81:A9:F0(1)(157, -
66.58)(161, -81.72)
*May 19 17:30:36.185: Airewave Director: 802.11a AP 00:1C:B1:07:FA:20(1) ch  56
(before -86.87, after -128.00)
*May 19 17:30:36.185: Airewave Director:         00:1C:B1:07:FA:20(1)( 20,
128.00)( 26, 128.00)( 36, -27.12)( 40, -43.49)
*May 19 17:30:36.186: Airewave Director:         00:1C:B1:07:FA:20(1)( 44, -
63.98)( 48, -66.87)( 52, -66.87)( 56, -86.87)
*May 19 17:30:36.186: Airewave Director:         00:1C:B1:07:FA:20(1)( 60, -
66.87)( 64, -66.91)(149, -48.76)(153, -42.78)
*May 19 17:30:36.186: Airewave Director:         00:1C:B1:07:FA:20(1)(157, -
45.79)(161, -25.91)
*May 19 17:30:36.186: Airewave Director: 802.11a AP 00:1E:13:06:F6:50(1) ch  36
(before -86.91, after -128.00)
*May 19 17:30:36.186: Airewave Director:         00:1E:13:06:F6:50(1)( 20,
128.00)( 26, 128.00)( 36, -86.91)( 40, -45.96)
*May 19 17:30:36.186: Airewave Director:         00:1E:13:06:F6:50(1)( 44, -
66.87)( 48, -63.98)( 52, -47.07)( 56, -27.12)
*May 19 17:30:36.186: Airewave Director:         00:1E:13:06:F6:50(1)( 60, -
47.07)( 64, -64.00)(149, -48.86)(153, -46.82)
*May 19 17:30:36.186: Airewave Director:         00:1E:13:06:F6:50(1)(157, -
63.76)(161, -59.47)
*May 19 17:30:36.186: Airewave Director: 802.11a AP 00:17:DF:A7:C7:40(1) ch 153
(before -86.87, after -128.00)
*May 19 17:30:36.187: Airewave Director:         00:17:DF:A7:C7:40(1)( 20,
128.00)( 26, 128.00)( 36, -46.82)( 40, -63.86)
*May 19 17:30:36.187: Airewave Director:         00:17:DF:A7:C7:40(1)( 44, -
66.83)( 48, -66.76)( 52, -61.38)( 56, -42.80)
*May 19 17:30:36.187: Airewave Director:         00:17:DF:A7:C7:40(1)( 60, -
61.38)( 64, -66.80)(149, -48.93)(153, -86.87)
*May 19 17:30:36.187: Airewave Director:         00:17:DF:A7:C7:40(1)(157, -
66.66)(161, -59.07)
```

Example 12-7   *Phase 2: The Controller Suggests a New Channel and Stores the Recommended Values*

```
*May 19 17:30:36.187: Airewave Director: Searching for better assignment for
802.11a with 4 unassigned lrads
*May 19 17:30:36.197: Airewave Director: Not using unsupported chan = 20 on AP
00:1C:B1:07:FA:20(1)
*May 19 17:30:36.197: Airewave Director: Not using unsupported chan = 26 on AP
00:1C:B1:07:FA:20(1)
*May 19 17:30:36.198: Airewave Director: worst radio changing to chan = (56,0) on
AP 00:1C:B1:07:FA:20(1)
*May 19 17:30:36.208: Airewave Director: Not using unsupported chan = 20 on AP
00:17:95:81:A9:F0(1)
*May 19 17:30:36.208: Airewave Director: Not using unsupported chan = 26 on AP
00:17:95:81:A9:F0(1)
*May 19 17:30:36.208: Airewave Director: worst radio changing to chan = (161,0) on
AP 00:17:95:81:A9:F0(1)
*May 19 17:30:36.219: Airewave Director: Not using unsupported chan = 20 on AP
00:1E:13:06:F6:50(1)
*May 19 17:30:36.219: Airewave Director: Not using unsupported chan = 26 on AP
00:1E:13:06:F6:50(1)
*May 19 17:30:36.219: Airewave Director: worst radio changing to chan = (36,0) on
AP 00:1E:13:06:F6:50(1)
*May 19 17:30:36.230: Airewave Director: Not using unsupported chan = 20 on AP
00:17:DF:A7:C7:40(1)
*May 19 17:30:36.230: Airewave Director: Not using unsupported chan = 26 on AP
00:17:DF:A7:C7:40(1)
*May 19 17:30:36.230: Airewave Director: worst radio changing to chan = (153,0) on
AP 00:17:DF:A7:C7:40(1)
*May 19 17:30:36.230: Airewave Director: 802.11a AP 00:17:95:81:A9:F0(1) ch 161
(before -81.72, after -128.00)
*May 19 17:30:36.230: Airewave Director:           00:17:95:81:A9:F0(1)( 20,
128.00)( 26, 128.00)( 36, -66.91)( 40, -66.87)
*May 19 17:30:36.231: Airewave Director:           00:17:95:81:A9:F0(1)( 44, -
66.87)( 48, -63.35)( 52, -45.88)( 56, -25.91)
*May 19 17:30:36.231: Airewave Director:           00:17:95:81:A9:F0(1)( 60, -
45.88)( 64, -63.37)(149, -48.93)(153, -66.87)
*May 19 17:30:36.231: Airewave Director:           00:17:95:81:A9:F0(1)(157, -
66.77)(161, -81.72)
*May 19 17:30:36.231: Airewave Director: 802.11a AP 00:1C:B1:07:FA:20(1) ch   56
(before -86.87, after -128.00)
*May 19 17:30:36.231: Airewave Director:           00:1C:B1:07:FA:20(1)( 20,
128.00)( 26, 128.00)( 36, -64.76)( 40, -45.96)
*May 19 17:30:36.231: Airewave Director:           00:1C:B1:07:FA:20(1)( 44, -
66.87)( 48, -66.87)( 52, -66.87)( 56, -86.87)
*May 19 17:30:36.231: Airewave Director:           00:1C:B1:07:FA:20(1)( 60, -
66.87)( 64, -66.91)(149, -48.93)(153, -66.87)
*May 19 17:30:36.231: Airewave Director:           00:1C:B1:07:FA:20(1)(157, -
66.87)(161, -66.91)
*May 19 17:30:36.231: Airewave Director: 802.11a AP 00:1E:13:06:F6:50(1) ch   36
(before -86.91, after -128.00)
```

```
*May 19 17:30:36.231: Airewave Director:         00:1E:13:06:F6:50(1)( 20,
128.00)( 26, 128.00)( 36, -86.91)( 40, -45.96)

*May 19 17:30:36.231: Airewave Director:         00:1E:13:06:F6:50(1)( 44, -
66.87)( 48, -63.98)( 52, -47.07)( 56, -27.12)

*May 19 17:30:36.231: Airewave Director:         00:1E:13:06:F6:50(1)( 60, -
47.07)( 64, -64.00)(149, -48.93)(153, -66.87)

*May 19 17:30:36.231: Airewave Director:         00:1E:13:06:F6:50(1)(157, -
66.68)(161, -59.48)

*May 19 17:30:36.231: Airewave Director: 802.11a AP 00:17:DF:A7:C7:40(1) ch 153
(before -86.87, after -128.00)

*May 19 17:30:36.231: Airewave Director:         00:17:DF:A7:C7:40(1)( 20,
128.00)( 26, 128.00)( 36, -46.82)( 40, -63.86)

*May 19 17:30:36.231: Airewave Director:         00:17:DF:A7:C7:40(1)( 44, -
66.83)( 48, -66.76)( 52, -61.38)( 56, -42.80)

*May 19 17:30:36.231: Airewave Director:         00:17:DF:A7:C7:40(1)( 60, -
61.38)( 64, -66.80)(149, -48.93)(153, -86.87)

*May 19 17:30:36.231: Airewave Director:         00:17:DF:A7:C7:40(1)(157, -
66.66)(161, -59.07)
```

Example 12-8 *Phase 3: The Controller Compares the Suggested Values to the Current Values*

```
*May 19 17:30:36.231: Airewave Director: Comparing old and new assignment for
802.11a

*May 19 17:30:36.231: Airewave Director: Not using unsupported chan = 20 on AP
00:17:95:81:A9:F0(1)

*May 19 17:30:36.231: Airewave Director: Not using unsupported chan = 26 on AP
00:17:95:81:A9:F0(1)

*May 19 17:30:36.231: Airewave Director: Not using unsupported chan = 20 on AP
00:1C:B1:07:FA:20(1)

*May 19 17:30:36.231: Airewave Director: Not using unsupported chan = 26 on AP
00:1C:B1:07:FA:20(1)

*May 19 17:30:36.231: Airewave Director: Not using unsupported chan = 20 on AP
00:1E:13:06:F6:50(1)

*May 19 17:30:36.231: Airewave Director: Not using unsupported chan = 26 on AP
00:1E:13:06:F6:50(1)

*May 19 17:30:36.232: Airewave Director: Not using unsupported chan = 20 on AP
00:17:DF:A7:C7:40(1)

*May 19 17:30:36.232: Airewave Director: Not using unsupported chan = 26 on AP
00:17:DF:A7:C7:40(1)

*May 19 17:30:36.232: Airewave Director: 802.11a AP 00:17:95:81:A9:F0(1) ch 161
(before -81.72, after -81.72)

*May 19 17:30:36.232: Airewave Director:         00:17:95:81:A9:F0(1)( 20, 128.00)(
26, 128.00)( 36, -59.48)( 40, -66.68)

*May 19 17:30:36.232: Airewave Director:         00:17:95:81:A9:F0(1)( 44, -
66.87)( 48, -63.35)( 52, -45.88)( 56, -25.91)

*May 19 17:30:36.232: Airewave Director:         00:17:95:81:A9:F0(1)( 60, -
45.88)( 64, -63.37)(149, -48.93)(153, -59.27)

*May 19 17:30:36.232: Airewave Director:         00:17:95:81:A9:F0(1)(157, -
66.58)(161, -81.72)
```

(continues)

Example 12-8   *Phase 3: The Controller Compares the Suggested Values to the Current Values (continued)*

```
*May 19 17:30:36.232: Airewave Director: 802.11a AP 00:1C:B1:07:FA:20(1) ch  56
(before -86.87, after -86.87)
*May 19 17:30:36.232: Airewave Director:        00:1C:B1:07:FA:20(1)( 20,
128.00)( 26, 128.00)( 36, -27.12)( 40, -43.49)
*May 19 17:30:36.232: Airewave Director:        00:1C:B1:07:FA:20(1)( 44, -
63.98)( 48, -66.87)( 52, -66.87)( 56, -86.87)
*May 19 17:30:36.232: Airewave Director:        00:1C:B1:07:FA:20(1)( 60, -
66.87)( 64, -66.91)(149, -48.76)(153, -42.78)
*May 19 17:30:36.232: Airewave Director:        00:1C:B1:07:FA:20(1)(157, -
45.79)(161, -25.91)
*May 19 17:30:36.232: Airewave Director: 802.11a AP 00:1E:13:06:F6:50(1) ch  36
(before -86.91, after -86.91)
*May 19 17:30:36.232: Airewave Director:        00:1E:13:06:F6:50(1)( 20,
128.00)( 26, 128.00)( 36, -86.91)( 40, -45.96)
*May 19 17:30:36.232: Airewave Director:        00:1E:13:06:F6:50(1)( 44, -
66.87)( 48, -63.98)( 52, -47.07)( 56, -27.12)
*May 19 17:30:36.232: Airewave Director:        00:1E:13:06:F6:50(1)( 60, -
47.07)( 64, -64.00)(149, -48.86)(153, -46.82)
*May 19 17:30:36.232: Airewave Director:        00:1E:13:06:F6:50(1)(157, -
63.76)(161, -59.47)
*May 19 17:30:36.232: Airewave Director: 802.11a AP 00:17:DF:A7:C7:40(1) ch 153
(before -86.87, after -86.87)
*May 19 17:30:36.232: Airewave Director:        00:17:DF:A7:C7:40(1)( 20,
128.00)( 26, 128.00)( 36, -46.82)( 40, -63.86)
*May 19 17:30:36.232: Airewave Director:        00:17:DF:A7:C7:40(1)( 44, -
66.83)( 48, -66.76)( 52, -61.38)( 56, -42.80)
*May 19 17:30:36.232: Airewave Director:        00:17:DF:A7:C7:40(1)( 60, -
61.38)( 64, -66.80)(149, -48.93)(153, -86.87)
*May 19 17:30:36.232: Airewave Director:        00:17:DF:A7:C7:40(1)(157, -
66.66)(161, -59.07)
```

Example 12-9   *Phase 4: The Controller Applies the Changes if Necessary*

```
*May 19 17:30:36.232: Airewave Director: Before — 802.11a energy worst -81.72,
average -85.59, best -86.91
*May 19 17:30:36.232: Airewave Director: After — 802.11a energy worst -81.72,
average -85.59, best -86.91
*May 19 17:30:36.232: Airewave Director: Assignment is not significantly better on
802.11a — discarding assignment
```

As you can see from the last line in this output, any suggested channel changes would not result in a significantly better RF environment, so no channel change takes place.

debug airewave-director detail Command Output

When you enable the aireware-director detail debug, you get a real-time view of how RRM is functioning on your controller.

Following are some common messages and their explanations:

■ **RF group keepalive:**

```
*May 19 14:49:35.140: Airewave Director: Sending keepalive packet to
802.11bg group members
```

```
*May 19 14:49:35.140: Airewave Director: Sending keepalive packet to 802.11a
group members
```

The RF group members exchange keepalive packets to maintain the group hierarchy.

■ **Neighbor pruning:**

```
*May 19 15:03:00.796: Airewave Director: Pruning stale RF neighbors 802.11a
AP 00:1E:13:06:F6:50(1)
```

■ **Processing noise, interference, and load statistics on neighbor APs:**

Noise and interference on 802.11a radio:

```
*May 19 15:01:31.137: Airewave Director: Processing Interference data on
802.11a AP 00:17:DF:A7:C7:40(1)
```

```
*May 19 15:01:31.139: Airewave Director: Processing noise data on 802.11a AP
00:17:DF:A7:C7:40(1)
```

Load on 802.11b/g:

```
*May 19 15:01:33.143: Airewave Director: Processing Load data on 802.11bg AP
00:1E:13:06:F6:50(0)
```

debug airewave-director manager Command Output

Enabling this debug allows you to see the RF grouping information. Following is the output of this debug from the RF group leader and an RF group member:

■ **RF group leader:** You can see that this controller is the RF group leader for both the 2.4- and 5-GHZ bands because the RRM state shows as **LEADER_IDLE**:

```
*May 19 16:59:31.994: Airewave Director: Group 802.11a action HELLO_TIMER in
state LEADER_IDLE
```

```
*May 19 16:59:31.994: Airewave Director: Group 802.11bg action HELLO_TIMER
in state LEADER_IDLE
```

```
*May 19 16:59:35.823: Airewave Director: Group 802.11a action CALC_TIMER in
state LEADER_IDLE
```

The RF grouping algorithms kick in, and the controller moves into the
LEADER_PREP state:

```
*May 19 16:59:35.824: Airewave Director: Group 802.11a trigger RF automatic
grouping

*May 19 16:59:35.824: Airewave Director: Group 802.11a trigger RF channel
assignment

*May 19 16:59:35.824: Airewave Director: Group 802.11a trigger RF transmit
power control

*May 19 16:59:35.824: Airewave Director: Group 802.11a change state from
LEADER_IDLE to LEADER_PREP

*May 19 16:59:35.824: Airewave Director: Group 802.11a action
TRANSMISSION_TIMER in state LEADER_PREP

*May 19 16:59:35.826: Airewave Director: Group 802.11a action CLIENT_DATA in
state LEADER_PREP

*May 19 16:59:36.781: Airewave Director: Group 802.11a action
TRANSMISSION_TIMER in state LEADER_PREP

*May 19 16:59:36.782: Airewave Director: Group 802.11a action CLIENT_DATA in
state LEADER_PREP

*May 19 16:59:37.737: Airewave Director: Group 802.11a action
TRANSMISSION_TIMER in state LEADER_PREP

*May 19 16:59:37.738: Airewave Director: Group 802.11a action CLIENT_DATA in
state LEADER_PREP

*May 19 16:59:37.739: Airewave Director: Group 802.11a action CLIENT_DATA in
state LEADER_PREP

*May 19 16:59:38.694: Airewave Director: Group 802.11a action
TRANSMISSION_TIMER in state LEADER_PREP

*May 19 16:59:38.696: Airewave Director: Group 802.11a action CLIENT_DATA in
state LEADER_PREP

*May 19 16:59:38.696: Airewave Director: Group 802.11a action CLIENT_DATA in
state LEADER_PREP

*May 19 16:59:39.650: Airewave Director: Group 802.11bg action CALC_TIMER in
state LEADER_IDLE

*May 19 16:59:39.651: Airewave Director: Group 802.11a action
TRANSMISSION_TIMER in state LEADER_PREP

*May 19 16:59:39.654: Airewave Director: Group 802.11a action CLIENT_DATA in
state LEADER_PREP

*May 19 16:59:39.655: Airewave Director: Group 802.11a action CLIENT_DATA in
state LEADER_PREP

*May 19 16:59:40.609: Airewave Director: Group 802.11a action
TRANSMISSION_TIMER in state LEADER_PREP

*May 19 16:59:40.611: Airewave Director: Group 802.11a action CLIENT_DATA in
state LEADER_PREP

*May 19 16:59:40.612: Airewave Director: Group 802.11a action CLIENT_DATA in
state LEADER_PREP
```

The LEADER_PREP state completes, and the controller transitions into LEADER_COMP to calculate the RF group leader:

```
*May 19 16:59:40.613: Airewave Director: Group 802.11a change state from
LEADER_PREP to LEADER_COMP

*May 19 16:59:40.702: Airewave Director: Group 802.11a action CALC_END in
state LEADER_COMP
```

After the LEADER_COMP state, the controller moves into the LEADER_ASSIGN state:

```
*May 19 16:59:40.702: Airewave Director: Group 802.11a change state from
LEADER_COMP to LEADER ASSIGN

*May 19 16:59:40.702: Airewave Director: Group 802.11a action
TRANSMISSION_TIMER in state LEADER ASSIGN

*May 19 16:59:40.704: Airewave Director: Group 802.11a action CLIENT_ACK in
state LEADER ASSIGN

*May 19 16:59:40.704: Airewave Director: Group 802.11a action CLIENT_ACK in
state LEADER ASSIGN

*May 19 16:59:41.565: Airewave Director: Group 802.11a action HELLO_TIMER in
state LEADER ASSIGN

*May 19 16:59:41.566: Airewave Director: Group 802.11bg action HELLO_TIMER
in state LEADER_IDLE

*May 19 16:59:41.567: Airewave Director: Group 802.11a action
TRANSMISSION_TIMER in state LEADER ASSIGN

*May 19 16:59:41.568: Airewave Director: Group 802.11a action CLIENT_ACK in
state LEADER ASSIGN

*May 19 16:59:41.568: Airewave Director: Group 802.11a action CLIENT_ACK in
state LEADER ASSIGN

*May 19 16:59:42.523: Airewave Director: Group 802.11a action
TRANSMISSION_TIMER in state LEADER ASSIGN

*May 19 16:59:42.524: Airewave Director: Group 802.11a action CLIENT_ACK in
state LEADER ASSIGN

*May 19 16:59:42.525: Airewave Director: Group 802.11a action CLIENT_ACK in
state LEADER ASSIGN

*May 19 16:59:43.480: Airewave Director: Group 802.11a action
TRANSMISSION_TIMER in state LEADER ASSIGN

*May 19 16:59:43.482: Airewave Director: Group 802.11a action CLIENT_ACK in
state LEADER ASSIGN

*May 19 16:59:43.482: Airewave Director: Group 802.11a action CLIENT_ACK in
state LEADER ASSIGN

*May 19 16:59:44.437: Airewave Director: Group 802.11a action
TRANSMISSION_TIMER in state LEADER ASSIGN

*May 19 16:59:44.438: Airewave Director: Group 802.11a action CLIENT_ACK in
state LEADER ASSIGN

*May 19 16:59:44.439: Airewave Director: Group 802.11a action CLIENT_ACK in
state LEADER ASSIGN
```

```
*May 19 16:59:45.394: Airewave Director: Group 802.11a action
TRANSMISSION_TIMER in state LEADER ASSIGN

*May 19 16:59:45.395: Airewave Director: Group 802.11a action CLIENT_ACK in
state LEADER ASSIGN

*May 19 16:59:45.396: Airewave Director: Group 802.11a action CLIENT_ACK in
state LEADER ASSIGN
```

The controller has the highest group ID and returns to the LEADER_IDLE state.
Then it starts sending HELLO packets to the other RF group members:

```
*May 19 16:59:45.396: Airewave Director: Group 802.11a change state from
LEADER ASSIGN to LEADER_IDLE

*May 19 16:59:49.223: Airewave Director: Group 802.11bg action CALC_TIMER in
state LEADER_IDLE

*May 19 16:59:51.138: Airewave Director: Group 802.11a action HELLO_TIMER in
state LEADER_IDLE

*May 19 16:59:51.138: Airewave Director: Group 802.11bg action HELLO_TIMER
in state LEADER_IDLE

*May 19 16:59:54.969: Airewave Director: Group 802.11a action CALC_TIMER in
state LEADER_IDLE

*May 19 16:59:58.801: Airewave Director: Group 802.11bg action CALC_TIMER in
state LEADER_IDLE

*May 19 17:00:00.715: Airewave Director: Group 802.11a action HELLO_TIMER in
state LEADER_IDLE

*May 19 17:00:00.715: Airewave Director: Group 802.11bg action HELLO_TIMER
in state LEADER_IDLE
```

You can tell that this particular controller is the current RF group leader for both the
802.11a and 802.11b/g networks because it sends HELLO packets in the LEADER
state.

■   **RF group member:** Here you can see the same debug output for a controller in the
    same 802.11a RF group as the preceding controller. Throughout the debug, you can
    see this controller sending HELLO packets in the GROUPIE RRM state for the
    802.11a network:

```
*May 19 16:58:30.351: Airewave Director: Group 802.11bg action HELLO_TIMER
in state LEADER_IDLE

*May 19 16:58:30.351: Airewave Director: Group 802.11bg action CALC_TIMER in
state LEADER_IDLE

*May 19 16:58:35.171: Airewave Director: Group 802.11a action HELLO_PKT in
state GROUPIE

*May 19 16:58:39.901: Airewave Director: Group 802.11bg action HELLO_TIMER
in state LEADER_IDLE

*May 19 16:58:39.901: Airewave Director: Group 802.11bg action CALC_TIMER in
state LEADER_IDLE
```

```
*May 19 16:58:39.902: Airewave Director: Group 802.11bg trigger RF automatic
grouping

*May 19 16:58:39.902: Airewave Director: Group 802.11bg trigger RF channel
assignment

*May 19 16:58:39.902: Airewave Director: Group 802.11bg trigger RF transmit
power control

*May 19 16:58:39.902: Airewave Director: Group 802.11bg change state from
LEADER_IDLE to LEADER_PREP

*May 19 16:58:39.902: Airewave Director: Group 802.11bg action TRANSMIS-
SION_TIMER in state LEADER_PREP

*May 19 16:58:39.902: Airewave Director: Group 802.11bg action CLIENT_DATA
in state LEADER_PREP

*May 19 16:58:39.903: Airewave Director: Group 802.11bg change state from
LEADER_PREP to LEADER_COMP

*May 19 16:58:39.924: Airewave Director: Group 802.11bg action CALC_END in
state LEADER_COMP

*May 19 16:58:39.924: Airewave Director: Group 802.11bg change state from
LEADER_COMP to LEADER ASSIGN

*May 19 16:58:39.924: Airewave Director: Group 802.11bg action TRANSMIS-
SION_TIMER in state LEADER ASSIGN

*May 19 16:58:39.924: Airewave Director: Group 802.11bg change state from
LEADER ASSIGN to LEADER_IDLE

*May 19 16:58:44.748: Airewave Director: Group 802.11a action HELLO_PKT in
state GROUPIE

*May 19 16:58:49.451: Airewave Director: Group 802.11bg action HELLO_TIMER
in state LEADER_IDLE
```

For the 802.11b/g network, however, this controller is the RF group leader. You can see the controller transition through the various RRM states and remain the 802.11b/g RF group leader for this RF group. After the RF grouping algorithm finishes, the controller starts to send HELLO packets in the LEADER_IDLE state.

Although these controllers are in the same RF group for the 802.11a network, they are both RF group leaders for the 802.11b/g network. The reason for this in this particular lab setup is because the 802.11b/g network is disabled on both controllers. Because the networks are disabled, the 2.4-GHz radios have no neighbors to form an RF group, so each controller assumes it is the RF group leader.

Summary

The RRM algorithm is a complex and constantly changing feature in the world of WLCs. RRM by far, can be one of the most complicated pieces to troubleshoot. One critical piece of information to remember is that it is not a replacement for a site survey. RRM cannot manufacture spectrum, but it achieves optimal balanced coverage for a given installation. In addition, RRM is constantly changing and improving from one version to the next. The version changes are the major revision, such as 4.x, 5.x, and 6.x. The only time you should see changes within version 6.x, for example, would be if it had bugs or major issues that required an immediate fix. The later version within first numeral depiction would obviously contain the fix if this were the case.

Another major factor to consider is your deployment. The changes you see are in direct relation to your physical and ever-changing RF environment. When you add all the factors—variables, conditions, exceptions—you have a complicated feature on the WLC. One of the major considerations if you suspect an RRM issue is to switch it to On Demand or Static so that you can see what RRM is trying to accomplish. It also points out potential trouble spots and areas you might want to focus on. In the end, RRM should always be utilized in medium to large deployments to compensate and correct the challenges a drastic RF environment can pose. Another key element to understand is that incorrect or nonoptimal AP placement can result in poor or suboptimal RRM calculations. RRM can only make changes based on what it collects within its environment. Feeding in AP placement from a good site survey can result in a much more efficient and accurate wireless infrastructure.

Chapter 13

H-REAP

With the advent of centralized wireless networking, you can take advantage of the benefits of a single point of administration for hundreds of APs. Using Wireless Control System (WCS) and WCS Navigator, you can centrally administer tens of thousands of APs from a single device. Wireless controllers, WCS, and Navigator, however, are expensive products. Should you need to implement a wireless solution at a remote office connected to your central network via a WAN, it can be cost prohibitive to install even a 2100 series controller to service only one or two APs.

Also, with Lightweight Access Point Protocol/Control and Provisioning of Wireless Access Points (LWAPP/CAPWAP), all the client traffic, even to the local network, would be tunneled back to the controller across the WAN, put back out on the network, only to go back across the WAN to reach its destination. This traffic flow pattern is inefficient and would eat up limited WAN bandwidth. Should you decide to install standalone access points (AP) in this situation, you lose the ease of central administration. The solution to this problem is to install a lightweight AP in Hybrid Remote Edge Access Point (H-REAP) mode at the remote location.

The H-REAP feature allows central administration of the APs and, depending on the configuration, keeps local traffic local. It also provides link resiliency in the event of a WAN outage. Should the WAN link between the AP and the controller be lost, an AP in local mode stops servicing clients even though the AP and the controller are operational. An AP in H-REAP mode, however, transitions to standalone mode and can continue to service existing, and even new, clients in certain cases until the WAN link is restored. This is a valuable feature if you have unreliable WAN links or an unscheduled WAN outage; it keeps the local users happy because they can continue working.

H-REAP Versus REAP

H-REAP is actually an enhanced version of the Remote Edge Access Point (REAP) feature. With REAP, you had centralized administration of the APs and link resiliency if the WAN link failed, but two fundamental limitations existed.

The first limitation was that only a single model of AP supported REAP mode: the 1030 series. The second limitation was that when the 1030 series AP lost communication to the controller across the WAN, it had no support for multiple wireless LANs (WLAN) or VLANs because of a lack of 802.1Q tagging support. The lack of VLAN tagging support exists because the 1000 series APs were never designed to be standalone units. The idea was that all traffic would be tunneled back to the controller and the controller would be responsible for bridging to the correct subnet.

If a controller was servicing three WLANs at the remote site and the WAN link was lost with a 1030 in REAP mode, only WLAN ID 1 would still be available and all client traffic would be on the same VLAN as the AP. Cisco introduced H-REAP in code Release 4.0 to overcome these limitations.

H-REAP supports multiple WLANs on different VLANs and is supported on 1130, 1140, 1240, 1250, and AP801 APs and all the controller platforms.

Split MAC Versus Local MAC Architecture

To fully understand how an H-REAP AP functions, you need to understand the difference between the Split MAC and Local MAC architectures.

With Split MAC, the 802.11 protocol functionality is divided between the wireless termination point (the AP) and the access controller (controller). Table 13-1 outlines the division of responsibility between the AP and controller with Split MAC.

As you can see from Table 13-1, the network distribution and integration functionality resides with the controller. This means that all the client data must be tunneled between the AP and the controller. The controller is also responsible for associations, reassociations, disassociations, and 802.1x/EAP and key management services. The AP, however, handles the beacons, probe responses, 802.11 encryption and decryption, and all other real-time 802.11 protocol services.

In a Local MAC architecture, however, the division of 802.11 protocol services is different. Table 13-2 outlines the Local MAC division of responsibility.

One of the first things you will notice in the Local MAC scenario is that every service except for 802.1x/EAP and key management resides with the AP. The 802.1x/EAP and key management service remain at the controller because the controller must be aware of any client mobility events between the APs. For the controller to be aware of mobility events, the AP must forward association requests to the controller.

The Local MAC mode of operation allows for the data frames to be either locally bridged (also known as *Local Switching*) or tunneled as 802.3 frames. The latter implies that the AP performs the 802.11 integration function. In either case, the Layer 2 wireless management frames are processed locally by the AP and then forwarded to the controller.

H-REAP APs take advantage of both Split MAC and Local MAC to provide wireless resiliency. So even though the AP may not be registered to a controller, it can service wireless clients.

Table 13-1   *Split MAC Architecture*

Function	Responsible Device
Distribution service	Controller
Integration service	Controller
Bcacons	AP
Probe response	AP
Power management/packet buffering	AP
Fragmentation/defragmentation	AP
Association/Reassociation/Disassociation	Controller
802.11e	
Classifying	Controller
Scheduling	Controller/AP
Queuing	AP
802.11i	
802.1x/EAP[1]	Controller
Key management	Controller
802.11 encrypt/decrypt	AP or controller

[1]EAP = Extensible Authentication Protocol

Table 13-2   *Local MAC Architecture*

Function	Responsible Device
Distribution service	AP
Integration service	AP
Beacons	AP
Probe response	AP
Power management/packet buffering	AP
Fragmentation/defragmentation	AP
Association/reassociation/disassociation	AP
802.11e	
Classifying	AP
Scheduling	AP
Queuing	AP
802.11i	
802.1x/EAP	Controller
Key management	Controller
802.11 encrypt/decrypt	AP

H-REAP Modes of Operation

A lightweight AP can be in any of several operating modes. By default, the AP is in local mode; this is not to be confused with Local MAC, as discussed earlier. When in local mode, should the AP not be connected to a controller, the AP cannot service wireless clients. When the AP is in H-REAP mode, however, depending on the WLAN and AP configuration (explained in detail next), clients can still use the wireless network.

H-REAP APs have two operating modes:

■ **Connected mode:** While in connected mode, the AP is registered to the controller across the WAN. The controller handles LWAPP/CAPWAP control traffic, authentication, and associations, and the AP bridges the client traffic to the local network depending on the VLAN mappings and WLAN settings.

■ **Standalone mode:** In standalone mode, the connection to the controller is down for one reason or another and the AP is operating on its own. While in standalone mode, the AP continues to service any existing clients and can even allow new client authentications and associations depending on the security parameters of the WLAN.

An H-REAP AP in standalone mode supports Open, Shared, static Wired Equivalent Privacy (WEP), Wi-Fi Protected Access (WPA)-PSK, WPA2-PSK, 802.1x, Cisco Centralized Key Management (CCKM), and local EAP authentication methods. Local EAP, CCKM, and 802.1x authentication methods are discussed later in the chapter in the "H-REAP Enhancements" section.

After the AP in standalone mode re-establishes a connection with the controller, it disconnects all clients, applies any new configuration information from the controller, and then allows client connectivity once again.

Central Versus Local Switching

When client traffic is centrally switched, the client traffic is passed between the AP and the controller in the LWAPP/CAPWAP tunnel, and the controller bridges the traffic to and from the network. Figure 13-1 illustrates central switching. This is the same process that an AP uses in local mode.

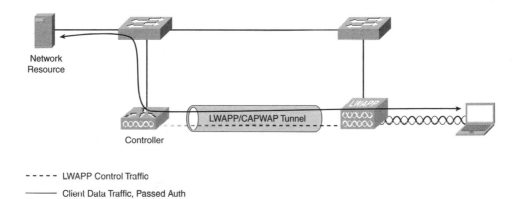

Figure 13-1   *Central Switching*

Local switching means that the client traffic is bridged to the local network directly by the AP on the locally connected switch and does not pass through the controller. Figure 13-2 shows local switching traffic flow.

It is important to remember that if your clients will be using Dynamic Host Configuration Protocol (DHCP), the DHCP service needs to be provided locally for each VLAN.

Figure 13-3 illustrates a mixed deployment of central and locally switched WLANs on the same H-REAP AP at a remote office.

On WLAN 1, which is centrally switched, Client 1 traffic is tunneled to and from the controller and the controller bridges that traffic. With WLAN 2 configured with local switching, after Client 2 has passed authentication, traffic to and from the client is bridged by the AP to the local network.

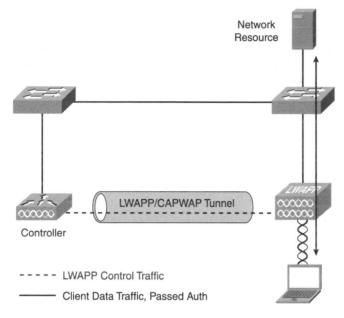

Figure 13-2   *Local Switching*

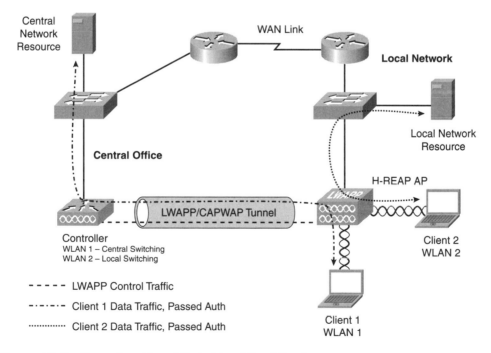

Figure 13-3   *Central and Local Switching Mixed Deployment*

H-REAP States of Operation

Along with configuring either central or local switching for a WLAN, H-REAP allows you to configure central or local authentication. Local authentications are handled "locally" by the AP. (Details follow in the "Local Authentication Local Switching" section.) The combination of the AP operating mode, central or local switching, and central or local authentication determines the operating state of the AP. The different combinations result in five operating states for H-REAP APs. Each state is explained in detail in the following sections.

Central Authentication Central Switching

With central authentication and central switching, the controller is responsible for client authentications, associations, and bridging the client traffic to the network. Central authentication with central switching is valid only when the AP is in connected mode.

When the AP changes to standalone mode, all clients are disconnected from the WLAN and no new clients are allowed on that WLAN until LWAPP/CAPWAP communications with the controller are restored and the AP returns to connected mode.

Central Authentication Local Switching

With central authentication local switching, the controller is responsible for the client authentication and associations, but the AP directly bridges client traffic to the local network. Web authentication is a good example of this. The guest users are redirected to the web auth page on the controller, pass authentication, and then the AP bridges the traffic to the local VLAN.

Central authentication local switching is valid only when the AP is in connected mode. Should the AP switch to standalone mode, any existing clients will continue to function until the WLAN session times out or the key session expires.

Local Authentication Local Switching

Local authentication local switching means that the AP can handle authentication configured on the WLAN. An example would be open (no authentication) or preshared key, such as WPA1-PSK and WPA2-PSK. The AP directly bridges client traffic to the local network.

When the AP is in connected mode, the controller still handles the authentications and associations. When the AP switches to standalone mode, the responsibility of authentication and association is transferred to the AP. Local authentication local switching is valid only when the AP is in standalone mode.

Authentication Down Local Switching

In this state, the H-REAP refuses any new client connections but continues to send beacons and probes so existing clients continue to function. You have an authentication down situation when 802.1X, WPA-802.1X, WPA2-802.1X, or CCKM is used on the WLAN, but no backup RADIUS servers are configured. This mode differs from central authentication local switching in that no new clients are allowed. After an existing client reaches the WLAN session timeout value, the AP will not allow that client to reauthenticate. When all existing clients have reached the WLAN session timeout and are disconnected, the AP transitions to the authentication down switching down state (discussed in the section that follows). Authentication down local switching is valid only in standalone mode.

Authentication Down Switching Down

With an authentication down switching down situation, the AP disconnects existing clients and stops sending beacons and probes. As mentioned earlier, the AP enters this state from authentication down local switching and when all clients have disconnected. This state is valid only in standalone mode.

H-REAP Wireless Security Support

Security support on the H-REAP locally switched WLANs depends on whether the AP is in connected or standalone mode. Security types, such as AirFortress, that require control over the data path do not work with traffic on locally switched WLANs because the client traffic is not tunneled back to the controller. The controller cannot control traffic that is not tunneled back to it. Any other security type works on either centrally or locally switched WLANs, provided the path between the H-REAP AP and the controller is up.

Table 13-3 outlines WLAN security configurations supported depending on the mode of the AP. Keep in mind that this table lists the configurations supported but not whether the authentication feature actually works in these modes. Table 13-4 under "H-REAP Guidelines and Limitations" outlines which authentication features work in each H-REAP operating mode.

Configuring H-REAP

To set up an H-REAP deployment, you need to complete several configuration steps:

Step 1.   Get the APs joined to the controller.

Step 2.   Configure the WLAN for central or local authentication.

Step 3.   Configure the WLAN for central or local switching.

Step 4.   Change the AP mode to H-REAP.

Step 5.   Configure local switching on the AP if desired.

Step 6.   Configure the local switch.

Controller Discovery

An H-REAP AP can use any of the usual AP discovery methods if they are available. If Layer 3 discovery methods are not feasible, you can statically configure the AP with the

Table 13-3 *WLAN Security Configurations: Dependent on H-REAP AP-Mode*

Security Type	Connected Mode (Centrally Switched)	Connected Mode (Locally Switched)	Standalone Mode (Locally Switched)
Open	Yes	Yes	Yes
Shared	Yes	Yes	Yes
WPA-PSK	Yes	Yes	Yes
WPA2-PSK	Yes	Yes	Yes
Client exclusion/ blacklisting	Yes	Yes	No
MAC address authentication (onboard or upstream)	Yes	Yes	No new authentications
Dynamic WEP (802.1X)	Yes	Yes	Yes (4.2 or higher)
WPA (802.1X)	Yes	Yes	Yes (4.2 or higher)
WPA2 (802.1X)	Yes	Yes	Yes (4.2 or higher)
CCKM	Yes	Yes	Yes (4.2 or higher)
IBNS[1]	Yes	Not supported	Not supported
NAC[2]	Yes	Yes	No new authentications
WebAuth (onboard or upstream)	Yes	Yes	No new authentications
VPN (onboard or upstream)	Yes	Not supported*	Not supported*
Cranite	Yes	Not supported*	Not supported*
AirFortress	Yes	Not supported*	Not supported*

[1]BNS = identity-based networking services

[2]NAC = network admission control

*These security methods require the controller to mandate all traffic flow through a given point on the network, that is, through AirFortress appliance, and so on. While in standalone mode, the controller cannot enforce these policies because the LWAPP/CAPWAP tunnel is down and the AP is not capable of enforcing the policies. If you want these security methods to be in place even when the AP is in standalone mode, the security resources must be present on the local network.

controller IP address you want it to try to join. See Chapter 8, "Access Point Registration," for more information on AP registration.

When you deploy APs at a remote location, it can be easy to strand an H-REAP AP because local tech support might not be available. There could be a misconfiguration of the AP, incorrect DHCP or Domain Name System (DNS) options, routing problems, and so on.

One method to recover a stranded AP is to enable protocol forwarding on the local Layer 3 switch. As long as the AP has an IP address in the correct subnet, you can enable protocol forwarding for User Datagram Protocol (UDP) port 12223 for LWAPP or 5246 for CAPWAP on the next local Layer 3 device where the AP is connected to the network. With protocol forwarding enabled, the Layer 3 discovery broadcast from the AP, sent to 255.255.255.255, is forwarded as a unicast using the protocol configured to the management interface IP address of the controller you desire using an ip helper-address on the Layer 3 interface by the Layer 3 network switch.

For example, if the management IP address of the LWAPP controller you want the H-REAP AP to join is 10.100.10.6 and the AP resides on VLAN 10 at the remote network, the Layer 3 next hop switch would have the configuration in Example 13-1.

Example 13-1   *Sample Switch Configuration to Forward AP Broadcast Discovery*

```
ip forward-protocol udp 12223
interface vlan10
 Description AP VLAN
 ip address 192.168.10.1 255.255.255.0
 ip helper-address 10.100.10.6
```

After the AP registers, you can remove the **ip forward-protocol** and **ip helper-address** commands from the next hop Layer 3 switch configuration.

Using IP protocol forwarding and ip helper-addresses is a great way to recover a stranded AP regardless of whether the AP is in H-REAP mode.

During the AP join process with an H-REAP AP, the AP sends its current H-REAP configuration, including the VLAN mappings for the locally switched WLANS, to the controller. Example 13-2 shows partial output from **debug capwap events** and **debug capwap packet** for a 1242 AP in H-REAP mode joining a controller running 5.2 code.

Example 13-2 *H-REAP AP Configuration During Join Process*

```
*Apr 06 10:46:57.557:
*Apr 06 10:46:57.557:          Type : CAPWAP_MSGELE_VENDOR_SPECIFIC_PAYLOAD, Length 25
*Apr 06 10:46:57.557:             Vendor Identifier  : 0x00409600
*Apr 06 10:46:57.557:
   IE            :   SPAM_VENDOR_SPECIFIC_PAYLOAD
*Apr 06 10:46:57.557:     IE Length    :   19
*Apr 06 10:46:57.557:          Type :   AP_VLAN_MAPPING_TYPE
*Apr 06 10:46:57.557:          Native Vlan ID : 1
*Apr 06 10:46:57.557:          Num of Entries : 2
*Apr 06 10:46:57.557:             vlan name: 02, Id: 12
*Apr 06 10:46:57.557:             vlan name: 03, Id: 20
*Apr 06 10:46:57.557:
*Apr 06 10:46:57.557:          Type : CAPWAP_MSGELE_VENDOR_SPECIFIC_PAYLOAD, Length 15
*Apr 06 10:46:57.557:             Vendor Identifier  : 0x00409600
*Apr 06 10:46:57.557:
   IE            :   SPAM_VENDOR_SPECIFIC_PAYLOAD
*Apr 06 10:46:57.557:     IE Length    :   9
*Apr 06 10:46:57.557:
*Apr 06 10:46:57.557:          Type : CAPWAP_MSGELE_VENDOR_SPECIFIC_PAYLOAD, Length 17
*Apr 06 10:46:57.557:             Vendor Identifier  : 0x00409600
*Apr 06 10:46:57.557:
   IE            :   SPAM_VENDOR_SPECIFIC_PAYLOAD
*Apr 06 10:46:57.557:     IE Length    :   11
*Apr 06 10:46:57.557: <<<<   End of CAPWAP Packet   >>>>
*Apr 06 10:46:57.557: 00:1e:13:06:f6:50 Configuration Status from
192.168.1.15:7645
*Apr 06 10:46:57.557: 00:1e:13:06:f6:50 Updating IP info for AP 00:1e:13:06:f6:50
— static 1, 192.168.1.15/255.255.255.0, gtw 192.168.1.1
*Apr 06 10:46:57.557: 00:1e:13:06:f6:50 Updated IP Domain info for AP
00:1e:13:06:f6:50 — set 0, Domain
*Apr 06 10:46:57.557: 00:1e:13:06:f6:50 Updating IP NamServer info for AP
00:1e:13:06:f6:50 — set 0, nameserver 0.0.0.0
*Apr 06 10:46:57.558: 00:1e:13:06:f6:50 Setting MTU to 1485
```

From this output, you can see that the native VLAN for the AP is VLAN 1, and WLAN IDs 2 and 3 are locally switched and mapped to local VLANs 12 and 20, respectively.

You can also see that the AP has a static IP address of 192.168.1.15 with a netmask of /24 and a default gateway of 192.168.1.1.

Remember that AP join packets are large and are always fragmented when they are sent to the controller. This can be important when you are trying to join APs across a WAN link.

Even though the maximum round trip network delay that the H-REAP APs can handle is 300 milliseconds (ms) (see "H-REAP Guidelines and Limitations"), packet fragments need to arrive within 100 ms of each other for the controller to able to reassemble them. It is also important to remember that the controller/AP can only handle four fragments. If a packet between the controller and the AP are broken up into more than four fragments, then they will not be able to reassemble it.

As an example of the affects of network delay during the AP join process, Figure 13-4 shows an AP is trying to join a controller across a slow WAN link. As you can see, the AP is sending the join request and the controller is responding with the join response, yet the AP is never able to successfully register.

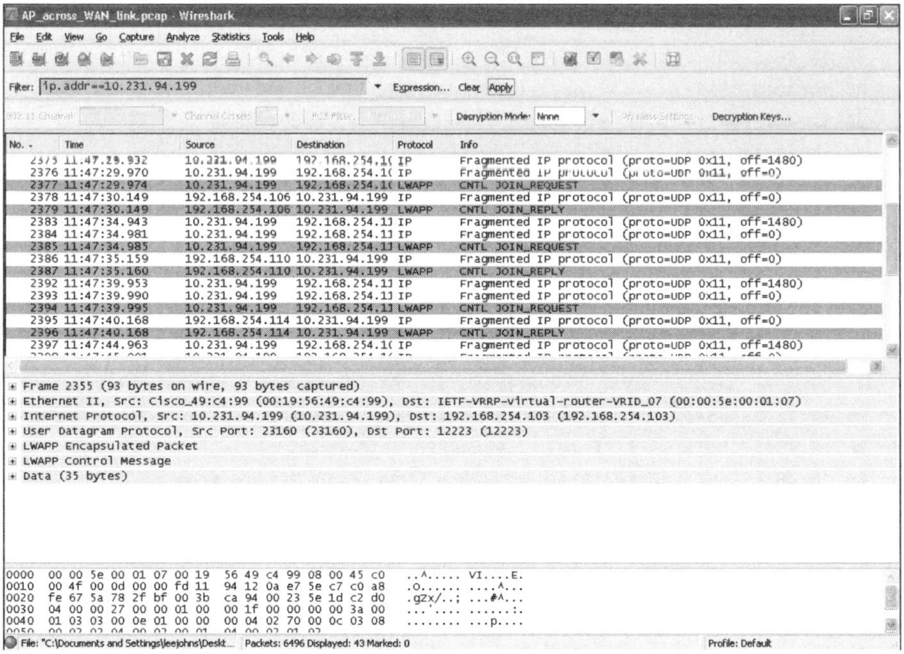

Figure 13-4   *Failed AP join process across a slow WAN link*

The reason the AP is not able to join the controller in Figure 13-4 is because the WAN link is causing a several hundred millisecond delay between the join request from the AP and the join response from the controller. The delay is large enough that the AP believes the controller did not respond and the process repeats over and over.

Configuring the WLAN

The default switching mode for a WLAN is central switching. So if you do want a particular WLAN to be locally switched, you need not change any of the configurations. If you do plan to locally switch a WLAN, select H-REAP local switching on the Advanced tab of the WLAN. Figure 13-5 shows the H-REAP selection check box.

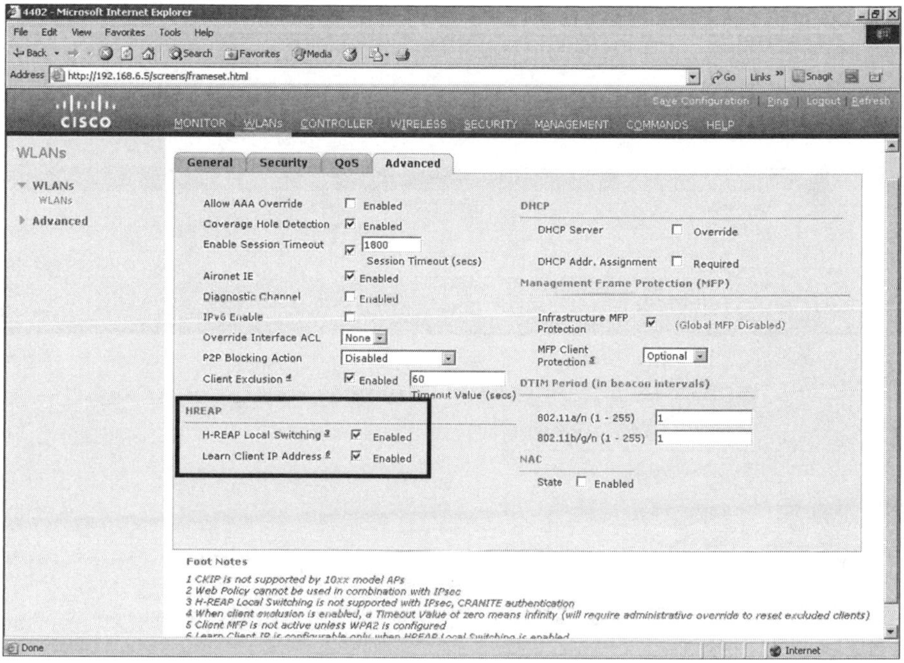

Figure 13-5   *Configuring H-REAP Local Switching on the WLAN*

When this feature is selected on the WLAN, an AP in H-REAP mode can bridge the client traffic directly to the local switch for the VLAN this WLAN is mapped to on the AP.

To configure the WLAN for H-REAP with local switching using the command-line interface (CLI), enter the following command:

```
config wlan h-reap local-switching wlan_id enable
```

A common misconception is that enabling H-REAP local switching on a WLAN affects non-H-REAP APs. This is not true. An AP in local mode ignores the H-REAP local switching setting. This means that you can easily have the same WLAN for both local and remote users. Along those same lines, an H-REAP AP ignores the local switching parameter for a WLAN unless local switching (VLAN support) is enabled.

In addition to the WLAN switching mode, you need to decide if you want to configure central or local authentication. Figure 13-6 shows the WLAN configured for WPA2-PSK, which is a local authentication method.

Also notice that, as part of the WLAN configuration, no mention was made of choosing an interface for the WLAN. Unless you will have APs in local mode servicing a WLAN configured for local switching in conjunction with H-REAP APs, the controller interface is irrelevant because the controller will not bridge the client traffic on the network. The H-REAP AP performs that function. Even if you will not be using any local mode APs, you must choose an interface to be associated with your WLAN. In this case, you could use the management interface or create a quarantine VLAN interface, for example if you do not want client traffic to be bridged by the controller if the client traffic is no longer locally switched.

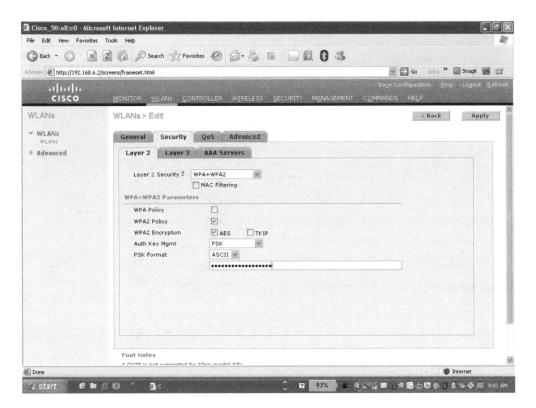

Figure 13-6 *WLAN Local Authentication*

Configuring the AP

The majority of configuring an H-REAP deployment is on the AP. You have to change the AP from the default AP-Mode of local to H-REAP mode (see Figure 13-7) and reboot the AP. After the AP rejoins the controller, you see the H-REAP configuration tab that is also shown in Figure 13-7. Under the H-REAP tab, you can configure the switching mode from the default of central switching. Using H-REAP groups, you configure local authentication settings if desired. H-REAP groups are covered later under the "H-REAP Enhancements" section.

To enable H-REAP mode on the AP from CLI, enter the following command:

```
config ap mode h-reap AP_name
```

Changing the switching mode of the AP from the default of central to local switching requires you to enable VLAN support on the AP. Select the native VLAN for the AP, and

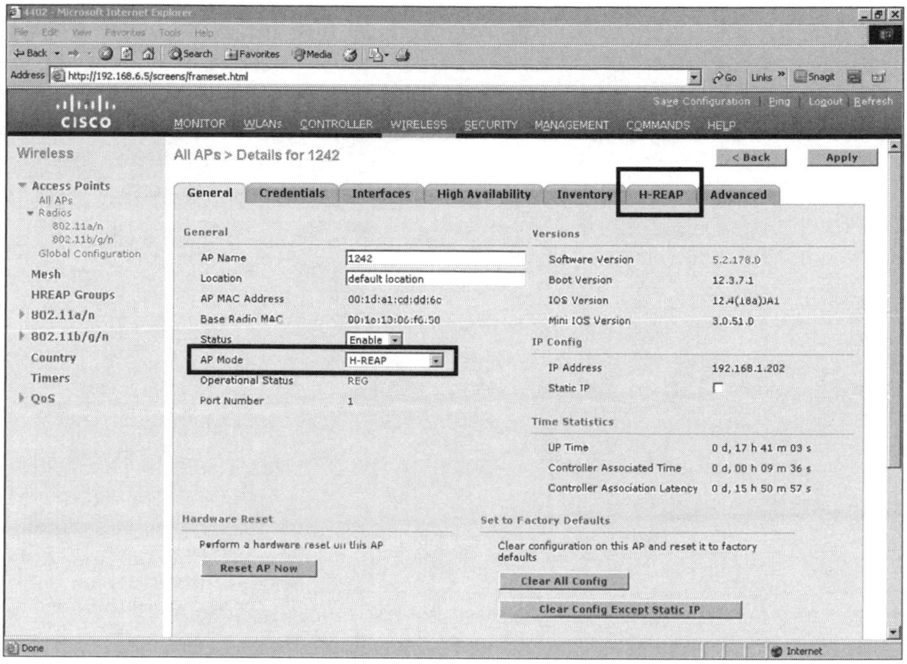

Figure 13-7   *H-REAP Mode and H-REAP Tab on the AP Configuration*

then map the H-REAP local switching enabled WLANs to the desired local VLAN. Figures 13-8 and 13-9 illustrate these steps from the controller graphical user interface (GUI).

To configure the native VLAN for the H-REAP AP from the CLI, enter the following commands:

```
config ap h-reap vlan {enable | disable} AP_name
config ap h-reap vlan native vlan-id AP_name
```

The native VLAN for the AP should match the native VLAN of the trunk port on the local switch.

To enable local switching for a WLAN, select the local VLAN you want a particular WLAN to use on the remote network. Remember that until you have configured at least one WLAN for local switching, you cannot map a WLAN to a local VLAN.

To map the WLANs to the local VLANs from the CLI, enter the following command:

```
config ap h-reap vlan wlan wlan_id vlan-id AP_name
```

Configuring the Local Switch

The configuration of the local network switch port that the H-REAP AP will be physically connected to depends on how you have configured the WLAN and H-REAP switching. If you are simply doing central switching, all you need is for the AP to be connected to an

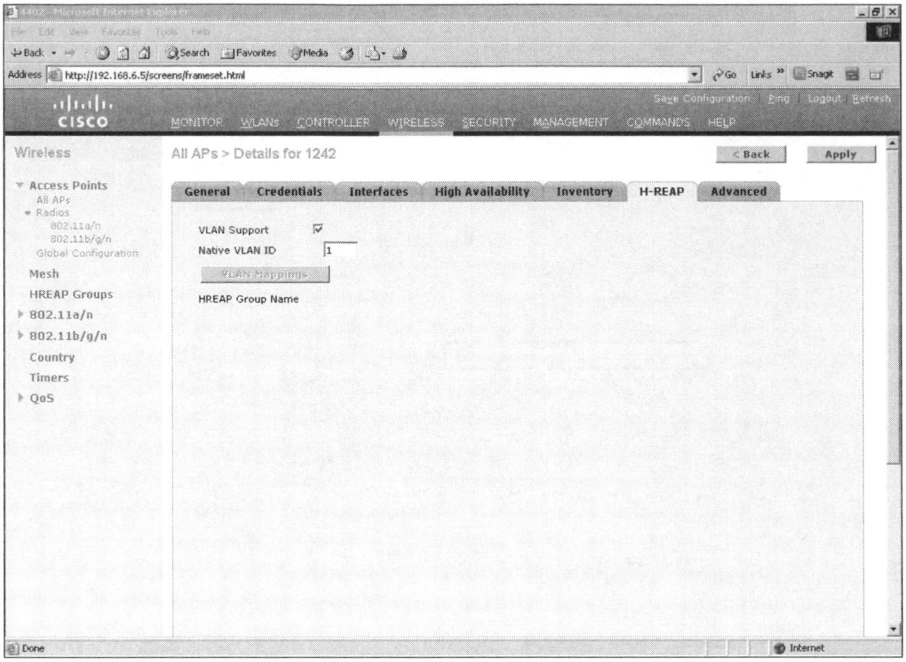

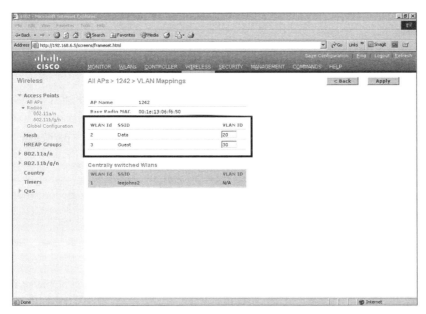

Figure 13-8 *Setting the Native VLAN*

Figure 13-9 *Mapping WLANs to Local VLANs*

access port in the correct VLAN (a VLAN that can route to the controller from the remote network). If you intend to only have a single locally switched WLAN or if multiple WLANs do not need wired side separation, you can use an access port. If you have multiple locally switched WLANs that need wired side separation or you do not want a single locally switched WLAN to use the same VLAN as the AP, configure an 802.1q trunk port instead.

Assume that you have a remote office with three VLANs. The remote network uses VLAN 10 for management, VLAN 20 for internal users, and VLAN 30 for guest traffic. The local Layer 3 switch also serves as the DHCP server (DHCP configuration not shown). You want the AP to be in VLAN 10 and have two WLANs on the controller that will be locally switched: one WLAN for internal users and one for guest users. To achieve this goal, the configuration for the local network switch should look like Example 13-3.

Example 13-3   *Local Switch Example Configuration*

```
interface Vlan10
 description Management VLAN
 ip address 10.10.10.1 255.255.255.0
interface Vlan20
 descriptin User VLAN
 ip address 10.10.20.1 255.255.255.0

interface Vlan30
 description Guest VLAN
 ip address 10.10.30.1 255.255.255.0

interface FastEthernet1/0/2
 description H-REAP AP Port
 switchport trunk encapsulation dot1q
 switchport trunk native vlan 10
 switchport trunk allowed vlan 10,20,30
 switchport mode trunk
 spanning-tree portfast trunk
```

The H-REAP AP would have its IP address in VLAN 10, either via DHCP or statically assigned, and this VLAN would be designated as the native VLAN for the AP on the controller. The management VLAN is the only VLAN at the remote location that needs to be routed across the WAN for the H-REAP AP to communicate with the controller.

H-REAP Guidelines and Limitations

You need to keep several guidelines and limitations in mind when deploying an H-REAP configuration on the network:

- A H-REAP AP can be deployed with either a static IP address or a DHCP address. In the case of DHCP, a DHCP server must be available locally and must be able to provide the IP address for the AP at bootup.

- As is true for all lightweight APs, the network link between the remote office and the controller network cannot be less than 128 kbps.

- H-REAP supports up to four fragmented packets or a minimum 500-byte maximum transmission unit (MTU) WAN link. This is the same value as an AP in local mode. With the introduction of CAPWAP for the controllers in 5.2 code, Path MTU Discovery is supported.

- Depending on the number of APs located at a remote site, Radio Resource Management (RRM) functionality may not work optimally. It takes at least four APs to trigger the Transmit Power Control algorithm. Dynamic Frequency Selection (DFS) and dynamic channel assignment (DCA) still function. See Chapter 12, "Radio Resource Management," for information.

- Roundtrip latency must not exceed 300 ms between the AP and the controller, and LWAPP/CAPWAP control packets must be prioritized over all other traffic.

- H-REAP APs can perform 802.11 authentication and association functions locally and then proxy that information up to the controller when in connected mode. Call Admission Control (CAC) and Traffic Specification (TSPEC) functions may not be desirable because of this. A client will likely be allowed to associate, but then, provided CAC or TSPEC limitations have already been met, the client connections may be severed as mandated by the controller.

- The advertised location accuracy of Cisco is not supported. The location algorithm accuracy increases with the number of APs, and the majority of H-REAP deployments will only have a few APs at a single location. This does not mean that location is not supported with H-REAP—only that the accuracy of the location might not be within 10 meters.

- True multicast is not supported when using locally switched WLANs. Only Multicast-Unicast is supported.

- To use CCKM fast roaming between H-REAP APs, you need to configure H-REAP groups.

- Roaming between H-REAP can take as long as 50 ms to 1500 ms. Keep in mind that all authentications while in connected mode must cross the WAN, be processed by the controller or external device (RADIUS, NAC, and so on), and the access-accept be sent back across the WAN to the AP. So if the WAN link is right at the limit of

300 ms round trip and the clients are using a form of EAP authentication in which you have lots of packet exchange, you can imagine how slow a roam might be before the client can pass traffic again. To help decrease the roaming times, all H-REAP APs should be configured with the same local VLAN mappings so roaming clients will not have to re-DHCP. The use of H-REAP groups and CCKM will help mitigate this.

■   H-REAP APs support a 1-1 Network Address Translation (NAT) configuration. They also support Port Address Translation (PAT) for all features except true multicast. Multicast is supported across NAT boundaries when configured using the Multicast-Unicast option on the controller. When Multicast-Unicast is enabled on the controller, the controller unicasts any multicast traffic to each AP joined to it. This means that if you had 100 APs joined, the controller would replicate a multicast packet 100 times instead of simply forwarding the traffic to the AP multicast address if you were using Multicast-Multicast instead. Multicast-Unicast can obviously be resource intensive on the controllers and is not a recommended configuration. H-REAP APs also support a many-to-one NAT/PAT boundary, except when you want true multicast to operate for all centrally switched WLANs. Keep in mind that the AP can be behind NAT/PAT, but the controller the AP is registered with cannot be behind a NAT/PAT network boundary.

■   PPTP is supported for locally switched traffic, provided that these security types are accessible locally at the AP.

■   H-REAP APs support multiple service set identifiers (SSID).

■   NAC out-of-band integration is supported only on WLANs configured for H-REAP central switching. It is not supported for use on WLANs configured for H-REAP local switching.

■   The primary and secondary controllers for an H-REAP AP must have the same configuration. Otherwise, the AP might lose its configuration, and certain features (such as WLAN override, AP group VLANs, and so on) might not operate correctly. In addition, make sure to duplicate the SSID of the H-REAP AP and its index number on both controllers as well as any other controller the AP can fail over to in the event of a controller failure.

Table 13-4 shows which security features are supported or partially supported with the different modes and states H-REAP operation.

Table 13-4   *H-REAP Supported Security Features*

Feature	Connected Mode (Centrally Switched)	Connected Mode (Locally Switched)	Standalone Mode (Locally Switched)
CCKM	Yes (if AP groups are used)	Yes (if AP groups are used)	Yes (if AP groups are used)
CAC and TSPEC	Yes	Yes	Not supported*
RFID[1]/location-based services	Yes	Yes	Not supported
Client load-balancing	Not supported	Not supported	Not supported
Peer-to-peer block-ing	Yes	Not supported	Not supported
WIDS[2]	Yes	Yes	Not supported
RLDP[3]	Yes	Yes	Not supported
RADIUS authenti-cation	Yes	Yes	Yes (4.2 and higher)
TACACS+ authenti-cation	Yes	Yes	Not supported
RADIUS/TACACS+ accounting	Yes	Yes	Not supported

*An AP in standalone mode does not follow CAC and TSPEC rules and allows all client connections.

[1]RFID = Radio Frequency Identification

[2]WIDS = Wireless Intrusion Detection Sytem

[3]RLDP = Rogue Location Discovery Protocol

H-REAP Enhancements

Since the introduction of H-REAP, several enhancements have been implemented to make it more robust and provide client access and authentication methods in the event the AP transitions to standalone mode.

Backup RADIUS Server

Starting in code Release 4.2, you can configure an H REAP AP with a backup RADIUS server. This allows the AP to perform full 802.1x EAP authentications using RADIUS while in standalone mode. The backup RADIUS server can be any RADIUS server on the network as long as the H-REAP AP still has network connectivity to that server during the network outage that caused it to enter standalone mode in the first place.

To configure an H-REAP AP with a backup RADIUS server, use the following command from the controller CLI:

```
config ap h-reap radius auth set {primary ¦ secondary} ip_address auth_port
secret AP_name
```

H-REAP Groups

H-REAP groups is another 4.2 feature that allows you to group APs that you want to share a common backup RADIUS server. If you had several H-REAP APs, for example, it is a lot less work to create an H-REAP group and then add the APs to that group rather than specifying the RADIUS servers on the individual APs. In later codes, you can also configure H-REAP groups for local authentication. An H-REAP AP can only be a member of one H-REAP group. You can configure up to 20 H-REAP Groups with 25 APs in each group per controller. Figure 13-10 shows an H-REAP group example.

H-REAP groups are required for CCKM fast roaming to work with H-REAP APs. CCKM fast roaming is achieved by caching a derivative of the master key from a full EAP authentication so that a simple and secure key exchange can occur when a wireless client roams to a different AP. This feature prevents the need to perform a full RADIUS EAP authentication as the client roams from one H-REAP AP to another within the same H-REAP group. If you create an H-REAP group comprising a limited number of APs (for example, you create a group for four APs in a remote office), the clients can roam only

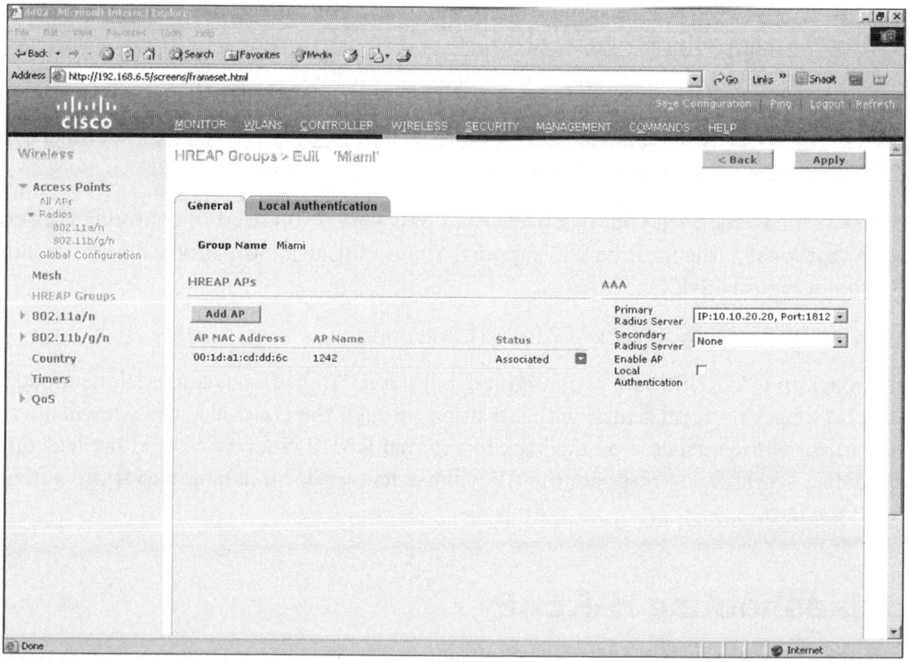

Figure 13-10   *H-REAP Group Configuration Example*

among those four APs, and the CCKM cache is distributed among those four APs only
when the clients associate to one of them.

Following is additional information on CCKM and H-REAP:

■   The H-REAP APs receive the CCKM cache keys from the controller.

■   The cache keys are stored on the AP. The AP can use the key in connected or stand-
     alone mode.

■   If an H-REAP AP boots up in the standalone mode, fast roaming is not supported
     because the AP cannot get the CCKM keys from the controller.

■   CCKM fast roaming is not supported between H-REAP and non-H-REAP APs. It is
     also not supported between different H-REAP groups. A client has to perform a full
     EAP authentication.

■   The controller distributes the cache key for a client to the APs in the configured H-
     REAP group the client is connected to.

■   CCKM cache key aging is based on the WLAN session timeout value.

■   CCKM cache keys are deleted when the client is removed from the system.

Local Authentication

With code Release 5.0 and higher, local authentication features were added to the H-
REAP group configuration. You can configure your H-REAP APs to perform Lightweight
Extensible Authentication Protocol (LEAP) or EAP-FAST using a local RADIUS server on
the AP. Originally, this was limited to 20 users, but with the 5.2 release of code, you can
configure up to 100 users. When an H-REAP AP joins the controller, it receives the list of
users. The AP only authenticates users present in its list. Figure 13-11 shows the local
authentication page of an H-REAP group.

After you have defined your usernames and passwords, you need to configure the protocols that local authentication will support. You do this using the Protocols tab, as illustrated in Figure 13-12.

As you can see, only LEAP or EAP-FAST is supported.

If a backup RADIUS server is configured and the AP transitions to standalone mode and
can no longer perform central authentication through the controller, the AP will always
try to authenticate a user via the backup external RADIUS server. Should the backup
RADIUS server fail to respond, the AP will use its own local database to try to authenticate the user.

Troubleshooting H-REAP

You can verify your H-REAP configuration on the controller and the AP with several
show and **debug** commands, as detailed in the sections that follow.

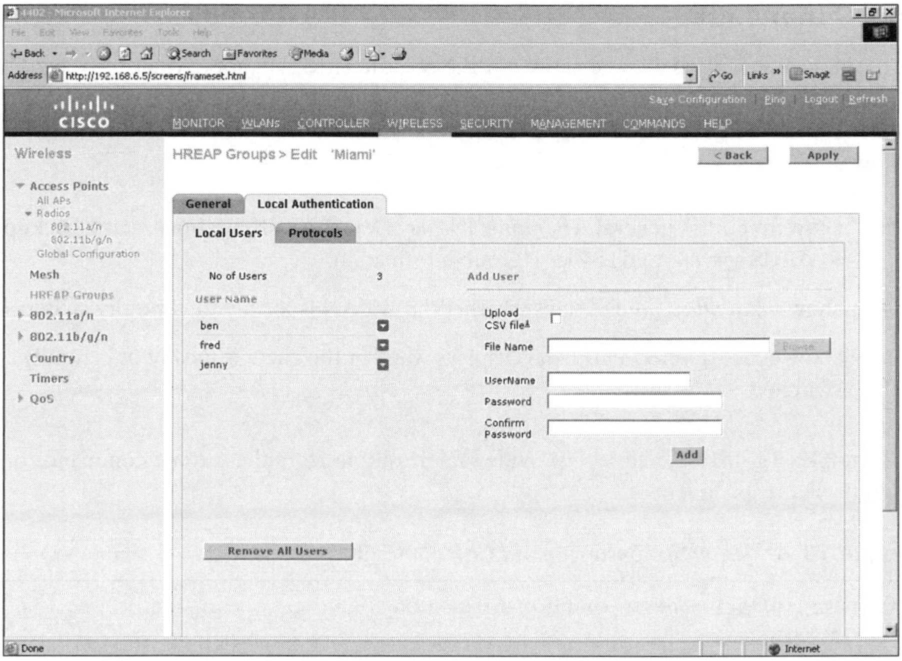

Figure 13-11   *Local Authentication with H-REAP Group Configuration Example*

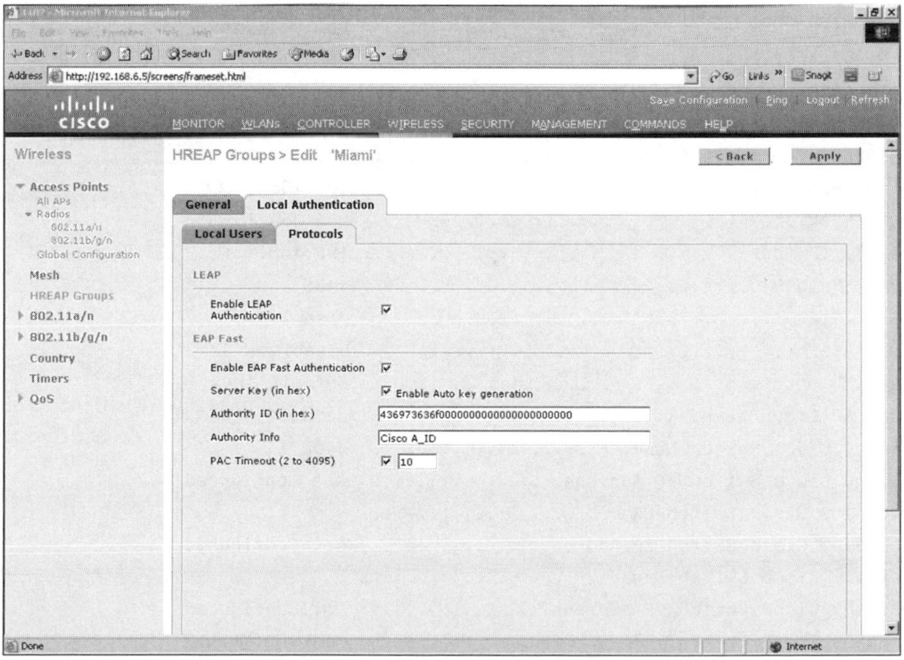

Figure 13-12   *Local Authentication with H-REAP Group Protocols Configuration Example*

show Commands

From the controller CLI, you can see if the AP is in H-REAP mode, what the local VLAN mappings are, its backup RADIUS servers, groups, and so on, and the state of a client associated with an H-REAP WLAN. The commands from the controller CLI are as follows:

- **show ap config general** *AP_name*: Displays VLAN configurations, static backup RADIUS servers, and H-REAP group information.

- **show wlan** *wlan_id*: Displays whether the WLAN is locally or centrally switched.

- **show client detail** *client_mac*: Displays whether the client is locally or centrally switched.

Examples 13-4, 13-5, and 13-6 provide sample output from these three commands on the controller respectively.

Example 13-4 *show ap config general Command Output*

```
(Cisco Controller)>show ap config general 1242
Cisco AP Identifier.............................. 2
Cisco AP Name.................................... 1242
Country code..................................... US  - United States
Regulatory Domain allowed by Country............. 802.11bg:-A    802.11a:-A
AP Country code.................................. US  - United States
AP Regulatory Domain............................. 802.11bg:-A    802.11a:-A
Switch Port Number .............................. 1
MAC Address...................................... 00:1d:a1:cd:dd:6c
IP Address Configuration......................... DHCP
IP Address....................................... 192.168.1.208
IP NetMask....................................... 255.255.255.0
Gateway IP Addr.................................. 192.168.1.1
CAPWAP Path MTU.................................. 1485
Telnet State..................................... Disabled
Ssh State........................................ Disabled
Cisco AP Location................................ default location
Cisco AP Group Name.............................. default-group
Primary Cisco Switch Name........................ 4402
Primary Cisco Switch IP Address.................. Not Configured
Secondary Cisco Switch Name......................
Secondary Cisco Switch IP Address................ Not Configured
Tertiary Cisco Switch Name.......................
Tertiary Cisco Switch IP Address................. Not Configured
Administrative State ............................ ADMIN_ENABLED
Operation State ................................. REGISTERED
```

```
Mirroring Mode ................................. Disabled
AP Mode ........................................ H-Reap
Public Safety .................................. Disabled
AP SubMode ..................................... Not Configured
Remote AP Debug ................................ Disabled
Logging trap severity level .................... informational
S/W  Version ................................... 5.2.178.0
Boot  Version .................................. 12.3.7.1
Mini IOS Version ............................... 3.0.51.0
Stats Reporting Period ......................... 180
LED State....................................... Enabled
PoE Pre-Standard Switch......................... Enabled
PoE Power Injector MAC Addr..................... Disabled
Power Type/Mode................................. Power injector / Normal mode
Number Of Slots................................. 2
AP Model........................................ AIR-AP1242AG-A-K9
AP Image........................................ C1240-K9W8-M
IOS Version..................................... 12.4(18a)JA1
Reset Button.................................... Enabled
--More-- or (q)uit
AP Serial Number................................ FTX114470HZ
AP Certificate Type............................. Manufacture Installed
H-REAP Vlan mode :.............................. Enabled
      Native ID :............................... 1
      WLAN 2 :.................................. 12
      WLAN 3 :.................................. 20
H-REAP Backup Auth Radius Servers :
  Static Primary Radius Server.................. Disabled
  Static Secondary Radius Server................ Disabled
  Group Primary Radius Server................... Enabled
          IP address: .......................... 192.168.1.10
          Port Number: ......................... 1812
  Group Secondary Radius Server................. Disabled
Management Frame Protection Validation.......... Enabled (Global MFP Disabled)
AP User Mode.................................... AUTOMATIC
AP User Name.................................... Not Configured
AP Dot1x User Mode.............................. Not Configured
AP Dot1x User Name.............................. Not Configured
Cisco AP System Logging Host.................... 255.255.255.255
AP Up Time...................................... 0 days, 00 h 03 m 58 s
AP LWAPP Up Time................................ 0 days, 00 h 03 m 03 s
Join Date and Time.............................. Wed Apr  1 03:52:23 2009
Join Taken Time................................. 0 days, 00 h 00 m 54 s
```

(continues)

Example 13-4 *show ap config general Command Output (continued)*

```
Ethernet Port Duplex............................ Auto
Ethernet Port Speed............................ Auto
AP Link Latency................................ Disabled
```

Example 13-5 *show wlan Command Output*

```
(Cisco Controller)>show wlan 3
WLAN Identifier................................. 3
Profile Name.................................... Guest
Network Name (SSID)............................. Guest
Status.......................................... Enabled
MAC Filtering................................... Disabled
Broadcast SSID.................................. Enabled
AAA Policy Override............................. Disabled
! output omitted for brevity
Security
   802.11 Authentication:....................... Open System
   Static WEP Keys.............................. Disabled
   802.1X....................................... Disabled
   Wi-Fi Protected Access (WPA/WPA2)............ Disabled
   CKIP ........................................ Disabled
   IP Security.................................. Disabled
   IP Security Passthru......................... Disabled
   Web Based Authentication..................... Disabled
   Web-Passthrough.............................. Enabled
    ACL......................................... Unconfigured
    Email Input................................. Disabled
   Conditional Web Redirect..................... Disabled
   Splash-Page Web Redirect..................... Disabled
   Auto Anchor.................................. Disabled
   H-REAP Local Switching....................... Enabled
   H-REAP Learn IP Address...................... Enabled
   Infrastructure MFP protection................ Enabled (Global Infrastructure
MFP Disabled)
   Client MFP................................... Optional but inactive (WPA2 not
configured)
   Tkip MIC Countermeasure Hold-down Timer....... 60
 Mobility Anchor List
 WLAN ID     IP Address           Status
 ------      -------------        ------
```

Example 13-6 *show client detail Command Output*

```
(Cisco Controller)>show client detail 00:40:96:a1:4a:f6
Client MAC Address............................... 00:40:96:a1:4a:f6
Client Username ................................. N/A
AP MAC Address................................... 00:1e:13:06:f6:50
Client State..................................... Associated
Client NAC  OOB State............................ Access
Wireless LAN Id.................................. 3
BSSID............................................ 00:1e:13:06:f6:5d
Connected For ................................... 48 secs
Channel.......................................... 161
IP Address....................................... 192.168.20.20
Association Id................................... 1
Authentication Algorithm......................... Open System
! output omitted for brevity
Encryption Cipher................................ None
Management Frame Protection...................... No
EAP Type......................................... Unknown
Data Switching................................... Local
Quarantine VLAN.................................. 0
Access VLAN...................................... 0
Client Capabilities:
      CF Pollable................................ Not implemented
      CF Poll Request............................ Not implemented
      Short Preamble............................. Not implemented
      PBCC....................................... Not implemented
      Channel Agility............................ Not implemented
      Listen Interval............................ 10
      Fast BSS Transition........................ Not implemented
! output omitted for brevity
```

The **show** commands on the H-REAP AP can show you the state of the AP, the configuration stored in nonvolatile RAM, whether the AP is in connected or standalone mode, the associated clients, traffic statistics, CCKM cache information, and high availability configurations, as well as mobile node (clients) while in connected mode.

The show commands on the AP are as follows:

- **show capwap/lwapp client rcb:** Displays AP radio control block information.

- **show capwap client ha:** Displays high availability configuration.

- **show capwap/lwapp client mn:** Displays mobile node information.

- **show capwap/lwapp client traffic:** Displays traffic statistics.

- **show capwap/lwapp reap association:** Displays associated clients.

- **show capwap/lwapp reap cckm:** Displays CCKM cache information.

- **show capwap/lwapp reap status:** Displays the status of the AP, connected or stand-alone, as well as any radar information.

The following examples provide the different outputs from these commands. Depending on whether the AP is in connected or standalone mode, the output can change. Example 13-7 shows the output from an AP in connected mode when the operation state is UP.

Example 13-7 *show capwap client rcb Command Output*

```
1242#show capwap client rcb
AdminState              :   ADMIN_ENABLED
SwVer                   :   5.2.178.0
NumFilledSlots          :   2
Name                    :   1242
Location                :   default location
MwarName                :   4402
MwarApMgrIp             :   192.168.6.6
MwarHwVer               :   0.0.0.0
ApMode                  :   Remote
ApSubMode               :   Not Configured
OperationState          :   UP
CAPWAP Path MTU         :   1485
LinkAuditing            :   disabled
```

Example 13-8 shows the same command output, but this time, the AP is in standalone mode and the operation state is DISCOVERY because the AP is trying to rejoin its controller.

Example 13-8 *show capwap client rcb Command Output*

```
1242#show client capwap client rcb
AdminState              :   ADMIN_ENABLED
SwVer                   :   5.2.178.0
NumFilledSlots          :   2
Name                    :   1242
Location                :   default location
MwarName                :   4402
MwarMacAddr             :   ffff.ffff.ffff
MwarHwVer               :   0.0.0.0
ApMode                  :   Remote
ApSubMode               :   Not Configured
OperationState          :   DISCOVERY
CAPWAP Path MTU         :   1485
LinkAuditing            :   disabled
```

To show whether the AP is in connected or standalone mode, use **show capwap/lwapp reap status**, as seen in Example 13-9.

Example 13-9 *show capwap reap status Command Output*

```
1242#show capwap reap status
 AP Mode:          REAP, Connected
 Radar detected on:
1242#show capwap reap status
 AP Mode:          REAP, Standalone


 Radar detected on:
```

To see the clients currently associated with the AP, use **show capwap/lwapp reap association**, as shown in Example 13-10.

Example 13-10 *show capwap reap association Command Output*

```
1242#show capwap reap association
Address            : 0040.96a1.4af6    Name              : LEEJOHNS-XP-TST
IP Address         : 192.168.20.20     Interface         : Dot11Radio 1
Device             : CB21AG/PI21AG     Software Version  : NONE
CCX Version        : 5                    Client MFP      : Off
State              : Assoc               Parent          : self
SSID               : Guest
WLAN               : 3
Hops to Infra      : 1                   Association Id   : 1
Clients Associated : 0                   Repeaters associated: 0
Tunnel Address     : 0.0.0.0
Key Mgmt type      : NONE                Encryption      : Off
Current Rate       : 54.0                Capability      : WMM
Supported Rates    : 6.0 9.0 12.0 18.0 24.0 36.0 48.0 54.0
Voice Rates        : disabled            Bandwidth       : 20 MHz
Signal Strength    : -52  dBm            Connected for   : 857 seconds
Signal to Noise    : 41   dB             Activity Timeout : 300 seconds
Power-save         : Off                 Last Activity   : 0 seconds ago
Apsd DE AC(s)      : NONE
Packets Input      : 3937                Packets Output  : 415
Bytes Input        : 160762              Bytes Output    : 255367
Duplicates Rcvd    : 13                  Data Retries    : 25
Decrypt Failed     : 0                   RTS Retries     : 0
MIC Failed         : 0                   MIC Missing     : 0
Packets Redirected : 0                   Redirect Filtered : 0
Session timeout    : 1800 seconds
Reauthenticate in  : never seconds
REAP Data Switching : Local
SSID: Data on Dot11Radio1
```

(continues)

Example 13-10 *show capwap reap association Command Output*   *(continued)*

```
  bssid: 001e.1306.f65e  Mode: 0x192, WLAN: 2 , VLAN name: 002    VLAN ID: 12
  Key Mgmt 4, Reap flags 0x1, Guest Yes, Current Users 0
SSID: Guest on Dot11Radio1
  bssid: 001e.1306.f65d  Mode: 0x192, WLAN: 3 , VLAN name: 003    VLAN ID: 20
  Key Mgmt 0, Reap flags 0x9, Guest Yes, Current Users 1, Open Auth
SSID: Data on Dot11Radio0
  bssid: 001e.1306.f651  Mode: 0x192, WLAN: 2 , VLAN name: 002    VLAN ID: 12
  Key Mgmt 4, Reap flags 0x1, Guest Yes, Current Users 0
```

To view CCKM cache entries, use **show capwap reap cckm,** as shown in Example 13-11.

Example 13-11 *show capwap reap cckm Command Output*

```
1242#show capwap reap cckm
CCKM Cache Entries:
HW Address        BSSID
Total number of cache entries = 0
```

When the AP is in connected mode, you can use **show capwap/lwapp client mn** to view the mobile node client information, the WLAN it is associated with, and the radio interface. When the AP is in standalone mode, the output is empty. Example 13-12 demonstrates the output from this command.

Example 13-12 *show capwap client mn Command Output*

```
1242#show capwap client mn
     CAPWAP mobile database
- - - - - - - - - - - - - - - - - - - - - - - - - - - - - - - - - - - - - - - - -
MAC                  State                    WLAN   Interface
0018.de74.b8b5       CAPWAP_MN_ST_ADDED         2     Dot11Radio1
0040.96a1.4af6       CAPWAP_MN_ST_ADDED         3     Dot11Radio1
! in standalone mode:
1242#show capwap client mn
     CAPWAP mobile database
- - - - - - - - - - - - - - - - - - - - - - - - - - - - - - - - - - - - - - - - -
MAC                  State                    WLAN   Interface
```

You can view the high availability configuration of the AP using **show capwap client ha,** as shown in Example 13-13. Notice that the IP address of the Primary Backup controller is listed in hex.

Example 13-13 *show capwap client ha Command Output*

```
1242#show capwap client ha
fastHeartbeatTmr          disabled
primaryDiscoverTmr(sec) 120
```

```
primaryBackupWlcIp          0xC0A80602
primaryBackupWlcName        leejohns
secondaryBackupWlcIp        0x0
secondaryBackupWlcName
DHCP renew try count        0
Fwd traffic stats get       0
Fast Heartbeat sent         0
Discovery attempt           0
Backup WLC array:
```

The output of **show capwap/lwapp client traffic**, as shown in Example 13-14, details traffic statistics for the AP.

Example 13-14   *show capwap client traffic Command Output*

```
1242#show capwap client traffic
 Traffic Statistics for CAPWAP Client of 192.168.6.6
 - - - - - - - - - - - - - - - - - - - - - - - - - - - - - - - - - - - - - - - -
Probe Rcvd:              2052;  Probe Fwd:              0
AssocReq Fwd:               3;  Beacon Rcvd:            0
unknown_mgmt_rcvd:          0;  mgmt_frame_dropped      171
data_frame_dropped          7;  unicast to CS:          418
unicast to MN              41;  multicast to MN         0
non capwap pkt:            14;  capwap ctrl rcvd:       123
capwap data rcvd:         45;  assoc resp rcvd:        3
Invalid slotid rcv         0;  capwap mgmt rcvd:       4
Fragments To AC:           0;  Not from AC:            4
Fragments to MN:           0;
Fragments no buf           0;  old fragments:          0
Too Many Reassembl         0;  Improper fragment       0
Overlap Reassembli         0;  Fragment no chunk:      0
Too Large Fragment         0;  Total reassembled       0
IP Fragments to MN         0;
IP Fragments no bu         0;  old IP fragments:       0
Too Many IP Reasse         0;  Improper IP fragme      0
Overlap IP Reassem         0;  IP Fragment no chu      0
Too Large IP Fragm         0;  Total IP reassembl      0
unknown client:            4;  otap_rcvd:              262
bcast from cs:             0;  no dup bcast:           0
drop_sniffer_disab         0;  pak_grow_err:           0
Downstream dot1p:          0;  Upstream dot1p:         0
mgmt2cs:                2056;  add_tsreq:              0
drop(not for us):          0;  old fragments:          0
mcast(not IGMP):           0;  mcast our grp(not       0
mcast rcvd:                0;  capwap data droppe      0
eap_pkts_rcvd:             0;  eap_pkts_sent:          0
```

(continues)

Example 13-14 *show capwap client traffic Command Output (continued)*

```
eap_pkts_qued:           0;   eap_pkts_dequed:        0
eap_pkts_dropped:        0;   eap_pkts_freed:         0
eap_pkts_noclient:       0;   runt capwap frags:      0
capwap too large f       0;   capwap invalid hea      0
```

debug Commands

To debug the H-REAP disassociation and joins on the controller, use the standard LWAPP/CAPWAP debugs outlined in Chapter 8.

Following are the main debugs:

■ debug **capwap/lwapp events**

■ debug **capwap/lwapp packet**

The debugs to view the more advanced features of H-REAP are as follows:

■ debug **hreap aaa** {event | error} {enable | disable}: Enables or disables debugging of H-REAP backup RADIUS server events or errors.

■ debug **hreap cckm** {enable | disable}: Enables or disables debugging of H-REAP CCKM.

■ debug **hreap group** {enable | disable}: Enables or disables debugging of H-REAP groups.

■ debug **pem state** {enable | disable}: Enables or disables debugging of the policy manager state machine.

■ debug **pem events** {enable | disable}: Enables or disables debugging of policy manager events.

Although having console or Telnet access to the remote AP is not always an option, you can gain a wealth of knowledge from the debugs you can run on the AP.

The H-REAP AP debugs are as follows:

■ debug **capwap reap:** Displays general H-REAP activities.

■ debug **capwap reap mgmt:** Displays client authentication and association messages.

■ debug **capwap reap load:** Displays payload activities, which are useful when the H-REAP AP boots in standalone mode.

■ debug **dot11 mgmt interface:** Displays 802.11 management interface events.

■ debug **dot11 mgmt msg:** Displays 802.11 management messages.

■ debug **dot11 mgmt ssid:** Displays SSID management events.

■ **debug dot11 mgmt state-machine:** Displays the 802.11 state machine.

■ **debug dot11 mgmt station:** Displays client events.

Example 13-15 shows the output from **debug capwap reap**. In this debug you can see the AP transition from connected to standalone mode. The AP sends a notification that it is closing the Datagram Transport Layer Security (DTLS) connection. When the controller is detected as being back up, the AP rejoins the controller, loads its configuration, and brings up its radios. Notice that the AP disables the IDS capability when it enters standalone mode.

Example 13-15 *debug capwap reap Output*

```
1242#debug capwap reap
CAPWAP REAP debugging is on
1242#
*Apr  1 08:23:17.635: REAP: REAP AP Switching to Standalone mode, Connected to
Controller 1
*Apr  1 08:23:17.636: REAP: set=1
*Apr  1 08:23:17.637: REAP: Radius First Time = 0
*Apr  1 08:23:17.637: %DTLS-5-SEND_ALERT: Send WARNING : Close notify Alert to
192.168.6.6
*Apr  1 08:23:17.747: %WIDS-6-DISABLED: IDS Signature is removed and disabled.
*Apr  1 08:23:17.749: %CAPWAP-5-CHANGED: CAPWAP changed state to DISCOVERY
*Apr  1 08:23:30.753:  capwapHandleDiscoveryTimer Expired
*Apr  1 08:23:43.757:  capwapHandleDiscoveryTimer Expired
*Apr  1 08:23:56.761:  capwapHandleDiscoveryTimer Expired
*Apr  1 08:24:09.765:  capwapHandleDiscoveryTimer Expired
*Apr  1 00:24:22.769:  capwapHandleDiscoveryTimer Expired
*Apr  1 08:24:35.773:  capwapHandleDiscoveryTimer Expired
*Apr  1 08:24:48.777:  capwapHandleDiscoveryTimer Expired
wtpDecodeDiscovery Response numOfCapwapDiscoveryResp = 0
*Apr  1 08:25:01.781:  capwapHandleDiscoveryTimer Expired
*Apr  1 08:25:02.000: %CAPWAP-5-DTLSREQSEND: DTLS connection request sent peer_ip:
192.168.6.6 peer_port: 5246
*Apr  1 08:25:03.409: %CAPWAP-5-DTLSREQSUCC: DTLS connection created sucessfully
peer_ip: 192.168.6.6 peer_port: 5246
*Apr  1 08:25:03.410: %CAPWAP-5-SENDJOIN: sending Join Request to 192.168.6.6
*Apr  1 08:25:03.410: %CAPWAP-5-CHANGED: CAPWAP changed state to JOIN
*Apr  1 08:25:03.568: REAP: lwapp_reap_load_cfg : Loading REAP Cfg, sizof of
Config is 40568, firsttime 0
*Apr  1 08:25:03.56
Configuration of vLAN subinterfaces and main
interface within the same bridge group is not permitted8: REAP:
lwapp_reap_load_cfg : Loading REAP Cfg, sizof of Config is 40568, firsttime 0
*Apr  1 08:25:03.570: %CAPWAP-5-CHANGED: CAPWAP changed state to CFG
*Apr  1 08:25:03.614: REAP: Getting into Connected REAP Mode, Zero out Payload
Save StandAlone Mode 1
```

(continues)

Example 13-15   *debug capwap reap Output (continued)*

```
*Apr  1 08:25:03.744: %LINK-5-CHANGED: Interface Dot11Radio0, changed state to
reset
*Apr  1 08:25:03.758: %CAPWAP-5-CHANGED: CAPWAP changed state to UP
*Apr  1 08:25:03.760: %LINK-3-UPDOWN: Interface Dot11Radio0, changed state to up
*Apr  1 08:25:03.767: REAP: Saving & Writing the LWAPP REAP CFG count 1
*Apr  1 08:25:03.767: REAP:  Saving REAP Cfg, sizof of Config is 40568
*Apr  1 08:25:03.809: %LINK-5-CHANGED: Interface Dot11Radio1, changed state to
reset
*Apr  1 08:25:04.614: %CAPWAP-5-JOINEDCONTROLLER: AP has joined controller 4402
*Apr  1 08:25:04.725: REAP: Switching to Connected REAP Mode 1, StandAlone Mode 1
*Apr  1 08:25:04.725: REAP: Switching to Connected mode
*Apr  1 08:25:04.727: REAP: Saving & Writing the LWAPP REAP CFG count 2
*Apr  1 08:25:04.727: REAP:  Saving REAP Cfg, sizof of Config is 40568
*Apr  1 08:25:04.831: %LINEPROTO-5-UPDOWN: Line protocol on Interface Dot11Radio1,
changed state to down
*Apr  1 08:25:04.972: REAP: Saving & Writing the LWAPP REAP CFG count 3
*Apr  1 08:25:04.972: REAP:  Saving REAP Cfg, sizof of Config is 40568
*Apr  1 08:25:05.212: REAP: Saving & Writing the LWAPP REAP CFG count 4
*Apr  1 08:25:05.212: REAP:  Saving REAP Cfg, sizof of Config is 40568
*Apr  1 08:25:06.059: REAP: Saving & Writing the LWAPP REAP CFG count 5
*Apr  1 08:25:06.059: REAP:  Saving REAP Cfg, sizof of Config is 40568
*Apr  1 08:25:06.302: REAP: Native VlanId for Slot 0 is 1, and Bridge-Group 1
*Apr  1 08:25:06.311: REAP: Native VlanId for Slot 1 is 1, and Bridge-Group 1
*Apr  1 08:25:06.344: REAP: Calling to Create Bridge-Group VlanId 12 for Name 02
*Apr  1 08:25:06.366: REAP: Calling to Create Bridge-Group VlanId 20 for Name 03
*Apr  1 08:25:06.388: REAP: Calling to Create Bridge-Group VlanId 12 for Name 02
*Apr  1 08:25:06.410: REAP: Calling to Create Bridge-Group VlanId 20 for Name 03
*Apr  1 08:25:06.411: REAP: Saving & Writing the LWAPP REAP CFG count 6
*Apr  1 08:25:06.411: REAP:  Saving REAP Cfg, sizof of Config is 40568
*Apr  1 08:25:06.643: %WIDS-6-ENABLED: IDS Signature is loaded and enabled
*Apr  1 08:25:06.645: REAP: Saving & Writing the LWAPP REAP CFG count 7
*Apr  1 08:25:06.645: REAP:  Saving REAP Cfg, sizof of Config is 40568
*Apr  1 08:25:07.842: %DOT11-6-FREQ_USED: Interface Dot11Radio1, frequency 5280
selected
*Apr  1 08:25:07.843: %LINK-3-UPDOWN: Interface Dot11Radio1, changed state to up
*Apr  1 08:25:07.853: %LINK-3-UPDOWN: Interface Dot11Radio0, changed state to down
*Apr  1 08:25:07.855: %LINK-5-CHANGED: Interface Dot11Radio0, changed state to
reset
*Apr  1 08:25:07.891: %LINK-3-UPDOWN: Interface Dot11Radio0, changed state to up
*Apr  1 08:25:07.897: %LINK-3-UPDOWN: Interface Dot11Radio1, changed state to down
*Apr  1 08:25:07.900: %LINK-5-CHANGED: Interface Dot11Radio1, changed state to
reset
*Apr  1 08:25:07.934: %LINK-3-UPDOWN: Interface Dot11Radio1, changed state to up
*Apr  1 08:25:08.843: %LINEPROTO-5-UPDOWN: Line protocol on Interface Dot11Radio1,
changed state to up
```

Example 13-16 shows the output from **debug dot11 mgmt station**, in which a client with MAC address 0018.de74.b8b5 is able to connect to a WLAN with SSID of data using WPA-PSK even though the AP just transitioned to standalone mode.

Example 13-16   *debug dot11 mgmt station Output*

```
1242#debug dot11 mgmt station
Dot11 Stations debugging is on
*Apr  1 09:34:08.993: dot11_mgmt: dot11_mgmt_sta_del_all_children sta_ptr
0x12A30FC
*Apr  1 09:34:08.993: dot11_mgmt: dot11_mgmt_sta_del_all_children sta_ptr
0x12A367C
*Apr  1 09:34:08.995: %DTLS-5-SEND_ALERT: Send WARNING : Close notify Alert to
192.168.6.6
*Apr  1 09:34:09.105: %WIDS-6-DISABLED: IDS Signature is removed and disabled.
*Apr  1 09:34:09.107: %CAPWAP-5-CHANGED: CAPWAP changed state to DISCOVERY
*Apr  1 09:34:22.112:   capwapHandleDiscoveryTimer Expired
1242#
*Apr  1 09:34:35.116:   capwapHandleDiscoveryTimer Expired
*Apr  1 09:34:48.120:   capwapHandleDiscoveryTimer Expired
*Apr  1 09:35:01.124:   capwapHandleDiscoveryTimer Expired
*Apr  1 09:35:14.128:   capwapHandleDiscoveryTimer Expired
*Apr  1 09:35:24.302: dot11_mgmt: add a new station 0018.de74.b8b5
*Apr  1 09:35:24.302: dot11_mgmt: dot11_mgmt_sta_add (ref=1, sta_ptr=0x1299D44,
mac=0018.de74.b8b5)
*Apr  1 09:35:24.302: dot11_mgmt: insert 0018.de74.b8b5 into ssid[] tree
*Apr  1 09:35:24.302: dot11_mgmt: dot11_mgmt_sta_ref (ref=1, sta_ptr=0x1299D44,
mac=0018.de74.b8b5)
*Apr  1 09:35:24.302: dot11_mgmt: dot11_mgmt_sta_ref (ref=2, sta_ptr=0x1299D44,
mac=0018.de74.b8b5)
*Apr  1 09:35:24.302: dot11_mgmt: dot11_mgmt_sta_deref (ref=3, sStation:
0018.de74.b8b5 roamed in with: First association to WLAN ta_ptr=0x1299D44,
mac=0018.de74.b8b5)
*Apr  1 09:35:24.303: dot11_mgmt: dot11_mgmt_sta_ref (ref=2, sta_ptr=0x1299D44,
mac=0018.de74.b8b5)
*Apr  1 09:35:24.303: dot11_mgmt: dot11_mgmt_sta_del_all_children sta_ptr
0x1299D44
*Apr  1 09:35:24.303: dot11_mgmt: dot11_mgmt_sta_tree_cont_cleanup, 0x1299D44
*Apr  1 09:35:24.303: dot11_mgmt: finish remove 0018.de74.b8b5 and its children
*Apr  1 09:35:24.303: dot11_mgmt: dot11_mgmt_sta_deref (ref=3, sta_ptr=0x1299D44,
mac=0018.de74.b8b5)
*Apr  1 09:35:24.304: dot11_mgmt: dot11_mgmt_sta_is_infra_client, flags 0x0
device 0x66
*Apr  1 09:35:24.304: dot11_mgmt: dot11_mgmt_sta_is_infra_client: false
*Apr  1 09:35:24.304: dot11_mgmt: dot11_mgmt_sta_is_infra_client, flags 0x0
device 0x66
*Apr  1 09:35:24.304: dot11_mgmt: dot11_mgmt_sta_is_infra_client: false
*Apr  1 09:35:24.304: dot11_mgmt: insert 0018.de74.b8b5 into ssid[Data] tree
```

(continues)

Example 13-16 *debug dot11 mgmt station Output (continued)*

```
*Apr  1 09:35:24.304: dot11_mgmt: dot11_mgmt_sta_ref (ref=2, sta_ptr=0x1299D44,
mac=0018.de74.b8b5)
*Apr  1 09:35:24.304: dot11_mgmt: dot11_mgmt_sta_is_infra_client, flags 0x0
device 0x66
*Apr  1 09:35:24.304: dot11_mgmt: dot11_mgmt_sta_is_infra_client: false
```

To troubleshoot backup RADIUS authentication and other events on the AP when it is in standalone mode, use the same IOS-based debugs you would use on an autonomous AP (see Appendix A, "Debugging Commands").

For example, in Example 13-17, which shows the output from **debug dot1x all**, **debug aaa authentication**, and **debug radius authentication**, you see a client with MAC address 000e.35f3.6073 authenticate using Protected Extensible Authentication Protocol (PEAP) to a backup RADIUS server while the AP is in standalone mode.

Example 13-17 *debug dot1x all, debug aaa all, and debug radius authentication Command Output on H-REAP AP in Standalone Mode*

```
1242#debug dot1x all
1242#debug aaa authentication
AAA Authentication debugging is on
1242#debug radius authentication
Radius protocol debugging is on
Radius protocol brief debugging is off
Radius protocol verbose debugging is off
Radius packet hex dump debugging is off
Radius packet protocol (authentication) debugging is on
Radius packet protocol (accounting) debugging is off
Radius elog debugging debugging is off
Radius packet retransmission debugging is off
Radius server fail-over debugging is off
Radius elog debugging debugging is off
1242#show capwap reap status
 AP Mode:          REAP, Standalone
 Radar detected on:
*Apr  2 06:59:09.754: AAA/BIND(00000005): Bind i/f
*Apr  2 06:59:09.890: dot1x-ev:dot1x_mgr_process_eapol_pak: dot1x eapol on dot11
interface
*Apr  2 06:59:09.890: dot1x-ev:dot1x_mgr_pre_process_eapol_pak: Role determination
not required on Dot11Radio0.2.
*Apr  2 06:59:09.890: dot1x-err:No dot1x subblock
*Apr  2 06:59:09.891: dot1x-packet:dot1x_mgr_process_eapol_pak: queuing an EAPOL
pkt on Authenticator Q
*Apr  2 06:59:09.891: AAA/AUTHEN/PPP (00000005): Pick method list
'reap_eap_methods'
*Apr  2 06:59:09.892: RADIUS/ENCODE(00000005):Orig. component type = DOT11
*Apr  2 06:59:09.892: RADIUS:   AAA Unsupported Attr: ssid          [265] 4
```

```
*Apr  2 06:59:09.892: RADIUS:    44 61                        for Radius-Server
192.168.1.10
*Apr  2 06:59:09.893: RADIUS(00000005): Send Access-Request to 192.168.1.10:1812
id 1645/19, len 140                        [Da]
*Apr  2 06:59:09.892: RADIUS:    AAA Unsu
*Apr  2 06:59:09.893: RADIUS:    authenticator 30 8B 8F 9B 07 80 08 C8 - 33 80 8E
8A 73 D8 70 44
*Apr  2 06:59:09.894: RADIUS:    User-Name        [1]    15   "LEESDESK\peap"
*Apr  2 06:59:09.894: RADIUS:    Framed-MTU       [12]   6    1400
*Apr  2 06:59:09.894: RADIUS:    Called-Station-Id  [30]  16   "001e.1306.f651"
*Apr  2 06:59:09.894: RADIUS:    Calling-Station-Id [31]  16   "000e.35f3.6073"
*Apr  2 06:59:09.894: RADIUS:    Service-Type     [6]    6    Login
[1]
*Apr  2 06:59:09.894: RADIUS:    Message-Authenticato[80]  18
*Apr  2 06:59:09.894: RADIUS:    01 1D 42 EB 69 BE 0A D4 4A 50 BB F7 24 F7 A7 61
[??B?i???JP??$??a]pported Attr: interface       [157] 3
*Apr  2 06:59:09.892US:   61 70                                            [ap]
*Apr  2 06:59:09.895: RADIUS:    NAS-Port-Type    [61]   6    802.11 wireless
[19]
*Apr  2 06:59:09.895: RADIUS:    NAS-Port         [5]    6    260
*Apr  2 06:59:09.895: RADIUS:    NAS-Port-Id      [87]   5    "260"
*Apr  2 06:59:09.895: RADIUS:    NAS-IP-Address   [4]    6    192.168.1.208
*Apr  2 06:59:09.904: RADIUS: Received from id 1645/19 192.168.1.10:1812, Access-
Challenge, len 76: RADIUS:    32
[2]
*Apr  2 06:59:09.905: RADIUS:    authenticator 58 6D 00 EF 70 0E 87 37 - 4C A0 D0
FF 79 1B 52 0F
*Apr  2 06:59:09.905: RADIUS:    Session-Timeout  [27]   6    30
*Apr  2 06:59:09.905: RADIUS:    EAP-Message      [79]   8
*Apr  2 06:59:09.905: RADIUS:    01 02 00 06 19 20
[????? ]
*Apr  2 06:59:09.905: RADIUS:    State            [24]   24
*Apr  2 06:59:09.905: RADIUS:    04 0B 00 67 00 00 01 37 00 01 03 03 03 03 00 00
[???g???7?????????]
*Apr  2 06:59:09.906: RADIUS:    00 01 00 00 00 20
[????? ]
*Apr  2 06:59:09.906: RADIUS:    Message-Authenticato[80]  18
*Apr  2 06:59:09.892: RADIUS(00000005): Config NAS IP: 0.0.0.0IUS(00000005):
Received from id 1645/19
*Apr  2 06:59:09.907: RADIUS/DECODE: EAP-Message fragments, 6, total 6 bytes
*Apr  2 06:59:09.946: dot1x-ev:dot1x_mgr_process_eapol_pak: dot1x eapol on dot11
interface
*Apr  2 06:59:09.946: dot1x-ev:dot1x_mgr_pre_process_eapol_pak: Role determination
not required on Dot11Radio0.2.
*Apr  2 06:59:09.946: dot1x-err:No dot1x subblock
*Apr  2 06:59:09.946: dot1x-packet:dot1x_mgr_process_eapol_pak: queuing an EAPOL
pkt on Authenticator Q
*Apr  2 06:59:09.893: RADIUS/ENCODE(00000005): acct_session_id
```

(continues)

Example 13-17 *debug dot1x all, debug aaa all, and debug radius authentication Command Output on H-REAP AP in Standalone Mode (continued)*

```
*Apr  2 06:59:09.946: AAA/AUTHEN/PPP (00000005): Pick method list
'reap_eap_methods'
*Apr  2 06:59:09.947: RADIUS/ENCODE(00000005):Orig. component type = DOT11
*Apr  2 06:59:09.947: RADIUS:  AAA Unsupported Attr: ssid          [265] 4
*Apr  2 06:59:09.947: RADIUS:   44 61
[Da]
*Apr  2 06:59:09.947: RADIUS:  AAA Unsupported Attr: interface     [157] 3
*Apr  2 06:59:09.948: RADIUS:   32
[2]
! output omitted for brevity
*Apr  2 06:59:30.116: RADIUS:  NAS-IP-Address      [4]   6   192.168.1.208
*Apr  2 06:59:31.036: RADIUS: Received from id 1645/35 192.168.1.10:1812, Access-
Challenge, len 259
*Apr  2 06:59:31.036: RADIUS:   authenticator 6F 41 26 DE 7A 96 A4 46 - 26 47 72
D6 73 0F E6 57
*Apr  2 06:59:31.039: RADIUS:   04 7B 62 40 34 80 DE 2D 39 D0 57 9B 3E 13 94 D0
[?{b@4??-9?W?>???]
*Apr  2 06:59:31.040: RADIUS(00000005): Received from id 1645/35
*Apr  2 06:59:31.041: RADIUS/DECODE: EAP-Message fragments, 38, total 38 bytes
*Apr  2 06:59:31.788: dot1x-ev:dot1x_mgr_process_eapol_pak: dot1x eapol on dot11
interface
*Apr  2 06:59:31.788: dot1x-ev:dot1x_mgr_pre_process_eapol_pak: Role determination
not required on Dot11Radio0.2.
*Apr  2 06:59:31.788: dot1x-err:No dot1x subblock
*Apr  2 06:59:31.788: dot1x-packet:dot1x_mgr_process_eapol_pak: queuing an EAPOL
pkt on Authenticator Q802.11 wireless           [19]
*Apr  2 06:59:31.793: RADIUS:  NAS-Port            [5]   6    260
*Apr  2 06:59:31.794: RADIUS:  NAS-Port-Id         [87]  5    "260"
*Apr  2 06:59:31.794: RADIUS:  State               [24]  24
*Apr  2 06:59:31.794: RADIUS:   04 0B 00 67 00 00 01 37 00 01 03 03 03 03 00 00
[???g?????????????]
*Apr  2 06:59:31.794: RADIUS:   00 01 00 00 00 20
[?????  ]
*Apr  2 06:59:31.794: RADIUS:  NAS-IP-Address      [4]   6   192.168.1.208
*Apr  2 06:59:32.692: RADIUS: Received from id 1645/36 192.168.1.10:1812, Access-
Accept, len 204
*Apr  2 06:59:32.693: RADIUS:  Class               [25]  32
*Apr  2 06:59:32.694: RADIUS:   2D 24 03 95 00 00 01 37 00 01 03 03 03 03 01 C9
[-$?????????????]
*Apr  2 06:59:32.694: RADIUS:   B1 4E 1B 5A 60 80 00 00 00 00 00 00 00 00 00 31
[?N?Z`????????1]
*Apr  2 06:59:32.694: RADIUS:  Message-Authenticato[80]  18
*Apr  2 06:59:32.694: RADIUS:   4B C5 F1 24 48 86 45 B5 88 71 10 CE 51 B0 9A C3
[K??$H?E??q??Q???]
*Apr  2 06:59:32.697: RADIUS(00000005): Received from id 1645/36
*Apr  2 06:59:32.697: RADIUS/DECODE: EAP-Message fragments, 4, total 4 bytes
```

After completing authentication, you can see the client is successfully authenticated on the AP, as demonstrated in Example 13-18.

Example 13-18 *show capwap reap association Command Output for a Backup RADIUS Client*

```
1242#show capwap reap association
Address          : 000e.35f3.6073    Name             : 1242
IP Address       : 192.168.12.103    Interface        : Dot11Radio 0
Device           : ccx-client        Software Version : NONE
CCX Version      : 3                 Client MFP       : Off
State            : EAP-Assoc         Parent           : self
SSID             : Data
WLAN             : 2
! output omitted for brevity
```

A packet capture from the H-REAP switch port shows the RADIUS request being sent directly from the AP. Figure 13-13 shows the RADIUS process and the Access-Accept from the RADIUS server.

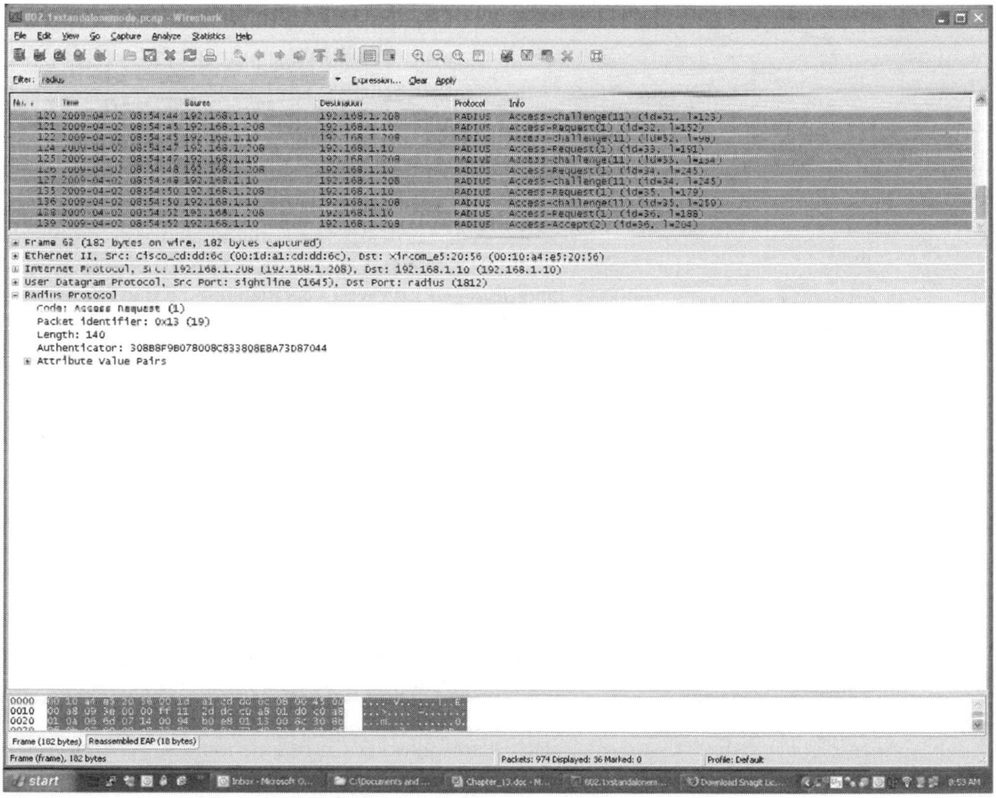

Figure 13-13 *Backup RADIUS 802.1x Authentication*

As you can see in the figure, the RADIUS packets are bridged directly to the local network from the AP and are not encapsulated in an LWAPP/CAPWAP tunnel.

Summary

The H-REAP feature available with the wireless LAN controllers is a robust and flexible solution for providing wireless network access for small, remote satellite offices. When using H-REAP local switching, after the wireless clients pass authentication, the client traffic is bridged directly onto the local network by the AP. Understanding how the traffic flows and what authentication method, static WEP, WPA1/2-PSK, 802.1x, and so on that you want to use will dictate what local network resources you will need to configure and have available while the AP is in both connected and standalone mode. H-REAP helps you save money by allowing wireless access at these smaller locations without having to purchase a dedicated controller. This solution also helps save precious WAN bandwidth as only LWAPP/CAPWAP control traffic and not client data is tunneled across the network link to the controller.

Chapter 14

Guest Networking

When a company provides a guest network for outside visitors, it allows those visitors access to the Internet using, usually, a segregated network subnet. This network segregation blocks internal network resources from the visitors but allows them to VPN to their own network, check their email, and so on.

Guest networking implies two things:

- Web authentication
- Centralized guest traffic flow

This chapter covers the basics of web authentication including how it works, how to configure it, how to troubleshoot it, as well as some features you can implement to fine-tune your visitor network. This chapter also discusses how you can centralize the traffic flow from your guest clients using auto-anchoring to help segregate that traffic from your internal wired corporate network.

Web Authentication

Web authentication, or web auth, is a Layer 3 security method that allows a client to pass Dynamic Host Configuration Protocol (DHCP) and Domain Name System (DNS) traffic only until they have passed some form of authentication. What makes web auth a great solution for wireless guest access is that no client-side configuration is required for it to work. A guest client needs only to associate to the guest WLAN and get an IP from DHCP. When the client tries to access the Internet, the controller redirects the client to the web authentication page. Here the client will accept a user agreement and, if authentication is configured, enter the correct username and password before being allowed network access.

Web Authentication Policies

A wireless controller has four authentication policies:

- Authentication
- Passthrough
- Conditional Web Redirect
- Splash Page Web Redirect (added in Release 5.0)

Figure 14-1 shows the authentication polices on the Layer 3 Security tab of the Wireless LANs (WLAN) configuration page.

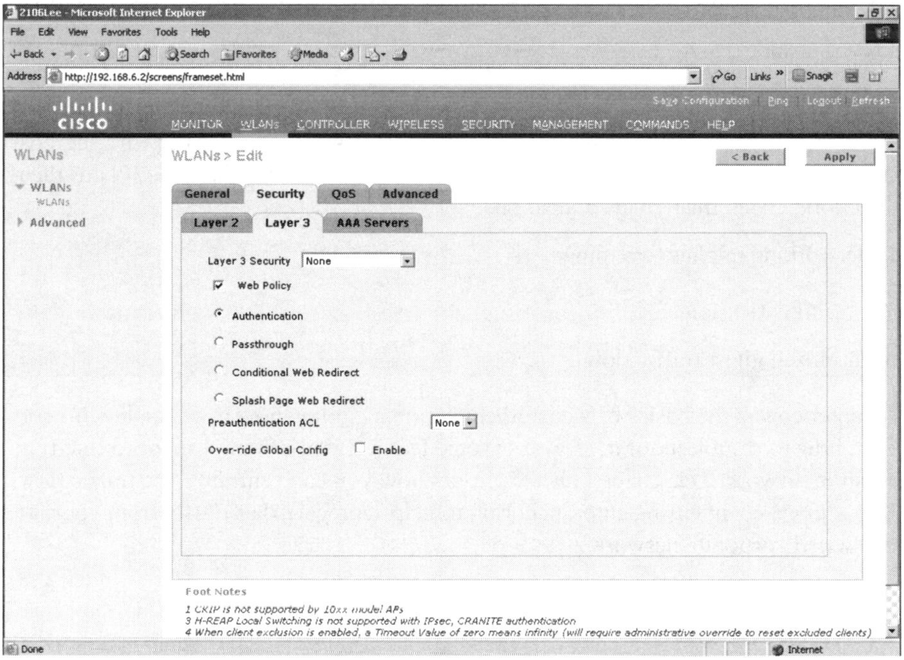

Figure 14-1 *Web Authentication Policies*

> **Note** You can also provide an open guest network with no security. To do this, you simply don't configure Layer 2 or Layer 3 security on the WLAN. Although this is easy to set up, it does allow any users, whether they are valid visitors or people out on the street, to use your wireless network and Internet access.

When you enable authentication, the controller presents a splash screen like the one in Figure 14-2 that you can configure to display a welcome message, terms of use agreement, or other legalese. The guest client has to enter a username and password to gain access to the guest network. Using authentication prevents someone off the street from using the wireless network of a company and taking up vital bandwidth that was intended for real guest users. The controller can authenticate the users using its local database, an external RADIUS, or Lightweight Directory Access Protocol (LDAP) server.

Figure 14-2 *Generic Web Auth Splash Page*

When using the passthrough policy, the guest client is presented with a splash screen just as with authentication. The difference between the two policies at this point is that clients need only to accept the agreement before gaining network access. Although the clients in this case are not authenticating with a username/password, the controller does not consider the clients authenticated to the network and blocks network access (except DHCP and DNS) until they click on the Submit/Accept button on the splash page. If desired, you can also use Layer 2 security methods in conjunction with web auth. This, of course, requires client-side configuration and can undermine the ease of guest access to visitors because they have to know what type of Layer 2 security to configure. Web auth supports open, open + WEP, and Wi-Fi Protected Access–Pre-Shared Key (WPA-PSK). It does not support 802.1x authentications like Lightweight Extensible Authentication Protocol (LEAP) and Protected Extensible Authentication Protocol (PEAP).

Controller code 4.2.61.0 introduced the Email Input option (see Figure 14-3). With Email Input selected, the guest user is prompted to enter an email address before proceeding. If you have Wireless Control System (WCS), you can run reports to see those email addresses. If you have configured RADIUS accounting on the guest WLAN, the email address entered is logged there as well. Administrators can then send emails to these users thanking them for visiting. You will only see the Email Input option when passthrough is selected.

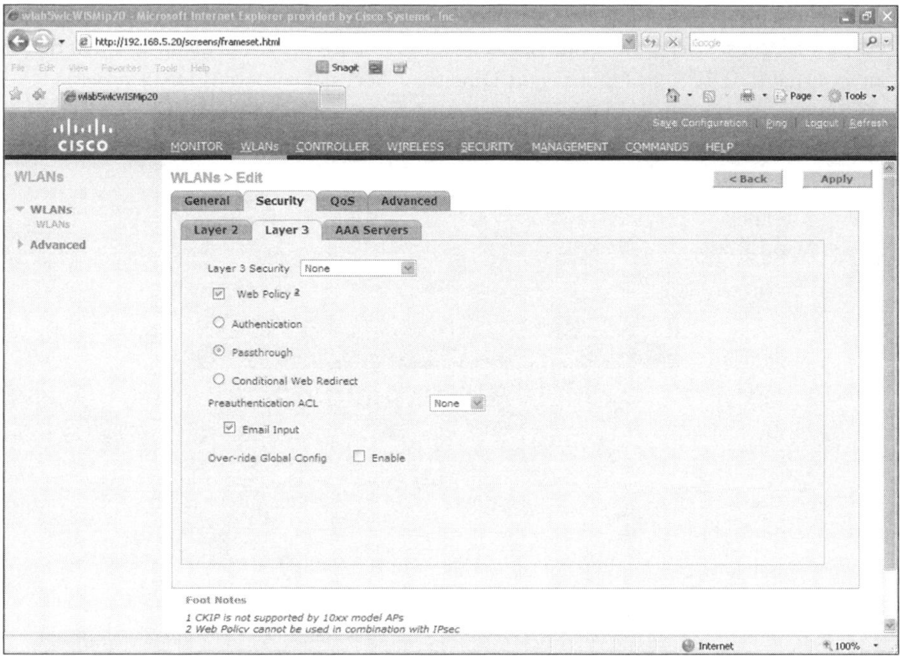

Figure 14-3 *Email Input Option with Passthrough Authentication*

> **Note**   Until controller Release 5.2.157.0, however, the format of the text entered was not veri-
> fied. This meant a guest user could choose not to enter anything, enter gibberish, or enter col-
> orful messages. Because the description of Email Input indicates that a user must enter an
> email address before proceeding, some administrators considered this a security violation.
> Cisco changed the code to ensure that text entered is in a valid format like
> name@company.com. A user can still enter bogus information because there is no way to vali-
> date the address, but at least it will be in the form of an email address before access is granted.

Cisco added this feature starting in 4.0.206.0 code. Conditional Web Redirect is commonly
used by businesses that are selling network access to users. There is now a Conditional
Web Redirect policy. When users log into the wireless network from the splash page, a
RADIUS server verifies their user credentials. Should certain conditions be met that
necessitate another redirect, the client is redirected to a new page. The conditions that
facilitate a redirect and the redirect URL are configured on the RADIUS server, not the
controller. An example of this is if the user needs to pay a bill and is redirected to a site
where it is possible to make that payment to continue having network access. The guest
WLAN must have some form of Layer 2 802.1x or WPA and WPA2 security configured
for Conditional Web Redirect to function. For more information on the Conditional
Redirect feature, please refer to Cisco.com.

With code Release 5.0, another web authentication policy was added, Splash Page Web
Redirect. With Splash Page Web Redirect, the user is redirected to a particular web page
after successfully completing 802.1X authentication. Once the redirect is complete, the

user has full access to the network. You can specify the redirect page on a RADIUS server. If the RADIUS server returns the Cisco AV-pair "url-redirect," then the user is redirected to the specified URL upon opening a browser. Even if the RADIUS server does not return a "url-redirect," the user is considered fully authorized at this point and is allowed to pass traffic. Just like the Conditional Web Redirect policy, Splash Page Web Redirect requires 802.1x or WPA + WPA2 Layer 2 security.

For more information on both Conditional Web Redirect and Splash Page Redirect, please refer to the wireless controller configuration guides at www.cisco.com.

Web Authentication Types

Three types of web authentication exist:

- **Internal:** Default web page from the internal web server of the controller.

- **Custom:** Customized web page using the internal web server of the controller.

- **External:** Uses an external web server to provide a customized splash page.

You can make your selection from the WLC graphical user interface (GUI) under **SECURITY > Web Auth > Configuration**, as illustrated in Figure 14-4.

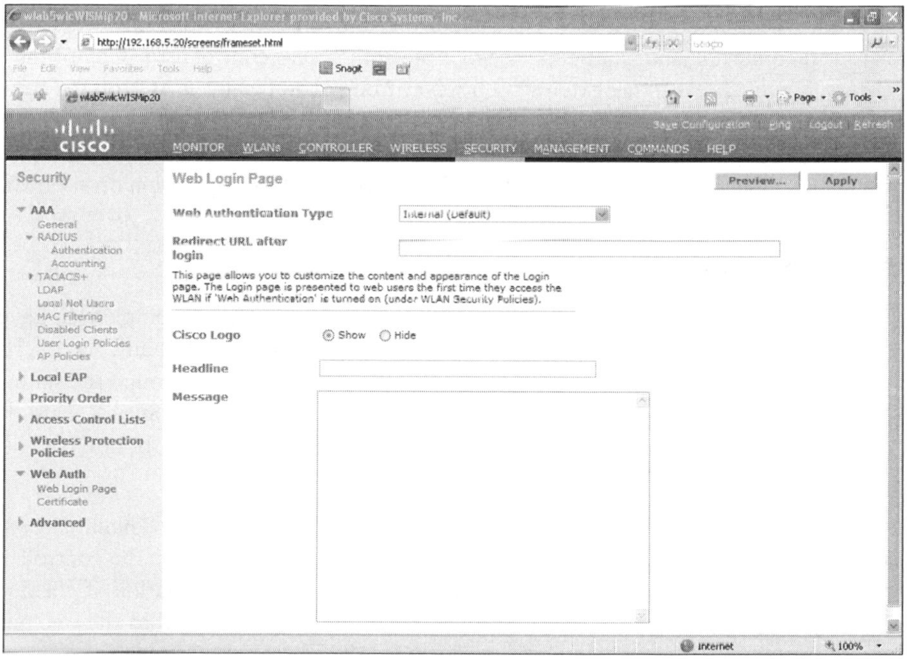

Figure 14-4   *Web Authentication Type Configuration*

If you want to use the most basic type, choose Internal web auth. Using Internal web auth allows you to hide the Cisco logo, enter a heading up to 127 characters, and enter up to 2047 characters of message text. If you want guest users to be redirected to a particular page after authentication, such as the company website, they can enter that address in the Redirect URL after login section.

> **Note**   Keep in mind that the redirect URL applies to all types of web authentication. In older code prior to 4.1.181.0, if you configured External or Custom web auth, the Redirect URL was not visible; the controller would still use that URL if configured.

Custom web auth allows you a lot more flexibility in the web auth splash page appearance. Using a web auth template login.html file, an HTML expert can modify the web auth splash page to include corporate logos, backgrounds, legalese, links to other pages, and so on within the custom web auth bundle. The web auth bundle is a GNU tar file that contains the HTML and GIF files. Custom web auth will be covered in more detail in the "Custom Web Auth Splash Pages" section later in this chapter.

If you want to use a network web server instead of the internal web server on the controller to service the web auth splash pages, select External web authentication and enter the address for the external web page. The use of the sample login.html file is required here as well to build the custom page that the network web server will use. Keep in mind that the external web server only provides the web page. The controller is still responsible for authenticating the guest user. The 2000, 2100, and WLCM series controllers have a hardware limitation and require the use of a pre-auth access control list (ACL) for the clients to gain access to the external web server. You would create an ACL on the controller allowing HTTP/HTTPs access to the external web server IP address and then apply that ACL under the Layer 3 Security under the WLAN configuration. Figure 14-3 shows the screen where you can access the Preauthentication ACL configuration drop-down list.

Web Authentication Process

Because web auth takes place at Layer 3, it only occurs after clients complete all Layer 2 authentications (WPA-PSK, static Wired Equivalent Privacy [WEP]), if any. As described in Chapter 10, "Troubleshooting Client-Related Issues," clients run through the state machine (see Figure 10-1). In that figure, you can see that web auth is State 8. This means that it happens after Layer 2 authentication and after DHCP-Required, but before clients enter the RUN state.

When clients associate to a web auth WLAN, they get an IP address, default gateway, and DNS server from DHCP. Web auth is the only security method on the controller that allows clients to obtain an IP before authentication. After association, if clients open a web browser and try to access a web page, they are redirected to the web auth splash page.

For this process to work, DNS resolution must be allowed on the guest VLAN. When a client browser opens a web page, that page has a friendly name, such as www.cisco.com. To the computer, however, it is really going to IP address 198.133.219.25. The client sends a DNS request and receives the DNS response telling it what IP to use. Without DNS, the client computer has no idea what IP address to send the HTTP GET to in order to pull up the www.cisco.com website. When the web server responds, the controller intercepts that packet and adds a URL redirect to either its own virtual interface IP address or that of the configured external web server so the guest client is presented with the web auth splash page.

The web authentication process is as follows:

Step 1.   The client enters the START machine state, completing any Layer 2 security if necessary.

Step 2.   After Layer 2 authentication state is complete, the client moves to DHCP-Required (DHCP_REQD).

Step 3.   The client receives IP, DNS, and so on from the DHCP server. The client opens the web browser and the PC sends a DNS query. In Figure 14-5 the client queries for webserver.lccsdesk.com.

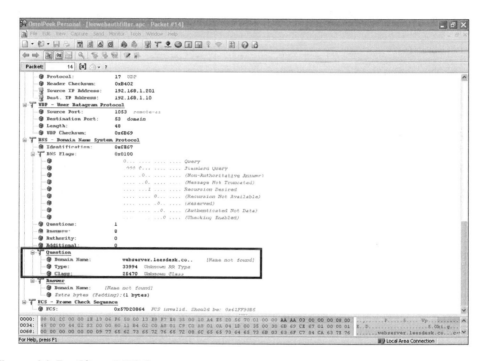

Figure 14-5   *Client DNS Query*

Step 4.   The controller forwards the DNS request.

Step 5.   The DNS server resolves webserver.leesdesk.com to 192.168.1.10 (see Figure 14-6).

Step 6.   The controller forwards the DNS reply.

Step 7.   The client sends HTTP GET to the web server, the destination host (see Figure 14-7). The client and the web server in this example are in the same domain, leesdesk.com.

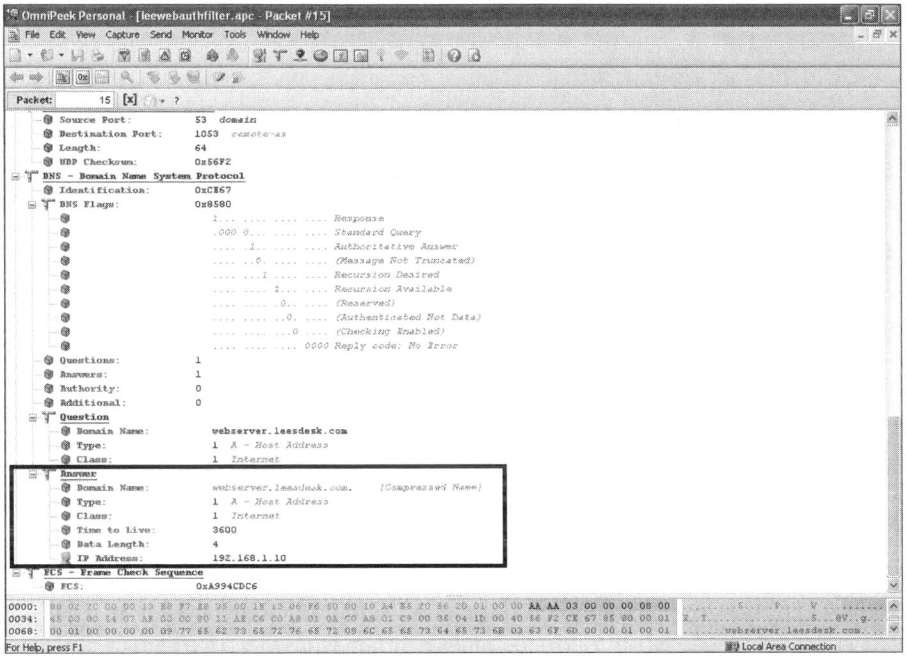

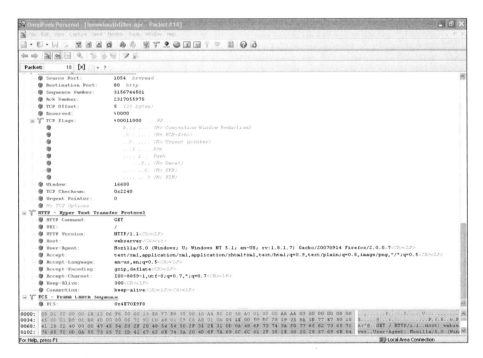

Figure 14-6 *DNS Response*

Figure 14-7 *Client HTTP GET*

Step 8.   The controller intercepts the returned web page from the destination web
server and sends a redirect to its own internal web server address
https://VIRTUAL-IP/login.html?redirect to the client. See Figure 14-8.

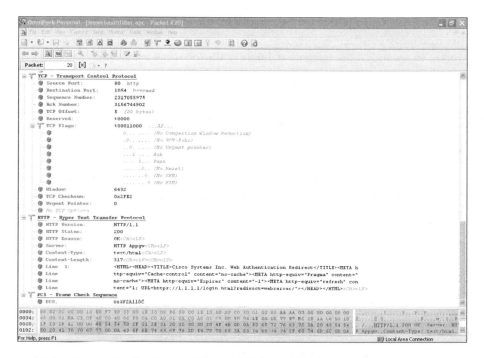

Figure 14-8   *Controller Redirect to Virtual IPAdress 1.1.1.1*

Step 9.   The client goes to the login page, passes web authentication, and enters the
RUN state on the controller.

Step 10.   The controller forwards the client browser to the original web page—
192.168.1.10/login.html.

Note   In this example the DNS server and the web host happen to be the same server.
That is why you see the same IP for both. Under non-lab conditions, these will typically
not be the same.

Before 4.0.206.0, a client associated to a web auth-enabled WLAN could sit indefinitely
without ever trying to authenticate. Knowing this, an attacker could initiate a denial-of-
service (DoS) attack on the guest network by using all the IP addresses in the DHCP
scope. To help mitigate this form of attack, Cisco added a web auth timeout. Should a

client associate and not authenticate after a 5-minute period, the controller will remove the client. The output of **debug client** *mac-addr* indicates when this time is reached:

```
Wed Feb 13 09:22:15 2009: 00:14:a5:d9:f6:d5 192.168.15.118 WEBAUTH_REQD (8) Web-
Auth Policy timeout
```

The web auth timeout value is not configurable, and until the 5.0 code release, you could not turn it off. In 5.0 and higher code, you can turn it off, but you must do that from the controller command-line interface (CLI) using the following command:

```
config wlan webauth-exclude WLAN ID disable
```

Troubleshooting Basic Web Authentication

Understanding how web auth works is key to troubleshooting it when it does not work. Common network issues that have nothing to do with wireless can stop web auth from working. The easiest way to test the guest WLAN is to remove the web auth security setting and see if the client can access the Internet. If it cannot, a network issue is likely to blame. You can also try performing an nslookup from the client or using the IP instead of the web address to see if the client gets the redirect page. If the DNS lookup fails but using the IP address works, the DNS is an issue. To verify that the redirect page on the controller is working, you can also enter https://1.1.1.1/login.html assuming that the IP of the virtual interface on the controller is 1.1.1.1.

The following is a list of common problems that can break web authentication:

■ The guest VLAN is not allowed on the controller trunk port.

■ The guest VLAN is not routed on the network.

■ DNS is blocked by a firewall or network ACLs.

■ The client is configured to use a proxy server. You might be able to make web auth work in conjunction with a network proxy server by performing the following two actions:

1. Add an exception to the client proxy configuration in the browser for the virtual interface IP address of the controller. The user must be a local admin to make this change. Keep in mind that corporate policies might not allow a user to change proxy settings.

2. Use the following command to add the proxy port (in this case port 8080) to the web auth redirect from the controller CLI:

```
config network web-auth-port proxy port
```

You must save and reboot for this to take effect. The output of the **show network summary** command will confirm the configuration:

```
(WLC1) >show network summary

RF-Network Name........................... West
```

```
Web Mode.................................. Enable
Secure Web Mode........................... Enable
Secure Web Mode Cipher-Option High......... Disable
Secure Web Mode Cipher-Option SSLv2........ Enable
Secure Shell (ssh)........................ Enable
Telnet.................................... Enable
Ethernet Multicast Mode................... Disable
Ethernet Broadcast Mode................... Disable
AP Multicast Mode......................... Unicast
IGMP snooping............................. Disabled
IGMP timeout.............................. 60 seconds
User Idle Timeout......................... 300 seconds
ARP Idle Timeout.......................... 300 seconds
Cisco AP Default Master................... Disable
AP Join Priority.......................... Enabled
Mgmt Via Wireless Interface............... Disable
Mgmt Via Dynamic Interface................ Disable
Bridge MAC filter Config.................. Enable
Bridge Security Mode...................... EAP
Mesh Full Sector DFS...................... Enable
—More— or (q)uit
Over The Air Provisioning of AP's......... Disable
Apple Talk ............................... Disable
AP Fallback .............................. Enable
Web Auth Redirect Ports .................. 80,8080
Fast SSID Change ......................... Disabled
802.3 Bridging ........................... Disable
IP/MAC Addr Binding Check ................ Enabled
```

■   The client browser does not, allow redirects. From Internet Explorer, **Tools > Internet Options > Security > Custom > Allow META-Refresh** should be enabled.

■   There is no DHCP on the guest VLAN.

- The client home page is HTTPS; HTTPS is not currently supported with web auth for the redirect. Hopefully this limitation will be removed in a future code release.

- A 2000 or 2100 series controller and external web authentication are used, but pre-auth ACL is missing or incorrect.

Debug information can be useful in determining where the redirect issue might lie if you have verified the underlying network configuration. The debug output is more informative with newer controller codes. Using these debugs, you can see the policy manager state of the client, whether the client received an IP address, the redirect, and so on. The most useful debugs for web auth are as follows:

- **debug mac addr** *client-MAC-address xx:xx:xx:xx:xx:xx*: Filters the output of other debugs based on the client MAC address.

- **debug aaa all enable:** Debugs authentication.

- **debug pem state enable:** Debugs policy manager State Machine.

- **debug pem events enable:** Debugs policy manager events.

- **debug dhcp message enable:** Debugs DHCP messages.

- **debug dhcp packet enable:** Debugs DHCP packets.

- **debug pm ssh-appgw enable:** Debugs application gateways.

- **debug pm ssh-tcp enable:** Debugs policy manager TCP handling.

Example 14-1 provides sample debug output of a successful web auth process using web authentication to the local user database or the controller.

Example 14-1 *Successful Web Authentication Debug Output*

```
! ! Client associates and is in DHCP_REQ state
Mon Sep 22 13:37:19 2008: 00:40:96:a1:4a:f6 Adding mobile on LWAPP AP
00:0b:85:65:59:10(1)
Mon Sep 22 13:37:19 2008: 00:40:96:a1:4a:f6 Scheduling deletion of Mobile Station:
(callerId: 23) in 5 seconds
Mon Sep 22 13:37:19 2008: 00:40:96:a1:4a:f6 apfProcessProbeReq (apf_80211.c:4072)
Changing state for mobile 00:40:96:a1:4a:f6 on AP 00:0b:85:65:59:10 from Idle to
Probe
Mon Sep 22 13:37:21 2008: 00:40:96:a1:4a:f6 Scheduling deletion of Mobile Station:
(callerId: 24) in 5 seconds
Mon Sep 22 13:37:21 2008: 00:40:96:a1:4a:f6 Scheduling deletion of Mobile Station:
(callerId: 24) in 5 seconds
Mon Sep 22 13:37:23 2008: 00:40:96:a1:4a:f6 Scheduling deletion of Mobile Station:
(callerId: 24) in 5 seconds
Mon Sep 22 13:37:23 2008: 00:40:96:a1:4a:f6 Association received from mobile on AP
00:0b:85:65:59:10
Mon Sep 22 13:37:23 2008: 00:40:96:a1:4a:f6 STA - rates (4): 2 4 11 22 0 0 0 0 0
0 0 0 0 0 0
```

```
Mon Sep 22 13:37:23 2008: 00:40:96:a1:4a:f6 0.0.0.0 START (0) Initializing policy
Mon Sep 22 13:37:23 2008: 00:40:96:a1:4a:f6 0.0.0.0 START (0) Change state to
AUTHCHECK (2) last state AUTHCHECK (2)
Mon Sep 22 13:37:23 2008: 00:40:96:a1:4a:f6 0.0.0.0 AUTHCHECK (2) Change state to
L2AUTHCOMPLETE (4) last state L2AUTHCOMPLETE (4)
Mon Sep 22 13:37:23 2008: 00:40:96:a1:4a:f6 0.0.0.0 L2AUTHCOMPLETE (4) Plumbed
mobile LWAPP rule on AP 00:0b:85:65:59:10
Mon Sep 22 13:37:23 2008: 00:40:96:a1:4a:f6 0.0.0.0 L2AUTHCOMPLETE (4) Change
state to DHCP_REQD (7) last state DHCP_REQD (7)
Mon Sep 22 13:37:23 2008: 00:40:96:a1:4a:f6 apfPemAddUser2 (apf_policy.c:209)
Changing state for mobile 00:40:96:a1:4a:f6 on AP 00:0b:85:65:59:10 from Probe to
Associated
Mon Sep 22 13:37:23 2008: 00:40:96:a1:4a:f6 Stopping deletion of Mobile Station:
(callerId: 48)
Mon Sep 22 13:37:23 2008: 00:40:96:a1:4a:f6 Sending Assoc Response to station on
BSSID 00:0b:85:65:59:10 (status 0)
Mon Sep 22 13:37:23 2008: 00:40:96:a1:4a:f6 apfProcessAssocReq (apf_80211.c:3853)
Changing state for mobile 00:40:96:a1:4a:f6 on AP 00:0b:85:65:59:10 from
Associated to Associated
Mon Sep 22 13:37:23 2008: 00:40:96:a1:4a:f6 0.0.0.0 DHCP_REQD (7) State Update
from Mobility-Incomplete to Mobility-Complete, mobility role=Local
Mon Sep 22 13:37:23 2008: 00:40:96:a1:4a:f6 0.0.0.0 DHCP_REQD (7) pemAdvanceState2
3949, Adding TMP rule
Mon Sep 22 13:37:23 2008: 00:40:96:a1:4a:f6 0.0.0.0 DHCP_REQD (7) Adding Fast
Path rule
  type = Airspace AP - Learn IP address
  on AP 00:0b:85:65:59:10, slot 1, interface = 29, QOS = 0
  ACL Id = 255, Jumbo Frames = NO, 802.1P = 0, DSCP = 0, TokenID = 5006
Mon Sep 22 13:37:23 2008: 00:40:96:a1:4a:f6 0.0.0.0 DHCP_REQD (7) Successfully
plumbed mobile rule (ACL ID 255)
Mon Sep 22 13:37:23 2008: 00:40:96:a1:4a:f6 0.0.0.0 Added NPU entry of type 9
! output omitted for brevity
! Client receives an IP and the controller places them into WEBAUTH_REQ
Mon Sep 22 13:37:24 2008: 00:40:96:a1:4a:f6 DHCP received op BOOTREPLY (2) (len
308, port 29, encap 0xec00)
Mon Sep 22 13:37:24 2008: 00:40:96:a1:4a:f6 DHCP option len (including the magic
cookie) 72
Mon Sep 22 13:37:24 2008: 00:40:96:a1:4a:f6 DHCP option: message type = DHCP ACK
Mon Sep 22 13:37:24 2008: 00:40:96:a1:4a:f6 DHCP option: 58 (len 4) - skipping
Mon Sep 22 13:37:24 2008: 00:40:96:a1:4a:f6 DHCP option: 59 (len 4) - skipping
Mon Sep 22 13:37:24 2008: 00:40:96:a1:4a:f6 DHCP option: lease time = 3600 seconds
Mon Sep 22 13:37:24 2008: 00:40:96:a1:4a:f6 DHCP option: server id = 192.168.1.20
Mon Sep 22 13:37:24 2008: 00:40:96:a1:4a:f6 DHCP option: netmask = 255.255.255.0
Mon Sep 22 13:37:24 2008: 00:40:96:a1:4a:f6 DHCP option: 15 (len 12) - skipping
Mon Sep 22 13:37:24 2008: 00:40:96:a1:4a:f6 DHCP option: gateway = 192.168.5.1
Mon Sep 22 13:37:24 2008: 00:40:96:a1:4a:f6 DHCP option: DNS server, cnt = 1,
first = 192.168.1.20
Mon Sep 22 13:37:24 2008: 00:40:96:a1:4a:f6 DHCP options end, len 72, actual 64
```

(continues)

Example 14-1 *Success Web Authentication Debug (continued)*

```
Mon Sep 22 13:37:24 2008: 00:40:96:a1:4a:f6 DHCP setting server from ACK (server
192.168.1.20, yiaddr 192.168.5.161)
Mon Sep 22 13:37:24 2008: 00:40:96:a1:4a:f6 192.168.5.161 DHCP_REQD (7) Change
state to WEBAUTH_REQD (8) last state WEBAUTH_REQD (8)
Mon Sep 22 13:37:24 2008: 00:40:96:a1:4a:f6 192.168.5.161 WEBAUTH_REQD (8)
pemAdvanceState2 4616, Adding TMP rule
Mon Sep 22 13:37:24 2008: 00:40:96:a1:4a:f6 192.168.5.161 WEBAUTH_REQD (8)
Replacing Fast Path rule
  type = Airespace AP Client - ACL passthru
  on AP 00:0b:85:65:59:10, slot 1, interface = 29, QOS = 0
  ACL Id = 255, Jumbo Frames = NO, 802.1P = 0, DSCP = 0, TokenID = 5006
Mon Sep 22 13:37:24 2008: 00:40:96:a1:4a:f6 192.168.5.161 WEBAUTH_REQD (8)
Successfully plumbed mobile rule (ACL ID 255)
! output omitted for brevity
! Client opens an Internet Browser and tries to access a web page at
192.168.5.151
Mon Sep 22 13:37:28 2008: SshPmAppgw/pm_appgw.c:1234/ssh_pm_appgw_request: New
application gateway request for `alg-http 192.168.5.161.2708 > 192.168.5.151.80
(nat: 192.168.5.151.80) tcp ft=0x00000000 tt=0x00000000
Mon Sep 22 13:37:28 2008: SshPmAppgw/pm_appgw.c:1239/ssh_pm_appgw_request: Packet
attributes: trigger_rule=0x4ebf, tunnel_id=0x0, trd_index=0xddffffff,
prev_trd_index=0xddffffff
Mon Sep 22 13:37:28 2008: SshPmAppgw/pm_appgw.c:1240/ssh_pm_appgw_request: Packet:
Mon Sep 22 13:37:28 2008: 00000000: 4500 0030 0340 4000 8006 6aff c0a8 05a1
E..0.@@...j.....
Mon Sep 22 13:37:28 2008: 00000010: c0a8 0597 0a94 0050 73f6 f8d2 0000 0000
.......Ps.......
Mon Sep 22 13:37:28 2008: 00000020: 7002 4000 3ee9 0000 0204 05b4 0101 0402
p.@.>..........
Mon Sep 22 13:37:28 2008: SshPmStAppgw/pm_st_appgw.c:403/ssh_pm_st_appgw_start:
Calling redirection callback
Mon Sep 22 13:37:28 2008: SshPmAppgw/pm_appgw.c:155/ssh_appgw_redirect:
Application gateway redirect: 192.168.5.151.80 -> 192.168.5.151.80
Mon Sep 22 13:37:28 2008: SshPmStAppgw/pm_st_appgw.c:445/ssh_pm_st_appgw_mappings:
Creating application gateway mappings: 192.168.5.161.2708 > 192.168.5.151.80
(192.168.5.151.80)
Mon Sep 22 13:37:28 2008: SshPmStAppgw/pm_st_appgw.c:102/ssh_pm_appgw_mappings_cb:
appgw connection cached: init flow_index=5850 resp flow_index=5849 event_cnt=379
Mon Sep 22 13:37:28 2008: SshPmStAppgw/pm_st_appgw.c:493/ssh_pm_st_appgw_map-
pings_done: NAT on initiator side
Mon Sep 22 13:37:28 2008:
SshPmStAppgw/pm_st_appgw.c:583/ssh_pm_st_appgw_tcp_responder_stream_done:
ssh_pm_st_appgw_tcp_responder_stream_done: conn->context.responder_stream=0x0
Mon Sep 22 13:37:28 2008:
SshPmStAppgw/pm_st_appgw.c:624/ssh_pm_st_appgw_tcp_responder_stream_done: Opening
initiator stream 192.168.5.151:47696 > 192.168.5.30:2006
Mon Sep 22 13:37:28 2008:
SshPmStAppgw/pm_st_appgw.c:154/ssh_pm_appgw_i_flow_enabled: Initiator flow mode
has now been set.
```

```
Mon Sep 22 13:37:28 2008: 00:40:96:a1:4a:f6 Orphan Packet from 192.168.5.161 on
mobile
Mon Sep 22 13:37:28 2008: 00:40:96:a1:4a:f6 Invalid MSCB state:
ipAddr=192.168.5.161, regType=2, Dhcp required!
Mon Sep 22 13:37:28 2008: SshPmAppgw/pm_appgw.c:507/ssh_appgw_tcp_listener_call-
back: New initiator stream: src=192.168.5.151:47696, dst=192.168.5.30:2006
Mon Sep 22 13:37:28 2008:
SshPmStAppgw/pm_st_appgw.c:646/ssh_pm_st_appgw_tcp_open_initiator_stream: Initiator
stream opened
Mon Sep 22 13:37:28 2008: SshAppgwHttp/appgw_http.c:531/ssh_appgw_http_conn_cb:
New TCP HTTP connection 192.168.5.161.2708 > 192.168.5.151.80
Mon Sep 22 13:37:28 2008: SshAppgwHttp/appgw_http.c:535/ssh_appgw_http_conn_cb:
Responder sees initiator as `192.168.5.30.2708'
Mon Sep 22 13:37:28 2008: SshAppgwHttp/appgw_http.c:539/ssh_appgw_http_conn_cb:
Initiator sees responder as `192.168.5.151.80'
Mon Sep 22 13:37:28 2008:
SshAppgwHttp/appgw_http.c:99/ssh_appgw_http_st_wait_input: entering state
st_wait_input: (i) reading_hdr 1 nmsgs 0
Mon Sep 22 13:37:28 2008:
SshAppgwHttpState/appgw_http_state.c:2077/ssh_appgw_http_handle_state: handling: 0
bytes:
Mon Sep 22 13:37:28 2008:
SshAppgwHttp/appgw_http.c:136/ssh_appgw_http_st_wait_input: read -1 bytes (offset
0 data 0)
Mon Sep 22 13:37:28 2008:
SshAppgwHttp/appgw_http.c:99/ssh_appgw_http_st_wait_input: entering state
st_wait_input: (r) reading_hdr 1 nmsgs 0
Mon Sep 22 13:37:28 2008:
SshAppgwHttpState/appgw_http_state.c:2077/ssh_appgw_http_handle_state: handling: 0
bytes:
Mon Sep 22 13:37:28 2008:
SshAppgwHttp/appgw_http.c:132/ssh_appgw_http_st_wait_input: appgw_http.c.132: io-
>src is NULL
Mon Sep 22 13:37:28 2008:
SshAppgwHttp/appgw_http.c:136/ssh_appgw_http_st_wait_input: read -1 bytes (offset
0 data 0)
Mon Sep 22 13:37:28 2008:
SshAppgwHttp/appgw_http.c:99/ssh_appgw_http_st_wait_input: entering state
st_wait_input: (i) reading_hdr 1 nmsgs 0
Mon Sep 22 13:37:28 2008:
SshAppgwHttpState/appgw_http_state.c:2077/ssh_appgw_http_handle_state: handling: 0
bytes:
Mon Sep 22 13:37:28 2008:
SshAppgwHttp/appgw_http.c:136/ssh_appgw_http_st_wait_input: read 240 bytes (offset
0 data 0)
! output omitted for brevity
! Here you see the HTTP GET from the client
Mon Sep 22 13:37:28 2008: 00000000: 4745 5420 2f20 4854 5450 2f31 2e31 0d0a  GET
/ HTTP/1.1..
Mon Sep 22 13:37:28 2008: 00000010: 4163 6365 7074 3a20 2a2f 2a0d 0a41 6363
Accept: */*..Acc
```

(continues)

Example 14-1   *Success Web Authentication Debug (continued)*

```
Mon Sep 22 13:37:28 2008: 00000020: 6570 742d 4c61 6e67 7561 6765 3a20 656e  ept-
Language: en
Mon Sep 22 13:37:28 2008: 00000030: 2d75 730d 0a41 6363 6570 742d 456e 636f  -
us..Accept-Enco
Mon Sep 22 13:37:28 2008: 00000040: 6469 6e67 3a20 677a 6970 2c20 6465 666c
ding: gzip, defl
Mon Sep 22 13:37:28 2008: 00000050: 6174 650d 0a55 7365 722d 4167 656e 743a
ate..User-Agent:
Mon Sep 22 13:37:28 2008: 00000060: 204d 6f7a 696c 6c61 2f34 2e30 2028 636f
Mozilla/4.0 (co
Mon Sep 22 13:37:28 2008: 00000070: 6d70 6174 6962 6c65 3b20 4d53 4945 2036
mpatible; MSIE 6
Mon Sep 22 13:37:28 2008: 00000080: 2e30 3b20 5769 6e64 6f77 7320 4e54 2035  .0;
Windows NT 5
Mon Sep 22 13:37:28 2008: 00000090: 2e31 3b20 5356 313b 202e 4e45 5420 434c  .1;
SV1; .NET CL
Mon Sep 22 13:37:28 2008: 000000a0: 5220 322e 302e 3530 3732 373b 202e 4e45  R
2.0.50727; .NE
Mon Sep 22 13:37:28 2008: 000000b0: 5420 434c 5220 312e 312e 3433 3232 290d  T
CLR 1.1.4322).
Mon Sep 22 13:37:28 2008: 000000c0: 0a48 6f73 743a 2031 3932 2e31 3638 2e35
.Host: 192.168.5
Mon Sep 22 13:37:28 2008: 000000d0: 2e31 3531 0d0a 436f 6e6e 6563 7469 6f6e
.151..Connection
Mon Sep 22 13:37:28 2008: 000000e0: 3a20 4b65 6570 2d41 6c69 7665 0d0a 0d0a  :
Keep-Alive....
Mon Sep 22 13:37:28 2008: SshAppgwHttpState/appgw_http_state.c:985/ssh_appgw_parse
_request_line: parsing request line GET / HTTP/1.1
Mon Sep 22 13:37:28 2008:
SshAppgwHttpState/appgw_http_state.c:1018/ssh_appgw_parse_request_line: internal
http version 3
Mon Sep 22 13:37:28 2008:
SshAppgwHttpState/appgw_http_state.c:1155/ssh_appgw_add_method: caching method 2
for reply 0
Mon Sep 22 13:37:28 2008:
SshAppgwHttpState/appgw_http_state.c:1604/ssh_appgw_check_msg: examining request
using service id 10
Mon Sep 22 13:37:28 2008:
SshAppgwHttpState/appgw_http_state.c:594/ssh_appgw_http_get_dst_host: destination
host: 192.168.5.151
! output omitted for brevity
! Here is the HTTP redirect and the guest user, fred, is authenticated
Mon Sep 22 13:37:35 2008: SshAppgwHttp/appgw_http.c:732/ssh_appgw_http_connec-
tion_terminate: service HTTP-REDIR: TCP HTTP connection 192.168.5.161.2708 >
192.168.5.151.80 terminated
Mon Sep 22 13:37:35 2008: SshPmStAppgw/pm_st_appgw.c:1094/ssh_pm_st_appgw termi-
nate: terminating appgw instance
Mon Sep 22 13:37:52 2008: 00:40:96:a1:4a:f6 Username entry (fred) created for
mobile
Mon Sep 22 13:37:52 2008: User fred authenticated
```

```
Mon Sep 22 13:37:52 2008: 00:40:96:a1:4a:f6 Returning AAA Success for mobile
00:40:96:a1:4a:f6
! output omitted for brevity
! Client is moved into RUN state
Mon Sep 22 13:37:52 2008: 00:40:96:a1:4a:f6 192.168.5.161 WEBAUTH_REQD (8) Change
state to WEBAUTH_NOL3SEC (14) last state WEBAUTH_NOL3SEC (14)
Mon Sep 22 13:37:52 2008: 00:40:96:a1:4a:f6 192.168.5.161 WEBAUTH_NOL3SEC (14)
Change state to RUN (20) last state RUN (20)
Mon Sep 22 13:37:52 2008: 00:40:96:a1:4a:f6 Session Timeout is 0 - not starting
session timer for the mobile
Mon Sep 22 13:37:52 2008: 00:40:96:a1:4a:f6 192.168.5.161 RUN (20) Reached PLUMB-
FASTPATH: from line 4536
Mon Sep 22 13:37:52 2008: 00:40:96:a1:4a:f6 192.168.5.161 RUN (20) Replacing Fast
Path rule
  type = Airespace AP Client
  on AP 00:0b:85:65:59:10, slot 1, interface = 29, QOS = 0
  ACL Id = 255, Jumbo Frames = NO, 802.1P = 0, DSCP = 0,    TokenID = 5006
```

Tip   When you upgrade controller code to 4.2.173.0 or higher, SSLv2 might become disabled and SSLv3 is only accepted by the controller for both web auth and administrative
access. You can see if SSLv2 is enabled using the command **show network summary**.
Some Internet browsers—Microsoft Internet Explorer 6 in particular—need to be configured to support SSLv3 because they may not by default. In this case, an IE 6 client, for
example, will receive a "404 Page cannot be displayed" message, whereas another browser
such as Firefox will work with no issues. If you run into this issue, you can enable SSLv2
on the controller from the CLI using the following command, saving, and rebooting:

```
config network secureweb cipher-option sslv2 enable
```

RADIUS and LDAP Authentication with Web Auth

If you want guest users to have to enter a valid username and password before gaining
network access and do not want to use the local user database on the controller, you can
set up a RADIUS server or connect directly to an LDAP server. This allows the guest user
account to be managed by someone other than the wireless engineers. The domain
administrator or other user with account management privileges on the network can manage the account and determine password changes, expiration dates, and so on.

It is important to remember that the controller checks the local user database first when
authenticating users. Should you have the same username in the local database as that of
the client on the RADIUS server and the password on the controller is incorrect, the user
will never pass authentication because the controller will not forward the request to the
RADIUS server after an access reject from the local database. You can configure the
order of Local, RADIUS, and LDAP that the WLAN should use for web auth.

If you have global RADIUS servers defined, the Network User option is selected (see Figure 14-9) on the controller, and the guest name does not exist in the local database, the controller sends a RADIUS request to the global RADIUS servers.

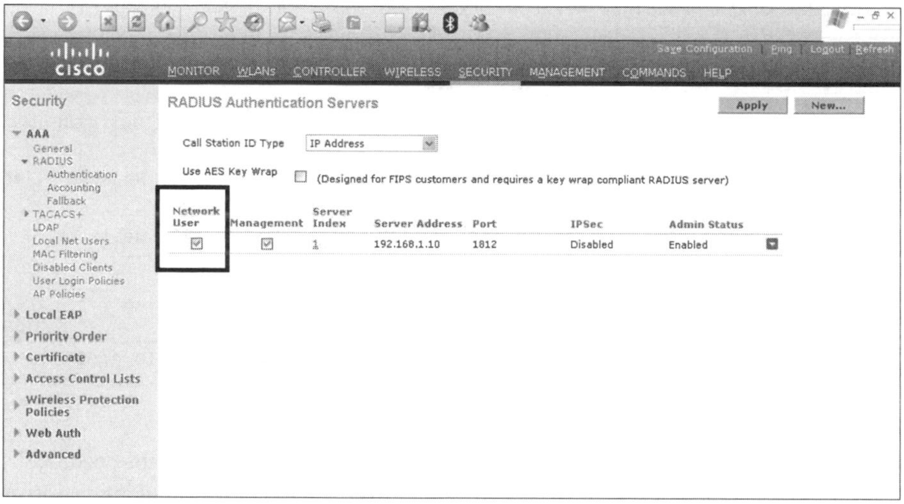

Figure 14-9   *RADIUS Configuration for Network User*

If you never want the controller to send a RADIUS request to an external RADIUS server that is configured on the controller, you can use the following commands from the controller CLI:

```
config wlan disable WLAN-id
config wlan RADIUS_server auth disable WLAN-id
config wlan enable WLAN-id
```

With auto-anchoring (discussed later in the chapter), the Anchor controller needs to be configured as a RADIUS client on the RADIUS server. Add the Management address of the Anchor controller as a AAA-Client on the AAA server in use.

Make sure you configure the Web RADIUS Authentication setting under CONTROLLER > General to match the supported protocol of your RADIUS server (see Figure 14-10).

If the RADIUS server is behind a network firewall, you need to make sure that the proper User Datagram Protocol (UDP) ports are open between the RADIUS server and the management interface of the controller. RADIUS servers typically use UDP port 1812/1645 for authentication messages and UDP port 1813/1646 for accounting messages, but you can change those ports on the server if you like.

Hybrid Remote Edge Access Point (H-REAP)–enabled APs (see Chapter 13, "H-REAP") also support RADIUS authentication with web auth. In a configuration in which the guest WLAN is H-REAP enabled, this would be central authentication with local switching. If the WLAN was not H-REAP enabled, you would have a central authentication with central switching configuration. Keep in mind that web auth is not supported when an H-REAP access point (AP) goes into standalone mode. When an H-REAP AP enters standalone modes, it implies that the AP has lost network connectivity to the controller. In this situation, there is no way for the controller to authenticate the guest user.

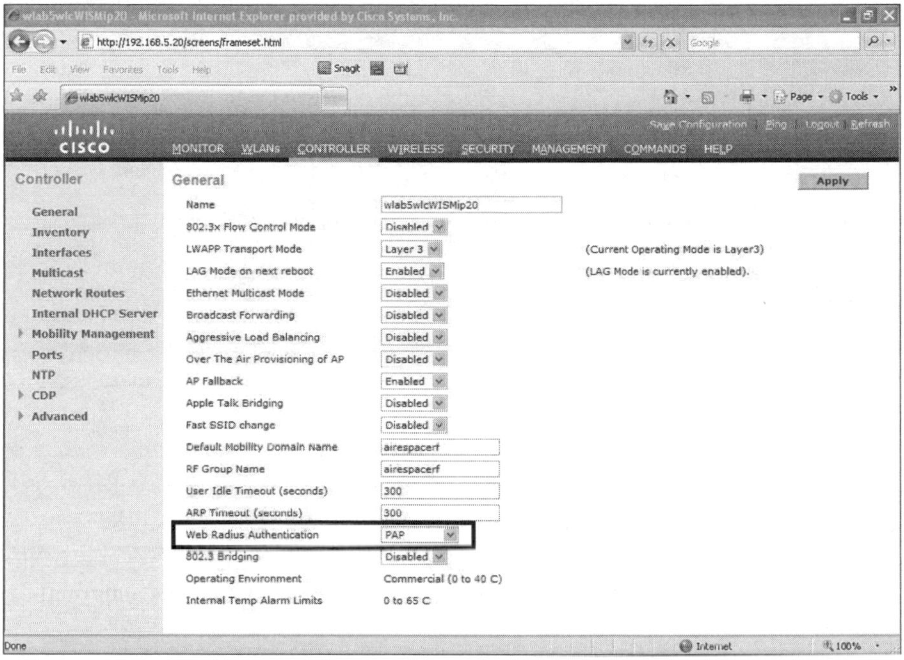

Figure 14-10 *Web RADIUS Authentication Protocol*

In the debug output from **debug aaa all enable**, you will want to look for access-accepts, access-rejects, server timeouts, and failed messages when using RADIUS authentication.

The 5.0 version of code introduced LDAP support for web authentication. The configuration of the controller for LDAP is quite simple. This is done by going to **SECURITY > AAA > LDAP** (see Figure 14-11), filling in the appropriate information for the LDAP server, and enabling it.

If you are unclear on the user base distinguished name, attribute, and object type, you can use an LDAP explorer program. You have numerous options, from high-end applications you can purchase to free programs on the Internet, that will show this information in the LDAP directory. Then on the AAA Servers tab for the guest WLAN, select the LDAP server you want you use.

The caveat with LDAP and web auth in earlier code is that the LDAP server must accept anonymous bind and pass the password in clear text. The controller cannot decrypt encrypted LDAP packets. In the 5.1 and higher code releases, authenticated binding is supported. A future code release will add support for LDAP using Secure Socket Layer (SSL), LDAP-S. For security and best practice purposes, you will want to set the base

Distinguished Name (DN) for searching for guest user accounts to a branch that is dedicated to guest users. By doing so, you prevent a corporate user from authenticating on the guest network and perhaps allowing them to circumvent company web use practices.

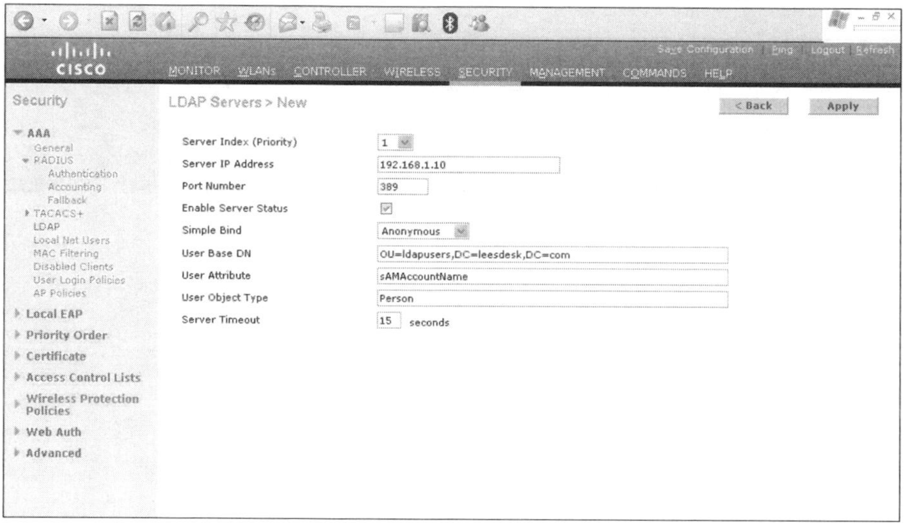

Figure 14-11   *LDAP Configuration*

You can verify your LDAP configuration using the following CLI commands on the controller:

■ **show ldap summary:** Displays a summary of the configured LDAP servers.

■ **show ldap detailed** *index*: Displays detailed LDAP server information.

■ **show ldap statistics:** Displays LDAP server statistics.

■ **show wlan** *wlan_id*: Displays the LDAP servers that are applied to a WLAN.

As with RADIUS authentication, you would be looking for success, rejects, timeouts, and failed messages in the web auth debugs if there is a problem with LDAP user authentications. Example 14-2 is a partial debug output showing a successful LDAP bind. You can also use wired sniffer captures to see the LDAP communication between the controller and the LDAP server if there is a problem.

Example 14-2   *Successful LDAP Bind*

```
*Jun 19 15:16:10.309: ldapAuthRequest [1] called lcapi_query base=
   "OU-ldapusers,DC=leesdesk,DC=com" type-"Person" attr="sAMAccountName"
   user="fred" (rc = 0 - Success)
*Jun 19 15:16:10.309: Attempting user bind with username
```

```
   CN=fred,OU=ldapusers,DC=leesdesk,DC=com
*Jun 19 15:16:10.335: LDAP ATTR> dn = CN=fred,OU=ldapusers,
   DC=leesdesk,DC=com (size 41)
*Jun 19 15:16:10.335: Handling LDAP response Success
*Jun 19 15:16:10.335: 00:40:96:a1:4a:f6  Returning AAA
   Success for mobile 00:40:96:a1:4a:f6
```

Guest User Accounts

Guest user accounts can reside locally on the controller, on an Access Control Server (ACS), or on a network domain controller. You can create the account on the controller using a read-write account from the CLI, the GUI (see Figure 14-12), or WCS. With WCS you can create guest users and schedule start and end dates and times for the guest account to be valid on the network. A guest user account created directly on the controller, not through WCS, is limited to a lifespan of 30 days. With WCS, you can schedule a guest user account to be valid up to 90 days.

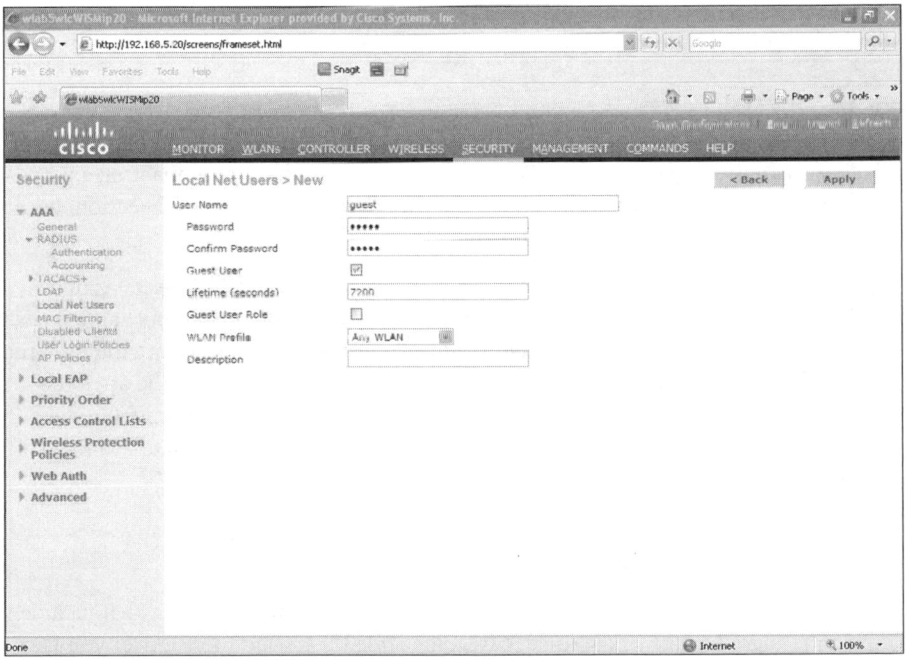

Figure 14-12   *Guest User Creation*

Using QoS roles, you can limit the download speeds based on the guest user account (see Figure 14-13). QoS roles have no impact on client upload speeds. Assigning a QoS role to a guest account prevents any user logged in with that account from using the same level of bandwidth as a regular user.

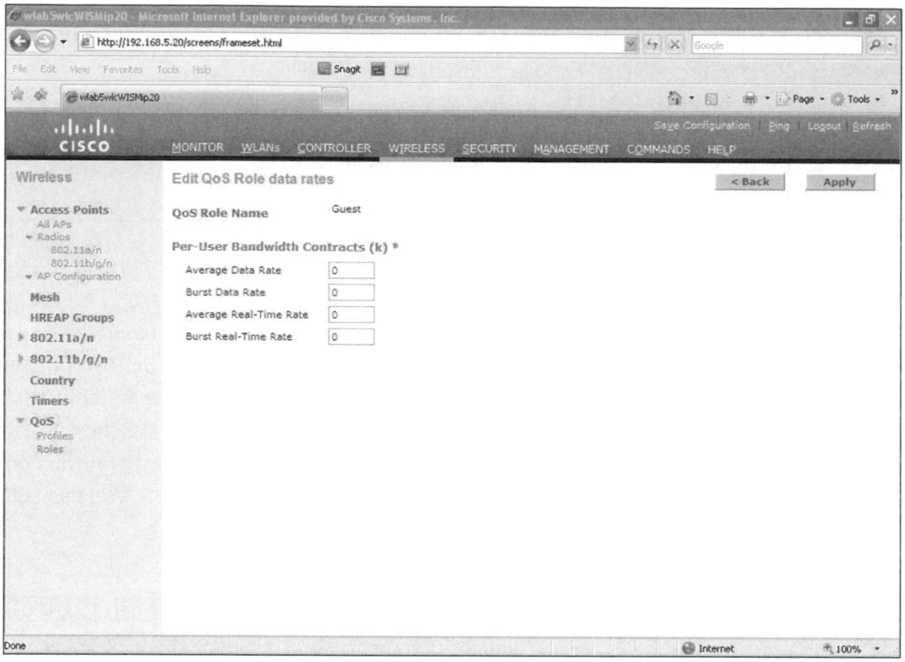

Figure 14-13 *QoS Roles*

QoS roles apply only to wireless guest user accounts and have no impact on a wired guest user (discussed later in this chapter in the "Wired Guest Access" section) because wired guest user traffic never traverses an AP.

It is also important to note that if you are authenticating your guest users against a RADIUS server and want to apply QoS roles to those accounts, you must assign the QoS role on the RADIUS server. You need to add a "guest-role" Airespace attribute on the RADIUS server with a datatype of "string" and a return value of 11. The attribute is sent to the controller during authentication. If a role with the name returned from the RADIUS server is configured on the controller, the bandwidth associated to that role is enforced for the guest user after successful authentication.

Custom Web Auth Splash Pages

Custom web auth splash pages allow you to create elaborate web pages that include your corporate logo, backgrounds, fonts, cascading style sheets and more. After you have created your HTML pages, you tar them up in a GNU standard tar file with your image files into a web auth bundle.

The main file in the web auth bundle is the login.html file. This file contains the HTML code for the Submit button that returns the control codes to the controller so it can process the authentication. You can get this code by copying it from the controller configurations guide web authentication chapter, downloading the login.tar file from WCS, or downloading sample custom web auth bundles from Cisco.com. Figure 14-2 shows a sample login.html page.

> **Tip** Copying the web auth page HTML code directly from the configuration guide does not work very well. The formatting of the page seems to have jumbled the Java code strings. Furthermore, the Submit button might not work correctly, and the user will never get past the splash page. The best practice is to use the sample files in the login.html from WCS or custom bundles files found on the Cisco website to avoid that issue.

The important thing to remember when creating the custom login.html file is not to edit the coding for the Submit button. You can change the text of the button so it says "Accept" or "I agree," for example, but an HTML expert should create the page because Cisco Technical Assistance Center (TAC) does not support the coding of a custom web auth page. Should you edit the sample file and it not work correctly, it is up to you to figure out why.

Web auth bundle guidelines include the following:

■ Name the login page login.html. The controller prepares the web authentication URL based on this name. If it does not find this file after the web auth bundle has been untarred, the bundle is discarded, and an error message appears.

■ Include input fields for both a username and password if you are creating a page for a WLAN with authentication. Passthrough does not require these fields. If you are using email input, you need to include a username/email field.

■ Retain the redirect URL as a hidden input item after extracting from the original URL.

■ Extract and set the action URL in the page from the original URL.

■ Include scripts to decode the return status code.

■ Make sure that all paths used in the main page (to refer to images, for example) are of relative type.

■ The maximum allowed total size of the files in their uncompressed state is 1 MB.

Global Override

Before the 4.2 release of controller code, every web auth-enabled WLAN on the controller displayed the same redirect page. With the addition of the global override feature and the support for 512 WLANs starting with the 5.2 code release, you now can configure up to 517 (512 WLAN and 5 Guest LAN) different splash pages. You would place all the different HTML pages, logos, and so on in a single web auth bundle. At least one of the HTML pages must be named login.html. The controller will use this file for the default web auth page. You can use more meaningful filenames, such as lobby.html or westguest.html, for the others.

When configuring web auth security for the guest WLAN, you will see the Override Global Config feature check box as illustrated in Figure 14-14. Select this and then choose the web auth policy and the desired login file.

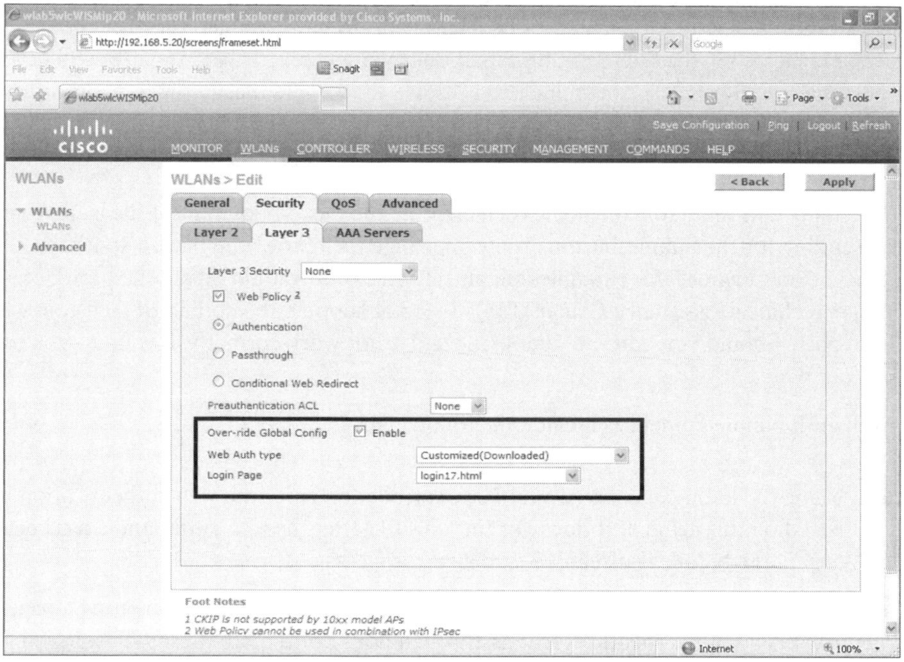

Figure 14-14   *Configuring Global Override*

Browser Security Warning

In a default configuration, the controller uses a self-signed certificate for the HTTPS redirect page. This causes the client browser to throw up a security alert about the validity of the website. To prevent your guest clients from receiving this warning, you have a couple of options.

The first option is one that most will not choose because it requires disabling SSL on the controller altogether. To do this, you would use the following commands from the controllers CLI:

```
config network webmode enable
config network secureweb disable
save config
reset system
```

Note   There is a strong following within Cisco to uncouple web auth pages from administrative access to the controller to allow an administrator to disable SSL for web auth but keep it enabled for administrative logins. Hopefully a future code release will bring about this change. If you do not want guest users accessing your internal DNS servers, you could set up a small Linux-based DNS server in your guest VLAN or DMZ that contained the A record for the controller's virtual interface for them to use instead.

The second option is to install a certificate on the controller from a Certificate Authority like VeriSign or Entrust. You would have the certificate issued for whatever DNS name you want to give the virtual interface IP address of the controller. The certificate signing request (CSR) for the controller is outlined in Cisco document ID 70584. You also need to have an A record in the local DNS server for that same name that points to the address of the virtual interface of the controller. Under the virtual interface configuration on the controller, you would enter the DNS hostname you set up in local DNS. It needs to be the Fully Qualified Domain Name (FQDN), as illustrated in Figure 14-15. You must reboot the controller for that configuration change to take effect. The guest client must use your internal DNS server, or it will never be able to resolve the IP address of the controller's virtual interface and the redirect will fail.

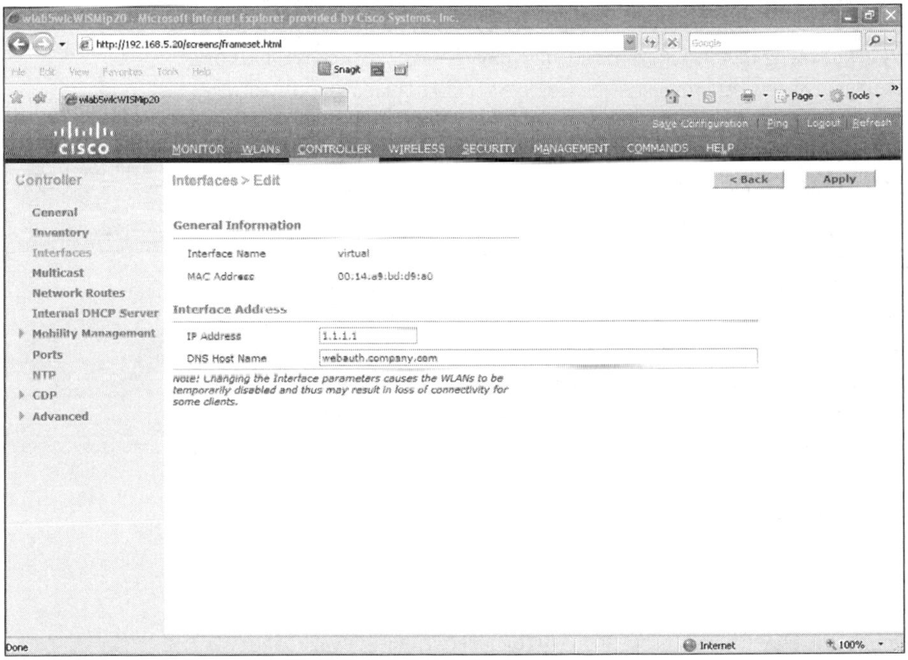

Figure 14-15   *Virtual Interface FQDN*

If you are able to obtain a root-level certificate as opposed to a chained or intermediate certificate, the process is easy. You need only follow the steps outlined in the CSR document. Because most certificate authorities are no longer issuing root-level certificates (VeriSign stopped the practice in 2008), the only other option is to use a chained or intermediate certificate. Web auth blocks all but DHCP and DNS traffic, so the client has no way of going up the certificate chain to validate an intermediate certificate, and you are back where you started. You could create a pre-auth ACL that allows the client to pass the traffic, but the preferred method is to build the final pem file that you will load on the controller so that it contains the certificate chain.

Example 14-3 shows what the PEM file content would be with multiple intermediate certificates.

Example 14-3   *Chained Certifcate PEM File*

```
Bag Attributes
    localKeyID: E5 9A 69 81 68 1E 2B 7F AD B5 5B A6 7D 00 7D 7D BF F9 50 87
subject=/C=US/ST=California/L=San Jose/O=Cisco Technology Inc/OU=Terms of use at
www.verisign.com/rpa (c)05/CN=www.wnbu-chain.cisco.com
issuer=/C=US/O=VeriSign, Inc./OU=VeriSign Trust Network/OU=Terms of use at
https://www.verisign.com/rpa (c)05/CN=VeriSign Class 3 Secure Server CA
— —-BEGIN CERTIFICATE— —-
MIIFOTCCBCGgAwIBAgIQBpUQkbj61LwTQ7PEsc8/JjANBgkqhkiG9w0BAQUFADCB
sDELMAkGA1UEBhMCVVMxFzAVBgNVBAoTDlZlcmlTaWduLCBJbmMuMR8wHQYDVQQL
ExZWZXJpU2lnbiBUcnVzdCBOZXR3b3JrMTswOQYDVQQLEzJUZXJtcyBvZiB1c2Ug
YXQgaHR0cHM6Ly93d3cudmVyaXNpZ24uY29tL3JwYSAoYykwNTEqMCgGA1UEAxMh
VmVyaVNpZ24gQ2xhc3MgMyBTZWN1cmUgU2VydmVyIENBMB4XDTA4MDYwNDAwMDAw
MFoXDTEwMDYwNDIzNTk1OVowgawxCzAJBgNVBAYTAlVTMRMwEQYDVQQIEwpDYWxp
Zm9ybmlhMREwDwYDVQQHFAhTYW4gSm9zZTEdMBsGA1UEChQUQ2lzY28gVGVjaG5v
bG9neSBJbmMxMzAxBgNVBAsUKlRlcm1zIG9mIHVzZSBhdCB3d3cudmVyaXNpZ24u
Y29tL3JwYSAoYykwNTEhMB8GA1UEAxQYd3d3LnduYnUtY2hhaW4uY2lzY28uY29t
MIGfMA0GCSqGSIb3DQEBAQUAA4GNADCBiQKBgQDvdYys7XU5rU3OCPw6m8eN47Dq
Ysv36zjQsXhjWtanrH+w0y9QpSLTG27NDY2rbbA/psjUmW1eXm7py3ZXd4zj8PsM
7D54oVFB2T6KfLQtl7jM+ltPd72KrykkGNLgjtM9/NVDrc8spaZuFUgRHCdoeR+G
2RcQ0Vo4lI8ZsoTiYQIDAQABo4IB0zCCAc8wCQYDVR0TBAIwADALBgNVHQ8EBAMC
BaAwRAYDVR0fBD0wOzA5oDegNYYzaHR0cDovL1NWUlNlY3VyZS1jcmwudmVyaXNp
Z24uY29tL1NWUlNlY3VyZTIwMDUuY3JsMEQGA1UdIAQ9MDswOQYLYIZIAYb4RQEH
FwMwKjAoBggrBgEFBQcCARYcaHR0cDovL3d3cudmVyaXNpZ24uY29tL3JwYTAd
BgNVHSUEFjAUBggrBgEFBQcDAQYIKwYBBQUHAwIwIwHwYDVR0jBBgwFoAUb+yvoN2K
pO/1KhBnLT9VgrzX7yUweQYIKwYBBQUHAQEEbTBrMCQGCCsGAQUFBzABhhhodHRw
Oi8vb2NzcC52ZXJpc2lnbi5jb20wQwYIKwYBBQUHMAKGN2h0dHA6Ly9TVlJJTZWN1
cmUtYWlhLnZlcmlzaWduLmNvbS9TVlJJTZWN1cmUyMDA1LWFpYS5jZXIwbgYIKwYB
BQUHAQwEYjBgoV6gXDBaMFgwVhYJaW1hZ2UvZ2lmMCEwHzAHBgUrDgMCGggUS2u5
KJYGDLvQUjibKaxLB4shBRgwJhYkaHR0cDovL2xvZ28udmVyaXNpZ24uY29tL3Zz
bG9nbzEuZ2lmMA0GCSqGSIb3DQEBBQUAA4IBAQBW8OsZmBgSROFyoZ70a2UtYuzU
w48RPAAkFdmbackkGB0fcyk06NeubEQqWUJIMwSKEhmt++ju1XFb2XcsAOu1XqSi
RycIsByP3VBCSgFih5g2mnMVhz7B0uro6WLltC0YBm+OsDqENgpLxGdWzuq5pIG9
aLVlhsIEnTxKPdCuBVtJh9ubrqUI5cLTI1FVwisV07mQS8nUIcn9TEsu2s+oVQN7
IaW+vEwjrq+Vl7J0TEQ4oktegtflGfw21fVA3io204Z70LrP+EfBRBz8UHw2dw2Q
j3dwA80dbKOmKTjoSxNotZmGVEhOVJrUoKnIJYcFIWgJvBa2dl6jn2C/hFO0
— —-END CERTIFICATE— —-
Bag Attributes: <No Attributes>
```

```
subject=/C=US/O=VeriSign, Inc./OU=VeriSign Trust Network/OU=Terms of use at
https://www.verisign.com/rpa (c)05/CN=VeriSign Class 3 Secure Server CA
issuer=/C=US/O=VeriSign, Inc./OU=Class 3 Public Primary Certification Authority
— —-BEGIN CERTIFICATE— —-
```

```
MIIEnDCCBAWgAwIBAgIQdTN9mrDhIzuuLX3kRpFi1DANBgkqhkiG9w0BAQUFADBf
MQswCQYDVQQGEwJVUzEXMBUGA1UEChMOVmVyaVNpZ24sIEluYy4xNzA1BgNVBAsT
LkNsYXNzIDMgUHVibGljIFByaW1hcnkgQ2VydGlmaWNhdGlvbiBBdXRob3JpdHkw
HhcNMDUwMTE5MDAwMDAwWhcNMTUwMTE4MjM1OTU5WjCBsDELMAkGA1UEBhMCVVMx
FzAVBgNVBAoTDlZlcmlTaWduLCBJbmMuMR8wHQYDVQQLExZWZXJpU2lnbiBUcnVz
dCBOZXR3b3JrMTswOQYDVQQLEzJUZXJtcyBvZiB1c2UgYXQgaHR0cHM6Ly93d3cu
dmVyaXNpZ24uY29tL3JwYSAoYykwNTEqMCgGA1UEAxMhVmVyaVNpZ24gQ2xhc3Mg
MyBTZWN1cmUgU2VydmVyIENBMIIBIjANBgkqhkiG9w0BAQEFAAOCAQ8AMIIBCgKC
AQEAlcMhEo5AxQ0BX3ZeZpTZcyxYGSK4yfx6OZAqd3J8HT732FXjr0LLhzAC3Fus
cOa4RLQrNeuT0hcFfstG1lxToDJRnXRkWPkMmgDqXkRJZHL0zRDihQr5NO6ziGap
paRa0A6Yf1gNK1K7hql+LvqySHyN2y1fAXWijQY7i7RhB8m+Ipn4G9G1V2YETTX0
kXGWtZkIJZuXyDrzILHdnpgMSmO3ps6wAc74k2rzDG6fsemEe4GYQeaB3D0s57Rr
4578CBbXs9W5ZhKZfG1xyE2+xw/j+zet1XWHIWuG0EQUW1R5OZZpVsm5Mc2JYVjh
2XYFBa33uQKvp/1HkaIiNFox0QIDAQABo4IBgTCCAX0wEgYDVR0TAQH/BAgwBgEB
/wIBADBEBgNVHSAEPTA7MDkGC2CGSAGG+EUBBxcDMCowKAYIKwYBBQUHAgEWHGh0
dHBzOi8vd3d3LnZlcmlzaWduLmNvbS9ycGEwMQYDVR0fBCowKDAmoCSgIoYgaHR0
cDovL2NybC52ZXJpc2lnbi5jb20vcGNhMy5jcmwwDgYDVR0PAQH/BAQDAgEGMBEG
CWCGSAGG+EIBAQQEAwIBBjApBgNVHREEIjAgpB4wHDEaMBgGA1UEAxMRQ2xhc3Mz
Q0EyMDQ4LTEtNDUwHQYDVR0OBBYEFG/sr6DdiqTv9SoQZy0/VYK81+8lMIGABgNV
HSMEeTB3oWOkYTBfMQswCQYDVQQGEwJVUzEXMBUGA1UEChMOVmVyaVNpZ24sIElu
Yy4xNzA1BgNVBAsTLkNsYXNzIDMgUHVibGljIFByaW1hcnkgQ2VydGlmaWNhdGlv
biBBdXRob3JpdHmCEHC65B0Q2Sk0tjjKewPMur8wDQYJKoZIhvcNAQEFBQADgYEA
w34IRl2RNs9n3Nenr6+4lsULBHTTsWC85v63RBKBWzFzFGNWxnIu0RoDQ1w4ClBK
Tc3athmo9JkNr+P32PF1KGX2av6b9L1S2T/L2hbLpZ4ujmZSeD0m+v6UNohKlV4q
TDnvbvqCPy0D79YoszcYz0KyNCFkR9MgazpM3OYDkAw=
```

```
— —-END CERTIFICATE— —-
Bag Attributes
    localKeyID: E5 9A 69 81 68 1E 2B 7F AD B5 5B A6 7D 00 7D 7D BF F9 50 87
Key Attributes: <No Attributes>
— —-BEGIN RSA PRIVATE KEY— —-
Proc-Type: 4,ENCRYPTED
DEK-Info: DES-EDE3-CBC,BD1E241BA56C16E2
```

```
DoYJrzfTX2oA8jmKGqWOfdcE6QvRHXc9Fw1MWRHuMi/cizbSzuqS8B9i4ISKY/Ld
Ys183dAVZcjHak/NJtv8o7tfCbcKagXIP0Mibpi+t1ylowuSN+edV4N20ZT8dYJV
zIi0/A8q5kEqyiSee66se/8E6WSbHEbg3USggRGce2IlSKW7AuciHKCJLV/7P5m3
9BPhRIXj1p3+OtfX3/0IDKdnGUcpDeuZDnaVk1/78cvaafgsVblWiAoldrVbyEaX
087GdtKo2Fk+P9+dJ5PEdlkW10BNDJqNN0om1Zidi65iXd1QF7X68GFfBQXZjyPz
3FzyD55ZQq9S/jacqbstYiUzFNkczDkcQlwcPmfRDg/gldEq8BZFGZq+HRRvlpZ4
BSXZ/38sx5hgioRuyQZnXtboSQKGSDxuabnnob0EhlsIrgVbVvdmH6uFSBZqcNCT
HNb3zCdRqPdoysLLO1C4rFx6RMT6zfo9PWP9QVMzm1yFwFrtcx24oUZTOSg00wRv
```

Example 14-3   *Chained Certifcate PEM File (continued)*

```
MBuRG1fPGD8w+hM8P3Ko1Ej45kDZ27nzhoeBK1zf3+O94PsLERBYRgnKjYcpE0am
aetsTzpuNmSa0KfwPDGoawue3dWkj3uJg976i21jV/l+cHZe1z4/8oSLIg1qrRlX
lue4t26/O+z1UICTc62PyiDaVrvRy3QGM/0hgVrnfQmwbV4YvBrpv+jXOVZ0qQuw
Gt1JAE/6nq7nZ70pzl3XJEUpteGlvOg8ywa4v6G1bLqCCNjBWI0tWtBjClqS7BQX
v9hwCkNLIg2KL6K/58zdwZFo8KkIKKxYcPx0XN5J6hYKvepWfsyxQA==
— — -END RSA PRIVATE KEY— — -
```

Notice that the root-level certificate is at the top of the file with each successive intermediate certificate until you get to the end of the chain. Cisco document 109597 covers
chained certificates for the controller.

> **Tip**   The CSR document states that chained certificates are not supported until the 5.1
> code release. The method of creating a final pem file with all the necessary certificates is
> valid for all code versions. There is no code change regarding this in the 5.1 code and above
> that allows a web auth client to validate a chained certificate.

If you are using an external web server for the web auth splash page, you will still see the
certificate security alert. Despite using an external web server, the client still passes
through the controller. If the external server web address is an HTTPS address, you will
need two certificates—one for the controller and one for the web server—to make the
warning go away. The guest client would need to be able to correctly resolve DNS for
both the controller virtual IP address and the external web server IP address.

Centralized Traffic Flow with Guest Access

As you learned in Chapter 9, "Mobility," you can use symmetric tunneling to force client
traffic to a single controller (Anchor), although the client is associated to an AP joined to
a different controller (Foreign). In normal mobility, the first controller the client associates with will become its anchor. The auto-anchor feature allows you to force all clients
accessing a specific WLAN to be tunneled to the same controller.

Auto-Anchor/Guest Tunneling

The auto-anchor/guest tunneling feature allows you to anchor the guest WLAN to a separate controller in the demilitarized zone (DMZ). Figure 14-16 shows a basic guest tunneling setup and the logical traffic flow. The anchor controller handles client DHCP and
authentication.

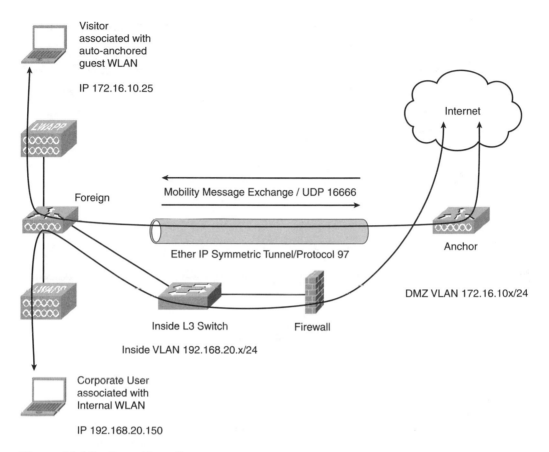

Figure 14-16 *Guest Tunneling*

In Figure 14-16, both the corporate user and the visitor are accessing Internet resources. The corporate user traffic is bridged by the controller directly onto the wired network. The visitor traffic, however, is sent to the anchor controller in the DMZ via an Ether IP tunnel, and the anchor controller bridges it to the DMZ network. The network firewall is configured to allow UDP 16666 and Protocol 97 traffic between the two controllers (covered in detail later in the "Troubleshooting Guest Tunneling" section of this chapter). Because the anchor controller handles client DHCP and authentication, the laptop of the visitor has an IP in the DMZ VLAN range. Figure 14-17 shows a client DHCP discovery Ether IP packet between a foreign and anchor controller.

A single anchor controller can support up to 40 simultaneous Ether IP tunnels at one time. This means you can have 50 foreign controllers anchored to a single anchor controller, but only 40 of the foreign controllers can have active Ether IP tunnels to the DMZ.

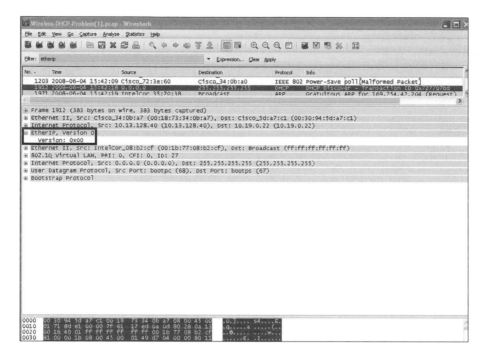

Figure 14-17   *Client DHCP in Ether IP, Packet 1912*

Configuring Auto-Anchor

Before you can designate a controller to be an auto-anchor for your guest WLAN, that particular controller needs to be listed in the mobility domain for the foreign controller. (See Chapter 9 for configuring mobility between controllers.) After you do that, to anchor your guest WLAN, first disable the WLAN and then go to **WLANS > Advanced > Mobility Anchors**. Then select the IP address of your anchor controller from the drop-down list and click on **Mobility Anchor Create**. The mobility anchor configuration page is shown in Figure 14-18.

An important configuration step that is often misunderstood is that the anchor controller should only have a mobility anchor configured as local. It should not have the foreign controllers configured as a mobility anchor. The foreign controller should only have the anchor controller(s) configured as mobility anchors for the WLAN. It should not have a local anchor configured. If this configuration is incorrect, you can create an anchoring loop as the controllers round-robin between the multiple controllers in the anchor list.

When multiple controllers are added as mobility anchors for a particular WLAN on a foreign controller to provide load balancing and redundancy, the foreign controller internally orders the anchors by their IP address and round-robins between them. The controller with the lowest IP is the first anchor. For example, 172.16.7.25 is first, 172.16.7.28 is second, and 192.168.5.15 is third. When the first client associates to the anchored WLAN of the foreign controller, that client database entry is sent to the first anchor controller in the list. The second client is sent to the second controller in the list, and so on until the

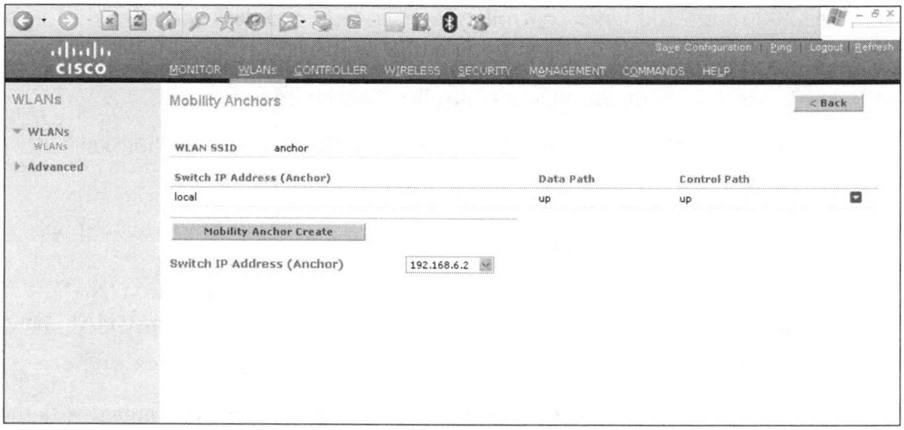

Figure 14-18 *Mobility Anchor Configuration*

end of the anchor list is reached. The process then begins again starting with the first anchor controller. Should one of the anchor controllers be detected as down, all the clients anchored to that particular anchor are deauthenticated by the foreign controller so that they go through the authentication and anchoring process again to a live anchor controller. You can verify the mobility configuration using the special ping commands eping and mping. These commands are described in detail in the next section.

Troubleshooting Guest Tunneling

In addition to all the possible issues mentioned earlier that can break web auth, added complexities are introduced with guest tunneling. Not only do you need to use the same debugs and troubleshooting methods outlined for basic web auth, you also need to incorporate the mobility debugs and troubleshooting guidelines outlined in Chapter 9.

For guest tunneling to function, certain guidelines need to be met:

- Controllers should run the same version of code. Starting with code Release 5.2, a foreign controller can have an anchor controller running 4.2 or higher code. This means a 6.0 controller can have auto-anchoring configured to controllers running 4.2, 5.0, 5.1, 5.2, and 6.0 code.

- The controllers need to be in the same mobility domain.

- The anchor and foreign controller do not need to be in the same mobility group.

- If a firewall is involved, ports 16666 (16667 if using secure mobility) and protocol 97 must be allowed bidirectionally between the IP addresses of the controller management interfaces.

- The guest WLAN configuration must match between the foreign and anchor; that is, if DHCP required is selected on the foreign guest WLAN, you should select it on the anchor guest WLAN as well.

- The 2000 and 2100 series controllers and network modules cannot be used as anchors but can be anchored to 4400 series controllers.

- The guest WLAN on the anchor controller is anchored to itself.

- The guest WLAN on the foreign controller is anchored to the anchor controller.

- Web auth is the only Layer 3 security supported.

- DHCP option 82 is not supported.

- Prior to 4.2, mobility did not work with Network Address Translation (NAT). Mobility group lookup has changed to use the MAC address because NAT changes the source IP in the IP header.

A common misconception is that the anchor controller needs to be configured with the same mobility group name for guest anchoring to function. This is not the case. In fact, for security reasons, you actually want the mobility group names to be different. When you are configuring mobility between the foreign and anchor controllers, the output of **show mobility summary** on the two controllers should look like that in Examples 14-4 and 14-5.

Example 14-4   *show mobility summary from Foreign Controller*

```
(testWLC) >show mobility summary
Symmetric Mobility Tunneling (current) .......... Disabled
Symmetric Mobility Tunneling (after reboot) ..... Disabled
Mobility Protocol  Port.......................... 16666
Mobility Security Mode.......................... Disabled
Default Mobility Domain......................... LAB
Mobility Keepalive interval..................... 10
Mobility Keepalive count........................ 3
Mobility Group members configured............... 5
Controllers configured in the Mobility Group
 MAC Address        IP Address        Group Name      Status
 00:0b:85:40:cf:a0   192.168.120.100   DMZ            Up
 00:14:a9:bd:d9:a0   192.168.5.20      LAB            Up
```

Example 14-5   *show mobility summary from Anchor Controller*

```
(DMZ) >show mobility summary
Symmetric Mobility Tunneling (current) .......... Disabled
Symmetric Mobility Tunneling (after reboot) ..... Disabled
Mobility Protocol  Port.......................... 16666
Mobility Security Mode.......................... Disabled
Default Mobility Domain......................... DMZ
Mobility Keepalive interval..................... 10
Mobility Keepalive count........................ 3
Mobility Group members configured............... 5
```

```
Controllers configured in the Mobility Group
 MAC Address          IP Address        Group Name  Status
 00:0b:85:40:cf:a0    192.168.120.100   DMZ         Up
 00:14:a9:bd:d9:a0    192.168.5.20      LAB         Up
```

Notice that the mobility group name configured for each controller in the other controller's mobility summary matches the default mobility name for that particular controller. When mobility messages are exchanged between the controllers, the receiving controller is expecting to receive the packet from a particular MAC address, IP address, and mobility name from the other controller.

You might have noticed in the output of **show mobility summary** from both the anchor and foreign controller that symmetric tunneling is disabled. Based on that configuration, you would expect reverse path forwarding (RPF) to be an issue. With auto-anchoring, however, RPF does not come into play because auto-anchoring always uses symmetric tunneling. The symmetric tunneling configuration option applies only to normal foreign and anchor mobility situations as a client roams between controllers.

Example 14-6 shows an incorrect mobility configuration on the anchor, which means anchoring will fail.

Example 14-6 *Incorrect Mobility Configuration on Anchor Controller*

```
(DMZ) >show mobility summary
Symmetric Mobility Tunneling (current) .......... Disabled
Symmetric Mobility Tunneling (after reboot) ..... Disabled
Mobility Protocol  Port.......................... 16666
Mobility Security Mode........................... Disabled
Default Mobility Domain.......................... DMZ
Mobility Keepalive interval...................... 10
Mobility Keepalive count......................... 3
Mobility Group members configured................ 5
Controllers configured in the Mobility Group
 MAC Address          IP Address        Group Name  Status
 00:0b:85:40:cf:a0    192.168.120.100   DMZ         Up
 00:14:a9:bd:d9:a0    192.168.5.20      DMZ         Control and Data Path Down
```

A common mistake is incorrect firewall rules blocking mobility and Ether IP traffic between the controllers. The firewall should allow UDP 16666 and protocol 97 and not port 97. Example 14-7 shows a sample ACL from an Adaptive Security Appliance (ASA).

Example 14-7   *Sample ASA ACL to Permit Mobility Anchoring Between Controllers*

```
ciscoasa(config)#access-list inbound extended permit UDP 199.199.199.0
255.255.255.0 10.0.10.0 255.255.255.0 eq 16666
ciscoasa(config)#access-list inbound extended permit UDP 199.199.199.0
255.255.255.0 10.0.10.0 255.255.255.0 eq 16667
ciscoasa(config)#access-list inbound extended permit 97 199.199.199.0
255.255.255.0 10.0.10.0 255.255.255.0
```

If the control path (UDP 16666/16667), data path (protocol 97), or both are down between the controllers, this is reflected in the mobility information. From the controller CLI, you can issue epings or mpings to test Ether IP and mobility, respectively. Packet captures, firewall logs, and TCP dumps can show if the epings and mpings are reaching the firewall, being passed to the DMZ controller, and vice versa. Mping and eping are not Internet Control Message Protocol (ICMP) pings; therefore, just because you can ping between the controllers does not mean that mping or eping should also work.

Example 14-8 shows sample output of control and data path issues on a controller.

Example 14-8   *show mobility summary Command Output Showing Some Mobility Issues*

```
(testWLC) >show mobility summary
Symmetric Mobility Tunneling (current) .......... Disabled
Symmetric Mobility Tunneling (after reboot) ..... Disabled
Mobility Protocol  Port......................... 16666
Mobility Security Mode.......................... Disabled
Default Mobility Domain......................... LAB
Mobility Keepalive interval..................... 10
Mobility Keepalive count........................ 3
Mobility Group members configured............... 5
Controllers configured in the Mobility Group
  MAC Address        IP Address       Group Name    Status
  00:0b:85:40:cf:a0  192.168.120.100  DMZ           Control Path Down
  00:14:a9:bd:d9:a0  192.168.5.20     LAB           Up
  00:14:a9:be:51:80  192.168.5.22     LAB           Up
  00:1d:45:f0:d2:c0  192.168.5.26     LAB           Control and Data Path Down
  00:23:33:b2:86:a0  192.168.5.32     LAB           Data Path Down
```

Mping sends mobility echo packets on UDP port 16666/16667, and eping sends Ether IP echo packets using protocol 97. To test mobility connectivity between your controllers, use the controller CLI and issue either an eping or mping (or both) to the IP address of the other controller, as shown in Example 14-9.

Example 14-9   *mping and eping from a Controller CLI*

```
(Cisco Controller) >mping 192.168.6.5
```

```
Send count=3, Receive count=3 from 192.168.6.5

(Cisco Controller) >eping 192.168.6.5

Send count=3, Receive count=3 from 192.168.6.5

(Cisco Controller) >
```

If **mping** or **eping** fails, you can investigate the appropriate rules on the firewall or network ACLs to find what is blocking that traffic.

> **Tip** It is important to make sure that the physical network connectivity for your controllers is configured properly. Speed and duplex settings on the switch or firewall ports that the controller is connected to need to be correct. If you are using link aggregation (LAG), you need to verify that the etherchannel load-balancing on the switch is src dst-ip. If you are not planning to use LAG but are going to connect multiple distribution ports on the controller, make sure you have an AP-Manager interface assigned to each port even though the anchor controller will not have APs joined to it. Failure to heed these basic setup guidelines will cause incorrect traffic flow into and out of the controller. Incorrect traffic flow will result in mobility issues—that is, epings work, but mpings don't—and break your auto-anchor configuration even if all the mobility, mobility anchor, and firewall configurations are correct. Even though the anchor controller usually has no APs joined to it, it must be in Layer 3 transport mode just like the foreign controller.

Additional debugs to help troubleshoot guest tunneling are used to investigate any mobility issues between the controllers.

The mobility debugs are as follows:

- **debug mobility handoff enable:** Debugs mobility packets.

- **debug mobility director enable:** Debugs mobility error messages.

- **debug mobility keepalive enable:** Shows what controllers are sending and receiving mobility keepalives and if they missed.

Example 14-10 presents sample output from these debugs showing sent and received keepalives as well as a down mobility member.

Example 14-10 *Sample Mobility Debug Output*

```
(testWLC) >Sun Mar  1 14:25:47 2009: EOIP Keepalive received from: 192.
168.120.100
Sun Mar  1 14:25:47 2009:  version : 02, opcode : ETHOIP_OP_REQ sequence no. 492
23 peerStatus: 0
Sun Mar  1 14:25:47 2009: EOIP Keepalive sent to: 192.168.120.100
```

(continues)

Example 14-10   *Sample Mobility Debug Output (continued)*

```
Sun Mar  1 14:25:47 2009:   version : 02, opcode : ETHOIP_OP_RESP sequence no. 49
223 peerStatus: 0
Sun Mar  1 14:25:52 2009: EOIP Keepalive sent to: 192.168.5.26
Sun Mar  1 14:25:52 2009:   version : 02, opcode : ETHOIP_OP_REQ sequence no.
812273 peerStatus: 0
Sun Mar  1 14:25:52 2009: EOIP Keepalive sent to: 192.168.5.26
Sun Mar  1 14:25:52 2009:   version : 01, opcode : ETHOIP_OP_REQ sequence no.
812274 peerStatus: 0
Sun Mar  1 14:25:52 2009: UDP Keepalive sent to ::
Sun Mar  1 14:25:52 2009:    192.168.5.26, port 16666
Sun Mar  1 14:25:52 2009:   type: 20(MobilityPingRequest)  subtype: 0  version: 1
xid: 144839  seq: 2094  len 36 flags 0
Sun Mar  1 14:25:52 2009:    group id: 30a33488 9524b58e 4a4d006c fcebcee8
Sun Mar  1 14:25:52 2009: Mobility Member 192.168.5.26 detected DOWN status 3,
cleaning up client entries
```

The output from these will also show any configuration issues between the guest WLANs on the controllers and whether mobility packets are being sent and received. Example 14-11 shows output that is indicative of a WLAN configuration mismatch.

Example 14-11   *Mobility Debug Output Indicating a WLAN Configuration issue*

```
mmAnchorExportRcv: 00:1f:f3:9f:07:f3 Ssid=Guest Security Policy=0x2000
mmAnchorExportRcv: WLAN Guest disabled or not found, ignore ExportAnchor msg.
Delete client 00:1f:f3:9f:07:f3
```

When the client entry is anchored to the controller in the DMZ, the WLAN security policy (think of this as the configuration of the WLAN) is such that the hex value is 0x2000. This means that the WLAN is anchored, but DHCP is not required. The different configuration options for the WLAN cause this security policy value to change. Therefore, if the WLAN is anchored, DHCP is required, and web auth is enabled, the security policy value would be 0x2050. This value is calculated by the following:

AutoAnchor (policy 0x02000) + Webauth (policy 0x00010) + DHCP Required (policy 0x00040) = 0x2050

The important aspect to take away from this is that the security policies must match between the foreign and anchor controllers. If not, the anchor will fail and you will see the preceding output in debugs.

When a successful mobility anchor takes place, the output of **show client detail** *client mac* should look like that in Example 14-12 for the foreign controller and Example 14-13 for the anchor controller.

Example 14-12   *Partial Client Detail Output from Foreign Controller*

```
Mobility State................................. Export Foreign
```

```
Mobility Anchor IP Address...................... 192.168.50.2
Mobility Move Count............................. 0
Security Policy Completed....................... Yes
Policy Manager State............................ RUN
```

Because the foreign controller is not responsible for authenticating the client, the state of the client on this controller is RUN.

Example 14-13 *Partial Client Detail Output from Anchor Controller*

```
Mobility State................................. Export Anchor
Mobility Foreign IP Address..................... 172.16.150.2
Mobility Move Count............................. 0
Security Policy Completed....................... No
Policy Manager State............................ WEBAUTH_REQD
```

Notice that the state of the client on the anchor in Example 14-13 is WEBAUTH_REQD, indicating that the client has yet to authenticate.

If the foreign controller shows the mobility state of the client as local, the mobility anchor is not working correctly. In this case, try the following:

Step 1.   Disable the guest WLAN on both the anchor and the foreign controller.

Step 2.   Remove the mobility anchor configuration from the WLAN on both controllers.

Step 3.   Save the configuration on both controllers.

Step 4.   Re-create the WLAN anchor on both controllers.

Step 5.   Enable the WLAN on both controllers.

Wired Guest Access

Wired guest access allows wired guest clients to use the controller for network access. This is useful in that a single device handles both wired and wireless guests. The controller supports up to five wired guest LANs.

To achieve this, the controller acts as a bridge between the wired client Layer 2 ingress VLAN and the Layer 3 egress VLAN. The wired client will have an IP address from the L3 VLAN and not the L2 VLAN. For example, if the wired guest VLAN is in VLAN 10 and the egress interface on the controller is in VLAN 12, the wired client will have a VLAN 12 IP address. The controller requires a Layer 2, or Guest LAN, interface in the wired guest VLAN to bridge the traffic. This is referred to as the ingress interface. Figure 14-19 shows a sample guest LAN interface.

Although the configuration is for wired clients, you still need a WLAN for those clients as seen in Figure 14-20 so you can configure the proper ingress and egress interfaces. When creating the wired WLAN, you would select guest LAN.

When you select Guest LAN when configuring the WLAN, the security tab changes to reflect the supported wired guest security settings.

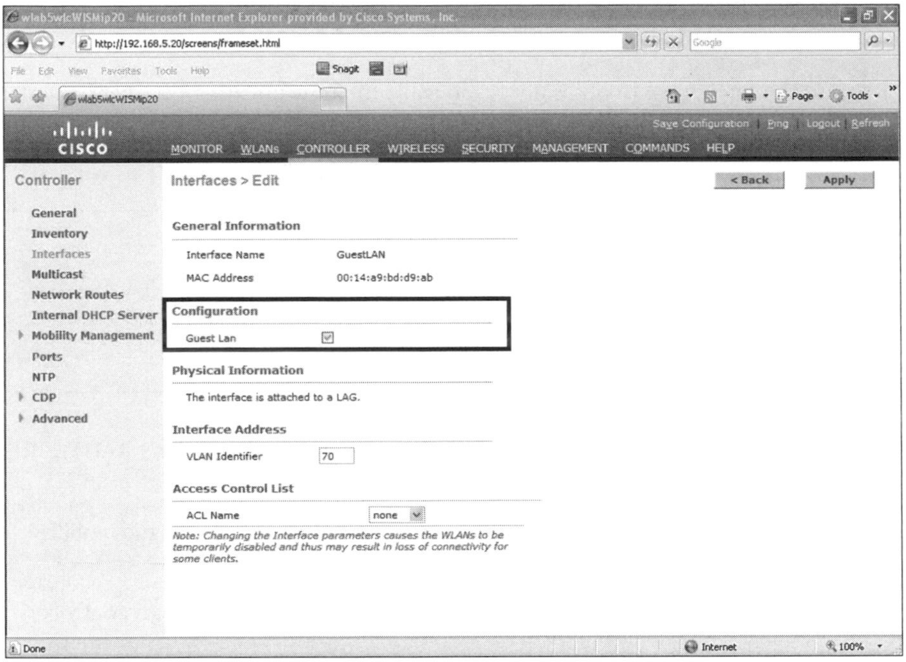

Figure 14-19 *Guest LAN Interface*

To set up a wired guest LAN from the controller GUI, follow these steps:

Step 1. Create your ingress and egress interfaces.

Step 2. The ingress interface is L2, so there is no IP address. Make sure you select the Guest LAN check box.

Step 3. Egress is any other dynamic (or management) interface you want to use. Wired and wireless can share the same egress interface.

Step 4. Under the WLAN tab, create the Guest LAN, not a WLAN as illustrated in Figure 14-20.

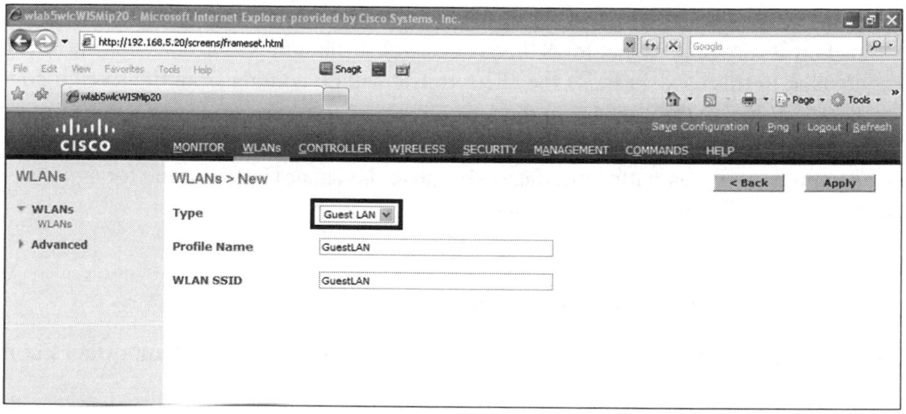

Figure 14-20   *Guest LAN Configuration*

Step 5.   Select the correct ingress and egress interfaces, as demonstrated in Figure 14-21.

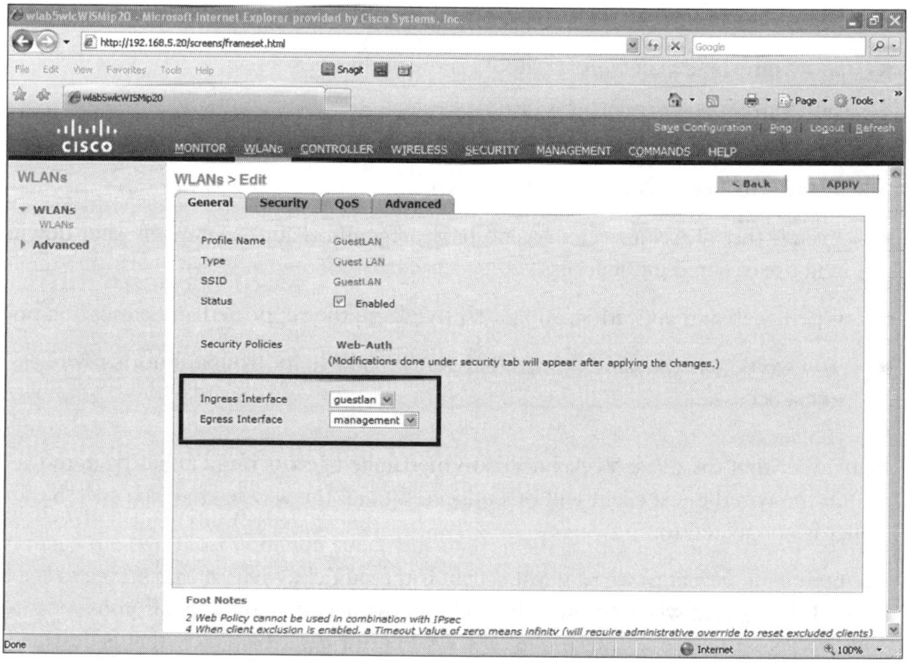

Figure 14-21   *Ingress and Egress Interface for Guest LAN*

Step 6.   Enable web auth security, and so on.

Tip   If more than one controller is on the network, you cannot have an ingress interface on both controllers for the same VLAN. Because the traffic is Layer 2, the client traffic can be picked up by either controller, and the client can see multiple authentications or other odd behavior.

Wired guest access is supported with guest tunneling as well. The setup for wired guest tunneling is the same as that for WLANs except for the ingress interface on the anchor controller. In this case, because the client traffic will be coming from the foreign controller via Ether IP the ingress interface would be set to none. Similar to wireless guest tunneling, the egress interface on the foreign controller can be anything—such as the management or a quarantine interface—because the client traffic on the foreign controller will never traverse that interface.

Troubleshooting Wired Guest Access

When configuring wired guest access, you need to remember several important points.

- The controller can support only five wired guest LANs.

- The ingress wired VLAN must be strictly L2. It can exist only in the VLAN database. There can be no Layer 3 interface for that VLAN on the switched network.

- **show vlan** should list the VLAN.

- **show interface vlan** *vlan ID* should show nothing:

  ```
  lab1sup720ip1#sh run int vlan 3
                    ^
  % Invalid input detected at '^' marker.
  ```

- Even if the VLAN interface has no IP address and is administratively shut down, it will break wired guest access.

- Open, web authentication, and passthrough are the supported authentication policies.

- You would use the same debugs that you would use for troubleshooting wireless guest access.

Remember that the guest VLAN needs to be trunked across all switches from the access switch the wired guest client will be connected to all the way back to the switch the controller is connected to.

An interesting caveat to wired guest access is the model of switch that serves as the core Layer 3 device and where the switch resides in the network topology. If you are using a 3500 series switch, for instance, the switch will not forward a packet that is destined to an SVI MAC address that it owns. This becomes a problem for wired guest access if the 3550 is between the wired client and the controller in the network (see Figure 14-22). The wired client will get a DHCP address, but when the browser is opened, the client will never see the redirect page. A packet capture will show that the DNS query by the client never makes it off the switch. This is because the DHCP request by the client is broadcast and the DNS query is unicast. The switch will flood a broadcast packet out all ports, but when the client sends a unicast packet, the switch will drop it because it owns the destination MAC address of the default gateway of the egress VLAN. This means DNS will fail because the controller cannot bridge the packet if it never receives it. With no DNS, the client will never send the HTTP GET and the controller will never send the redirect.

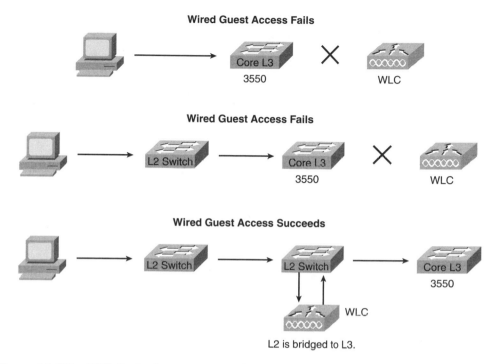

Figure 14-22   *3550 Series Impact on Wired Guest Access*

Larger multilayer switches like the Catalyst 6500 are not subject to this issue because those switches handle their SVI MAC addresses differently.

Notice that in the third example (in Figure 14-22), the controller is connected to a switch on the same side of the core switch as the wired guest client. With this topology, the controller is able to bridge the unicast traffic from the client to the Layer 3 egress VLAN before it gets to the core switch. In this case, wired guest accounts will succeed.

Summary

The wireless controllers allow you to centralize guest traffic on your network and authenticate guest users. Depending on your goals, you can provide a completely open guest network, authenticate guests against the local WLC database, or use external RADIUS or LDAP servers for authentication. It is important to understand how web auth works and what network resources, such as DNS and correct firewall configurations, are required to allow the feature to function properly. You must also be aware of the physical devices on the network, such as your switching infrastructure, that could inadvertently block wired guest access to the controller. If you are going to implement auto-anchoring, you need to correctly configure both the anchor and foreign controllers to correctly tunnel and load-balance the guest traffic through the network. When all of this comes together correctly, you will have a robust and secure guest solution for both your wired and wireless guest users.

Chapter 15

Mesh

The wireless mesh deployment access points (AP), along with the wireless controllers, allow you to provide a secure wireless solution for outdoor environments such as a college campus or an entire city. The mesh feature allows you to place APs in areas where you have no wired Ethernet network connection. A mesh deployment consists of a root AP (RAP) and one or more mesh APs (MAP). The RAP provides the wired link back to the controller for the MAPs. In order to avoid confusion throughout the rest of the chapter, when referring to the mesh series of APs, they will be called 'mesh APs', whereas the term 'MAP' will refer to a mesh AP that is connected to the controller wirelessly through a RAP.

Originally, only the 1500 and 1520 series APs, outdoor mesh APs, supported mesh deployments. In later code releases, however, Cisco introduced Enterprise Mesh, indoor mesh APs, which allows you to use 1130 and 1240 series APs to install a mesh wireless network indoors.

MAPs use their 802.11a radios as a wireless backhaul to join the controller and send client traffic to the wired network through the RAP. The wireless clients in a mesh network associate to the mesh AP's 802.11b/radio.

Currently, you can find four different models of outdoor mesh APs in the field:

- 1505
- 1510
- 1522
- 1524

The 1505 model is a 802.11b/g only radio, so client access and the backhaul use the single radio. The 1510 model has both an 802.11a and 802.11b/g radio, which allows the AP to have a dedicated radio for the backhaul and a dedicated radio for client access. The 1505 and 1510 series APs are difficult to troubleshoot because they do not have LEDs or standard console cable access. Therefore, without taking the units down and connecting them in a lab environment, it would be nearly impossible to determine if the APs were actually powered up and working. The 1500 series models are end of sale and no longer available for purchase. In November 2013, Cisco will no longer support the 1500 series APs.

The 152x series APs are a dramatic improvement over the 1500s. They have LEDs and standard console connections. You can even enable remote Telnet on the APs and run debug and show commands directly on the APs to help with problem analysis.

Mesh Code Releases

Before the 4.2 release of code, mesh features were included in the main code base for all controllers. Mesh development, bug fixes, and features, however, were being delayed because of mainline code release timelines. To facilitate the development of mesh and get bug fixes to customers faster, Cisco split mesh into its own code branch. The original mesh-only branch uses the 4.1 code base and retains the 4.1 naming convention with an M at the end. An example is 4.1.192.22M.

Although splitting the mesh and mainline code into two separate code bases allowed Cisco to release mesh enhancements and bug fixes faster, it introduced two limitations:

- With the early mesh releases, only the 1500 and 1520 series APs were supported. This meant that if you had other APs models, you had to have two controllers: one for mesh and one for the indoor APs. With mesh Release 4.1.191.24M, Cisco added support for the 1000, 1100, 1200, 1230, 1130, 1240, and 1300 series APs.

- Because the base code is 4.1, 1250, 1140, and 801 series APs are not supported.

Starting with the 5.2 release of code, Cisco merged the mesh-only and mainline code releases. The 1500 series APs are not supported on 5.2 code. To address security vulnerabilities inherent in the 4.1 code base for customers who have deployed 1500 series APs, Cisco released 4.2.176.51M code in June 2009.

Mesh Deployments

You can use mesh APs in various deployment scenarios:

- Point-to-point
- Point-to-multipoint
- Mesh

In a point-to-point mesh deployment, you would have a RAP and a single MAP bridging two wired networks using their 802.11a radios (see Figure 15-1).

With a point-to-multipoint mesh installation, you have a single RAP acting as a root bridge with two or more MAPs connecting their respective wired networks. Figure 15-2 shows a typical point-to-multipoint deployment.

If you plan to enable Ethernet bridging (discussed later in the "Ethernet Bridging" section) with a point-to-multipoint installation, it is recommended that you disable VLAN

Trunking Protocol (VTP) on any switch with a connected MAP. VTP can reconfigure the trunked VLANs across the mesh network, making the RAP lose its connection to the controller and bring down the wireless network.

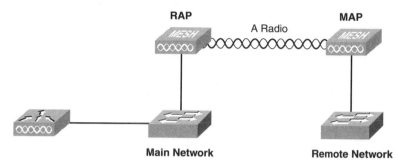

Figure 15-1   *Mesh Point-to-Point Deployment*

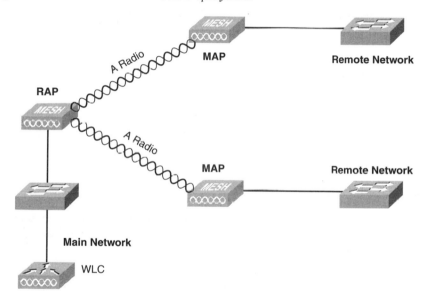

Figure 15-2   *Mesh Point-to-Multipoint Deployment*

In a true mesh deployment, you would have a RAP, or several RAPs if the deployment is large, as well as MAPs deployed across the outdoor space. The MAPs would form parent-child relationships using the 802.11a backhaul (see Figure 15-3). The 802.11b/g radios would service your wireless clients.

As you can see in Figure 15-3, the MAPs relay their wireless connections using their 802.11a backhaul radios to the RAP. The RAP sends that traffic to the controller through the Lightweight Access Point Protocol (LWAPP)/Control and Provisioning of Wireless Access Points (CAPWAP) tunnel to the controller. The 802.11b/g radios on the APs provide client access to the wireless network. Although its not shown in Figure 15-3, clients can connect to the 802.11b/g radio on the RAP as well.

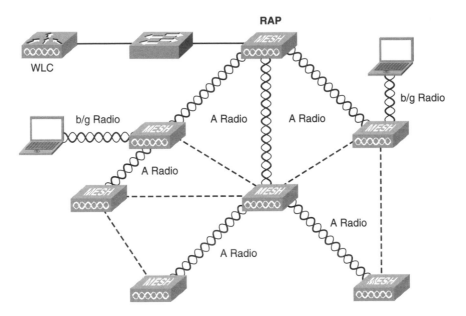

Figure 15-3   *Mesh Deployment*

> **Note**   Although you can enable client access on the mesh backhaul, this feature is not rec-
> ommended. Client access on the 802.11a radios takes away precious bandwidth from the
> MAP backhaul and can severely degrade the performance of the mesh network.

How Mesh Works

Mesh is a fairly complex feature that relies on a wireless routing protocol, Cisco Adaptive
Wireless Path Protocol (AWPP), that allows the MAPs to determine the best parent to
relay their traffic to the RAP.

AWPP is designed specifically for wireless mesh networking in that its path decisions are
based on link quality and number of hops. AWPP is also designed to provide ease of
deployment, fast convergence, and minimal resource consumption. AWPP takes advantage of the LWAPP/CAPWAP wireless LAN (WLAN), where client traffic is tunneled to
the controller and hidden from the AWPP process. Also, the advanced radio management
features in the LWAPP/CAPWAP WLAN solution are available to the wireless mesh network and do not have to be built into AWPP.

When a MAP comes up in a mesh network, the AP is authenticated (bridge authentication). Two possible security modes are available for the bridge authentication: Extensible
Authentication Protocol (EAP) and Pre-Shared Key. There is a four-way handshake using
this primary key to establish an Advanced Encryption Standard (AES) session. Next, the
new AP establishes an LWAPP/CAPWAP tunnel to the controller and is authenticated
against the MAC filter list of the controller.

The controller then pushes the bridge shared secret key to the AP via LWAPP/CAPWAP,
after which it re-establishes the AES session with the parent AP.

As previously described, the wireless mesh bridges traffic between the MAPs and the RAPs. The traffic can be from wired devices being bridged by the wireless mesh or wireless client traffic that is encapsulated in LWAPP/CAPWAP-Data and LWAPP/CAP-WAP-Control traffic from the MAPs.

The AES encryption is established as part of the MAP establishing neighbor relationships with other MAPs (bridge authentication). The bridge shared secret is used to establish unique encryption keys between mesh neighbors. All APs establish an LWAPP/CAPWAP connection to the controller through AES-encrypted backhaul tunnels between the APs.

Mesh Bootup and Join Process

When a mesh AP first boots up, it must determine whether it is a RAP. This decision-making process is as follows:

Step 1.   Upon boot, an AP checks its state; if it is a RAP, it enters the Maintain state.

Step 2.   If it is not a RAP, the AP scans all the channels for Bridge Group Names (BGN).

Step 3.   The AP actively solicits neighboring APs (Seek state).

Step 4.   The AP selects the best parent from the available list.

Step 5.   The AP authenticates to the Mesh network.

Step 6.   The AP then enters the Maintain state and is willing to respond to solicitations. Solicitation allows for faster convergence, leaving more time for data transfer.

Figure 15-4 illustrates the Mesh Machine state.

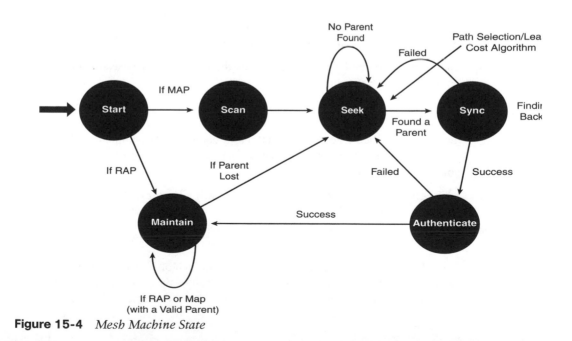

Figure 15-4   *Mesh Machine State*

A mesh AP become a RAP if it can communicate with an LWAPP/CAPWAP controller through its Ethernet interface. All 1500 and 1520 series mesh APs ship as MAPs. If the mesh AP is a RAP, it can go straight to the Maintain state. In the Maintain state, the mesh AP has established an LWAPP/CAPWAP connection to the controller, so it does not need to seek other APs; rather, it simply responds to solicitations. If the mesh AP is not a RAP, it starts a scan process where it scans all available channels and solicits information from other mesh APs.

This behavior has two main implications:

■ The RAP does not change channels; therefore, the channel used to build the mesh from a RAP is defined in the RAP configuration. By default, the RAP uses channel 161 if it is an outdoor AP.

■ The mesh is built from the RAP out, because initially only the RAP can respond to solicitations.

If the AP is not a RAP, it follows the state diagram in Figure 15-4 in the following modes:

■ **Scan:** The AP scans all the backhaul channels using mesh beaconing. This mechanism is similar to the 802.11 beaconing mechanisms used by wireless access networks, except the protocol frames conform to the AWPP frames on the backhaul. The frame used for beaconing is a broadcast NEIGHBOR_RESPONSE called NEIGHBOR_ UPDATE and is sent unsolicited.

Essentially, the network advertises NEIGHBOR_UPDATE frames so that new nodes can scan and quickly discover neighbors. The generation rule is that each RAP and MAP broadcast NEIGHBOR_UPDATE frames after being connected to the network (via a controller). Any neighbor updates with signal-to-noise ratios (SNR) lower than 10 dB are discarded. This process is called *passive scanning*.

The AP looks for mesh beacons advertising the same BGN as what was configured on the AP when you primed it.

If the AP hasn't been preconfigured or primed (joined to the controller on the wire, AP role, BGN set, and so on), or if the BGN it has been configured to is not seen in mesh beacons, the AP goes into default mode and proceeds with joining. This allows you to "catch" an AP in case of a config issue. Nevertheless, Cisco recommends that you always prime the APs with the BGN.

■ **Seek:** After the AP decides to join a mesh network it has located, bridge authentication takes place. This is done based on PSK or EAP. The AP solicits members of the mesh network. Successful responses to these solicitations become neighbors. These neighbors must have the same bridge group name and same shared secret.

■ **Sync:** The MAP learns the path information from each of its neighbors, and the neighbor with the greatest ease becomes the parent of the soliciting MAP. If the neighbors report multiple RAPs, the RAP with the greatest ease is chosen.

- **Authenticate:** The MAP authenticates to the controller through a connection established through its parent AP. This AP authentication is standard LWAPP/CAPWAP AP authentication, and the MAP is already part of the mesh and using the mesh to communicate with its controller.

  Because MAPs are always in bridge mode, in addition to the standard LWAPP/CAPWAP authentication (bridge authentication during the Seek state), the controller requires mandatory MAC address authorization. Should you fail to add the AP's MAC address to the controller's MAC filter list (see Figure 15-6), the AP will not be able to proceed beyond the Authenticate state.

- **Maintain:** The MAP responds to other MAP solicitations and regularly solicits to determine any changes in the mesh. It is only after entering the Maintain state that the MAP is visible to the controller and Wireless Control System (WCS). Note that in the Maintain state, the solicitations occur only on the channel defined by the RAP, whereas a MAP in seek mode solicits on all channels, only stopping when it has found a parent AP.

AWPP uses ease to determine the best path. Ease can be considered the opposite of cost, and the preferred path is the path with the higher ease.

Ease is calculated using the SNR and hop value of each neighbor and applying a multiplier based on various SNR thresholds. The purpose of this multiplier is to apply a spreading function to the SNRs that reflects various link qualities.

In Figure 15-5, MAP2 prefers the path through MAP1 because the adjusted ease (436906) though this path is greater than the ease value (262144) of the direct path from MAP2 to RAP.

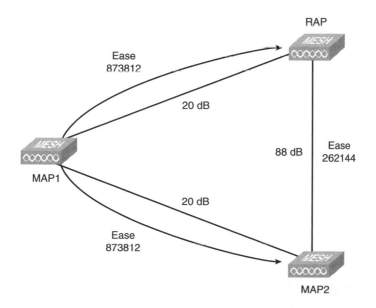

Figure 15-5 *Mesh Parent Selection*

A parent AP is chosen by using the adjusted ease, which is the ease of each neighbor divided by the number of hops to the RAP:

$$\text{Adjusted ease} = \frac{\min\ (ease\ at\ each\ hop)}{\text{Hop count}}$$

So in Figure 15-5, the adjusted case for MAP2 through MAP1 is 873812/2 = 436906.

Configuring Mesh

Configuring the controller to support mesh is quite simple. All you need to do is add the MAC address of the mesh AP to the MAC Filter list of the controller (see Figure 15-6). For 152x outdoor mesh APs, use the Bridge-Group Virtual Interface (BVI) MAC address of the mesh AP. For 1130 and 1240 series indoor mesh APs, you would use the Ethernet MAC address. If you do not know the MAC of the AP and it is not on the exterior of the unit, you can use the console to determine the BVI and Ethernet MAC addresses using the command **sh int | i Hardware**. You can also run **debug pm pki enable** from the controller command-line interface (CLI) to see the MAC address of the AP that is trying to join, as demonstrated in Example 15-1. The description for the AP in the MAC filter list is simply a text string you enter; it has nothing to do with actually configuring the AP.

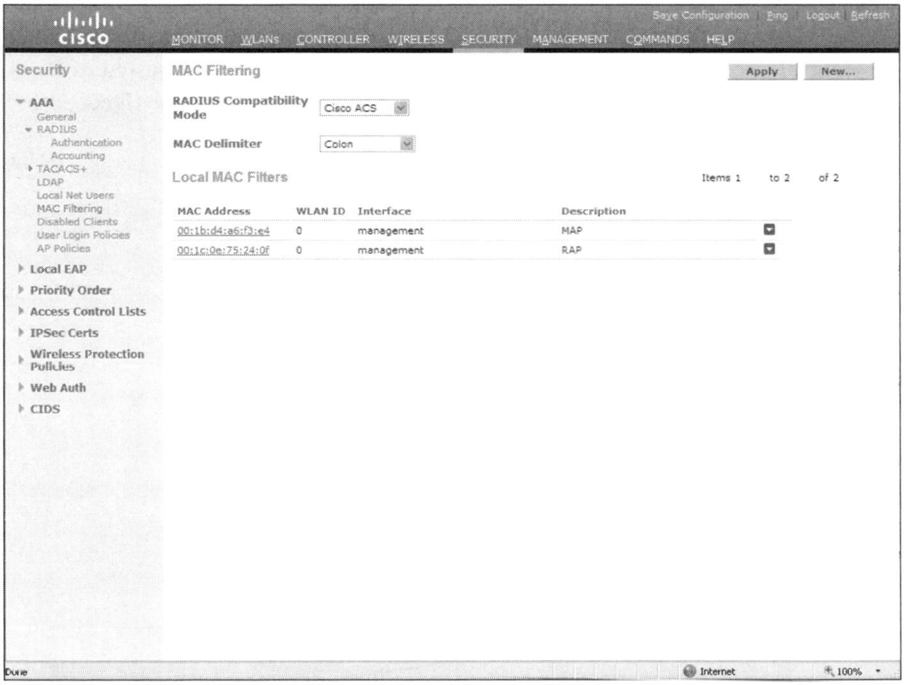

Figure 15-6 *MAC Filter List for MAPs*

Example 15-1 *debug pm pki enable Command Output*

```
Fri Jul 10 17:55:37 2009: spamMeshRadiusProcessResponse: AP Authorization failure
for 00:0b:85:6f:9b:90
```

If the APs' MAC address is not listed, the AP fails authentication and cannot join the controller. This is true for both the indoor and outdoor mesh APs. When the AP rejoins the controller, set its role to be either a RAP or MAP (see Figure 15-7) using the Mesh tab. For the indoor APs, change the AP mode to Bridge and reboot it (see Figure 15-8) before you can configure the mesh-specific settings. When the AP reboots in bridge mode, you see the Mesh tab on the AP configuration page.

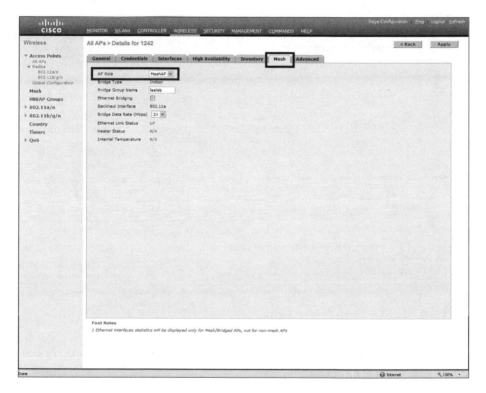

Figure 15-7 *Mesh AP Role*

The Mesh tab is where you will set the AP role as well as the BGN and backhaul data rates. This is true for both outdoor and indoor MAPs.

Caution The recommended backhaul data rate for 1510 series APs is 18 Mbps, whereas the recommended backhaul data rate for the 152x series is 24 Mbps. Use caution if you decide to change the backhaul data rate from the recommended values. You should have a site survey confirming that the wireless link between the MAPs is good enough to maintain a stable backhaul connection at the different rate; otherwise, you risk stranding your MAPs. Should you decide to alter the backhand data rate, always start with the MAP that is furthest away and work back toward the RAP.

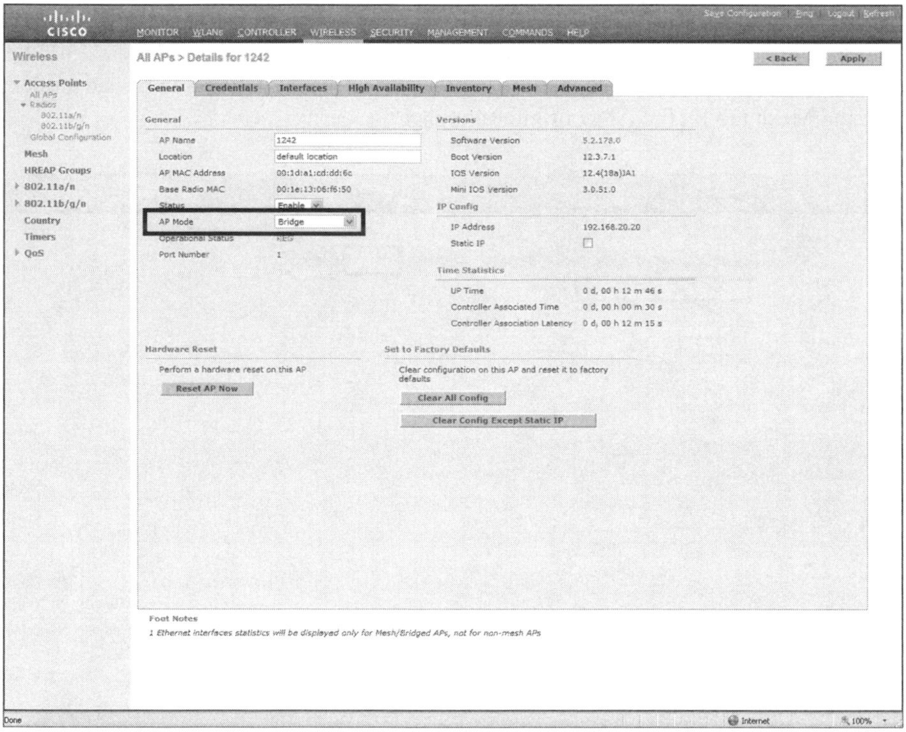

Figure 15-8 *Indoor Mesh Bridge Setting*

You can use the BGN to break large mesh deployments into sectors so that only certain APs will form parent-child relationships.

Note   Remember to record the Ethernet MAC address of the indoor mesh AP so you can add it to the MAC filter list on the controller. Otherwise, it will fail authentication and not be able to join the controller.

By default, the security mode for bridge authentication is EAP. This is done using manufacturer-installed certificates and therefore does not need configuring. Should you want to change the security mode to PSK or use a RADIUS server to authenticate the mesh APs, you can configure those settings from the controller GUI under **Wireless > Mesh**, as shown in Figure 15-9.

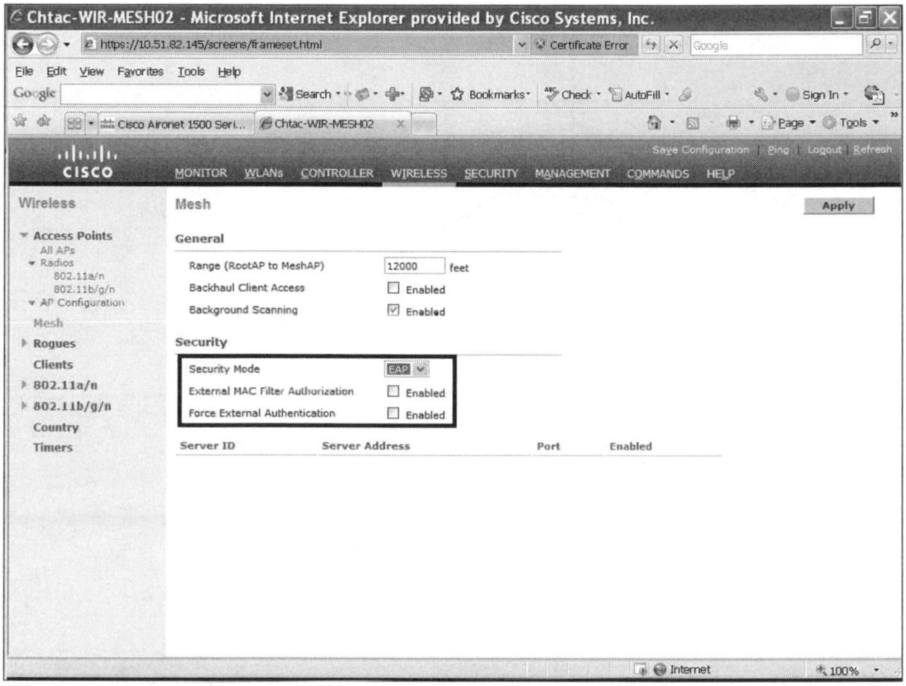

Figure 15-9 *Mesh Bridge Security Configuration*

Ethernet Bridging

Ethernet bridging allows you to connect remote wired networks to each other using the Ethernet port of the MAPs. A common use for Ethernet bridging is installing video cameras or street poles with the mesh APs. For bridging to work, every MAP and RAP in the path must have Ethernet bridging enabled.

Prior to code Release 5.2, Ethernet bridging only allowed the extension of the Layer 2 network in which the MAPs resided. So if the APs had IP addresses in VLAN 5, for example, you could only extend VLAN 5 to the remote wired network. The 5.2 release allows you to bridge multiple VLANs. Like the earlier feature, every AP in the mesh path back to the RAP and including the RAP must support bridging the same VLANs as the MAP with the wired connection. Figure 15-10 illustrates this concept.

If you do not allow the desired VLANs on all the MAPs, then in the event of a failure within the mesh network it is possible to break the bridging feature if a MAP in the new path to the RAP does not support a particular VLAN. In Figure 15-10, if MAP1 were to go down and MAP3 changed its parent to MAP2, the Ethernet bridging on MAP3 would fail for VLAN 2 because MAP2 does not support bridging VLAN 2.

After you have enabled Ethernet bridging support on your mesh APs you need to configure the VLAN tagging. Figure 15-11 shows the Ethernet configuration of an indoor RAP, and Figure 15-12 shows the Ethernet configuration on the indoor MAP.

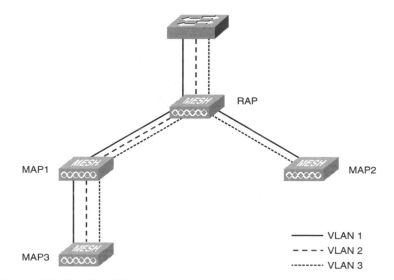

Figure 15-10   *VLAN Tagging Support Example Within a Mesh Network*

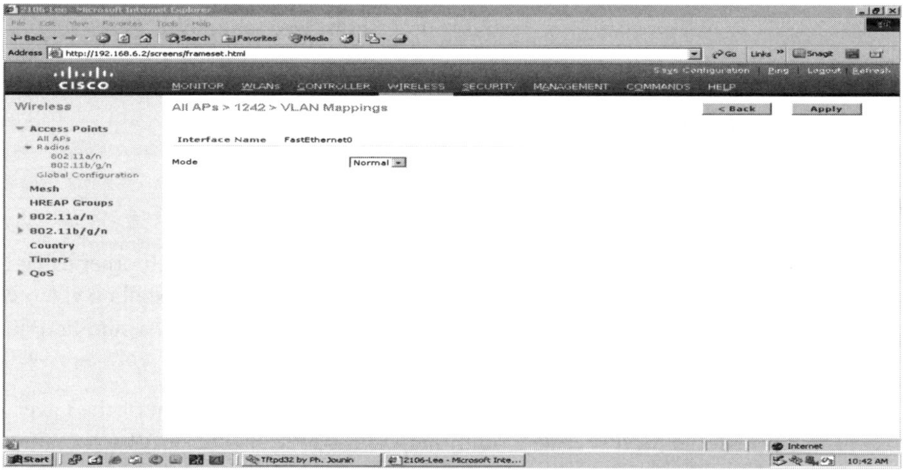

Figure 15-11   *RAP VLAN Tagging Configuration*

Figure 15-12   *MAP VLAN Tagging Configuration*

Notice that the RAP Ethernet interface mode in Figure 15-11 is left as Normal. By default, the wired Ethernet Interface of the RAP will pass all VLAN traffic. This is because the wired connection between the RAP and the switch is the primary backhaul interface to the WLC. Even though you can configure this interface with VLAN tagging, those settings will not be applied until that interface is no longer being used as the backhaul. Since this interface passes all VLAN traffic, it is important to remember to configure the network switch port the RAP is using to only allow the correct VLANs. If not, any VLAN traffic received that is not on any of the bridged VLANs within the mesh network, the RAP will inject those packets into the native VLAN, VLAN 1, in the mesh network. This can corrupt the mesh routing protocol.

Because the MAP is only bridging VLAN 12 in this case, the Ethernet port mode is Access. The AP tags the incoming untagged packet and forwards it to the RAP. Any tagged packets are dropped.

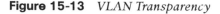

Figure 15-13 *VLAN Transparency*

Mesh APs use VLAN transparency to perform Ethernet bridging when extending the Layer 2 network. To allow multiple VLAN bridging/tagging, you must disable VLAN transparency (see Figure 15-13) under the **Wireless>Mesh>Ethernet Bridging** section on the controller. When VLAN transparency is enabled, VLAN processing does not occur. This assumes that all traffic is destined to and from the same VLAN with no 802.1 tagging.

After you have disabled VLAN transparency, reboot the mesh APs for that setting to take effect.

It is important to understand the traffic flow when using Ethernet bridging. Figure 15-14 shows the traffic flow for both wired and wireless clients within the mesh network with Ethernet bridging enabled.

As you can see, with Ethernet bridging enabled, the traffic flow for wireless clients is unchanged. The wireless client packets are sent using LWAPP/CAPWAP data, which is sent through the encrypted backhaul to the controller. The controller then bridges that traffic to the wired network. The bridged wired client traffic, however, is bridged directly into the backhaul toward the RAP. The RAP then bridges the traffic directly onto the wired network. The wired bridged traffic is not sent back to the controller.

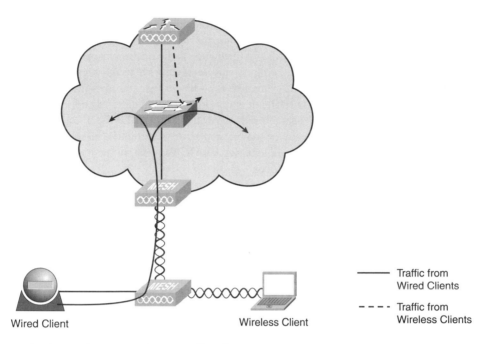

Figure 15-14   *Ethernet Bridging Traffic Flow*

Several guidelines exist in addition to disabling VLAN transparency that allow the correct VLANs on the APs when you use the Ethernet bridging and VLAN tagging feature
in 5.2 code:

- For security reasons, the Ethernet port on a mesh AP (RAP and MAP) is disabled by
  default. It is enabled by configuring Ethernet bridging on the MAP port.

- Ethernet bridging must be enabled on all the APs in the mesh network to allow
  Ethernet VLAN tagging to operate.

- VLAN mode must be set as non-VLAN transparent (global mesh parameter).

  VLAN transparent is enabled by default. To set as non-VLAN transparent, you must
  uncheck the VLAN transparent option in the global mesh parameters window.

- VLAN configuration on a mesh AP is applied only if all the uplink MAPs are able to
  support that VLAN.

- If uplink APs are not able to support the VLAN, the configuration is stored rather
  than applied.

- VLAN tagging can be configured only on Ethernet interfaces.

  On 152x mesh APs, three of the four ports can be used as *secondary Ethernet
  interfaces*: *port 0-PoE in*, *port 1-PoE out*, and *port 3- fiber. Port 2 - cable* cannot
  be configured as a secondary Ethernet interface.

In Ethernet VLAN tagging, *port 0-PoE in* on the RAP connects to the trunk port of the switch of the wired network. *Port 1-PoE out* on the MAP connects to external devices such as video cameras.

■ Backhaul interfaces (802.11a radios) act as *primary Ethernet interfaces*. Backhauls function as trunks in the network and carry all VLAN traffic between the wireless and wired network. No configuration of primary Ethernet interfaces is required.

■ The switch port in the wired network that is attached to the RAP (*port 0-PoE in*) must be configured to accept tagged packets on its trunk port. The RAP forwards all tagged packets received from the mesh network to the wired network.

■ No configuration is required to support VLAN tagging on an 802.11a backhaul Ethernet interface within the mesh network. This includes the RAP uplink Ethernet port. The required configuration happens automatically using a registration mechanism. Any configuration changes to an 802.11a Ethernet link acting as a backhaul are ignored and a warning results. When the Ethernet link no longer functions as a backhaul, the modified configuration is applied.

■ VLAN configuration is not allowed on a port-02-cable modem port of an 152x AP. VLANs can be configured on ports 0 (PoE-in), 1 (PoE-out), and 3 (fiber).

■ If you are bridging between two MAPs, enter the distance (mesh range) between the two APs that are bridging. (This is not applicable to applications in which you are forwarding traffic connected to the MAP or to the RAP access mode.)

■ Up to 16 VLANs are supported on each sector. Therefore, the cumulative number of VLANs supported by RAP's children (MAPs) cannot exceed 16.

■ Ethernet ports on APs function as either *access* or *trunk* ports within an Ethernet tagging deployment.

■ In Access mode, only untagged packets are accepted. All packets are tagged with a user-configured VLAN called access VLAN. For this mode to take effect, the global VLAN mode should be non-VLAN transparent. This option is used for applications in which information is collected from devices connected to the MAP, such as cameras or PCs, and then forwarded to the RAP. The RAP then applies tags and forwards traffic to a switch on the wired network.

■ Trunk mode requires the user to configure a native VLAN and an allowed VLAN list (no defaults). In this mode, both tagged and untagged packets are accepted. Untagged packets are always accepted and are tagged with the user-specified native VLAN. Tagged packets are accepted if they are tagged with a VLAN in the allowed VLAN list. For this mode to take effect, the global VLAN mode should be non-VLAN transparent. This option is used for bridging applications such as forwarding traffic between two MAPs residing in separate buildings within a campus.

- The switch port connected to the RAP must be a trunk.

  The trunk port configuration on the switch and the RAP trunk port must match.

- A configured VLAN on a MAP Ethernet port cannot function as a management VLAN.

- The RAP must always connect to the native VLAN (ID 1) on a switch.

  The RAP's primary Ethernet interface is by default the native VLAN of 1.

Troubleshooting Mesh

Mesh deployments add an extra level of complexity to troubleshooting because the connection between the MAPs and the controller is wireless. The MAPs need to have good signal strength to their parent AP. You do not want the SNR up and SNR down to differ by more than 10 dTS. The Fresnel zone between the APs also needs to be clear to prevent obstructions from interfering with the connection. You want to make sure that the APs are mounted correctly according to the installation guides and have similar heights. Mesh APs can transmit as far as 25 miles, so depending on the distance between them and the type of antenna, you might need to use a laser or other professional alignment tool.

AP Join Problems

Just like any controller-based AP, mesh APs have to be joined to a controller before they can start to service clients. Before the mesh network can come up, you need to have at least one RAP with a wired connection to the controller. After the RAP is joined, the MAPs can start to join the controller through the 802.11a radio of the RAP.

To troubleshoot mesh AP join issues, you can use the standard LWAPP/CAPWAP debugs on the controller that you would use for a non-MAP such as a 1242. In addition to those debugs, you can run the following debugs on the controller:

- **debug mesh security events enable**
- **debug mesh security message enable**
- **debug dot1x events enable**
- **debug dot1x packet enable**

The output of these debugs shows you if you have AP authentication issues. Example 15-2 shows sample output for **debug mesh security all**. (The **all** keyword includes events and messages.)

Example 15-2 *debug mesh security all Command Output*

```
*May 03 13:36:00.846:  00:1C:B1:07:FA:20 MESH_ASSOC_REQUEST_PAYLOAD in Association
Request for AP 00:0B:85:65:51:60
*May 03 13:36:00.846:  00:1C:B1:07:FA:20 Mesh assoc request for known AP
00:0b:85:65:51:60
```

```
*May 03 13:36:00.846:  00:1C:B1:07:FA:20 Mesh assoc request :child :
00:0b:85:65:51:60 NextHop : 00:23:5d:f1:9d:41  LradIp 192.168.1.200  vlanid: 0
mwarPort: 5246  lradPort: 35184
*May 03 13:36:00.846:  00:1C:B1:07:FA:20 Request MAC authorization for AP Child
Addr:  00:0b:85:65:51:60 AP Identity: 00:0b:85:65:51:60 AWPP Identity:
00:1c:b1:07:fa:2f
*May 03 13:36:00.847: MAC Validation of Mesh Assoc Request for00:0b:85:65:51:60 is
-4, Mode is : 0
(Cisco Controller) >*May 03 13:36:00.847: MAC authoriztion fail. REsetting MSCB
state for 00:0b:85:65:51:60 to 9
```

From this output, you can tell that the MAP that is trying to join is failing MAC authorization. The root cause might be a missing or incorrect MAC address in the MAC filter list of the controller or a similar problem on a RADIUS server if you are using Authentication, Authorization, and Accounting (AAA) to authenticate the APs. The controller traplogs also contain valuable information about any AP join issues:

```
Mesh Node '00:0b:85:65:51:60' failed to join controller, MAC address not in MAC
filter list
```

If you have console access to the AP that is not joining the controller (152x and indoor mesh-APs), you can enable the following debugs:

- **debug mesh adjacency**

- **debug mesh event**

- **debug mesh link**

Using these debugs on the MAP closest to the AP that is not joining (the RAP if no MAPs are joining), you can see the adjacencies and events. Example 15-3 shows sample output from **debug mesh adjacency** and **mesh event**.

Example 15-3 *debug mesh adjacency and debug mesh event Command Output*

```
*May  3 16:54:36.582: ADJ:Processing child adjacency from 001e.1306.f65f channel 64
*May  3 16:54:36.582: mesh_adj_add_association: client exists 001e.1306.f65f
*May  3 16:54:36.863: mesh_adj_current_backhaul: Dot11Radio1
*May  3 16:56:22.662: ADJ:Child 001e.1306.f65f timed out
*May  3 16:56:22.662: %MESH-6-LINK_UPDOWN: Mesh station 001e.1306.f65f link Down
*May  3 16:56:22.663: MESH_EVENT:mesh_lwapp_link_down: link 001e.1306.f65f
*May  3 16:56:22.665: MESH_EVENT:received mesh_lwapp_handle_request type LINK_DOWN
```

The sample output in Example 15-3 from a RAP shows the child adjacency timing out and a mesh link down event.

If the mesh APs are not in the same VLAN as the management interface of the controller, be sure to check your discovery methods. Incorrect DHCP options, for example, prevent the APs from learning the correct controller IP. Table 15-1 outlines the correct Vendor Class

Identifiers (VCI) for the different outdoor mesh APs should you decide to use DHCP options for controller discovery.

Table 15-1   *Outdoor Mesh APs DHCP VCI Strings*

MAP	Code Release	VCI String
Any 1500	4.1	Cisco AP c1500
1500 OAP	4.0	Cisco AP.OAP1500
1505	4.0	Cisco AP.LAP1505
1510	4.0	Cisco AP.LAP1510
Any 1500	3.2	Airespace.AP1200
1520	4.1M or 5.2	Cisco AP c1520

An interesting behavior for the 1500 series APs with older code is that if they cannot join a controller for an extensive period of time, they can revert to a previously installed image. Therefore, an AP that was running 4.0 code could fall back to a 3.2 image. If this happens, the VCI you had set up would no longer be valid. You would need to get a wired packet capture to determine the VCI string the AP was sending to the DHCP server. The APs no longer exhibit this image fallback behavior in the 4.1 mesh-only releases and higher.

Another mesh behavior that can result in long join times is that, by design, a mesh AP gives precedence to its wired port on bootup if it detects a signal. This is common when using Ethernet bridging. Only after several failed attempts does it try to use the 802.11a radio as the primary backhaul when the Ethernet port is live. To decrease the join time, you can disconnect the device connected to the Ethernet port of the MAP.

Make sure you are using the correct APs for RAPs and MAPs. Although most mesh APs can be a RAP or MAP to a different AP model, the 1505 APs can mesh only with each other.

If you are using BGNs, a blank or incorrect BGN prevents a MAP from staying joined to the controller. If an AP has a blank BGN, it remains joined for approximately 30 minutes before it drops off the network. You need to correct the BGN during this time to prevent it from continuously dropping off the network. Should you ever want to change the BGN or backhaul data rate (not recommended), you should always start with the farthest out MAP to prevent stranding an AP.

Note   A MAP with a wired connection to the controller will not participate in the mesh network. Some users will use a single 151x or 152x series AP as a regular outdoor AP by configuring the AP as a wired MAP. If you enable client backhaul access, clients would have use of both the 802.11a and 802.11b/g radios.

> **Tip** If you prime all your APs on the wire first, you will have much better success when deploying the mesh network. When you add the AP to the network on the wire first, you can verify that the hardware is good, let the AP download the code from the controller, and configure the AP role and BGN. It is much easier to determine a problem with the AP at your desk or lab than have to climb a light pole or rent a bucket truck to retrieve a problematic AP.

RF Issues

Just like the radio frequency (RF) environment can affect wireless clients, it can disrupt a mesh network. High-channel utilization, interference, and radar can wreak havoc on a mesh network.

Wireless radios that operate in the UNII-2 and UNII-2 Extended bands must adhere to Dynamic Frequency Selection (DFS) and change channels when the AP detects radar on that channel. The controllers automatically enable DFS on 15 channels (52 through 140). If an AP detects radar on the channel it is currently using, it scans for a new channel and waits 60 seconds to make sure no radar is on that channel before it starts using it. An AP avoids trying to use the previous channel for 30 minutes. Even if you hard-code the AP channel and do not use Auto-RF, the AP must change channels when it detects radar.

> **Note** With statically assigned 802.11a channels, if the AP had to change channels because of a DFS event, the AP would rescan the preferred channel after 30 minutes. If no radar is detected, the AP would move back to the configured channel.

As demonstrated in Example 15-4, when an AP detects radar and changes channels, it announces the change to any child APs. The radio change event also generates trap logs to let you know why the AP changed channels.

Example 15-4 *DFS Radar Event SNMP Trap Log*

```
Mon Feb 9 13:07:00 2009 Channel changed for Base Radio MAC: 00:1d:46:24:43:a0 on
802.11a radio. Old Channel: 60. New Channel: 161. Why: Radar. Energy
before/after change:
0/0. Noise before/after change: 0/0. Interference before/after change: 0/0.
Mon Feb 9 13:07:00 2009 Radar signals have been detected on channel 60 by 802.11a
radio with MAC: 00:1d:46:24:43:a0 and slot 1
```

A radar event requires your mesh network to change, which causes outages until the network converges after the channel changes.

Besides radar, you might see poor throughput for various other reasons. Table 15-2 outlines some common RF issues, their cause, and potential resolutions.

The number of hops from a MAP to a RAP is also a factor. With the half-duplex nature of wireless, you are cutting your backhaul rates essentially in half with each hop. For example, the maximum throughput for an 18 Mbps backhaul is approximately 10 Mbps for the first hop, 5 Mbps for the second hop, and 2.5 Mbps for the third hop. Although 8 hops is the backhaul hop limit for outdoor mesh APs, Cisco recommends no more than 4 hops from RAP to MAP.

Table 15-2   *Common RF Symptoms and Resolutions*

Symptom	Possible Causes	Potential Solution
Throughput is low; link test Rx is significantly less than Tx	Tx power is low	Check Tx power level
	Antenna alignment is poor	Realign antennas
	LOS[1] is obstructed or Fresnel zone is not clear	Remove obstruction or raise or move APs/antennas
Throughput is low; link test Rx is significantly higher than Tx	RF has interference	Change radio channel
SNR uplink and downlink are off by 10 dB or more	RF has interference, LOS is obstructed, or hardware is bad	Change radio channel, check LOS, check hardware

[1]*LOS = line of sight*

Note   Indoor MAPs have a maximum hop count of 4, with a recommendation of 3.

Tip   Make sure that no autonomous APs (aIOS) are on the same VLAN as any of your RAPs. The Inter-Access Point Protocol (IAPP) messages from aIOS APs will corrupt the mesh forwarding tables and cause problems such as poor client throughput and MAP join problems that essentially bring down the entire mesh network.

show Commands

Several **show** commands are available on the controllers that you can use to see the state of your mesh deployment and help pinpoint a problem area.

Example 15-5 reveals the mesh **show** commands.

Example 15-5   *show mesh Command List*

```
(MeshController) >show mesh ?
env                Show mesh environment.
neigh              Show AP neigh list.
path               Show AP path.
astools            show mesh astools list
stats              Show AP stats.
secbh-stats        Show Mesh AP secondary backhaul stats.
per-stats          Show AP Neighbor Packet Error Rate stats.
```

```
queue-stats            Show AP local queue stats.
security-stats         Show AP security stats.
ap                     Show mesh AP information.
config                 Show mesh configurations.
secondary-backhaul     Show mesh secondary-backhaul
client-access          Show mesh backhaul with client access.
public-safety          Show mesh public safety.
background-scanning    Show mesh background-scanning state.
cac                    Show mesh cac.
bhrateadapt            Show Mesh Backhaul Rate Adaptation State.
```

Example 15-6 shows some sample output from the **show mesh neigh summary** command.

Example 15-6 *show mesh neigh summary Command Output*

```
(Cisco Controller) >show mesh neigh summary 1131
AP Name/Radio Mac   Channel Snr-Up Snr-Down Link-Snr Flags     State
-----------------   ------- ------ -------- -------- -------   -----
00:18:74:FB:1E:FF   36      13     13       13       0x860     BEACON
00:1C:F9:05:9D:DF   36      13     13       13       0x860     BEACON
00:1D:A1:CD:DD:6C   64      53     53       53       0x960     CHILD BEACON
```

With **show mesh neigh**, you can see the information from any child or parent APs as well as any other surrounding APs the AP hears. Here you can see three neighbors, one of which is a child AP.

To see more detailed information about the neighbors of an AP, use **show mesh neigh detail**, as demonstrated in Example 15-7.

Example 15-7 *show mesh neigh detail Command Output*

```
(Cisco Controller) >show mesh neigh detail 1131
AP MAC : 00:0B:85:65:51:60
FLAGS : 1160 CHILD DEFAULT
worstDv 255, Ant 0, channel 64, biters 0, ppiters 10
Numroutes 0, snr 0, snrUp 13, snrDown 13, linkSnr 13
adjustedEase 0, unadjustedEase 0
txParent 0, rxParent 0
poorSnr  0
lastUpdate    1241358733 (Sun May  3 13:52:13 2009)
parentChange 0
Per antenna smoothed snr values: 0 0 0 0
Vector through 00:0B:85:65:51:60
AP MAC : 00:18:74:FB:1E:FF
```

(continues)

Example 15-7   *show mesh neigh detail Command Output (continued)*

```
FLAGS : 860 BEACON
worstDv 255, Ant 0, channel 36, biters 0, ppiters 0
Numroutes 0, snr 0, snrUp 13, snrDown 13, linkSnr 13
adjustedEase 0, unadjustedEase 0
txParent 0, rxParent 0
poorSnr  0
lastUpdate   1241358199 (Sun May  3 13:43:19 2009)
parentChange 0
Per antenna smoothed snr values: 0 0 0 0
Vector through 00:18:74:FB:1E:FF
AP MAC : 00:1C:F9:05:9D:DF
FLAGS : 860 BEACON
worstDv 255, Ant 0, channel 36, biters 0, ppiters 0
Numroutes 0, snr 0, snrUp 13, snrDown 13, linkSnr 13
adjustedEase 0, unadjustedEase 0
txParent 0, rxParent 0
poorSnr  0
lastUpdate   1241358199 (Sun May  3 13:43:19 2009)
parentChange 0
Per antenna smoothed snr values: 0 0 0 0
Vector through 00:1C:F9:05:9D:DF
AP MAC : 00:1D:A1:CD:DD:6C
FLAGS : 860 BEACON
worstDv 255, Ant 0, channel 64, biters 0, ppiters 0
Numroutes 0, snr 0, snrUp 0, snrDown 0, linkSnr 0
adjustedEase 0, unadjustedEase 0
txParent 0, rxParent 0
poorSnr  0
lastUpdate   1241358245 (Sun May  3 13:44:05 2009)
parentChange 0
Per antenna smoothed snr values: 0 0 0 0
Vector through 00:1D:A1:CD:DD:6C
```

Using **show mesh ap tree**, as demonstrated in Example 15-8, you can see the logical parent child mappings, the hop count, the SNR, and the BGN.

Example 15-8   *show mesh ap tree Command Output*

```
(Cisco Controller) >show mesh ap tree
  ========================================================
|¦   AP Name [Hop Counter, Link SNR, Bridge Group Name] ¦|
  ========================================================
[Sector 1]
— — — — —
```

```
1131[0,0,leelab]
  ¦-1242[1,50,leelab]
 _ _ _ _ _ _ _ _ _ _ _ _ _ _ _ _ _ _ _ _ _ _ _ _ _ _
Number of Mesh APs.............................. 2
Number of RAPs.................................. 1
Number of MAPs.................................. 1
```

As demonstrated in Example 15-9, the **show mesh path** command displays the path through the mesh network to the AP you specify.

Example 15-9 *show mesh path Command Output*

```
(Cisco Controller) >show mesh path 1242
AP Name/Radio Mac  Channel Snr-Up Snr-Down Link-Snr Flags    State
-----------------  ------- ------ -------- -------- -------  -----
1131               64      61     54       51       0x86e    NEIGH PARENT BEACON
1131               is a Root AP.
```

This output also displays the channel in use and the SNR values. The MAP 1242 in this case is directly connected to the RAP 1131.

Remote Telnet and AP Debugs

You can gain a wealth of information from running **show** commands on the MAPs.

For the 1500 series APs, you need to run remote **debug** commands. To enable remote debugs for an AP, use the following command from the controller CLI:

```
debug ap enable AP_name
```

After you enable remote debugging on the AP, you can run debug commands to pull information directly from the AP:

debug ap command `"command"` `AP_name`

Some of the commands you can run on the 1500s are as follows:

- **printRadar():** Displays radar information
- **printBsnRateTable(1):** Displays valid radio data rates
- **apCfgRadioChannelGet(0):** Displays current radio channel
- **keyShow(0):** Displays encryption key entries per radio
- **apPrintForwardList:** Displays client transmit statistics
- **sibSmeShow(0):** Displays association table
- **sibStationShow(0,3):** Displays association table details

- **sibShow(0,3):** Displays additional client information

- **sibAgingShow():** Displays queue/frame information per MAC

- **dumpMeshSecBhStats(0):** Displays mesh backhaul stats

- **dumpAp():** Displays MAP info

- **dumpAdjs():** Displays mesh adjacencies

- **spamPrintRcb:** Displays AP control block information

- **ifShow:** Displays interface information and AP IP address

- **bsnPrintCrashData():** Displays AP crash data

- **SpamPrintCfgFile():** Displays current AP configuration

Example 15-10 demonstrates some sample output from **debug ap command dumpAdjs()**.

Example 15-10   *debug ap command dumpAdjs()Command Output*

```
(MeshController) >debug ap command "dumpAdjs()" lab5map1510
(MeshController) >Sun May  3 09:07:46 2009: lab5map1510: Calling "dumpAdjs" with
args 0x0, 0x0, 0x0, 0x0
Sun May  3 09:07:46 2009: lab5map1510: ADJ 1 Identity 001b.d4a6.f3e4 MA: 001c.0e
75.240f version 0x20 Error/10K txpkts 6181
Sun May  3 09:07:46 2009: lab5map1510: Flags: CHILD BEACON
Sun May  3 09:07:46 2009: lab5map1510:   Minor ver: 32, worstDv 255 Ant 0, channe
l 0, biters 0, ppiters 10
Sun May  3 09:07:46 2009: lab5map1510:   Numroutes 0, snr 0, snrUp 8 snrDown 0 li
nkSnr 0 blistExp 3 bliters 0
Sun May  3 09:07:46 2009: lab5map1510:   adjustedEase 0 unadjustedEase 0 txParent
0 rxParent 0
Sun May  3 09:07:46 2009: lab5map1510:   Secondary backhaul channel: 0 BGN  Last
exclusion cause:0
Sun May  3 09:07:46 2009: lab5map1510:   Vector through 001c.0e75.240f:
Sun May  3 09:07:46 2009: lab5map1510:   Per antenna smoothed snr values: 0 0 0 0
Sun May  3 09:07:46 2009: lab5map1510:   Subordinate neighbors: 001b.d4a6.f3e4
Sun May  3 09:07:46 2009: lab5map1510:   Time since last update: 0 Days, 00:00:02
Sun May  3 09:07:46 2009: lab5map1510: dumpAdjs Returns: 0
```

This output shows you the uplink and downlink SNRs for any parent or child AP as well as any other neighbors the AP hears. This particular AP is RAP with no children.

Obviously, remembering these commands and what they do is difficult. You could run several other commands from the controller CLI to get information on the different quality of service (QoS) queues, Differentiated Services Code Point (DSCP), Cisco Discovery Protocol (CDP), and more. In the 4.2 mesh release of code, Cisco has added new commands specific to the 1510 series APs, as the output in Example 15-11 reveals.

Example 15-11   *show mesh 1510-ap Commands*

```
(Cisco Controller) >show mesh 1510-ap ?
QoS-info - Displays various Queues on Mesh Backhaul
mesh-entries - Displays Mesh Association Table Entries
backhaul-stats - Displays Mesh Backhaul Statistics
client-stats - Displays Access Radio and Client information
mesh-aging - Displays Mesh Aging Parameters
11h-info - Displays 802.11h Management Frame Parameters
secBh-stats - Displays Secondary Backhaul Statistics
mesh-adjs - Displays Mesh Adjacencies
interface-info - Displays Ethernet and Loopback Interface Information
lwapp-config - Displays LWAPP Configuration
```

These new commands make viewing 1510 information easier because they are easier to remember and can combine several commands into one. For example, **QoS-info** includes **dDetails**, **qShow**, **showQreset**, and **dumpQueueDrops** output.

For the 1520 series APs, you can enable Telnet or run remote debugs from the controller:

```
debug ap enable AP_name
debug ap command "test mesh enable telnet" AP_name
```

Once Telnet is enabled, you can Telnet to the AP's IP address and run commands directly on the AP instead of remotely through the controller like on the 1510s. You can run the following commands on the 152x AP:

- **show mesh adj all:** Displays mesh adjacencies

- **show mesh dfs history:** Displays radar history

- **show mesh dfs channel** *channel*: Displays the current DFS channel

- **show controllers dot111:** Displays A radio

- **show controllers dot110:** Displays B/G radio

- **show interface dot111:** Displays A radio stats

- **show interface dot110:** Displays B/G radio stats

- **show ip int brief:** Displays IP information

- **config mesh linktest** *src AP name dst AP name* **18 100:** Runs a link test with a backhaul rate of 18 and 100 pps

Ethernet Bridging Troubleshooting

Before the 5.2 code release, troubleshooting Ethernet bridging with mesh APs was almost impossible. You had to rely on packet captures and Ethernet interface statistics.

Cisco added several **show** and **debug** commands with the 5.2 release to help troubleshoot and view VLAN tagging information.

From the controller, you can verify your VLAN tagging configuration using the following commands:

■ **show ap config ethernet** *AP_name*

■ **show mesh config**

The **show ap config ethernet** command shows you the mode of the Ethernet port, the native VLAN, and any allowed VLANs, as demonstrated in Example 15-12.

Example 15-12 *show ap config ethernet Command Output*

```
Cisco Controller) >show ap config ethernet 1131
Vlan Tagging Information For AP 1131
Ethernet 0
Mode: TRUNK
                                                      Native Vlan 12

Allowed Vlans:
```

The **show mesh config** command shows the status of VLAN transparency mode, as demonstrated in Example 15-13.

Example 15-13 *show mesh config Command Output*

```
(Cisco Controller) >show mesh config
Mesh Range...................................... 12000
Backhaul with client access status.............. disabled
Background Scanning State....................... enabled
Mesh Security
    Security Mode............................... EAP
    External-Auth............................... disabled
    Use MAC Filter in External AAA server........ disabled
    Force External Authentication................ disabled
Mesh Alarm Criteria
    Max Hop Count............................... 4
    Recommended Max Children for MAP............. 10
    Recommended Max Children for RAP............. 20
    Low Link SNR................................ 12
    High Link SNR............................... 60
    Max Association Number...................... 10
    Association Interval........................ 60 minutes
    Parent Change Numbers....................... 3
    Parent Change Interval...................... 60 minutes
    Mesh Multicast Mode......................... In-Out
    Mesh Full Sector DFS........................ enabled
    Mesh Ethernet Bridging VLAN Transparent Mode..... disabled
```

As you can see in Example 15-13, **show mesh config** shows the entire mesh configuration for a controller.

> **Tip** One configuration that confuses most users is the Mesh Range setting. In the controller GUI, this setting is the RAP to MAP distance. Most think that this is the distance from the RAP to the first MAP, but that is incorrect; this value merely adjusts a timer to tell the APs how long they should wait to receive an ACK from a child AP. The higher the value (in feet), the longer the sending AP waits for a response. The general rule of thumb is that the Mesh Distance should be set to the farthest distance between any two APs in the mesh network.

Here are the **mesh ap debug** commands:

- **debug mesh ethernet bridging:** Debugs Ethernet bridging
- **debug mesh ethernet config:** Debugs access and trunk port configuration
- **debug mesh ethernet registration:** Debugs VLAN registration protocol
- **debug mesh forwarding table:** Debugs forwarding table containing bridge groups
- **debug mesh forwarding packet bridge-group:** Debugs the bridge group packet forwarding

Here are the **mesh ap show** commands:

- **show mesh forwarding table:** Shows all the bridges with their mac-table entries.
- **show mesh forwarding vlan mode:** Displays VLAN-Transparent mode.
- **show mesh forwarding vlan statistics:** Displays VLAN forwarding statistics.
- **show mesh forwarding vlans:** Shows all the supported VLANs.
- **show mesh forwarding interfaces:** Displays the bridge groups and the interfaces contained in them. Useful for troubleshooting the bridge group membership.
- **show mesh ethernet vlan statistics:** Shows Ethernet subinterface statistics.

Example 15-14 demonstrates output from the **show mesh forwarding table** command.

Example 15-14 *show mesh forwarding table Command Output*

```
(Cisco Controller) >debug ap command "show mesh forwarding table" 1242
(Cisco Controller) >*May 03 13:13:49.219: 1242:
*May 03 13:13:49.219: 1242: Mesh Forwarding Table Entries
```

(continues)

Example 15-14 *show mesh forwarding table Command Output (continued)*

```
*May 03 13:13:49.219: 1242:
*May 03 13:13:49.219: 1242: Bridge Group 1    Vlan 1 :
*May 03 13:13:49.219: 1242:    0023.5df1.9d40, nh 001c.b107.fa2f, swif Virtual-
Dot11Radio1:BACKHAUL: 43 : 8
*May 03 13:13:49.219: 1242:    0023.5df1.9d06, nh 001c.b107.fa2f, swif Virtual-
Dot11Radio1:BACKHAUL: 43 : 8
*May 03 13:13:49.219: 1242:    001c.b107.fa2f, nh 001c.b107.fa2f, swif Virtual-
Dot11Radio1:AWPP: 23 : 8
*May 03 13:13:49.219: 1242:    001c.58dc.97b0, nh 001c.b107.fa2f, swif Virtual-
Dot11Radio1:BACKHAUL: 43 : 7
*May 03 13:13:49.219: 1242:    0010.a4e5.2056, nh 001c.b107.fa2f, swif Virtual-
Dot11Radio1:BACKHAUL: 43 : 8
*May 03 13:13:49.219: 1242:    0001.0386.1991, nh 001c.b107.fa2f, swif Virtual-
Dot11Radio1:BACKHAUL: 43 : 8
*May 03 13:13:49.219: 1242:
*May 03 13:13:49.219: 1242: Bridge Group 2    Vlan 12 :
*May 03 13:13:49.219: 1242:
*May 03 13:13:49.219: 1242: Table size: 128, count 3
*May 03 13:13:49.219: 1242:    0023.5df1.9d06 Virtual-Dot11Radio1 LEARNED (life 300)
*May 03 13:13:49.219: 1242:    000f.b049.5898 FastEthernet0 LEARNED (life 300)
*May 03 13:13:49.219: 1242:    0023.5df1.9d43 Virtual-Dot11Radio1 LEARNED (life 300)
```

From this output you can see that this AP has two bridge groups: one for VLAN 1 and the other for VLAN 12. There is a wired client in VLAN 12 with the MAC address of 000f.b049.5898.

The output from **show mesh forwarding vlan mode** tells you whether VLAN transparency is enabled or disabled on the AP, as demonstrated in Example 15-15.

Example 15-15 *show mesh forwarding vlan mode Command Output*

```
(Cisco Controller) >debug ap command "show mesh forwarding vlan mode" 1242
(Cisco Controller) >*May 03 13:15:53.025: 1242:
*May 03 13:15:53.025: 1242:  Vlan Transparent mode DISABLED
To see the VLANs that the AP is bridging, use show mesh forwarding vlan:
(Cisco Controller) >*May 03 13:15:17.697: 1242:
*May 03 13:15:17.697: 1242: Mesh Forwarding Vlans
*May 03 13:15:17.697: 1242: Vlan: 1      Supporting Bridge Group: 1
*May 03 13:15:17.697: 1242: Vlan: 12     Supporting Bridge Group: 2
```

To see transmit and receive stats for the bridged VLANs, use **show mesh ethernet vlan statistics**, as demonstrated in Example 15-16.

Example 15-16   *show mesh ethernet vlan statistics Command Output*

```
(Cisco Controller) >debug ap command "show mesh ethernet vlan statistics" 1242
Interface             Rx Packets  Tx Packets  Tbridge Reject
FastEthernet0               119          41                0
```

This output is helpful in determining whether traffic is passing over the bridge links.

To troubleshoot bridge group membership, use **show mesh forwarding interfaces**, as demonstrated in Example 15-17.

Example 15-17   *show mesh forwarding interfaces Output*

```
(Cisco Controller) >debug ap command "show mesh forwarding interfaces" 1242
(Cisco Controller) >*May 03 13:19:26.714: 1242: Bridge Group 1: Ethernet
Bridging enabled
*May 03 13:19:26.714: 1242:    Virtual-Dot11Radio1: Virtual-Dot11Radio1(state is
OPEN)
*May 03 13:19:26.714: 1242:        Node 001c.b107.fa2f
*May 03 13:19:26.714: 1242: Bridge Group 2: Ethernet Bridging enabled
*May 03 13:19:26.714: 1242:    FastEthernet0: FastEthernet0(state is OPEN)
*May 03 13:19:26.714: 1242:        Node 0083.e574.0b0d
*May 03 13:19:26.714: 1242:    Virtual-Dot11Radio1: Virtual-Dot11Radio1(state is
OPEN)
*May 03 13:19:26.714: 1242:        Node 001c.b107.fa2f
```

Here you can see that Ethernet bridging is enabled for bridge group 1 and 2. The FastEthernet port 0 is in bridge group 2. With the preceding output of **show mesh forwarding vlan,** you know that bridge group 2 is forwarding VLAN 12.

> **Note**   The switch trunk port should not allow any VLAN other than the VLANs configured on the mesh APs. Because of a bug, CSCsr87215, the packets from any non-configured VLANs are accepted in the native-VLAN through the RAP backhaul Ethernet interface. You can easily avoid this by carefully configuring the switch port.

Summary

Wireless mesh deployments are becoming more and more popular as colleges, towns, police and fire departments, and cities strive to provide wireless access. When installing a mesh network, it is important to remember to prime the APs on the wired network because this small step lets you know if the APs are functioning properly before you install them 40 or 50 feet off the ground on a light pole or the side of a building. You need to know what VLANs need to be trunked across the mesh network if you are going to enable Ethernet bridging. You also need to make sure all the APs in the mesh path are configured to support those VLANs. You should conduct a proper site survey to ensure that your AP placement allows for good SNR links between the APs and that the line of sight and Fresnel zones are clear. Depending on the physical distance between your APs, you might have to use laser devices to properly align the antennas. Keeping these factors in mind will help you deploy a fast and stable wireless mesh network.

Debugging Commands

A major tool for troubleshooting Cisco Wireless LAN Controllers (WLC) is the **debug** command executed on the controller command-line interface (CLI). This appendix provides a comprehensive overview of the available **debug** commands and their uses.

WLC Debugs

The tables in the sections that follow outline all the possible debugs that you can run on the WLC. Keep in mind that some of these debugs might not be available in certain versions. The lists of debugs are those available from Release 5.2.x.x and earlier.

Existing Debugs in Software Version 5.0 and Earlier

Table A-1 lists all the Authentication, Authorization, and Accounting (AAA) **debug** options used to troubleshoot interactions between the controller and external authentication servers in web authentication and similar setups.

Table A-1 *AAA Debug Options*

Command	Description
**debug aaa all [enable	disable]**	Specifies debugging of all AAA messages.
**debug aaa detail [enable	disable]**	Specifies debugging of AAA errors.
**debug aaa events [enable	disable]**	Specifies debugging of AAA events.
**debug aaa packet [enable	disable]**	Specifies debugging of AAA packets.
**debug aaa ldap [enable	disable]**	Specifies debugging of the AAA LDAP[1] events.

[1]LDAP = Lightweight Directory Access Protocol

Table A-2 lists all the AAA local authentication debug options.

Table A-2 *AAA Local Authentication Debug Options*

Command	Description
debug aaa local-auth db [enable | disable]	Configures debugging of the AAA local authentication backend messages and events.
debug aaa local-auth eap framework all [enable | disable]	Configures debugging of all the AAA local EAP[1] authentication.
debug aaa local-auth eap framework errors [enable | disable]	Configures debugging of the AAA local EAP authentication errors.
debug aaa local-auth eap framework events [enable | disable]	Configures debugging of the AAA local EAP authentication events.
debug aaa local-auth eap framework packets [enable | disable]	Configures debugging of the AAA local EAP authentication packets.
debug aaa local-auth eap framework sm [enable | disable]	Configures debugging of the AAA local EAP authentication state machine.
debug aaa local-auth eap method all [enable | disable]	Configures debugging of all local EAP methods.
debug aaa local-auth eap method errors [enable | disable]	Configures debugging of local EAP method errors.
debug aaa local-auth eap method events [enable | disable]	Configures debugging of local EAP method events.
debug aaa local-auth eap method packets [enable | disable]	Configures debugging of local EAP method packets.
debug aaa local-auth eap method sm [enable | disable]	Configures debugging of the local EAP method state machine.
debug aaa local-auth shim [enable | disable]	Configures debugging of local EAP method shim layer events.

[1]EAP = Extensible Authentication Protocol

Table A-3 lists all the AAA TACACS+ **debug** options used for controller administrator authentication issues.

Table A-3 *AAA TACACS+ Debug Options*

Command	Description
debug aaa tacacs [enable | disable]	Specifies debugging of the AAA TACACS+ events.

Table A-4 lists all the Airewave Director **debug** options. Those are the debugs needed for troubleshooting Radio Resource Management (RRM) issues and other RF-related details such as radar events.

Table A-4   *Airewave Director Debug Options*

Command	Description
debug airewave-director all [enable | disable]	Configures debugging of all Airewave Director logs.
debug airewave-director channel [enable | disable]	Configures debugging of the Airewave Director channel assignment protocol.
debug airewave-director error [enable | disable]	Configures debugging of Airewave Director error logs.
debug airewave-director detail [enable | disable]	Configures debugging of Airewave Director detail logs.
debug airewave-director group [enable | disable]	Configures debugging of the Airewave Director grouping protocol.
debug airewave-director manager [enable | disable]	Configures debugging of the Airewave Director manager.
debug airewave-director message [enable | disable]	Configures debugging of Airewave Director messages.
debug airewave-director packet [enable | disable]	Configures debugging of Airewave Director packets.
debug airewave-director power [enable | disable]	Configures debugging of the Airewave Director power assignment protocol and coverage hole detection.
debug airewave-director radar [enable | disable]	Configures debugging of the Airewave Director radar detection/avoidance protocol.
debug airewave-director rf-change [enable | disable]	Configures debugging of Airewave Director RF changes.
debug airewave-director profile [enable | disable]	Configures debugging of Airewave Director profile events.

Table A-5 lists all the Address Resolution Protocol (ARP) debug options. Those debugs are useful if an 802.11 link is established but basic IP connectivity is not working, such as failing Dynamic Host Configuration Protocol (DHCP) and similar issues.

Table A-5   *ARP Debug Options*

Command	Description
debug arp all [enable | disable]	Configures debugging of all ARP logs.
debug arp error [enable | disable]	Configures debugging of ARP errors.
debug arp message [enable | disable]	Configures debugging of ARP messages.
debug arp detail [enable | disable]	Configures debugging of ARP detail messages.

Table A-6 lists all the broadcast **debug** options. These debugs are used while troubleshooting packet forwarding issues on the controller, in conjunction with multicast setups or in case of packet flood issues.

Table A-6   *Broadcast Debug Options*

Command	Description
debug bcast all [enable | disable]	Configures debugging of all broadcast logs.
debug bcast error [enable | disable]	Configures debugging of broadcast errors.
debug bcast message [enable | disable]	Configures debugging of broadcast messages.
debug bcast igmp [enable | disable]	Configures debugging of broadcast messages.
debug bcast detail [enable | disable]	Configures debugging of broadcast detailed messages.

Table A-7 lists all the Call Admission Control (CAC) debug options. These debugs are used in voice setups, quality of service (QoS), and Wi-Fi Multimedia (WMM) issues.

Table A-7   *CAC Debug Options*

Command	Description
debug cac all [enable | disable]	Configures debugging of all CAC messages.
debug cac event [enable | disable]	Configures debugging of CAC events.
debug cac packet [enable | disable]	Configures debugging of CAC packets.

Table A-8 lists all the Cisco Centralized Key Management (CCKM) debug options. CCKM debugs are used to troubleshoot client roaming and (re)association issues.

Table A-8   *CCKM Debug Options*

Command	Description
debug cckm client [enable | disable]	Configures a debug of CCKM.
debug cckm detailed [enable | disable]	Configures a detailed debug of CCKM.

Table A-9 lists all the Cisco Compatible Extension (CCX) debug options. These debugs are used to troubleshoot interoperability issues with CCX wireless clients as well as details of CCX radio measurement message exchanges such as client location calibration activities.

Table A-9   *CCX Debug Options*

Command	Description
debug ccxdiag all [enable | disable]	Configures a debug of all CCX diagnostic messages.
debug ccxdiag event [enable | disable]	Configures a debug of CCX diagnostic event events.
debug ccxdiag error [enable | disable]	Configures a debug of CCX diagnostic error events.
debug ccxdiag packet [enable | disable]	Configures a debug of CCX diagnostic packet events.
debug ccxrm all [enable | disable]	Configures a debug of all CCX client location calibration activity messages.
debug ccxrm detail [enable | disable]	Configures a debug of CCX_RM detail.
debug ccxrm error [enable | disable]	Configures a debug of CCX_RM error events.
debug ccxrm location-calibration [enable | disable]	Configures a debug of CCX_RM location calibration.
debug ccxrm message [enable | disable]	Configures a debug of CCX_RM message events.
debug ccxrm packet [enable | disable]	Configures a debug of CCX_RM packets.
debug ccxrm warning [enable | disable]	Configures a debug of CCX_RM warning events.

Table A-10 lists all the Cisco Discovery Protocol (CDP) debug options.

Table A-10 *CDP Debug Options*

Command	Description
debug cdp events [enable | disable]	Configures a debug of CDP events.
debug cdp packets [enable | disable]	Configures a debug of CDP packets.

Table A-11 shows how to enable the command **debug client** *mac_address*. This **debug** command is a macro that enables eight **debug** commands, plus a filter on the MAC address provided, so only messages that contain the specified MAC address are shown. The eight **debug** commands show the most important details on client association and authentication. The filter helps with situations in which there are multiple wireless clients—situations such as when too much output is generated or the controller is over-loaded when debugging is enabled without the filter.

Table A-11 *Common Client-Related Debug Options*

Command	Description
debug client mac_address	This command enables the following debugs for the MAC address specified with "MAC_addr" and applies a MAC filter for the further client debugs added afterward: ■ dhcp packet enabled ■ dot11 mobile enabled ■ dot11 state enabled ■ dot1x events enabled ■ dot1x states enabled ■ pem events enabled ■ pem state enabled ■ CCKM client debug enabled

Table A-12 lists all the Hardware Crypto debug options. The VPN termination hardware module is the module that was used in pre-4.0 setups that were installed on the controller, whereas any WLCs that run version 4.0 or later do not support such a module. Therefore, the only VPN feature supported in versions later than 4.0 is VPN Pass-through.

Table A-12 *Hardware Crypto Debug Options*

Command	Description
debug crypto all [enable | disable]	Configures a debug of all hardware crypto messages.
debug crypto sessions [enable | disable]	Configures a debug of hardware crypto sessions.
debug crypto trace [enable | disable]	Configures a debug of hardware crypto sessions.
debug crypto warnings [enable | disable]	Configures a debug of hardware crypto sessions.

Table A-13 lists all the DHCP debug options. Use this debug for the internal DHCP server of the controller and if the controller is acting as DHCP proxy and DHCP activities on the service port.

Table A-13   *DHCP Debug Options*

Command	Description
debug dhcp message [enable | disable]	Configures a debug of DHCP error messages.
debug dhcp packet [enable | disable]	Configures a debug of DHCP packets.
debug dhcp service-port [enable | disable]	Enables/disables debugging of DHCP packets on the service port.

Table A-14 lists all the 802.1x debug options. These debugs are useful for troubleshooting key-handshake issues as well as complete EAP authentications. Using these **debug** command options, it is possible to isolate which identity involved in an EAP authentication is breaking.

Table A-14   *802.1x Debug Options*

Command	Description
debug dot1x aaa [enable | disable]	Configures a debug of 802.1X AAA interactions.
debug dot1x all [enable | disable]	Configures a debug of all 802.1x messages.
debug dot1x events [enable | disable]	Configures a debug of 802.1x events.
debug dot1x packet [enable | disable]	Configures a debug of 802.1x packets.
debug dot1x states [enable | disable]	Configures a debug of 802.1x mobile state transitions.

Table A-15 lists all the 802.11 event debug options. These debugs are important while troubleshooting wireless client connectivity and mobility issues and other 802.11-related activities such as rogue location discovery.

Table A-15 *802.11 Events Debug Options*

Command	Description
debug dot11 all [enable | disable]	Configures a debug of all 802.11 messages.
debug dot11 load-balancing [enable | disable]	Configures a debug of 802.11 load balancing events.
debug dot11 management [enable | disable]	Configures a debug of 802.11 MAC management messages.
debug dot11 mobile [enable | disable]	Configures a debug of 802.11 mobile events.
debug dot11 rldp [enable | disable]	Configures a debug of 802.11 Rogue Location Discovery.
debug dot11 rogue [enable | disable]	Configures a debug of 802.11 rogue events.
debug dot11 rogue rule [enable | disable]	Configures a debug of 802.11 rogue rule events.
debug dot11 state [enable | disable]	Configures a debug of 802.11 mobile state transitions.

Table A-16 lists all the WEB debug options. Those debugs are used when you have issues with the controller-embedded web server.

Table A-16 *WEB Debug Options*

Command	Description
debug emweb server [enable | disable]	Configures a debug of the WEB server.
debug emweb web [enable | disable]	Configures a debug of WEB application code.

Table A-17 lists all the 802.11r debug options. 802.11r is the IEEE proposal for a fast-roaming standard.

Table A-17 *802.11r Debug Options*

Command	Description
debug ft events [enable | disable]	Configures a debug of 802.11r events.
debug ft keys [enable | disable]	Configures a debug of 802.11r key generation.
debug ft all [enable | disable]	Configures a debug of all 802.11r events.

Table A-18 lists all the guest-lan error message debug options.

Table A-18   *guest-lan Error Message Debug Options*

Command	Description
debug guest-lan client [enable | disable]	Configures a debug of guest-lan client error messages.

Table A-19 lists all the Hybrid Remote Edge Access Point (H-REAP) debug options. Use these debugs when troubleshooting H-REAP backup RADIUS server events or errors and H-REAP configuration issues.

Table A-19   *H-REAP Debug Options*

Command	Description
debug hreap aaa event [enable | disable]	Configures a debug of H-REAP AAA events.
debug hreap aaa error [enable | disable]	Configures a debug of H-REAP AAA errors.
debug hreap group [enable | disable]	Configures a debug of the H-REAP group.

Table A-20 lists all the H-REAP CCKM debug options. This command is used while troubleshooting roaming and (re)association issues on a remote side while access points (AP) are in local mode.

Table A-20   *H-REAP CCKM Options*

Command	Description
debug hreap cckm [enable | disable]	Configures a debug of H-REAP CCKM.

Table A-21 lists all the Inter Access Point Protocol (IAPP) debug options.

Table A-21   *IAPP Debug Options*

Command	Description
debug iapp all [enable | disable]	Configures a debug of all IAPP messages.
debug iapp error [enable | disable]	Configures a debug of IAPP error events.
debug iapp locp [enable | disable]	Configures a debug of IAPP Narrative Media Streaming Protocol (NMSP) events.
debug iapp packet [enable | disable]	Configures a debug of IAPP packets.

Table A-22 lists all the Location Control Protocol (LOCP) aggregate event debug options. It is used in location appliance setups.

Table A-22 *LOCP Aggregate Event Debug Options*

Command	Description
**debug locp aggregate [enable	disable]**	Configures a debug of LOCP aggregate events.
**debug locp all [enable	disable]**	Configures a debug of all LOCP messages.
**debug locp detail [enable	disable]**	Configures a debug of LOCP detailed events.
**debug locp error [enable	disable]**	Configures a debug of LOCP error messages.
**debug locp event [enable	disable]**	Configures a debug of LOCP events.
**debug locp packet [enable	disable]**	Configures debug of LOCP packet events.

Table A-23 lists all the Lightweight Access Point Protocol (LWAPP) debug options. These are the crucial debugs when troubleshooting LWAPP join problems. (For more details see Chapter 3, "Introduction to LWAPP.")

Table A-23 *LWAPP Debug Options*

Command	Description
**debug lwapp events [enable	disable]**	Configures a debug of LWAPP events and errors.
**debug lwapp errors [enable	disable]**	Configures a debug of LWAPP errors.
**debug lwapp detail [enable	disable]**	Configures a debug of LWAPP detail.
**debug lwapp packet [enable	disable]**	Configures a debug of LWAPP packet trace.

Table A-24 lists all the Layer 2 ROAM debug options.

Table A-24 *Layer 2 Roam Debug Options*

Command	Description
**debug l2roam all [enable	disable]**	Configures a debug of all L2ROAM messages.
**debug l2roam detail [enable	disable]**	Configures a debug of L2ROAM detail events.
**debug l2roam error [enable	disable]**	Configures a debug of L2ROAM error events.
**debug l2roam packet [enable	disable]**	Configures a debug of L2ROAM packet events.

Table A-25 lists all the MAC debug options. Use this command to limit the output of the subsequent **debug** command to a single MAC address. LWAPP or Control and Provisioning of Wireless Access Points Protocol (CAPWAP) debugs, for example, can be limited to a specific AP when using **debug mac addr** AP's wired MAC address before enabling the CAPWAP/LWAPP debugs.

Table A-25   *MAC Debug Options*

Command	Description
debug mac disable	Disables MAC debugging.
debug mac addr *MAC_addr*	Enables MAC debugging.

Table A-26 lists all the mesh debug options.

Table A-26   *Mesh Debug Options*

Command	Description
debug mesh security all [enable | disable]	Configures a debug of all mesh security messages.
debug mesh security events [enable | disable]	Configures a debug of mesh security event messages.
debug mesh security errors [enable | disable]	Configures a debug of mesh security error messages.
debug mesh message env [enable | disable]	Configures a debug of mesh message environment update.
debug mesh message neigh [enable | disable]	Configures a debug of mesh message neigh update.
debug mesh message node [enable | disable]	Configures a debug of mesh message node update.
debug mesh message stats [enable | disable]	Configures a debug of mesh message stats update.

Table A-27 lists all the mobility debug options. These are the debugs needed while troubleshooting client inter-controller roaming.

Table A-27 *Mobility Debug Options*

Command	Description
debug mobility directory [enable | disable]	Configures a debug of mobility error messages.
debug mobility handoff [enable | disable]	Configures a debug of mobility packets.
debug mobility multicast [enable | disable]	Configures a debug of multicast mobility packets.
debug mobility keep-alive [enable | disable]	Configures a debug of mobility keep-alive messages.

Table A-28 lists all the Network Admission Control (NAC) debug options.

Table A-28 *NAC Debug Options*

Command	Description
debug nac packet [enable | disable]	Configures a debug of NAC packets.
debug nac events [enable | disable]	Configures a debug of NAC events.

Table A-29 lists all the detailed Network Time Protocol (NTP) message debug options.

Table A-29 *NTP Message Debug Options*

Command	Description
debug ntp detail [enable | disable]	Configures a debug of detailed NTP messages.
debug ntp low [enable | disable]	Configures a debug of NTP messages.
debug ntp packet [enable | disable]	Configures a debug of NTP packets.

Table A-30 lists all the policy enforcement module (PEM) debug options. This module is explained in Chapter 10, "Troubleshooting Client-Related Issues". The debug is important when troubleshooting client association, authentication, and connectivity issues.

Table A-30 *Policy Manager Debug Options*

Command	Description
debug pem events [enable | disable]	Configures a debug of policy manager events.
debug pem state [enable | disable]	Configures a debug of the policy manager state machine.

Table A-31 lists all the security policy manager module debug options. This debug is used while troubleshooting security-related issues such as certificate validation that are passed between the AP and the WLC.

Table A-31 *Security Policy Manager Module Debug Options*

Command	Description
debug pm all [enable | disable]	Disables all debugs in policy manager module.
debug pm init [enable | disable]	Configures a debug of policy manager initialization events.
debug pm config [enable | disable]	Configures a debug of policy manager configuration.
debug pm rules [enable | disable]	Configures a debug of Layer 3 policy events.
debug pm message [enable | disable]	Configures a debug of policy manager message queue events.
debug pm pki [enable | disable]	Configures a debug of PKI[1]-related events. Shows the debug of certificate messages that are passed between the AP and the WLC.
debug pm sa-export [enable | disable]	Configures a debug of SA[2] export (mobility).
debug pm sa-import [enable | disable]	Configures a debug of SA import (mobility).
debug pm hwcrypto [enable | disable]	Configures a debug of hardware offload events.

(continues)

Table A-31   *Security Policy Manager Module Debug Options (continued)*

Command	Description
debug pm rng [enable | disable]	Configures a debug of random number generation.
debug pm ssh-pmgr [enable | disable]	Configures a debug of the policy manager.
debug pm ssh-engine [enable | disable]	Configures a debug of the policy manager engine.
debug pm ssh-int [enable | disable]	Configures a debug of the policy manager interceptor.
debug pm ssh-appgw [enable | disable]	Configures a debug of application gateways.
debug pm ssh-tcp [enable | disable]	Configures a debug of policy manager TCP[3] handling.
debug pm ssh-l2tp [enable | disable]	Configures a debug of policy manager l2tp handling.
debug pm ssh-ppp [enable | disable]	Configures a debug of policy manager PPP[4] handling.
debug pm list [enable | disable]	Configures a debug of policy manager list management.
debug pm ikemsg [enable | disable]	Configures a debug of IKE[5] messages.

[1]PKI = Public Key Infrastructure
[2]SA = Security Association
[3]TCP = Transmission Control Protocol
[4]PPP = Point-to-Point Protocol
[5]IKE = Internet Key Exchange

Table A-32 lists all the Router Blade Configuration Protocol (RBCP) debug options.

Table A-32   *RBCP Debug Options*

Command	Description
debug rbcp all [enable | disable]	Configures a debug of RBCP.
debug rbcp errors [enable | disable]	Configures a debug of RBCP errors.
debug rbcp detail [enable | disable]	Configures a debug of RBCP detail.
debug rbcp packet [enable | disable]	Configures a debug of RBCP packet trace.

Table A-33 lists all the Simple Network Management Protocol (SNMP) debug options.

Table A-33 *SNMP Debug Options*

Command	Description
debug snmp all [enable | disable]	Configures a debug of all SNMP messages.
debug snmp agent [enable | disable]	Configures a debug of SNMP agent.
debug snmp mib [enable | disable]	Configures a debug of SNMP MIB[1].
debug snmp trap [enable | disable]	Configures a debug of SNMP traps.
debug snmp engine [enable | disable]	Configures a debug of the SNMP engine.

[1]MIB = management information base

Table A-34 lists all the transfer debug options. These debugs are used when troubleshooting a data transfer to and from the controller, such as a TFTP copy from a new image.

Table A-34 *Transfer Debug Options*

Command	Description
debug transfer all [enable | disable]	Configures a debug of all transfer messages.
debug transfer tftp [enable | disable]	Configures a debug of TFTP transfers.
debug transfer trace [enable | disable]	Configures a debug of a transfer/upgrade.

Table A-35 lists all the WLAN Control Protocol (WCP) debug options. WCP is the protocol running on the backplane to communicate with a Cisco Wireless Integrated Service Module (WiSM).

Table A-35 *WCP Debug Options*

Command	Description
debug wcp packet [enable | disable]	Configures a debug of WCP packets.
debug wcp events [enable | disable]	Configures a debug of WCP events.

Table A-36 lists all the Management Frame Protection (MFP) debug options.

Table A-36   *Management Frame Debug Options*

Command	Description
debug wps mfp client [enable | disable]	Configures a debug of Client MFP messages.
debug wps mfp lwapp [enable | disable]	Configures a debug of MFP messages.
debug wps mfp detail [enable | disable]	Configures a detailed debug of MFP LWAPP messages.
debug wps mfp report [enable | disable]	Configures a debug of MFP reporting.
debug wps mfp mm [enable | disable]	Configures a debug of MFP mobility (inter-controller) messages.
debug wps sig event [enable | disable]	Debugs signature events.
debug wps sig error [enable | disable]	Debugs signature errors.
debug wps cids [enable | disable]	Configures a debug of CIDS[1] integration.

[1]CIDS = Connection Identification

Debugs Introduced in Software Version 5.1

Table A-37 lists all the CCX S60 Power Measurement Loss message debug options.

Table A-37   *CCX S60 Power Measurement Loss Message Debug Options*

Command	Description
debug airewave-director plm [enable | disable]	Configures a debug of CCX S60 Power Measurement Loss messages.

Table A-38 lists all the licensing debug options.

Table A-38   *Licensing Debug Options*

Command	Description
debug license errors [enable | disable]	Configures debugging of licensing errors.
debug license events [enable | disable]	Configures debugging of licensing events.
debug license core errors [enable | disable]	Configures debugging of licensing core errors.
debug license core events [enable | disable]	Configures debugging of licensing core events.
debug license core all [enable | disable]	Configures debugging of licensing core all.
debug license agent errors [enable | disable]	Configures debugging of license agent errors.
debug license agent all [enable | disable]	Configures debugging of license agent all.

Table A-39 lists all the CCX S69 debug options.

Table A-39   *CCX S69 Debug Options*

Command	Description
debug ccxs69 all [enable | disable]	Configures a debug of all CCX S69 messages.
debug ccxs69 event [enable | disable]	Configures a debug of CCX S69 events.
debug ccxs69 error [enable | disable]	Configures a debug of CCX error events.

Table A-40 lists all the radio frequency identification (RFID) debug options.

Table A-40   *RFID Debug Options*

Command	Description
debug rfid all [enable | disable]	Configures a debug of all RFID messages.
debug rfid detail [enable | disable]	Configures a debug of RFID detailed events.
debug rfid error [enable | disable]	Configures a debug of RFID error messages.
debug rfid nmsp [enable | disable]	Configures a debug of RFID NMSP[1] messages.
debug rfid receive [enable | disable]	Configures a debug of RFID tag messages.

[1]NMSP=Network Mobility Services Protocol (NMSP)

Table A-41 lists all the Fixed Mobile Convergence Handover Service (FMCHS) debug options.

Table A-41 *FMCHS Debug Options*

Command	Description
debug fmchs all [enable	disable]	Configures a debug of all FMCHS messages.
debug fmchs error [enable	disable]	Configures a debug of FMCHS error events.
debug fmchs locp [enable	disable]	Configures a debug of FMCHS LOCP events.
debug fmchs packet [enable	disable]	Configures a debug of FMCHS packets.
debug fmchs event [enable	disable]	Configures a debug of FMCHS events.

Table A-42 lists all the location debug options.

Table A-42 *Location Debug Options*

Command	Description
debug location plm [enable	disable]	Configures a debug of location PLM messages.
debug location client [enable	disable]	Configures a debug of location client messages.

Debugs Introduced in Software Version 6.0

Table A-43 lists all the CAPWAP events and state debug options. Refer to Chapter 4, "The CAPWAP Protocol," for CAPWAP protocol details and how to use these debugs.

Table A-43 *CAPWAP Events and State Debug Options*

Command	Description
debug capwap events [enable	disable]	Configures a debug of CAPWAP events and states.
debug capwap errors [enable	disable]	Configures a debug of CAPWAP errors.
debug capwap detail [enable	disable]	Configures a debug of CAPWAP details.
debug capwap info [enable	disable]	Configures a debug of CAPWAP information.
debug capwap payload [enable	disable]	Configures a debug of CAPWAP payloads.
debug capwap hexdump [enable	disable]	Configures a debug of CAPWAP payloads.

Table A-44 lists all the AP monitor service debug options.

Table A-44 *AP Monitor Service Debug Options*

Command	Description
debug service ap-monitor all [enable | disable]	Configures a debug of all AP monitor messages.
debug service ap-monitor error [enable | disable]	Configures a debug of AP monitor error events.
debug service ap-monitor event [enable | disable]	Configures a debug of AP monitor events.
debug service ap-monitor nmsp [enable | disable]	Configures a debug of AP monitor NMSP events.
debug service ap-monitor packet [enable | disable]	Configures a debug of AP monitor packets.

Table A-45 lists all the Datagram Transport Layer Security (DTLS) message-related debug options. These debugs are used in conjunction with CAPWAP troubleshooting. See Chapter 4 for more details about the conjunction.

Table A-45 *DTLS Message-Related Debug Options*

Command	Description
debug dtls all [enable | disable]	Configures a debug of all DTLS messages.
debug dtls event [enable | disable]	Configures a debug of DTLS event events.
debug dtls trace [enable | disable]	Configures a debug of DTLS event events.
debug dtls packet [enable | disable]	Configures a debug of DTLS packet events.

Table A-46 lists all the wireless LAN (WLAN) AP group–related debug options.

Table A-46 *WLAN AP Group–Related Debug Options*

Command	Description
debug group [enable | disable]	Configures a debug of WLAN AP group.

Table A-47 lists all the mesh-related debug options.

Table A-47   *Mesh-Related Debug Options*

Command	Description
debug mesh astools troubleshoot *MAC_addr* **start**	Enables debugging of mesh astools for the specified AP (by b/g radio MAC address of the stranded AP).
debug mesh astools troubleshoot *MAC_addr* **stop**	Disables debugging of mesh astools for the specified AP (by b/g radio MAC address of the stranded AP).
debug mesh alarms [enable | disable]	Configures the mesh alarms debug options.

Table A-48 lists all the NMSP debug options, used in context-aware mobility solutions.

Table A-48   *NMSP Debug Options*

Command	Description
debug nmsp all [enable | disable]	Configures a debug of all NMSP messages.
debug nmsp connection [enable | disable]	Configures a debug of NMSP connection events.
debug nmsp detail [enable | disable]	Configures a debug of NMSP detailed events.
debug nmsp error [enable | disable]	Configures a debug of NMSP error messages.
debug nmsp event [enable | disable]	Configures a debug of NMSP event events.
debug nmsp message rx [enable | disable]	Configures a debug of NMSP receive messages.
debug nmsp message tx [enable | disable]	Configures a debug of NMSP transmit messages.
debug nmsp packet [enable | disable]	Configures a debug of NMSP packet events.

Table A-49 lists all the Wireless Intrusion Prevention Service (WIPS) debug options.

Table A-49   *WIPS Debug Options*

Command	Description
debug wips all [enable | disable]	Configures a debug of all WIPS messages.
debug wips error [enable | disable]	Configures a debug of WIPS error events.
debug wips event [enable | disable]	Configures a debug of WIPS events.
debug wips nmsp [enable | disable]	Configures a debug of WIPS NMSP events.
debug wips packet [enable | disable]	Configures a debug of WIPS packets.

Table A-50 shows how to disable all active debugs. When the CLI is flooded with debug output, it is almost impossible to "search" for a debug using the question mark; therefore, it is highly recommended that you memorize this debug.

Table A-50   *Disable All Debugs*

Command	Description
debug disable-all	Disables all debug messages.

Debug Packet Logging

Packet logging, also known as the debug facility, enables you to display all packets going to and from the controller CPU. You can enable it for received packets, transmitted packets, or both. By default, all packets received by the debug facility are displayed. However, you can define access control lists (ACL) to filter packets before they are displayed. Packets not passing the ACLs are discarded without being displayed.

Each ACL includes an action (permit, deny, or disable) and one or more fields that can be used to match the packet.

Use the following steps to work with the packet logging debugging.

Step 1.   Enable the debug facility by entering the command **debug packet logging enable** {rx | tx | all} *packet_count display_size*.

Step 2.   Configure packet-logging ACLs according to Table A-51.

Step 3.   Configure the format of the debug output by entering the command **debug packet logging format** {hex2pcap | text2pcap}.

Step 4.   To remove all configured ACLs, enter this command: **debug packet logging acl clear-all**.

The debug facility provides ACLs that operate at the following levels and on the following values:

- Driver ACL

   NPU encapsulation type

   Port

- Ethernet header ACL

   Destination address

   Source address

   Ethernet type

   VLAN ID

Table A-51   *How to Configure Packet-Logging ACLs*

Command	Parameter Description
debug packet logging acl driver *rule_index action npu_encap port*	*rule_index* is a value between 1 and 6 (inclusive). action is permit, deny, or disable. *npu_encap* specifies the NPU encapsulation type, which determines how packets are filtered. The possible values include dhcp, dot11-mgmt, dot11-probe, dot1x, eoip-ping, iapp, ip, lwapp, multicast, orphan-from-sta, orphan-to-sta, rbcp, wired-guest, or any. *port* is the physical port for packet transmission or reception.
debug packet logging acl eth *rule_index action dst src type vlan*	*rule_index* is a value between 1 and 6 (inclusive). *action* is permit, deny, or disable. *dst* is the destination MAC address. *src* is the source MAC address. *type* is the two-byte type code (such as 0x800 for IP, 0x806 for ARP). This parameter also accepts a few common string values, such as "ip" (for 0x800) or "arp" (for 0x806). *vlan* is the two-byte VLAN ID.
debug packet logging acl ip *rule_index action src dst proto src_port dst_port*	*rule_index* is a value between 1 and 6 (inclusive). *action* is permit, deny, or disable. *proto* is a numeric or any string recognized by getprotobyname(). The controller supports the following strings: ip, icmp, igmp, ggp, ipencap, st, tcp, egp, pup, udp, hmp, xns-idp, rdp, iso-tp4, xtp, ddp, idpr-cmtp, rspf, vmtp, ospf, ipip, and encap. *src_port* is the UDP/TCP 2-byte source port (for example, Telnet, 23) or "any." The controller accepts a numeric or any string recognized by getservbyname(). The controller supports the following strings: tcpmux, echo, discard, systat, daytime, netstat, qotd, msp, chargen, ftp-data,ftp, fsp, ssh, telnet, smtp, time, rlp, nameserver, whois, re-mail-ck, domain, mtp, bootps, bootpc, tftp, gopher, rje, finger, www, link, kerberos, supdup, hostnames, iso-tsap, csnet-ns, 3com-tsmux,

rtelnet, pop-2, pop-3, sunrpc, auth, sftp, uucp-path, nntp, ntp, net-bios-ns, netbios-dgm, netbios-ssn, imap2, snmp, snmp-trap, cmip-man, cmip-agent, xdmcp, nextstep, bgp, prospero, irc, smux, at-rtmp, at-nbp, at-echo, at-zis, qmtp, z3950, ipx, imap3, ulistserv, https, snpp, saft, npmp-local, npmp-gui, and hmmp-ind.

dst_port is the UDP/TCP 2-byte destination port (for example, Telnet, 23) or "any." The controller accepts a numeric or any string recognized by getservbyname(). The controller supports the same strings as those for the src_port.

debug packet logging acl eoip-eth *rule_index action dst src type vlan*	The parameters of this command are the same as the parameters from the previous listed commands.
debug packet logging acl eoip-ip *rule_index action src dst proto src_port dst_port*	The parameters of this command are the same as the parameters from the previous listed commands.
debug packet logging acl lwapp-dot11 *rule_index action dst src bssid snap_type*	*bssid* is the BSSID. *snap_type* is the Ethernet type. The remaining parameters of this command are the same as the parameters from the previous listed commands.
debug packet logging acl lwapp-ip *rule_index action src dst proto src_port dst_port*	The parameters of this command are the same as the parameters from the previous listed commands.

- IP header ACL

  Source address

  Destination address

  Protocol

  Source port (if applicable)

  Destination port (if applicable)

- Ethernet over IP (EoIP) payload Ethernet header ACL

  Destination address

  Source address

  Ethernet type

  VLAN ID

- EoIP payload IP header ACL

  Source address

  Destination address

  Protocol

  Source port (if applicable)

  Destination port (if applicable)

- LWAPP payload 802.11 header ACL

  Destination address

  Source address

  Basic service set identifier (BSSID)

  Subnetwork Access Protocol (SNAP) header type

- LWAPP payload IP header ACL

  Source address

  Destination address

  Protocol

  Source port (if applicable)

  Destination port (if applicable)

AP Debugs

Although most debugging is done on the controller, the unified WLAN solution also allows you to run specific **debug** and **show** commands on an AP. You can achieve this in two ways:

- Accessing the AP via the console and executing the **debug/show** commands like you used to do on every IOS device.

- Executing the **show/debug** commands from the controller using the AP remote-debug feature.

The first method is the one you are used to from IOS devices, although it is not always possible to use this method. That is because the console port from APs is not always physically cabled, and APs are often mounted at places based on a good RF coverage rather than comfortable console access.

To execute an AP **show/debug** command via the controller console, you first need to enable remote debugging on the AP. The following commands needs to be executed using **debug ap** *Cisco_AP*. After this, you can execute every IOS command using **debug ap command** *command Cisco_AP syntax.* Example A-1 shows how to display the contents of logging buffers of the AP with the name **SE.AP-01-1240** using the remote debugs on the controller CLI. Example A-2 shows how to enable CAPWAP event debugs on the AP with the name **SE.AP-01-1240** using the remote debugs on the controller CLI.

Example A-1   *Collecting "show logging" Using the remote-AP-debug Feature*

```
(Cisco Controller) >show ap summary

Number of APs.................................... 1

Global AP User Name............................. Not Configured
Global AP Dot1x User Name....................... Not Configured

AP Name             Slots  AP Model             Ethernet MAC         Port  Country
-----------------   -----  ------------------   -----------------    ----  -------
SE.AP-01-1240         2    AIR-LAP1242AG-E-K9   00:1d:a1:fc:0d:14    29     CH

(Cisco Controller) >debug ap enable SE.AP-01-1240
(Cisco Controller) >debug ap command "show logging" SE.AP-01-1240
```

Example A-2   *Running debug capwap client events Using the remote-AP-debug Feature*

```
(Cisco Controller) >show ap summary

Number of APs................................... 1

Global AP User Name............................. Not Configured
Global AP Dot1x User Name....................... Not Configured

AP Name               Slots  AP Model              Ethernet MAC         Port  Country
----------------      -----  -----------------     ------------------   ------------
SE.AP-01-1240           2    AIR-LAP1242AG-E-K9    00:1d:a1:fc:0d:14    29    CH

(Cisco Controller) >debug ap enable SE.AP-01-1240



(Cisco Controller) > debug ap command "debug capwap client event" SE.AP-01-1240
```

Example A-3 demonstrates how to verify that remote debugging is enabled on a specific AP.

Example A-3   *Verifying That Remote Debugging Is Enabled on a Specific AP*

```
(Cisco Controller) >show  ap config general SE.AP-01-1240

Cisco AP Identifier............................. 71
Cisco AP Name................................... SE.AP-01-1240
Country code.................................... CH  - Switzerland
Regulatory Domain allowed by Country............ 802.11bg:-E    802.11a:-E
AP Country code................................. CH  - Switzerland
AP Regulatory Domain............................ 802.11bg:-E    802.11a:-E
Switch Port Number ............................. 29
MAC Address..................................... 00:1d:a1:fc:0d:14
IP Address Configuration........................ DHCP
IP Address...................................... 10.0.102.117
IP NetMask...................................... 255.255.255.0
Gateway IP Addr................................. 10.0.102.1
CAPWAP Path MTU................................. 1485
Telnet State.................................... Disabled
Ssh State....................................... Disabled
Cisco AP Location............................... default location
Cisco AP Group Name............................. default-group
Primary Cisco Switch Name....................... Chtac-WIR-WLC02
Primary Cisco Switch IP Address................. Not Configured
Secondary Cisco Switch Name.....................
Secondary Cisco Switch IP Address............... Not Configured
```

```
Tertiary Cisco Switch Name......................
Tertiary Cisco Switch IP Address................ Not Configured
Administrative State ........................... ADMIN_ENABLED
Operation State ................................ REGISTERED
Mirroring Mode ................................. Disabled
AP Mode ........................................ Local
Public Safety .................................. Disabled
AP SubMode ..................................... Not Configured
Remote AP Debug ................................ Disabled
Logging trap severity level .................... informational
S/W  Version ................................... 5.2.178.0
Boot  Version .................................. 12.3.7.1
Mini IOS Version ............................... 3.0.51.0
Stats Reporting Period ......................... 180
LED State....................................... Enabled
PoE Pre-Standard Switch......................... Disabled
PoE Power Injector MAC Addr..................... Disabled
Power Type/Mode................................. Power injector / Normal mode
Number Of Slots................................. 2
AP Model........................................ AIR-LAP1242AG-E-K9
AP Image........................................ C1240-K9W8-M
IOS Version..................................... 12.4(18a)JA1
Reset Button.................................... Enabled
```

Table A-52 lists several useful remote debugs for the APs.

Table A-52   *Remote Debugs*

Command	Description
debug ap command "show capwap client rcb" *AP_Name*	Displays the RCB of the AP.
debug ap command "show capwap reap association" *AP_Name*	Displays CAPWAP REAP association information from an AP in H-REAP mode.
debug ap command "show capwap reap status" *AP_Name*	Displays the AP mode and its connection state.
debug ap command "debug dtls client events" *AP_Name*	Enables DTLS event debugs on an AP.
debug ap command "debug dtls client error" *AP_Name*	Enables DTLS error debugs on an AP.

(continues)

Table A-52 *Remote Debugs (continued)*

Command	Description
debug ap command "debug capwap client events" *AP_Name*	Enables CAPWAP event debugs on an AP.
debug ap command "debug capwap client error" *AP_Name*	Enables CAPWAP error debugs on an AP.
debug ap command "show memory debug leaks" *AP_Name*	Runs the leak detector on an AP.
debug ap command "show buffers address *DataArea*" *AP_Name*	Displays the buffer at a given address on an AP.
debug ap command "show buffers input-interface G0 dump" *AP_Name*	Displays the buffer assigned to an input interface on an AP.
debug ap command "show buffers all dump" *AP_Name*	Show the buffer header and all data on an AP.
debug ap command "show memory processor dead" *AP_Name*	Displays memory owned by dead processes on an AP.
debug ap command "show interfaces FastEthernet 0 " *AP_Name*	Displays the interface status and configuration on an AP.

Note The main purpose of remote AP debugs is to provide a tool for finding configuration issues in a comfortable way without needing to physically access the AP via console. Extensive debug commands, such as radio firmware debugs, are not forwarded to the controller CLI. In such scenarios, console access to the AP is still needed.

Table A-53 lists the AP remote debugs for the 1000 series APs.

Table A-53 *1000 Series Remote AP Debugs*

Command	Description
config wlan	Configures the specified wlan.
del acl	Delete the ACL.
del key	Delete the encryption key.
find bss	Find the BSS[1].

find channel	Find the available channel.
find all	Find all BSS.
get acl	Display the ACL.
get aging	Display the aging interval.
get aifs	Display AIFS[2].
get antenna	Display antenna diversity.
get association	Display the association table.
get authentication	Display the authentication type.
get autochannelselect	Display auto channel select.
get beaconinterval	Display the beacon interval.
get cfpperiod	Display the contention-free period interval.
get cfpmaxduration	Display the contention-free period max duration.
get cfpstatus	Display the contention-free period status.
get channel	Display the radio channel.
get cipher	Display the encryption cipher.
get config	Display the current AP configuration.
get countrycode	Display the country code.
get cwmin	Display the minimum contention window.
get domainsuffix	Display the DNS[3] suffix.
get dtim	Display the DTIM.
get encryption	Display the encryption mode.
get fragmentthreshold	Display the fragment threshold.
get frequency	Display the radio frequency (MHz).
get gateway	Display the gateway IP address.
get groupkeyupdate	Display the group key update interval (in seconds).
get hardware	Display the hardware revisions.

(continues)

Table A-53   *1000 Series Remote AP Debugs (continued)*

Command	Description
get hostipaddr	Display the host IP address.
get ipaddr	Display the IP address.
get ipmask	Display the IP subnet mask.
get key	Display the encryption key.
get keyentrymethod	Display the encryption key entry method.
get keysource	Display the source of encryption keys.
get login	Display the login username.
get nameaddr	Display the IP address of the name server.
get power	Display the transmit power setting.
get radiusname	Display the RADIUS server name or IP address.
get radiusport	Display the RADIUS port number.
get rate	Display the data rate.
get rtsthreshold	Display the RTS/CTS[4] threshold.
get ssid	Display the SSID[5].
get ssidsuppress	Display the SSID suppress mode.
get station	Display the station status.
get switch	Display the Airespace switch parameters.
get systemname	Display the AP system name.
get telnet	Display the Telnet mode.
get timeout	Display the Telnet timeout.
get tzone	Display the time zone setting.
get uptime	Display the uptime.
get wirelessmode	Display the WLAN mode.
get wlanstate	Display the WLAN state.
help	Display the CLI command list.
ping	Ping.

reboot	Reboot the AP.
quit	Log off.
set acl	Set the ACL.
set aging	Set the aging interval.
set aifs	Set the AIFS.
set antenna	Set the antenna.
set authentication	Set the authentication type.
set autochannelselect	Set the auto channel selection.
set beaconinterval	Modify the beacon interval.
set cfpperiod	Set the contention-free period interval.
set cfpmaxduration	Set the contention-free period max duration.
set cfpstatus	Set the contention-free period status.
set channel	Set the radio channel.
set cipher	Set the cipher.
set countrycode	Set the country code.
set cwmin	Set the minimum contention window.
set domainsuffix	Set the DNS suffix.
set dtim	Set the data beacon rate (DTIM).
set encryption	Set the encryption mode.
set factorydefault	Restore to default factory settings.
set fragmentthreshold	Set the fragment threshold.
set frequency	Set the radio frequency (MHz).
set gateway	Set the gateway IP address.
set groupkeyupdate	Set the group key update interval (in seconds).
set hostipaddr	Set the host IP address.
set ipaddr	Set the IP address.
set ipmask	Set the IP subnet mask.

(continues)

Table A-53 *1000 Series Remote AP Debugs (continued)*

Command	Description
set key	Set the encryption key.
set keyentrymethod	Select the encryption key entry method.
set keysource	Select the source of encryption keys.
set login	Modify the login username.
set nameaddress	Set the name server IP address.
set password	Modify the password.
set passphrase	Modify the passphrase.
set power	Set the transmit power.
set radiusname	Set the RADIUS name or IP address.
set radiusport	Set the RADIUS port number.
set radiussecret	Set the RADIUS shared secret.
set rate	Set the data rate.
set rtsthreshold	Set the RTS/CTS threshold.
set ssid	Set the SSID.
set ssidsuppress	Set the SSID suppress mode.
set switch	Set the Airespace switch parameters.
set systemname	Set the AP system name.
set telnet	Set the Telnet mode.
set timeout	Set the Telnet timeout.
set tzone	Set the time zone setting.
set wlanstate	Set the WLAN state.
set wirelessmode	Set the WLAN mode.
Timeofday	Display the current time of day.
Version	Software version.

[1]BSS = Basic Service Set

[2]AIFS = Arbitration Interframe Space

[3]DNS = Domain Name System

[4]RTS/CTS = Ready To Send/Clear To Send

[5]SSID = service set identifier

Appendix B

LWAPP and CAPWAP Payloads

The existing Lightweight Access Point Protocol (LWAPP) payloads will be reused if there is no corresponding Control and Provisioning of Wireless Access Points (CAPWAP) payload and will be sent as vendor-specific payloads. Table B-1 outlines all CAPWAP/LWAPP message elements. For a packet format description and more detailed explanation, please refer to the section "802.11 Bindings and Payloads" in Chapter 4, "The CAPWAP Protocol."

Table B-1 *CAPWAP/LWAPP Message Elements*

Type #	LWAPP Payload	CAPWAP Payload
1	NOP_PAYLOAD	Not required in CAPWAP; used in LWAPP for encryption
2	RESULT_CODE	Result Code
3	MWAR_ADDR_PAYLOAD	Vendor-specific payload
4	RAD_PAYLOAD	WTP descriptor
5	RAD_SLOT_PAYLOAD	IEEE 802.11 WTP radio information
6	RAD_NAME_PAYLOAD	WTP name
7	MWAR_PAYLOAD	AC descriptor
8	VAP_PAYLOAD DELETE_VAP_PAYLOAD UPDATE_VAP_PAYLOAD	IEEE 802.11 WLAN configuration request; things like AironetIE and 7920 support details will go as vendor-specific payloads

(continues)

Table B-1 *CAPWAP/LWAPP Message Elements (continued)*

Type #	LWAPP Payload	CAPWAP Payload
9	STATION_CFG_PAYLOAD	Vendor-specific payload
10	OPERATION_RATE_SET_PAYLOAD	IEEE 802.11 rate set
11	MULTI_DOMAIN_CAPABILITY_PAYLOAD	Vendor-specific payload
12	MAC_OPERATION_PAYLOAD	Vendor-specific payload
13	PHY_TX_POWER_PAYLOAD	Vendor-specific payload
14	PHY_TX_POWER_LEVEL_PAYLOAD	IEEE 802.11 Tx power level
15	PHY_DSSS_PAYLOAD	Vendor-specific payload
16	PHY_OFDM_PAYLOAD	Vendor-specific payload
17	SUPPORTED_RATES_PAYLOAD	IEEE 802.11 supported rates
18	AUTH_PAYLOAD	Vendor-specific payload
19	TEST_PAYLOAD	Not required in CAPWAP
20	RRM_NEIGHBOR_CTRL_PAYLOAD	Vendor-specific payload
21	RRM_NOISE_CTRL_PAYLOAD	Vendor-specific payload
22	RRM_NOISE_DATA_PAYLOAD	Vendor-specific payload
23	RRM_INTERFERENCE_CTRL_PAYLOAD	Vendor-specific payload
24	RRM_INTERFERENCE_DATA_PAYLOAD	Vendor-specific payload
25	RRM_LOAD_CTRL_PAYLOAD	Vendor-specific payload
26	RRM_LOAD_DATA_PAYLOAD	Vendor-specific payload
27	CHANGE_STATE_EVENT_PAYLOAD	Radio operational state
28	ADMIN_STATE_PAYLOAD	Radio administrative state
30	ADD_MOBILE_PAYLOAD	Vendor-specific payload

Table B-1 *CAPWAP/LWAPP Message Elements*

Type #	LWAPP Payload	CAPWAP Payload
30	ADD_MOBILE_PAYLOAD	Vendor-specific payload
31	DELETE_MOBILE_PAYLOAD	Station configuration request, which includes delete station
32	MWAR_NAME_PAYLOAD	AC name
33	IMAGE_DOWNLOAD_PAYLOAD	
34	IMAGE_DATA_PAYLOAD	
36	LOCATION_DATA_PAYLOAD	Location data
37	RRM_LOAD_GEN_CTRL_PAYLOAD	Vendor-specific payload
38	STAT_TMR_PAYLOAD	Statistics timer
39	STAT_PAYLOAD	IEEE 802.11 statistics
40	DECRYPT_ERR_REPORT_PERIOD	Decryption error report period
41	DECRYPT_ERR_REPORT	Decryption error report exists, but it is not sufficient; you can use a vendor-specific payload if this is not changed in CAPWAP
42	ANTENNA_PAYLOAD	IEEE 802.11 antenna "twiceExternalAntennaGain" is not there in this payload, so this might be sent as a vendor-specific payload
43	RRM_COVERAGE_CTRL_PAYLOAD	Vendor-specific payload
44	RRM_COVERAGE_DATA_PAYLOAD	Vendor-specific payload
45	CERTIFICATE_PAYLOAD	Not required in CAPWAP
46	SESSION_PAYLOAD	Session ID
47	SPAM_CRYPTO_PAYLOAD	Not required in CAPWAP

(continues)

Table B-1   *CAPWAP/LWAPP Message Elements (continued)*

Type #	LWAPP Payload	CAPWAP Payload
48	PERFORMANCE_PROFILE_PAYLOAD	Vendor-specific payload
49	SPAM_CFPSTATUS_PAYLOAD	Not actually sent in LWAPP; need to see if this can be removed
50	ROGUE_AP_REPORT	Vendor-specific payload
51	BOARD_DATA_PAYLOAD	WTP board data
52	BCAST_SSID_MODE_PAYLOAD	Vendor-specific payload
53	DATA_TRANSFER_PAYLOAD	Data transfer data
54	DATA_TRANSFER_DATA_PAYLOAD	
55	AP_MODE_AND_TYPE_PAYLOAD	Check whether WTP MAC type will suffice
56	APF_ROGUE_CONTAINMENT_PAYLOAD	Vendor-specific payload
57	RRM_NEIGHBOR_LIST_PAYLOAD	Vendor-specific payload
58	AP_QOS_PAYLOAD	IEEE 802.11 WTP quality of service; for things like "ACM & CBR," vendor-specific information can be used
59	DISCOVERY_TYPE_PAYLOAD	Discovery type
60	MWAR_LIST_PAYLOAD	Vendor-specific payload
61	STATUS_PAYLOAD	May not be required in CAPWAP
62	SPAM_MIC_COUNTERMEASURE_PAYLOAD	IEEE 802.11 MIC countermeasures

Table B-1 *CAPWAP/LWAPP Message Elements*

Type #	LWAPP Payload	CAPWAP Payload
63	WLAN_OVERRIDE_MODE_PAYLOAD	Vendor-specific payload
64	ADD_LOCAL_WLAN_PAYLOAD	Vendor-specific payload
65	DELETE_LOCAL_WLAN_PAYLOAD	Vendor-specific payload
66	ADD_BLACKLIST_ENTRY	Vendor-specific payload
67	DELETE_BLACKLIST_ENTRY	Vendor-specific payload
68	AP_REBOOT_STAT_PAYLOAD	WTP reboot statistics
69	AP_TIMER_PAYLOAD	CAPWAP timers
70	ROGUE_CLIENT_REPORT	Vendor-specific payload
71	ADD_STATIC_BLACKLIST_ENTRY	Vendor-specific payload
72	DELETE_STATIC_BLACKLIST_ENTRY	Vendor-specific payload
73	CLIENT_AUTO_HANDOFF_PAYLOAD	Vendor-specific payload
74	DATA_TRANSFER_LOG_DATA_PAYLOAD	Not used in LWAPP
75	REMOTE_AP_DEBUG_ENABLE_DISABLE	Vendor-specific payload
76	REMOTE_AP_DEBUG_FUNCTION_CALL	Vendor-specific payload
77	REMOTE_AP_DEBUG_VAR_SET	Vendor-specific payload
78	SPAM_DUPLICATE_IP_ADDR_PAYLOAD	Duplicate IPv4 address
79	SPAM_AP_BEING_CONTAINED_PAYLOAD	Vendor-specific payload
80	SPAM_NOT_USED_PAYLOAD_THERE_FOR_BACKWARD_COMPATABILITY	Vendor-specific payload

(continues)

Table B-1 *CAPWAP/LWAPP Message Elements (continued)*

Type #	LWAPP Payload	CAPWAP Payload
81	SPAM_MIC_ERROR_REPORT_FROM_MS	Vendor-specific payload
82	RRM_RECEIVER_CTRL_PAYLOAD	Vendor-specific payload
83	RRM_COVERAGE_QUERY_PAYLOAD	Vendor-specific payload
84	AP_IP_ADDR_PAYLOAD	WTP static IP address information
85	SPAM_ADD_SIG_PAYLOAD	Vendor-specific payload
86	SPAM_DEL_SIG_PAYLOAD	Vendor-specific payload
87	SPAM_SIG_REPORT_PAYLOAD	Vendor-specific payload
88	SPAM_SIG_TOGGLE_PAYLOAD	Vendor-specific payload
89	AIRESPACE_CAPABILITY_PAYLOAD	Vendor-specific payload
90	ROGUE_TABLE_UPDATE	Vendor-specific payload
91	SPAM_ROGUE_ON_NET	Vendor-specific payload
92	MWAR_NAME_WITH_INDEX_PAYLOAD	AC name with index
93	AP_FALLBACK_ENABLED_PAYLOAD	WTP fallback
94	MM_SWITCH_INFO_PAYLOAD	AC IPv4 list
95	RFID_TAG_STATUS_PAYLOAD	Vendor-specific payload
96	SPAM_AP_RADIO_FAIL_ALARM_PAYLOAD	IEEE 802.11 WTP radio fail alarm indication

Table B-1   *CAPWAP/LWAPP Message Elements*

Type #	LWAPP Payload	CAPWAP Payload
97	SPAM_DOMAIN_SECRET_PAYLOAD	Vendor-specific payload
98	IDLE_TIMEOUT_PAYLOAD	Idle timeout
99	SNIFFER_ENABLE_DISABLE_PAYLOAD	Vendor-specific payload
100	SPAM_AP_MGR_IP_ADDR	CAPWAP control IPv4 address
101	MD5_CHKSUM_DATA_PAYLOAD	Not required in CAPWAP
102	ADD_TS_PAYLOAD	Vendor-specific payload
103	DELETE_TS_PAYLOAD	Vendor-specific payload
104	SPAM_80211_MANAGEMENT_TRAFFIC_LIMIT_PAYLOAD	Vendor-specific payload
105	SPAM_VENDOR_SPECIFIC_PAYLOAD	CAPWAP vendor-specific payload
106	AP_ROLE_PAYLOAD	Vendor-specific payload
107	MESH_NEIGH_PAYLOAD	Vendor-specific payload
108	MESH_STATS_PAYLOAD	Vendor-specific payload
109	MESH_LINKRATE_PAYLOAD	Vendor-specific payload
110	MESH_LINK_PARA_PAYLOAD	Vendor-specific payload
111	MESH_NODE_UPDATE_PAYLOAD	Vendor-specific payload
112	MESH_NEIGHS_UPDATE_PAYLOAD	Vendor-specific payload
113	AP_BACKHAUL_PAYLOAD	Vendor-specific payload

(continues)

Table B-1 *CAPWAP/LWAPP Message Elements (continued)*

Type #	LWAPP Payload	CAPWAP Payload
114	AP_BHRATE_PAYLOAD	Vendor-specific payload
115	AP_CFGROLE_PAYLOAD	Vendor-specific payload
116	LINKTEST_CFG_PAYLOAD	Vendor-specific payload
117	LINKTEST_RESULTS_PAYLOAD	Vendor-specific payload
118	BRIDGE_GROUPNAME_PAYLOAD	Vendor-specific payload
119	BMK_RSP_PAYLOAD	Vendor-specific payload
120	COMPRESSED_CERTIFICATE_PAYLOAD	Not used in LWAPP
121	NONCE_PAYLOAD	Not required in CAPWAP—used in LWAPP in discovery response and join request
122	AUTH_STRING_PAYLOAD	Used for bridged APs (check if needed); use vendor-specific payload if needed
123	GOODNEIGH_PAYLOAD	Not used in LWAPP
124	AP_GROUP_NAME_PAYLOAD	Vendor-specific payload
125	SPAM_BIG_NAV_ATTACK_PAYLOAD	Vendor-specific payload
126	SPAM_AP_LED_STATE_CONFIG_PAYLOAD	Vendor-specific payload
127	AP_REGULATORY_DOMAIN_PAYLOAD	Vendor-specific payload
128	SPAM_AP_MODEL_PAYLOAD	Not used in LWAPP
129	SPAM_AP_RESET_BUTTON_STATE_PAYLOAD	Vendor-specific payload

Table B-1   *CAPWAP/LWAPP Message Elements*

Type #	LWAPP Payload	CAPWAP Payload
130	SPAM_AP_TFTP_DOWNGRADE_PAYLOAD	Not used in LWAPP
131	REMOTE_AP_DEBUG_COMMAND	Vendor-specific payload
132	SPAM_AP_RADIO_CORE_DUMP_NOTIFICATION	Vendor-specific payload
133	AP_DOT11H_PAYLOAD	Vendor-specific payload
134	RRM_RADAR_DATA_PAYLOAD	Vendor-specific payload
135	LWAPP_CHANNEL_PWR_PAYLOAD	Vendor-specific payload
136	AP_MEMORY_COREDUMP_CONFIG_PAYLOAD	Vendor-specific payload
137	SPAM_MGMT_FRAME_DELIVERY_NOTIFICATION_PAYLOAD	Vendor-specific payload
138	SPAM_AP_PRE_STD_SWITCH_CONFIG_PAYLOAD	Not used in LWAPP
139	SPAM_AP_POWER_INJECTOR_CONFIG_PAYLOAD	Not used in LWAPP
140	AP_MANAGER_CONTROL_IPv6_ADDRESS_PAYLOAD	Not used in LWAPP
141	AP_MANAGER_DATA_IPv4_ADDRESS_PAYLOAD	Not used in LWAPP
142	AP_MANAGER_DATA_IPv6_ADDRESS_PAYLOAD	Not used in LWAPP
143	CLIENT_QOS_PROFILE_PAYLOAD	Not used in LWAPP
144	CONTROLLER_IPv6_ADDRESS_LIST_PAYLOAD	Not used in LWAPP
145	AP_BRIDGE_STATE_PAYLOAD	Vendor-specific payload
146	AP_DTPC_PAYLOAD	Vendor-specific payload

(continues)

Table B-1   *CAPWAP/LWAPP Message Elements (continued)*

Type #	LWAPP Payload	CAPWAP Payload
147	AP_CISCO_7920_VSIE_PAYLOAD	Vendor-specific payload
148	AP_DFS_CHANNEL_LIST	Vendor-specific payload
149	AP_MULTICAST_GROUP_PAYLOAD	Vendor-specific payload
150	AP_MINIOS_VERSION_PAYLOAD	Vendor-specific payload
151	AP_MINIOS_UPGRADE_PAYLOAD	Vendor-specific payload
152	AP_TIMESYNC_PAYLOAD	Vendor-specific payload
153	STATION_STATS_PAYLOAD	Not used in LWAPP; needs to be removed
154	AP_TSM_CONFIG_PAYLOAD	Vendor-specific payload
155	CCX_LINKTEST_START_PAYLOAD	Vendor-specific payload
156	CCX_LINKTEST_REPORT_PAYLOAD	Vendor-specific payload

LWAPP and CAPWAP Message Payloads

Table B-2 details the payloads (message elements) sent in LWAPP control messages and the corresponding ones that will be sent in CAPWAP control messages. For packet format description and more detailed explanation, please refer to the "802.11 Bindings and Payloads" section in Chapter 4.

Table B-2 *LWAPP/CAPWAP Control Message Payloads*

Message	LWAPP Message Elements	CAPWAP Message Elements
Discovery Request	DISCOVERY_TYPE_PAYLOAD BOARD_DATA_PAYLOAD RAD_PAYLOAD RAD_SLOT_PAYLOAD	Discovery type WTP board data WTP descriptor IEEE 802.11 WTP radio information WTP frame tunnel mode WTP MAC type
Discovery Response	MWAR_PAYLOAD MWAR_NAME_PAYLOAD NONCE_PAYLOAD SPAM_AP_MGR_IP_ADDR	AC descriptor AC name Vendor-specific payload for "NONCE_PAYLOAD" CAPWAP control IPv4 address IEEE 802.11 WTP radio information
Primary Discovery Request	RAD_PAYLOAD RAD_SLOT_PAYLOAD BOARD_DATA_PAYLOAD	WTP descriptor IEEE 802.11 WTP radio information WTP board data Discovery type WTP frame tunnel mode WTP MAC type
Primary Discovery Response	MWAR_PAYLOAD MWAR_NAME_PAYLOAD	AC descriptor AC name CAPWAP control IPv4 address IEEE 802.11 WTP radio information

(continues)

Table B-2   *LWAPP/CAPWAP Control Message Payloads (continued)*

Message	LWAPP Message Elements	CAPWAP Message Elements
Join Request	MWAR_ADDR_PAYLOAD RAD_PAYLOAD RAD_NAME_PAYLOAD BOARD_DATA_PAYLOAD NONCE_PAYLOAD AUTH_STRING_PAYLOAD LOCATION_DATA_PAYLOAD RAD_SLOT_PAYLOAD CERTIFICATE_PAYLOAD SESSION_PAYLOAD TEST_PAYLOAD	Vendor-specific payload for "MWAR_ADDR_PAYLOAD" WTP descriptor WTP name WTP board data Vendor-specific payload for "NONCE_PAYLOAD" Vendor-specific payload for "AUTH_STRING_PAYLOAD" Location data IEEE 802.11 WTP radio information N/A Session ID N/A WTP IPv4 IP address WTP frame tunnel mode WTP MAC type
Join Response	RESULT_CODE CERTIFICATE_PAYLOAD SPAM_CRYPTO_PAYLOAD TEST_PAYLOAD	Result code N/A N/A N/A AC descriptor AC name CAPWAP control IPv4 address IEEE 802.11 WTP radio information
Echo Request	None	None
Echo Response	None	None

Table B-2   *LWAPP/CAPWAP Control Message Payloads*

Message	LWAPP Message Elements	CAPWAP Message Elements
Configuration Status	ADMIN_STATE_PAYLOAD MWAR_NAME_PAYLOAD MWAR_NAME_WITH_INDEX_PAYLOAD BOARD_DATA_PAYLOAD AP_REGULATORY_DOMAIN_PAYLOAD Vendor-specific payload for MFP config AP_GROUP_NAME_PAYLOAD Vendor-specific payload for CDP ADMIN_STATE_PAYLOAD STATION_CFG_PAYLOAD MULTI_DOMAIN_CAPABILITY_PAYLOAD MAC_OPERATION_PAYLOAD PHY_TX_POWER_LEVEL_PAYLOAD PHY_TX_POWER_PAYLOAD PHY_DSSS_PAYLOAD ANTENNA_PAYLOAD SUPPORTED_RATES_PAYLOAD PERFORMANCE_PROFILE_PAYLOAD Vendor-specific payload for CCX RM config SPAM_CFPSTATUS_PAYLOAD WLAN_OVERRIDE_MODE_PAYLOAD SNIFFER_ENABLE_DISABLE_PAYLOAD ADD_LOCAL_WLAN_PAYLOAD SPAM_AP_LED_STATE_CONFIG_PAYLOAD LWAPP_CHANNEL_PWR_PAYLOAD AP_DFS_CHANNEL_LIST Vendor-specific payload for MFP capabilities STAT_TMR_PAYLOAD AP_MODE_AND_TYPE_PAYLOAD AP_REBOOT_STAT_PAYLOAD AP_IP_ADDR_PAYLOAD LOCATION_DATA_PAYLOAD AP_ROLE_PAYLOAD AP_CFGROLE_PAYLOAD AP_BACKHAUL_PAYLOAD AP_BHRATE_PAYLOAD BRIDGE_GROUPNAME_PAYLOAD AP_BRIDGE_STATE_PAYLOAD	Radio administrative state AC name AC name with index WTP board data Vendor-specific payload for "AP_REGULATORY_DOMAIN_PAYLOAD" Vendor-specific payload for MFP config Vendor-specific payload for "AP_GROUP_NAME_PAYLOAD" Vendor-specific payload for CDP Radio administrative state IEEE 802.11 WTP radio configuration + vendor-specific IEEE 802.11 multidomain capability IEEE 802.11 MAC operation Statistics timer WTP reboot statistics

(continues)

Table B-2   *LWAPP/CAPWAP Control Message Payloads (continued)*

Message	LWAPP Message Elements	CAPWAP Message Elements
Configure Response	AP_TIMESYNC_PAYLOAD SPAM_DOMAIN_SECRET_PAYLOAD STATION_CFG_PAYLOAD OPERATION_RATE_SET_PAYLOAD MULTI_DOMAIN_CAPABILITY_PAYLOAD MAC_OPERATION_PAYLOAD PHY_TX_POWER_PAYLOAD PHY_DSSS_PAYLOAD ANTENNA_PAYLOAD DECRYPT_ERR_REPORT_PERIOD AP_QOS_PAYLOAD AIRESPACE_CAPABILITY_PAYLOAD CHANGE_STATE_EVENT_PAYLOAD APF_ROGUE_CONTAINMENT_PAYLOAD SNIFFER_ENABLE_DISABLE_PAYLOAD AP_DOT11H_PAYLOAD AP_DTPC_PAYLOAD AP_TSM_CONFIG_PAYLOAD AP_CISCO_7920_VSIE_PAYLOAD AP_MULTICAST_GROUP_PAYLOAD BCAST_SSID_MODE_PAYLOAD AP_TIMER_PAYLOAD CLIENT_AUTO_HANDOFF_PAYLOAD SPAM_80211_MANAGEMENT_TRAFFIC_LIMIT_PAYLOAD MWAR_LIST_PAYLOAD AP_FALLBACK_ENABLED_PAYLOAD MM_SWITCH_INFO_PAYLOAD AP_MINIOS_UPGRADE_PAYLOAD RFID_TAG_STATUS_PAYLOAD IDLE_TIMEOUT_PAYLOAD Management IP Address payload–vendor-specific for HREAPs MESH_LINK_PARA_PAYLOAD BMK_RSP_PAYLOAD MFP Config vendor-specific payload CDP Config vendor-specific payload AP user and password vendor-specific payload	AC IPv4 List CAPWAP timers Decryption error report period Idle timeout WTP fallback
Image Data Request	IMAGE_DOWNLOAD_PAYLOAD	Image data Image data identifier

Table B-2 *LWAPP/CAPWAP Control Message Payloads*

Message	LWAPP Message Elements	CAPWAP Message Elements
Image Data Response	IMAGE_DATA_PAYLOAD	Result code Image data request
Change State Event Request	CHANGE_STATE_EVENT_PAYLOAD	Radio operational state Result code
Change State Event Response	None	None

Index

E

F-G

M

N

·ı|ı.ı|ı.
CISCO™

ciscopress.com: Your Cisco Certification and Networking Learning Resource

Subscribe to the monthly Cisco Press newsletter to be the first to learn about new releases and special promotions.

Visit **ciscopress.com/newsletters.**

While you are visiting, check out the offerings available at your finger tips.

–Free Podcasts from experts:
  · OnNetworking
  · OnCertification
  · OnSecurity

Podcasts

View them at **ciscopress.com/podcasts.**

–Read the latest author **articles** and **sample chapters** at ciscopress.com/articles.

–Bookmark the Certification Reference Guide available through our partner site at **informit.com/certguide.**

Connect with Cisco Press authors and editors via Facebook and Twitter, visit **informit.com/socialconnect.**

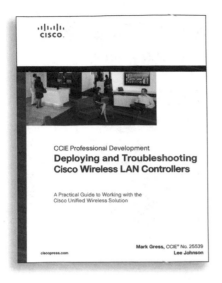

FREE Online Edition

Your purchase of **Deploying and Troubleshooting Cisco Wireless LAN Controllers** includes access to a free online edition for 45 days through the Safari Books Online subscription service. Nearly every Cisco Press book is available online through Safari Books Online, along with more than 5,000 other technical books and videos from publishers such as Addison-Wesley Professional, Exam Cram, IBM Press, O'Reilly, Prentice Hall, Que, and Sams.

SAFARI BOOKS ONLINE allows you to search for a specific answer, cut and paste code, download chapters, and stay current with emerging technologies.

Activate your FREE Online Edition at www.informit.com/safarifree

> **STEP 1:** Enter the coupon code: AXKFREH.

> **STEP 2:** New Safari users, complete the brief registration form.
> Safari subscribers, just log in.

If you have difficulty registering on Safari or accessing the online edition, please e-mail customer-service@safaribooksonline.com